Brief Table of Contents

focus on...the Cover

How do you feel when you look at this cover? We hope the image on the book conveys a feeling of relaxation and overall peace of mind—both achieved by developing a solid financial plan. From cover to cover, this text's goal is to actively help you gain the financial literacy and personal finance skills you need to make sound financial decisions for life. Use this book as a tool to help you gain peace of mind about your financial future!

focus on
personal finance

an active approach to help you
develop successful financial skills

2nd edition

KAPOOR   DLABAY   HUGHES

The McGraw-Hill/Irwin Series in Finance, Insurance and Real Estate

Stephen A. Ross
Franco Modigliani Professor of Finance and Economics
Sloan School of Management
Massachusetts Institute of Technology
Consulting Editor

FINANCIAL MANAGEMENT

Adair
Excel Applications for Corporate Finance
First Edition

Block and Hirt
Foundations of Financial Management
Twelfth Edition

Brealey, Myers, and Allen
Principles of Corporate Finance
Ninth Edition

Brealey, Myers, and Allen
Corporate Finance, Brief Edition
First Edition

Brealey, Myers and Marcus
Fundamentals of Corporate Finance
Fifth Edition

Brooks
FinGame Online 5.0

Bruner
Case Studies in Finance: Managing for Corporate Value Creation
Fifth Edition

Chew
The New Corporate Finance: Where Theory Meets Practice
Third Edition

DeMello
Cases in Finance
Second Edition

Grinblatt (editor)
Stephen A. Ross, Mentor: Influence through Generations

Grinblatt and Titman
Financial Markets and Corporate Strategy
Second Edition

Helfert
Techniques of Financial Analysis: A Guide to Value Creation
Eleventh Edition

Higgins
Analysis for Financial Management
Eighth Edition

Kester, Ruback, and Tufano
Case Problems in Finance
Twelfth Edition

Ross, Westerfield and Jaffe
Corporate Finance
Eighth Edition

Ross, Westerfield, Jaffe and Jordon
Corporate Finance: Core Principles and Applications
First Edition

Ross, Westerfield and Jordan
Essentials of Corporate Finance
Sixth Edition

Ross, Westerfield and Jordan
Fundamentals of Corporate Finance
Eighth Edition

Shefrin
Behavioral Corporate Finance: Decisions that Create Value
First Edition

White
Financial Analysis with an Electronic Calculator
Sixth Edition

INVESTMENTS

Adair
Excel Applications for Investments
First Edition

Bodie, Kane and Marcus
Essentials of Investments
Seventh Edition

Bodie, Kane and Marcus
Investments
Eighth Edition

Hirt and Block
Fundamentals of Investment Management
Ninth Edition

Hirschey and Nofsinger
Investments: Analysis and Behavior
First Edition

Jordan and Miller
Fundamentals of Investments: Valuation and Management
Fourth Edition

FINANCIAL INSTITUTIONS AND MARKETS

Rose and Hudgins
Bank Management and Financial Services
Seventh Edition

Rose and Marquis
Money and Capital Markets: Financial Institutions and Instruments in a Global Marketplace
Tenth Edition

Saunders and Cornett
Financial Institutions Management: A Risk Management Approach
Sixth Edition

Saunders and Cornett
Financial Markets and Institutions: An Introduction to the Risk Management Approach
Third Edition

INTERNATIONAL FINANCE

Eun and Resnick
International Financial Management
Fourth Edition

Kuemmerle
Case Studies in International Entrepreneurship: Managing and Financing Ventures in the Global Economy
First Edition

REAL ESTATE

Brueggeman and Fisher
Real Estate Finance and Investments
Thirteenth Edition

Corgel, Ling and Smith
Real Estate Perspectives: An Introduction to Real Estate
Fourth Edition

Ling and Archer
Real Estate Principles: A Value Approach
Second Edition

FINANCIAL PLANNING AND INSURANCE

Allen, Melone, Rosenbloom and Mahoney
Retirement Plans: 401(k)s, IRAs, and Other Deferred Compensation Approaches
Tenth Edition

Altfest
Personal Financial Planning
First Edition

Harrington and Niehaus
Risk Management and Insurance
Second Edition

Kapoor, Dlabay, and Hughes
Focus on Personal Finance: An active approach to help you develop successful financial skills
Second Edition

Kapoor, Dlabay and Hughes
Personal Finance
Eighth Edition

Focus on Personal Finance

An Active Approach to Help You Develop
Successful Financial Skills

SECOND EDITION

To my father, Ram Kapoor, and the memory of my mother, Sheila; my wife, Theresa, and my children, Karen, Kathryn, and Dave

To my mother, Mary Dlabay, and the memory of my father, Les; to my wife, Linda, and my children, Carissa and Kyle

To my mother, Barbara Y. Hughes; and my wife, Peggy

Focus on Personal Finance

*An Active Approach to Help You Develop
Successful Financial Skills*

SECOND EDITION

Jack R. Kapoor
COLLEGE OF DUPAGE

Les R. Dlabay
LAKE FOREST COLLEGE

Robert J. Hughes
DALLAS COUNTY COMMUNITY COLLEGES

**McGraw-Hill
Irwin**

Boston   Burr Ridge, IL   Dubuque, IA   New York   San Francisco   St. Louis
Bangkok   Bogotá   Caracas   Kuala Lumpur   Lisbon   London   Madrid   Mexico City
Milan   Montreal   New Delhi   Santiago   Seoul   Singapore   Sydney   Taipei   Toronto

 **McGraw-Hill
Irwin**

FOCUS ON PERSONAL FINANCE: AN ACTIVE APPROACH TO HELP YOU DEVELOP
SUCCESSFUL FINANCIAL SKILLS

ISBN 978-0-07-353063-5
MHID 0-07-353063-8

VP/Editor-in-chief: *Brent Gordon*
Executive editor: *Michele Janicek*
Development editor: *Elizabeth Hughes*
Marketing director: *Dan Silverburg*
Associate producer, media technology: *Xin Zhu*
Manager of publishing tools: *Mary Conzachi*
Lead production supervisor: *Michael R. McCormick*
Senior designer: *Cara David*
Senior media project manager: *Matthew Perry*
Typeface: *10/12 Times Roman*
Compositor: *ICC Macmillan Inc.*
Printer: *Quebecor World Versailles Inc.*

Library of Congress Cataloging-in-Publication Data

Kapoor, Jack R., 1937-
    Focus on personal finance : an active approach to help you develop successful
financial skills / Jack R. Kapoor, Les R. Dlabay, Robert J. Hughes.—2nd ed.
        p. cm. — (The Mcgraw-Hill/Irwin series in finance, insurance, and real estate)
    Includes index.
    ISBN-13: 978-0-07-353063-5 (alk. paper)
    ISBN-10: 0-07-353063-8 (alk. paper)
    1. Finance, Personal. 2. Investments. I. Dlabay, Les R. II. Hughes, Robert
James, 1946- III. Title.
HG179.K368 2008
332.024'01—dc22

                                                        2007023842

www.mhhe.com

Focus on ... the Authors

Jack R. Kapoor, *College of DuPage*

Jack Kapoor is a professor of business and economics in the Business and Technology Division of the College of DuPage, Glen Ellyn, Illinois, where he has taught business and economics since 1969. He received his BA and MS from San Francisco State College and his EdD from Northern Illinois University. He previously taught at Illinois Institute of Technology's Stuart School of Management, San Francisco State University's School of World Business, and other colleges. Professor Kapoor was awarded the Business and Technology Division's Outstanding Professor Award for 1999–2000. He served as an assistant national bank examiner for the U.S. Treasury Department and has been an international trade consultant to Bolting Manufacturing Co., Ltd., Bombay, India.

Dr. Kapoor is known internationally as a co-author of several textbooks, including *Business: A Practical Approach* (Rand McNally), *Business* (Houghton Mifflin), *Business and Personal Finance* (Glencoe), and *Personal Finance* (McGraw-Hill). He served as a content consultant for the popular national television series *The Business File: An Introduction to Business* and developed two full-length audio courses in Business and Personal Finance. He has been quoted in many national newspapers and magazines, including *USA Today, U.S. News & World Report,* the *Chicago Sun-Times, Crain's Small Business,* the *Chicago Tribune,* and other publications.

Dr. Kapoor has traveled around the world and has studied business practices in capitalist, socialist, and communist countries.

Les R. Dlabay, *Lake Forest College*

Sharing resources with the less fortunate is an ongoing financial goal of Les Dlabay, professor of business at Lake Forest College, Lake Forest, Illinois. Through child sponsorship programs, world hunger organizations, and community service activities, he believes the extensive wealth in our society should be used to help others. In addition to writing several textbooks, Dr. Dlabay teaches various international business courses. His "hobbies" include collecting cereal packages from over 100 countries and paper currency from 200 countries, which are used to teach about economic, cultural, and political aspects of foreign business environments. Professor Dlabay also uses many field research activities with his students, conducting interviews, surveys, and observations of business activities.

Robert J. Hughes, *Dallas County Community Colleges*

Financial literacy! Only two words, but Bob Hughes, professor of business at Dallas County Community Colleges, believes that these two words can literally change people's lives. Whether you want to be rich or just manage the money you have, the ability to analyze financial decisions and gather financial information are skills that can always be improved. In addition to writing several textbooks, Dr. Hughes has taught personal finance, introduction to business, business math, small business management, small business finance, and accounting since 1972. He also served as a content consultant for two popular national television series, *It's Strictly Business* and *Dollars & Sense: Personal Finance for the 21st Century,* and is the lead author for a business math project utilizing computer-assisted instruction funded by the ALEKS Corporation. He received his BBA from Southern Nazarene University and his MBA and EdD from the University of North Texas. His hobbies include writing, investing, collecting French antiques, art, and travel.

What Are Your Financial Goals?

Owning a huge house and a luxury car?
Retiring at age 45 and traveling the world?
Having a sense of freedom from financial worries?

Though the first two suggestions are very appealing, most of you would welcome the third—being able to go out to dinner, occasionally splurging at a sale at your favorite store, just paying bills and credit cards in full—and avoiding arguments that many people experience because they never seem to have enough money. Enjoying *peace of mind* with regard to your financial situation is a very attainable goal, and you took the first step by enrolling in a personal finance course and purchasing this book.

Focus on Personal Finance is all about you—this text will not only get you thinking about your current situation and your financial goals, but it will encourage you to put these in writing to use as a guide and revise over the course of your life. The more you involve yourself in the Getting Personal self-assessments, the in-chapter exercises, and, most important, Your Personal Financial Plan worksheets, the more you will discover about your current habits and how to improve them for greater financial freedom. The fact is that there is no better time to start than now.

No matter your age, gender, family status, economic status, or stage of life, being financially literate—having the ability to make informed choices about spending, saving, borrowing, and investing—is critical. This book won't give you the hottest stock tips, tell you where you can get the best deal on a car, or offer secrets for instant wealth, but you will learn basic concepts that will increase your comfort in financial situations. These concepts include advantages and disadvantages of different investments, tips you need to know before purchasing a car, suggestions for financing a home, and how to calculate how much money you will need to retire comfortably. Not every topic will apply to your life right now, but this book will be a valuable reference when you do need to apply for credit or a loan, purchase insurance, or plan your estate.

Be sure to check the cover foldout for ways to use the many learning resources available and to get the most out of this text, and Web site at www.mhhe.com/kdh. We hope that your active involvement with this text and the resulting financial plan bring you closer to peace of mind and the many financial goals you select for yourself!

Jack Kapoor
kapoorj@cod.edu

Les Dlabay
dlabay@lakeforest.edu

Bob Hughes
bhughes@dcccd.edu

Focus on ... Learning

Getting Personal

Fill it in and get personal! Each chapter starts with a personal assessment questionnaire focusing on your current personal financial habits for the topics that will be covered in that chapter. Each assessment contains four to six questions that ask you to fill in, circle, or rate your answer.

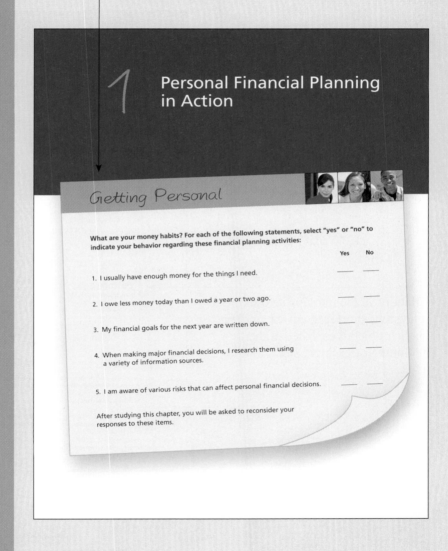

1

Personal Financial Planning in Action

Getting Personal

What are your money habits? For each of the following statements, select "yes" or "no" to indicate your behavior regarding these financial planning activities:

	Yes	No
1. I usually have enough money for the things I need.	___	___
2. I owe less money today than I owed a year or two ago.	___	___
3. My financial goals for the next year are written down.	___	___
4. When making major financial decisions, I research them using a variety of information sources.	___	___
5. I am aware of various risks that can affect personal financial decisions.	___	___

After studying this chapter, you will be asked to reconsider your responses to these items.

Objectives and Why Is This Important?

As each chapter begins, a list of the chapter objectives and why they are important is boxed off for easy reference. The objectives are also used to organize the end-of-chapter summary.

Your Personal Financial Plan Sheets

A list of all of the *Your Personal Financial Plan* worksheets for each chapter is presented at the start of each chapter for easy reference.

Your Personal Financial Plan Sheets
1. Personal financial data.
2. Setting personal financial goals.
3. Achieving financial goals using time value of money.
4. Planning your career.

Objectives

In this chapter, you will learn to:

1. Identify social and economic influences on personal financial goals and decisions.
2. Develop personal financial goals.
3. Assess personal and financial opportunity costs associated with financial decisions.
4. Implement a plan for making personal financial and career decisions.

Why is this important?

Each year, more than a million people declare bankruptcy, and Americans lose more than $1.2 billion in fraudulent investments. Both of these common difficulties result from poor personal financial planning. Your ability to make wise money decisions is a foundation for your current and long-term well-being.

Making Financial Decisions

OBJECTIVE 1
Identify social and economic influences on personal financial goals and decisions.

Money is a constant topic of conversation in our society. People everywhere talk about money.

Most people want to handle their finances so that they get full satisfaction from each available dollar. Typical financial goals may include buying a new car or a larger home, pursuing advanced career training, contributing to charity, traveling extensively, and ensuring self-sufficiency during working and retirement years. To achieve these and other goals, people need to identify and set priorities. Financial and personal satisfaction are the result of an organized process that is commonly referred to as *personal money management* or *personal financial planning*.

Your Life Situation and Financial Planning

personal financial planning The process of managing your money to achieve personal economic satisfaction.

financial plan A formalized report that summarizes your current financial situation, analyzes your financial needs, and recommends future financial activities.

Personal financial planning is the process of managing your money to achieve personal economic satisfaction. This planning process allows you to control your financial situation. Every person, family, or household has a unique situation; therefore, financial decisions must be planned to meet specific needs and goals.

A comprehensive financial plan can enhance the quality of your life and increase your satisfaction by reducing uncertainty about your future needs and resources. A **financial plan** is a formalized report that summarizes your current financial situation, analyzes your financial needs, and recommends future financial activities. You can create this document on your own (by using the sheets at the end of each chapter) or you can seek assistance from a financial planner or use a money management software package.

Objective References

Citations in the margins next to the relevant text refer to corresponding chapter objectives, listed at the beginning of each chapter.

Key Terms

Key terms appear in bold type within the text and are defined in the margins. A list of key terms and page references is located at the end of each chapter.

did you know?

If you invest $2,000 a year (at 9 percent) from ages 31 to 65, these funds will grow to $470,249 by age 65. However, if you save $2,000 a year (at 9 percent) for only 9 years (ages 22 to 30), at age 65 this fund will be worth $579,471! Most important: Start investing something now!

The sooner you make deposits, the greater the future value will be. Depositing $1,000 in a 5 percent account at age 40 will give you $3,387 at age 65. However, making the $1,000 deposit at age 25 would result in an account balance of $7,040 at age 65.

FUTURE VALUE OF A SERIES OF DEPOSITS

Many savers and investors make regular deposits. An *annuity* is a series of equal deposits or payments. To determine the future value of equal yearly savings deposits, use Exhibit 1–3B. For this table to be used, the deposits must earn a constant interest rate. If you deposit $50 a year at 7 percent for six years, starting at the end of the first year, you will have $357.65 at the end of that time ($50 × 7.153). The Figure It Out box on this page presents examples of using future value to achieve financial goals.

present value The current value for a future amount based on a certain interest rate and a certain time period; also referred to as *discounting.*

PRESENT VALUE OF A SINGLE AMOUNT

Another aspect of the time value of money involves determining the current value of an amount desired in the future. **Present value** is the current value for a future amount based on a certain interest rate and a certain time period. Present value computations, also called *discounting,* allow you to determine how much to deposit now to obtain a desired total in the future. Present value tables (Exhibit 1–3C) can be used to make the computations. If you want $1,000 five years from now and you earn 5 percent on your savings, you need to deposit $784 ($1,000 × 0.784). The present value of the amount you want in the future will always be less than the future value. Note that all of the factors in Exhibit 1–3C are less than 1 and interest earned will increase the present value amount to the desired future amount.

Did You Know?

Did you know each chapter contains several *did you know?* yellow "sticky-notes" containing fun facts, information, and financial planning assistance you can use in creating your personal financial plan?

From the Pages of . . . Kiplinger's Personal Finance

This one-page chapter feature presents an article from the well-known *Kiplinger's Personal Finance Magazine* related to a chapter topic. Each article presents a personal finance issue for you to debate and solve, using the questions at the bottom of the page. This is an excellent tool to develop critical thinking and writing skills!

An immigrant couple weigh alternate futures. By *Jeffrey R. Kosnett*

Pushing your FINANCIAL CLOCK ahead

For Sneha and Kaushal Joshi, New York City is nirvana. They love its energy and they have good jobs there. They've even circumvented the legendary housing crunch by buying a town-house in Jersey City, N.J., a quick train ride from their offices in Manhattan.

But the young couple also love India, where they were born and raised. They're thinking of resettling in Sneha's hometown of Bangalore or Kaushal's native Bombay in about six years. India's bright economy will surely offer opportunities for Sneha, 29, a credit analyst, and Kaushal, a 32-year-old IT consultant, both of whom have MBAs. But, Sneha says, if you're paid in rupees, "the earnings are not so great, even in our

professions." Their combined income of $130,000 would plunge.

But their expenses probably wouldn't. Western-style homes and conveniences in Indian cities are costly. Sneha and Kaushal also hope to start a family in a year or two and expect that their children will also attend American universities. So they're eager to accumulate as much money as possible while in the U.S. **Unusual "early retirement."** If the Joshis decide to return to India, they'll need to push their financial clocks ahead. The Joshis' position will be similar to that of a couple in their late 50s–the age at which you start to fret about losing the hefty paychecks.

Sneha and Kaushal are off to a good start. They have about

$100,000 in 401(k) savings and $40,000 in bank savings, mutual funds and a few stocks. They have $125,000 in equity in the New Jersey home and $20,000 in equity in a rental house in Bangalore. The Joshis say they can invest $4,500 a month on top of their 401(k) contributions. Because they are young, they'd normally be wise to place 90% in stocks and stock funds and keep bonds and cash to a minimum. But Sneha and Kaushal will need plenty of cash for the transition given the prospect of reduced income, says Doug Taylor, of Taylor Wealth Management, in Torrance, Cal. He advises them to amass at least $100,000 in a ladder of certificates of deposit.

If the Joshis earmark $2,500 a month for CDs, they can still

put $2,000 into growth investments. Time is short, so they should not be timid. They've begun investing in high-octane funds, such as CGM Focus and Bridgeway Aggressive Investors 2. To those solid choices they should add an international fund or two. Then, when the time comes, they could enroll in 529 college-savings plans.

In general, the couple should avoid new long-term obligations in the U.S. until they firm up their plans. They've thought about a larger house in New Jersey and whole life insurance. If they stay in the States, both could make sense. For now, the timing is wrong.

Source: Reprinted by permission from the June issue of *Kiplinger's Personal Finance.* Copyright © 2006 The Kiplinger Washington Editors, Inc.

1. What wise financial planning decisions are suggested by the actions of Sneha and Kaushal?

2. Describe actions you might take based on the financial planning activities of Sneha and Kaushal.

3. What information is available at www.kiplinger.com that might be of value when making personal financial decisions?

Concept Checks

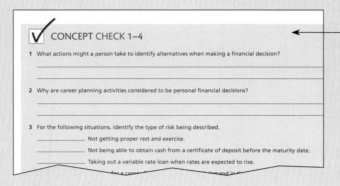

Concept Checks at the end of each numbered section provide fill-in-the-blank questions to help you assess your knowledge of the main ideas covered in that section. You'll know whether you have mastered the concepts and are ready to move on, or if you should stop and revisit certain topics.

Your Personal Financial Plan Sheet References

The integrated use of the *Your Personal Financial Plan* sheets is highlighted with an icon in the margin. This visual, near the text material needed to complete each worksheet, helps you better integrate this study resource into your learning process and continue to track your personal financial habits.

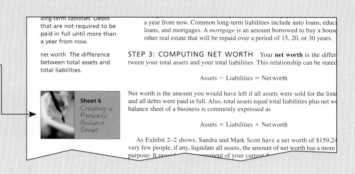

Apply Yourself!

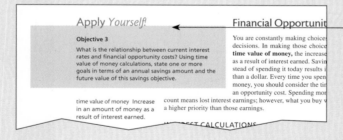

Boxed activities, listed by chapter objectives, ask you to perform activities that apply concepts learned to your life situations.

Exhibits and Tables

Throughout the text, exhibits and tables help to visually illustrate important personal finance concepts and processes.

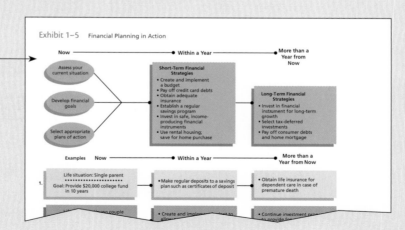

Personal Finance in Practice

› Selecting a Budgeting System

Although your checkbook will give you a fairly complete record of your expenses, it does not serve the purpose of planning for spending. A budget requires that you outline how you will spend available income. Described below are
budgeting systems. For each, list a benefit and concern of this method, and explain who might use this system.

Type of budgeting system	What are the benefits? What are the concerns?	Who might use this sy
A *mental budget* exists only in a person's mind. This simple system may be appropriate if you have limited resources and minimal financial responsibilities.		
A *physical budget* involves envelopes, folders, or containers to hold the money or slips of paper. Envelopes would contain the amount of cash or a note listing the amount to be used for "Food," "Rent," "Auto Payment," and other expenses.		
A *written budget* can be kept on notebook paper or on specialized budgeting paper available in office supply stores.		

...d budgeting systems use a ...

Personal Finance in Practice

These boxes offer information that
can assist you when faced with special
situations and unique financial planning
decisions. They challenge you to apply the
concepts you have learned to your life and
record personal responses.

Figure It Out!

This boxed feature presents a variety
of important mathematical applications
relevant to personal finance situations
and concepts.

Figure It Out!

› Ratios for Evaluating Financial Progress

Financial ratios provide guidelines for measuring the changes in your financial situation. These relationships can indicate
progress toward an improved financial position.

Ratio	Calculation	Example	Interpretation
Debt ratio	Liabilities divided by net worth	$25,000/$50,000 = 0.5	Shows relationship between debt and net worth; a low debt ratio is best.
Current ratio	Liquid assets divided by current liabilities	$4,000/$2,000 = 2	Indicates $2 in liquid assets for every $1 of current liabilities; a high current ratio is desirable to have cash available to pay bills.
Liquidity ratio	Liquid assets divided by monthly expenses	$10,000/$4,000 = 2.5	Indicates the number of months in which living expenses can be paid if an emergency arises; a high liquidity ratio is desirable.
Debt-payments ratio	Monthly credit payments divided by take-home pay	$540/$3,600 = 0.15	Indicates how much of a person's earnings goes for debt payments (excluding a home mortgage); most financial advisers recommend a debt/payments ratio of less than 20 percent.
Savings ratio	Amount saved each month divided by gross income	$648/$5,400 = 0.12	Financial experts recommend monthly savings of at least 10 percent.

Annotated Web Links

Web sites that are relevant to a section or
concept in the text are presented in the
margins.

increase based on a certain
interest rate and a certain
time period; also referred to
as *compounding*.

*Key Web Sites for Time Value
of Money*

www.moneychimp.com/
calculator
www.rbccentura.com/tools
www.dinkytown.net

deposited in a 6 percent account for one year will grow to $106. This amount is com-
puted as follows:

$$\text{Future value} = \$100 + (\$100 \times 0.06 \times 1 \text{ year}) = \$106$$

Original amount   Amount of
in savings   interest earned

The same process could be continued for a second, third, and fourth year, but the
computations would be time-consuming. Future value tables simplify the process (see
Exhibit 1–3). To use a future value table, multiply the amount deposited by the factor
for the desired interest rate and time period. For example, $650 at 8 percent for 10 years
would have a future value of $1,403.35 ($650 × 2.159). The future value of an amount
will always be greater than the original amount. As Exhibit 1–3A shows, all the future
value factors are larger than 1. Future value computations may be referred to as *compounding*, since interest is earned on previously earned interest. Compounding allows
the future value of a deposit to grow faster than it would if interest were paid only on
the original deposit.

back to Getting Personal

1. Reconsider your responses to the Getting Personal questions at the beginning of the chapter. What did you learn in this chapter that might affect your answers to these questions in the future?

   _____

   _____

2. List one of your personal financial goals for the next few months or years.

   _____

   _____

3. Describe how the three main financial statements from this chapter could be used to (a) achieve the financial goal you stated above, and (b) improve your daily money management activities.

Financial Statement Use	Balance Sheet	Cash Flow Statement	Budget
a. How could each financial statement be used to achieve your personal financial goal?			
b. How could your daily money management activities be improved with information from these financial statements?			

Chapter Summary

Objective 1 Successful money management requires a coordination of personal financial records, personal financial statements, and budgeting activities. An organized system of financial records and documents should provide ease of access as well as security for financial documents that may be impossible to replace.

Objective 2 A personal balance sheet, also known as a *net worth statement*, is prepared by listing all items of value (assets) and all amounts owed to others (liabilities). The difference between your total assets and your total liabilities is your net worth. A cash flow statement, also called a *personal income and expenditure statement*, is a summary of cash receipts and payments for a given period, such as a month or a year.

Objective 3 The budgeting process consists of seven steps: (1) set financial goals; (2) estimate income; (3) budget an emergency fund and savings; (4) budget fixed expenses; (5) budget variable expenses; (6) record spending amounts; and (7) review spending and saving patterns.

Objective 4 The relationship among the personal balance sheet, cash flow statement, and budget provides the basis for achieving long-term financial security. Future value and present value calculations may be used to compute the increased value of savings for achieving financial goals.

Back to Getting Personal

Now, what would you do differently? At the end of each chapter, you are asked to revisit your initial responses to the chapter opening self-assessment, *Getting Personal*. Having read the chapter, you are now challenged to rethink your personal financial habits and record what you'd do differently and why.

iPod Content

At the end of each chapter, this icon indicates that various study tools are available in iPod format. Don't have an iPod? You can still use the tools on your PC. See www.mhhe.com/kdh for more information.

Chapter Summary

Organized by chapter objective, this concise summary of each chapter is a great study and self-assessment tool, located conveniently at the end of chapters.

Problems

A variety of problems that allow you to put your quantitative analysis of personal financial decisions for each chapter to work in the spaces provided!

Key Terms

adult life cycle 4	future value 12	present value 14
bankruptcy 8	inflation 6	time value of money 12
economics 4	opportunity cost 11	values 4
financial plan 3	personal financial planning 3	

Problems

(Note: Some of these problems require the use of the time value of money tables in the chapter appendix.)

1. Using the rule of 72, approximate the following amounts.
   a. If the value of land in an area is increasing 6 percent a year, how long will it take for property values to double?

   b. If you earn 10 percent on your investments, how long will it take for your money to double?

   c. At an annual interest rate of 5 percent, how long will it take for your savings to double?

2. In the early 2000s, selected automobiles had an average cost of $15,000. The average cost of those same automobiles is now $18,000. What was the rate of increase for these automobiles between the two time periods?

$34,000 a year for living expenses. If ___ increase by 4 percent a year for the next ___

Questions

1. In your opinion, what is the main benefit of wise financial planning?

2. What factors in an economy might affect the level of interest rates?

3. Describe risks that you might encounter when making financial decisions over the next few years.

4. What are possible drawbacks associated with seeking advice from a financial planning professional? How might these concerns be minimized?

5. Talk with several people about their career choices. How have their employment situations affected their financial planning activities?

Internet Connection

RESEARCHING ECONOMIC CONDITIONS AFFECTING FINANCIAL DECISIONS

For these two major economic indicators: (1) obtain current information and (2) determine how the current trend might affect your future financial planning activities.

Inflation Web sources

1. Current findings:

2. Possible influence on your financial decisions

Interest Rates Web sources

1. Current findings:

2. Possible influence on your financial decisions

www.mhhe.com/kdh

Questions

A set of questions that tests your qualitative analysis of personal finance.

Internet Connection

This end-of-chapter Web exercise asks you to apply concepts just learned to real-life situations and institutions by surfing the Web. Directions are given to help guide the way, and spaces are provided to record your findings for reference or for a class project.

Case in Point

You are given a hypothetical personal finance dilemma and data to work through to practice concepts just learned from a chapter. A series of questions reinforces your successful mastery and application of these chapter topics!

Continuing Case

This feature allows students to apply course concepts in a life situation. This feature encourages students to evaluate the changes that affect a family and then respond to the resulting shift in needs, resources, and priorities through the questions at the end of each case.

Case in Point

STUCK IN THE MIDDLE

Until recently, Fran and Ed Blake's personal finances ran smoothly. Both had well-paying jobs while raising two children. The Blakes have a daughter who is completing her freshman year of college and a son three years younger. Currently they have $22,000 in various savings and investment funds set aside for the children's education. With education costs increasing faster than inflation, they are uncertain whether this amount is adequate.

In recent months, Fran's mother has required extensive medical attention and personal care assistance. Unable to live alone, she is now a resident of a long-term care facility. The cost of this service is $2,650 a month, with annual increases of about 4 percent. While a major portion of the cost is covered by her Social Security and pension, Fran's mother is unable to cover the entire cost. Their desire to help adds to the Blakes' financial burden.

The Blakes are like millions of other Americans who have financial responsibilities for both dependent children and aging parents. Commonly referred to as the "sandwich generation," this group is squeezed on one side by the cost of raising and educating children and on the other side by the financial demands of caring for aging parents.

Finally, the Blakes, ages 47 and 43, are als saving for their own retirement. While they made annual deposits to a retirement fund, va cial demands may force them to access some

Questions

1. What actions have the Blakes taken that ered wise financial planning choices?

2. What actions might be appropriate to ad faced by the Blake household?

3. Conduct an Internet search to obtain addi that might be of value to the Blakes.

Continuing Case

GETTING STARTED

Life Situation
Single
Age 22
Starting a career
No dependents

Financial Data
Monthly income $2,600
Living expenses $2,180
Assets $8,200
Liabilities $3,470
Emergency fund $530

While in college, Pam Jenkins worked part-time and was never concerned about long-term financial planning. Rat budget, she used her checkbook and savings account (which usually had a very low balance) to handle her financia

After completing college, Pam began her career as a sales representative for a clothing manufacturer located i one year, her assets consist of a 1999 automobile, a television set, some electronic entertainment equipment, and personal belongs, with a total value of about $8,200.

www.mhhe.com/kdh

Video Case

In connection with the BusinessWeek videos, a Video Case at the end of every chapter builds upon a particular topic and provides questions to support how it relates to chapter concepts.

Daily Spending Diary

At the end of each chapter a series of questions asks you to analyze your individual spending diary sheets (see Appendix C.)

Your Personal Financial Plan Sheets

Listed at the beginning of each chapter and with in-text icons, at the end of each chapter are several worksheets—each asking you to work through the application and record your own personal financial plan answers. These sheets apply concepts learned to your personal situation and serve as a roadmap to your personal financial future. Fill them out, rip them out, submit them for homework, and keep them filed in a safe spot for future reference!

Also, key Web sites are given to help you devise your personal financial plan, and the "What's Next for Your Personal Financial Plan?" section at the end of each sheet challenges you to use your responses to plan the next level, as well as foreshadowing upcoming concepts.

Comprehensive Teaching and Learning Package

INSTRUCTOR SUPPLEMENTS

Instructor's CD-ROM ISBN 0073282065

Keep all the supplements in one place! This CD contains all the necessary supplements—Instructor's Manual, Solutions, Test Bank, Computerized Test Bank, and Power-Point—all in one useful product in an electronic format.

- **Instructor's Manual (IM)** Created by the authors, the *Instructor's Manual* includes a "Course Planning Guide" with instructional strategies, course projects, supplementary resource lists and sample syllabi. The "Chapter Teaching Materials" section of the Instructor's Manual provides a chapter overview, the chapter objectives with summaries, introductory activities, and detailed lecture outlines with teaching suggestions.

  This section also includes concluding activities, ready-to-duplicate quizzes, supplementary lecture materials and activities, and answers to concept checks, end-of-chapter questions and problems and cases. A print version of the Instructor's Manual 0073282057 is also available through your McGraw-Hill/Irwin representative.

- **Test Bank** The *Test Bank,* also created by the authors, consists of approximately 2,000 multiple-choice, true-false, and essay questions. These test items are organized by the objectives for each chapter. This resource also includes answers, text page references, and an indication of difficulty level.

- **Computerized Test Bank (Windows)** Create your own tests in a snap! The Test Bank questions are also in McGraw-Hill's EZ Test testing software to quickly create customized exams. This user-friendly program allows instructors to sort questions by format; edit existing questions or add new ones; and scramble questions for multiple versions of the same test.

- **PowerPoint Presentation** Created by Samira Hussein, Johnson County Community College, it offers more than 350 visual presentations that may be edited and manipulated to fit a particular course format.

Video (DVD Format) ISBN 007328209X

New videos by BusinessWeek! Each 5–10 minute video highlights issues relevant to today's personal finance student, showcasing real-world application. Topics include taxes, consumer credit, insurance and investing.

Assurance of Learning

Many educational institutions today are focused on the notion of assurance of learning, an important element of some accreditation standards. *Focus on Personal Finance* is designed specifically to support your assurance of learning initiatives with a simple, yet powerful, solution.

Each test bank question for *Focus on Personal Finance* maps to a specific chapter learning outcome/objective listed in the text. You can use the test bank software to easily query for learning outcomes/objectives that directly relate to the learning objectives for your course. You can then use the reporting features of the software to aggregate student results in similar fashion, making the collection and presentation of assurance of learning data simple and easy.

The Online Learning Center (OLC) contains FREE access to additional Web-based study and teaching aids created for this text, such as:

- **Student Support** A great resource for those seeking additional practice, students can access self-grading quizzes, electronic flashcards, self-study software, Web Exercises, Your Personal Financial Plan sheets in Excel format, and much more to help master the fundamentals of personal finance!
- **Teaching Support** Along with having access to all of the same material your students can view on the book's OLC, you also have password protected access to the Instructor's Manual, solutions to end-of-chapter problems, and Instructor's PowerPoint.

Enhanced Cartridges

Enhanced WebCT and Blackboard course cartridges allow instructors to manage their course and administer online examinations. Some of the new features include:

- **Narrated PowerPoint** Each chapter's slides follow the chapter topics and provide steps and explanations for how to solve those topics using real-life examples. Knowing that each student learns differently, a quick click on each slide and the slide will "talk through" its contents with students! Students can view these slides via computer or download them onto their video iPod (see details below).
- **iPod Content** Harness the power of one of the most popular technology tools students use today, the Apple iPod® Our innovative approach enables students to download Narrated PowerPoints and quizzes right into their iPod and take learning materials with them wherever they go. This makes review and study time as easy as putting on headphones!
- **Chapter Overviews** Concise recap of what students should learn from each chapter. A great reading prep assignment.
- **Pretest and Posttest Question Banks** Administer comprehensive and chapter-specific pretest and posttests to evaluate student understanding.
- **Online Glossary** Key terms and their definitions in a ready to use format. Distribute to students for a study tool, or mix and match to create a quiz.

Ask your McGraw-Hill representative for more details about Enhanced Cartridges today!

McGraw-Hill's Homework Manager and Homework Manager Plus™

Are you looking for a way to spend less time grading and to have more flexibility with the problems you assign as homework and tests? McGraw-Hill's Homework Manager is an exciting package option developed for this text! Homework Manager is a Web-based tool for instructors and students for delivering, answering, and grading end-of-chapter problems and tests, and providing a limitless supply of self-graded practice for students.

Applicable end-of-chapter Questions and Problems are loaded into Homework Manager, and instructors can choose to assign the exact problems as stated in the book, or algorithmic versions of them so each student has a unique set of variables for the problems. You create the assignments and control parameters such as do you want your students to receive hints, is this a graded assignment or practice, etc. The test bank is also available in Homework Manager, giving you the ability to use those questions for online tests. Both the problems and the tests are automatically graded and the results are stored in a private grade book, which is created when you set up your class. Detailed results let you see at a glance how each student does on an assignment or an individual problem—you can even see how many tries it took them to solve it. If you order this special package, students will receive a Homework Manager User's Guide and an access code packaged with their text.

There is also an enhanced version of McGraw-Hill's Homework Manager through the Homework Manager Plus package option. If you order the text packaged with Homework Manager Plus, your students will receive Homework Manager as described above, but with an integrated online text included. When students are in Homework Manager and need more help to solve a problem, there will be a link that takes them to the section of the text online that explains the concept they are struggling with. All of McGraw-Hill's media assets, such as videos, narrated lectures, and additional online quizzing, are also integrated at the appropriate places of the online text to provide students with a full learning experience. If you order this special package, students will receive the Homework Manager Plus card packaged with their text, which gives them access to all of these products.

McGraw-Hill's Homework Manager is powered by Brownstone.

Thank You!

We express our deepest appreciation for the efforts of the colleagues who provided extensive comments that helped to shape and create this text and contributed to the quality of the book you are using.

Chris A. Austin, *Normandale Community College*
Gail H. Austin, *Rose State College*
Tom Bilyeu, *Southwestern Illinois College*
Ross Blankenship, *State Fair Community College*
William F. Blosel, *California University of Pennsylvania*
John Bockino, *Suffolk County Community College*
Karen Bonding, *University of Virginia*
Jennifer Brewer, *Butler County Community College*
Peg Camp, *University of Nebraska–Kearney*
Stephen Chambers, *Johnson County Community College*
It-Keong Chew, *University of Kentucky*
Julie Douthit, *Abilene Christian University*
Bill Dowling, *Savannah State University*
Dorsey Dyer, *Davidson County Community College*
John D. Farlin, *Ohio Dominican University*
Garry Fleming, *Roanoke College*
Paula G. Freston, *Merced College*
Robert Friederichs, *Alexandria Technical College*
Caroline S. Fulmer, *University of Alabama*
Dwight Giles, *Jefferson State Community College*
Michael Gordinier, *Washington University*
Shari Gowers, *Dixie State College*
Michael P. Griffin, *University of Massachusetts–Dartmouth*
Ward Hooker, *Orangeburg–Calhoun Tech College*
Ishappa S. Hullur, *Morehead State University*
Samira Hussein, *Johnson County Community College*
Dorothy W. Jones, *Northwestern State University*
Jeanette Klosterman, *Hutchinson Community College*
Robert Kozub, *University of Wisconsin–Milwaukee*
Margo Kraft, *Heidelberg College*
John Ledgerwood, *Bethune-Cookman College*
Richard "Lee" Kitchen, *Tallahassee Community College*
Marc LeFebvre, *Creighton University*
Nolan Lickey, *Utah Valley State College*
Joseph T. Marchese, *Monroe Community College*

Kenneth L. Mark, *Kansas City Kansas Community College*
Paul S. Marshall, *Widener University*
Jennifer Morton, *Ivy Tech Community College of Indiana*
Allan O'Bryan, *Rochester Community & Tech College*
Carl Parker, *Fort Hays State University*
David M. Payne, *Ohio University*
Aaron Phillips, *California State University–Bakersfield*
Padmaja Pillutla, *Western Illinois University*
Brenda Rice, *Ozarks Technical Community College*
Carla Rich, *Pensacola Junior College*
John Roberts, *Florida Metropolitan University*
Sammie Root, *Texas State University–San Marcos*
Joan Ryan, *Clackamas Community College*
Tim Samolis, *Pittsburgh Technical Institute*
Steven R. Scheff, *Florida Gulf Coast University*
James T. Schiermeyer, *Texas Tech University*
Joseph Simon, *Casper College*
Vernon Stauble, *San Bernardino Valley College*
Lea Timpler, *College of the Canyons*
Dick Verrone, *University of North Carolina–Wilmington*
Randall Wade, *Rogue Community College*
Kent Weilage, *McCook Community College*
Sally Wells, *Columbia College*
Micheline West, *New Hampshire Tech*
Bob Willis, *Rogers State University*
Glen Wood, *Broome Community College*

Many talented professionals at McGraw-Hill/Irwin have contributed to the development of *Focus on Personal Finance.* We are especially grateful to Michele Janicek, Elizabeth Hughes, Jennifer Rizzi, Mary Conzachi, and Cara David.

In addition, Jack Kapoor expresses special appreciation to Theresa and Dave Kapoor, Kathryn Thumme, and Karen Tucker for their typing, proofreading, and research assistance. Finally, we thank our wives and families for their patience, understanding, encouragement, and love throughout this project.

Contents

Appendix

Focus on Personal Finance

*An Active Approach to Help You Develop
Successful Financial Skills*

SECOND EDITION

1 Personal Financial Planning in Action

Getting Personal

What are your money habits? For each of the following statements, select "yes" or "no" to indicate your behavior regarding these financial planning activities:

	Yes	No
1. I usually have enough money for the things I need.	⎯⎯	⎯⎯
2. I owe less money today than I owed a year or two ago.	⎯⎯	⎯⎯
3. My financial goals for the next year are written down.	⎯⎯	⎯⎯
4. When making major financial decisions, I research them using a variety of information sources.	⎯⎯	⎯⎯
5. I am aware of various risks that can affect personal financial decisions.	⎯⎯	⎯⎯

After studying this chapter, you will be asked to reconsider your responses to these items.

Your Personal Financial Plan Sheets

1. Personal financial data.
2. Setting personal financial goals.
3. Achieving financial goals using time value of money.
4. Planning your career.

Objectives

In this chapter, you will learn to:

1. Identify social and economic influences on personal financial goals and decisions.
2. Develop personal financial goals.
3. Assess personal and financial opportunity costs associated with financial decisions.
4. Implement a plan for making personal financial and career decisions.

Why is this important?

Each year, more than a million people declare bankruptcy, and Americans lose more than $1.2 billion in fraudulent investments. Both of these common difficulties result from poor personal financial planning. Your ability to make wise money decisions is a foundation for your current and long-term well-being.

Making Financial Decisions

OBJECTIVE 1
Identify social and economic influences on personal financial goals and decisions.

Money is a constant topic of conversation in our society. People everywhere talk about money.

Most people want to handle their finances so that they get full satisfaction from each available dollar. Typical financial goals may include buying a new car or a larger home, pursuing advanced career training, contributing to charity, traveling extensively, and ensuring self-sufficiency during working and retirement years. To achieve these and other goals, people need to identify and set priorities. Financial and personal satisfaction are the result of an organized process that is commonly referred to as *personal money management* or *personal financial planning*.

Your Life Situation and Financial Planning

personal financial planning The process of managing your money to achieve personal economic satisfaction.

financial plan A formalized report that summarizes your current financial situation, analyzes your financial needs, and recommends future financial activities.

Personal financial planning is the process of managing your money to achieve personal economic satisfaction. This planning process allows you to control your financial situation. Every person, family, or household has a unique situation; therefore, financial decisions must be planned to meet specific needs and goals.

A comprehensive financial plan can enhance the quality of your life and increase your satisfaction by reducing uncertainty about your future needs and resources. A **financial plan** is a formalized report that summarizes your current financial situation, analyzes your financial needs, and recommends future financial activities. You can create this document on your own (by using the sheets at the end of each chapter) or you can seek assistance from a financial planner or use a money management software package.

Some of the advantages of personal financial planning include

- Increased effectiveness in obtaining, using, and protecting your financial resources throughout your life.
- Increased control of your financial affairs by avoiding excessive debt, bankruptcy, and dependence on others.
- Improved personal relationships resulting from well-planned and effectively communicated financial decisions.
- A sense of freedom from financial worries obtained by looking to the future, anticipating expenses, and achieving personal economic goals.

Many factors influence daily financial decisions, ranging from age and household size to interest rates and inflation. People in their 20s spend money differently from those in their 50s. Personal factors such as age, income, household size, and personal beliefs influence your spending and saving patterns. Your life situation or lifestyle is created by a combination of factors.

As our society changes, different types of financial needs evolve. Today people tend to get married at a later age, and more households have two incomes. Many households are headed by single parents. More than 2 million women provide care for both dependent children and parents. We are also living longer; over 80 percent of all Americans now living are expected to live past age 65.

adult life cycle The stages in the family situation and financial needs of an adult.

As Exhibit 1–1 shows, the **adult life cycle**—the stages in the family and financial needs of an adult—is an important influence on your financial activities and decisions. Your life situation is also affected by events such as graduation, dependent children leaving home, changes in health, engagement and marriage, divorce, birth or adoption of a child, retirement, a career change or a move to new area, or the death of a spouse, family member, or other dependent.

values Ideas and principles that a person considers correct, desirable, and important.

In addition to being defined by your family situation, you are defined by your **values**—the ideas and principles that you consider correct, desirable, and important. Values have a direct influence on such decisions as spending now versus saving for the future or continuing school versus getting a job.

Financial Planning in Our Economy

economics The study of how wealth is created and distributed.

Daily economic activities have a strong influence on financial planning. **Economics** is the study of how wealth is created and distributed. The economic environment includes various institutions, principally business, labor, and government, that work together to satisfy our needs and wants.

Apply *Yourself!*

Objective 1

Using Web research and discussion with others, calculate the inflation rate that reflects the change in price for items frequently bought by you and your family.

While various government agencies regulate financial activities, the Federal Reserve System, our nation's central bank, has significant responsibility in our economy. *The Fed,* as it is called, is concerned with maintaining an adequate money supply. It achieves this by influencing borrowing, interest rates, and the buying or selling of government securities. The Fed attempts to make adequate funds available for consumer spending and business expansion while keeping interest rates and consumer prices at an appropriate level.

GLOBAL INFLUENCES   The global economy can influence financial activities. The U.S. economy is affected by both foreign investors and competition from foreign companies. American businesses compete against foreign companies for the spending dollars of American consumers. When the level of exports of U.S.-made goods is

Exhibit 1–1   Financial Planning Influences, Goals, and Activities

Life Situation Factors Affect Financial Planning Activities

Age	Marital Status	Number and Age of Household Members	Employment Situation
• 18–24 • 25–34 • 35–44 • 45–54 • 55–64 • 65 and over	• single • married • separated/divorced • widowed	• no other household members • preschool children • elementary and secondary school children • college students • dependent adults • nondependent adults	• full-time student • not employed • full-time employment or volunteer work • part-time employment or volunteer work

COMMON FINANCIAL GOALS AND ACTIVITIES

- Obtain appropriate career training.
- Create an effective financial recordkeeping system.
- Develop a regular savings and investment program.
- Accumulate an appropriate emergency fund.
- Purchase appropriate types and amounts of insurance coverage.
- Create and implement a flexible budget.
- Evaluate and select appropriate investments.
- Establish and implement a plan for retirement goals.
- Make a will and develop an estate plan.

Life Situation	Specialized Financial Activities
Young, single (18–35)	• Establish financial independence. • Obtain disability insurance to replace income during prolonged illness. • Consider home purchase for tax benefit.
Young couple with children under 18	• Carefully manage the increased need for the use of credit. • Obtain an appropriate amount of life insurance for the care of dependents. • Use a will to name guardian for children.
Single parent with children under 18	• Obtain adequate amounts of health, life, and disability insurance. • Contribute to savings and investment fund for college. • Name a guardian for children and make other estate plans.
Young dual-income couple, no children	• Coordinate insurance coverage and other benefits. • Develop savings and investment program for changes in life situation (larger house, children). • Consider tax-deferred contributions to retirement fund.
Older couple (+50), no dependent children at home	• Consolidate financial assets and review estate plans. • Obtain health insurance for postretirement period. • Plan retirement housing, living expenses, recreational activities, and part-time work.
Mixed-generation household (elderly individuals and children under 18)	• Obtain long-term health care insurance and life/disability income for care of younger dependents. • Use dependent care service if needed. • Provide arrangements for handling finances of elderly if they become ill. • Consider splitting of investment cost, with elderly getting income while alive and principal going to surviving relatives.
Older (+50), single	• Arrange for long-term health care coverage. • Review will and estate plan. • Plan retirement living facilities, living expenses, and activities.

Key Web Sites for Global Business
www.businessweek.com/
globalbiz
www.globalfinancialdata.com

inflation A rise in the general level of prices.

lower than the level of imported goods, more U.S. dollars leave the country than the dollar value of foreign currency coming into the United States. This reduces the funds available for domestic spending and investment. Also, if foreign companies decide not to invest in the United States, the domestic money supply is reduced. This reduced money supply can cause higher interest rates.

INFLATION   Most people are concerned with the buying power of their money. **Inflation** is a rise in the general level of prices. In times of inflation, the buying power of the dollar decreases. For example, if prices increased 5 percent during the last year, items that cost $100 then would now cost $105. This means it now takes more money to buy the same amount of goods and services.

Inflation is most harmful to people living on fixed incomes. Due to inflation, retired people and others whose incomes do not change are able to afford fewer goods and services. Inflation can also adversely affect lenders of money. Unless an adequate interest rate is charged, amounts repaid by borrowers in times of inflation have less buying power than the money they borrowed.

Inflation rates vary. During the late 1950s and early 1960s, the annual inflation rate was in the 1 to 3 percent range. During the late 1970s and early 1980s, the cost of living increased 10 to 12 percent annually. At a 12 percent annual inflation rate, prices double (and the value of the dollar is cut in half) in about six years. To find out how fast prices (or your savings) will double, use the *rule of 72:* Just divide 72 by the annual inflation (or interest) rate.

EXAMPLE: RULE OF 72

An annual inflation rate of 4 percent, for example, means prices will double in 18 years (72 ÷ 4 = 18). Regarding savings, if you earn 6 percent, your money will double in 12 years (72 ÷ 6 = 12).

---

did you know?

Consumer prices can change by very significant amounts over time. The general price level in the United States between 1970 and 1980 nearly doubled. However, between 1990 and 2000, average consumer prices rose about 34 percent.

More recently, the reported annual price increase for goods and services as measured by the consumer price index has been in the 2 to 4 percent range. The *consumer price index (CPI),* computed and published by the Bureau of Labor Statistics, is a measure of the average change in the prices urban consumers pay for a fixed "basket" of goods and services.

Inflation rates can be deceptive since the index is based on items calculated in a predetermined manner. Many people face *hidden* inflation since the cost of necessities (food, gas, health care), on which they spend the greatest proportion of their money, may rise at a higher rate than nonessential items, which could be dropping in price. This results in a reported inflation rate much lower than the actual cost-of-living increase being experienced by consumers.

INTEREST RATES   In simple terms, interest rates represent the cost of money. Like everything else, money has a price. The forces of supply and demand influence interest rates. When consumer saving and investing increase the supply of money, interest rates tend to decrease. However, as borrowing by consumers, businesses, and government increases, interest rates are likely to rise.

Interest rates can have a major effect on financial planning. The earnings you receive as a saver or an investor reflect current interest rates as well as a *risk premium* based on such factors as the length of time your funds will be used by others, expected inflation, and the extent of uncertainty about getting your money back. Risk is also a factor in the interest rate you pay as a borrower. People with poor credit ratings pay a higher interest rate than people with good credit ratings. Interest rates influence many financial decisions.

Financial Planning Activities

To achieve a successful financial situation, you must coordinate various components through an organized plan and wise decision making. Exhibit 1–2 presents an overview of the eight major personal financial planning areas.

OBTAINING   You obtain financial resources from employment, investments, or ownership of a business. Obtaining financial resources is the foundation of financial planning, since these resources are used for all financial activities.

PLANNING   Planned spending through budgeting is the key to achieving goals and future financial security. Efforts to anticipate expenses along with making certain financial decisions can help reduce taxes.

SAVING   Long-term financial security starts with a regular savings plan for emergencies, unexpected bills, replacement of major items, and the purchase of special goods

Key Web Sites for Economic Conditions
www.westegg.com/inflation
www.bls.gov
www.federalreserve.gov
www.bloomberg.com

Key Web Sites for Obtaining
www.rileyguide.com
www.monster.com

Key Web Sites for Planning
www.americasaves.org
www.irs.gov

Key Web Sites for Savings
www.bankrate.com
www.fdic.gov

Exhibit 1–2   Components of Personal Financial Planning

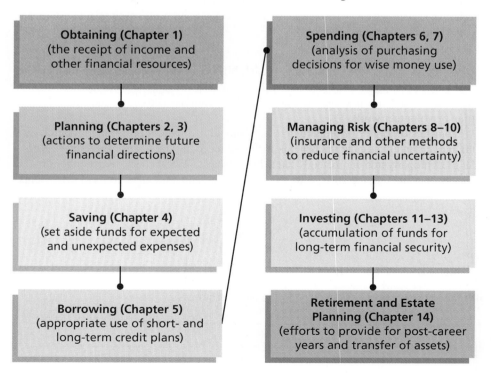

Obtaining (Chapter 1)
(the receipt of income and other financial resources)

Planning (Chapters 2, 3)
(actions to determine future financial directions)

Saving (Chapter 4)
(set aside funds for expected and unexpected expenses)

Borrowing (Chapter 5)
(appropriate use of short- and long-term credit plans)

Spending (Chapters 6, 7)
(analysis of purchasing decisions for wise money use)

Managing Risk (Chapters 8–10)
(insurance and other methods to reduce financial uncertainty)

Investing (Chapters 11–13)
(accumulation of funds for long-term financial security)

Retirement and Estate Planning (Chapter 14)
(efforts to provide for post-career years and transfer of assets)

and services, such as a college education, a boat, or a vacation home. Once you have established a basic savings plan, you may use additional money for investments that offer greater financial growth.

Key Web Sites for Borrowing

www.finance-center.com

www.debtadvice.com

bankruptcy A set of federal laws allowing you to either restructure your debts or remove certain debts.

BORROWING   Maintaining control over your credit-buying habits will contribute to your financial goals. The overuse and misuse of credit may cause a situation in which a person's debts far exceed the resources available to pay those debts. **Bankruptcy** is a set of federal laws allowing you to either restructure your debts or remove certain debts. The people who declare bankruptcy each year may have avoided this trauma with wise spending and borrowing decisions. Chapter 5 discusses bankruptcy in detail.

Key Web Sites for Spending

www.consumer.gov

www.autoweb.com

SPENDING   Financial planning is designed not to prevent your enjoyment of life but to help you obtain the items you want. Too often, however, people make purchases without considering the financial consequences. Some people shop compulsively, creating financial difficulties. You should detail your living expenses and your other financial obligations in a spending plan. Spending less than you earn is the only way to achieve long-term financial security.

Key Web Sites for Managing Risk

www.insure.com

www.insweb.com

MANAGING RISK   Adequate insurance coverage is another component of personal financial planning. Certain types of insurance are commonly overlooked in financial plans. For example, the number of people who suffer disabling injuries or diseases at age 50 is greater than the number who die at that age, so people may need disability insurance more than they need life insurance. Yet surveys reveal that most people have adequate life insurance but few have needed disability insurance.

Key Web Sites for Investing

www.fool.com

www.cbsmarketwatch.com

INVESTING   Although many types of investments are available, people invest for two primary reasons. Those interested in *current income* select investments that pay regular dividends or interest. In contrast, investors who desire *long-term growth* choose stocks, mutual funds, real estate, and other investments with potential for increased value in the future. You can achieve investment diversification by including a variety of assets in your *portfolio*—these may include stocks, bond mutual funds, real estate, and collectibles such as rare coins.

Key Web Sites for Retirement and Estate Planning

www.ssa.gov

www.aarp.org/financial/

RETIREMENT AND ESTATE PLANNING   Most people desire financial security upon completion of full-time employment. But retirement planning also involves thinking about your housing situation, your recreational activities, and possible part-time or volunteer work.

Transfers of money or property to others should be timed, if possible, to minimize the tax burden and maximize the benefits for those receiving the financial resources. Knowledge of property transfer methods can help you select the best course of action for funding current and future living costs, educational expenses, and retirement needs of dependents.

Sheet 1
Personal Financial Data

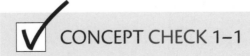

✓ CONCEPT CHECK 1–1

1 What personal and economic factors commonly affect personal financial decisions?

2 For each of the following situations, indicate if the person would tend to "suffer" or tend to "benefit" from inflation. (Circle your answer)

A person with money in a savings account.   suffer   benefit

A person who is borrowing money.   suffer   benefit

A person who is lending money.   suffer   benefit

A person receiving a fixed income amount.   suffer   benefit

3 Listed here are the eight main components of personal financial planning. Circle one or more areas and describe an action that you might need to take in the next few months or years.

1. Obtaining 2. Planning 3. Saving 4. Borrowing		5. Spending 6. Managing risk 7. Investing 8. Retirement estate planning	

Developing and Achieving Financial Goals

Why do so many Americans—living in one of the richest countries in the world—have money problems? The answer can be found in two main factors. The first is poor planning and weak money management habits in areas such as spending and the use of credit. The other factor is extensive advertising, selling efforts, and product availability that encourage overbuying. Achieving personal financial satisfaction starts with clear financial goals.

> **OBJECTIVE 2**
> Develop personal financial goals.

Types of Financial Goals

What would you like to do tomorrow? Believe it or not, that question involves goal setting, which may be viewed in three time frames:

- *Short-term goals* will be achieved within the next year or so, such as saving for a vacation or paying off small debts.
- *Intermediate goals* have a time frame of two to five years.
- *Long-term goals* involve financial plans that are more than five years off, such as retirement, money for children's college education, or the purchase of a vacation home.

Long-term goals should be planned in coordination with short-term and intermediate goals. Setting and achieving short-term goals is commonly the basis for moving toward success of long-term goals. For example, saving for a down payment to buy a house is a short-term goal that can be a foundation for a long-term goal: owning your own home.

Apply *Yourself!*

Objective 2

Ask friends, relatives, and others about their short-term and long-term financial goals. What are some of the common goals for various personal situations?

Personal Finance in Practice

› Creating Financial Goals

Based on your current situation or expectations for the future, create two financial goals—one short-term and one long-term—using the following guidelines:

Goal-setting Actions	Short-term Goal	Long-term Goal
Step 1. Create realistic goals based on your life situation.		
Step 2. State your goals in specific, measurable terms.		
Step 3. Describe the time frame for accomplishing your goals.		
Step 4. Indicate an action to be taken to achieve your goals.		

A goal of obtaining increased career training is different from a goal of saving money to pay a semiannual auto insurance premium. *Consumable-product goals* usually occur on a periodic basis and involve items that are used up relatively quickly, such as food, clothing, and entertainment. *Durable-product goals* usually involve infrequently purchased, expensive items such as appliances, cars, and sporting equipment; these consist of tangible items. In contrast, many people overlook *intangible-purchase goals*. These goals may relate to personal relationships, health, education, community service, and leisure.

Goal-Setting Guidelines

An old saying goes, "If you don't know where you're going, you might end up somewhere else and not even know it." Goal setting is central to financial decision making. Your financial goals are the basis for planning, implementing, and measuring the progress of your spending, saving, and investing activities. Exhibit 1–1 on page 5 offers typical goals and financial activities for various life situations.

Effective financial goals should be:

- *Realistic,* based on your income and life situation. For example, if you are a full-time student, expecting to buy a new car each year is probably not realistic.
- *Stated in specific, measurable terms,* since having exact goals will help you create a plan to achieve them. For example, the goal of "accumulating $5,000 in an investment fund within three years" is a clearer guide to planning than the goal of "putting money into an investment fund."

CAUTION!

A survey conducted by the Consumer Federation of America (CFA) estimates that over 60 million American households will probably fail to realize one or more of their major life goals largely due to a lack of a comprehensive financial plan. In households with annual incomes of less than $100,000, savers who say they have financial plans report about twice as much savings and investments as savers without plans.

- *Based on a time frame,* such as a goal to be achieved in three years. A time frame helps you measure your progress toward your financial goals.
- *Action oriented,* because your financial goals are the basis for the various financial activities you will undertake. For example, "reducing credit card debt" will likely mean a decreased use of credit.

Sheet 2
Setting Personal Financial Goals

✓ CONCEPT CHECK 1–2

1 What are some examples of long-term goals?

_____

_____

2 What are the main characteristics of useful financial goals?

_____

_____

3 Match the following common goals to the life situation of the people listed.

a. Pay off student loans

b. Start a college savings fund

c. Increase retirement contributions

d. Finance long-term care

_____ A young couple without children.

_____ An older person living alone.

_____ A person who just completed college.

_____ A single mother with a preschool daughter.

Opportunity Costs and the Time Value of Money

OBJECTIVE 3
Assess personal and financial opportunity costs associated with financial decisions.

Have you noticed that you always give up something when you make choices? In every financial decision, you sacrifice something to obtain something else that you consider more desirable. For example, you might forgo current buying to invest funds for future purchases or long-term financial security. Or you might gain the use of an expensive item now by making credit payments from future earnings.

Opportunity cost is what you give up by making a choice. This cost, commonly referred to as the *trade-off* of a decision, cannot always be measured in dollars. Opportunity costs should be viewed in terms of both personal and financial resources.

opportunity cost What a person gives up by making a choice.

Personal Opportunity Costs

An important personal opportunity cost involves time that when used for one activity cannot be used for other activities. Time used for studying, working, or shopping will not be available for other uses. Other personal opportunity costs relate to health. Poor eating habits, lack of sleep, or avoiding exercise can result in illness, time away from school or work, increased health care costs, and reduced financial security. Like financial resources, your personal resources (time, energy, health, abilities, knowledge) require planning and wise management.

time value of money Increase in an amount of money as a result of interest earned.

Financial Opportunity Costs

You are constantly making choices among various financial decisions. In making those choices, you must consider the **time value of money,** the increases in an amount of money as a result of interest earned. Saving or investing a dollar instead of spending it today results in a future amount greater than a dollar. Every time you spend, save, invest, or borrow money, you should consider the time value of that money as an opportunity cost. Spending money from your savings account means lost interest earnings; however, what you buy with that money may have a higher priority than those earnings.

INTEREST CALCULATIONS   Three amounts are used to calculate the time value of money for savings in the form of interest earned:

- The amount of the savings (commonly called the *principal*).
- The annual interest rate.
- The length of time the money is on deposit.

These three items are multiplied to obtain the amount of interest. Simple interest is calculated as follows:

For example, $500 on deposit at 6 percent for six months would earn $15 ($500 × 0.06 × 6/12, or ½ year).

You can calculate the increased value of your money from interest earned in two ways: You can calculate the total amount that will be available later (future value), or you can determine the current value of an amount desired in the future (present value).

FUTURE VALUE OF A SINGLE AMOUNT   Deposited money earns interest that will increase over time. **Future value** is the amount to which current savings will increase based on a certain interest rate and a certain time period. For example, $100 deposited in a 6 percent account for one year will grow to $106. This amount is computed as follows:

future value The amount to which current savings will increase based on a certain interest rate and a certain time period; also referred to as *compounding*.

$$\text{Future value} \;=\; \underset{\substack{\uparrow \\ \text{Original amount} \\ \text{in savings}}}{\$100} \;+\; (\$100 \;\times\; \underset{\substack{\uparrow \\ \text{Amount of} \\ \text{interest earned}}}{0.06} \;\times\; 1\text{ year}) \;=\; \$106$$

The same process could be continued for a second, third, and fourth year, but the computations would be time-consuming. Future value tables simplify the process (see Exhibit 1–3). To use a future value table, multiply the amount deposited by the factor for the desired interest rate and time period. For example, $650 at 8 percent for 10 years would have a future value of $1,403.35 ($650 × 2.159). The future value of an amount will always be greater than the original amount. As Exhibit 1–3A shows, all the future value factors are larger than 1. Future value computations may be referred to as *compounding,* since interest is earned on previously earned interest. Compounding allows the future value of a deposit to grow faster than it would if interest were paid only on the original deposit.

Key Web Sites for Time Value of Money

www.moneychimp.com/calculator

www.rbccentura.com/tools

www.dinkytown.net

A. Future Value of $1 (single amount)

Year	PERCENT				
	5%	6%	7%	8%	9%
5	1.276	1.338	1.403	1.469	1.539
6	1.340	1.419	1.501	1.587	1.677
7	1.407	1.504	1.606	1.714	1.828
8	1.477	1.594	1.718	1.851	1.993
9	1.551	1.689	1.838	1.999	2.172
10	1.629	1.791	1.967	2.159	2.367

B. Future Value of a Series of Annual Deposits (annuity)

Year	PERCENT				
	5%	6%	7%	8%	9%
5	5.526	5.637	5.751	5.867	5.985
6	6.802	6.975	7.153	7.336	7.523
7	8.142	8.394	8.654	8.923	9.200
8	9.549	9.897	10.260	10.637	11.028
9	11.027	11.491	11.978	12.488	13.021
10	12.578	13.181	13.816	14.487	15.193

C. Present Value of $1 (single amount)

Year	PERCENT				
	5%	6%	7%	8%	9%
5	0.784	0.747	0.713	0.681	0.650
6	0.746	0.705	0.666	0.630	0.596
7	0.711	0.665	0.623	0.583	0.547
8	0.677	0.627	0.582	0.540	0.502
9	0.645	0.592	0.544	0.500	0.460
10	0.614	0.558	0.508	0.463	0.422

D. Present Value of a Series of Annual Deposits (annuity)

Year	PERCENT				
	5%	6%	7%	8%	9%
5	4.329	4.212	4.100	3.993	3.890
6	5.076	4.917	4.767	4.623	4.486
7	5.786	5.582	5.389	5.206	5.033
8	6.463	6.210	5.971	5.747	5.535
9	7.108	6.802	6.515	6.247	5.995
10	7.722	7.360	7.024	6.710	6.418

Note: See the appendix at the end of this chapter for more complete future value and present value tables.

Exhibit 1–3

Time Value of Money Tables (condensed)

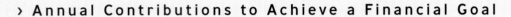

Figure It Out!

› Annual Contributions to Achieve a Financial Goal

Achieving specific financial goals often requires regular deposits to a savings or investment account. By using time value of money calculations, you can determine the amount you should save or invest to achieve a specific goal for the future.

EXAMPLE 1

Jonie Emerson has two children who will start college in 10 years. She plans to set aside $1,500 a year for her children's college educations during that period and estimates she will earn an annual interest rate of 5 percent on her savings. What amount can Jonie expect to have available for her children's college educations when they start college?

CALCULATION:

$1,500 × Future value of a series of deposits, 5%, 10 years

$1,500 × 12.578 (Exhibit 1–3B) = $18,867

EXAMPLE 2

Don Calder wants to accumulate $50,000 over the next 10 years as a reserve fund for his parents' retirement living expenses and health care. If he earns an average of 8 percent on his investments, what amount must he invest each year to achieve this goal?

CALCULATION:

$50,000 ÷ Future value of a series of deposits, 8%, 10 years

$50,000 ÷ 14.487 (Exhibit 1–3B) = $3,452.80

Don needs to invest approximately $3,450 a year for 10 years at 8 percent to achieve the desired financial goal.

---

did you know?

If you invest $2,000 a year (at 9 percent) from ages 31 to 65, these funds will grow to $470,249 by age 65. However, if you save $2,000 a year (at 9 percent) for only 9 years (ages 22 to 30), at age 65 this fund will be worth $579,471! Most important: Start investing something now!

The sooner you make deposits, the greater the future value will be. Depositing $1,000 in a 5 percent account at age 40 will give you $3,387 at age 65. However, making the $1,000 deposit at age 25 would result in an account balance of $7,040 at age 65.

FUTURE VALUE OF A SERIES OF DEPOSITS

Many savers and investors make regular deposits. An *annuity* is a series of equal deposits or payments. To determine the future value of equal yearly savings deposits, use Exhibit 1–3B. For this table to be used, the deposits must earn a constant interest rate. If you deposit $50 a year at 7 percent for six years, starting at the end of the first year, you will have $357.65 at the end of that time ($50 × 7.153). The Figure It Out box on this page presents examples of using future value to achieve financial goals.

present value The current value for a future amount based on a certain interest rate and a certain time period; also referred to as *discounting.*

PRESENT VALUE OF A SINGLE AMOUNT   Another aspect of the time value of money involves determining the current value of an amount desired in the future. **Present value** is the current value for a future amount based on a certain interest rate and a certain time period. Present value computations, also called *discounting,* allow you to determine how much to deposit now to obtain a desired total in the future. Present value tables (Exhibit 1–3C) can be used to make the computations. If you want $1,000 five years from now and you earn 5 percent on your savings, you need to deposit $784 ($1,000 × 0.784). The present value of the amount you want in the future will always be less than the future value. Note that all of the factors in Exhibit 1–3C are less than 1 and interest earned will increase the present value amount to the desired future amount.

PRESENT VALUE OF A SERIES OF DEPOSITS   You may also use present value computations to determine how much you need to deposit so that you can take a certain amount out of the account for a desired number of years. For example, if you want to take $400 out of an investment account each year for nine years and your money is earning an annual rate of 8 percent, you can see from Exhibit 1–3D that you would need to make a current deposit of $2,498.80 ($400 × 6.247).

The formulas for calculating future and present values, as well as tables covering additional interest rates and time periods, are presented in the appendix to this chapter. Computer programs and financial calculators may also be used for calculating time value of money.

Sheet 3
Achieving Financial Goals Using Time Value of Money

✓ CONCEPT CHECK 1–3

1 What are some examples of personal opportunity costs?

_____

_____

2 What does time value of money measure?

_____

_____

3 Use the time value of money tables in Exhibit 1–3 to calculate the following:

a. The future value of $100 at 7 percent in 10 years.

_____

b. The future value of $100 a year for six years earning 6 percent.

_____

c. The present value of $500 received in eight years with an interest rate of 8 percent.

_____

A Plan for Personal Financial Planning

We all make hundreds of decisions each day. Most of these decisions are quite simple and have few consequences. However, some are complex and have long-term effects on our personal and financial situations. While everyone makes decisions, few people consider how to make better decisions. As Exhibit 1–4 shows, the financial planning process can be viewed as a six-step procedure.

OBJECTIVE 4
Implement a plan for making personal financial and career decisions.

Step 1: Determine Your Current Financial Situation

In this first step, determine your current financial situation regarding income, savings, living expenses, and debts. Preparing a list of current asset and debt balances and amounts spent for various items gives you a foundation for financial planning activities. The personal financial statements discussed in Chapter 2 will provide the information needed in this phase of financial decision making.

Exhibit 1–4   The Financial Planning Process

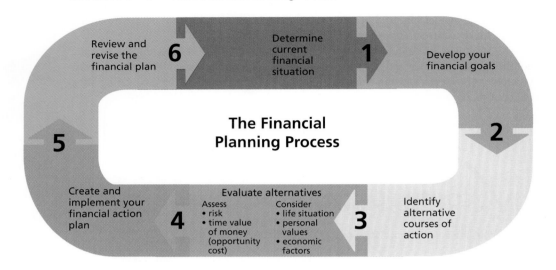

> **STEP 1 EXAMPLE**
>
> Carla Elliot plans to complete her college degree in the next two years. She works two part-time jobs in an effort to pay her educational expenses. Currently, Carla has $700 in a savings account and existing debt that includes a $640 balance on her credit card and $2,300 in student loans. What additional information should Carla have available when planning her personal finances?
>
> _____
>
> **EXAMPLE FROM YOUR LIFE**
>
> What actions have you taken to determine your current financial situation?
>
> _____

Step 2: Develop Your Financial Goals

You should periodically analyze your financial values and goals. The purpose of this analysis is to differentiate your needs from your wants. Specific financial goals are vital to financial planning. Others can suggest financial goals for you; however, *you* must decide which goals to pursue. Your financial goals can range from spending all of your current income to developing an extensive savings and investment program for your future financial security.

> **STEP 2 EXAMPLE**
>
> The main financial goals of Carla Elliot for the next two years are to complete her college degree and to maintain or reduce the amounts owed. What other goals might be appropriate for Carla?
>
> _____
>
> *(Continued)*

EXAMPLE FROM YOUR LIFE

Describe some short-term or long-term goals that might be appropriate for your life situation.

_____

_____

Step 3: Identify Alternative Courses of Action

Developing alternatives is crucial when making decisions. Although many factors will influence the available alternatives, possible courses of action usually fall into these categories:

- *Continue the same course of action.* For example, you may determine that the amount you have saved each month is still appropriate.
- *Expand the current situation.* You may choose to save a larger amount each month.
- *Change the current situation.* You may decide to use a money market account instead of a regular savings account.
- *Take a new course of action.* You may decide to use your monthly saving budget to pay off credit card debts.

Not all of these categories will apply to every decision; however, they do represent possible courses of action. For example, if you want to stop working full time to go to school, you must generate several alternatives under the category "Take a new course of action." Creativity in decision making is vital to effective choices. Considering all of the possible alternatives will help you make more effective and satisfying decisions. For instance, most people believe they must own a car to get to work or school. However, they should consider other alternatives such as public transportation, carpooling, renting a car, shared ownership of a car, or a company car.

Remember, when you decide not to take action, you elect to "do nothing," which can be a dangerous alternative.

did you know?

According to the National Endowment for Financial Education, 70 percent of major lottery winners end up with financial difficulties. These winners often squander the funds awarded them, while others overspend and many end up declaring bankruptcy. Having more money does not automatically mean making better financial planning choices.

Apply *Yourself!*

Objective 4

Prepare a list of questions that might be asked of a financial planning professional by *(a)* a young person just starting out on his or her own, *(b)* a young couple planning for their children's education and for their own retirement, and *(c)* a person nearing retirement.

STEP 3 EXAMPLE

To achieve her goals, Carla Elliot has several options available. She could reduce her spending, seek a higher-paying part-time job, or use her savings to pay off some of her debt. What additional alternatives might she consider?

_____

EXAMPLE FROM YOUR LIFE

List various alternatives for achieving the financial goals you identified in the previous step.

_____

Step 4: Evaluate Your Alternatives

You need to evaluate possible courses of action, taking into consideration your life situation, personal values, and current economic conditions. How will the ages of dependents affect your saving goals? How do you like to spend leisure time? How will changes in interest rates affect your financial situation?

CONSEQUENCES OF CHOICES   Every decision closes off alternatives. For example, a decision to invest in stock may mean you cannot take a vacation. A decision to go to school full-time may mean you cannot work full-time. *Opportunity cost* is what you give up by making a choice. These *trade-offs* cannot always be measured in dollars. However, the resources you give up (money or time) have a value that is lost.

EVALUATING RISK   Uncertainty is also a part of every decision. Selecting a college major and choosing a career field involve risk. What if you don't like working in this field or cannot obtain employment in it? Other decisions involve a very low degree of risk, such as putting money in an insured savings account or purchasing items that cost only a few dollars. Your chances of losing something of great value are low in these situations.

In many financial decisions, identifying and evaluating risk are difficult. Common risks to consider include:

- Inflation risk, due to rising prices that cause lost buying power.
- Interest rate risk, resulting from changes in the cost of money, which can affect your costs (when you borrow) and benefits (when you save or invest).
- Income risk may result from a loss of a job or encountering illness.
- Personal risk involves tangible and intangible factors that create a less than desirable situation, such as health or safety concerns.
- Liquidity risk, when savings and investments that have potential for higher earnings are difficult to convert to cash or to sell without significant loss in value.

did you know?

The main sources from which people get their money advice are financial professionals, friends and family, printed materials from work, newspapers and magazines, the Internet, and television and radio.

The best way to consider risk is to gather information based on your experience and the experiences of others and to use financial planning information sources.

FINANCIAL PLANNING INFORMATION SOURCES
Relevant information is required at each stage of the decision-making process. In addition to this book, common sources available to help you with your financial decisions include (1) the Internet; (2) financial institutions, such as banks, credit unions, and investment companies; (3) media sources, such as newspapers, magazines, television, and radio; and (4) financial specialists, such as financial planners, insurance agents, investment advisers, credit counselors, lawyers, and tax preparers.

STEP 4 EXAMPLE

As Carla Elliot evaluates her alternative courses of action, she should consider both her short-term and long-term situations. What risks and trade-offs should Carla consider?

_____

EXAMPLE FROM YOUR LIFE

In your life, what types of risks might be encountered when planning and implementing various personal financial activities?

_____

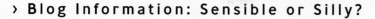

Personal Finance in Practice

› Blog Information: Sensible or Silly?

Web logs, commonly called "blogs," offer commentaries, news, and observations on various subjects. These online journals communicate experiences along with other thoughts and information. Blog readers are usually also allowed to "post" comments with their experiences, opinions, complaints, or news items.

Blogs for personal finance are available on all topics. The sources of blog postings can range from an economist at the Tax Foundation to a dissatisfied customer. Blog users should be cautious before believing or acting on postings. Always compare information with other sources. In an effort to become a sensible user of personal finance blogs, take action on one or more of these activities:

---

1. Locate a blog that discusses various financial planning mistakes.

   a. What are some recent postings?

   b. What is a reaction you might post on this blog?

2. Locate a blog with tax tips or tax planning experiences.

   a. Describe an idea from this source that might be of value to you in the future.

   b. Explain what actions you might take to verify the validity of this information.

3. Locate a blog reporting the experiences people who have used various types of credit. Describe how an idea from this source might be of value to you in the future.

   a. How valuable is the information presented on this blog?

   b. What authority does the source of the blog information have on this topic area?

4. Assume you are creating a blog designed to assist people when planning and using a budget.

   a. What types of information might be included in the blog?

   b. What actions might be taken to establish credibility for your blog?

What guidelines would you follow when accessing and using information from a blog related to personal finance?

Step 5: Create and Implement Your Financial Action Plan

You are now ready to develop an action plan to identify ways to achieve your goals. For example, you can increase your savings by reducing your spending or by increasing your income through extra time on the job. If you are concerned about year-end tax payments, you may increase the amount withheld from each paycheck, file quarterly tax payments, or shelter current income in a tax-deferred retirement program.

To implement your financial action plan, you may need assistance from others. For example, you may use the services of an insurance agent to purchase property insurance or the services of an investment broker to purchase stocks, bonds, or mutual funds. Exhibit 1–5 offers a framework for developing and implementing a financial plan, along with examples for several life situations.

Exhibit 1–5   Financial Planning in Action

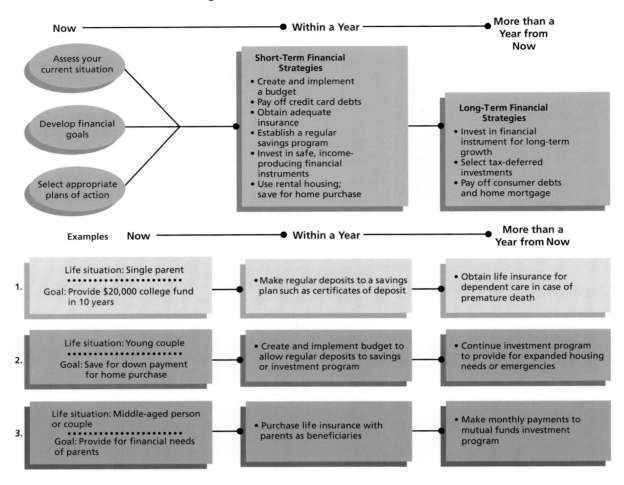

STEP 5 EXAMPLE

Carla has decided to reduce her course load and work longer hours in an effort both to reduce her debt level and to increase the amount she has in savings. What are the benefits and drawbacks of this choice?

_____

EXAMPLE FROM YOUR LIFE

Describe the benefits and drawbacks of a financial situation you have encountered during the past year.

_____

Step 6: Review and Revise Your Plan

Financial planning is a dynamic process that does not end when you take a particular action. You need to regularly assess your financial decisions. You should do a complete review of your finances at least once a year. Changing personal, social, and economic factors may require more frequent assessments.

An immigrant couple weigh alternate futures. By *Jeffrey R. Kosnett*

Pushing your FINANCIAL CLOCK ahead

For Sneha and Kaushal Joshi, New York City is nirvana. They love its energy and they have good jobs there. They've even circumvented the legendary housing crunch by buying a town-house in Jersey City, N.J., a quick train ride from their offices in Manhattan.

But the young couple also love India, where they were born and raised. They're thinking of resettling in Sneha's hometown of Bangalore or Kaushal's native Bombay in about six years. India's bright economy will surely offer opportunities for Sneha, 29, a credit analyst, and Kaushal, a 32-year-old IT consultant, both of whom have MBAs. But, Sneha says, if you're paid in rupees, "the earnings are not so great, even in our professions." Their combined income of $130,000 would plunge.

But their expenses probably wouldn't. Western-style homes and conveniences in Indian cities are costly. Sneha and Kaushal also hope to start a family in a year or two and expect that their children will also attend American universities. So they're eager to accumulate as much money as possible while in the U.S.

Unusual "early retirement." If the Joshis decide to return to India, they'll need to push their financial clocks ahead. The Joshis' position will be similar to that of a couple in their late 50s—the age at which you start to fret about losing the hefty paychecks.

Sneha and Kaushal are off to a good start. They have about $100,000 in 401(k) savings and $40,000 in bank savings, mutual funds and a few stocks. They have $125,000 in equity in the New Jersey home and $20,000 in equity in a rental house in Bangalore. The Joshis say they can invest $4,500 a month on top of their 401(k) contributions. Because they are young, they'd normally be wise to place 90% in stocks and stock funds and keep bonds and cash to a minimum. But Sneha and Kaushal will need plenty of cash for the transition given the prospect of reduced income, says Doug Taylor, of Taylor Wealth Management, in Torrance, Cal. He advises them to amass at least $100,000 in a ladder of certificates of deposit.

If the Joshis earmark $2,500 a month for CDs, they can still put $2,000 into growth investments. Time is short, so they should not be timid. They've begun investing in high-octane funds, such as CGM Focus and Bridgeway Aggressive Investors 2. To those solid choices they should add an international fund or two. Then, when the time comes, they could enroll in 529 college-savings plans.

In general, the couple should avoid new long-term obligations in the U.S. until they firm up their plans. They've thought about a larger house in New Jersey and whole life insurance. If they stay in the States, both could make sense. For now, the timing is wrong.

1. What wise financial planning decisions are suggested by the actions of Sneha and Kaushal?

2. Describe actions you might take based on the financial planning activities of Sneha and Kaushal?

3. What information is available at www.kiplinger.com that might be of value when making personal financial decisions?

When life events affect your financial needs, this financial planning process will provide a vehicle for adapting to those changes. A regular review of this decision-making process will help you make priority adjustments that will bring your financial goals and activities in line with your current life situation.

STEP 6 EXAMPLE

Over the next 6 to 12 months, Carla Elliot should reassess her financial, personal, and educational situation. What types of circumstances might occur that could require that Carla take a different approach to her personal finances?

_____

EXAMPLE FROM YOUR LIFE

What factors in your life might affect your personal financial situation and decisions in the future?

_____

Career Choice and Financial Planning

Have you ever wondered why some people find great satisfaction in their work while others only put in their time? As with other personal financial decisions, career selection and professional growth require planning. The average person changes jobs seven times during a lifetime. Most likely, therefore, you will reevaluate your choice of a job on a regular basis. The lifework you select is a key to your financial well-being and personal satisfaction.

Like other decisions, career choice and professional development alternatives have risks and opportunity costs. In recent years, many people have placed family and personal fulfillment above monetary reward and professional recognition. Career choices require periodic evaluation of trade-offs related to personal, social, and economic factors.

In addition, changing personal and social factors will require you to continually assess your work situation. The steps of the financial planning process can provide an approach to career planning, advancement, and career change. Your career goals will affect how you use this process. If you desire more responsibility on the job, for example, you may decide to obtain advanced training or change career fields. Appendix A provides a plan for obtaining employment and professional advancement.

Sheet 4
Planning Your Career

YOUR CAREER PLANNING DECISIONS

Based on the your current or future career situation, describe how you might use the Financial Planning Process (Exhibit 1–4, p. 16) to plan and implement an employment decision.

_____

_____

✓ CONCEPT CHECK 1–4

1 What actions might a person take to identify alternatives when making a financial decision?

_____

_____

2 Why are career planning activities considered to be personal financial decisions?

_____

_____

3 For the following situations, identify the type of risk being described.

_____ Not getting proper rest and exercise.

_____ Not being able to obtain cash from a certificate of deposit before the maturity date.

_____ Taking out a variable rate loan when rates are expected to rise.

_____ Training for a career field with low potential demand in the future.

4 For the following main sources of personal finance information, list a specific Web site, organization, or person whom you might contact in the future.

Type of information	Specific source	Contact information
Web site		
Financial institution		
Media source		
Financial specialist		

www.mhhe.com/kdh

back to *Getting Personal*

1. Reconsider your responses to the Getting Personal questions at the beginning of the chapter. Have any of your answers changed as a result of your learning or changing financial activities?

_____

_____

2. What did you learn in this chapter that might affect your answers to these questions in the future?

_____

_____

3. Describe one of your financial goals. What actions will you take to achieve this goal?

_____

_____

4. Explain a situation in which you assessed the risk when making a financial decision.

_____

_____

Chapter Summary

Objective 1 Financial decisions are affected by a person's life situation (income, age, household size, health), personal values, and economic factors (prices, interest rates, and employment opportunities). The major elements of financial planning are obtaining, planning, saving, borrowing, spending, managing risk, investing, and retirement and estate planning.

Objective 2 Financial goals should (1) be realistic; (2) be stated in specific, measurable terms; (3) have a time frame; and (4) indicate the type of action to be taken.

Objective 3 Every decision involves a trade-off with things given up. Personal opportunity costs include time, effort, and health. Financial opportunity costs are based on the time value of money. Future value and present value calculations enable you to measure the increased value (or lost interest) that results from a saving, investing, borrowing, or purchasing decision.

Objective 4 Personal financial planning involves the following process: (1) determine your current financial situation; (2) develop financial goals; (3) identify alternative courses of action; (4) evaluate alternatives; (5) create and implement a financial action plan; and (6) review and revise the financial plan.

Key Terms

adult life cycle   4
bankruptcy   8
economics   4
financial plan   3

future value   12
inflation   6
opportunity cost   11
personal financial planning   3

present value   14
time value of money   12
values   4

Problems

(Note: Some of these problems require the use of the time value of money tables in the chapter appendix.)

1. Using the rule of 72, approximate the following amounts.
   a. If the value of land in an area is increasing 6 percent a year, how long will it take for property values to double?

   b. If you earn 10 percent on your investments, how long will it take for your money to double?

   c. At an annual interest rate of 5 percent, how long will it take for your savings to double?

2. In the early 2000s, selected automobiles had an average cost of $15,000. The average cost of those same automobiles is now $18,000. What was the rate of increase for these automobiles between the two time periods?

3. A family spends $34,000 a year for living expenses. If prices increase by 4 percent a year for the next three years, what amount will the family need for their living expenses after three years?

4. Ben Collins plans to buy a house for $120,000. If that real estate is expected to increase in value by 5 percent each year, what will its approximate value be seven years from now?

5. What would be the yearly earnings for a person with $6,000 in savings at an annual interest rate of 5.5 percent?

6. Using time value of money tables (Exhibit 1–3 or chapter appendix tables), calculate the following.
   a. The future value of $450 six years from now at 7 percent.

   b. The future value of $800 saved each year for 10 years at 8 percent.

c. The amount a person would have to deposit today (present value) at a 6 percent interest rate to have $1,000 five years from now.

d. The amount a person would have to deposit today to be able to take out $500 a year for 10 years from an account earning 8 percent.

7. If you desire to have $10,000 for a down payment for a house in five years, what amount would you need to deposit today? Assume that your money will earn 5 percent.

8. Pete Morton is planning to go to graduate school in a program of study that will take three years. Pete wants to have $10,000 available each year for various school and living expenses. If he earns 4 percent on his money, how much must he deposit at the start of his studies to be able to withdraw $10,000 a year for three years?

9. Carla Lopez deposits $3,000 a year into her retirement account. If these funds have an average earning of 8 percent over the 40 years until her retirement, what will be the value of her retirement account?

10. If a person spends $10 a week on coffee (assume $500 a year), what would be the future value of that amount over 10 years if the funds were deposited in an account earning 4 percent?

Questions

1. In your opinion, what is the main benefit of wise financial planning?

2. What factors in an economy might affect the level of interest rates?

3. Describe risks that you might encounter when making financial decisions over the next few years.

4. What are possible drawbacks associated with seeking advice from a financial planning professional? How might these concerns be minimized?

5. Talk with several people about their career choices. How have their employment situations affected their financial planning activities?

Internet Connection

RESEARCHING ECONOMIC CONDITIONS AFFECTING FINANCIAL DECISIONS

For these two major economic indicators: (1) obtain current information and (2) determine how the current trend might affect your future financial planning activities.

Inflation Web sources

_____

_____

1. Current findings:

_____

2. Possible influence on your financial decisions

_____

_____

Interest Rates Web sources

_____

_____

1. Current findings:

_____

2. Possible influence on your financial decisions

_____

_____

Case in Point

STUCK IN THE MIDDLE

Until recently, Fran and Ed Blake's personal finances ran smoothly. Both had well-paying jobs while raising two children. The Blakes have a daughter who is completing her freshman year of college and a son three years younger. Currently they have $22,000 in various savings and investment funds set aside for the children's education. With education costs increasing faster than inflation, they are uncertain whether this amount is adequate.

In recent months, Fran's mother has required extensive medical attention and personal care assistance. Unable to live alone, she is now a resident of a long-term care facility. The cost of this service is $2,650 a month, with annual increases of about 4 percent. While a major portion of the cost is covered by her Social Security and pension, Fran's mother is unable to cover the entire cost. Their desire to help adds to the Blakes' financial burden.

The Blakes are like millions of other Americans who have financial responsibilities for both dependent children and aging parents. Commonly referred to as the "sandwich generation," this group is squeezed on one side by the cost of raising and educating children and on the other side by the financial demands of caring for aging parents.

Finally, the Blakes, ages 47 and 43, are also concerned about saving for their own retirement. While they have consistently made annual deposits to a retirement fund, various current financial demands may force them to access some of this money.

Questions

1. What actions have the Blakes taken that would be considered wise financial planning choices?

2. What actions might be appropriate to address the concerns faced by the Blake household?

3. Conduct an Internet search to obtain additional information that might be of value to the Blakes.

Continuing Case

GETTING STARTED

Life Situation	*Financial Data*
Single	Monthly income $2,600
Age 22	Living expenses $2,180
Starting a career	Assets $8,200
No dependents	Liabilities $3,470
	Emergency fund $530

While in college, Pam Jenkins worked part-time and was never concerned about long-term financial planning. Rather than creating a budget, she used her checkbook and savings account (which usually had a very low balance) to handle her financial needs.

After completing college, Pam began her career as a sales representative for a clothing manufacturer located in California. After one year, her assets consist of a 1999 automobile, a television set, some electronic entertainment equipment, and clothing and other personal belongs, with a total value of about $8,200.

QUESTIONS

1. List various personal financial decisions that Pam might be thinking about at this point in her life.

2. What are some short-term, intermediate, and long-term financial goals that Pam might want to develop?

3. Explain which sections of *Your Personal Financial Plan* sheets 1–4 could be useful for Pam.

Video Case

CFA VS. CPA: PICKING A FINANCIAL ADVISER

Several types of financial advisers with various certifications are available to assist you with different aspects of personal financial planning. Consumers should investigate the background, training, fees, and services offered before turning to someone to help you with managing your finances.

Questions

1. What are some types of financial advisers available to assist people with money management and investment activities?

2. What cautions should you consider when using the services of a financial adviser?

3. Conduct an online search to obtain additional information about using the services of a financial adviser.

Spending Diary

"I FIRST THOUGHT THIS PROCESS WOULD BE A WASTE OF TIME, BUT THE INFORMATION HAS HELPED ME BECOME MUCH MORE CAREFUL OF HOW I SPENT MY MONEY."

Nearly everyone who has made the effort to keep a daily spending diary has found it beneficial. While at first the process may seem tedious, after a while recording this information becomes easier and faster.

Directions

Using the Daily Spending Diary sheets provided at the end of the book, record *every cent* of your spending each day in the categories provided. Or you may create your own format to monitor your spending. You can indicate the use of a credit card with (CR). This experience will help you better understand your spending patterns and identify desired changes you might want to make in your spending habits.

Questions

1. What did your daily spending diary reveal about your spending habits? What areas of spending might you consider changing?

2. How might your daily spending diary assist you when identifying and achieving financial goals?

www.mhhe.com/kdh

Personal Financial Data

Financial Planning Activities: Complete the information request to provide a quick reference for vital household data.

Suggested Web Sites: www.money.com   www.kiplinger.com

Name	_____ _____
Birthdate	_____ _____
Marital Status	_____ _____
Address	_____ _____
Phone	_____ _____
e-mail	_____ _____
Social Security No.	_____ _____
Drivers License No.	_____ _____
Place of Employment	_____ _____
Address	_____ _____
Phone	_____ _____
Position	_____ _____
Length of Service	_____ _____
Checking Acct. No.	_____ _____
Financial Inst.	_____ _____
Address	_____ _____
Phone	_____ _____

Dependent Data

Name	Birthdate	Relationship	Social Security No.
_____	_____	_____	_____
_____	_____	_____	_____
_____	_____	_____	_____
_____	_____	_____	_____

What's Next for Your Personal Financial Plan?

- Identify financial planning experts (insurance agent, banker, investment adviser, tax preparer, others) you might contact for financial planning information or assistance.
- Discuss with other household members various financial planning priorities.

Setting Personal Financial Goals

Financial Planning Activities: Based on personal and household needs and values, identify specific goals that require action for your life.

Suggested Web Sites: www.financialplan.about.com   www.money.com

Short-Term Monetary Goals (less than two years)

Description	Amount needed	Months to achieve	Action to be taken	Priority
Example: pay off credit card debt	$850	12	Use money from pay raise	High

Intermediate and Long-Term Monetary Goals

Description	Amount needed	Months to achieve	Action to be taken	Priority

Nonmonetary Goals

Description	Time frame	Actions to be taken
Example: set up file for personal financial records and documents	next 2–3 months	locate all personal and financial records and documents; set up files for various spending, saving, borrowing categories

What's Next for Your Personal Financial Plan?

- Based on various financial goals, calculate the savings deposits necessary to achieve those goals.
- Identify current economic trends that might influence various saving, spending, investing, and borrowing decisions.

Achieving Financial Goals Using Time Value of Money

Financial Planning Activities: Calculate future and present value amounts related to specific financial goal using time value of money tables, a financial calculator, spreadsheet software, or an online calculator.

Suggested Web Sites: www.moneychimp.com/calculator   www.rbccentura.com/tools

Future Value of a Single Amount

1. To determine future value of a single amount
2. To determine interest lost when cash purchases in made

(Use Exhibit 1–A in Chapter 1 appendix.)

current amount	times	future value factor	equals	future value amount
$ _____	×	$ _____	=	$ _____

Future Value of a Series of Deposits

1. To determine future values of regular savings deposits
2. To determine future value of regular retirement deposits

(Use Exhibit 1–B in Chapter 1 appendix.)

regular deposit amount	times	future value of annuity factor	equals	future value amount
$ _____	×	$ _____	=	$ _____

Present Value of a Single Amount

1. To determine an amount to be deposited now that will grow to desired amount

(Use Exhibit 1–C in Chapter 1 appendix.)

future amount desired	times	present value factor	equals	present value amount
$ _____	×	$ _____	=	$ _____

Present Value of a Series of Deposits

1. To determine an amount that can be withdrawn on a regular basis

(Use Exhibit 1–D in Chapter 1 appendix.)

regular amount to be withdrawn	times	present value of annuity factor	equals	present value amount
$ _____	×	$ _____	=	$ _____

What's Next for Your Personal Financial Plan?

- Describe some situations in which you could use time value of money calculations for achieving various personal financial goals.
- What specific actions are you taking to achieve various financial goals?

Planning Your Career

Financial Planning Activities: Research and plan various actions related to obtaining employment.

Suggested Web Sites: www.monster.com   www.careerjournal.com

Career area, job titles	
Useful career information sources—Web sites, books	
Career contacts (name, title, organization, address, phone, e-mail, organization Web site)	
Informational interview questions about the career field, industry	1. 2. 3.
Key items to include in my résumé	1. 2. 3.
Key points to emphasize in my cover letters	1. 2.
Interview questions I should practice answering	1. 2. 3.
Interview questions to ask the organization	1. 2.
Other career planning, job search ideas	

What's Next for Your Personal Financial Plan?

- Talk with various people who have worked in the career fields of interest to you.
- Outline a plan for long-term professional development and career advancement.

Appendix   Time Value of Money

- "If I deposit $10,000 today, how much will I have for a down payment on a house in five years?"
- "Will $2,000 saved each year give me enough money when I retire?"
- "How much must I save today to have enough for my children's college education?"

The *time value of money,* more commonly referred to as *interest,* is the cost of money that is borrowed or lent. Interest can be compared to rent, the cost of using an apartment or other item. The time value of money is based on the fact that a dollar received today is worth more than a dollar that will be received one year from today, because the dollar received today can be saved or invested and will be worth more than a dollar a year from today. Similarly, a dollar that will be received one year from today is currently worth less than a dollar today.

The time value of money has two major components: future value and present value. *Future value* computations, which are also referred to as *compounding,* yield the amount to which a current sum will increase based on a certain interest rate and period of time. *Present value,* which is calculated through a process called *discounting,* is the current value of a future sum based on a certain interest rate and period of time.

In future value problems, you are given an amount to save or invest and you calculate the amount that will be available at some future date. With present value problems, you are given the amount that will be available at some future date and you calculate the current value of that amount. Both future value and present value computations are based on basic interest rate calculations.

Interest Rate Basics

Simple interest is the dollar cost of borrowing or earnings from lending money. The interest is based on three elements:

- The dollar amount, called the *principal.*
- The *rate of interest.*
- The amount of *time.*

The formula for computing interest is

$$\text{Interest} = \text{Principal} \times \text{Rate of interest} \times \text{Time}$$

The interest rate is stated as a percentage for a year. For example, you must convert 12 percent to either 0.12 or 12/100 before doing your calculations. The time element must also be converted to a decimal or fraction. For example, three months would be shown as 0.25 or 1/4 of a year. Interest for 2½ years would involve a time period of 2.5.

Example A

Suppose you borrow $1,000 at 5 percent and will repay it in one payment at the end of one year. Using the simple interest calculation, the interest is $50, computed as follows:

$$\$50 = \$1,000 \times 0.05 \times 1 \text{ (year)}$$

Example B

If you deposited $750 in a savings account paying 8 percent, how much interest would you earn in nine months? You would compute this amount as follows:

$$\text{Interest} = \$750 \times 0.08 \times 3/4 \text{ (or 0.75 of a year)}$$
$$= \$45$$

Sample Problem 1

How much interest would you earn if you deposited $300 at 6 percent for 27 months?

(Answers to sample problems are on page 37.)

Sample Problem 2

How much interest would you pay to borrow $670 for eight months at 12 percent?

Future Value of a Single Amount

The future value of an amount consists of the original amount plus compound interest. This calculation involves the following elements:

$$FV = \text{Future value}$$
$$PV = \text{Present value}$$
$$i = \text{Interest rate}$$
$$n = \text{Number of time periods}$$

The formula for the future value of a single amount is

$$FV = PV(1 + i)^n$$

Example C

The future value of $1 at 10 percent after three years is $1.33. This amount is calculated as follows:

$$\$1.33 = \$1.00(1 + 0.10)^3$$

Future value tables are available to help you determine compounded interest amounts (see Exhibit 1–A on page 39). Looking at Exhibit 1–A for 10 percent and three years, you can see that $1 would be worth $1.33 at that time. For other amounts, multiply the table factor by the original amount.

This may be viewed as follows:

Example D

If your savings of $400 earn 12 percent, compounded *monthly,* over a year and a half, use the table factor for 1 percent for 18 time periods. The future value of this amount is $478.40, calculated as follows:

$$\$478.40 + \$400(1.196)$$

Sample Problem 3

What is the future value of $800 at 8 percent after six years?

_____

Sample Problem 4

How much would you have in savings if you kept $200 on deposit for eight years at 8 percent, compounded *semiannually?*

_____

Future Value of a Series of Equal Amounts (an Annuity)

Future value may also be calculated for a situation in which regular additions are made to savings. The following formula is used:

$$FV = \frac{(1 + i)^n - 1}{I}$$

This formula assumes that (1) each deposit is for the same amount, (2) the interest rate is the same for each time period, and (3) the deposits are made at the end of each time period.

Example E

The future value of three $1 deposits made at the end of the next three years, earning 10 percent interest, is $3.31. This is calculated as follows:

$$\$3.31 = \$1\frac{(1 + 0.10)^3 - 1}{0.10}$$

This may be viewed as follows:

Future value (rounded)	$1	$1	$2.10	FV = $3.31
		Deposit $1 Interest 0	Deposit $1 Interest $0.10	Deposit $1 Interest $0.21
After year	0	1	2	3

Using Exhibit 1–B on page 40, you can find this same amount for 10 percent for three time periods. To use the table for other amounts, multiply the table factors by the annual deposit.

Example F

If you plan to deposit $40 a year for 10 years, earning 8 percent compounded annually, use the table factor for 8 percent for 10 time periods. The future value of this amount is $579.48, calculated as follows:

$$\$579.48 = \$40(14.487)$$

Sample Problem 5

What is the future value of an annual deposit of $230 earning 6 percent for 15 years?

_____

Sample Problem 6

What amount would you have in a retirement account if you made annual deposits of $375 for 25 years earning 12 percent, compounded annually?

_____

Present Value of a Single Amount

If you want to know how much you need to deposit now to receive a certain amount in the future, use the following formula:

$$PV = \frac{1}{(I + i)^n}$$

Example G

The present value of $1 to be received three years from now based on a 10 percent interest rate is $0.75. This amount is calculated as follows:

$$\$0.75 = \frac{\$1}{(1 + 0.10)^3}$$

This may be viewed as follows:

Present value tables are available to assist you in this process (see Exhibit 1–C on page 41). Notice that $1 at 10 percent for three years has a present value of $0.75. For amounts other than $1, multiply the table factor by the amount involved.

Example H

If you want to have $300 seven years from now and your savings earn 10 percent, compounded *semiannually,* use the table factor for 5 percent for 14 time periods. In this situation, the present value is $151.50, calculated as follows:

$$\$151.50 = \$300(0.505)$$

Sample Problem 7

What is the present value of $2,200 earning 15 percent for eight years?

Sample Problem 8

To have $6,000 for a child's education in 10 years, what amount should a parent deposit in a savings account that earns 12 percent, compounded *quarterly?*

Present Value of a Series of Equal Amounts (an Annuity)

The final time value of money situation allows you to receive an amount at the end of each time period for a certain number of periods. This amount is calculated as follows:

$$PV = \frac{1 - \frac{1}{(1+i)^n}}{i}$$

Example I

The present value of a $1 withdrawal at the end of the next three years would be $2.49, calculated as follows:

$$\$2.49 = \$1 \left[\frac{1 - \frac{1}{(1 + 0.10)^n}}{0.10} \right]$$

This may be viewed as follows:

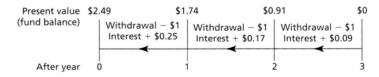

This same amount appears in Exhibit 1–D on page 42 for 10 percent and three time periods. To use the table for other situations, multiply the table factor by the amount to be withdrawn each year.

Example J

If you wish to withdraw $100 at the end of each year for 10 years from an account that earns 14 percent, compounded annually, what amount must you deposit now? Use the table factor for 14 percent for 10 time periods. In this situation, the present value is $521.60, calculated as follows:

$$\$521.60 = \$100(5.216)$$

Sample Problem 9

What is the present value of a withdrawal of $200 at the end of each year for 14 years with an interest rate of 7 percent?

Sample Problem 10

How much would you have to deposit now to be able to withdraw $650 at the end of each year for 20 years from an account that earns 11 percent?

Using Present Value to Determine Loan Payments

Present value tables (Exhibit 1–D) can also be used to determine installment payments for a loan as follows:

$$\frac{\text{Amount borrowed}}{\text{Present value of a series table factor}} = \text{Loan payment}$$

Example K

If you borrow $1,000 with a 6 percent interest rate to be repaid in three equal payments at the end of the next three years, the payments will be $374.11. This is calculated as follows:

$$\frac{\$1,000}{2.673} = \$374.11$$

Sample Problem 11

What would be the annual payment amount for a $20,000, ten-year loan at 7 percent?

Answers To Sample Problems

1. $300 × 0.06 × 2.25 years (27 months) = $40.50.
2. $670 × 0.12 × 2/3 (of a year) = $53.60.
3. $800(1.587) = $1,269.60. (Use Exhibit 1–A, 8%, 6 periods.)
4. $200(1.873) = $374.60. (Use Exhibit 1–A, 4%, 16 periods.)
5. $230(23.276) = $5,353.48. (Use Exhibit 1–B, 6%, 15 periods.)
6. $375(133.33) = $49,998.75. (Use Exhibit 1–B, 12%, 25 periods.)
7. $2,200(0.327) = $719.40. (Use Exhibit 1–C, 15%, 8 periods.)
8. $6,000(0.307) = $1,842. (Use Exhibit 1–C, 3%, 40 periods.)
9. $200(8.745) = $1,749. (Use Exhibit 1–D, 7%, 14 periods.)
10. $650(7.963) = $5,175.95. (Use Exhibit 1–D, 11%, 20 periods.)
11. $20,000/7.024 = $2,847.38. (Use Exhibit 1–D, 7%, 10 periods.)

Time Value of Money Calculation Methods: A Summary

The time value of money may be calculated using a variety of techniques. When achieving specific financial goals requires regular deposits to a savings or investment account, the computation may occur in one of several ways. For example, Jonie Emerson plans to deposit $10,000 in an account for the next 10 years. She estimates these funds will earn an annual rate of 5 percent. What amount can Jonie expect to have available after 10 years?

Method	Process, Results
Formula Calculation The most basic method of calculating the time value of money involves using a formula.	For this situation, the formula would be: $$PV(1 = i)^n = FV$$ The result sould be $$\$10,000 \ (1 + 0.05)^{10} = \$16,288.95$$
Time Value of Money Tables Instead of calculating with a formula, time value of money tables are available. The numeric factors presented ease the computational process.	Using the table in Exhibit 1–8A: $10,000 × Future value of $1, 5%, 10 years $10,000 × 1.629 = $16,290
Financial Calculator A variety of handheld financial calculators are programmed with various financial functions. Both future value and present value calculations may be performed using the appropriate keystrokes.	Using a financial calculator, the keystrokes would be: Amount $\qquad$ −10000 PV Time periods $\qquad$ 10 N Interest rate $\qquad$ 5 I Result $\qquad$ FV $16,288.94
Spreadsheet Software Excel and other software programs have built-in formulas for various financial computations, including time value of money.	When using a spreadsheet program, this type of calculation would require this format: = *FV*(rate, periods, amount per period, single amount) The results of this example would be: = *FV*(0.05, 10, 0, −10000) = $16,288.95
Time Value of Money Web Sites Many time-value-of-money calculators are also available online. These Web-based programs perform calculations for the future value of savings as well as determining amounts for loan payments.	Some easy-to-use calculators for computing the time value of money and other financial computations are located at • www.kiplinger.com/tools • www.dinkytown.net • www.rbccentura.com/tools • cgi.money.cnn.com/tools

Note: The slight differences in answers are the result of rounding.

Exhibit 1–A   Future Value (Compounded Sum) of $1 after a Given Number of Time Periods

Period	1%	2%	3%	4%	5%	6%	7%	8%	9%	10%	11%
1	1.010	1.020	1.030	1.040	1.050	1.060	1.070	1.080	1.090	1.100	1.110
2	1.020	1.040	1.061	1.082	1.103	1.124	1.145	1.166	1.188	1.210	1.232
3	1.030	1.061	1.093	1.125	1.158	1.191	1.225	1.260	1.295	1.331	1.368
4	1.041	1.082	1.126	1.170	1.216	1.262	1.311	1.360	1.412	1.464	1.518
5	1.051	1.104	1.159	1.217	1.276	1.338	1.403	1.469	1.539	1.611	1.685
6	1.062	1.126	1.194	1.265	1.340	1.419	1.501	1.587	1.677	1.772	1.870
7	1.072	1.149	1.230	1.316	1.407	1.504	1.606	1.714	1.828	1.949	2.076
8	1.083	1.172	1.267	1.369	1.477	1.594	1.718	1.851	1.993	2.144	2.305
9	1.094	1.195	1.305	1.423	1.551	1.689	1.838	1.999	2.172	2.358	2.558
10	1.105	1.219	1.344	1.480	1.629	1.791	1.967	2.159	2.367	2.594	2.839
11	1.116	1.243	1.384	1.539	1.710	1.898	2.105	2.332	2.580	2.853	3.152
12	1.127	1.268	1.426	1.601	1.796	2.012	2.252	2.518	2.813	3.138	3.498
13	1.138	1.294	1.469	1.665	1.886	2.133	2.410	2.720	3.066	3.452	3.883
14	1.149	1.319	1.513	1.732	1.980	2.261	2.579	2.937	3.342	3.797	4.310
15	1.161	1.346	1.558	1.801	2.079	2.397	2.759	3.172	3.642	4.177	4.785
16	1.173	1.373	1.605	1.873	2.183	2.540	2.952	3.426	3.970	4.595	5.311
17	1.184	1.400	1.653	1.948	2.292	2.693	3.159	3.700	4.328	5.054	5.895
18	1.196	1.428	1.702	2.026	2.407	2.854	3.380	3.996	4.717	5.560	6.544
19	1.208	1.457	1.754	2.107	2.527	3.026	3.617	4.316	5.142	6.116	7.263
20	1.220	1.486	1.806	2.191	2.653	3.207	3.870	4.661	5.604	6.727	8.062
25	1.282	1.641	2.094	2.666	3.386	4.292	5.427	6.848	8.623	10.835	13.585
30	1.348	1.811	2.427	3.243	4.322	5.743	7.612	10.063	13.268	17.449	22.892
40	1.489	2.208	3.262	4.801	7.040	10.286	14.974	21.725	31.409	45.259	65.001
50	1.645	2.692	4.384	7.107	11.467	18.420	29.457	46.902	74.358	117.390	184.570

Period	12%	13%	14%	15%	16%	17%	18%	19%	20%	25%	30%
1	1.120	1.130	1.140	1.150	1.160	1.170	1.180	1.190	1.200	1.250	1.300
2	1.254	1.277	1.300	1.323	1.346	1.369	1.392	1.416	1.440	1.563	1.690
3	1.405	1.443	1.482	1.521	1.561	1.602	1.643	1.685	1.728	1.953	2.197
4	1.574	1.630	1.689	1.749	1.811	1.874	1.939	2.005	2.074	2.441	2.856
5	1.762	1.842	1.925	2.011	2.100	2.192	2.288	2.386	2.488	3.052	3.713
6	1.974	2.082	2.195	2.313	2.436	2.565	2.700	2.840	2.986	3.815	4.827
7	2.211	2.353	2.502	2.660	2.826	3.001	3.185	3.379	3.583	4.768	6.276
8	2.476	2.658	2.853	3.059	3.278	3.511	3.759	4.021	4.300	5.960	8.157
9	2.773	3.004	3.252	3.518	3.803	4.108	4.435	4.785	5.160	7.451	10.604
10	3.106	3.395	3.707	4.046	4.411	4.807	5.234	5.696	6.192	9.313	13.786
11	3.479	3.836	4.226	4.652	5.117	5.624	6.176	6.777	7.430	11.642	17.922
12	3.896	4.335	4.818	5.350	5.936	6.580	7.288	8.064	8.916	14.552	23.298
13	4.363	4.898	5.492	6.153	6.886	7.699	8.599	9.596	10.699	18.190	30.288
14	4.887	5.535	6.261	7.076	7.988	9.007	10.147	11.420	12.839	22.737	39.374
15	5.474	6.254	7.138	8.137	9.266	10.539	11.974	13.590	15.407	28.422	51.186
16	6.130	7.067	8.137	9.358	10.748	12.330	14.129	16.172	18.488	35.527	66.542
17	6.866	7.986	9.276	10.761	12.468	14.426	16.672	19.244	22.186	44.409	86.504
18	7.690	9.024	10.575	12.375	14.463	16.879	19.673	22.091	26.623	55.511	112.460
19	8.613	10.197	12.056	14.232	16.777	19.748	23.214	27.252	31.948	69.389	146.190
20	9.646	11.523	13.743	16.367	19.461	23.106	27.393	32.429	38.338	86.736	190.050
25	17.000	21.231	26.462	32.919	40.874	50.658	62.669	77.388	95.396	264.700	705.640
30	29.960	39.116	50.950	66.212	85.850	111.070	143.370	184.680	237.380	807.790	2,620.000
40	93.051	132.780	188.880	267.860	378.720	533.870	750.380	1,051.700	1,469.800	7,523.200	36,119.000
50	289.000	450.740	700.230	1,083.700	1,670.700	2,566.200	3,927.400	5,988.900	9,100.400	70,065.000	497,929.000

Exhibit 1–B Future Value (Compounded Sum) of $1 Paid in at the End of Each Period for a Given Number of Time Periods (an Annuity)

Period	1%	2%	3%	4%	5%	6%	7%	8%	9%	10%	11%
1	1.000	1.000	1.000	1.000	1.000	1.000	1.000	1.000	1.000	1.000	1.000
2	2.010	2.020	2.030	2.040	2.050	2.060	2.070	2.080	2.090	2.100	2.110
3	3.030	3.060	3.091	3.122	3.153	3.184	3.215	3.246	3.278	3.310	3.342
4	4.060	4.122	4.184	4.246	4.310	4.375	4.440	4.506	4.573	4.641	4.710
5	5.101	5.204	5.309	5.416	5.526	5.637	5.751	5.867	5.985	6.105	6.228
6	6.152	6.308	6.468	6.633	6.802	6.975	7.153	7.336	7.523	7.716	7.913
7	7.214	7.434	7.662	7.898	8.142	8.394	8.654	8.923	9.200	9.487	9.783
8	8.286	8.583	8.892	9.214	9.549	9.897	10.260	10.637	11.028	11.436	11.859
9	9.369	9.755	10.159	10.583	11.027	11.491	11.978	12.488	13.021	13.579	14.164
10	10.462	10.950	11.464	12.006	12.578	13.181	13.816	14.487	15.193	15.937	16.722
11	11.567	12.169	12.808	13.486	14.207	14.972	15.784	16.645	17.560	18.531	19.561
12	12.683	13.412	14.192	15.026	15.917	16.870	17.888	18.977	20.141	21.384	22.713
13	13.809	14.680	15.618	16.627	17.713	18.882	20.141	21.495	22.953	24.523	26.212
14	14.947	15.974	17.086	18.292	19.599	21.015	22.550	24.215	26.019	27.975	30.095
15	16.097	17.293	18.599	20.024	21.579	23.276	25.129	27.152	29.361	31.772	34.405
16	17.258	18.639	20.157	21.825	23.657	25.673	27.888	30.324	33.003	35.950	39.190
17	18.430	20.012	21.762	23.698	25.840	28.213	30.840	33.750	36.974	40.545	44.501
18	19.615	21.412	23.414	25.645	28.132	30.906	33.999	37.450	41.301	45.599	50.396
19	20.811	22.841	25.117	27.671	30.539	33.760	37.379	41.446	46.018	51.159	56.939
20	22.019	24.297	26.870	29.778	33.066	36.786	40.995	45.762	51.160	57.275	64.203
25	28.243	32.030	36.459	41.646	47.727	54.865	63.249	73.106	84.701	98.347	114.410
30	34.785	40.588	47.575	56.085	66.439	79.058	94.461	113.280	136.310	164.490	199.020
40	48.886	60.402	75.401	95.026	120.800	154.760	199.640	259.060	337.890	442.590	581.830
50	64.463	84.579	112.800	152.670	209.350	290.340	406.530	573.770	815.080	1,163.900	1,668.800

Period	12%	13%	14%	15%	16%	17%	18%	19%	20%	25%	30%
1	1.000	1.000	1.000	1.000	1.000	1.000	1.000	1.000	1.000	1.000	1.000
2	2.120	2.130	2.140	2.150	2.160	2.170	2.180	2.190	2.200	2.250	2.300
3	3.374	3.407	3.440	3.473	3.506	3.539	3.572	3.606	3.640	3.813	3.990
4	4.779	4.850	4.921	4.993	5.066	5.141	5.215	5.291	5.368	5.766	6.187
5	6.353	6.480	6.610	6.742	6.877	7.014	7.154	7.297	7.442	8.207	9.043
6	8.115	8.323	8.536	8.754	8.977	9.207	9.442	9.683	9.930	11.259	12.756
7	10.089	10.405	10.730	11.067	11.414	11.772	12.142	12.523	12.916	15.073	17.583
8	12.300	12.757	13.233	13.727	14.240	14.773	15.327	15.902	16.499	19.842	23.858
9	14.776	15.416	16.085	16.786	17.519	18.285	19.086	19.923	20.799	25.802	32.015
10	17.549	18.420	19.337	20.304	21.321	22.393	23.521	24.701	25.959	33.253	42.619
11	20.655	21.814	23.045	24.349	25.733	27.200	28.755	30.404	32.150	42.566	56.405
12	24.133	25.650	27.271	29.002	30.850	32.824	34.931	37.180	39.581	54.208	74.327
13	28.029	29.985	32.089	34.352	36.786	39.404	42.219	45.244	48.497	68.760	97.625
14	32.393	34.883	37.581	40.505	43.672	47.103	50.818	54.841	59.196	86.949	127.910
15	37.280	40.417	43.842	47.580	51.660	56.110	60.965	66.261	72.035	109.690	167.290
16	42.753	46.672	50.980	55.717	60.925	66.649	72.939	79.850	87.442	138.110	218.470
17	48.884	53.739	59.118	65.075	71.673	78.979	87.068	96.022	105.930	173.640	285.010
18	55.750	61.725	68.394	75.836	84.141	93.406	103.740	115.270	128.120	218.050	371.520
19	63.440	70.749	78.969	88.212	98.603	110.290	123.410	138.170	154.740	273.560	483.970
20	72.052	80.947	91.025	102.440	115.380	130.030	146.630	165.420	186.690	342.950	630.170
25	133.330	155.620	181.870	212.790	249.210	292.110	342.600	402.040	471.980	1,054.800	2,348.800
30	241.330	293.200	356.790	434.750	530.310	647.440	790.950	966.700	1,181.900	3,227.200	8,730.000
40	767.090	1,013.700	1,342.000	1,779.100	2,360.800	3,134.500	4,163.210	5,529.800	7,343.900	30,089.000	120,393.000
50	2,400.000	3,459.500	4,994.500	7,217.700	10,436.000	15,090.000	21,813.000	31,515.000	45,497.000	80,256.000	165,976.000

Exhibit 1–C   Present Value of $1 to Be Received at the End of a Given Number of Time Periods

Period	1%	2%	3%	4%	5%	6%	7%	8%	9%	10%	11%	12%
1	0.990	0.980	0.971	0.962	0.952	0.943	0.935	0.926	0.917	0.909	0.901	0.893
2	0.980	0.961	0.943	0.925	0.907	0.890	0.873	0.857	0.842	0.826	0.812	0.797
3	0.971	0.942	0.915	0.889	0.864	0.840	0.816	0.794	0.772	0.751	0.731	0.712
4	0.961	0.924	0.885	0.855	0.823	0.792	0.763	0.735	0.708	0.683	0.659	0.636
5	0.951	0.906	0.863	0.822	0.784	0.747	0.713	0.681	0.650	0.621	0.593	0.567
6	0.942	0.888	0.837	0.790	0.746	0.705	0.666	0.630	0.596	0.564	0.535	0.507
7	0.933	0.871	0.813	0.760	0.711	0.665	0.623	0.583	0.547	0.513	0.482	0.452
8	0.923	0.853	0.789	0.731	0.677	0.627	0.582	0.540	0.502	0.467	0.434	0.404
9	0.914	0.837	0.766	0.703	0.645	0.592	0.544	0.500	0.460	0.424	0.391	0.361
10	0.905	0.820	0.744	0.676	0.614	0.558	0.508	0.463	0.422	0.386	0.352	0.322
11	0.896	0.804	0.722	0.650	0.585	0.527	0.475	0.429	0.388	0.350	0.317	0.287
12	0.887	0.788	0.701	0.625	0.557	0.497	0.444	0.397	0.356	0.319	0.286	0.257
13	0.879	0.773	0.681	0.601	0.530	0.469	0.415	0.368	0.326	0.290	0.258	0.229
14	0.870	0.758	0.661	0.577	0.505	0.442	0.388	0.340	0.299	0.263	0.232	0.205
15	0.861	0.743	0.642	0.555	0.481	0.417	0.362	0.315	0.275	0.239	0.209	0.183
16	0.853	0.728	0.623	0.534	0.458	0.394	0.339	0.292	0.252	0.218	0.188	0.163
17	0.844	0.714	0.605	0.513	0.436	0.371	0.317	0.270	0.231	0.198	0.170	0.146
18	0.836	0.700	0.587	0.494	0.416	0.350	0.296	0.250	0.212	0.180	0.153	0.130
19	0.828	0.686	0.570	0.475	0.396	0.331	0.277	0.232	0.194	0.164	0.138	0.116
20	0.820	0.673	0.554	0.456	0.377	0.312	0.258	0.215	0.178	0.149	0.124	0.104
25	0.780	0.610	0.478	0.375	0.295	0.233	0.184	0.146	0.116	0.092	0.074	0.059
30	0.742	0.552	0.412	0.308	0.231	0.174	0.131	0.099	0.075	0.057	0.044	0.033
40	0.672	0.453	0.307	0.208	0.142	0.097	0.067	0.046	0.032	0.022	0.015	0.011
50	0.608	0.372	0.228	0.141	0.087	0.054	0.034	0.021	0.013	0.009	0.005	0.003

Period	13%	14%	15%	16%	17%	18%	19%	20%	25%	30%	35%	40%	50%
1	0.885	0.877	0.870	0.862	0.855	0.847	0.840	0.833	0.800	0.769	0.741	0.714	0.667
2	0.783	0.769	0.756	0.743	0.731	0.718	0.706	0.694	0.640	0.592	0.549	0.510	0.444
3	0.693	0.675	0.658	0.641	0.624	0.609	0.593	0.579	0.512	0.455	0.406	0.364	0.296
4	0.613	0.592	0.572	0.552	0.534	0.515	0.499	0.482	0.410	0.350	0.301	0.260	0.198
5	0.543	0.519	0.497	0.476	0.456	0.437	0.419	0.402	0.320	0.269	0.223	0.186	0.132
6	0.480	0.456	0.432	0.410	0.390	0.370	0.352	0.335	0.262	0.207	0.165	0.133	0.088
7	0.425	0.400	0.376	0.354	0.333	0.314	0.296	0.279	0.210	0.159	0.122	0.095	0.059
8	0.376	0.351	0.327	0.305	0.285	0.266	0.249	0.233	0.168	0.123	0.091	0.068	0.039
9	0.333	0.300	0.284	0.263	0.243	0.225	0.209	0.194	0.134	0.094	0.067	0.048	0.026
10	0.295	0.270	0.247	0.227	0.208	0.191	0.176	0.162	0.107	0.073	0.050	0.035	0.017
11	0.261	0.237	0.215	0.195	0.178	0.162	0.148	0.135	0.086	0.056	0.037	0.025	0.012
12	0.231	0.208	0.187	0.168	0.152	0.137	0.124	0.112	0.069	0.043	0.027	0.018	0.008
13	0.204	0.182	0.163	0.145	0.130	0.116	0.104	0.093	0.055	0.033	0.020	0.013	0.005
14	0.181	0.160	0.141	0.125	0.111	0.099	0.088	0.078	0.044	0.025	0.015	0.009	0.003
15	0.160	0.140	0.123	0.108	0.095	0.084	0.074	0.065	0.035	0.020	0.011	0.006	0.002
16	0.141	0.123	0.107	0.093	0.081	0.071	0.062	0.054	0.028	0.015	0.008	0.005	0.002
17	0.125	0.108	0.093	0.080	0.069	0.060	0.052	0.045	0.023	0.012	0.006	0.003	0.001
18	0.111	0.095	0.081	0.069	0.059	0.051	0.044	0.038	0.018	0.009	0.005	0.002	0.001
19	0.098	0.083	0.070	0.060	0.051	0.043	0.037	0.031	0.014	0.007	0.003	0.002	0
20	0.087	0.073	0.061	0.051	0.043	0.037	0.031	0.026	0.012	0.005	0.002	0.001	0
25	0.047	0.038	0.030	0.024	0.020	0.016	0.013	0.010	0.004	0.001	0.001	0	0
30	0.026	0.020	0.015	0.012	0.009	0.007	0.005	0.004	0.001	0	0	0	0
40	0.008	0.005	0.004	0.003	0.002	0.001	0.001	0.001	0	0	0	0	0
50	0.002	0.001	0.001	0.001	0	0	0	0	0	0	0	0	0

Exhibit 1–D   Present Value of $1 Received at the End of Each Period for a Given Number of Time Periods (an Annuity)

Period	1%	2%	3%	4%	5%	6%	7%	8%	9%	10%	11%	12%
1	0.990	0.980	0.971	0.962	0.952	0.943	0.935	0.926	0.917	0.909	0.901	0.893
2	1.970	1.942	1.913	1.886	1.859	1.833	1.808	1.783	1.759	1.736	1.713	1.690
3	2.941	2.884	2.829	2.775	2.723	2.673	2.624	2.577	2.531	2.487	2.444	2.402
4	3.902	3.808	3.717	3.630	3.546	3.465	3.387	3.312	3.240	3.170	3.102	3.037
5	4.853	4.713	4.580	4.452	4.329	4.212	4.100	3.993	3.890	3.791	3.696	3.605
6	5.795	5.601	5.417	5.242	5.076	4.917	4.767	4.623	4.486	4.355	4.231	4.111
7	6.728	6.472	6.230	6.002	5.786	5.582	5.389	5.206	5.033	4.868	4.712	4.564
8	7.652	7.325	7.020	6.733	6.463	6.210	5.971	5.747	5.535	5.335	5.146	4.968
9	8.566	8.162	7.786	7.435	7.108	6.802	6.515	6.247	5.995	5.759	5.537	5.328
10	9.471	8.983	8.530	8.111	7.722	7.360	7.024	6.710	6.418	6.145	5.889	5.650
11	10.368	9.787	9.253	8.760	8.306	7.887	7.499	7.139	6.805	6.495	6.207	5.938
12	11.255	10.575	9.954	9.385	8.863	8.384	7.943	7.536	7.161	6.814	6.492	6.194
13	12.134	11.348	10.635	9.986	9.394	8.853	8.358	7.904	7.487	7.103	6.750	6.424
14	13.004	12.106	11.296	10.563	9.899	9.295	8.745	8.244	7.786	7.367	6.982	6.628
15	13.865	12.849	11.939	11.118	10.380	9.712	9.108	8.559	8.061	7.606	7.191	6.811
16	14.718	13.578	12.561	11.652	10.838	10.106	9.447	8.851	8.313	7.824	7.379	6.974
17	15.562	14.292	13.166	12.166	11.274	10.477	9.763	9.122	8.544	8.022	7.549	7.102
18	16.398	14.992	13.754	12.659	11.690	10.828	10.059	9.372	8.756	8.201	7.702	7.250
19	17.226	15.678	14.324	13.134	12.085	11.158	10.336	9.604	8.950	8.365	7.839	7.366
20	18.046	16.351	14.877	13.590	12.462	11.470	10.594	9.818	9.129	8.514	7.963	7.469
25	22.023	19.523	17.413	15.622	14.094	12.783	11.654	10.675	9.823	9.077	8.422	7.843
30	25.808	22.396	19.600	17.292	15.372	13.765	12.409	11.258	10.274	9.427	8.694	8.055
40	32.835	27.355	23.115	19.793	17.159	15.046	13.332	11.925	10.757	9.779	8.951	8.244
50	39.196	31.424	25.730	21.482	18.256	15.762	13.801	12.233	10.962	9.915	9.042	8.304

Period	13%	14%	15%	16%	17%	18%	19%	20%	25%	30%	35%	40%	50%
1	0.885	0.877	0.870	0.862	0.855	0.847	0.840	0.833	0.800	0.769	0.741	0.714	0.667
2	1.668	1.647	1.626	1.605	1.585	1.566	1.547	1.528	1.440	1.361	1.289	1.224	1.111
3	2.361	2.322	2.283	2.246	2.210	2.174	2.140	2.106	1.952	1.816	1.696	1.589	1.407
4	2.974	2.914	2.855	2.798	2.743	2.690	2.639	2.589	2.362	2.166	1.997	1.849	1.605
5	3.517	3.433	3.352	3.274	3.199	3.127	3.058	2.991	2.689	2.436	2.220	2.035	1.737
6	3.998	3.889	3.784	3.685	3.589	3.498	3.410	3.326	2.951	2.643	2.385	2.168	1.824
7	4.423	4.288	4.160	4.039	3.922	3.812	3.706	3.605	3.161	2.802	2.508	2.263	1.883
8	4.799	4.639	4.487	4.344	4.207	4.078	3.954	3.837	3.329	2.925	2.598	2.331	1.922
9	5.132	4.946	4.772	4.607	4.451	4.303	4.163	4.031	3.463	3.019	2.665	2.379	1.948
10	5.426	5.216	5.019	4.833	4.659	4.494	4.339	4.192	3.571	3.092	2.715	2.414	1.965
11	5.687	5.453	5.234	5.029	4.836	4.656	4.486	4.327	3.656	3.147	2.752	2.438	1.977
12	5.918	5.660	5.421	5.197	4.988	4.793	4.611	4.439	3.725	3.190	2.779	2.456	1.985
13	6.122	5.842	5.583	5.342	5.118	4.910	4.715	4.533	3.780	3.223	2.799	2.469	1.990
14	6.302	6.002	5.724	5.468	5.229	5.008	4.802	4.611	3.824	3.249	2.814	2.478	1.993
15	6.462	6.142	5.847	5.575	5.324	5.092	4.876	4.675	3.859	3.268	2.825	2.484	1.995
16	6.604	6.265	5.954	5.668	5.405	5.162	4.938	4.730	3.887	3.283	2.834	2.489	1.997
17	6.729	6.373	6.047	5.749	5.475	5.222	4.988	4.775	3.910	3.295	2.840	2.492	1.998
18	6.840	6.467	6.128	5.818	5.534	5.273	5.033	4.812	3.928	3.304	2.844	2.494	1.999
19	6.938	6.550	6.198	5.877	5.584	5.316	5.070	4.843	3.942	3.311	2.848	2.496	1.999
20	7.025	6.623	6.259	5.929	5.628	5.353	5.101	4.870	3.954	3.316	2.850	2.497	1.999
25	7.330	6.873	6.464	6.097	5.766	5.467	5.195	4.948	3.985	3.329	2.856	2.499	2.000
30	7.496	7.003	6.566	6.177	5.829	5.517	5.235	4.979	3.995	3.332	2.857	2.500	2.000
40	7.634	7.105	6.642	6.233	5.871	5.548	5.258	4.997	3.999	3.333	2.857	2.500	2.000
50	7.675	7.133	6.661	6.246	5.880	5.554	5.262	4.999	4.000	3.333	2.857	2.500	2.000

2 Money Management Skills

Getting Personal

What are your money management habits? For each of the following statements, circle the choice that best describes your current situation:

1. My system for organizing personal financial records could be described as
   a. Nonexistent . . . I have documents that are missing in action!
   b. Basic . . . I can find most stuff when I need to!
   c. Very efficient . . . better than the Library of Congress!

2. How often do you prepare a personal balance sheet?
   a. Every few months.
   b. Every year.
   c. Never.

3. The details of my cash flow statement are
   a. Simple . . . "money coming in" and "money going out."
   b. Appropriate for my needs . . . enough information for me.
   c. Very informative . . . I know where my money goes.

4. My budgeting activities could be described as
   a. "I don't have enough money to worry about where it goes."
   b. "I keep track of my spending in my checkbook."
   c. "I have a written plan for spending and paying my bills on time."

After studying this chapter, you will be asked to reconsider your responses to these items.

Your Personal Financial Plan Sheets

5. Financial documents and records.
6. Creating a personal balance sheet.
7. Creating a personal cash flow statement.
8. Developing a personal budget.

Objectives

In this chapter, you will learn to:

1. Identify the main components of wise money management.
2. Create a personal balance sheet and cash flow statement.
3. Develop and implement a personal budget.
4. Connect money management activities with saving for personal financial goals.

Why is this important?

The average person in the United States saves less than three cents of every dollar earned. This lack of saving results in not having adequate funds for long-term financial security. Effectively planning your spending and saving decisions provides a foundation for wise money management today and financial prosperity in the future.

A Successful Money Management Plan

OBJECTIVE 1
Identify the main components of wise money management.

money management Day-to-day financial activities necessary to manage current personal economic resources while working toward long-term financial security.

"Each month I have too much month and not enough money. If the month were only 20 days long, budgeting would be easy."

Daily spending and saving decisions are at the center of your financial planning activities. You must coordinate these decisions with your needs, goals, and personal situation. Maintaining financial records and planning your spending are essential skills for successful personal financial management. The time and effort you devote to these activities will yield many benefits. **Money management** refers to the day-to-day financial activities necessary to manage current personal economic resources while working toward long-term financial security.

Components of Money Management

As shown here, three major money management activities are interrelated:

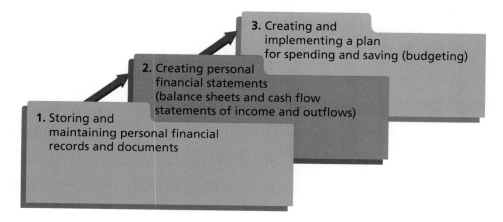

3. Creating and implementing a plan for spending and saving (budgeting)

2. Creating personal financial statements (balance sheets and cash flow statements of income and outflows)

1. Storing and maintaining personal financial records and documents

First, personal financial records and documents are the foundation of systematic resource use. These provide written evidence of business transactions, ownership of property, and legal matters. Next, personal financial statements enable you to measure and assess your financial position and progress. Finally, your spending plan, or *budget,* is the basis for effective money management.

A System for Personal Financial Records

Invoices, credit card statements, insurance policies, and tax forms are the basis of financial recordkeeping and personal economic choices. An organized system of financial records provides a basis for (1) handling daily business activities, such as bill paying;

Exhibit 2–1   Where to Keep Your Financial Records

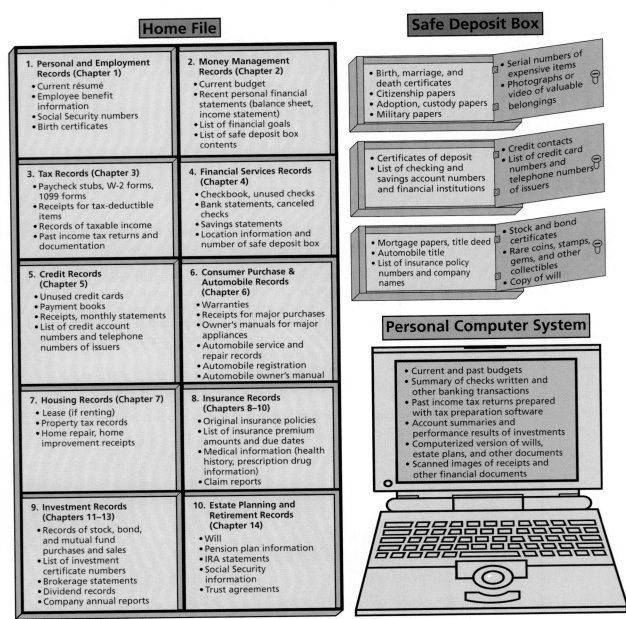

Home File

1. Personal and Employment Records (Chapter 1)
- Current résumé
- Employee benefit information
- Social Security numbers
- Birth certificates

2. Money Management Records (Chapter 2)
- Current budget
- Recent personal financial statements (balance sheet, income statement)
- List of financial goals
- List of safe deposit box contents

3. Tax Records (Chapter 3)
- Paycheck stubs, W-2 forms, 1099 forms
- Receipts for tax-deductible items
- Records of taxable income
- Past income tax returns and documentation

4. Financial Services Records (Chapter 4)
- Checkbook, unused checks
- Bank statements, canceled checks
- Savings statements
- Location information and number of safe deposit box

5. Credit Records (Chapter 5)
- Unused credit cards
- Payment books
- Receipts, monthly statements
- List of credit account numbers and telephone numbers of issuers

6. Consumer Purchase & Automobile Records (Chapter 6)
- Warranties
- Receipts for major purchases
- Owner's manuals for major appliances
- Automobile service and repair records
- Automobile registration
- Automobile owner's manual

7. Housing Records (Chapter 7)
- Lease (if renting)
- Property tax records
- Home repair, home improvement receipts

8. Insurance Records (Chapters 8–10)
- Original insurance policies
- List of insurance premium amounts and due dates
- Medical information (health history, prescription drug information)
- Claim reports

9. Investment Records (Chapters 11–13)
- Records of stock, bond, and mutual fund purchases and sales
- List of investment certificate numbers
- Brokerage statements
- Dividend records
- Company annual reports

10. Estate Planning and Retirement Records (Chapter 14)
- Will
- Pension plan information
- IRA statements
- Social Security information
- Trust agreements

Safe Deposit Box

- Birth, marriage, and death certificates
- Citizenship papers
- Adoption, custody papers
- Military papers
- Serial numbers of expensive items
- Photographs or video of valuable belongings

- Certificates of deposit
- List of checking and savings account numbers and financial institutions
- Credit contacts
- List of credit card numbers and telephone numbers of issuers

- Mortgage papers, title deed
- Automobile title
- List of insurance policy numbers and company names
- Stock and bond certificates
- Rare coins, stamps, gems, and other collectibles
- Copy of will

Personal Computer System

- Current and past budgets
- Summary of checks written and other banking transactions
- Past income tax returns prepared with tax preparation software
- Account summaries and performance results of investments
- Computerized version of wills, estate plans, and other documents
- Scanned images of receipts and other financial documents

(2) planning and measuring financial progress; (3) completing required tax reports; (4) making effective investment decisions; and (5) determining available resources for current and future spending.

As Exhibit 2–1 shows, most financial records are kept in one of three places: a home file, a safe deposit box, or a home computer. A home file should be used to keep records for current needs and documents with limited value. Your home file may be a series of folders, a cabinet with several drawers, or even a box. Whatever method you use, it is most important that your home file be organized to allow quick access to needed documents and information.

Important financial records and valuable articles should be kept in a location that provides better security than a home file. A **safe deposit box** is a private storage area at a financial institution with maximum security for valuables and difficult-to-replace documents. Items commonly kept in a safe deposit box include stock certificates, contracts, a list of insurance policies, and valuables such as rare coins and stamps.

The number of financial records and documents may seem overwhelming; however, they can easily be organized into 10 categories (see Exhibit 2–1). These groups correspond to the major topics covered in this book. You may not need to use all of these records and documents at present. As your financial situation changes, you will add others.

How long should you keep personal finance records? Records such as birth certificates, wills, and Social Security data should be kept permanently. Records on property and investments should be kept as long as you own these items. Federal tax laws dictate the length of time you should keep tax-related information. Copies of tax returns and supporting data should be saved for seven years. Normally, an audit will go back only three years; however, under certain circumstances, the Internal Revenue Service may request information from further back. Financial experts also recommend keeping documents related to the purchase and sale of real estate indefinitely.

Apply *Yourself!*

Objective 1

Working with two or three others in your class, develop a system for filing and maintaining personal financial records.

safe deposit box A private storage area at a financial institution with maximum security for valuables.

 CAUTION!

In the United States, people keep various documents and valuables in 30 million safe deposit boxes in banks and other financial institutions. While these boxes are usually very safe, each year a few people lose the contents of their safe deposit boxes through theft, fire, or natural disasters. Such losses are usually, but not always, covered by the financial institution's insurance.

Sheet 5
Financial Documents and Records

✓ CONCEPT CHECK 2–1

1 What are the three major money management activities?

_____

_____

2 What are the benefits of an organized system of financial records and documents?

_____

_____

(continued)

3 For each of the following records, check the column to indicate the length of time the item should be kept. "Short time period" refers to less than five years.

Document	Short time period	Longer time period
Credit card statements		
Mortgage documents		
Receipts for furniture, clothing		
Retirement account information		
Will		

Personal Financial Statements

OBJECTIVE 2

Create a personal balance sheet and cash flow statement.

Every journey starts somewhere. You need to know where you are before you can go somewhere else. Personal financial statements tell you the starting point of your financial journey. Most financial documents come from financial institutions, businesses, or the government. However, two documents you create yourself are the personal balance sheet and the cash flow statement, also called *personal financial statements*.

These reports provide information about your current financial position and present a summary of your income and spending. The main purposes of personal financial statements are to (1) report your current financial position; (2) measure your progress toward financial goals; (3) maintain information about your financial activities; and (4) provide data for preparing tax forms or applying for credit.

Your Personal Balance Sheet: The Starting Point

balance sheet A financial statement that reports what an individual or a family owns and owes; also called a *net worth statement* or *statement of financial position*.

The current financial position of an individual or family is a common starting point for financial planning. A **balance sheet,** also called a *net worth statement* or *statement of financial position,* reports what you own and what you owe. You prepare a personal balance sheet to determine your current financial position using the following process:

| Items of value (what you own) | − | Amounts owed (what you owe) | = | Net worth (your wealth) |

For example, if your possessions are worth $4,500 and you owe $800 to others, your net worth is $3,700. As shown in Exhibit 2–2, preparation of a balance sheet involves three main steps.

STEP 1: LISTING ITEMS OF VALUE   Available cash and money in bank accounts combined with other items of value are the foundation of your current financial position. **Assets** are cash and other tangible property with a monetary value. The balance sheet for Sandra and Mark Scott lists their assets in four categories:

assets Cash and other property with a monetary value.

liquid assets Cash and items of value that can easily be converted to cash.

1. **Liquid assets** are cash and items of value that can easily be converted to cash. Money in checking and savings accounts is *liquid* and is available to the Scott family for current spending. The cash value of their life insurance may be borrowed if needed. While assets other than liquid assets can also be converted into cash, the process is not quite as easy.

Exhibit 2–2   Creating a Personal Balance Sheet

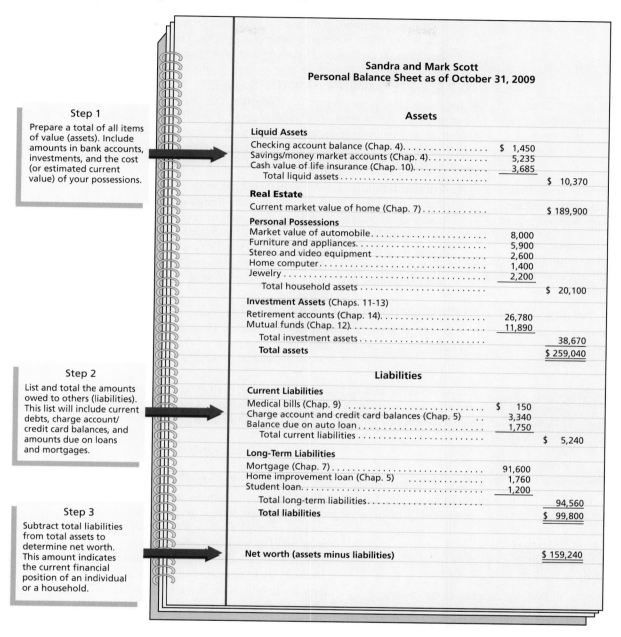

Step 1

Prepare a total of all items of value (assets). Include amounts in bank accounts, investments, and the cost (or estimated current value) of your possessions.

Step 2

List and total the amounts owed to others (liabilities). This list will include current debts, charge account/credit card balances, and amounts due on loans and mortgages.

Step 3

Subtract total liabilities from total assets to determine net worth. This amount indicates the current financial position of an individual or a household.

Sandra and Mark Scott
Personal Balance Sheet as of October 31, 2009

Assets

Liquid Assets

Checking account balance (Chap. 4)................	$ 1,450	
Savings/money market accounts (Chap. 4)............	5,235	
Cash value of life insurance (Chap. 10)...............	3,685	
Total liquid assets................................		$ 10,370

Real Estate

Current market value of home (Chap. 7)............	$ 189,900

Personal Possessions

Market value of automobile......................	8,000	
Furniture and appliances........................	5,900	
Stereo and video equipment	2,600	
Home computer.................................	1,400	
Jewelry	2,200	
Total household assets		$ 20,100

Investment Assets (Chaps. 11-13)

Retirement accounts (Chap. 14)...................	26,780	
Mutual funds (Chap. 12).........................	11,890	
Total investment assets........................		38,670
Total assets		$ 259,040

Liabilities

Current Liabilities

Medical bills (Chap. 9)	$ 150	
Charge account and credit card balances (Chap. 5) ..	3,340	
Balance due on auto loan........................	1,750	
Total current liabilities		$ 5,240

Long-Term Liabilities

Mortgage (Chap. 7).............................	91,600	
Home improvement loan (Chap. 5)	1,760	
Student loan...................................	1,200	
Total long-term liabilities......................		94,560
Total liabilities		$ 99,800

Net worth (assets minus liabilities)	$ 159,240

2. *Real estate* includes a home, a condominium, vacation property, or other land that a person or family owns.
3. *Personal possessions* are a major portion of assets for most people. Included in this category are automobiles and other personal belongings. Although these items have value, they may be difficult to convert to cash. You may decide to list your possessions on the balance sheet at their original cost. However, these values probably need to be revised over time, since a five-year-old television set, for example, is worth less now than when it was new. Thus you may wish to list your possessions at their current value (also referred to as *market value*).

did you know?

According to the Bureau of the Census, U.S. Department of Commerce, the assets most frequently held by households are motor vehicles, homes, savings accounts, U.S. savings bonds, certificates of deposit, mutual funds, stocks, corporate bonds, and retirement accounts.

4. *Investment assets* are funds set aside for long-term financial needs. The Scott family will use their investments for such things as financing their children's education, purchasing a vacation home, and planning for retirement. Since investment assets usually fluctuate in value, the amounts listed should reflect their value at the time the balance sheet is prepared.

STEP 2: DETERMINING AMOUNTS OWED   After looking at the total assets of the Scott family, you might conclude that they have a strong financial position. However, their debts must also be considered. **Liabilities** are amounts owed to others but do not include items not yet due, such as next month's rent. A liability is a debt you owe now, not something you may owe in the future. Liabilities fall into two categories:

liabilities Amounts owed to others.

1. **Current liabilities** are debts you must pay within a short time, usually less than a year. These liabilities include such things as medical bills, tax payments, insurance premiums, cash loans, and charge accounts.
2. **Long-term liabilities** are debts you do not have to pay in full until more than a year from now. Common long-term liabilities include auto loans, educational loans, and mortgages. A *mortgage* is an amount borrowed to buy a house or other real estate that will be repaid over a period of 15, 20, or 30 years.

current liabilities Debts that must be paid within a short time, usually less than a year.

long-term liabilities Debts that are not required to be paid in full until more than a year from now.

STEP 3: COMPUTING NET WORTH   Your **net worth** is the difference between your total assets and your total liabilities. This relationship can be stated as

net worth The difference between total assets and total liabilities.

$$\text{Assets} - \text{Liabilities} = \text{Net worth}$$

Net worth is the amount you would have left if all assets were sold for the listed values and all debts were paid in full. Also, total assets equal total liabilities plus net worth. The balance sheet of a business is commonly expressed as

$$\text{Assets} = \text{Liabilities} + \text{Net worth}$$

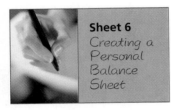

Sheet 6
Creating a Personal Balance Sheet

As Exhibit 2–2 shows, Sandra and Mark Scott have a net worth of $159,240. Since very few people, if any, liquidate all assets, the amount of net worth has a more practical purpose: It provides a measurement of your current financial position.

A person may have a high net worth but still have financial difficulties. Having many assets with low liquidity means not having the cash available to pay current expenses. **Insolvency** is the inability to pay debts when they are due; it occurs when a person's liabilities far exceed available assets.

Individuals and families can increase their net worth by (1) increasing their savings; (2) reducing spending; (3) increasing the value of investments and other possessions; and (4) reducing amounts owed. Remember, your net worth is *not* money available to use, but an indication of your financial position on a given date.

insolvency The inability to pay debts when they are due because liabilities far exceed the value of assets.

cash flow The actual inflow and outflow of cash during a given time period.

Your Cash Flow Statement: Inflows and Outflows

Each day, financial events can affect your net worth. When you receive a paycheck or pay living expenses, your total assets and liabilities change. **Cash flow** is the actual inflow and outflow of cash during a given time period. Income from employment will probably represent your most important *cash inflow;* however, other income, such as interest earned on a savings account, should also be considered. In contrast, payments for items such as rent, food, and loans are *cash outflows.*

Figure It Out!

› Ratios for Evaluating Financial Progress

Financial ratios provide guidelines for measuring the changes in your financial situation. These relationships can indicate progress toward an improved financial position.

Ratio	Calculation	Example	Interpretation
Debt ratio	Liabilities divided by net worth	$25,000/$50,000 = 0.5	Shows relationship between debt and net worth; a low debt ratio is best.
Current ratio	Liquid assets divided by current liabilities	$4,000/$2,000 = 2	Indicates $2 in liquid assets for every $1 of current liabilities; a high current ratio is desirable to have cash available to pay bills.
Liquidity ratio	Liquid assets divided by monthly expenses	$10,000/$4,000 = 2.5	Indicates the number of months in which living expenses can be paid if an emergency arises; a high liquidity ratio is desirable.
Debt-payments ratio	Monthly credit payments divided by take-home pay	$540/$3,600 = 0.15	Indicates how much of a person's earnings goes for debt payments (excluding a home mortgage); most financial advisers recommend a debt/payments ratio of less than 20 percent.
Savings ratio	Amount saved each month divided by gross income	$648/$5,400 = 0.12	Financial experts recommend monthly savings of at least 10 percent.

Based on the following information, calculate the ratios requested:

- Liabilities $12,000
- Liquid assets $2,200
- Monthly credit payments $150
- Monthly savings $130

(1) Debt ratio _____

(2) Debt-payments ratio _____

- Net worth $36,000
- Current liabilities $550
- Take-home pay $900
- Gross income $1,500

(3) Current ratio _____

(4) Savings ratio _____

A **cash flow statement,** also called a *personal income and expenditure statement* (Exhibit 2–3), is a summary of cash receipts and payments for a given period, such as a month or a year. This report provides data on your income and spending patterns, which will be helpful when preparing a budget.

A checking account can provide information for your cash flow statement. Deposits to the account are your *inflows;* checks written, cash withdrawals, and debit card payments are your *outflows.* Of course, in using this system, when you do not deposit entire amounts received, you must also note the spending of these nondeposited amounts in your cash flow statement.

The process for preparing a cash flow statement involves three steps:

cash flow statement A financial statement that summarizes cash receipts and payments for a given period; also called a *personal income and expenditure statement.*

Total cash received during the time period	—	Cash outflows during the time period	=	Cash surplus or deficit

Exhibit 2–3   Creating a Cash Flow Statement

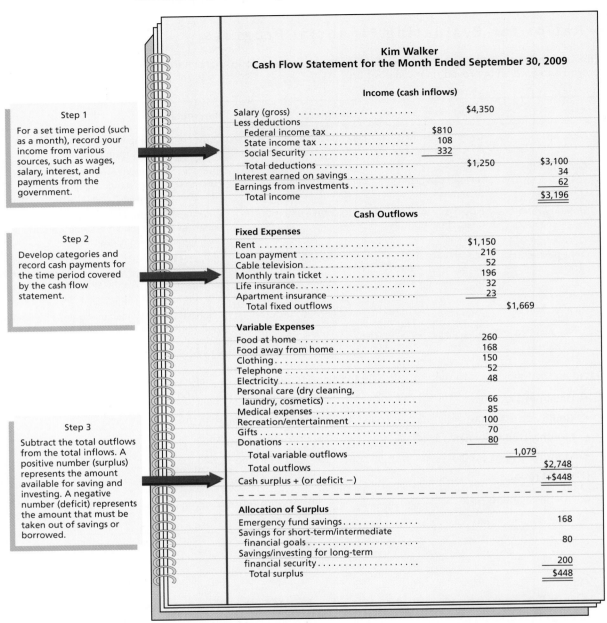

Step 1

For a set time period (such as a month), record your income from various sources, such as wages, salary, interest, and payments from the government.

Step 2

Develop categories and record cash payments for the time period covered by the cash flow statement.

Step 3

Subtract the total outflows from the total inflows. A positive number (surplus) represents the amount available for saving and investing. A negative number (deficit) represents the amount that must be taken out of savings or borrowed.

Kim Walker
Cash Flow Statement for the Month Ended September 30, 2009

Income (cash inflows)

Salary (gross)		$4,350	
Less deductions			
Federal income tax	$810		
State income tax	108		
Social Security	332		
Total deductions	$1,250	$3,100	
Interest earned on savings		34	
Earnings from investments		62	
Total income		$3,196	

Cash Outflows

Fixed Expenses

Rent	$1,150	
Loan payment	216	
Cable television	52	
Monthly train ticket	196	
Life insurance	32	
Apartment insurance	23	
Total fixed outflows	$1,669	

Variable Expenses

Food at home	260	
Food away from home	168	
Clothing	150	
Telephone	52	
Electricity	48	
Personal care (dry cleaning, laundry, cosmetics)	66	
Medical expenses	85	
Recreation/entertainment	100	
Gifts	70	
Donations	80	
Total variable outflows	1,079	
Total outflows	$2,748	
Cash surplus + (or deficit −)	+$448	

Allocation of Surplus

Emergency fund savings	168	
Savings for short-term/intermediate financial goals	80	
Savings/investing for long-term financial security	200	
Total surplus	$448	

income Inflows of cash to an individual or a household.

take-home pay Earnings after deductions for taxes and other items; also called *disposable income*.

STEP 1: RECORD INCOME   To create a cash flow statement, start by identifying the funds received. **Income** is the inflows of cash for an individual or a household. For most people, the main source of income is money received from a job. Other common income sources include commissions, self-employment income, interest, dividends, gifts, grants, scholarships, government payments, pensions, retirement income, alimony, and child support.

In Exhibit 2–3, notice that Kim Walker's monthly salary (or *gross income*) of $4,350 is her main source of income. However, she does not have use of the entire amount. **Take-home pay,** also called *net pay,* is a person's earnings after deductions for taxes and other items. Kim's deductions for federal, state, and Social Security taxes are $1,250. Her take-home pay is $3,100. This amount, plus earnings from savings and investments, is the income she has available for use during the current month.

Take-home pay is also called *disposable income,* the amount a person or household has available to spend. **Discretionary income** is money left over after paying for housing, food, and other necessities. Studies report that discretionary income ranges from less than 5 percent for people under age 25 to more than 40 percent for older people.

discretionary income Money left over after paying for housing, food, and other necessities.

STEP 2: RECORD CASH OUTFLOWS   Cash payments for living expenses and other items make up the second component of a cash flow statement. Kim Walker divides her cash outflows into two major categories: fixed expenses and variable expenses. Every individual and household has different cash outflows, but these main categories, along with the subcategories Kim uses, can be adapted to most situations.

1. *Fixed expenses* are payments that do not vary from month to month. Rent or mortgage payments, installment loan payments, cable television service fees, and a monthly train ticket for commuting to work are examples of constant or fixed cash outflows. For Kim, another type of fixed expense is the amount she sets aside each month for payments due once or twice a year. For example, Kim pays $384 every March for life insurance. Each month, she records a fixed outflow of $32 for deposit in a special savings account so that the money will be available when her insurance payment is due.

2. *Variable expenses* are flexible payments that change from month to month. Common examples of variable cash outflows are food, clothing, utilities (such as electricity and telephone), recreation, medical expenses, gifts, and donations. The use of a checkbook or some other recordkeeping system is necessary for an accurate total of cash outflows.

> *did you know?*
>
> The most common advice from financial planners: "Save more." "Save all you can." "Cut your spending so you can save more."

STEP 3: DETERMINE NET CASH FLOW   The difference between income and outflows can be either a positive (*surplus*) or a negative (*deficit*) cash flow. A deficit exists if more cash goes out than comes in during a given month. This amount must be made up by withdrawals from savings or by borrowing.

When you have a cash surplus, as Kim did (Exhibit 2–3), this amount is available for saving, investing, or paying off debts. Each month, Kim sets aside money for her *emergency fund* in a savings account that she would use for unexpected expenses or to pay living costs if she did not receive her salary. She deposits the rest of the surplus in savings and investment plans that have two purposes. The first is the achievement of short-term and intermediate financial goals, such as a new car, a vacation, or reenrollment in school; the second is long-term financial security—her retirement. A cash flow statement provides the foundation for preparing and implementing a spending, saving, and investment plan.

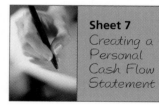

Sheet 7
Creating a Personal Cash Flow Statement

✓ CONCEPT CHECK 2–2

1 What are the main purposes of personal financial statements?

_____

_____

2 What does a personal balance sheet tell you about your financial situation?

_____

_____

(continued)

3 For the following items, identify each as an asset (A), liability (L), cash inflow (CI), or cash outflow (CO):

_____ monthly rent   _____ automobile loan

_____ interest on savings account   _____ collection of rare coins

_____ retirement account   _____ mortgage amount

_____ electric bill   _____ market value of automobile

4 Jan Franks has liquid assets of $6,300 and monthly expenses of $2,100. Based on the liquidity ratio, she has _____ months in which living expenses could be paid if an emergency arises.

A Plan for Effective Budgeting

<table>
<tr><td>

OBJECTIVE 3

Develop and implement a personal budget.

</td></tr>
</table>

budget A specific plan for spending income; also called a *spending plan.*

A **budget,** or *spending plan,* is necessary for successful financial planning. The common financial problems of overusing credit, lacking a regular savings program, and failing to ensure future financial security can be minimized through budgeting. The main purposes of a budget are to help you live within your income, spend your money wisely, reach your financial goals, prepare for financial emergencies, and develop wise financial management habits. Budgeting may be viewed in seven main steps.

Step 1: Set Financial Goals

Future plans are an important dimension for deciding your financial direction. Financial goals are plans for activities that require you to plan your spending, saving, and investing. As discussed in Chapter 1, financial goals should (1) be realistic; (2) be stated in measurable terms; (3) have a definite time frame; and (4) imply the type of action to be taken. Exhibit 2–4 gives examples of common financial goals based on life situation and time.

Step 2: Estimate Income

As Exhibit 2–5 shows, after setting goals, you need to estimate available money for a given time period. A common budgeting period is a month, since many payments, such as rent or mortgage, utilities, and credit cards, are due each month. In determining

Exhibit 2–4   Common Financial Goals

Personal Situation	Short-Term Goals (less than 2 years)	Intermediate Goals (2–5 years)	Long-Term Goals (over 5 years)
Single person	• Complete college • Pay off auto loan	• Take a vacation to Europe • Pay off education loan • Attend graduate school	• Buy a vacation home in the mountains • Provide for retirement income
Married couple (no children)	• Take an annual vacation • Buy a new car	• Remodel home • Build a stock portfolio	• Buy a retirement home • Provide for retirement income
Parent (young children)	• Increase life insurance • Increase savings	• Increase investments • Buy a new car	• Accumulate a college fund for children • Move to a larger home

Exhibit 2–5   Developing a Monthly Budget

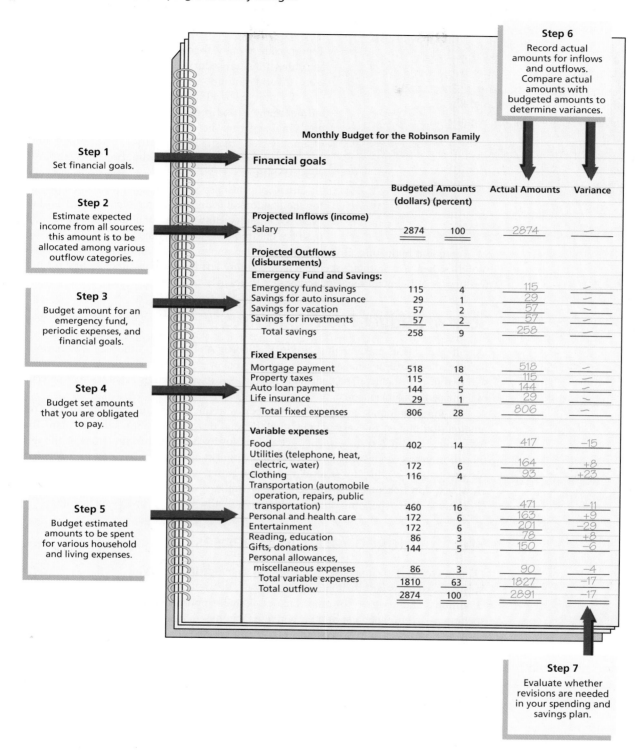

Step 1
Set financial goals.

Step 2
Estimate expected income from all sources; this amount is to be allocated among various outflow categories.

Step 3
Budget amount for an emergency fund, periodic expenses, and financial goals.

Step 4
Budget set amounts that you are obligated to pay.

Step 5
Budget estimated amounts to be spent for various household and living expenses.

Step 6
Record actual amounts for inflows and outflows. Compare actual amounts with budgeted amounts to determine variances.

Step 7
Evaluate whether revisions are needed in your spending and savings plan.

Monthly Budget for the Robinson Family

Financial goals

	Budgeted Amounts (dollars)	(percent)	Actual Amounts	Variance
Projected Inflows (income)				
Salary	2874	100	2874	—
Projected Outflows (disbursements)				
Emergency Fund and Savings:				
Emergency fund savings	115	4	115	—
Savings for auto insurance	29	1	29	—
Savings for vacation	57	2	57	—
Savings for investments	57	2	57	—
Total savings	258	9	258	—
Fixed Expenses				
Mortgage payment	518	18	518	—
Property taxes	115	4	115	—
Auto loan payment	144	5	144	—
Life insurance	29	1	29	—
Total fixed expenses	806	28	806	—
Variable expenses				
Food	402	14	417	−15
Utilities (telephone, heat, electric, water)	172	6	164	+8
Clothing	116	4	93	+23
Transportation (automobile operation, repairs, public transportation)	460	16	471	−11
Personal and health care	172	6	163	+9
Entertainment	172	6	201	−29
Reading, education	86	3	78	+8
Gifts, donations	144	5	150	−6
Personal allowances, miscellaneous expenses	86	3	90	−4
Total variable expenses	1810	63	1827	−17
Total outflow	2874	100	2891	−17

available income, include only money that you are sure you'll receive. Bonuses, gifts, or unexpected income should not be considered until the money is actually received.

Budgeting income may be difficult if your earnings vary by season or your income is irregular, as with sales commissions. In these situations, estimate your income on the low side to help avoid overspending and other financial difficulties.

Step 3: Budget an Emergency Fund and Savings

To set aside money for unexpected expenses as well as future financial security, the Robinsons have budgeted several amounts for savings and investments (see Exhibit 2–5). Financial advisers suggest that an emergency fund representing three to six months of living expenses be established for use in periods of unexpected financial difficulty. This amount will vary based on a person's life situation and employment stability.

The Robinsons also set aside an amount each month for their automobile insurance payment, which is due every six months. Both this amount and the emergency fund are put into a savings account.

A frequent budgeting mistake is to save the amount you have left at the end of the month. When you do that, you often have *nothing* left for savings. Since saving is vital for long-term financial security, remember to always "pay yourself first."

Step 4: Budget Fixed Expenses

Definite obligations make up this portion of a budget. As Exhibit 2–5 shows, the Robinsons have fixed expenses for housing, taxes, and loan payments. They make a monthly payment of $29 for life insurance. The budgeted total for their fixed expenses is $806, or 28 percent of estimated available income.

Assigning amounts to spending categories requires careful consideration. The amount you budget for various items will depend on your current needs and plans for the future. Exhibit 2–6 suggests budget allocations for different life situations. Although this information can be of value when creating budget categories, maintaining a detailed record of your spending for several months is a better source for your personal situation. However, don't become discouraged. Use a simple system, such as a notebook or your checkbook. This "spending diary" will help you know where your money is going.

Step 5: Budget Variable Expenses

Planning for variable expenses is not as easy as budgeting for savings or fixed expenses. Variable expenses will fluctuate by household situation, time of year, health, economic conditions, and a variety of other factors. A major portion of the Robinsons' planned spending—over 60 percent of their budgeted income—is for variable living costs. They base their estimates on past spending as well as expected changes in their cost of living.

Step 6: Record Spending Amounts

budget variance The difference between the amount budgeted and the actual amount received or spent.

deficit The amount by which actual spending exceeds planned spending.

surplus The amount by which actual spending is less than planned spending.

After having established a spending plan, you will need to keep track of your actual income and expenses. This process is similar to preparing a cash flow statement. In Exhibit 2–5, notice that the Robinsons estimated specific amounts for income and expenses. These are presented under "Budgeted Amounts." The family's actual spending was not always the same as planned. A **budget variance** is the difference between the amount budgeted and the actual amount received or spent. The total variance for the Robinsons was a $17 **deficit,** since their actual spending exceeded their planned spending by this amount. They would have had a **surplus** if their actual spending had been less than they had planned.

Exhibit 2–6   Typical After-Tax Budget Allocations

Budget Category	Student	Working Single (no dependents)	Couple (children under 18)	Single Parent (young children)	Parents (children over 18 in college)	Couple (over 55, no dependent children)
Housing (rent or mortgage payment; utilities; furnishings and appliances)	0–25%	30–35%	25–35%	20–30%	25–30%	25–35%
Transportation	5–10	15–20	15–20	10–18	12–18	10–18
Food (at home and away from home)	15–20	15–25	15–25	13–20	15–20	18–25
Clothing	5–12	5–15	5–10	5–10	4–8	4–8
Personal and health care (including child care)	3–5	3–5	4–10	8–12	4–6	6–12
Entertainment and recreation	5–10	5–10	4–8	4–8	6–10	5–8
Reading and education	10–30	2–4	3–5	3–5	6–12	2–4
Personal insurance and pension payments	0–5	4–8	5–9	5–9	4–7	6–8
Gifts, donations, and contributions	4–6	5–8	3–5	3–5	4–8	3–5
Savings	0–10	4–15	5–10	5–8	2–4	3–5

Sources: Bureau of Labor Statistics (http://stats.bls.gov); *American Demographics; Money; The Wall Street Journal.*

Variances for income should be viewed as the opposite of variances for expenses. Less income than expected would be a deficit, whereas more income than expected would be a surplus. Spending more than planned for an item may be justified by reducing spending for another item or putting less into savings. However, revising your budget and financial goals may be necessary.

Step 7: Review Spending and Saving Patterns

Like most decision-making activities, budgeting is a circular, ongoing process. You will need to review and perhaps revise your spending plan on a regular basis.

REVIEW YOUR FINANCIAL PROGRESS   The results of your budget may be obvious: having extra cash in checking or falling behind in your bill payments. However, such obvious results may not always be present. Occasionally, you will have to review areas where spending has been more or less than expected. You can prepare an annual summary to compare actual spending with budgeted amounts for each month. A spreadsheet program can be useful for this purpose. This summary will help you see areas where changes in your budget may be necessary. This review process is vital to both successful short-term money management and long-term financial security.

Apply *Yourself!*

Objective 3

Ask two or three friends or relatives about their budgeting systems. Obtain information on how they maintain their spending records. Create a visual presentation (video or slide presentation) that communicates wise budgeting techniques.

Personal Finance in Practice

› Selecting a Budgeting System

Although your checkbook will give you a fairly complete record of your expenses, it does not serve the purpose of planning for spending. A budget requires that you outline how you will spend available income. Described below are various budgeting systems. For each, list a benefit and concern of this method, and explain who might use this system.

Type of budgeting system	What are the benefits? What are the concerns?	Who might use this system?
A *mental budget* exists only in a person's mind. This simple system may be appropriate if you have limited resources and minimal financial responsibilities.		
A *physical budget* involves envelopes, folders, or containers to hold the money or slips of paper. Envelopes would contain the amount of cash or a note listing the amount to be used for "Food," "Rent," "Auto Payment," and other expenses.		
A *written budget* can be kept on notebook paper or on specialized budgeting paper available in office supply stores.		
Computerized budgeting systems use a spreadsheet program or specialized software such as Microsoft Money (www.msn.com/money) or Quicken (www.quicken.com).		

What would you do? Describe your current budgeting system. Are there any recordkeeping activities you might do differently?

REVISE YOUR GOALS AND BUDGET ALLOCATIONS What should you cut first when a budget shortage occurs? This question doesn't have easy answers, and answers will vary for different households. The most common overspending areas are entertainment and food, especially away-from-home meals. Purchasing less expensive brand items, buying quality used products, and avoiding credit card purchases are common budget adjustment techniques. At this point in the budgeting process, you may also revise your financial goals. Are you making progress toward achieving your objectives? Have changes in personal or economic conditions affected the desirability of certain goals? Have new goals surfaced that should be given a higher priority? Addressing these issues while creating an effective saving method will help ensure accomplishment of your financial goals.

CHARACTERISTICS OF SUCCESSFUL BUDGETING Having a spending plan will not eliminate financial worries. A budget will work only if you follow it.

did you know?

For years, co-workers were amused by a woman who carried a brown bag to lunch each day. That woman later retired in financial comfort and lived her later years in beachfront property. A daily coffee and muffin can add up to over $1,300 a year.

Changes in income, living expenses, and goals will require changes in your spending plan. Successful budgets are commonly viewed as being:

- *Well planned.* A good budget takes time and effort to prepare and should involve everyone affected by it.
- *Realistic.* If you have a moderate income, don't immediately expect to save enough money for an expensive car. A budget is designed not to prevent you from enjoying life but to help you achieve what you want most.
- *Flexible.* Unexpected expenses and life situation changes will require a budget that you can easily revise.
- *Clearly communicated.* Unless you and others involved are aware of the spending plan, it will not work. The budget should be written and available to all household members.

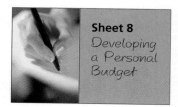

Sheet 8
Developing a Personal Budget

✓ CONCEPT CHECK 2–3

1 What are the main purposes of a budget?

_____

_____

2 How does a person's life situation affect goal setting and amounts allocated for various budget categories?

_____

_____

3 For each of the following household expenses, indicate if the item is a FIXED or a VARIABLE expense.

_____ food away from home   _____ cable television

_____ rent   _____ electricity

_____ health insurance premium   _____ auto repairs

4 The Nollin family has budgeted expenses for a month of $4,560 and actual spending of $4,480. This would result in a budget SURPLUS or DEFICIT (circle one) of $ _____ .

Money Management and Achieving Financial Goals

Your personal financial statements and budget allow you to achieve your financial goals with

1. Your balance sheet: reporting your current financial position—where you are now.
2. Your cash flow statement: telling you what you received and spent over the past month.
3. Your budget: planning spending and saving to achieve financial goals.

Many people prepare a balance sheet on a periodic basis, such as every three or six months. Between those points in time, your budget and cash flow statement help you

OBJECTIVE 4

Connect money management activities with saving for personal financial goals.

SOFTWARE | The latest money management programs have bells and whistles, and are easy to use. *By Jeff Bertolucci*

Quicken Stays a Step Ahead

Less has become more in the battle for supremacy in personal-finance software. Intuit's Quicken and Microsoft's Money both have dozens of money-management tools, slick integration with banking sites for paying bills and tracking accounts, and a dazzling array of charts and graphs. But we suspect only an obsessive-compulsive actuary would appreciate the details.

In a comparison between the recently released 2007 versions of the two programs, Intuit quicken wins top honors, thanks in large part to its redesigned—and vastly simplified—navigation. The first screen you see when the program launches has undergone a dramatic makeover that eliminates gratuitous charts and graphs and focuses on what really matters: cash flow. The home

page displays three large boxes: In, Out, and What's Left. The first box lists income and deposits; the second, bills and other expenses; and the third, available cash. What could be easier? Kudos to Intuit for using everyday language.

If you want the full range of bells and whistles, you'll need Microsoft Money Premium or Quicken Premier. Both sell for $80, but rebates knock the price down to $50 and $60 respectively. If you just want to focus on the basics, such as paying bills, balancing your checkbook and tracking credit card use, buy Microsoft Money Essentials ($20) or Quicken Basic ($30).

For many users, the difference between Microsoft's and Intuit's products may boil down to taste. Money 2007's My Money home page is pretty much unchanged from last year's model.

It's well organized (although perhaps a bit less intuitive than Quicken's minimalist setup) and provides a bird's-eye view of your finances.

What's new. The improvements in both versions are evolutionary, not revolutionary. Take Quicken's ability to attach electronic images of checks and other financial documents to records, for example. This feature, introduced last year, was clumsy to use at times, particularly when it came to attaching scanned records. But you can now scan multiple-page statements, bills or even warranties directly into Quicken.

Another worthwhile improvement: Quicken 2007 lets you download financial data from multiple sites with just one mouse click. With the previous version, you had to connect to each bank separately.

Money 2007 has its upgrades too, albeit nothing dramatic. We particularly like the new Savings and Spending Budget, a financial planner that helps you set aside 60 percent of your gross income for "committed expenses," such as food, insurance, and taxes. And the improved Tax Estimator is handy for a preview of your April tax bill or refund. However, for nitty-gritty details and more exact estimates, you're better off with a full-fledged tax program, such as H&R Block TaxCut or Intuit's TurboTax.

Quicken 2007's setup has a light edge because it takes fewer steps to create an account. Money users are forced to sign up for a free Windows Live ID account to use all its features. (A Hot-mail or MSN e-mail account will allow access to Money's features too.)

1. What factors might be considered when evaluating money management software before buying?

2. Describe money management software features that could be of most value to you.

3. Go to www.kiplinger.com to obtain additional information about budgeting and wise money management. Summarize your findings.

plan and measure spending and saving activities. For example, you might prepare a balance sheet on January 1, June 30, and December 31. Your budget would serve to plan your spending and saving between these points in time, and your cash flow statement of income and outflows would document your actual spending and saving. This relationship may be illustrated in this way:

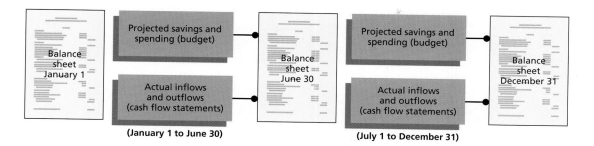

Changes in your net worth result from cash inflows and outflows. In periods when your outflows exceed your inflows, you must draw on savings or borrow (buy on credit). When this happens, lower assets (savings) or higher liabilities (due to the use of credit) result in a lower net worth. When inflows exceed outflows, putting money into savings or paying off debts will result in a higher net worth.

Apply *Yourself!*

Objective 4

Interview a young single person, a young couple, and a middle-aged person about their financial goals and savings habits. What actions do they take to determine and achieve various financial goals?

Selecting a Saving Technique

Traditionally, the United States ranks low among industrial nations in savings rate. Low savings affect personal financial situations. Studies reveal that the majority of Americans do not set aside an adequate amount for emergencies.

Since most people find saving difficult, financial advisers suggest these methods to make it easier:

1. Write a check each payday and deposit it in a savings account not readily available for regular spending. This savings deposit can be a percentage of income, such as 5 or 10 percent, or a specific dollar amount.
2. *Payroll deduction* is available at many places of employment. Under a *direct deposit* system, an amount is automatically deducted from your salary and deposited in savings.
3. Saving coins or spending less on certain items can help you save. Each day, put your change in a container. You can also increase your savings by taking a sandwich to work instead of buying lunch or by refraining from buying snacks or magazines.

How you save is far less important than making regular periodic savings deposits that will help you achieve financial goals. Small amounts of savings can grow faster than most people realize.

Calculating Savings Amounts

To achieve your financial objectives, you should convert your savings goals into specific amounts. Your use of a savings or investment plan is vital to the growth of your money. As Exhibit 2–7 shows, using the time value of money calculations, introduced in Chapter 1, can help you calculate progress toward achieving your financial goals.

Exhibit 2–7   Using Savings to Achieve Financial Goals

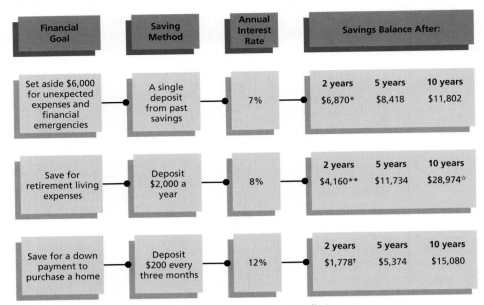

Financial Goal	Saving Method	Annual Interest Rate	Savings Balance After:		
			2 years	5 years	10 years
Set aside $6,000 for unexpected expenses and financial emergencies	A single deposit from past savings	7%	$6,870*	$8,418	$11,802
Save for retirement living expenses	Deposit $2,000 a year	8%	$4,160**	$11,734	$28,974☆
Save for a down payment to purchase a home	Deposit $200 every three months	12%	$1,778†	$5,374	$15,080

* Based on the future value of $1 tables in Chapter 1 and Appendix A.
** Based on the future value of a series of deposits tables in Chapter 1 and Appendix A.
☆ With annual $2,000 deposits, this same retirement account would grow to over $500,000 in 40 years.
† Based on quarterly compounding, explained in Chapter 4.

✔ CONCEPT CHECK 2–4

1 What relationship exists among personal financial statements, budgeting, and achieving financial goals?

_____

_____

2 What are some suggested methods to make saving easy?

_____

_____

3 If you wanted to obtain the following types of information, check the box for the document that you would find most useful.

Financial information needed	Balance sheet	Cash flow statement	Budget
Amounts owed for medical expenses			
Spending patterns for the past few months			
Planned spending patterns for the next month			
Current value of investment accounts			
Amounts to deposit in savings accounts			

back to *Getting Personal*

1. Reconsider your responses to the Getting Personal questions at the beginning of the chapter. What did you learn in this chapter that might affect your answers to these questions in the future?

_____

_____

2. List one of your personal financial goals for the next few months or years.

_____

_____

3. Describe how the three main financial statements from this chapter could be used to (a) achieve the financial goal you stated above, and (b) improve your daily money management activities.

Financial Statement Use	Balance Sheet	Cash Flow Statement	Budget
a. How could each financial statement be used to achieve your personal financial goal?			
b. How could your daily money management activities be improved with information from these financial statements?			

Chapter Summary

Objective 1   Successful money management requires a coordination of personal financial records, personal financial statements, and budgeting activities. An organized system of financial records and documents should provide ease of access as well as security for financial documents that may be impossible to replace.

Objective 2   A personal balance sheet, also known as a *net worth statement,* is prepared by listing all items of value (assets) and all amounts owed to others (liabilities). The difference between your total assets and your total liabilities is your net worth. A cash flow statement, also called a *personal income and expenditure statement,* is a summary of

cash receipts and payments for a given period, such as a month or a year.

Objective 3   The budgeting process consists of seven steps: (1) set financial goals; (2) estimate income; (3) budget an emergency fund and savings; (4) budget fixed expenses; (5) budget variable expenses; (6) record spending amounts; and (7) review spending and saving patterns.

Objective 4   The relationship among the personal balance sheet, cash flow statement, and budget provides the basis for achieving long-term financial security. Future value and present value calculations may be used to compute the increased value of savings for achieving financial goals.

Key Terms

assets   48

balance sheet   48

budget   54

budget variance   56

cash flow   50

cash flow statement   51

current liabilities   50

deficit   56

discretionary income   53

income   52

insolvency   50

liabilities   50

liquid assets   48

long-term liabilities   50

money management   45

net worth   50

safe deposit box   47

surplus   56

take-home pay   52

Problems

1. Based on the following data, determine the amount of total assets, total liabilities, and net worth.

    Liquid assets, $3,670

    Current liabilities, $2,670

    Long-term liabilities, $76,230

    Investment assets, $8,340

    Household assets, $89,890

    a. Total assets $ _____

    b. Total liabilities $ _____

    c. Net worth $ _____

2. Using the following balance sheet items and amounts, calculate the total liquid assets and total current liabilities:

    Money market account $2,600

    Mortgage $158,000

    Retirement account $86,700

    Medical bills $232

    Checking account $780

    Credit card balance $489

    a. Total liquid assets $ _____

    b. Total current liabilities $ _____

3. Use the following items to determine the total assets, total liabilities, net worth, total cash inflows, and total cash outflows.

    Rent for the month, $650

    Spending for food, $345

    Savings account balance, $1,890

    Current value of automobile, $7,800

    Credit card balance, $235

    Auto insurance, $230

    Stereo equipment, $2,350

    Lunches/parking at work, $180

    Home computer, $1,500

    Clothing purchase, $110

    Monthly take-home salary, $1,950

    Cash in checking account, $450

    Balance of educational loan, $2,160

    Telephone bill paid for month, $65

    Loan payment, $80

    Household possessions, $3,400

    Payment for electricity, $90

    Donations, $70

    Value of stock investment, $860

    Restaurant spending, $130

    a. Total assets $ _____

    b. Total liabilities $ _____

    c. Net worth $ _____

    d. Total cash inflows $ _____

    e. Total cash outflows $ _____

4. For each of the following situations, compute the missing amount.

  a. Assets $45,000; liabilities $16,000; net worth $ _____

  b. Assets $76,500; liabilities $ _____; net worth $18,700

  c. Assets $34,280; liabilities $12,965; net worth $ _____

  d. Assets $ _____; liabilities $38,345; net worth $52,654

5. Based on this financial data, calculate the ratios requested:

  Liabilities, $8,000   Net worth, $58,000
  Liquid assets, $4,600   Current liabilities, $1,300
  Monthly credit payments, $640   Take-home pay, $2,600
  Monthly savings, $130   Gross income, $2,850

  a. Debt ratio _____

  b. Current ratio _____

  c. Debt-payments ratio _____

  d. Savings ratio _____

6. For the following situations, calculate the cash surplus or deficit:

Cash inflows	Cash Outflows	Difference (surplus or deficit)
$3,400	$3,218	$_____ _____
4,756	4,833	$_____ _____
4,287	4,218	$_____ _____

7. The Brandon household has a monthly income of $5,630 on which to base their budget. They plan to save 10 percent and spend 32 percent on fixed expenses and 56 percent on variable expenses.
  a. What amount do they plan to set aside for each major budget section?

  Savings $_____
  Fixed expenses $_____
  Variable expenses $_____

  b. After setting aside these amounts, what amount would remain for additional savings or for paying off debts?

8. Fran Powers created the following budget and reported the actual spending listed. Calculate the variance for each of these categories, and indicate whether it was a *deficit* or a *surplus*.

Item	Budgeted	Actual	Variance	Deficit/Surplus
Food	$350	$298	_____	_____
Transportation	320	337	_____	_____
Housing	950	982	_____	_____
Clothing	100	134	_____	_____
Personal	275	231	_____	_____

9. Use future value and present value calculations (see tables in the appendix for Chapter 1) to determine the following:
  a. The future value of a $500 savings deposit after eight years at an annual interest rate of 7 percent.

   b. The future value of saving $1,500 a year for five years at an annual interest rate of 8 percent.

   c. The present value of a $2,000 savings account that will earn 6 percent interest for four years.

10. Ed Weston recently lost his job. Before unemployment occurred, the Weston household (Ed; wife, Alice; two children, ages 12 and 9) had a monthly take-home income of $3,165. Each month, the money went for the following items; $880 for rent, $180 for utilities, $560 for food, $480 for automobile expenses, $300 for clothing, $280 for insurance, $250 for savings, and $235 for personal and other items. After the loss of Ed's job, the household's monthly income is $1,550, from his wife's wages and his unemployment benefits. The Westons also have savings accounts, investments, and retirement funds of $28,000.

   a. What budget items might the Westons consider reducing to cope with their financial difficulties?

   b. How should the Westons use their savings and retirement funds during this financial crisis? What additional sources of funds might be available to them during this period of unemployment?

Questions

1. Describe some common money management mistakes that can cause long-term financial concerns.

2. What do you believe to be the major characteristics of an effective system to keep track of financial documents and records?

3. How might financial ratios be used when planning and implementing financial activities?

4. Discuss with several people how a budget might be changed if a household faced a decline in income. What spending areas might be reduced first?

5. What are long-term effects of low savings for both individuals and the economy of a country?

Internet Connection

COMPARING ONLINE MONEY MANAGEMENT ADVICE

Conduct an Internet search to locate two Web sites that provide information on budgeting and other money management activities. Compare the advice provided for the following categories:

Money management topic areas	Web site	Web site
1. What budget guidelines are provided for suggested spending amounts for food, housing, transportation, and other living expenses?		
2. How can a person avoid financial problems and money management difficulties?		
3. What suggestions are provided for saving and investing to achieve financial goals?		

What similarities and differences exist in the advice given by these Web sites? Which sites do you believe provide the most useful and reliable information?

www.mhhe.com/kdh

Case in Point

A LITTLE BECOMES A LOT

Can you imagine saving 25 cents a week and having it grow to more than $30,000?

As hard as that may be to believe, that's exactly what Ken Lopez was able to do. Putting aside a quarter a week starting in second grade, he built up a small savings account. These funds were then invested in various stocks and mutual funds. While in college, Ken was able to pay for his education while continuing to save between $50 and $100 a month. He closely monitored spending. Ken realized that the few dollars here and there for snacks and other minor purchases quickly add up.

Today, at age 27, Ken works as a customer service manager for an online sales division of a retailing company. He lives with his wife, Alicia, and their two young children. The family's spending plan allows for all their needs and also includes regularly saving and investing for the children's education and for retirement. Recently, Ken was asked by a co-worker, Brian, "How come you and Alicia never seem to have financial stress in your household?"

Ken replied, "Do you know where your money is going each month?"

"Not really," was Brian's response.

"You'd be surprised by how much is spent on little things you might do without," Ken responded.

"I guess so, I just don't want to have to go around with a notebook writing down every amount I spend," Brian said in a troubled voice.

"Well, you have to take some action if you want your financial situation to change," Ken said in an encouraging voice.

Brian conceded with, "All right, what would you recommend?"

Questions

1. What money management behaviors did Ken practice that most people neglect?

2. Based on information at www.kiplinger.com, www.money.com, or www.asec.org, describe money management and financial planning advice that would be appropriate for Brian.

3. What additional goals might be appropriate for Ken, Alicia, and their children?

Continuing Case

MONEY MANAGEMENT ACTIVITIES

Life Situation:

Single

Age 22

Starting a career

No dependents

Financial Date:

Monthly income $2,600

Living expenses $2,180

Assets $8,200

Liabilities $3,470

Emergency fund $530

Since the major portion of Pam's income is based on commission, her earnings vary from one month to the next. This situation makes it difficult for her to establish a realistic budget. During lean months, she has had to resort to using her credit card to make ends meet. In fact, her credit card debt, $3,470, is at a fairly high level. In addition, she has not been able to save much for various unexpected expenses and for her long-term financial security.

Questions

1. How might Pam budget for fluctuations in her income caused by commission earnings?

2. What are financial actions and revised goals Pam might want to consider at this time?

3. Explain Pam's potential uses of *Your Personal Financial Plan* sheets 5–8 for her money management and budgeting activities.

Video Case

FINANCIAL FITNESS

Various suggestions are available to better manage your daily finances and to obtain long-term financial security. Consumers are warned to assess the dangers of changing interest rates in relation to mortgages and credit-card use.

Questions

1. What actions would help a person to better manage daily spending?

2. How might credit card offers and adjustable rate mortgages affect spending and budgeting activities?

3. Conduct an online search to obtain additional suggestions for avoiding dangers of day-to-day overspending.

Spending Diary

"I AM AMAZED HOW LITTLE THINGS CAN ADD UP . . . HOWEVER, SINCE KEEPING TRACK OF ALL MY SPENDING, I REALIZE THAT I NEED TO CUT DOWN ON SOME ITEMS SO I CAN PUT SOME MONEY AWAY INTO SAVINGS."

Directions

Continue or start using the Daily Spending Diary sheets provided at the end of the book, or create your own format, to record *every cent* of your spending in the categories provided. This experience will help you better understand your spending patterns and help you plan for achieving financial goals.

Questions

1. What information from your daily spending diary might encourage you to reconsider various money management actions?

2. How can your daily spending diary assist you when planning and implementing a budget?

Financial Documents and Records

Financial Planning Activities: Indicate the location of the following records, and create files for the eight major categories of financial documents.

Suggested Web Sites: www.money.com   www.kiplinger.com

Item	Home file	Safe deposit box	Other (specify)
Money management records • budget, financial statements			
Personal/employment records • current résumé, social security card			
• educational transcripts			
• birth, marriage, divorce certificates			
• citizenship, military papers			
• adoption, custody papers			
Tax records **Financial services/consumer credit records** • unused, canceled checks			
• savings, passbook statements			
• savings certificates			
• credit card information, statements			
• credit contracts			
Consumer purchase, housing, and automobile records • warranties, receipts			
• owner's manuals			
• lease or mortgage papers, title deed, property tax info			
• automobile title			
• auto registration			
• auto service records			
Insurance records • insurance policies			
• home inventory			
• medical information (health history)			
Investment records • broker statements			
• dividend reports			
• stock/bond certificates			
• rare coins, stamps, and collectibles			
Estate planning and retirement • will			
• pension, social security info			

What's Next for Your Personal Financial Plan?

- Select a location for storing your financial documents and records.
- Decide if various documents may no longer be needed.

Your Personal Financial Plan

Name: _____   Date: _____

Creating a Personal Balance Sheet

Financial Planning Activities: List current values of the assets; amounts owed for liabilities; subtract total liabilities from total assets to determine net worth.

Suggested Web Sites: www.kiplinger.com   www.money.com

Balance sheet as of _____

Assets

Liquid assets

Checking account balance _____

Savings/money market accounts, funds _____

Cash value of life insurance _____

Other _____ _____

Total liquid assets _____

Household assets & possessions

Current market value of home _____

Market value of automobiles _____

Furniture _____

Stereo, video, camera equipment _____

Jewelry _____

Other _____ _____

Other _____ _____

Total household assets _____

Investment assets

Savings certificates _____

Stocks and bonds _____

Individual retirement accounts _____

Mutual funds _____

Other _____ _____

Total investment assets

Total Assets .... _____

Liabilities

Current liabilities

Charge account and credit card balances _____

Loan balances _____

Other _____ _____

Other _____ _____

Total current liabilities _____

Long-term liabilities

Mortgage

Other _____

Total long-term liabilities _____

Total Liabilities .... _____

Net Worth (assets minus liabilities) _____

What's Next for Your Personal Financial Plan?

- Compare your net worth to previous balance sheets.
- Decide how often you will prepare a balance sheet.

Creating a Personal Cash Flow Statement

Financial Planning Activities: Record inflows and outflows of cash for a one- (or three-) month period.

Suggested Web Sites: www.americasaves.org   www.money.com

For month ending _____

Cash Inflows
Salary (take-home) _____
Other income: _____
Other income: _____
Total Income _____

Cash Outflows
Fixed expenses
Mortgage or rent _____
Loan payments _____
Insurance _____
Other _____ _____
Other _____ _____
Total fixed outflows _____
Variable expenses _____
Food _____
Clothing _____
Electricity _____
Telephone _____
Water _____
Transportation _____
Personal care _____
Medical expenses _____
Recreation/entertainment _____
Gifts _____
Donations _____
Other _____ _____
Other _____ _____
Total variable outflows _____
Total Outflows _____
Surplus/Deficit _____

Allocation of surplus
Emergency fund savings _____
Financial goals savings _____
Other savings _____ _____

What's Next for Your Personal Financial Plan?

- Decide which areas of spending need to be revised.
- Evaluate your spending patterns for preparation of a budget.

Developing a Personal Budget

Financial Planning Activities: Estimate projected spending based on your cash flow statement, and maintain records for actual spending for these same budget categories.

Suggested Web Sites: www.betterbudgeting.com   www.asec.org

	Budgeted amounts		Actual amounts	Variance
Income	**Dollar**	**Percent**		
Salary				
Other _____				
Total income		100%		
Expenses				
Fixed expenses Mortgage or rent				
Property taxes				
Loan payments				
Insurance				
Other _____				
Total fixed expenses				
Emergency fund/savings Emergency fund				
Savings for _____				
Savings for _____				
Total savings				
Variable expenses Food				
Utilities				
Clothing				
Transportation costs				
Personal care				
Medical and health care				
Entertainment				
Education				
Gifts/donations				
Miscellaneous				
Other _____				
Other _____				
Total variable expenses				
Total expenses		100%		

What's Next for Your Personal Financial Plan?

- Evaluate the appropriateness of your budget for your life situation.
- Assess whether your budgeting activities are helping you achieve your financial goals.

3

Taxes in Your Financial Plan

Getting Personal

For each of the following statements, select "agree" or "disagree" to reflect your current behavior regarding these tax planning activities:

	Agree	Disagree
1. My tax records are organized to allow me to easily find needed information.	_____	_____
2. I have tax withheld from my pay to make sure I get a refund every year.	_____	_____
3. I am able to file my taxes on time each year.	_____	_____
4. My tax returns have never been questioned by the Internal Revenue Service.	_____	_____
5. Every few months, I learn new tax information to make filing easier and to reduce the amount of taxes owed.	_____	

After studying this chapter, you will be asked to reconsider your responses to these items.

Taxes in Your Financial Plan

OBJECTIVE 1

Identify the major taxes paid by people in our society.

Taxes are an everyday financial fact of life. You pay taxes when you get a paycheck or make a purchase. However, most people concern themselves with taxes only immediately before April 15.

Planning Your Tax Strategy

Each year, the Tax Foundation determines how long the average person works to pay taxes. In recent years, "Tax Freedom Day" came in early May. This means that the time that elapsed from January 1 until early May represents the portion of the year people work to pay their taxes.

Tax planning starts with knowing current tax laws. Next, maintain complete and appropriate tax records. Then, make purchase and investment decisions that can reduce your tax liability. Your primary goal should be to pay your fair share of taxes while taking advantage of appropriate tax benefits.

Apply *Yourself!*

Objective 1

Prepare a list of taxes that people commonly encounter in your geographic region.

Types of Tax

Most people pay taxes in four major categories: taxes on purchases, taxes on property, taxes on wealth, and taxes on earnings.

TAXES ON PURCHASES   You probably pay *sales tax* on many purchases. Many states exempt food and drugs from sales tax to reduce the financial burden on low-income households. In recent years, all but five states (Alaska, Delaware, Montana,

excise tax A tax imposed on specific goods and services, such as gasoline, cigarettes, alcoholic beverages, tires, and air travel.

New Hampshire, and Oregon) had a general sales tax. An **excise tax** is imposed by the federal and state governments on specific goods and services, such as gasoline, cigarettes, alcoholic beverages, tires, air travel, and telephone service.

TAXES ON PROPERTY

Real estate property tax is a major source of revenue for local governments. This tax is based on the value of land and buildings. Some areas impose a *personal property tax* on the value of automobiles, boats, furniture, and farm equipment.

TAXES ON WEALTH

estate tax A tax imposed on the value of a person's property at the time of death.

An **estate tax** is imposed on the value of a person's property at the time of death. This federal tax is based on the fair market value of the deceased person's investments, property, and bank accounts less allowable deductions and other taxes.

Money and property passed on to heirs may be subject to a state tax. An **inheritance tax** is levied on the value of property bequeathed by a deceased person. This tax is paid for the right to acquire the inherited property.

inheritance tax A tax levied on the value of property bequeathed by a deceased person.

Individuals are allowed to give money or items valued at $12,000 or less in a year to a person without being subject to taxes. Gift amounts greater than $12,000 are subject to federal tax. Amounts given for tuition payments or medical expenses are not subject to gift taxes.

TAXES ON EARNINGS

The two main taxes on wages and salaries are Social Security and income taxes. The Federal Insurance Contributions Act (FICA) created the Social Security tax to fund the old-age, survivors, and disability insurance portion of the Social Security system and the hospital insurance portion (Medicare).

Income tax is a major financial planning factor for most people. Some workers are subject to federal, state, and local income taxes. Currently, only seven states do not have a state income tax.

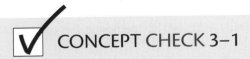

did you know?

According to the Tax Foundation (www.taxfoundation.org), Alaska, New Hampshire, Tennessee, Colorado, and South Dakota were the most "tax-friendly" states. In contrast, Maine, New York, Wisconsin, Vermont, and Hawaii had the highest taxes as a percentage of income.

Throughout the year, your employer will withhold income tax payments from your paycheck, or you may be required to make estimated tax payments if you own your own business. Both types of payments are only estimates; you may need to pay an additional amount, or you may get a tax refund. The following sections will assist you in preparing your federal income tax return and planning your future tax strategies.

✓ **CONCEPT CHECK 3–1**

1 What are the four major categories of taxes?

_____

_____

2 For each of the following situations, list the type of tax that is being described.

Financial planning situation	Type of tax
a. A tax on the value of a person's house.	
b. The additional charge for gasoline and air travel.	
c. Payroll deductions for federal government retirement benefits.	
d. Amount owed on property received from a deceased person.	
e. Payroll deductions for a direct tax on earnings.	

The Basics of Federal Income Tax

Each year, millions of Americans are required to pay their share of income taxes to the federal government. As shown in Exhibit 3–1, this process involves several steps.

Step 1: Determining Adjusted Gross Income

This process starts with steps to determine **taxable income,** which is the net amount of income, after allowable deductions, on which income tax is computed.

OBJECTIVE 2
Calculate taxable income and the amount owed for federal income tax.

taxable income The net amount of income, after allowable deductions, on which income tax is computed.

Exhibit 3–1   Computing Taxable Income and Your Tax Liability

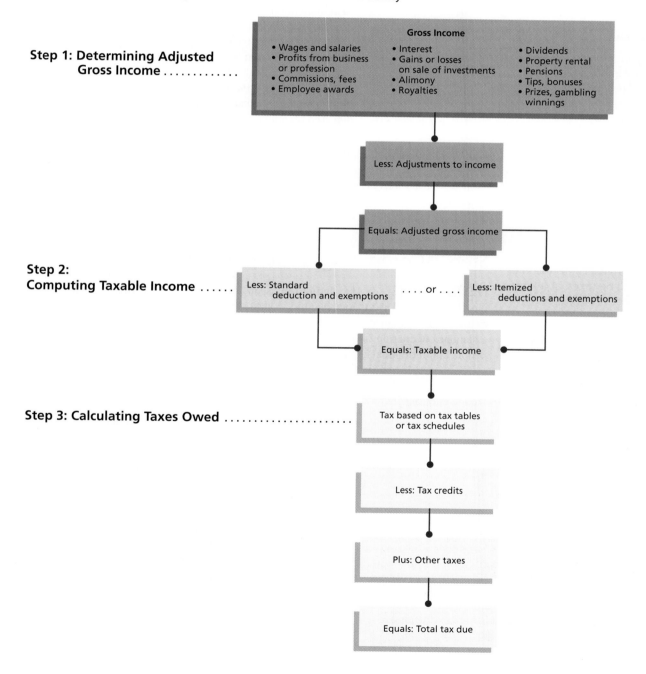

Step 1: Determining Adjusted Gross Income . . . .

Gross Income
- Wages and salaries
- Profits from business or profession
- Commissions, fees
- Employee awards
- Interest
- Gains or losses on sale of investments
- Alimony
- Royalties
- Dividends
- Property rental
- Pensions
- Tips, bonuses
- Prizes, gambling winnings

Less: Adjustments to income

Equals: Adjusted gross income

Step 2: Computing Taxable Income . . . . . .

Less: Standard deduction and exemptions   . . . . or . . . .   Less: Itemized deductions and exemptions

Equals: Taxable income

Step 3: Calculating Taxes Owed . . . .

Tax based on tax tables or tax schedules

Less: Tax credits

Plus: Other taxes

Equals: Total tax due

earned income Money received for personal effort, such as wages, salary, commission, fees, tips, or bonuses.

investment income Money received in the form of dividends, interest, or rent from investments; also called *portfolio income.*

Apply *Yourself!*

passive income Income resulting from business activities in which you do not actively participate.

exclusion An amount not included in gross income.

tax-exempt income Income that is not subject to tax.

tax-deferred income Income that will be taxed at a later date.

adjusted gross income (AGI) Gross income reduced by certain adjustments, such as contributions to an individual retirement account (IRA) and alimony payments.

CAUTION!

Each year, taxpayers are deceived with bogus opportunities such as a home-based business to qualify for a "home office" deduction, increased refunds for a "tax consultant" fee, prepayment for prizes you have won, and an offer to obtain a refund of Social Security taxes paid during your lifetime for a "paperwork" fee of $100. Information on these and other tax frauds are available at www.ustreas.gov/tigta.

TYPES OF INCOME   Most, but not all, income is subject to taxation. Your gross, or total, income can consist of three main components:

1. **Earned income** is usually in the form of wages, salary, commission, fees, tips, or bonuses.
2. **Investment income** (sometimes referred to as *portfolio income*) is money received in the form of dividends, interest, or rent from investments.
3. **Passive income** results from business activities in which you do not actively participate, such as a limited partnership.

Other types of income subject to federal income tax include alimony, awards, lottery winnings, and prizes. For example, cash and prizes won on television game shows are subject to both federal and state taxes.

Total income is also affected by exclusions. An **exclusion** is an amount not included in gross income. For example, the foreign income exclusion allows U.S. citizens working and living in another country to exclude a certain portion ($80,000) of their income from federal income taxes.

Exclusions may also be referred to as **tax-exempt income,** or income that is not subject to tax. For example, interest earned on most state and city bonds is exempt from federal income tax. **Tax-deferred income** is income that will be taxed at a later date.

ADJUSTMENTS TO INCOME   **Adjusted gross income (AGI)** is gross income after certain reductions have been made. These reductions, called *adjustments to income*, include contributions to an IRA or a Keogh retirement plan, penalties for early withdrawal of savings, and alimony payments. Adjusted gross income is used as the basis for computing various income tax deductions, such as medical expenses.

Step 2: Computing Taxable Income

DEDUCTIONS   A **tax deduction** is an amount subtracted from adjusted gross income to arrive at taxable income. Every taxpayer receives at least the **standard deduction,** a set amount on which no taxes are paid. As of 2006, single people receive a standard deduction of $5,150 (married couples filing jointly receive $10,300). Blind people and individuals 65 and older receive higher standard deductions.

Many people qualify for more than the standard deduction. **Itemized deductions** are expenses a taxpayer is allowed to deduct from adjusted gross income. Common itemized deductions include:

- *Medical and dental expenses*—physician fees, prescription medications, hospital expenses, medical insurance premiums, hearing aids, eyeglasses, and medical travel that has not been reimbursed or paid by others. The amount of this deduction is the medical and dental expenses that exceed 7.5 percent (as of 2007) of adjusted gross income.
- *Taxes*—state and local income tax, real estate property tax, and state or local personal property tax.
- *Interest*—mortgage interest, home equity loan interest, and investment interest expense up to an amount equal to investment income.
- *Contributions*—cash or property donated to qualified charitable organizations. Contribution totals greater than 20 percent of adjusted gross income are subject to limitations.

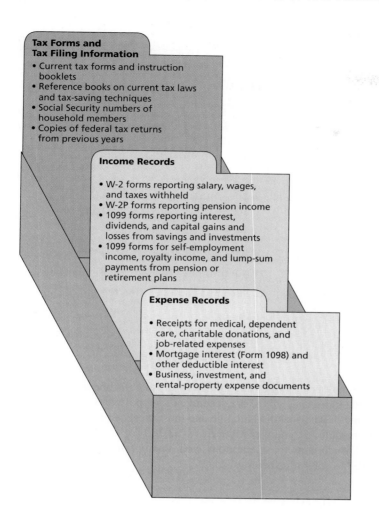

Exhibit 3–2

A Tax Recordkeeping System

Tax Forms and Tax Filing Information
- Current tax forms and instruction booklets
- Reference books on current tax laws and tax-saving techniques
- Social Security numbers of household members
- Copies of federal tax returns from previous years

Income Records
- W-2 forms reporting salary, wages, and taxes withheld
- W-2P forms reporting pension income
- 1099 forms reporting interest, dividends, and capital gains and losses from savings and investments
- 1099 forms for self-employment income, royalty income, and lump-sum payments from pension or retirement plans

Expense Records
- Receipts for medical, dependent care, charitable donations, and job-related expenses
- Mortgage interest (Form 1098) and other deductible interest
- Business, investment, and rental-property expense documents

- *Casualty and theft losses*—financial losses resulting from natural disasters, accidents, or unlawful acts.
- *Moving expenses*—costs incurred for a change in residence associated with a new job that is at least 50 miles farther from your former home than your old main job location.
- *Job-related and other miscellaneous expenses*—unreimbursed job travel, union dues, required continuing education, work clothes or uniforms, investment expenses, tax preparation fees, safe deposit box rental (for storing investment documents), and so on. The total of these expenses must exceed 2 percent of adjusted gross income to qualify as a deduction.

The standard deduction *or* total itemized deductions, along with the value of your exemptions (see next section), are subtracted from adjusted gross income to obtain your taxable income.

You are required to maintain records to document tax deductions, such as a home filing system (Exhibit 3–2). Canceled checks and receipts serve as proof of payment for deductions such as charitable contributions, medical expenses, and business-related expenses. Travel expenses can be documented in a daily log with records of mileage, tolls, parking fees, and away-from-home costs.

Generally, you should keep tax records for three years from the date you file your return. However, you may be held responsible for providing back documentation up to six years. Records such as past tax returns and housing documents should be kept indefinitely.

EXEMPTIONS   An **exemption** is a deduction from adjusted gross income for yourself, your spouse, and qualified dependents. A dependent must not earn more than

tax deduction An amount subtracted from adjusted gross income to arrive at taxable income.

standard deduction A set amount on which no taxes are paid.

itemized deductions Expenses that can be deducted from adjusted gross income, such as medical expenses, real estate property taxes, home mortgage interest, charitable contributions, casualty losses, and certain work-related expenses.

exemption A deduction from adjusted gross income for yourself, your spouse, and qualified dependents.

Personal Finance in Practice

› Is It Taxable Income? Is It Deductible?

Certain financial benefits individuals receive are not subject to federal income tax. Indicate whether each of the following items would or would not be included in taxable income when you compute your federal income tax.

Indicate whether each of the following items would or would not be deductible when you compute your federal income tax.

Is it taxable income . . . ?	Yes	No
1. Lottery winnings	____	____
2. Child support received	____	____
3. Worker's compensation benefits	____	____
4. Life insurance death benefits	____	____
5. Municipal bond interest earnings	____	____
6. Bartering income	____	____

Is it deductible . . . ?	Yes	No
7. Life insurance premiums	____	____
8. Cosmetic surgery for improved looks	____	____
9. Fees for traffic violations	____	____
10. Mileage for driving to volunteer work	____	____
11. An attorney's fee for preparing a will	____	____
12. Income tax preparation fee	____	____

Note: These taxable income items and deductions are based on the 2007 tax year and may change due to changes in the tax code.

Answers: 1, 6, 10, 12—yes; 2, 3, 4, 5, 7, 8, 9, 11—no.

a set amount unless he or she is under age 19 or is a full-time student under age 24; you must provide more than half of the dependent's support; and the dependent must reside in your home or be a specified relative and must meet certain citizenship requirements. For 2006, taxable income was reduced by $3,300 for each exemption claimed. After deducting the amounts for exemptions, you obtain your taxable income, which is the amount used to determine taxes owed.

Step 3: Calculating Taxes Owed

Your taxable income is the basis for computing the amount of tax owed.

TAX RATES Use your taxable income in conjunction with the appropriate tax table or tax schedule. For 2006, the six-rate system for federal income tax was as follows:

Rate on Taxable Income	Single Taxpayers	Married Taxpayers Filing Jointly	Heads of Households
10%	Up to $7,550	Up to $15,100	Up to $10,750
15	$7,550–$30,650	$15,100–$61,300	$10,750–$41,050
25	$30,650–$74,200	$61,300–$123,700	$41,050–$106,000
28	$74,200–$154,800	$123,700–$188,450	$106,000–$171,650
33	$154,800–$336,550	$188,450–$336,550	$171,650–$336,550
35	Over $336,550	Over $336,550	Over $336,550

marginal tax rate The rate used to calculate tax on the last (and next) dollar of taxable income.

A separate tax rate schedule also exists for married persons who file separate income tax returns.

The 10, 15, 25, 28, and 35 percent rates are referred to as **marginal tax rates.** These rates are used to calculate tax on the last (and next) dollar of taxable income. After deductions and exemptions, a person in the 35 percent tax bracket pays 35 cents in taxes for every dollar of taxable income in that bracket.

Figure it Out!

› Tax Credits versus Tax Deductions

Many people confuse *tax credits* with *tax deductions.* Is one better than the other? A tax *credit,* such as eligible child care or dependent care expenses, results in a dollar-for-dollar reduction in the amount of taxes owed. A tax *deduction,* such as an itemized deduction in the form of medical expenses, mortgage interest, or charitable contributions, reduces the taxable income on which your taxes are based.

Here is how a $100 tax credit compares with a $100 tax deduction:

As your might expect, tax credits are less readily available than tax deductions. To qualify for a $100 child care tax credit, you may have to spend $500 in child care expenses. In some situations, spending on deductible items may be more beneficial than qualifying for a tax credit. A knowledge of tax law and careful financial planning will help you use both tax credits and tax deductions to maximum advantage.

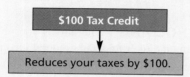

$100 Tax Credit
Reduces your taxes by $100.

$100 Tax Deduction
Reduces your taxable income by $100. The amount of your tax reduction depends on your tax bracket. Your taxes will be reduced by $15 if you are in the 15 percent tax bracket and by $28 if you are in the 28 percent tax bracket.

CALCULATIONS

1. If a person in a 30 percent tax bracket received a $1,000 tax deduction, how much would the person's taxes be reduced? $_____

2. If a person in a 27 percent tax bracket received a $200 tax credit, how much would the person's taxes be reduced? $_____

In contrast, the **average tax rate** is based on the total tax due divided by taxable income. Except for taxpayers in the 10 percent bracket, this rate is less than a person's marginal tax rate. For example, a person with taxable income of $40,000 and a total tax bill of $4,200 would have an average tax rate of 10.5 percent ($4,200 ÷ $40,000).

average tax rate Total tax due divided by taxable income.

Taxpayers with high amounts of certain deductions and various types of income may be subject to an additional tax. The *alternative minimum tax (AMT)* is designed to ensure that those who receive tax breaks also pay their fair share of taxes. The AMT was originally designed tax to prevent those with high incomes from using special tax breaks to pay little in taxes. However, in recent years, this tax is affecting many taxpayers, with nearly 4 million people subject to the AMT. This number could exceed 20 million if no changes are made in the tax laws. Some of the tax situations that can result in a person paying the AMT include high levels of deductions for state and local taxes, interest on second mortgages, medical expenses, and other deductions. Other items that can trigger the AMT are incentive stock options, long-term capital gains, and tax-exempt interest. Additional information about the AMT may be obtained at www.irs.gov.

TAX CREDITS   The tax owed may be reduced by a **tax credit,** an amount subtracted directly from the amount of taxes owed. One example of a tax credit is the credit given for child care and dependent care expenses. Another tax credit for low-income workers is the *earned-income credit (EIC),* for working parents with taxable income under a certain amount. Families that do not earn enough to owe federal income taxes are also eligible for the EIC and receive a check for the amount of their credit. A *tax credit* differs from a deduction in that a tax credit has a full dollar effect in lowering taxes, whereas a *deduction* reduces the taxable income on which the tax liability is computed.

tax credit An amount subtracted directly from the amount of taxes owed.

Recent tax credits also included:

- Foreign tax credit to avoid double taxation on income taxes paid to another country.
- Retirement tax credit to encourage investment contributions to individual and employer-sponsored retirement plans by low- and middle-income taxpayers.
- Adoption tax credit to cover expenses when adopting a child under age 18.
- Hope Scholarship and Lifetime Learning tax credits to help offset college education expenses.

Step 4: Making Tax Payments

did you know?

Each year more than 90,000 taxpayers do not receive their refunds. The undeliverable checks total over $60 million, an average of more than $600 per check. These refund checks were returned by the post office because it was unable to deliver them. Taxpayers due a refund may contact the IRS at 1-800-829-1040.

You pay federal income taxes through either payroll withholding or estimated tax payments.

WITHHOLDING   The pay-as-you-go system requires an employer to deduct federal income tax from your pay. The withheld amount is based on the number of exemptions and the expected deductions claimed. For example, a married person with children would have less withheld than a single person with the same salary, since the married person will owe less tax.

After the end of the year, you will receive a W-2 form, which reports your annual earnings and the amounts deducted for taxes. The difference between the amount withheld and the tax owed is either the additional amount to pay or your refund. Students and low-income individuals may file for exemption from withholding if they paid no federal income tax last year and do not expect to pay any in the current year.

Many taxpayers view an annual tax refund as a "windfall," extra money they count on each year. These taxpayers are forgetting the opportunity cost of withholding excessive amounts. Others view their extra tax withholding as "forced savings." However, a payroll deduction plan for savings could serve the same purpose while also earning interest on your funds.

ESTIMATED PAYMENTS   Income from savings, investments, independent contracting, royalties, and pension payments is reported on Form 1099. People who receive such income may be required to make tax payments during the year (April 15, June 15, September 15, and January 15 as the last payment for the previous tax year). These payments are based on an estimate of taxes due at year-end. Underpayment or failure to make estimated payments can result in penalties and interest charges.

Step 5: Watching Deadlines and Avoiding Penalties

Most people are required to file a federal income tax return by April 15. If you are not able to file on time, you can use Form 4868 to obtain an automatic four-month extension.

This extension is for the 1040 form and other documents, but it does not delay your payment liability. You must submit the estimated amount owed along with Form 4868 by April 15. Failure to file on time can result in a penalty for being just one day late. Underpayment of quarterly estimated taxes may require paying interest on the amount you should have paid. Underpayment due to negligence or fraud can result in penalties of 50 to 75 percent.

The good news is that if you claim a refund several months or years late, the IRS will pay you interest. However, refunds must be claimed within three years of filing the return or within two years of paying the tax.

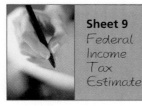
Sheet 9 Federal Income Tax Estimate

CONCEPT CHECK 3–2

1 How does tax-exempt income differ from tax-deferred income?

_____

2 When would you use the standard deduction instead of itemized deductions?

_____

_____

3 What is the difference between your marginal tax rate and your average tax rate?

_____

4 For each of the following, indicate if the item is a _tax deduction_ or a _tax credit_.

Check the appropriate box to indicate if this is . . .	a tax deduction or . . .	a tax credit.
_a._ State personal income taxes paid		
_b._ Charitable donations		
_c._ Child care costs		
_d._ Moving expenses		

Filing Your Federal Income Tax Return

As you prepare to do your taxes, you must first determine whether you are required to file a return. Next, you need to decide which tax form best serves you and if you are required to submit supplementary schedules or forms.

OBJECTIVE 3
Prepare a federal income tax return.

Who Must File?

Every citizen or resident of the United States and every U.S. citizen who is a resident of Puerto Rico is required to file a federal income tax return if his or her income is above a certain amount. The amount is based on the person's _filing status_ and other factors such as age. For example, single persons under 65 had to file a return on April 15, 2007 (for tax year 2006) if their gross income exceeded $8,450. If your gross income is less than this amount but taxes were withheld, you should file a return to obtain your refund.

Your filing status is affected by marital status and dependents. The five filing status categories are:

- _Single_—never-married, divorced, or legally separated individuals with no dependents.
- _Married, filing joint return_—combines the spouses' incomes.
- _Married, filing separate returns_—each spouse is responsible for his or her own tax. Under certain conditions, a married couple can benefit from this filing status.
- _Head of household_—an unmarried individual or a surviving spouse who maintains a household (paying for more than half of the costs) for a child or a dependent relative.
- _Qualifying widow or widower_—an individual whose spouse died within the past two years and who has a dependent; this status is limited to two years after the death of the spouse.

In some situations, you may have a choice of filing status. In such cases, compute your taxes under the alternatives to determine the most advantageous filing status.

Personal Finance in Practice

FORM 1040EZ

You may use Form 1040EZ if:

- You are single or married filing a joint return, under age 65, and claim no dependents.
- Your income consisted only of wages, salaries, and tips and not more than $1,500 of taxable interest.
- Your taxable income is less than $100,000.
- You do not itemize deductions or claim any adjustments to income or any tax credits.

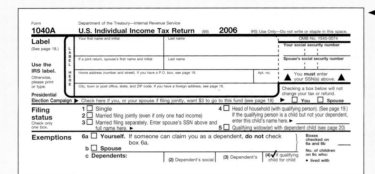

FORM 1040A

This form would be used by people who have less that $100,000 in taxable income from wages, salaries, tips, unemployment compensation, interest, or dividends and use the standard deduction. With Form 1040A, you can also take deductions for individual retirement account (IRA) contributions and a tax credit for child care and dependent care expenses. If you qualify for either Form 1040EZ or Form 1040A, you may wish to use one of them to simplify filing your tax return. You may not want to use either the Form 1040EZ or Form 1040A if Form 1040 allows you to pay less tax.

FORM 1040

Form 1040 is an expanded version of Form 1040A that includes sections for all types of income. You are required to use this form if your income is over $50,000 or if you can be claimed as a dependent on your parents return *and* you had interest or dividends over a set limit.

Form 1040 allows you to itemize your deductions. You can list various allowable expenses (medical costs, home mortgage interest, real estate property taxes) that will reduce taxable income and the amount you owe the government. You should learn about all the possible adjustments to income, deductions, and tax credits for which you may qualify.

FORM 1040X

This form is used to amend a previously filed tax return. If you discover income that was not reported, or if you find additional deductions, you should file Form 1040X to pay the additional tax or obtain a refund.

Apply *Yourself!*

Objective 3

Create a visual presentation (video or slide presentation) that demonstrates actions a person might take to reduce errors when filing a federal tax return.

Which Tax Form Should You Use?

Although about 400 federal tax forms and schedules exist, you have a choice of three basic forms when filing your income tax (see "Personal Finance in Practice" above). Recently about 20 percent of taxpayers used Form 1040EZ or Form 1040A; about 60 percent used the regular Form 1040. Your decision in this matter will depend on your type of income, the amount of your income, the number of your deductions, and the complexity of your tax situation. Most tax preparation software programs will guide you in selecting the appropriate 1040 form.

What Is the Process for Completing the Federal Income Tax Return?

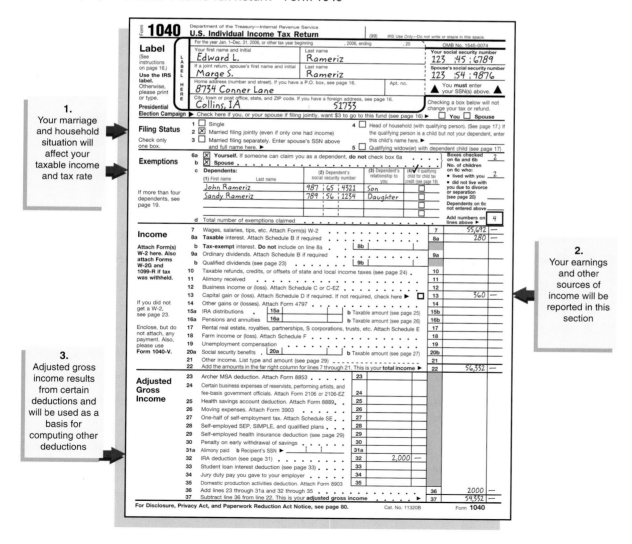

did you know?

The Internal Revenue Service oversees more than 17,000 pages of laws and regulations with about 500 different tax forms.

The major sections of Form 1040 (see Exhibit 3–3) correspond to tax topics discussed in the previous sections of this chapter:

1. *Filing status and exemptions.* Your tax rate is determined by your filing status and allowances for yourself, your spouse, and each person you claim as a dependent.
2. *Income.* Earnings from your employment (as reported by your W-2 form) and other income, such as savings and investment income, are reported in this section of Form 1040.
3. *Adjustments to income.* As discussed later in the chapter, if you qualify, you may deduct contributions (up to a certain amount) to an individual retirement account (IRA) or other qualified retirement program.

Exhibit 3–3   Federal Income Tax Return—Form 1040

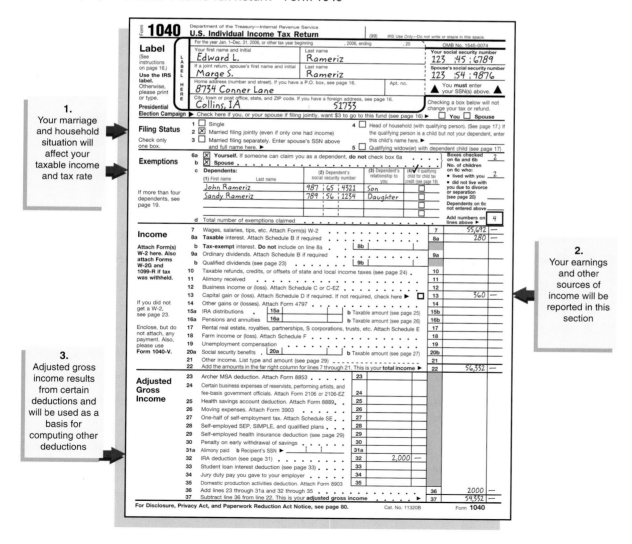

Exhibit 3–3   (concluded)

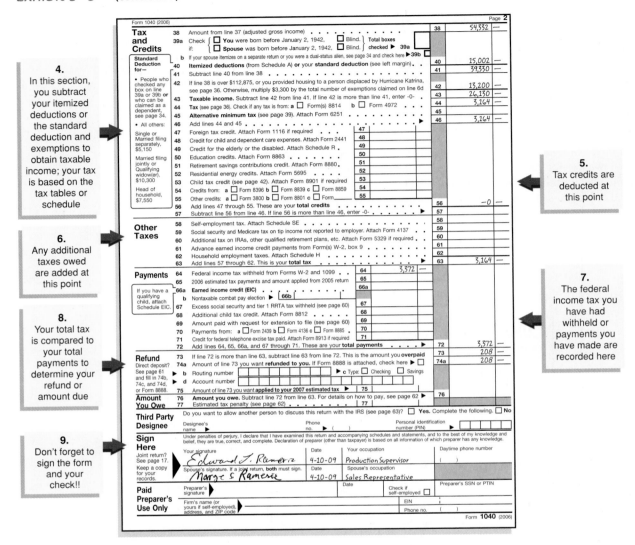

4.
In this section, you subtract your itemized deductions or the standard deduction and exemptions to obtain taxable income; your tax is based on the tax tables or schedule

6.
Any additional taxes owed are added at this point

8.
Your total tax is compared to your total payments to determine your refund or amount due

9.
Don't forget to sign the form and your check!!

5.
Tax credits are deducted at this point

7.
The federal income tax you have had withheld or payments you have made are recorded here

Note: These forms were used in a recent year; the current forms may not be exactly the same. Obtain current income tax forms and current tax information from your local IRS office, post office, public library, or at www.irs.gov.

4. *Tax computation.* In this section, your adjusted gross income is reduced by your itemized deductions (see Exhibit 3–4) or by the standard deduction for your tax situation. In addition, an amount is deducted for each exemption to arrive at your taxable income. That income is the basis for determining the amount of your tax (see Exhibit 3–5).

5. *Tax credits.* Any tax credits for which you qualify are subtracted at this point.

6. *Other taxes.* Any special taxes, such as self-employment tax, are included at this point.

7. *Payments.* Your total withholding and other payments are indicated in this section.

8. *Refund or amount you owe.* If your payments exceed the amount of income tax you owe, you are entitled to a refund. If the opposite is true, you must make an additional payment. Taxpayers who want their refunds sent directly to a bank can provide the necessary account information directly on Form 1040, 1040A, or 1040EZ.

9. *Your signature.* Forgetting to sign a tax return is one of the most frequent filing errors.

Exhibit 3–4   Schedule A for Itemized Deductions—Form 1040

Health care expenses (not covered by insurance) are listed here, but must exceed 7.5% of adjusted gross income to be deductible	
Deductible interest payments are listed here	
A variety of other expenses may qualify under these deduction categories	

Certain other taxes may be deducted

Donations and charitable contributions are reported here

The total of your itemized deductions is transferred to form 1040 in the "Tax Computation" section

SCHEDULES A&B (Form 1040)	**Schedule A—Itemized Deductions** (Schedule B is on back) OMB No. 1545-0074
Department of the Treasury Internal Revenue Service (99)	▶ Attach to Form 1040. ▶ See Instructions for Schedules A&B (Form 1040). Attachment Sequence No. 07

Name(s) shown on Form 1040   Your social security number 123 | 45 | 6789

Medical and Dental Expenses
Caution. Do not include expenses reimbursed or paid by others.
1 Medical and dental expenses (see page A-1) ... 1 2,676 —
2 Enter amount from Form 1040, line 38 2 53,132 —
3 Multiply line 2 by 7.5% (.075) ... 3 3,985 —
4 Subtract line 3 from line 1. If line 3 is more than line 1, enter -0- 4 — 0 —

Taxes You Paid
(See page A-3.)
5 State and local income taxes ... 5 822 —
6 Real estate taxes (see page A-3) ... 6 2,840 —
7 Personal property taxes ... 7
8 Other taxes. List type and amount ▶ _____ 8
9 Add lines 5 through 8 ... 9 3,662 —

Interest You Paid
(See page A-3.)
Note. Personal interest is not deductible.
10 Home mortgage interest and points reported to you on Form 1098 10 6,870 —
11 Home mortgage interest not reported to you on Form 1098. If paid to the person from whom you bought the home, see page A-3 and show that person's name, identifying no., and address ▶ 11
12 Points not reported to you on Form 1098. See page A-4 for special rules ... 12
13 Investment interest. Attach Form 4952 if required. (See page A-4.) ... 13
14 Add lines 10 through 13 ... 14 6,870 —

Gifts to Charity
If you made a gift and got a benefit for it, see page A-4.
15 Gifts by cash or check. If you made any gift of $250 or more, see page A-5 ... 15 4,470 —
16 Other than by cash or check. If any gift of $250 or more, see page A-5. You must attach Form 8283 if over $500 16
17 Carryover from prior year ... 17
18 Add lines 15 through 17 ... 18 4,470 —

Casualty and Theft Losses
19 Casualty or theft loss(es). Attach Form 4684. (See page A-6.) ... 19

Job Expenses and Certain Miscellaneous Deductions
(See page A-6.)
20 Unreimbursed employee expenses—job travel, union dues, job education, etc. Attach Form 2106 or 2106-EZ if required. (See page A-6.) ▶ _____ 20 850 —
21 Tax preparation fees ... 21
22 Other expenses—investment, safe deposit box, etc. List type and amount ▶ _Continuing Education_ 22
23 Add lines 20 through 22 ... 23 850 —
24 Enter amount from Form 1040, line 38 24 53,132
25 Multiply line 24 by 2% (.02) ... 25 1,063 —
26 Subtract line 25 from line 23. If line 25 is more than line 23, enter -0- ... 26 — 0 —

Other Miscellaneous Deductions
27 Other—from list on page A-7. List type and amount ▶ _____ 27

Total Itemized Deductions
28 Is Form 1040, line 38, over $150,500 (over $75,250 if married filing separately)?
☐ No. Your deduction is not limited. Add the amounts in the far right column for lines 4 through 27. Also, enter this amount on Form 1040, line 40.
☐ Yes. Your deduction may be limited. See page A-7 for the amount to enter. ▶ 28 15,002 —
29 If you elect to itemize deductions even though they are less than your standard deduction, check here ▶ ☐

For Paperwork Reduction Act Notice, see Form 1040 instructions.   Cat. No. 11330X   Schedule A (Form 1040)

How Do I File My State Tax Return?

All but seven states (Alaska, Florida, Nevada, South Dakota, Texas, Washington, and Wyoming) have a state income tax. In most states, the tax rate ranges from 1 to 10 percent. For further information about the income tax in your state, contact the state department of revenue. States usually require income tax returns to be filed when the federal income tax return is due. For planning your tax activities, see Exhibit 3–6 on page 89.

How Do I File My Taxes Online?

Software packages such as *TaxCut* and *TurboTax* allow you to complete needed tax forms and schedules and either print for mailing or file online. Electronic filing of federal taxes now exceeds 60 million returns annually. With e-file, taxpayers usually receive their refunds within three weeks. The cost for this service is usually between $15 and $40.

TAX PREPARATION SOFTWARE   Today, most taxpayers use personal computers for tax recordkeeping and tax form preparation. A spreadsheet program can be helpful in maintaining and updating income and expense data. Software packages such

Exhibit 3–5   Tax Tables and Tax Rate Schedules

Tax Table

If line 43 (taxable income) is—		And you are—			
At least	But less than	Single	Married filing jointly *	Married filing sepa-rately	Head of a house-hold
			Your tax is—		

26,000

At least	But less than	Single	Married filing jointly	Married filing separately	Head of household
26,000	26,050	3,526	3,149	3,526	3,366
26,050	26,100	3,535	3,156	3,534	3,374
26,100	26,150	3,541	3,164	3,541	3,381
26,150	26,200	3,549	3,171	3,549	3,389
26,200	26,250	3,556	3,179	3,556	3,396
26,250	26,300	3,564	3,186	3,564	3,404
26,300	26,350	3,571	3,194	3,571	3,411
26,350	26,400	3,579	3,201	3,579	3,419
26,400	26,450	3,586	3,209	3,586	3,426
26,450	26,500	3,594	3,216	3,594	3,434
26,500	26,550	3,601	3,224	3,601	3,441
26,550	26,600	3,609	3,231	3,609	3,449
26,600	26,650	3,616	3,239	3,616	3,456
26,650	26,700	3,624	3,246	3,624	3,464
26,700	26,750	3,631	3,254	3,631	3,471
26,750	26,800	3,639	3,261	3,639	3,479
26,800	26,850	3,646	3,269	3,646	3,486
26,850	26,900	3,654	3,276	3,654	3,494
26,900	26,950	3,661	3,284	3,661	3,501
26,950	27,000	3,669	3,291	3,669	3,509

* This column must also be used by a qualifying widow(er).

Tax Rate Schedules

Schedule Y-1—Use if your filing status is Married filing jointly or Qualifying widow(er)

If your taxable income is:		The tax is:	of the amount over—
Over—	But not over—		
$0	$15,100	.... 10%	$0
15,100	61,300	$1,510.00 + 15%	15,100
61,300	123,700	8,440.00 + 25%	61,300
123,700	188,450	24,040.00 + 28%	123,700
188,450	336,550	42,170.00 + 33%	188,450
336,550	....	91,043.00 + 35%	336,550

Use **only** if your taxable income (Form 1040, line 41) is $100,000 or more. If less, use the **Tax Table.** Even though you cannot use the Tax Rate Schedules below if your taxable income is less than $100,000, all levels of taxable income are shown so taxpayers can see the tax rate that applies to each level.

Note: These were the federal income tax rates for a recent year. Current rates may vary due to changes in the tax code and adjustments for inflation. Obtain current income tax booklets from your local IRS office, post office, bank, public library, or at www.irs.gov.

as *TaxCut* and *TurboTax* allow you to complete needed tax forms and schedules to either print mailing or file online.

Using tax software can save you 10 or more hours when preparing your Form 1040 and accompanying schedules. When selecting tax software, consider the following factors:

1. Your personal situation—are you employed or do you operate your own business?
2. Special tax situations with regard to types of income, unusual deductions, and various tax credits.
3. Features in the software, such as "audit check," future tax planning, and filing your federal and state tax forms online.
4. Technical aspects, such as the hardware and operating system requirements, and online support that is provided.
5. Purchase location—will you buy from a local store or from an online retailer?

did you know?

Electronically filed federal income tax returns have an accuracy rate of 99 percent, compared to 81 percent for paper returns. Most electronic filing programs do your calculations and signal potential errors before you file.

ELECTRONIC FILING   In recent years, the IRS has made online filing easier and less expensive. Through the Free File Alliance, online tax preparation and e-filing are available free to millions of taxpayers. This partnership between the IRS and the tax software industry encourages more e-filing. The online filing process involves the following steps:

Step 1   Go to the "Free File" page at www.irs.gov and click "Start Now" to view the various Free File companies.

Step 2   Determine your eligibility with a particular company. A brief description of the criteria for each is provided. Some companies limit service to taxpayers in certain states; others target filers by age (younger than 21 or older than 61). Many of the services are limited to

January
• Establish a recordkeeping system for your tax information.
• If you expect a refund, file your tax return for the previous year.
• Make your final estimated quarterly payment for the previous year for income not covered by withholding.

February
• Check to make sure you received W-2 and 1099 forms from all organizations from which you had income during the previous year; these should have been received by January 31; if not, contact the organization.

March
• Organize your records and tax information in preparation for filing your tax return; if you expect a refund, file as soon as possible.

April
• April 15 is the deadline for filing your federal tax return; if it falls on a weekend, you have until the next business day (usually Monday).
• If necessary, file for an automatic extension for filing your tax forms.

May
• Review your tax return to determine whether any changes in withholding, exemptions, or marital status have not been reported to your employer.

June
• The second installment for estimated tax is due June 15 for income not covered by withholding.

July
• With the year half over, consider or implement plans for a personal retirement program such as an IRA or a Keogh.

August
• Tax returns are due August 15 for those who received the automatic four-month extension.

September
• The third installment for estimated tax is due September 15 for income not covered by withholding.

October
• Determine the tax benefits of selling certain investments by year-end.
• Prepare a preliminary tax form to determine the most advantageous filing status.

November
• Make any last-minute changes in withholding by your employer to avoid penalties for too little withholding.
• Determine if you qualify for an IRA; if so, consider opening one.

December
• Determine if it would be to your advantage to make payments for next year before December 31 of the current year.
• Decide if you can defer income for the current year until the following year.

Exhibit 3–6

Tax-Planner Calendar

Note: Children born before the end of the year give you a full-year exemption, so plan accordingly!

lower-income taxpayers, and some offer: "No restrictions. Everyone qualifies." A "Guide Me to a Service" option is available to help you narrow down the possible companies offering free preparation and e-filing for you.

Step 3   Next, connect to the company's Web site to begin the preparation of your tax return.

Step 4   Finally, use the company's online software to prepare your return. Your federal tax return is then filed electronically and your tax data is stored at the vendor's site. Taxpayers who do not qualify for the Free File Alliance program may still be able to file online for a nominal fee. You don't have to purchase the software; simply go to the software company's Internet site and pay a fee to use the tax program.

Taxpayers who use the Free File Alliance are cautioned to be careful consumers. A company may attempt to sell other financial products to inexperienced taxpayers, such as expensive refund anticipation loans. Also, taxpayers using the free file service must be aware that their state tax return might not be included in the free program.

Telefile is a file-by-phone system that has been tested in various geographic areas. It allows taxpayers to call a toll-free number, using a touch-tone phone, to file their tax returns. A follow-up written or voice "signature" confirmation is required.

What Tax Assistance Sources Are Available?

As with other aspects of personal financial planning, many tax resources are available to assist you.

did you know?

An IRS study of visits to its tax assistance centers found that 19 of 26 tax returns (83 percent) had been incorrectly prepared by IRS employees. The agency reported that 17 of the 19 inaccurately prepared fictitious returns would have resulted in incorrect refunds totaling nearly $32,000.

IRS SERVICES   If you prepare your own tax return or desire tax information, the IRS can assist in four ways:

1. *Publications.* The IRS offers hundreds of free booklets and pamphlets that can be obtained at a local IRS office, by mail request, or by telephone. Especially helpful is *Your Federal Income Tax* (IRS Publication 17). IRS publications and tax forms are available by phone at 1-800-TAX-FORM, online at www.irs.gov, or by fax at 703-368-9694.
2. *Recorded messages.* The IRS Tele-Tax system gives you 24-hour access to about 150 recorded tax tips at 1-800-829-4477.
3. *Phone hot line.* Information about specific problems is available through an IRS-staffed phone line at 1-800-829-1040.
4. *Walk-in service.* You can visit a local IRS office (400 are available) to obtain tax assistance.

TAX PUBLICATIONS   Each year, several tax guides are published and offered for sale. Publications such as *J. K. Lasser's Your Income Tax* and *The Ernst & Young Tax Guide* can be purchased online or at local stores.

THE INTERNET   As with other personal finance topics, extensive information may be found on Web sites such as those listed at the start of the chapter.

Tax Preparation Services

Over 40 million U.S. taxpayers pay someone to do their income taxes. The fee for this service can range from $40 at a tax preparation service for a simple return to more than $2,000 to a certified public accountant for a complicated return.

TYPES OF TAX SERVICES   Doing your own taxes may not be desirable, especially if you have sources of income other than salary. The sources available for professional tax assistance include the following:

- Tax services range from local, one-person operations to national firms with thousands of offices, such as H&R Block.
- Enrolled agents—government-approved tax experts—prepare returns and provide tax advice. You may contact the National Association of Enrolled Agents at 1-800-424-4339 for information about enrolled agents in your area.
- Many accountants offer tax assistance along with other business services. A certified public accountant (CPA) with special training in taxes can help with tax planning and the preparation of your annual tax return.
- Attorneys usually do not complete tax returns; however, you can use an attorney's services when you are involved in a tax-related transaction or when you have a difference of opinion with the IRS.

EVALUATING TAX SERVICES   When planning to use a tax preparation service, consider these factors:

- What training and experience does the tax professional possess?
- How will the fee be determined? (Avoid preparers who earn a percentage of your refund.)
- Does the preparer suggest you report various deductions that might be questioned?
- Will the preparer represent you if your return is audited?
- Is tax preparation the main business activity, or does it serve as a front for selling other financial products and services?

Additional information about tax preparers may be obtained at the Web sites for the National Association of Enrolled Agents (www.naea.org) and the National Association of Tax Professionals (www.natptax.com).

TAX SERVICE WARNINGS   Even if you hire a professional tax preparer, you are responsible for supplying accurate and complete information. Hiring a tax preparer will not guarantee that you pay the *correct* amount. A study conducted by *Money* magazine of 41 tax preparers reported fees ranging from $375 to $3,600, with taxes due ranging from $31,846 to $74,450 for the same fictional family. If you owe more tax because your return contains errors or you have made entries that are not allowed, it is your responsibility to pay that additional tax, plus any interest and penalties.

Beware of tax preparers and other businesses that offer your refund in advance. These "refund anticipation loans" frequently charge very high interest rates for this type of consumer credit. Studies reveal interest rates sometimes exceeding 300 percent (on an annualized basis).

What If Your Return Is Audited?

The Internal Revenue Service reviews all returns for completeness and accuracy. If you make an error, your tax is automatically refigured and you receive either a bill or a refund. If you make an entry that is not allowed, you will be notified by mail. A **tax audit** is a detailed examination of your tax return by the IRS. In most audits, the IRS requests more information to support your tax return. Be sure to keep accurate records. Receipts, canceled checks, and other evidence can verify amounts that you claim. Avoiding common filing mistakes helps to minimize your chances of an audit (see Exhibit 3–7).

tax audit A detailed examination of your tax return by the Internal Revenue Service.

WHO GETS AUDITED?   About 0.6 percent of all tax filers—fewer than 1 million people—are audited each year. Although the IRS does not reveal its basis for auditing returns, several indicators are evident. People who claim large or unusual deductions increase their chances of an audit. Tax advisers suggest including a brief explanation or a copy of receipts for deductions that may be questioned.

TYPES OF AUDITS   The simplest and most frequent type of audit is the *correspondence audit*. This mail inquiry requires you to clarify or document minor questions. The *office audit* requires you to visit an IRS office to clarify some aspect of your tax return.

The *field audit* is more complex. An IRS agent visits you at your home, your business, or the office of your accountant so you have access to records. A field audit may be done to verify whether an individual has a home office if this is claimed.

The IRS also conducts more detailed audits for about 50,000 taxpayers. These range from random requests to document various tax return items to line-by-line reviews by IRS employees.

Exhibit 3–7   How to Avoid Common Filing Errors

- Organize all tax-related information for easy access.

- Follow instructions carefully. Many people deduct total medical and dental expenses rather than the amount of these expenses that exceeds 7.5 percent of adjusted gross income.

- Use the proper tax rate schedule or tax table column.

- Be sure to claim the correct number of exemptions and correct amounts of standard deductions.

- Consider the alternative minimum tax that may apply to your situation. Be sure to pay self-employment tax and tax on early IRA withdrawals.

- Check your arithmetic several times.

- Sign your return (both spouses must sign a joint return), or the IRS won't process it.

- Be sure to include the correct Social Security number(s) and to record amounts on the correct lines.

- Attach necessary documentation such as your W-2 forms and required supporting schedules.

- Make the check payable to "United States Treasury."

- Put your Social Security number, the tax year, and a daytime telephone number on your check—and be sure to sign the check!

- Keep a photocopy of your return.

- Put the proper postage on your mailing envelope.

- Finally, check everything again—and file on time! Care taken when you file your income tax can result in "many happy returns."

YOUR AUDIT RIGHTS   When you receive an audit notice, you have the right to request time to prepare. Also, you can ask the IRS for clarification of items being questioned. When audited, follow these suggestions:

- Decide whether you will bring your tax preparer, accountant, or lawyer.
- Be on time for your appointment; bring only relevant documents.
- Present tax evidence in a logical, calm, and confident manner; maintain a positive attitude.
- Make sure the information you present is consistent with the tax law.
- Keep your answers aimed at the auditor's questions. Answer questions clearly and completely. Be as brief as possible. The five best responses to questions during an audit are "Yes," "No," "I don't recall," "I'll have to check on that," and "What specific items do you want to see?"

If you disagree with the results of an audit, you may request a conference at the Regional Appeals Office. Although most differences of opinion are settled at this stage, some taxpayers take their cases further. A person may go to the U.S. tax court, the U.S. claims court, or the U.S. district court. Some tax disputes have gone to the U.S. Supreme Court.

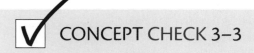 CONCEPT CHECK 3–3

1 In what ways does your filing status affect preparation of your federal income tax return?

_____

_____

2 What are the main sources available to help people prepare their taxes?

_____

_____

3 What actions can reduce the chances of an IRS audit?

_____

_____

4 Which 1040 form should each of the following individuals use? (Check one for each situation.)

Tax situation	1040EZ	1040A	1040
a. A high school student with an after-school job and interest earnings of $480 from savings accounts.			
b. A college student who, because of ownership of property, is able to itemize deductions rather than take the standard deduction.			
c. A young, entry-level worker with no dependents and income only from salary.			

Using Tax Planning Strategies

For people to pay their fair share of taxes—no more, no less—they should practice **tax avoidance,** the use of legitimate methods to reduce one's taxes. In contrast, **tax evasion** is the use of illegal actions to reduce one's taxes. To minimize taxes owed, follow these guidelines:

> **OBJECTIVE 4**
> Select appropriate tax strategies for various life situations.

- If you expect to have the *same* or a *lower* tax rate next year, *accelerate deductions* into the current year. Pay real estate property taxes or make charitable donations by December 31.
- If you expect to have a *lower* or the *same* tax rate next year, *delay the receipt of income* until next year so the funds will be taxed at a lower rate or at a later date.
- If you expect to have a *higher* tax rate next year, consider *delaying deductions,* since they will have a greater benefit. A $1,000 deduction at 25 percent lowers your taxes $250; at 28 percent, your taxes are lowered $280.
- If you expect to have a *higher* tax rate next year, *accelerate the receipt of income* to have it taxed at the current lower rate.

tax avoidance The use of legitimate methods to reduce one's taxes.

tax evasion The use of illegal actions to reduce one's taxes.

When considering financial decisions in relation to your taxes, remember that purchasing, investing, and retirement planning are the areas most heavily affected by tax laws.

Consumer Purchasing

The buying decisions most directly affected by taxes are the purchase of a residence, the use of credit, and job-related expenses.

PLACE OF RESIDENCE   Owning a home is one of the best tax shelters. Both real estate property taxes and interest on the mortgage are deductible (as itemized deductions) and thus reduce your taxable income.

CONSUMER DEBT   Current tax laws allow homeowners to borrow for consumer purchases. You can deduct interest on loans (of up to $100,000) secured by your

Figure It Out!

› Short-Term and Long-Term Capital Gains

You will pay a lower tax rate on the profits from stocks and other investments if you hold the asset for more than 12 months. As of 2007, a taxpayer in the 28 percent tax bracket would pay $280 in taxes on a $1,000 short-term capital gain (assets held for one year or less). However, that same taxpayer would pay only $150 on the $1,000 (a 15 percent capital gains tax) If the investment were held for more than a year.

	Short-Term Capital Gain (Assets held for one year or less)	Long-Term Capital Gain (Assets held for more than one year)
Capital Gain	$1,000	$1,000
Capital Gains Tax Rate	28%	15%
Capital Gains Tax	$ 280	$ 150
Tax Savings		$ 130

primary or secondary home up to the actual dollar amount you have invested in it—the difference between the market value of the home and the amount you owe on it. These *home equity loans,* which are *second mortgages,* allow you to use that line of credit for various purchases. Some states place restrictions on home equity loans.

JOB-RELATED EXPENSES   As previously mentioned, certain work expenses, such as union dues, some travel and education costs, business tools, and job search expenses, may be included as itemized deductions.

HEALTH CARE EXPENSES   *Flexible spending account (FSA),* also called *health savings accounts* and expense reimbursement accounts, allow you to reduce your taxable income when paying for medical expenses or child care costs. Workers are allowed to put pretax dollars into these employer-sponsored programs. These "deposits" result in a lower taxable income. Then, the funds in the FSA may be used to pay for various medical expenses and dependent care costs.

Investment Decisions

A major area of tax planning involves decisions related to investing.

TAX-EXEMPT INVESTMENTS   Interest income from municipal bonds, which are issued by state and local governments, and other tax-exempt investments is not subject to federal income tax. Although municipal bonds have lower interest rates than other investments, the *after-tax* income may be higher. For example, if you are in the 27 percent tax bracket, earning $100 of tax-exempt income would be worth more to you than earning $125 in taxable investment income. The $125 would have an after-tax value of $91—$125 less $34 (27 percent of $125) for taxes.

TAX-DEFERRED INVESTMENTS   Although tax-deferred investments, with income taxed at a later date, are less beneficial than tax-exempt investments, they give you the advantage of paying taxes in the future rather than now. Examples of tax-deferred investments include:

- *Tax-deferred annuities,* usually issued by insurance companies. These investments are discussed in Chapter 10.

- *Section 529 savings plans* are state-run, tax-deferred plans to set aside money for a child's education. The 529 is like a prepaid tuition plan in which you invest to cover future education costs. The 529 plans differ from state to state.
- *Retirement plans* such as IRA, Keogh, or 401(k) plans. The next section discusses the tax implications of these plans.

Capital gains, profits from the sale of a capital asset such as stocks, bonds, or real estate, are also tax deferred; you do not have to pay the tax on these profits until the asset is sold. In recent years, *long-term* capital gains (on investments held more than a year) have been taxed at a lower rate.

The sale of an investment for less than its purchase price is, of course, a *capital loss.* Capital losses can be used to offset capital gains and up to $3,000 of ordinary income. Unused capital losses may be carried forward into future years to offset capital gains or ordinary income up to $3,000 per year.

capital gains Profits from the sale of a capital asset such as stocks, bonds, or real estate.

SELF-EMPLOYMENT
Owning your own business can have tax advantages. Self-employed persons may deduct expenses such as health and certain life insurance as business costs. However, business owners have to pay self-employment tax (Social Security) in addition to the regular tax rate.

CHILDREN'S INVESTMENTS
A child under 14 with investment income of more than $1,500 is taxed at the parent's top rate. For investment income under $1,500, the child receives a deduction of $750 and the next $750 is taxed at his or her own rate, which is probably lower than the parent's rate. This restriction does not apply to children 14 and older.

Retirement Plans

A major tax strategy of benefit to working people is the use of tax-deferred retirement plans such as individual retirement arrangements (IRAs), Keogh plans, and 401(k) plans.

Apply *Yourself!*

Objective 4

Survey friends and relatives about their tax planning strategies. Do most people get a federal tax refund or owe taxes each year? Is their situation (refund or payment) planned?

TRADITIONAL IRA
The regular IRA deduction is available only to people who do not participate in employer-sponsored retirement plans or who have an adjusted gross income under a certain amount. As of 2007, the IRA contribution limit was $4,000. Older workers, age 50 and over, were allowed to contribute up to $4,500 as a "catch up" to make up for lost time saving for retirement.

In general, amounts withdrawn from deductible IRAs are included in gross income. An additional 10 percent penalty is usually imposed on withdrawals made before age 59½ unless the withdrawn funds are on account of death or disability, for medical expenses, or for qualified higher education expenses.

ROTH IRA
The Roth IRA also allows a $3,000 annual contribution, which is not tax deductible; however, the earnings on the account are tax free after five years. The funds from the Roth IRA may be withdrawn before age 59½ if the account owner is disabled, or for the purchase of a first home ($10,000 maximum). Like the regular IRA, the Roth IRA is limited to people with an adjusted gross income under a certain amount.

Deductible IRAs provide tax relief up front as contributions reduce current taxes. However, taxes must be paid when the withdrawals are made from the deductible IRA. In contrast, the Roth IRA does not have immediate benefits, but the investment grows in value on a tax-free basis. Withdrawals from the Roth IRA are exempt from federal and state taxes.

EDUCATION IRA
The Education Savings Account is designed to assist parents in saving for the college education of their children. Once again, the annual contribution (limited to $2,000) is not tax deductible and is limited to taxpayers with an adjusted

gross income under a certain amount. However, as with the Roth IRA, the earnings accumulate tax free.

KEOGH PLAN   If you are self-employed and own your own business, you can establish a Keogh plan. This retirement plan, also called an HR10 plan, may combine a profit-sharing plan and a pension plan of other investments purchased by the employee. In general, with a Keogh, people may contribute 25 percent of their annual income, up to a maximum of $30,000, to this tax-deferred retirement plan.

401(K) PLAN   The part of the tax code called 401(k) authorizes a tax-deferred retirement plan sponsored by an employer. This plan allows you to contribute a greater tax-deferred amount ($15,000 in 2007) than you can contribute to an IRA. Older workers, age 50 and over, are allowed to contribute up to $14,000. However, most companies set a limit on your contribution, such as 15 percent of your salary. Some employers provide a matching contribution in their 401(k) plans. For example, a company may contribute 50 cents for each $1 contributed by an employee. This results in an immediate 50 percent return on your investment.

Tax planners advise people to contribute as much as possible to a Keogh or 401(k) plan since (1) the increased value of the investment accumulates on a tax-free basis until the funds are withdrawn and (2) contributions reduce your adjusted gross income for computing your current tax liability.

Changing Tax Strategies

Sheet 10
Tax Planning Activities

Each year, the IRS modifies the tax form and filing procedures. In addition, Congress frequently passes legislation that changes the tax code. These changes require that you regularly determine how to take best advantage of the tax laws for personal financial planning. Also, carefully consider changes in your personal situation and your income level. You should carefully monitor your personal tax strategies to best serve both your daily living needs and your long-term financial goals.

✓ CONCEPT CHECK 3–4

1 How does tax avoidance differ from tax evasion?

_____

_____

2 What common tax-saving methods are available to most individuals and households?

_____

_____

3 For the following tax situations, indicate if this item refers to tax-exempt income or tax-deferred income.

	Tax-exempt	Tax-deferred
a. Interest earned on municipal bonds		
b. Earnings on an individual retirement account		
c. Education IRA earnings used for college expenses		
d. Income of U.S. citizens working in another country		

An overlooked way to **SHEAR** your taxes

L IKE MOST people, Tom Berry wants to pay less tax. Tom, a retired 63-year-old computer engineer from Edwardsville, Ill., has a plan that may enable him to do just that: He's considering converting his $165,000 traditional IRA to a Roth IRA.

Traditional IRA distributions are taxable; Roth distributions aren't. Tom must begin taking distributions from his traditional IRA at age 70½. At that point, Tom figures, the combination of taxable withdrawals, pension income and Social Security would push him and his wife, Paula, into the 25% federal tax bracket. Converting his IRA to a Roth now could keep him in a lower tax bracket later. "Why waste that 15% bracket?" Tom asks.

Tom says he has no pressing financial needs and does not intend to draw on his traditional IRA until the law requires him to. Tom, who could live into his nineties based on his family history, invests in an assortment of mutual funds, with about two-thirds in stock funds. Assuming a 7% annual return, Tom's traditional IRA could reach nearly $300,000 by the time he's 70½. Tom would have to take out a minimum of about $11,000 that year, based on an IRS schedule designed to deplete the account over 27 years.

Beyond the sweet smell of tax-free withdrawals in retirement, converting to a Roth is appealing because Tom could avoid those mandatory withdrawals. The original owner of a Roth never has to tap the account, so investments can grow indefinitely. To be eligible to convert to a Roth, your income (on a single or joint return) must be less than $100,000. Tom qualifies. (The $100,000 limit disappears in 2010.)

The drawback with Tom's plan is that he would have to pay taxes on all of the money he moves from his traditional IRA to a Roth. And if Tom switched all the money at once, he would catapult from the 15% bracket to the 33% bracket, and he'd lose one-third of his $165,000 kitty. But there's a way to limit the pain. Tom can convert to a Roth gradually so that he's not pushed into a higher tax bracket in any given year.

It's important to figure out how much you can convert each year without "pushing yourself into an outrageous tax bracket," says Curtis Chen, a financial planner in Belmont, Cal. That amount will vary with your other income and with tweaks in tax brackets.

Test case. If Tom and Paula's taxable income this year before any Roth conversion is, say, $50,000, Tom could move $11,300 to a Roth before tripping into the 25% bracket. Want to try Tom's strategy yourself? For an idea of your own "conversion capacity," compare your estimated taxable income for the year with the income stepping stones in the tax brackets. (To find the latest brackets, search "tax rates" at www.irs.gov.)

Converting to a Roth also holds promise for your heirs: Avoiding mandatory payouts means there might be more money left for them. Even better, money in an inherited Roth IRA is tax-free while cash in a traditional IRA is taxed in the beneficiary's top tax bracket. "If you want to leave money to someone, you'll leave a bigger amount" with a Roth because the taxes have already been paid, says Donald Duncan, a planner with D3 Financial Counselors, in Downers Grove, Ill. He adds that the conversion strategy works best if you pay the taxes on the converted money from other sources rather than from the IRA. That enables more of your money to grow tax-free.

from the pages of . . . **Kiplinger's Personal Finance**

(December 2006, p. 28)

1. What actions could be taken to reduce the amount a person pays in taxes?

2. How might you benefit from this information?

3. Locate and prepare a short summary of other current tax information at www.kiplinger.com.

back to *Getting Personal*

1. Reconsider your responses to the Getting Personal questions at the beginning of the chapter. What did you learn in this chapter that might affect your answers to these questions in the future?

_____

_____

2. What actions have you taken in recent years for effective tax preparation and tax planning?

_____

_____

3. Describe potential tax planning actions for each of these areas that you might consider within (*a*) the next year, and (*b*) the next three to five years:

Tax Planning Activities	Actions within the Next Year	Actions within Three to Five Years
Create tax document filing system or online tax recordkeeping system		
Prepare summary of itemized deductions		
Make regular contributions to tax-deferred retirement plan		
Investigate tax preparation software		

Chapter Summary

Objective 1   Tax planning can influence spending, saving, borrowing, and investing decisions. An awareness of income taxes, sales taxes, excise taxes, property taxes, estate taxes, inheritance taxes, gift taxes, and Social Security taxes is vital for successful financial planning.

Objective 2   Taxable income is determined by subtracting adjustments to income, deductions, and allowances for exemptions from gross income. Your total tax liability is based on the published tax tables or tax schedules, less any tax credits.

Objective 3   The major sections of Form 1040 provide the basic framework for filing your federal income tax return. The main sources of tax assistance are IRS services and publications, other publications, the Internet, computer software, and professional tax preparers such as commercial tax services, enrolled agents, accountants, and attorneys.

Objective 4   You may reduce your tax burden through careful planning and making financial decisions related to consumer purchasing, and the use of debt, investments, and retirement planning.

Key Terms

adjusted gross income (AGI) 78	inheritance tax 76	tax avoidance 93
average tax rate 81	investment income 78	tax credit 81
capital gains 95	itemized deductions 79	tax deduction 79
earned income 78	marginal tax rate 80	tax-deferred income 78
estate tax 76	passive income 78	tax evasion 93
excise tax 76	standard deduction 79	tax-exempt income 78
exclusion 78	taxable income 77	
exemption 79	tax audit 91	

Problems

1. Thomas Franklin arrived at the following tax information:

   Gross salary, $41,780   Interest earnings, $225
   Dividend income, $80   One personal exemption, $2,650
   Itemized deductions, $3,890   Adjustments to income, $1,150

   What amount would Thomas report as taxable income?

2. If Lola Harper had the following itemized deductions, should she use Schedule A or the standard deduction? The standard deduction for her tax situation is $6,050.

   Donations to church and other charities, $1,980
   Medical and dental expenses exceeding 7.5 percent of adjusted gross income, $430
   State income tax, $690
   Job-related expenses exceeding 2 percent of adjusted gross income, $1,610

3. What would be the average tax rate for a person who paid taxes of $4,864.14 on a taxable income of $39,870?

4. Based on the following data, would Ann and Carl Wilton receive a refund or owe additional taxes?

   Adjusted gross income, $43,190   Itemized deductions, $11,420
   Child care tax credit, $80   Federal income tax withheld, $6,784
   Amount for personal exemptions, $7,950   Tax rate on taxable income, 15 percent

5. Using the tax table in Exhibit 3–5 (p. 88), determine the amount of taxes for the following situations:
   a. A head of household with taxable income of $26,210.

   b. A single person with taxable income of $26,888.

   c. A married person filing a separate return with taxable income of $26,272.

7. Would you prefer a fully taxable investment earning 10.7 percent or a tax-exempt investment earning 8.1 percent? Why? (Assume a 28 percent tax rate.)

8. On December 30, you decide to make a $1,000 charitable donation.
   a. If you are in the 27 percent tax bracket, how much will you save in taxes for the current year?

   b. If you deposit that tax savings in a savings account for the next five years at 8 percent, what will be the future value of that account?

9. Elaine Romberg prepares her own income tax return each year. A tax preparer would charge her $60 for this service. Over a period of 10 years, how much does Elaine gain from preparing her own tax return? Assume she can earn 3 percent on her savings.

10. Jeff Perez deposits $2,000 each year in a tax-deferred retirement account. If he is in a 27 percent tax bracket, what amount would his tax be reduced over a 20-year time period?

Questions

1. What factors might be considered when creating a tax that is considered fair by most people in a society?

2. How might tax-exempt income and tax credits be used by government to stimulate economic growth?

3. What tax information sources would you be most likely to use? Why?

4. Use IRS publications and other reference materials to answer a specific tax question. Contact an IRS office to obtain an answer for the same question. What differences, if any, exist between the information sources?

5. What are some tax advantages and disadvantages of owning your own business?

Internet Connection

COMPARING TAX INFORMATION SOURCES

Visit the Web sites of three commonly used tax information sources: (1) the Internal Revenue Service, (2) a tax preparation service, and (3) a financial planning information service, such as Kiplinger.com, Money.com, or Turbotax.com. Obtain information for the following items:

Areas of analysis	Internal Revenue Service	Tax preparation service	Financial planning service
Web site	www.irs.gov		
Major emphasis of information			
Availability of current tax forms			
Coverage of latest tax law changes			
Other information and services			
E-file information and cost			

Case in Point

A SINGLE FATHER'S TAX SITUATION

Ever since his wife's death, Eric Stanford has faced difficult personal and financial circumstances. His job provides him with a fairly good income but keeps him away from his daughters, ages 8 and 10, nearly 20 days a month. This requires him to use in-home child care services that consume a major portion of his income. Since the Stanfords live in a small apartment, this arrangement has been very inconvenient.

Due to the costs of caring for his children, Eric has only a minimal amount withheld from his salary for federal income taxes. Thus more money is available during the year, but for the last few years he has had to make a payment in April—another financial burden.

Although Eric has created an investment fund for his daughters' college education and for his retirement, he has not sought to select investments that offer tax benefits. Overall, he needs to look at several aspects of his tax planning activities to find strategies that will best serve his current and future financial needs.

Eric has assembled the following information for the current tax year:

Earnings from wages, $42,590

Interest earned on savings, $125

IRA deduction, $2,000

Checking account interest, $65

Three exemptions at $2,750 each

Current standard deduction for filing status, $6,350

Amount withheld for federal income tax, $3,178

Tax credit for child care, $400

Filing status: head of household

Questions

1. What are Eric's major financial concerns in his current situation?

2. In what ways might Eric improve his tax planning efforts?

3. Calculate the following:
   a. What is Eric's taxable income? (Refer to Exhibit 3–1, page 77.)

   b. What is his total tax liability? (Use Exhibit 3–5, page 88.) What is his average tax rate?

   c. Based on his withholding, will Eric receive a refund or owe additional tax? What is the amount?

Continuing Case

TAXES

Life Situation	*Financial Data*
Single	Monthly income $2,600
Age 22	Living expenses $2,180
Starting a career	Assets $8,200
No dependents	Liabilities $3,470
	Emergency fund $530

During the year, Pam has had tax withholding greater than her actual tax liability. As a result, Pam is expecting a fairly large tax refund. In the past, she has always used tax refunds to finance major purchases (a vacation or furniture) or pay off credit card debt. Currently, she is also considering saving some of the money.

Questions

1. Assume Pam's federal tax refund is $1,100. Given her current situation, what should she do with the refund?

2. Based on her current and future life situation, what tax planning activities might Pam consider?

3. In what ways might *Your Personal Financial Plan* sheets 9–10 be useful to Pam for her tax planning activities?

Video Case

YEAR-END TAX TIPS

At the end of each year, various actions can result in a reduced tax bill. Various types of deductions, deposits to tax-deferred plans, and investment losses should be considered. Taxpayers should also be aware of how the alternative minimum tax (AMT) might affect their financial situation.

Questions

1. What tax planning actions might be appropriate for you now or in the near future?

2. How can the alternative minimum tax (AMT) affect people in various income levels?

3. Conduct an online search to obtain additional information about the AMT and suggestions for wise tax planning.

Spending Diary

"SALES TAX ON VARIOUS PURCHASES CAN REALLY INCREASE THE AMOUNT OF MY TOTAL SPENDING."

Directions

Continue your Daily Spending Diary to record and monitor your spending in various categories. Your comments should reflect what you have learned about your spending patterns and help you consider possible changes you might want to make in your spending habits.

Questions

1. What taxes do you usually pay that are reflected (directly or indirectly) in your daily spending diary?

2. How might your spending habits be revised to better control or reduce the amount you pay in taxes?

Federal Income Tax Estimate

Financial Planning Activities: Based on last year's tax return, estimates for the current year, and current tax regulations and rates, estimate your current tax liability.

Suggested Web Sites: www.irs.gov   www.taxlogic.com

Your Personal Financial Plan

9

Gross income (wages, salary, investment income, and other ordinary income		$
Less Adjustments to income (see current tax regulations)		− $
Equals Adjusted gross income		= $
Less Standard deduction or	Itemized deduction	
	medical expenses (exceeding 7.5% of AGI)	$
	state/local income, property taxes	$
	mortgage, home equity loan	$
	interest	$
	contributions	$
	casualty and theft losses	$
	moving expenses, job-related and miscellaneous expenses (exceeding 2% of AGI)	$
Amount − $	**Total**	− $
Less Personal exemptions		− $
Equals Taxable income		= $
Estimated tax (based on current tax tables or tax schedules)		$
Less Tax credits		− $
Plus Other taxes		+ $
Equals Total tax liability		= $
Less Estimated withholding and payments		− $
Equals Tax due (or refund)		= $

What's Next for Your Personal Financial Plan?

- Develop a system for filing and storing various tax records related to income, deductible expenses, and current tax forms.
- Using the IRS and other Web sites, identify recent changes in tax laws that may affect your financial planning decisions.

Name: _____ **Date:** _____

Tax Planning Activities

Financial Planning Activities: To determine which of the following actions are appropriate for your tax situation to prevent penalties and obtain tax savings.

Suggested Web Sites: www.turbotax.com   http://taxes.about.com

	Action to be taken (if applicable)	Completed
Filing status/withholding • Change filing status or exemptions due to changes in life situation		
• Change amount of withholding due to changes in tax situations		
• Plan to make estimated tax payments (due the 15th of April, June, September, and January)		
Tax records/documents • Organize home files for ease of maintaining and retrieving data		
• Send current mailing address and correct Social Security number to IRS, place of employment, and other income sources		
Annual tax activities • Be certain all needed data and current tax forms are available well before deadline		
• Research tax code changes and uncertain tax areas		
Tax-savings actions • Consider tax-exempt and tax-deferred investments		
• If you expect to have the same or lower tax rate next year, accelerate deductions into the current year		
• If you expect to have the same or lower tax rate next year, delay the receipt of income until next year		
• If you expect to have a higher tax rate next year, delay deductions since they will have a greater benefit		
• If you expect to have a higher tax rate next year, accelerate the receipt of income to have it taxed at the current lower rate		
• Start or increase use of tax-deferred retirement plans		
• Other		

What's Next for Your Personal Financial Plan?

- Identify saving and investing decisions that would minimize future income taxes.
- Develop a plan for actions to take related to your current and future tax situation.

4 Savings and Payment Services

Getting Personal

What are your attitudes toward financial services? For each of the following statements, circle the choice that best describes your current situation.

1. The financial service about which I'm least informed is
   a. Online banking.
   b. Certificates of deposit and other savings plans.
   c. Checking accounts and other payment methods.

2. My primary financial service activities involve the use of
   a. A bank or credit union.
   b. Online payments and ATMs.
   c. A check-cashing outlet.

3. When selecting a savings plan, my main concern is
   a. Bank location and availability of cash machines.
   b. Federal deposit insurance coverage.
   c. Rate of return.

4. My checking account records are
   a. Updated by me after every check written and deposit made.
   b. Based on a rough estimate in my checkbook.
   c. Known only by my financial institution.

After studying this chapter, you will be asked to reconsider your responses to these items.

Your Personal Financial Plan Sheets

11. Planning the use of financial services.
12. Comparing savings plans.
13. Using savings plans to achieve financial goals.
14. Comparing payment methods; bank reconciliation.

Objectives

In this chapter, you will learn to:

1. Identify commonly used financial services.
2. Compare the types of financial institutions.
3. Assess various types of savings plans.
4. Evaluate different types of payment methods.

Why is this important?

ATM fees can range from nothing to as high as $3 per cash withdrawal. If you are charged two $1 transaction fees a week and could invest your money at 5 percent, this convenience will cost you more than $570 over a five-year period.

What Financial Services Do You Need?

OBJECTIVE 1
Identify commonly used financial services.

More than 20,000 banks, savings and loan associations, credit unions, and other financial institutions provide various payment, savings, and credit services. Today a trip to "the bank" may mean a visit to a credit union, a stop at an ATM at the mall, or a transfer of funds online. While some financial decisions relate directly to goals, your daily activities require different financial services. Exhibit 4–1 is an overview of financial services for managing cash flows and moving toward specific financial goals.

Meeting Daily Money Needs

Buying groceries, paying the rent, and completing other routine spending activities require a cash management plan. Cash, check, credit card, and debit card are the common payment choices. Mistakes made frequently when managing current cash needs include (1) overspending as a result of impulse buying and using credit; (2) having insufficient liquid assets to pay current bills; (3) using savings or borrowing to pay for current expenses; (4) failing to put unneeded funds in an interest-earning savings account or investment plan.

Sources of Quick Cash

No matter how carefully you manage your money, at some time you will need more cash than you have available. To cope in that situation, you have two basic choices: liquidate savings or borrow. A savings account, certificate of deposit, mutual fund, or other investment may be accessed when you need funds. Or a credit card cash advance or a personal loan may be appropriate. Remember, however, that both using savings and increasing borrowing reduce your net worth and your potential to achieve long-term financial security.

Exhibit 4–1

Financial Services
for Managing Cash
Flow and Reaching
Financial Goals

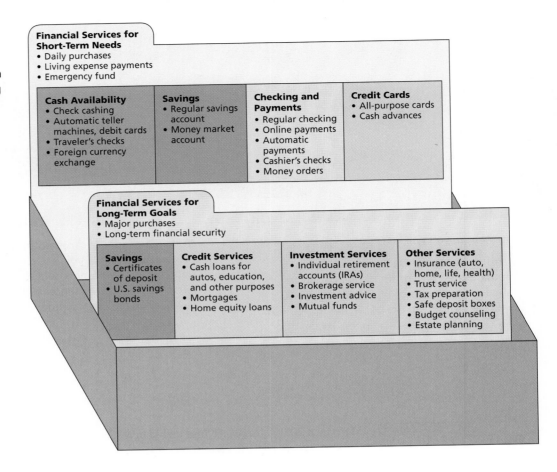

**Financial Services for
Short-Term Needs**
• Daily purchases
• Living expense payments
• Emergency fund

Cash Availability
• Check cashing
• Automatic teller
  machines, debit cards
• Traveler's checks
• Foreign currency
  exchange

Savings
• Regular savings
  account
• Money market
  account

**Checking and
Payments**
• Regular checking
• Online payments
• Automatic
  payments
• Cashier's checks
• Money orders

Credit Cards
• All-purpose cards
• Cash advances

**Financial Services for
Long-Term Goals**
• Major purchases
• Long-term financial security

Savings
• Certificates
  of deposit
• U.S. savings
  bonds

Credit Services
• Cash loans for
  autos, education,
  and other purposes
• Mortgages
• Home equity loans

Investment Services
• Individual retirement
  accounts (IRAs)
• Brokerage service
• Investment advice
• Mutual funds

Other Services
• Insurance (auto,
  home, life, health)
• Trust service
• Tax preparation
• Safe deposit boxes
• Budget counseling
• Estate planning

Types of Financial Services

Banks and other financial institutions offer services to meet a variety of needs. These services may be viewed in into four main categories:

1. *Savings* provides safe storage of funds for future use. Commonly referred to as *time deposits,* money in savings accounts and certificates of deposit are examples of savings plans.

2. *Payment services* offer an ability to transfer money to others for daily business activities. Checking accounts and other payment methods are generally called *demand deposits.*

3. *Borrowing* is used by most people at some time during their lives. Credit alternatives range from short-term accounts, such as credit cards and cash loans, to long-term borrowing, such as a home mortgage.

4. *Other financial services* include insurance, investments, tax assistance, and financial planning. A **trust** is a legal agreement that provides for the management and control of assets by one party for the benefit of another. This type of arrangement is usually created through a commercial bank or a lawyer. Parents who want to set aside certain funds for their children's education may use a trust.

To simplify financial services, many financial businesses offer all-purpose accounts. An **asset management account,** also called a *cash management account,* provides a complete financial services program for a single fee. Investment companies and others offer this type of account, with checking, an ATM card, a credit card, online banking, and a line of credit as well as access for buying stocks, bonds, mutual funds, and other investments.

Apply *Yourself!*

Objective 1

Survey several people to determine awareness and use of various financial services such as online banking.

trust A legal agreement that provides for the management and control of assets by one party for the benefit of another.

asset management account An all-in-one account that includes savings, checking, borrowing, investing, and other financial services for a single fee; also called a *cash management account.*

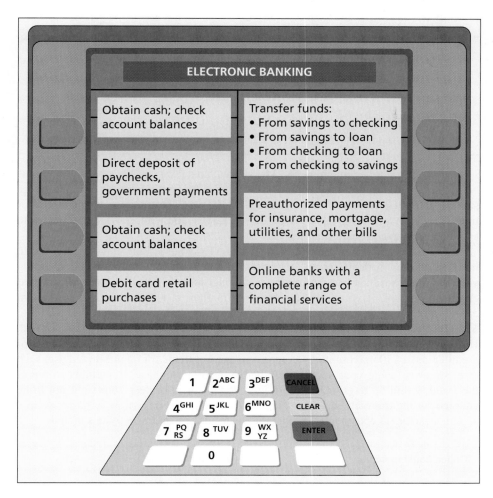

Exhibit 4–2

Electronic Banking Services

Electronic and Online Banking

Banking online and through electronic systems continues to expand (see Exhibit 4–2). While most traditional financial institutions offer online banking services, Web-only banks have also become strong competitors. For example, E*Trade Bank operates online while also providing customers with access to ATMs. These "e-banks" and "e-branches" provide nearly every needed financial service:

Category	Online Services Available	Sample Providers
Savings plans	• Deposits to savings accounts, money market accounts, certificates of deposit (CDs), and retirement accounts • Direct deposit of paychecks and government payments	www.Netbank.com www.INGdirect.com www.hsbcdirect.com
Payment services and cash access	• Online payments including automatic transfers funds for rent, mortgage, utilities, loans, and investment deposits • ATM (cash machine) access for various banking activities • Payments for online purchases	www.usbank.com www.etradebank.com www.paypal.com www.paytrust.com

(continued)

Category	Online Services Available	Sample Providers
Borrowing	• Comparison of current loan rates • Online application and approval for auto loans, credit cards, mortgages, and other loans	www.eloan.com www.chase.com www.citibankdirect.com
Other services	• Online rates and applications for various types of insurance coverage • Buy, sell, monitor investments (stocks, bonds, mutual funds, and other securities)	www.insure.com www.wachovia.com www.etrade.com www.schwab.com

automatic teller machine (ATM) A computer terminal used to conduct banking transactions; also called a *cash machine.*

debit card A plastic access card used in computerized banking transactions; also called a *cash card.*

An **automatic teller machine (ATM),** also called a *cash machine,* provides various banking activities and other types of transactions such as buying transit passes, postage stamps, and gift certificates. To minimize ATM fees, compare several financial institutions. Use your own bank's ATM to avoid surcharges, and withdraw larger amounts to avoid fees on several small transactions.

The **debit card,** or *cash card,* that activates ATM transactions may also be used to make purchases. A debit card is in contrast to a *credit card,* since you are spending your own funds rather than borrowing additional money. A lost or stolen debit card can be expensive. If you notify the financial institution within two days of the lost card, your liability for unauthorized use is $50. After that, you can be liable for up to $500 of unauthorized use for up to 60 days. Beyond that, your liability is unlimited. However, some card issuers use the same rules for lost or stolen debit cards as for credit cards: a $50 maximum. Of course, you are not liable for unauthorized use, such as a con artist using your account number to make a purchase. Remember to report the fraud within 60 days of receiving your statement to protect your right not to be charged for the transaction.

Other factors to consider when planning your online banking activities include:

Online Banking Benefits	Online Banking Concerns
• Time and money savings	• Potential privacy, security violations
• Convenience for transactions, comparing rates	• ATM fees can become costly
• No paper trail for identity thieves	• Difficulty depositing cash, checks
• Transfer access for loans, investments	• Overspending due to ease of access
• E-mail notices of due dates	• Online scams, "phishing," and e-mail spam

Sheet 11
Planning the Use of Financial Services

CAUTION!

"Phishing" is a scam that uses e-mail spam or pop-up messages to deceive you into revealing your credit card number, bank account information, Social Security number, passwords, or other private information. These e-mails usually look official, like they are coming from a legitimate bank or other financial institution. Never disclose personal data online or by phone to a questionable source.

Financial Services and Economic Conditions

Changing interest rates, rising consumer prices, and other economic factors influence financial services. For successful financial planning, be aware of the current trends and future prospects for interest rates (see Exhibit 4–3). You can learn about these trends and prospects by reading *The Wall Street Journal* (www.wsj.com), *The Financial Times* (www.ft.com), the business section of daily newspapers, and business periodicals such as *Business-Week* (www.businessweek.com), *Forbes* (www.forbes.com), and *Fortune* (www.fortune.com).

CREDIT | Online banking is convenient but not foolproof. *By Joan Goldwasser*

Electronic bill-paying SNAFUS

WHEN EMILY and Greg Martinez moved from Philadelphia to Los Angeles earlier this year, they thought that transferring their online bank account would be a snap. They were wrong. Because they didn't notify Sprint in time, their monthly cellphone bill was paid twice—once from their Philadelphia account and again from their new Los Angeles bank account.

Other online bill-payers have had bills that narrowly escaped being paid late, or weren't paid at all. One couple failed to notify Check-free, their bill-paying service, that their mortgage lender had changed addresses.

Their mortgage check was forwarded and ended up arriving on time. However, a young teacher wasn't so fortunate. He assumed that his car payments would be automatically debited from his checking account. But he neglected to sign the necessary documents, and after several missed payments, he had to scramble to fix the problem—after his car had been repossessed in the middle of the night.

If you're among the two-thirds of U.S. consumers who no longer worry about writing checks or running out of stamps thanks to automatic bill-paying services, you still need to monitor your bills. After you sign up with

a vendor or your bank, review your account statements on a regular basis, advises Mike Herd of Nacha, the electronic-payments association. And make sure that your payee mailing addresses are up-to-date.

When you sign up for automatic bill-paying with an individual vendor or with your bank, you can generally decide whether you want the funds debited from your checking account or charged to a credit card. You can change the amount, or even cancel the payment, sometimes as late as the day before your bill is due.

If you have a problem with unauthorized payments—which happens to about 25

out of every 100,000 transactions, according to Nacha—be sure to notify your bank or credit-card company immediately. Nacha rules require the financial institution to reimburse your account if a transaction is unauthorized. Neither Visa nor MasterCard holds consumers liable for unintended charges to their accounts.

In a rare instance, automatic bill-paying can be too efficient. Take the case of the Canadian man who died in his Winnipeg apartment but wasn't discovered for nearly two years. No one noticed because all of his monthly bills had been paid on time.

1. What concerns may be associated with online bill paying activities?

_____

_____

2. Describe actions you should take to avoid online banking problems.

_____

3. Locate additional information about online banking at www.kiplinger.com or www.bankrate.com that might be of value when making personal financial decisions.

_____

_____

Exhibit 4–3

Changing Interest Rates and
Financial Service Decisions

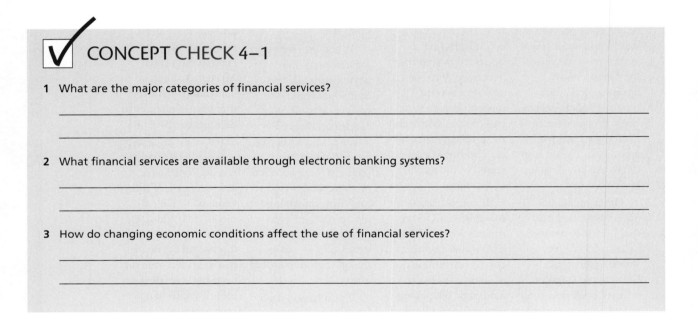

**When interest
rates are rising...**

• Use long-term loans to take
  advantage of current low rates.
• Select short-term savings
  instruments to take advantage
  of higher rates when they
  mature.

• Use short-term loans to take
  advantage of lower rates when
  you refinance the loans.
• Select long-term savings
  instruments to "lock in"
  earnings at current high rates.

**When interest
rates are falling...**

✔ CONCEPT CHECK 4–1

1 What are the major categories of financial services?

_____

_____

2 What financial services are available through electronic banking systems?

_____

_____

3 How do changing economic conditions affect the use of financial services?

_____

_____

Sources of Financial Services

OBJECTIVE 2
Compare the types of
financial institutions.

Many types of businesses, including insurance companies, investment brokers, and credit card companies, offer financial services that were once exclusive to banks. Companies such as General Motors, Sears, and AT&T issue credit cards. Banks have also expanded their activities to provide investments, insurance, and real estate services.

Comparing Financial Institutions

The basic questions to ask when selecting a financial service provider are simple:

• Where can I get the best return on my savings?
• How can I minimize the cost of checking and payments services?
• Will I be able to borrow money if I need it?

As you use financial services, decide what you want from the organization that will serve your needs. With the financial marketplace constantly changing, plan to continually consider various factors before selecting an organization.

The services offered by the financial institution will likely be a major factor. In addition, personal service may be important to you. Convenience may take the form of branch

Exhibit 4–4   Who Provides Financial Services?

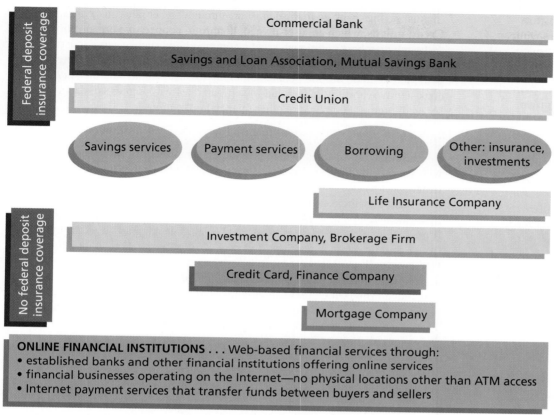

Note: The actual services offered by specific organizations may vary.

office and ATM locations as well as online services. Remember, convenience and service have a cost; be sure to compare fees and other charges at several financial institutions.

Finally, also consider safety and rates. Obtain information about earnings you will receive on savings and checking accounts and the rate you will pay for borrowed funds. Most financial institutions have deposit insurance to protect customers against losses; however, not all of them are insured by federal government programs.

Types of Financial Institutions

Despite changes in the banking environment, many familiar financial institutions still serve your needs. As shown in Exhibit 4–4, many organizations offer a range of financial services while others provide specialized assistance. Be aware that distinctions among the various types of financial institutions are disappearing. For example, today, people can buy investments through their bank and credit union as well as from an investment company or brokerage firm.

Deposit institutions serve as intermediaries between suppliers (savers) and users (borrowers) of funds. The most common of these traditional organizations are:

- **Commercial banks,** which offer a full range of financial services, including checking, savings, lending, and most other services. Commercial banks are organized as corporations, with investors (stockholders) contributing the needed capital to operate.
- **Savings and loan associations (S&Ls),** which traditionally specialized in savings accounts and mortgages. Today, many of these organizations have expanded to offer financial services comparable to those of a bank.

commercial bank A financial institution that offers a full range of financial services to individuals, businesses, and government agencies.

savings and loan association (S&L) A financial institution that traditionally specialized in savings accounts and mortgage loans.

mutual savings bank A financial institution that is owned by depositors and specializes in savings accounts and mortgage loans.

credit union A user-owned, nonprofit, cooperative financial institution that is organized for the benefit of its members.

money market fund A savings–investment plan offered by investment companies, with earnings based on investments in various short-term financial instruments.

- **Mutual savings banks,** which are owned by depositors, also specialize in savings and mortgages. Located mainly in the northeastern United States, the profits of a mutual savings bank go to the depositors through higher rates on savings.
- **Credit unions,** which are user-owned, nonprofit, cooperative organizations. Although members traditionally had a common bond such as work location, church, or community affiliation, credit union membership today is more flexible, with more than 80 million people belonging to one. Annual banking studies consistently report lower fees and lower loan rates with higher satisfaction levels for credit unions compared to other financial institutions.

Nondeposit institutions offer various financial services. These institutions include:

- Life insurance companies, which provide financial security for dependents with various life insurance policies, some containing savings and investment features. Expanded activities of life insurance companies include investment and retirement planning services.
- Investment companies, also called *mutual funds,* which offer a **money market fund**—a combination savings–investment plan. The company uses the money from many investors to purchase a variety of short-term financial instruments. However, unlike accounts at most deposit institutions, investment company accounts are not covered by federal deposit insurance.
- Brokerage firms, which often employ investment advisers, serve as an agent between the buyer and seller for stocks, bonds, and other investment securities. These companies obtain their earnings through the commissions and fees charged for various services.
- Credit card companies, which specialize in funding short-term retail lending. However, these networks, including VISA, MasterCard, and Discover, have also expanded into various other banking and investing services.
- Finance companies, which provide loans to consumers and small businesses. These loans have short and intermediate terms with higher rates than most other lenders charge. Most finance companies also offer other financial planning services.
- Mortgage companies, which are organized primarily to provide loans for home purchases. The services of mortgage companies are presented in Chapter 7.

These and other types of financial institutions compete for your business. More and more of these companies are offering a combination of services (saving, checking, credit, insurance, investments) from one source. These one-stop financial service operations are sometimes referred to as *financial supermarkets.*

did you know?

7-Eleven and other retailers are expanding to offer various financial services. The electronic kiosks in their stores will allow cashing of paychecks, paying utility bills, and obtaining money orders.

Problematic Financial Businesses

Would you pay $8 to cash a $100 check? Or pay $20 to borrow $100 for two weeks? Many people without ready access to financial services (especially low-income consumers) use pawnshops, check-cashing outlets, loan stores, and rent-to-own centers.

Apply *Yourself!*

Objective 2

Using the Web site for the Credit Union National Association (www.cuna.org) or other sources, obtain information about joining a credit union and the services offered by this type of financial institution.

PAWNSHOPS   Pawnshops make loans based on the value of tangible possessions such as jewelry or other valuable items. Many low- and moderate-income families use these organizations to obtain cash loans quickly. Pawnshops charge higher fees than other financial institutions. Thousands of consumers are increasingly in need of small loans—usually $50 to $75, to be repaid in 30 to 45 days. Pawnshops have become the "neighborhood bankers" and the "local shopping malls," since they provide both lending and retail shopping services, selling items that owners do not redeem. While states regulate the interest rates charged by pawnshops, 3 percent a month or higher is common.

CHECK-CASHING OUTLETS   Most financial institutions will not cash a check unless you have an account. The more than 6,000 check-cashing outlets (CCOs) charge anywhere from 1 to 20 percent of the face value of a check; the average cost is 2 to 3 percent. However, for a low-income family, that can be a significant portion of the total household budget. CCOs, sometimes called a currency exchanges, also offer services, including electronic tax filing, money orders, private postal boxes, utility bill payment, and the sale of transit tokens. A person can usually obtain most of these services for less at other locations.

> *did you know?*
>
> To avoid check-cashing fees, some employees receive a prepaid debit card rather than a paper paycheck. People without checking accounts are able to access an ATM and avoid check-cashing outlets.

PAYDAY LOANS   Many consumer organizations caution against using payday loans, also referred to as *cash advances, check advance loans, postdated check loans,* and *delayed deposit loans.* Desperate borrowers pay annual interest rates of as much as 780 percent and more to obtain needed cash from payday loan companies. These enterprises have increased to more than 8,000. The most frequent users of payday loans are workers who have become trapped by debts or who have been driven into debt by misfortune.

In a typical payday loan, a consumer writes a personal check for $115 to borrow $100 for 14 days. The payday lender agrees to hold the check until the next payday. This $15 finance charge for the 14 days translates into an annual percentage rate of 391 percent. Some consumers "roll over" their loans, paying another $15 for the $100 loan for the next 14 days. After a few rollovers, the finance charge can exceed the amount borrowed. The Chicago Department of Consumer Services has reported annual rates ranging from 659 to 1,300 percent for some payday loans.

RENT-TO-OWN CENTERS   Years ago, people who rented furniture and appliances found few deluxe items available. Today rental businesses offer big-screen televisions, seven-piece cherrywood bedroom sets, and personal computers. The rent-to-purchase industry is defined as stores that lease products to consumers who can own the item if they complete a certain number of monthly or weekly payments.

In Wisconsin, more than 10,000 customers of the Rent-A-Center chain became part of a class action lawsuit seeking refunds of finance charges for rented merchandise. The suit accused the rental chain of illegally charging interest rates as high as 100 percent to rent televisions and other appliances, often to customers in low-income areas.

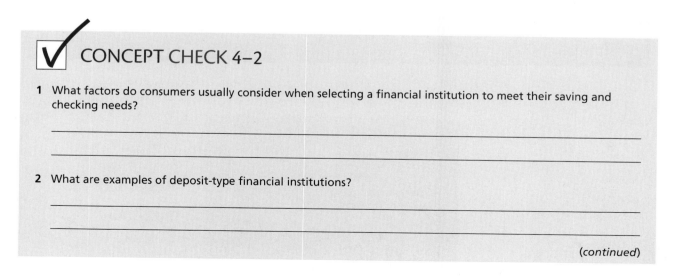

✔ CONCEPT CHECK 4–2

1 What factors do consumers usually consider when selecting a financial institution to meet their saving and checking needs?

_____

_____

2 What are examples of deposit-type financial institutions?

_____

_____

(continued)

3 Match the following descriptions with the appropriate financial institution.

a. commercial bank   _____ Commonly used by people without a bank account.

b. credit union   _____ Investment services accompany main business focus.

c. life insurance company   _____ Traditionally provides widest range of financial services.

d. check-cashing outlet   _____ Offers lower fee costs for members.

Comparing Savings Plans

OBJECTIVE 3

Assess various types of savings plans.

A savings plan is vital to attain financial goals. A range of savings alternatives exist (Exhibit 4–5). The many types of savings plans can be grouped into the following main categories.

Exhibit 4–5

Savings Alternatives

Regular Savings Accounts

Benefits
- Low minimum balance
- Ease of withdrawal
- Insured

Drawback
- Low rate of return

more liquidity   less liquidity

Money Market Account/Funds

Benefits
- Favorable rate of return (based on current interest rates)
- Allows limited number of checks to be writen
- Insured (money market accounts)

Drawbacks
- Higher minimum balance than regular savings accounts
- Service charge and/or lower rate if below certain balance
- Not insured (money market funds)

Certificates of Deposit (CDs)

Benefits
- Guaranteed rate of return for time of CD
- Insured (when purchased from bank or comparable financial institution)

Drawbacks
- Possible penalty (reduced interest) for early withdrawal
- Minimum deposit

U.S. Savings Bonds

Benefits
- Rate varies with interest rates (I-bonds)
- Low minimum deposit
- Government guaranteed
- Exempt from state, local income taxes

Drawback
- Lower rate when redeemed within first five years

Regular Savings Accounts

Regular savings accounts, also called *passbook* or *statement accounts,* usually involve a low or no minimum balance and allow you to withdraw money as needed. Banks, savings and loan associations, and other financial institutions offer regular savings accounts. At a credit union, these savings plans are called *share accounts.*

Certificates of Deposit

Higher earnings are available to savers when they leave money on deposit for a set time period. A **certificate of deposit (CD)** is a savings plan requiring that a certain amount be left on deposit for a stated time period (ranging from 30 days to five or more years) to earn a specific rate of return. These time deposits can be an attractive and a safe savings alternative. However, most financial institutions impose a penalty for early withdrawal of CD funds.

certificate of deposit (CD) A savings plan requiring that a certain amount be left on deposit for a stated time period to earn a specified interest rate.

TYPES OF CDS   Financial institutions offer certificates of deposit with various features:

- *Rising-rate* or *bump-up CDs* have higher rates at various intervals. However, this rate may be in effect for only a couple of months.
- *Stock-indexed CDs* have earnings based on the stock market with higher earnings in times of strong stock performance. At other times, you may earn no interest and may even lose part of your savings.
- *Callable CDs* start with higher rates and long-term maturities. However, the bank may "call" the account after a stipulated period, such as one or two years, if interest rates drop. When the call option is exercised, the saver receives the original investment principal and any interest that has been earned.
- *Promotional CDs* attempt to attract savers with gifts or special rates. A Boulder, Colorado, bank offered Rolex watches, archery equipment, and Zodiac inflatable boats in lieu of interest. Compare the value of the item to the lost interest.

MANAGING CDS   When first buying or *rolling over* a CD (buying a new one at maturity), investigate potential earnings and costs. Do not allow your financial institution to automatically roll over your money into another CD for the same term. If interest rates have dropped, you might consider a shorter maturity. Or if you believe rates are at a peak and you won't need the money for some time, obtain a CD with a longer term.

Consider creating a CD *portfolio* with CDs maturing at different times, for example, $2,000 in a three-month CD, $2,000 in a six-month CD, $2,000 in a one-year CD, and $2,000 in a two-year CD. This will give you some degree of liquidity and flexibility when you reinvest your funds.

Interest-Earning Checking Accounts

Checking accounts frequently have a savings feature. These interest-earning accounts usually pay a low interest rate.

Money Market Accounts and Funds

To provide savers with higher interest rates, a savings plan with a floating interest rate was created. A **money market account** is a savings account that requires a minimum balance and has earnings based on the changing market level of interest rates. Money market accounts may allow a limited number of checks to be written and generally impose a fee when the account balance goes below the required minimum, usually $1,000.

money market account A savings account offered by banks, savings and loan associations, and credit unions that requires a minimum balance and has earnings based on market interest rates.

Apply *Yourself!*

Objective 3

Conduct online research to obtain past and current data on various interest rates (such as prime rate, T-bill rate, mortgage rate, corporate bond rate, and six-month CD rate). Information may be obtained at www.federalreserve.gov and other Web sites. How do these rates affect various personal financial decisions?

Both money market accounts and money market funds offer earnings based on current interest rates, and both have minimum-balance restrictions and allow check writing. The major difference is in safety. Money market *accounts* at banks and savings and loan associations are covered by federal deposit insurance. This is not true of money market *funds*, which are a product of investment and insurance companies. Since money market funds invest mainly in short-term (less than a year) government and corporate securities, however, they are usually quite safe.

U.S. Savings Bonds

Years ago, the low return on savings bonds made their purchase a patriotic act rather than a wise saving choice. In recent years, however, the Treasury Department has offered various programs to make buying savings bonds more attractive.

EE BONDS   Series EE bonds (called Patriot Bonds after the September 11, 2001, terrorist attacks) may be purchased for amounts ranging from $25 to $5,000 (face values of $50 to $10,000, respectively). Electronic EE bonds are purchased at face value; for example, you pay $50 for a $50 bond. These bonds may be purchased in amounts of $25 or more.

EE bonds increase in value every month as interest accrues monthly and compounds semiannually. If you redeem EE bonds before five years, you forfeit the latest three months of interest; after five years, you are not penalized. A bond must be held for one year before it can be cashed.

EE bonds purchased between May 1997 and April 30, 2005, earned market-based interest. Since that time, a fixed interest rate has been paid. Series EE bonds continue to earn interest for 30 years, well beyond the time at which the face value is reached. The main tax advantages of Series EE bonds are that (1) the interest earned is exempt from state and local taxes and (2) you do not have to pay federal income tax on earnings until the bonds are redeemed.

Redeemed Series EE bonds may be exempt from federal income tax if the funds are used to pay tuition and fees at a college, university, or qualified technical school for yourself or a dependent. The bonds must be purchased by an individual who is at least 24 years old, and they must be issued in the names of one or both parents. These provisions have been designed to assist low- and middle-income households; people whose incomes exceed a certain amount do not qualify for the exemption.

HH BONDS   Series HH bonds are *current-income* bonds, which earn interest every six months. The interest is deposited electronically to your bank account. This interest is taxed as current income. The semiannual interest payments of HH bonds make them a popular source of retirement income.

You can redeem your HH bonds at any time after six months from the issue date. The value of HH bonds doesn't change, so when redeemed, you get back your original investment. HH bonds were available in denominations of $500, $1,000, $5,000, and $10,000. As of 2004, investors are no longer able to reinvest HH bonds or exchange EE bonds for HH bonds.

I BONDS   The I bond earns a combined rate consisting of (1) a fixed rate for the life of the bond, and (2) an inflation rate that changes twice a year. Every six months a new, fixed base rate is set for new bonds. The additional interest payment is recalculated twice a year, based on the current annual inflation rate. I bonds are sold in the same denominations as EE bonds, but are purchased at face value, not discount. Also, as with EE bonds, the minimum holding period is one year.

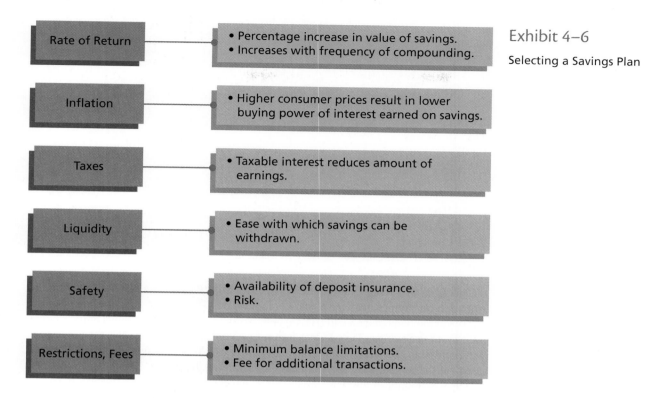

Exhibit 4–6

Selecting a Savings Plan

A person may purchase up to $15,000 ($30,000 maturity face) of U.S. savings bonds a year. This amount applies to any person, so parents may buy an additional $15,000 in each child's name. Banks and other financial institutions sell U.S. savings bonds; they may also be purchased online. Lost, stolen, or destroyed savings bonds will be replaced by the government free of charge. Additional information and current value calculations for savings bonds' values may be obtained at www.savingsbonds.gov.

Key Web Site for Savings Bonds
www.savingsbonds.gov.

Evaluating Savings Plans

Selection of a savings plan is usually influenced by the rate of return, inflation, tax considerations, liquidity, safety, restrictions, and fees (see Exhibit 4–6).

RATE OF RETURN   Earnings on savings can be measured by the **rate of return,** or *yield,* the percentage of increase in the value of your savings from earned interest. For example, a $100 savings account that earned $5 after a year would have a rate of return, or yield, of 5 percent. This rate of return was determined by dividing the interest earned ($5) by the amount in the savings account ($100). The yield on your savings usually will be greater than the stated interest rate.

rate of return The percentage of increase in the value of savings as a result of interest earned; also called *yield.*

   Compounding refers to interest that is earned on previously earned interest. Each time interest is added to your savings, the next interest amount is computed on the new balance in the account. The more frequent the compounding, the higher your rate of return will be. For example, $100 in a savings account that earns 6 percent compounded annually will increase $6 after a year. But the same $100 in a 6 percent account compounded daily will earn $6.19 for the year. Although this difference may seem slight, large amounts held in savings for long periods of time will result in far higher differences (see Exhibit 4–7).

compounding A process that calculates interest based on previously earned interest.

Exhibit 4–7

Compounding Frequency Affects the Saving Yield

Shorter compounding periods result in higher yields. This chart shows the growth of $10,000, earning a rate of 8 percent, but with different compounding methods.

End of year	COMPOUNDING METHOD			
	Daily	Monthly	Quarterly	Annually
1	$10,832.78	$10,830.00	$10,824.32	$10,800.00
2	11,743.91	11,728.88	11,716.59	11,664.00
3	12,712.17	12,702.37	12,682.41	12,597.12
4	13,770.82	13,756.66	13,727.85	13,604.89
5	14,917.62	14.898.46	14,859.46	14,693.28
Annual yield	8.33%	8.30%	8.24%	8.00%

annual percentage yield (APY) The percentage rate expressing the total amount of interest that would be received on a $100 deposit based on the annual rate and frequency of compounding for a 365-day period.

The *Truth in Savings Act* requires financial institutions to disclose the following information on savings account plans: (1) fees on deposit accounts; (2) the interest rate; (3) the annual percentage yield (APY); and (4) other terms and conditions of the savings plan. Truth in Savings (TIS) defines **annual percentage yield (APY)** as the percentage rate expressing the total amount of interest that would be received on a $100 deposit based on the annual rate and frequency of compounding for a 365-day period. APY reflects the amount of interest a saver should expect to earn.

INFLATION   The rate of return you earn on your savings should be compared with the inflation rate. When inflation was over 10 percent, people with money in savings accounts earning 5 or 6 percent were experiencing a loss in the buying power of that money. In general, as the inflation rate increases, the interest rates offered to savers also increase.

TAXES   Like inflation, taxes reduce interest earned on savings. For example, a 10 percent return for a saver in a 28 percent tax bracket means a real return of 7.2 percent (the Figure It Out box shows how to compute the after-tax savings rate of return). As discussed in Chapter 3, several tax-exempt and tax-deferred savings plans and investments can increase your real rate of return.

did you know?

As of April 2006, the Federal Deposit Insurance Corporation (FDIC) and the National Credit Union Administration (NCUA) increased deposit coverage for certain retirement accounts from $100,000 to $250,000. The higher insurance coverage applies to traditional and Roth IRAs, Simplified Employee Pension (SEP) IRAs, and Savings Incentive Match Plans for Employees (SIMPLE) IRAs. Also included are self-directed Keogh accounts and various plans for state government employees. This coverage applies only to retirement accounts in financial institutions insured by the FDIC and NCUA.

LIQUIDITY   *Liquidity* allows you to withdraw your money on short notice without a loss of value or fees. Some savings plans impose penalties for early withdrawal or have other restrictions. With certain types of savings certificates and accounts, early withdrawal may be penalized by a loss of interest or a lower earnings rate. Consider the degree of liquidity you desire in relation to your savings goals. To achieve long-term financial goals, many people trade off liquidity for a higher return.

SAFETY   Most savings plans at banks, savings and loan associations, and credit unions are insured by agencies affiliated with the federal government. This protection prevents a loss of money due to the failure of the insured institution. While a few financial institutions have failed in recent years, savers with deposits covered

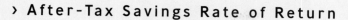

Figure It Out!

› After-Tax Savings Rate of Return

The taxability of interest on your savings reduces your real rate of return. In other words, you lose some portion of your interest to taxes. This calculation consists of the following steps:

1. Determine your top tax bracket for federal income taxes.

2. Subtract this rate, expressed as a decimal, from 1.0.

3. Multiply the result by the yield on your savings account.

4. This number, expressed as a percentage, is your after-tax rate of return.

For example,

1. You are in the 28 percent tax bracket.

2. $1.0 - 0.28 = 0.72$.

3. If the yield on your savings account is 6.25 percent, $0.0625 \times 0.72 = 0.045$.

4. Your after-tax rate of return is 4.5 percent.

You may use the same procedure to determine the *real rate of return* on your savings based on inflation. For example, if you are earning 6 percent on savings and inflation is 5 percent, your real rate of return (after inflation) is 5.7 percent: $0.06 \times (1 - 0.05) = 0.057$.

CALCULATIONS

1. What would be the after-tax return for a person who is receiving 4 percent on savings and is in a 15 percent tax bracket? _____%

2. What would be the after-tax value of $100 earned in interest for a person who is in a 31 percent tax bracket? $_____

by federal insurance have not lost any money. Depositors of failed organizations either have been paid the amounts in their accounts or have had the accounts taken over by a financially stable institution.

The Federal Deposit Insurance Corporation (FDIC) administers separate insurance funds: the Bank Insurance Fund and the Savings Association Insurance Fund (SAIF). Credit unions may obtain deposit insurance through the National Credit Union Association (NCUA). Some state-chartered credit unions have opted for a private insurance program.

The FDIC insures deposits of up to $100,000 per person per financial institution; a joint account is considered to belong proportionally to each name on the account. For example, if you have a $70,000 individual account and an $80,000 joint account with a relative in the same financial institution, $10,000 of your savings will not be covered by federal deposit insurance ($70,000 plus one-half of $80,000 exceeds the $100,000 limit). However, by using combinations of individual, joint, and trust accounts in different financial institutions, it is possible to have federal deposit insurance cover amounts that exceed $100,000. Remember, the maximum coverage of federal deposit insurance is based on each depositor, not on each account. The best advice is to never keep more than $100,000 in one financial institution. Be careful, however, since different branch offices count as the same institution. Also, mergers in the financial service industry may bring accounts from different banks together.

RESTRICTIONS AND FEES Other limitations can affect your choice of a savings program. For example, there may be a delay between the time interest is earned and the time it is added to your account. This means the interest will not be available for your immediate use. Also, some institutions charge a transaction fee for each deposit or withdrawal. Some financial institutions offer a "free gift" when a certain savings amount is deposited. To receive this gift, you have to leave your money on deposit for a certain time period, or you may receive less interest, since some of the earnings are used to cover the cost of the "free" items.

Sheet 12
Comparing Savings Plans

Sheet 13
Using Savings Plans to Achieve Financial Goals

✓ CONCEPT CHECK 4–3

1 What are the main types of savings plans offered by financial institutions?

_____

_____

2 How does a money market *account* differ from a money market *fund?*

_____

_____

3 What are the benefits of U.S. savings bonds?

_____

4 How do inflation and taxes affect earnings on savings?

_____

_____

5 In the following financial situations, check the box that is the major influence for the person when selecting a savings plan:

Financial planning situation	Rate of return	Inflation	Taxes	Liquidity	Safety
a. An older couple needs easy access to funds for living expenses.					
b. A person is concerned with loss of buying power of funds on deposit.					
c. A saver desires to maximize earnings from the savings plan.					
d. A middle-aged person wants assurance that the funds are safe.					

Comparing Payment Methods

OBJECTIVE 4
Evaluate different types of payment methods.

Each year, paper checks account for a smaller and smaller portion of payments in our society. While check writing is being used less, checking accounts are still the common source for most debit card transactions and online payments. As shown in Exhibit 4–8, payment alternatives may be viewed in three main categories.

Exhibit 4–8

Payment Alternatives

Electronic Payments	Checking Accounts	Other Payment Methods
Debit (cash) and credit cards	Regular checking account	Certified check
Online payments, transfer	Activity checking account	Cashier's check
Smart cards ("electronic wallet")	Interest-earning account	Traveler's checks
Stored-value (prepaid) cards		Money order

Electronic Payments

Transactions not involving cash, checks, or credit cards have expanded with technology, improved security, and increased consumer acceptance.

DEBIT CARD TRANSACTIONS   Most retail stores, restaurants, and other businesses accept debit cards, also called check cards, issued by Visa and MasterCard. When the debit card transaction is processed, the amount of the purchase is deducted from your checking account. Most debit cards can be used two ways: (1) with your signature, like a credit card, or (2) with your personal identification number (PIN), like an ATM card.

ONLINE PAYMENTS   Banks and Internet companies are serving as third parties to facilitate online bill payments. Some of these Internet companies are www.paypal.com, www.checkfree.com, and www.paytrust.com. When using these services, be sure to consider the monthly charge as well as online security and customer service availability. Also on the Web are "cyber cash" services creating their own *e-money* that serves as a medium of exchange for online transactions.

STORED-VALUE CARDS   Prepaid cards for telephone service, transit fares, highway tolls, laundry service, and school lunches are common. Some of these stored-value cards are disposable; others can be reloaded with an additional amount.

SMART CARDS   These "electronic wallets" are similar to other ATM cards. However, the imbedded microchip stores prepaid amounts as well as information with account balances, transaction records, insurance information, and medical history.

Checking Accounts

Despite increased use of electronic payment systems, a checking account is still a necessity for most people. Checking accounts fall into three major categories: regular checking accounts, activity accounts, and interest-earning checking accounts.

REGULAR CHECKING ACCOUNTS   *Regular checking accounts* usually have a monthly service charge that you may avoid by keeping a minimum balance in the account. Some financial institutions will waive the monthly fee if you keep a certain amount in savings. Avoiding the monthly service charge can be beneficial. For example, a monthly fee of $7.50 results in $90 a year. However, you lose interest on the minimum-balance amount in a non-interest-earning account.

ACTIVITY ACCOUNTS   *Activity accounts* charge a fee for each check written and sometimes a fee for each deposit in addition to a monthly service charge. However, you do not have to maintain a minimum balance. An activity account is most appropriate for people who write only a few checks each month and are unable to maintain the required minimum balance.

INTEREST-EARNING CHECKING   *Interest-earning checking accounts* usually require a minimum balance. If the account balance goes below this amount, you may not earn interest and will likely incur a service charge. These are called *share draft accounts* at credit unions.

Apply *Yourself!*

Objective 4

Observe customers making payments in a retail store. How often are cash, checks, credit cards, or debit cards used?

did you know?

Mobile payment systems through cell phones and other wireless devices are expanding. This usually occurs through an existing bank account. Most banking activities accessed by computer will soon also occur via cell phone. Some future transactions may bypass banks with charges on your phone bill.

Exhibit 4–9

Checking Account Selection Factors

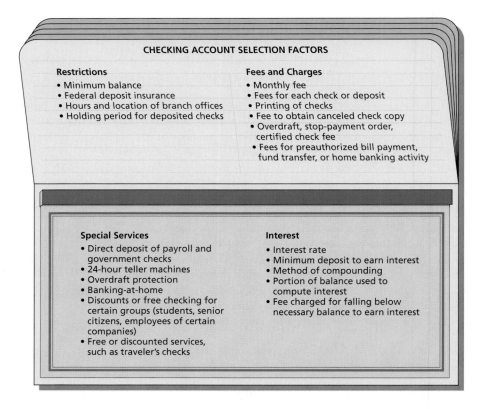

CHECKING ACCOUNT SELECTION FACTORS

Restrictions
- Minimum balance
- Federal deposit insurance
- Hours and location of branch offices
- Holding period for deposited checks

Fees and Charges
- Monthly fee
- Fees for each check or deposit
- Printing of checks
- Fee to obtain canceled check copy
- Overdraft, stop-payment order, certified check fee
- Fees for preauthorized bill payment, fund transfer, or home banking activity

Special Services
- Direct deposit of payroll and government checks
- 24-hour teller machines
- Overdraft protection
- Banking-at-home
- Discounts or free checking for certain groups (students, senior citizens, employees of certain companies)
- Free or discounted services, such as traveler's checks

Interest
- Interest rate
- Minimum deposit to earn interest
- Method of compounding
- Portion of balance used to compute interest
- Fee charged for falling below necessary balance to earn interest

Evaluating Checking and Payment Accounts

Would you rather have a checking account that pays interest and requires a $1,000 minimum balance or an account that doesn't pay interest and requires a $300 minimum balance? This decision requires evaluating factors such as restrictions, fees and charges, interest, and special services (see Exhibit 4–9).

RESTRICTIONS   The most common limitation on a checking account is the required amount that must be kept on deposit to earn interest or avoid a service charge. In the past, financial institutions placed restrictions on the holding period for deposited checks. A waiting period was usually required before you could access the funds. The Check Clearing for the 21st Century Act (known as Check 21) shortens the processing time. This law establishes the *substitute check,* which is a digital reproduction of the original paper check, and is considered a legal equivalent of the original check.

CAUTION!

A bounced check may result in not only a fee of $30 or more but also restrictions on the acceptance of your checks in the future. Some check-approval systems may keep your name on a "restricted" list for a period of six months to five years.

FEES AND CHARGES   Nearly all financial institutions require a minimum balance or impose service charges for checking accounts. When using an interest-bearing checking account, compare your earnings with any service charge or fee. Also, consider the cost of lost or reduced interest resulting from maintaining the minimum balance. Checking account fees have increased in recent years. Items such as check printing, overdraft fees, and stop-payment orders have doubled or tripled in price at some financial institutions.

INTEREST   The interest rate, the frequency of compounding, and the interest computation method will affect the earnings on your checking account.

SPECIAL SERVICES   Many financial institutions attempting to reduce costs do not return canceled checks. Copies of a canceled check may be retrieved online by customers or by the financial institution from its microfilm file for a fee.

Overdraft protection is an automatic loan made to checking customers for checks written in excess of their balance. This service is convenient but costly. Most overdraft plans make loans based on $50 or $100 increments. An overdraft of just $1 might trigger a $50 loan and corresponding finance charges of perhaps 18 percent. But overdraft protection can be less costly than the fee charged for a check you write when you do not have enough money on deposit to cover it. That fee may be $20 or more. Many financial institutions will allow you to cover checking account overdrafts with an automatic transfer from a savings account for a nominal fee.

Beware of checking accounts packaged with several services (safe deposit box, traveler's checks, low-rate loans, and travel insurance) for a single monthly fee. This may sound like a good value; however, financial experts observe that only a small group of people make use of all services in the package.

overdraft protection An automatic loan made to checking account customers to cover the amount of checks written in excess of the available balance in the checking account.

Other Payment Methods

A *certified check* is a personal check with guaranteed payment. The amount of the check is deducted from your balance when the financial institution certifies the check. A *cashier's check* is a check of a financial institution. You may purchase one by paying the amount of the check plus a fee. You may purchase a *money order* in a similar manner from financial institutions, post offices, and stores. Certified checks, cashier's checks, and money orders allow you to make a payment that the recipient knows is valid.

Traveler's checks allow you to make payments when you are away from home. This payment form requires you to sign each check twice. First, you sign the traveler's checks when you purchase them. Then, to identify you as the authorized person, you sign them again as you cash them. Electronic traveler's checks, in the form of a prepaid travel card, are also available. The card allows travelers visiting other nations to get local currency from an ATM.

did you know?

Biometry, the analysis of biological observations, is expanding in use for banking security. Fingerprint verification is being used by Bank of America to give individuals access to their online banking services. Iris scanning of the characteristics of your eyeball may be used as a bank account password. A voice-activated response system is being used by the American Savings Bank in Hawaii for customers to obtain an account balance or make a money transfer.

Managing Your Checking Account

Obtaining and using a checking account involves several activities.

OPENING A CHECKING ACCOUNT   First, decide who the owner of the account is. Only one person is allowed to write checks on an *individual account*. A *joint account* has two or more owners. Both an individual account and a joint account require a signature card. This document is a record of the official signatures of the person or persons authorized to write checks on the account.

MAKING DEPOSITS   A *deposit ticket* is used for adding funds to your checking account. On this document, you list the amounts of cash and checks being deposited. Each check you deposit requires an *endorsement*—your signature on the back of the check—to authorize the transfer of the funds into your account. The three common endorsement forms are:

- A *blank endorsement* is just your signature, which should be used only when you are actually depositing or cashing a check, since a check may be cashed by anyone once it has been signed.
- A *restrictive endorsement* consists of the words *for deposit only,* followed by your signature, which is especially useful when you are depositing checks.
- A *special endorsement* allows you to transfer a check to someone else with the words *pay to the order of* followed by the name of the other person and then your signature.

Personal Finance in Practice

› Are You Avoiding Identity Theft?

People who put their Social Security and driver's license numbers on their checks are making identity theft fairly easy. With one check, a con artist could know your Social Security, driver's license, and bank account numbers as well as your address, phone number, and perhaps even a sample of your signature.

An attorney had his wallet stolen. Within a week, the thieves ordered an expensive monthly cell phone package, applied for a Visa credit card, had a credit line approved to buy a Gateway computer, and received a PIN number from the Department of Motor Vehicles to change his driving record information online.

Identity fraud can range from passing bad checks and using stolen credit cards to theft of another person's total financial existence. The following quiz can help you avoid becoming one of the more than 1,000 people who each day have their identities stolen by con artists.

If you are a victim of identity theft, take the following actions:

- File a police report immediately in the area where the item was stolen. This proves you were diligent and is a first step toward an investigation (if there ever is one).

- Call the three national credit reporting organizations *immediately* to place a fraud alert on your name and Social Security number. The numbers are: Equifax, 1-800-525-6285; Experian (formerly TRW), 1-888-397-3742; and Trans Union, 1-800-680-7289.

- Contact the Social Security Administration fraud line at 1-800-269-0271.

Additional information on financial privacy and identity theft is available at www.identitytheft.org, www.idfraud.org, www.privacyrights.org.

Which of the following actions have you taken to avoid identity theft?	Yes	No	Action needed
1. I have only my initials and last name on my checks so a person will not know how I sign my checks.			
2. I do not put the full account number on my checks when paying a bill; I put only the last four numbers.			
3. I have my work phone and a P.O. box (if applicable) on my checks instead of home information.			
4. I don't put my Social Security number on any document unless it is legally required.			
5. I shred or burn financial information containing account or Social Security numbers.			
6. I use passwords other than maiden names.			
7. I do not mail bills from my home mailbox, especially if it is out by the street.			
8. I check my credit report once or twice a year to make sure it is correct.			
9. I ask to have my name removed from mailing lists operated by credit agencies and companies offering credit promotions.			
10. I have a photocopy of the contents of my wallet (both sides of each item) as a record to cancel accounts if necessary.			

WRITING CHECKS   Before writing a check, record the information in your check register and deduct the amount of the check from your balance. Many checking account customers use duplicate checks to maintain a record of their current balance.

The procedure for proper check writing has the following steps: (1) record the date; (2) write the name of the person or organization receiving the payment; (3) record the amount of the check in numerals; (4) write the amount of the check in words; checks for less than a dollar should be written as "only 79 cents," for example, and cross out the word *dollars* on the check; (5) sign the check; (6) note the reason for payment.

A *stop-payment order* may be necessary if a check is lost or stolen. Most banks do not honor checks with "stale" dates, usually six months old or older. The fee for a stop-payment commonly ranges from $20 to more than $30. If several checks are missing or you lose your checkbook, closing the account and opening a new one is likely to be less costly than paying several stop-payment fees.

RECONCILING YOUR CHECKING ACCOUNT   Each month you will receive a *bank statement* summarizing deposits, checks paid, ATM withdrawals, interest earned, and fees such as service charges and printing of checks. The balance reported on the statement will usually differ from the balance in your checkbook. Reasons for a difference may include checks that have not yet cleared, deposits not received by the bank, and interest earned.

To determine the correct balance, prepare a *bank reconciliation,* to account for differences between the bank statement and your checkbook balance. This process involves the following steps:

1. Compare the checks written with those reported as paid on the statement. Use the canceled checks, or compare your check register with the check numbers reported on the bank statement. *Subtract* from the *bank statement balance* the total of the checks written but not yet cleared.
2. Determine whether any deposits made are not on the statement; *add* the amount of the outstanding deposits to the *bank statement balance.*
3. *Subtract* fees or charges on the bank statement and ATM withdrawals from your *checkbook balance.*
4. *Add* any interest earned to your *checkbook balance.*

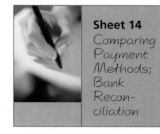

Sheet 14
Comparing Payment Methods; Bank Reconciliation

At this point, the revised balances for both the checkbook and the bank statement should be the same. If the two do not match, check your math; make sure every check and deposit was recorded correctly.

✓ CONCEPT CHECK 4–4

1   Are checking accounts that earn interest preferable to regular checking accounts? Why or why not?

_____

_____

2   What factors are commonly considered when selecting a checking account?

_____

_____

3   For the following situations, select and describe a payment method that would be appropriate for the needs of the person.

Payment situation	Suggested payment method
a. A need to send funds for a purchase from an organization that requires guaranteed payment.	
b. Traveling to Asia, you desire to be able to access funds in the local currencies of various countries.	
c. A desire to pay bills using your home computer instead of writing checks.	
d. You write only a few checks a month and you want to minimize your costs.	

(continued)

4 Based on the following information, determine the true balance in your checking account.

Balance in your checkbook, $356   Balance on bank statement, $472

Service charge and other fees, $15   Interest earned on the account, $4

Total of outstanding checks, $187   Deposits in transit, $60

back to Getting Personal

1. Reconsider your responses to the Getting Personal questions at the beginning of the chapter. Have any of your answers changed as a result of your learning or changing financial activities?

2. On which types of financial services are you least informed?

3. For each of the main types of financial services, what actions might you take to increase earnings or reduce costs?

Type of Financial Service	Actions to Increase Earnings or Reduce Costs
a. Savings plans	
b. Payment services	
c. Borrowing	
d. Online banking	

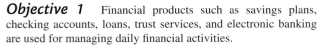

www.mhhe.com/kdh

Chapter Summary

Objective 1   Financial products such as savings plans, checking accounts, loans, trust services, and electronic banking are used for managing daily financial activities.

Objective 2   Commercial banks, savings and loan associations, mutual savings banks, credit unions, life insurance companies, investment companies, finance companies, mortgage companies, pawnshops, and check-cashing outlets may be compared on the basis of services offered, rates and fees, safety, convenience, and special programs available to customers.

Objective 3   Commonly used savings plans include regular savings accounts, certificates of deposit, interest-earning check-

ing accounts, money market accounts, money market funds, and U.S. savings bonds. Savings plans may be evaluated on the basis of rate of return, inflation, tax considerations, liquidity, safety, restrictions, and fees.

Objective 4   Debit cards, online payment systems, and stored-value cards are increasing in use for payment activities. Regular checking accounts, activity accounts, and interest-earning checking accounts can be compared with regard to restrictions (such as a minimum balance), fees and charges, interest, and special services.

Key Terms

annual percentage yield (APY)   120
asset management account   108
automatic teller machine (ATM)   110
certificate of deposit (CD)   117
commercial bank   113
compounding   119

credit union   114
debit card   110
money market account   117
money market fund   114
mutual savings bank   114

overdraft protection   125
rate of return   119
savings and loan association
    (S&L)   113
trust   108

Problems

1. An ATM with a service fee of $2 is used by a person 100 times in a year. What would be the future value in 10 years (use a 4 percent rate) of the annual amount paid in ATM fees?

2. What might be a savings goal for a person who buys a five-year CD paying 4.67 percent instead of an 18-month savings certificate paying 3.29 percent?

3. For each of these situations, determine the savings amount. Use the time value of money tables in Chapter 1 (Exhibit 1–3) or in the Chapter 1 appendix.
   a. What would be the value of a savings account started with $500, earning 6 percent (compounded annually) after 10 years?

   b. Brenda Young desires to have $10,000 eight years from now for her daughter's college fund. If she will earn 7 percent (compounded annually) on her money, what amount should she deposit now? Use the present value of a single amount calculation.

   c. What amount would you have if you deposited $1,500 a year for 30 years at 8 percent (compounded annually)?

4. What would be the annual percentage yield for a savings account that earned $56 in interest on $800 over the past 365 days?

5. With a 28 percent marginal tax rate, would a tax-free yield of 7 percent or a taxable yield of 9.5 percent give you a better return on your savings? Why?

6. Janie has $40,000 in a money market account, $20,000 in a savings certificate, and has a joint account with her mother with a balance of $93,000. Based on $100,000 of Federal Deposit Insurance Corporation coverage, what amount of Janie's savings would not be covered by deposit insurance?

7. What is the annual *opportunity cost* of a checking account that requires a $350 minimum balance to avoid service charges? Assume an interest rate of 3 percent.

8. Compare the costs and benefits of these two checking accounts:
   Account 1: A regular checking account with a monthly fee of $6 when the balance goes below $300.

   Account 2: An interest-earning checking account (paying 1.2 percent), with a monthly charge of $3 if the balance goes below $100.

9. A bank that provides overdraft protection charges 12 percent for each $100 (or portion of $100) borrowed when an overdraft occurs.
   a. What amount of interest would the customer pay for a $188 overdraft? (Assume the interest is for the full amount borrowed for whole year.)

b. How much would be saved by using the overdraft protection loan if a customer has three overdraft charges of $30 each during the year?

10. What would be the net *annual* cost of the following checking accounts?
   a. Monthly fee, $3.75; processing fee, 25 cents per check; checks written, an average of 14 a month.

   b. Interest earnings of 4 percent with a $500 minimum balance; average monthly balance, $600; monthly service charge of $15 for falling below the minimum balance, which occurs three times a year (no interest earned in these months).

Questions

1. How has online banking changed the way consumers select and use various financial services?

2. What relationship exists between changing interest rates and the rates of return for various savings accounts, money market accounts, and certificates of deposit of various lengths?

3. What actions would you recommend to someone who was considering using the services of a pawnshop, check-cashing outlet, or payday loan company?

4. What fees and deductions may be overlooked when balancing your checking account?

5. a. What are potential benefits of an overdraft protection service for your checking account?

   b. What costs should a person consider before deciding to use the overdraft protection service?

Internet Connection

COMPARING ONLINE PAYMENT SYSTEMS

Compare the online bill payment services for (1) a bank, (2) a bill payment service (such as www.bills.com or www.paytrust.com), and (3) money management software.

	Online bank	Internet payment service	Software (MS Money, Quicken)
Name, Web site			
Description of online payment services; types of payments			
Cost (per month or per transaction)			
Security measures			
Potential concerns			

Case in Point

BEWARE OF HIDDEN BANKING FEES

"Wow! My account balance is a little lower than I expected," commented Lisa Cross as she reviewed her monthly bank statement. "Wait a minute! There's nearly $20 in fees for ATM withdrawals and other service charges," she cried out.

Many people do not realize the amount they pay each month for various bank fees. These charges result from various services that give customers convenience, reliability, and safety.

"Oh no! I also went below the minimum balance required for my *free* checking account," Lisa groaned. "That cost me $7.50!"

Lisa is not alone in her frustration with fees paid for financial services. While careless money management caused many of these charges, others could be reduced or eliminated by comparing costs at various financial institutions.

Many consumers are also upset with slow customer service and long waits in lines. These drawbacks have caused many customers to consider the use of online banking services. Whether using the Internet services of your current financial institution or starting an account with a "Web bank," you can gain faster access to your account. Other benefits may also be present. Often, costs of online banking services are lower than those in traditional settings. Online banking can also offer access to an expanded array of financial services. For example, some online bank accounts include low-cost online investment trading and instant loan approval.

Lisa believes that online banking services provide her with an opportunity to better control her financial service costs. However, she also has concerns about introductory low costs, privacy, and security of transaction information.

Questions

1. What benefits might Lisa gain when using online banking services?

2. Based on information at www.bankrate.com, describe how Lisa could reduce her checking account costs and other banking fees.

3. What concerns might be associated with using online banking services?

Continuing Case

BANKING SERVICES

Life Situation

Recently married couple

Pam, 26

Josh, 28

Renting an apartment

Financial Data

Monthly income	$5,840
Living expenses	$3,900
Assets	$13,500
Liabilities	$4,800
Emergency fund	$1,000

Pam Jenkins recently married Josh Brock. Pam continues to work as a sales representative for a clothing manufacturer, and her monthly income has averaged $2,840 a month over the past year. Josh is employed as a computer programmer and earns $3,000 a month. Their combined monthly income allows them to live comfortably. Yet they have been unable to save any money for emergencies.

According to Josh, "It's hard to believe, but we don't even have a savings account because we spend almost everything we make." Every month, they deposit each of their paychecks in separate checking accounts. Josh pays the rent and makes the car payment. Pam buys the groceries and pays the utilities. They use the money left over to purchase new clothes and the other "necessities" for enjoying life.

Questions

1. What is the minimum amount that the Brocks should have in an emergency fund? What actions might be taken to increase the amount in this fund?

2. What other money management and financial planning activities would you recommend for the Brocks?

3. Which of *Your Personal Financial Plan* sheets could be useful for planning and using financial services by Pam and Josh?

Video Case

ATM FEES ADDING UP

The fees for using a cash machine continue to rise. ATM charges can cost a person several hundred dollars a year. Some simple actions are possible to avoid these fees.

Questions

1. What actions can be taken to reduce ATM fees?

2. Other than increased earnings, how do banks benefit from the fees charged for ATM services?

3. Conduct an online search to obtain current information about ATM charges and actions to minimize these fees.

Spending Diary

"MY CASH WITHDRAWALS HAVE RESULTED IN MANY ATM FEES THAT TAKE AWAY MONEY FROM OTHER BUDGET ITEMS."

Directions

Start (or continue) your Daily Spending Diary or use your own format to record and monitor spending in various categories. Your comments should reflect what you have learned about your spending patterns and help you consider possible changes you might want to make in your spending habits.

Questions

1. Are there any banking fees that you encounter each month? What actions might be taken to reduce or eliminate these cash outflows?

2. What other areas of your daily spending might be reduced or revised?

Planning the Use of Financial Services

Financial Planning Activities: List (1) currently used services with financial institution information (name, address, phone); and (2) services that are likely to be needed in the future.

Suggested Web Sites: www.bankrate.com   www.banking.about.com

Types of financial services	Current financial services used	Additional financial services needed
Payment services (checking, ATM, online bill payment, money orders)	Financial Institution	
Savings services (savings account, money market account, certificate of deposit, savings bonds)	Financial Institution	
Credit services (credit cards, personal loans, mortgage)	Financial Institution	
Other financial services (investments, trust account, tax planning)	Financial Institution	

What's Next for Your Personal Financial Plan?

- Assess whether the current types and sources of your financial services are appropriate.
- Determine additional financial services you may wish to make use of in the future.

Your Personal Financial Plan

Comparing Savings Plans

Financial Planning Activities: Obtain information online and from various financial institutions to compare savings plans on the factors listed below.

Suggested Web Sites: www.bankrate.com   www.banx.com

Type of savings plan (regular passbook account, special accounts, savings certificate, money market account, other)			
Financial institution			
Address/phone			
Web site			
Annual interest rate			
Annual percentage yield (APY)			
Frequency of compounding			
Insured by FDIC, NCUA, other			
Maximum amount insured			
Minimum initial deposit			
Minimum time period savings must be on deposit			
Penalties for early withdrawal			
Service charges/transaction fees, other costs, fees			
Additional services, other information			

What's Next for Your Personal Financial Plan?

- Based on this savings plan analysis, determine the best types for your current and future financial situation.
- When analyzing savings plans, what factors should you carefully investigate?

Using Savings Plans to Achieve Financial Goals

Financial Planning Activities: Record savings plan information along with the amount of your balance or income on a periodic basis.

Suggested Web Sites: www.savingsbonds.gov   www.fdic.gov

Regular savings account

Acct. No. _____
Financial institution
_____
Address _____
_____
Phone _____

Savings goal/Amount needed/Date needed: _____

Initial deposit: Date _____ $ _____
Balance: Date _____ $ _____
Date _____ $ _____
Date _____ $ _____
Date _____ $ _____

Certificate of deposit

Acct. No. _____
Financial institution
_____
Address _____
_____
Phone _____

Savings goal/Amount needed/Date needed: _____

Initial deposit: Date _____ $ _____
Balance: Date _____ $ _____
Date _____ $ _____
Date _____ $ _____
Date _____ $ _____

Money market/fund acct.

Acct. No. _____
Financial institution
_____
Address _____
_____
Phone _____

Savings goal/Amount needed/Date needed: _____

Initial deposit: Date _____ $ _____
Balance: Date _____ $ _____
Date _____ $ _____
Date _____ $ _____
Date _____ $ _____

U.S. savings bonds

Purchase location _____
_____
Address _____
_____
Phone _____

Savings goal/Amount needed/Date needed: _____

Purchase date: _____   Maturity date: _____
Amount: _____   Maturity date: _____

Purchase date: _____   Maturity date: _____
Amount: _____   Maturity date: _____

Other savings

Acct. No. _____
Financial institution
_____
Address _____
_____
Phone _____

Savings goal/Amount needed/Date needed: _____

Initial deposit: Date _____ $ _____
Balance: Date _____ $ _____
Date _____ $ _____
Date _____ $ _____
Date _____ $ _____

What's Next for Your Personal Financial Plan?

- Assess your current progress toward achieving various savings goals. Evaluate existing and new savings goals.
- Plan actions to expand the amount you are saving toward various savings goals.

Name: _____   **Date:** _____

Comparing Payment Methods; Bank Reconciliation

Financial Planning Activities: Compare checking accounts and payment services at various financial institutions (banks, savings and loan associations, credit unions, Web banks).

Suggested Web Sites: www.bankrate.com   www.kiplinger.com

Institution name			
Address			
Phone			
Web site			
Type of account (regular checking, activity account, bill payment service)			
Minimum balance			
Monthly charge below balance			
"Free" checking for students?			
Online banking services			
Branch/ATM locations			
Banking hours			
Other fees/costs			
Printing of checks			
Stop-payment order			
Overdrawn account			
Certified check			
ATM, other charges			
Other information			

Checking Account Reconciliation

Statement date:		**Statement Balance:**	$_____
Step 1: Compare the checks written with those paid on statement. *Subtract* total of outstanding checks from the bank balance.	Check No.	Amount	−$_____
Step 2: Determine whether any deposits are not on the statement; *add* the amount of the outstanding deposits to the *bank statement balance.*	Deposit date	Amount	+$_____
	Adjusted Balance		=$_____
	Checkbook Balance		
Step 3: *Subtract* fees or charges on the bank statement and ATM withdrawals from your *checkbook balance.*	Item	Amount	−$_____
Step 4: *Add* interest or direct deposits earned to your *checkbook balance.*			+$_____
Note: The two adjusted balances should be the same; if not, carefully check your math and check to see that deposits and checks recorded in your checkbook and on your statement are for the correct amounts.	**Adjusted Balance**		=$_____

5 Consumer Credit: Advantages, Disadvantages, Sources, and Costs

Getting Personal

Do you know how to use credit wisely? For each of the following statements, select the letter to indicate your answers regarding these statements:

1. I pay any bills I have when they are due _____.
   a. always
   b. most of the time
   c. sometimes

2. If I need more money for my expenses, I borrow it _____.
   a. never
   b. sometimes
   c. often

3. If I want to see a copy of my credit report, I can contact _____.
   a. a credit reporting agency
   b. a bank
   c. the principal of my school

4. If I default (do not repay) on a loan, it will stay on my credit report for _____.
   a. 7 years
   b. 2 years
   c. 6 months

5. If I have serious credit problems, I should _____.
   a. contact my creditors to explain the problem
   b. contact only the most persistent creditors
   c. not contact my creditors and hope they will forget about me

6. I can begin building a good rating by _____.
   a. opening a savings account and making regular monthly deposits
   b. paying most of my bills on time
   c. opening a checking account and bouncing checks

Source: *How to Be Credit Smart* (Washington, DC: Consumer Education Foundation, 1994).

Objectives

In this chapter, you will learn to:

1. Analyze advantages and disadvantages of using consumer credit.
2. Assess the types and sources of consumer credit.
3. Determine whether you can afford a loan and how to apply for credit.
4. Determine the cost of credit by calculating interest using various interest formulas.
5. Develop a plan to protect your credit and manage your debts.

Why is this important?

Understanding the advantages and disadvantages of consumer credit as well as the types of credit that are available will enable you to make wise decisions regarding credit now and in the future. Understanding the costs involved in obtaining credit will give you the tools to acquire the best source of credit.

What Is Consumer Credit?

OBJECTIVE 1
Analyze advantages and disadvantages of using consumer credit.

credit An arrangement to receive cash, goods, or services now and pay for them in the future.

consumer credit The use of credit for personal needs (except a home mortgage).

Credit is an arrangement to receive cash, goods, or services now and pay for them in the future. **Consumer credit** refers to the use of credit for personal needs (except a home mortgage) by individuals and families, in contrast to credit used for business purposes.

Consumer credit is based on trust in people's ability and willingness to pay bills when due. It works because people by and large are honest and responsible. But how does consumer credit affect our economy, and how is it affected by our economy?

The Importance of Consumer Credit in Our Economy

Consumer credit dates back to colonial times. Although credit was originally a privilege of the affluent, farmers came to use it extensively. No direct finance charges were imposed; instead, the cost of credit was added to the prices of goods. With the advent of the automobile in the early 1900s, installment credit, in which the debt is repaid in equal installments over a specified period of time, exploded on the American scene.

All economists now recognize consumer credit as a major force in the American economy. Any forecast or evaluation of the economy includes consumer spending trends and consumer credit as a sustaining force. To paraphrase an old political expression, as the consumer goes, so goes the U.S. economy.

Uses and Misuses of Credit

Using credit to purchase goods and services may allow consumers to be more efficient or more productive or to lead more satisfying lives. Many valid reasons can be found for using credit. A medical emergency may leave a person strapped for funds. A homemaker returning to the workforce may need a car. An item may cost less money now than it will cost later. Borrowing for a college education is another valid reason. But borrowing for everyday living expenses or financing a Corvette on credit when a Ford Escort is all your budget allows is probably not reasonable.

Using credit increases the amount of money a person can spend to purchase goods and services now. But the trade-off is that it decreases the amount of money that will be available to spend in the future. However, many people expect their incomes to increase and therefore expect to be able to make payments on past credit purchases and still make new purchases.

Here are some questions you should consider before you decide how and when to make a major purchase, for example, a car:

- Do I have the cash I need for the down payment?
- Do I want to use my savings for this purchase?
- Does the purchase fit my budget?
- Could I use the credit I need for this purchase in some better way?
- Could I postpone the purchase?
- What are the opportunity costs of postponing the purchase (alternative transportation costs, a possible increase in the price of the car)?
- What are the dollar costs and the psychological costs of using credit (interest, other finance charges, being in debt and responsible for making a monthly payment)?

If you decide to use credit, make sure the benefits of purchasing now (increased efficiency or productivity, a more satisfying life, etc.) outweigh the costs (financial and psychological) of using credit. Thus, credit, when effectively used, can help you have more and enjoy more. When misused, credit can result in default, bankruptcy, and loss of creditworthiness.

Apply *Yourself!*

Objective 1

Using Web research and discussion with family members and friends, prepare a list of advantages and disadvantages of using credit.

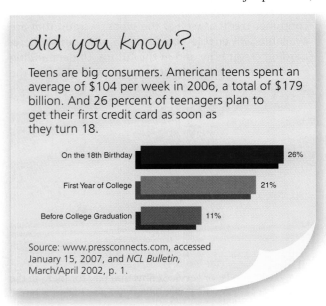

did you know?

Teens are big consumers. American teens spent an average of $104 per week in 2006, a total of $179 billion. And 26 percent of teenagers plan to get their first credit card as soon as they turn 18.

On the 18th Birthday — 26%
First Year of College — 21%
Before College Graduation — 11%

Source: www.pressconnects.com, accessed January 15, 2007, and *NCL Bulletin*, March/April 2002, p. 1.

Advantages of Credit

Consumer credit enables people to enjoy goods and services now—a car, a home, an education, emergencies—and pay for them through payment plans based on future income.

Credit cards permit the purchase of goods even when funds are low. Customers with previously approved credit may receive other extras, such as advance notice of sales and the right to order by phone or to buy on approval. In addition, many shoppers believe that returning merchandise purchased on account is easier than returning cash purchases. Credit cards also provide shopping convenience and the efficiency of paying for several purchases with one monthly payment.

Credit is more than a substitute for cash. Many of the services it provides are taken for granted. Every time you turn on the water tap, click the light switch, or telephone a friend, you are using credit.

Using credit is safe, since charge accounts and credit cards let you shop and travel without carrying a large amount of cash. It offers convenience, since you need a credit card to make a hotel reservation, rent a car, and shop by phone or Internet. You may also use credit cards for identification when cashing checks, and the use of credit provides you with a record of expenses.

The use of credit cards can provide up to a 50-day "float," the time lag between when you make the purchase and when the lender deducts the balance from your checking

Key Web Sites for Money Management

www.moneymanagement.com
www.moneypage.com

account when payment is due. This float, offered by many credit card issuers, includes a grace period of 20 to 25 days. During the grace period, no finance charges are assessed on current purchases if the balance is paid in full each month within 25 days after billing.

Some corporations, such as General Electric Company and General Motors Corporation, issue their own Visa and MasterCard and offer rebates on purchases. In the late 1990s, however, some corporations began to eliminate these cards.

Finally, credit indicates stability. The fact that lenders consider you a good risk usually means you are a responsible individual. However, if you do not repay your debts in a timely manner, you will find that credit has many disadvantages.

Key Web Sites for Consumer Credit

www.abcguides.com
www.lendingtree.com

Disadvantages of Credit

Perhaps the greatest disadvantage of using credit is the temptation to overspend, especially during periods of inflation. Buying today and paying tomorrow, using cheaper dollars, seems ideal. But continual overspending can lead to serious trouble.

Whether or not credit involves *security*—something of value to back the loan—failure to repay a loan may result in loss of income, valuable property, and your good reputation. It can even lead to court action and bankruptcy. Misuse of credit can create serious long-term financial problems, damage to family relationships, and a slowing of progress toward financial goals. Therefore, you should approach credit with caution and avoid using it more extensively than your budget permits.

Although credit allows immediate satisfaction of needs and desires, it does not increase total purchasing power. Credit purchases must be paid for out of future income; therefore, credit ties up the use of future income. Furthermore, if your income does not increase to cover rising costs, your ability to repay credit commitments will diminish. Before buying goods and services on credit, consider whether they will have lasting value, whether they will increase your personal satisfaction during present and future income periods, and whether your current income will continue or increase.

Finally, credit costs money. It is a service for which you must pay. Paying for purchases over a period of time is more costly than paying for them with cash. Purchasing with credit rather than cash involves one obvious trade-off: The items purchased will cost more due to monthly finance charges and the compounding effect of interest on interest.

✔ CONCEPT CHECK 5–1

1 What is consumer credit?

_____

_____

2 Why is consumer credit important to our economy?

_____

_____

3 For each of following situations, check "yes" if a valid reason to borrow, or "no" if not.

	Yes	No
a. A medical emergency.	_____	_____
b. Borrowing for college education.	_____	_____

(continued)

c. Borrowing for everyday living expenses.   _____   _____

d. Borrowing to finance a luxury car.   _____   _____

4 For each of the following statements, check "yes" if an advantage, "no" if a disadvantage of using credit.

	Yes	No

a. It is easier to return merchandise if it is purchased on credit.   _____   _____

b. Credit cards provide shopping convenience.   _____   _____

c. Credit tempts people to overspend.   _____   _____

d. Failure to repay a loan may result in loss of income.   _____   _____

Types of Credit

OBJECTIVE 2
Assess the types and sources of consumer credit.

Two basic types of consumer credit exist: closed-end and open-end credit. With **closed-end credit,** you pay back one-time loans in a specified period of time and in payments of equal amounts. With **open-end credit,** loans are made on a continuous basis and you are billed periodically for at least partial payment. Exhibit 5–1 shows examples of closed-end and open-end credit.

Closed-End Credit

closed-end credit One-time loans that the borrower pays back in a specified period of time and in payments of equal amounts.

open-end credit A line of credit in which loans are made on a continuous basis and the borrower is billed periodically for at least partial payment.

Closed-end credit is used for a specific purpose and involves a specified amount. Mortgage loans, automobile loans, and installment loans for purchasing furniture or appliances are examples of closed-end credit. Generally, the seller holds title to the merchandise until the payments have been completed.

The three most common types of closed-end credit are installment sales credit, installment cash credit, and single lump-sum credit. *Installment sales credit* is a loan that allows you to receive merchandise, usually high-priced items such as large appliances or furniture. You make a down payment and usually sign a contract to repay the balance, plus interest and service charges, in equal installments over a specified period.

Installment cash credit is a direct loan of money for personal purposes, home improvements, or vacation expenses. You make no down payment and make payments in specified amounts over a set period.

Single lump-sum credit is a loan that must be repaid in total on a specified day, usually within 30 to 90 days. Lump-sum credit is generally, but not always, used to purchase a single item. As Exhibit 5–2 shows, consumer installment credit reached over $2.3 trillion in 2006.

Exhibit 5–1

Examples of Closed-End and Open-End Credit

Closed-End Credit	**Open-End Credit**
• Mortgage loans • Automobile loans • Installment loans (installment sales contract, installment cash credit, single lump-sum credit)	• Cards issued by department stores, bank cards (Visa, MasterCard, American Express) • Travel and Entertainment (T&E) • Overdraft protection

Exhibit 5–2   Volume of Consumer Credit

All economists now recognize consumer credit as a major force in the American economy.

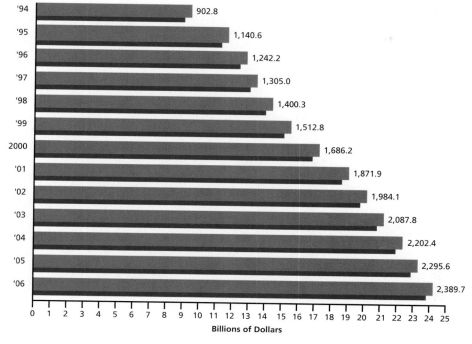

Source: www.federalreserve.gov/RELEASES/g19/currentg/19.htm, accessed January 10, 2007.

Open-End Credit

Using a credit card issued by a department store, using a bank credit card (Visa, Master-Card) to make purchases at different stores, charging a meal at a restaurant, and using overdraft protection are examples of open-end credit. As you will soon see, you do not apply for open-end credit to make a single purchase, as you do with closed-end credit. Rather, you can use open-end credit to make any purchases you wish if you do not exceed your **line of credit,** the maximum dollar amount of credit the lender has made available to you. You may have to pay **interest,** a periodic charge for the use of credit, or other finance charges. Some creditors allow you a grace period of 20 to 25 days to pay a bill in full before you incur any interest charges.

Many retailers use open-end credit. Customers can purchase goods or services up to a fixed dollar limit at any time. Usually you have the option to pay the bill in full within 30 days without interest charges or to make set monthly installments based on the account balance plus interest.

Many banks extend **revolving check credit.** Also called a *bank line of credit,* this is a prearranged loan for a specified amount that you can use by writing a special check. Repayment is made in installments over a set period. The finance charges are based on the amount of credit used during the month and on the outstanding balance.

line of credit The dollar amount, which may or may not be borrowed, that a lender makes available to a borrower.

interest A periodic charge for the use of credit.

revolving check credit A prearranged loan from a bank for a specified amount; also called a *bank line of credit.*

Sources of Consumer Credit

Many sources of consumer credit are available, including commercial banks and credit unions. Exhibit 5–3 summarizes the major sources of consumer credit. Study and compare the differences to determine which source might best meet your needs and requirements.

Exhibit 5–3 Sources of Consumer Credit

Credit Source	Type of Loan	Lending Policies
Commercial banks	Single-payment loan Personal installment loans Passbook loans Check-credit loans Credit card loans Second mortgages	• Seek customers with established credit history • Often require collateral or security • Prefer to deal in large loans, such as vehicle, home improvement, and home modernization, with the exception of credit card and check-credit plans • Determine repayment schedules according to the purpose of the loan • Vary credit rates according to the type of credit, time period, customer's credit history, and the security offered • May require several days to process a new credit application
Consumer finance companies	Personal installment loans Second mortgages	• Often lend to consumers without established credit history • Often make unsecured loans • Often vary rates according to the size of the loan balance • Offer a variety of repayment schedules • Make a higher percentage of small loans than other lenders • Maximum loan size limited by law • Process applications quickly, frequently on the same day the application is made
Credit unions	Personal installment loans Share draft-credit plans Credit-card loans Second mortgages	• Lend to members only • Make unsecured loans • May require collateral or cosigner for loans over a specified amount • May require payroll deductions to pay off loan • May submit large loan applications to a committee of members for approval • Offer a variety of repayment schedules
Life insurance companies	Single-payment or partial-payment loans	• Lend on cash value of life insurance policy • No date or penalty on repayment • Deduct amount owed from the value of policy benefit if death or other maturity occurs before repayment
Federal savings banks (savings and loan associations)	Personal installment loans (generally permitted by state-chartered savings associations) Home improvement loans Education loans Savings account loans Second mortgages	• Will lend to all creditworthy individuals • Often require collateral • Loan rates vary depending on size of loan, length of payment, and security involved

Consumer credit is available from several types of sources. *Which sources seem to offer the widest variety of loans?*

Loans

Loans involve borrowing money with an agreement to repay it, as well as interest, within a certain amount of time. If you were considering taking out a loan, your immediate thought might be to go to your local bank. However, you might want to explore some other options first.

Figure It Out!

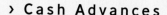

› Cash Advances

A cash advance is a loan billed to your credit card. You can obtain a cash advance with your credit card at a bank or an automated teller machine (ATM) or by using checks linked to your credit card account.

Most cards charge a special fee when a cash advance is taken out. The fee is based on a percentage of the amount borrowed, usually about 2 or 3 percent.

Some credit cards charge a minimum cash advance fee, as high as $5. You could get $20 in cash and be charged $5, a fee equal to 25 percent of the amount you borrowed.

Most cards do not have a grace period on cash advances. This means you pay interest every day until you repay the cash advance, even if you do not have an outstanding balance from the previous statement.

On some cards, the interest rate on cash advances is higher than the rate on purchases. Be sure you check the details on the contract sent to you by the card issuer.

Here is an example of charges that could be imposed for a $200 cash advance that you pay off when the bill arrives:

Cash advance fee = $4(2% of $200)

Interest for one month = $3(18% APR on $200)

Total cost for one month = $7($4 + $3)

In comparison, a $200 purchase on a card with a grace period could cost $0 if paid off promptly in full.

The bottom line: It is usually much more expensive to take out a cash advance than to charge a purchase to your credit card. Use cash advances only for real emergencies.

INEXPENSIVE LOANS   Parents or other family members are often the source of the least expensive loans—loans with low interest. They may charge only interest they would have earned on the money if they had deposited it in a savings account. They may even give you a loan without interest. Be aware, however, that loans can complicate family relationships.

MEDIUM-PRICED LOANS   Often you can obtain medium-priced loans—loans with moderate interest—from commercial banks, savings and loan associations, and credit unions. Borrowing from credit unions has several advantages. They provide personalized service, and usually they're willing to be patient with borrowers who can provide good reasons for late or missed payments. However, you must be a member of a credit union in order to get a loan.

EXPENSIVE LOANS   The easiest loans to obtain are also the most expensive. Finance companies and retail stores that lend to consumers will frequently charge high interest rates, ranging from 12 to 25 percent. Banks also lend money to their credit card holders through cash advances—loans that are billed to the customer's credit card account. Most cards charge higher interest for a cash advance and charge interest from the day the cash advance is made. As a result, taking out a cash advance is much more expensive than charging a purchase to a credit card. Read the nearby Figure It Out box to learn why you should avoid such cash advances.

HOME EQUITY LOANS   A home equity loan is a loan based on your home equity—the difference between the current market value of your home and the amount you still owe on the mortgage. Unlike interest on most other types of credit, the interest you pay on a home equity loan is tax-deductible. You should use these loans only for major items such as education, home improvements, or medical bills, and you must use them with care. If you miss payments on a home equity loan, the lender can take your home.

Key Web Sites for Consumer Credit

www.consumercredit.com
www.practicalmoneyskills.com
www.Bankrate.com

Apply *Yourself!*

Objective 2

Research three credit card companies. List their fees and any advantages they offer. Record your findings.

Credit Cards

Credit cards are extremely popular. The average cardholder has more than nine credit cards, including bank, retail, gasoline, and telephone cards. Cardholders who pay off their balances in full each month are often known as *convenience* users. Cardholders who do not pay off their balances every month are known as *borrowers*.

Most credit card companies offer a grace period, a time period during which no finance charges will be added to your account. A **finance charge** is the total dollar amount you pay to use credit. Usually, if you pay your entire balance before the due date stated on your monthly bill, you will not have to pay a finance charge. Borrowers carry balances beyond the grace period and pay finance charges.

The cost of a credit card depends on the type of credit card you have and the terms set forth by the lender. As a cardholder, you may have to pay interest or other finance charges. Some credit card companies charge cardholders an annual fee, usually about $20. However, many companies have eliminated annual fees in order to attract more customers. If you are looking for a credit card, be sure to shop around for one with no annual fee. The nearby Personal Finance in Practice box offers some other helpful hints for choosing a credit card.

finance charge The total dollar amount paid to use credit.

Key Web Sites for Credit Cards

www.cardratings.com
www.bankrate.com

DEBIT CARDS   Don't confuse credit cards with debit cards. Although they may look alike, they're very different. A debit card electronically subtracts money from your savings or checking account to pay for goods and services. A credit card extends credit and delays your payment. Debit cards are most frequently used at automatic teller machines (ATMs). More and more, however, they are also used to purchase goods in stores and to make other types of payments.

STORED VALUE (or GIFT) CARDS   Stored-value cards, gift cards, or prepaid cards resemble a typical debit card, using magnetic stripe technology to store information and track funds. However, unlike traditional debit cards, stored value cards are prepaid, providing you with immediate money. By the mid-1990s, large retailers began issuing stored value cards instead of traditional paper gift certificates. Over the past decade, the stored value cards have grown rapidly. Today, gift cards are being used for many purposes, including payroll, general spending, travel expenses, government benefit payments, and employee benefit and reward payments.

did you know?

In 2008, an estimated 188 million debit card holders will use 293 million cards for 34 trillion transactions amounting to over $1.6 trillion.

Source: *Statistical Abstract of the United States 2006*, Table 1175, p. 766.

SMART CARDS   Some lenders are starting to offer a new kind of credit card called a smart card. A smart card is a plastic card equipped with a computer chip that can store 500 times as much data as a normal credit card. Smart cards can combine credit card balances, a driver's license, health care identification, medical history, and other information all in one place. A smart card, for example, can be used to buy an airline ticket, store it digitally, and track frequent flyer miles.

TRAVEL AND ENTERTAINMENT CARDS   Travel and entertainment (T&E) cards are really not credit cards because the balance is due in full each month. However, most people think of T&E cards—such as Diners Club or American Express cards—as credit cards because they don't pay for goods or service when they purchase them.

Personal Finance in Practice

› Choosing a Credit Card

When you choose a credit card, shopping around can yield big returns. Follow these suggestions to find the card that best meets your needs and to use it wisely:

1. Department stores and gasoline companies are good places to obtain your first credit card.

2. Bank credit cards are offered through banks and savings and loan associations. Annual fees and finance charges vary widely, so shop around.

3. If you plan on paying off your balance every month, look for a card that has a grace period and carries no annual fee or a low annual fee. You might have a higher interest rate, but you plan to pay little or no interest anyway.

4. Watch out for creditors that offer low or no annual fees but instead charge a transaction fee every time you use the card.

5. If you plan to carry a balance, look for a card with a low monthly finance charge. Be sure that you understand how the finance charge is calculated.

6. To avoid delays that may result in finance charges, follow the card issuer's instructions as to where, how, and when to make bill payments.

7. Beware of offers of easy credit. No one can guarantee to get you credit.

8. If your card offers a grace period, take advantage of it by paying off your balance in full each month. With a grace period of 25 days, you actually get a free loan when you pay bills in full each month.

9. If you have a bad credit history and have trouble getting a credit card, look for a savings institution that will give you a secured credit card. With this type of card, your line of credit depends on how much money you keep in a savings account that you open at the same time.

10. Travel and entertainment cards often charge higher annual fees than most credit cards. Usually, you must make payment in full within 30 days of receiving your bill, or no further purchases will be approved on the account.

11. Be aware that debit cards are not credit cards but simply a substitute for a check or cash. The amount of the sale is subtracted from your checking account.

12. Think twice before you make a telephone call to a 900 number to request a credit card. You will pay from $2 to $50 for the 900 call and may never receive a credit card.

Before you enter the world of credit, you need to understand the various options that are available to you. *Which of the preceding factors would be most important in your choice of a credit card?*

Sources: American Institute of Certified Public Accountants. U.S. Office of Consumer Affairs. Federal Trade Commission.

✓ CONCEPT CHECK 5–2

1 What are two types of consumer credit? _____ _____

2 Match the following key terms with the appropriate definition.

   a. closed-end credit   _____ A line of credit in which loans are made on a continuous basis.

   b. open-end credit   _____ One-time loan paid back in a specified time in payments of equal amounts.

   c. line of credit   _____ The dollar amount that a lender makes available to a borrower.

   d. interest   _____ The total dollar amount paid to use the credit.

   e. finance charge   _____ A periodic charge for the use of credit.

3 What are the major sources of:

Inexpensive loans	Medium-priced loans	Expensive loans
_____	_____	_____
_____	_____	_____
_____	_____	_____

(continued)

4 What is the difference between a credit and a debit card?

_____

_____

Applying for Credit

OBJECTIVE 3

Determine whether you
can afford a loan and how
to apply for credit.

Can You Afford a Loan?

The only way to determine how much credit you can assume is to first learn how to make an accurate and sensible personal or family budget.

Before you take out a loan, ask yourself whether you can meet all of your essential expenses and still afford the monthly loan payments. You can make this calculation in two ways. One is to add up all your basic monthly expenses and then subtract this total from your take-home pay. If the difference will not cover the monthly payment and still leave funds for other expenses, you cannot afford the loan.

A second and more reliable method is to ask yourself what you plan to give up to make the monthly loan payment. If you currently save a portion of your income that is greater than the monthly payment, you can use these savings to pay off the loan. But if you do not, you will have to forgo spending on entertainment, new appliances, or perhaps even necessities. Are you prepared to make this trade-off? Although precisely measuring your credit capacity is difficult, you can follow certain rules of thumb.

General Rules of Credit Capacity

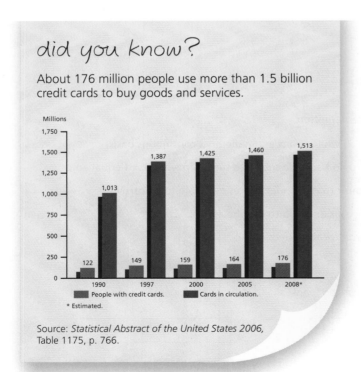

did you know?

About 176 million people use more than 1.5 billion credit cards to buy goods and services.

Millions

	1990	1997	2000	2005	2008*
People with credit cards	122	149	159	164	176
Cards in circulation	1,013	1,387	1,425	1,460	1,513

* Estimated.

Source: _Statistical Abstract of the United States 2006_, Table 1175, p. 766.

DEBT PAYMENTS-TO-INCOME RATIO   The debt payments-to-income ratio is calculated by dividing your monthly debt payments (not including house payment, which is long-term liability) by your net monthly income. Experts suggest that you spend no more than 20 percent of your net (after-tax) income on consumer credit payments. Thus, as Exhibit 5–4 shows, a person making $1,068 per month after taxes should spend no more than $213 on credit payments per month.

The 20 percent is the maximum; however, 15 percent or less is much better. The 20 percent estimate is based on the average family, with average expenses; it does not take major emergencies into account. If you are just beginning to use credit, you should not consider yourself safe if you are spending 20 percent of your net income on credit payments.

DEBT-TO-EQUITY RATIO   The debt-to-equity ratio is calculated by dividing your total liabilities by your net worth. In calculating this ratio, do not include the value of your home and the amount of its mortgage. If your debt-to-equity ratio is about 1—that is, if your consumer installment debt roughly equals your net worth (not including your home or the mortgage)—you have probably reached the upper limit of debt obligations.

Monthly gross income	$1,500
Less:	
All taxes	270
Social Security	112
Monthly IRA contribution	50
Monthly net income	$1,068
Monthly installment credit payments:	
Visa	25
MasterCard	20
Discover card	15
Education loan	—
Personal bank loan	—
Auto loan	153
Total monthly payments	$ 213
Debt payments-to-income ratio ($213/$1,068)	19.94%

Exhibit 5–4

How to Calculate Debt Payments-to-Income Ratio
Spend no more than 20 percent of your net (after-tax) income on credit payments.

None of the above methods is perfect for everyone; the limits given are only guidelines. Only you, based on the money you earn, your obligations, and your financial plans for the future, can determine the exact amount of credit you need and can afford. You must be your own credit manager.

The Five Cs of Credit

When you're ready to apply for a loan or a credit card, you should understand the factors that determine whether a lender will extend credit to you.

When a lender extends credit to consumers, it takes for granted that some people will be unable or unwilling to pay their debts. Therefore, lenders establish policies for determining who will receive credit. Most lenders build such policies around the "five Cs of credit": character, capacity, capital, collateral, and conditions.

Sheet 15
Consumer Credit Usage Patterns

CHARACTER: WILL YOU REPAY THE LOAN?
Creditors want to know your **character**—what kind of person they are lending money to. They want to know that you're trustworthy and stable. They may ask for personal or professional references, and they may check to see whether you have a history of trouble with the law. Some questions a lender might ask to determine your character are:

character The borrower's attitude toward his or her credit obligations.

- Have you used credit before?
- How long have you lived at your present address?
- How long have you held your current job?

CAPACITY: CAN YOU REPAY THE LOAN?
Your income and the debts you already have will affect your **capacity**—your ability to pay additional debts. If you already have a large amount of debt in proportion to your income, lenders probably won't extend more credit to you. Some questions a creditor may ask about your income and expenses are:

capacity The borrower's financial ability to meet credit obligations.

- What is your job, and how much is your salary?
- Do you have other sources of income?
- What are your current debts?

CAPITAL: WHAT ARE YOUR ASSETS AND NET WORTH?
Assets are any items of value that you own, including cash, property, personal possessions, and investments. Your **capital** is the amount of your assets that exceed your liabilities, or the

capital The borrower's assets or net worth.

Apply *Yourself!*

Objective 3

Talk to a person who has cosigned a loan. What experiences did this person have as a cosigner?

debts you owe. Lenders want to be sure that you have enough capital to pay back a loan. That way, if you lost your source of income, you could repay your loan from your savings or by selling some of your assets. A lender might ask:

- What are your assets?
- What are your liabilities?

COLLATERAL: WHAT IF YOU DON'T REPAY THE LOAN?

Creditors look at what kinds of property or savings you already have, because these can be offered as **collateral** to secure the loan. If you fail to repay the loan, the creditor may take whatever you pledged as collateral. A creditor might ask:

collateral A valuable asset that is pledged to ensure loan payments.

- What assets do you have to secure the loan (such as a vehicle, your home, or furniture)?
- Do you have any other valuable assets (such as bonds or savings)?

CONDITIONS: WHAT IF YOUR JOB IS INSECURE?   General economic **conditions,** such as unemployment and recession, can affect your ability to repay a loan. The basic question focuses on security—of both your job and the firm that employs you.

conditions The general economic conditions that can affect a borrower's ability to repay a loan.

The information gathered from your application and the credit bureau establishes your credit rating. A *credit rating* is a measure of a person's ability and willingness to make credit payments on time. The factors that determine a person's credit rating are income, current debt, information about character, and how debts have been repaid in the past. If you always make your payments on time, you will probably have an excellent credit rating. If not, your credit rating will be poor, and a lender probably won't extend credit to you. A good credit rating is a valuable asset that you should protect.

Creditors use different combinations of the five Cs to reach their decisions. Some creditors set unusually high standards, and others simply do not offer certain types of loans. Creditors also use various rating systems. Some rely strictly on their own instincts and experience. Others use a credit scoring or statistical system to predict whether an applicant is a good credit risk. When you apply for a loan, the lender is likely to evaluate your application by asking questions such as those included in the checklist in the Personal Finance in Practice box.

The information in your credit report is used to calculate your FICO credit score—a number generally between 350 and 850 that rates how risky a borrower is. The higher the score, the less risk you pose to creditors. Your FICO score is available from www.myfico.com for a fee. Free credit reports do not contain your credit score. Exhibit 5–5 shows a numerical depiction of your creditworthiness and how you can improve your credit score.

You should also know what factors a lender cannot consider, according to the law. The *Equal Credit Opportunity Act* (ECOA) gives all credit applicants the same basic rights. It states that race, nationality, age, sex, marital status, and certain other factors may not be used to discriminate against you in any part of a credit dealing.

Other Factors Considered in Determining Creditworthiness

AGE   The Equal Credit Opportunity Act is very specific about how a person's age may be used as a factor in credit decisions. A creditor may request that you state your age on an application, but if you're old enough to sign a legal contract (usually 18–21 years

Personal Finance in Practice

› The Five Cs of Credit

Here is what lenders look for in determining your credit-worthiness.

CREDIT HISTORY

1. Character: Will you repay the loan?   Yes   No

Do you have a good attitude toward
credit obligations?   _____   _____

Have you used credit before?   _____   _____

Do you pay your bills on time?   _____   _____

Have you ever filed for bankruptcy?   _____   _____

Do you live within your means?   _____   _____

STABILITY

How long have you lived at your
present address?   _____ yrs.

Do you own your home?   _____   _____

How long have you been employed
by your present employer?   _____ yrs.

INCOME

2. Capacity: Can you repay the loan?

Your salary and occupation? $_____; _____

Place of occupation?   _____

How reliable is your
income?   Reliable _____; Not reliable _____

Any other sources of income? $_____

EXPENSES

Number of dependents?   _____

Do you pay any alimony or
child support?   Yes _____; No _____

Current debts? $_____

NET WORTH

3. Capital: What are your assets and net worth?

What are your assets? $_____

What are your liabilities? $_____

What is your net worth? $_____

LOAN SECURITY

4. Collateral: What if you don't repay the loan?

What assets do you have to secure
the loan? (Car, home, furniture?)   _____

What sources do you have besides
income? (Savings, stocks, bonds,
insurance?)   _____

JOB SECURITY

**5. Conditions: What general economic conditions can
affect your repayment of the loan?**

How secure is
your job?   Secure _____; Not secure _____

How secure is the firm
you work for?   Secure _____; Not secure _____

Source: Adapted from William M. Pride, Robert J. Hughes, and Jack R. Kapoor, *Business*, 9th ed. (Boston: Houghton Mifflin, 2008), pp. 648–649.

old, depending on state law), a creditor may not turn you down or decrease your credit because of your age. Creditors may not close your credit account because you reach a certain age or retire.

PUBLIC ASSISTANCE   You may not be denied credit because you receive Social Security or public assistance. However, certain information related to this source of income can be considered in determining your creditworthiness.

HOUSING LOANS   The ECOA also covers applications for mortgages or home improvement loans. In particular, it bans discrimination against you based on the race or nationality of the people in the neighborhood where you live or want to buy your home, a practice called *redlining*.

Exhibit 5–5   TransUnion Personal Credit Score
The higher your FICO score, the less risk you pose to creditors.

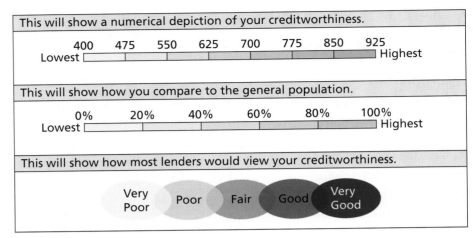

Your Credit Score is:

Score created on:
02/18/2005

You can purchase your credit score for $5.95 by calling 1-866-SCORE-TU or 1-866-726-7388.

This will show a numerical depiction of your creditworthiness.

Lowest   400   475   550   625   700   775   850   925   Highest

This will show how you compare to the general population.

Lowest   0%   20%   40%   60%   80%   100%   Highest

This will show how most lenders would view your creditworthiness.

Very Poor   Poor   Fair   Good   Very Good

- **How can I Improve my credit score?**

A credit score is a snapshot of the contents of your credit report at the time it is calculated. The first step in improving your score is to review your credit report to ensure it is accurate. Long-term, responsible credit behavior is the most effective way to improve future scores. Pay bills on time, lower balances and use credit wisely to improve your score over time.

What If Your Application Is Denied?

If your credit application is denied, the ECOA gives you the right to know the reasons. If the denial is based on a credit report from the credit bureau, you're entitled to know the specific information in the report that led to the denial. After you receive this information, you can contact the credit bureau and ask for a copy of your credit report. The bureau cannot charge a fee for this service as long as you ask to see your files within 60 days of notification that your credit application has been denied. You're entitled to ask the bureau to investigate any inaccurate or incomplete information and correct its records (see Exhibit 5–6).

Your Credit Report

When you apply for a loan, the lender will review your credit history very closely. The record of your complete credit history is called your *credit report*, or *credit file*. Your credit records are collected and maintained by credit bureaus. Most lenders rely heavily on credit reports when they consider loan applications. Exhibit 5–7 provides a checklist for building and protecting your credit history.

CREDIT BUREAUS   A credit bureau is an agency that collects information on how promptly people and businesses pay their bills. The three major credit bureaus are Experian, Trans Union, and Equifax. Each of these bureaus maintains more than 200 million credit

did you know?

What age group has the best credit rating in America?

According to Experian, the average credit score for Americans is 675 out of a possible 830. Credit scores are based on financial behavior (debt, credit usage, paying bills on time).

Age group	Score
70–plus	747
60–69	722
50–59	697
40–49	675
30–39	654
18–29	637

Source: Experian (www.NationalScoreIndex.com), accessed January 15, 2007.

Exhibit 5–6   **What If You Are Denied Credit?**
Steps you can take if you are denied credit

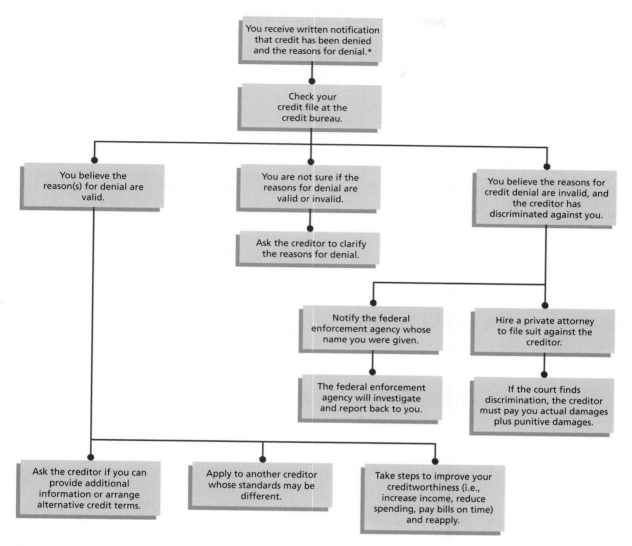

*If a creditor receives no more than 150 applications during a calendar year, the disclosures may be oral.

Source: Reprinted courtesy of Office of Public Information, Federal Reserve Bank of Minneapolis, Minneapolis, MN 55480.

files on individuals, based on information they receive from lenders. Several thousand smaller credit bureaus also collect credit information about consumers. These firms make money by selling the information they collect to creditors who are considering loan applications.

Credit bureaus get their information from banks, finance companies, stores, credit card companies, and other lenders. These sources regularly transmit information about the types of credit they extend to customers, the amounts and terms of the loans, and the customer's payment habits. Credit bureaus also collect some information from other sources, such as court records.

CAUTION!

www.annualcreditreport.com is the only online source authorized to provide a free credit report at your request. Beware of other sites that may look and sound similar.

Exhibit 5–7   Checklist for Building and Protecting Your Credit History

It is simple and sensible to build and protect your own credit history. Here are some steps to get you started:

- Open a checking or savings account, or both.
- Apply for a local department store credit card.
- Take out a small loan from your bank. Make payments on time.

A Creditor Must . . .	**Remember that a Creditor Cannot . . .**
1. Evaluate all applicants on the same basis	1. Refuse you individual credit in your own name if you are creditworthy
2. Consider income from part-time employment	2. Require your spouse to cosign a loan. Any creditworthy person can be your cosigner if one is required
3. Consider the payment history of all joint accounts, if this accurately reflects your credit history	3. Ask about your family plans or assume that your income will be interrupted to have children
4. Disregard information on accounts if you can prove that it doesn't affect your ability or willingness to repay	4. Consider whether you have a telephone listing in your name

If you want a good credit rating, you must use credit wisely. *Why is it a good idea to apply for a local department store credit card or a small loan from your bank?*

Source: Reprinted by permission of the Federal Reserve Bank of Minneapolis.

WHAT'S IN YOUR CREDIT FILES?   A typical credit bureau file contains your name, address, Social Security number, and birth date. It may also include the following information:

- Your employer, position, and income
- Your previous address
- Your previous employer
- Your spouse's name, Social Security number, employer, and income
- Whether you rent or own your home
- Checks returned for insufficient funds

did you know?

The Fair Credit Reporting Act requires each of the nation wide consumer reporting companies—Experian, Equifax, and TransUnion—to provide you with a free copy of your credit report annually. Call 1-877-322-8228.

In addition, your credit file contains detailed credit information. Each time you use credit to make a purchase or take out a loan of any kind, a credit bureau is informed of your account number and the date, amount, terms, and type of credit. Your file is updated regularly to show how many payments you've made, how many payments were late or missed, and how much you owe. Any lawsuits or judgments against you may appear as well. Federal law protects your rights if the information in your credit file is incorrect.

FAIR CREDIT REPORTING   Fair and accurate credit reporting is vital to both creditors and consumers. In 1971 the U.S. Congress enacted the Fair Credit Reporting Act, which regulates the use of credit reports. This law requires the deletion of out-of-date information and gives consumers access to their files as well as the right to correct any misinformation that the files may include. The act also places limits on who can obtain your credit report.

WHO CAN OBTAIN A CREDIT REPORT?

Your credit report may be issued only to properly identified persons for approved purposes. It may be supplied in response to a court order or by your own written request. A credit report may also be provided for use in connection with a credit transaction, underwriting of insurance, or some legitimate business need. Friends, neighbors, and other individuals cannot be given access to credit information about you. In fact, if they even request such information, they may be subject to a fine, imprisonment, or both.

TIME LIMITS ON UNFAVORABLE DATA

Most of the information in your credit file may be reported for only seven years. However, if you've declared personal bankruptcy, that fact may be reported for 10 years. A credit reporting agency can't disclose information in your credit file that's more than 7 or 10 years old unless you're being reviewed for a credit application of $75,000 or more, or unless you apply to purchase life insurance of $150,000 or more.

INCORRECT INFORMATION IN YOUR CREDIT FILE

Credit bureaus are required to follow reasonable procedures to ensure that the information in their files is correct. Mistakes can and do occur, however. If you think that a credit bureau may be reporting incorrect data from your file, contact the bureau to dispute the information. The credit bureau must check its records and change or remove the incorrect items. If you challenge the accuracy of an item on your credit report, the bureau must remove the item unless the lender can verify that the information is accurate.

If you are denied credit, insurance, employment, or rental housing based on the information in a credit report, you can get a free copy of your report. Remember to request it within 60 days of notification that your application has been denied.

WHAT ARE YOUR LEGAL RIGHTS?

You have legal rights to sue a credit bureau or creditor that has caused you harm by not following the rules established by the Fair Credit Reporting Act.

Key Web Sites for Credit Reporting

www.experian.com
www.ftc.gov

✓ CONCEPT CHECK 5–3

1 What are the two general rules of measuring credit capacity? How is it calculated?

_____

_____

2 Match the following key terms with the appropriate definition.

a. character   _____ An asset pledged to obtain a loan.

b. capacity   _____ The borrower's attitude toward credit obligations.

c. capital   _____ Financial ability to meet credit obligations.

d. collateral   _____ The borrower's assets or net worth.

e. conditions   _____ General economic conditions that affect your ability to repay a loan.

3 What are the factors a lender cannot consider according to the law?

_____

(*continued*)

4 What is a credit bureau? _____

5 Write the steps you should take if you are denied credit.

_____

_____

The Cost of Credit

OBJECTIVE 4

Determine the cost of credit by calculating interest using various interest formulas.

annual percentage rate (APR) The percentage cost (or relative cost) of credit on a yearly basis. The APR yields a true rate of interest for comparisons with other sources of credit.

If you are thinking of borrowing money or opening a credit account, your first step should be to figure out how much it will cost you and whether you can afford it. Then you should shop for the best terms. Two key concepts that you should remember are the finance charge and the annual percentage rate.

Finance Charge and Annual Percentage Rate

Credit costs vary. If you know the finance charge and the annual percentage rate you can compare credit prices from different sources. The *finance charge* is the total dollar amount you pay to use credit. It includes interest costs and sometimes other costs such as service charges, credit-related insurance premiums, or appraisal fees.

For example, borrowing $100 for a year might cost you $10 in interest. If there is also a service charge of $1, the finance charge will be $11. The **annual percentage rate (APR)** is the percentage cost (or relative cost) of credit on a yearly basis. The APR is your key to comparing costs, regardless of the amount of credit or how much time you have to repay it.

Suppose you borrow $100 for one year and pay a finance charge of $10. If you can keep the entire $100 for one year and then pay it all back at once, you are paying an APR of 10 percent.

Amount Borrowed	Month Number	Payment Made	Loan Balance
$100	1	$ 0	$100
	2	0	100
	3	0	100
	.	.	.
	.	.	.
	.	.	.
	12	$100	0

(plus $10 interest)

On average, you had full use of $100 throughout the year. To calculate the average use, add the loan balance during the first and last month, then divide by 2:

$$\text{Average balance} = \frac{\$100 + \$100}{2} = \$100$$

But if you repay the $100 and the finance charge (a total of $110) in 12 equal monthly payments, you don't get use of $100 for the whole year. In fact, as shown next, you get use of increasingly less of that $100 each month. In this case, the $10 charge for credit amounts to an APR of 18.5 percent.

Amount Borrowed	Month Number	Payment Made	Loan Balance
$100	1	$ 0	$100.00
	2	8.33	91.67
	3	8.33	83.34
	4	8.33	75.01
	5	8.33	66.68
	6	8.33	58.35
	7	8.33	50.02
	8	8.33	41.69
	9	8.33	33.36
	10	8.33	25.03
	11	8.33	16.70
	12	8.33	8.37

Note that you are paying 10 percent interest even though you had use of only $91.67 during the second month, not $100. During the last month, you owed only $8.37 (and had use of $8.37), but the $10 interest is for the entire $100. As calculated in the previous example, the average use of the money during the year is $100 + $8.37 ÷ 2, or $54.18.

Tackling the Trade-Offs

When you choose your financing, there are trade-offs between the features you prefer (term, size of payments, fixed or variable interest, or payment plan) and the cost of your loan. Here are some major trade-offs you should consider.

TERM VERSUS INTEREST COSTS   Many people choose longer term financing because they want smaller monthly payments, but the longer the term for a loan at a given interest rate, the greater the amount you must pay in interest charges. Consider the following analysis of the relationship between the term and interest costs.

Suppose you're buying a $7,500 used car. You put $1,500 down, and you need to borrow $6,000. Compare the following three credit arrangements:

	APR	Length of Loan	Monthly Payment	Total Finance Charge	Total Cost
Creditor A	14%	3 years	$205.07	$1,382.52	$7,382.52
Creditor B	14	4 years	163.96	1,870.08	7,870.08
Creditor C	15	4 years	166.98	2,015.04	8,015.04

How do these choices compare? The answer depends partly on what you need. The lowest cost loan is available from creditor A. If you are looking for lower monthly payments, you should repay the loan over a longer period of time. However, you would have to pay more in total costs. A loan from creditor B—also at a 14 percent APR, but for four years—would add about $488 to your finance charge.

If that four-year loan were available only from creditor C, the APR of 15 percent would add another $145 to your finance charges. Other terms, such as the size of the down payment, will also make a difference. Be sure to look at all the terms before you make your choice.

LENDER RISK VERSUS INTEREST RATE   You may prefer financing that requires low fixed payments with a large final payment or only a minimum of up-front cash. But both of these requirements can increase your cost of borrowing because they create more risk for your lender.

If you want to minimize your borrowing costs, you may need to accept conditions that reduce your lender's risk. Here are a few possibilities:

- *Variable interest rate.* A variable interest rate is based on fluctuating rates in the banking system, such as the prime rate. With this type of loan, you share the interest rate risks with the lender. Therefore, the lender may offer you a lower initial interest rate than it would with a fixed-rate loan.
- *A secured loan.* If you pledge property or other asset as collateral, you'll probably receive a lower interest rate on your loan.
- *Up-front cash.* Many lenders believe you have a higher stake in repaying a loan if you pay cash for a large portion of what you are financing. Doing so may give you a better chance of getting the other terms you want.
- *A shorter term.* As you have learned, the shorter the period of time for which you borrow, the smaller the chance that something will prevent you from repaying and the lower the risk to the lender. Therefore, you may be able to borrow at a lower interest rate if you accept a shorter-term loan, but your payments will be higher.

In the next section, you will see how the foregoing trade-offs can affect the cost of closed-end and open-end credit.

Calculating the Cost of Credit

The most common method of calculating interest is the simple interest formula. Other methods, such as simple interest on the declining balance and add-on interest, are variations of this formula.

simple interest Interest computed on principal only and without compounding.

SIMPLE INTEREST   **Simple interest** is the interest computed only on the principal, the amount that you borrow. It is based on three factors: the principal, the interest rate, and the amount of time for which the principal is borrowed. To calculate simple interest on a loan, multiply the principal by the interest rate and by the amount of time (in years) for which the money is borrowed. For example, suppose you convinced your aunt to lend you $1,000 to purchase a laptop computer. She agreed to charge only 5 percent simple interest and you agreed to repay the loan at the end of one year. How much interest will you pay for the year? Using the formula above, you simply multiply $1,000 by 5 percent and the term of one year ($1,000 $\times$ 5% $\times$ 1 = $50).

Key Web Sites for Cost of Credit
www.pirg.org/consumer/credit
www.econsumer.equifax.com

SIMPLE INTEREST ON THE DECLINING BALANCE   When simple interest is paid back in more than one payment, the method of computing interest is known as the declining balance method. You pay interest only on the amount of principal that you have not yet repaid. The more often you make payments, the lower the interest you'll pay. Most credit unions use this method.

ADD-ON INTEREST With the add-on interest method, interest is calculated on the full amount of the original principal, no matter how frequently you make payments. When you pay off the loan with one payment, this method produces the same annual percentage rate (APR) as the simple interest method. However, if you pay in installments, your actual rate of interest will be higher than the stated rate. Interest payments on this type of loan do not decrease as the loan is repaid. The longer you take to repay the loan, the more interest you'll pay.

CAUTION!

Many banks will increase the interest rate because of one late payment. They'll also slap on a penalty fee, which can run as high as $50 a pop.

COST OF OPEN-END CREDIT The Truth in Lending Act requires that open-end creditors inform consumers as to how the finance charge and the APR will affect their costs. For example, they must explain how they calculate the finance charge. They must also inform you when finance charges on your credit account begin to accrue, so that you know how much time you have to pay your bills before a finance charge is added.

Sheet 16
Credit Card/Charge Account Comparison

COST OF CREDIT AND EXPECTED INFLATION Inflation reduces the buying power of money. Each percentage point increase in inflation means a decrease of about 1 percent in the quantity of goods and services you can buy with the same amount of money. Because of this, lenders incorporate the expected rate of inflation when deciding how much interest to charge.

Remember the earlier example in which you borrowed $1,000 from your aunt at the bargain rate of 5 percent for one year? If the inflation rate was 4 percent that year, your aunt's actual rate of return on the loan would have been only 1 percent (5 percent stated interest minus 4 percent inflation rate). A professional lender who wanted to receive 5 percent interest on your loan might have charged you 9 percent interest (5 percent interest plus 4 percent anticipated inflation rate).

AVOID THE MINIMUM MONTHLY PAYMENT TRAP On credit card bills and with certain other forms of credit, the *minimum monthly payment* is the smallest amount you can pay and remain a borrower in good standing. Lenders often encourage you to make the minimum payment because it will then take you longer to pay off the loan. However, if you are paying only the minimum amount on your monthly statement, you need to plan your budget more carefully. The longer it takes for you to pay off a bill, the more interest you pay. The finance charges you pay on an item could end up being more than the item is worth.

Apply *Yourself!*

Objective 4

Use the Internet to obtain information about the costs of closed-end and open-end credit.

Consider the following examples. In each example, the minimum payment is based on 1/36 of the outstanding balance or $20, whichever is greater.

EXAMPLE 1

You are buying new books for college. If you spend $500 on textbooks using a credit card charging 19.8 percent interest and make only the minimum payment, it will take you more than 2½ years to pay off the loan, adding $150 in interest charges to the cost of your purchase. The same purchase on a credit card charging 12 percent interest will cost only $78 extra.

(continued)

Sheet 17
*Consumer
Loan
Comparison*

EXAMPLE 2

You purchase a $2,000 stereo system using a credit card with 19 percent interest and a 2 percent minimum payment. If you pay just the minimum every month, it will take you 265 months—over 22 years—to pay off the debt and will cost you nearly $4,800 in interest payments. Doubling the amount paid each month to 4 percent of the balance owed would allow you to shorten the payment time to 88 months from 265 months—or 7 years as opposed to 22 years—and save you about $3,680.

✔ CONCEPT CHECK 5–4

1 What are the two key concepts to remember when you borrow money?

_____

2 What are the three major trade-offs you should consider as you take out a loan?

_____

3 Using terms from the following list, complete the sentences below. Write the term you have chosen in the space provided.

> finance charge
> annual percentage rate
> simple interest
> minimum monthly payment
> add-on interest method

a. The _____ is the cost of credit on a yearly basis expressed as a percentage.

b. The total dollar amount paid to use credit is the _____ .

c. The smallest amount a borrower can pay on a credit card bill and remain a borrower in good standing is the _____ .

d. With the _____, interest is calculated on the full amount of the original principal, no matter how often you make payments.

e. _____ is the interest computed only on the principal, the amount that you borrow.

Protecting Your Credit

OBJECTIVE 5

Develop a plan to protect your credit and manage your debts.

Have you ever received a bill for merchandise you never bought or that you returned to the store or never received? Have you ever made a payment that was not credited to your account or been charged twice for the same item? If so, you are not alone.

Billing Errors and Disputes

The **Fair Credit Billing Act (FCBA),** passed in 1975, sets procedures for promptly correcting billing mistakes, refusing to make credit card or revolving credit payments on defective goods, and promptly crediting your payments.

Follow these steps if you think that a bill is wrong or want more information about it. First notify your creditor in writing, and include any information that might support your case. (A telephone call is not sufficient and will not protect your rights.) Then pay the portion of the bill that is not in question.

Your creditor must acknowledge your letter within 30 days. Then, within two billing periods (but not longer than 90 days), the creditor must adjust your account or tell you why the bill is correct. If the creditor made a mistake, you don't have to pay any finance charges on the disputed amount. If no mistake is found, the creditor must promptly send you an explanation of the situation and a statement of what you owe, including any finance charges that may have accumulated and any minimum payments you missed while you were questioning the bill.

PROTECTING YOUR CREDIT RATING   According to law, a creditor may not threaten your credit rating or do anything to damage your credit reputation while you're negotiating a billing dispute. In addition, the creditor may not take any action to collect the amount in question until your complaint has been answered.

DEFECTIVE GOODS AND SERVICES   Theo used his credit card to buy a new mountain bike. When it arrived, he discovered that some of the gears didn't work properly. He tried to return it, but the store would not accept a return. He asked the store to repair or replace the bike—but still he had no luck. According to the Fair Credit Billing Act, he may tell his credit card company to stop payment for the bike because he has made a sincere attempt to resolve the problem with the store.

Identity Crisis: What to Do If Your Identity Is Stolen

"I don't remember charging those items. I've never been in that store." Maybe you never charged those goods and services, but someone else did—someone who used your name and personal information to commit fraud. When imposters use your personal information for their own purposes, they are committing a crime.

The biggest problem? You may not know that your identity has been stolen until you notice that something is wrong: You may get bills for a credit card account you never opened, or you may see charges to your account for things that you didn't purchase.

If you think that your identity has been stolen and that someone is using it to charge purchases or obtain credit in some other way, the Federal Trade Commission recommends that you take the following three actions immediately:

1. *Contact the credit bureaus.* Tell them to flag your file with a fraud alert, including a statement that creditors should call you for permission before they open any new accounts in your name.
2. *Contact the creditors.* Contact the creditors for any accounts that have been tampered with or opened fraudulently. Follow up in writing.
3. *File a police report.* Keep a copy of the police report in case your creditors need proof of the crime. If you're still having identity problems, stay alert to new instances of identity theft. You can also contact the Privacy Rights Clearinghouse. Call 1-619-298-3396.

Fair Credit Billing Act (FCBA) Sets procedures for promptly correcting billing mistakes, refusing to make credit card payments on defective goods, and promptly crediting payments.

Key Web Sites for Protecting Credit
www.consumer-action.org
www.ftc.gov/ogc/stats.htm

Apply *Yourself!*

Objective 5

Use an Internet search engine to find branches of the Consumer Credit Counseling Service across the country. Choose one in your area and one in another part of the country. Visit the Web sites to find out who funds the offices.

Key Web Sites for Identity Theft
www.consumer.gov/idtheft/index
www.econsumer.equifax.com

CAUTION!

If you see an error on your credit report, contact the three major credit bureaus immediately: Equifax (1-800-685-1111), Experian (1-888-397-3742) and TransUnion (1-800-916-880).

Protecting Your Credit from Theft or Loss

Some thieves will pick through your trash in the hope of coming across your personal information. You can prevent this from happening by tearing or shredding any papers that contain personal information before you throw them out.

If you believe that an identity thief has accessed your bank accounts, close the accounts immediately. If your checks have been stolen or misused, stop payment on them. If your debit card has been lost or stolen, cancel it and get another with a new personal identification number (PIN).

Lost credit cards are a key element in credit card fraud. To protect your card, you should take the following actions:

- Be sure that your card is returned to you after a purchase. Unreturned cards can find their way into the wrong hands.
- Keep a record of your credit card number. You should keep this record separate from your card.
- Notify the credit card company immediately if your card is lost or stolen. Under the Consumer Credit Protection Act, the maximum amount that you must pay if someone uses your card illegally is $50. However, if you manage to inform the company before the card is used illegally, you have no obligation to pay at all.

Protecting Your Credit Information on the Internet

The Internet is becoming almost as important to daily life as the telephone and television. Increasing numbers of consumers use the Internet for financial activities, such as investing, banking, and shopping.

When you make purchases online, make sure that your transactions are secure, that your personal information is protected, and that your "fraud sensors" are sharpened. Although you can't control fraud or deception on the Internet, you can take steps to recognize it, avoid it, and report it. Here's how:

- Use a secure browser.
- Keep records of your online transactions.
- Review your monthly bank and credit card statements.
- Read the privacy and security policies of Web sites you visit.
- Keep your personal information private.
- Never give your password to anyone online.
- Don't download files sent to you by strangers.

Cosigning a Loan

If a friend or relative ever asks you to cosign a loan, think twice. *Cosigning* a loan means that you agree to be responsible for loan payments if the other party fails to make them. When you cosign, you're taking a chance that a professional lender will not take. The lender would not require a cosigner if the borrower were considered a good risk.

If you cosign a loan and the borrower does not pay the debt, you may have to pay up to the full amount of the debt as well as any late fees or collection costs. The creditor can even collect the debt from you without first trying to collect from the borrower. The creditor can use the same collection methods against you that can be used against the borrower. If the debt is not repaid, that fact will appear on your credit record.

Complaining about Consumer Credit

If you believe that a lender is not following the consumer credit protection laws, first try to solve the problem directly with the lender. If that fails, use formal complaint procedures. This section describes how to file a complaint with the federal agencies that administer credit protection laws.

Consumer Credit Protection Laws

did you know?

OPTING OUT
You can stop preapproved credit card offers by calling 1-888-567-8688.

If you have a particular problem with a bank in connection with any of the consumer credit protection laws, you can get advice and help from the Federal Reserve System. You don't need to have an account at the bank to file a complaint. You may also take legal action against a creditor. If you decide to file a lawsuit, you should be aware of the various consumer credit protection laws described below.

TRUTH IN LENDING AND CONSUMER LEASING ACTS   If a creditor fails to disclose information as required under the Truth in Lending Act or the Consumer Leasing Act, or gives inaccurate information, you can sue for any money loss you suffer. You can also sue a creditor that does not follow rules regarding credit cards. In addition, the Truth in Lending Act and the Consumer Leasing Act permit class action of all the people who have suffered the same injustice.

EQUAL CREDIT OPPORTUNITY ACT (ECOA)   If you think that you can prove that a creditor has discriminated against you for any reason prohibited by the ECOA, you may sue for actual damages plus punitive damages—a payment used to punish the creditor who has violated the law—up to $10,000.

FAIR CREDIT BILLING ACT   A creditor that fails to follow the rules that apply to correcting any billing errors will automatically give up the amount owed on the item in question and any finance charges on it, up to a combined total of $50. This is true even if the bill was correct. You may also sue for actual damages plus twice the amount of any finance charges.

FAIR CREDIT REPORTING ACT   You may sue any credit bureau or creditor that violates the rules regarding access to your credit records, or that fails to correct errors in your credit file. You're entitled to actual damages plus any punitive damages the court allows if the violation is proven to have been intentional.

CONSUMER CREDIT REPORTING REFORM ACT   The Consumer Credit Reporting Reform Act of 1977 places the burden of proof for accurate credit information on the credit bureau rather than on you. Under this law, the creditor must prove that disputed information is accurate. If a creditor or the credit bureau verifies incorrect data, you can sue for damages.

Key Web Sites for Credit Protection Laws
www.federalreserve.gov
www.uschamber.com

Your Rights under Consumer Credit Laws

If you believe that you've been refused credit because of discrimination, you can take one or more of the following steps:

- Complain to the creditor. Let the creditor know that you are aware of the law.
- File a complaint with the government. You can report any violations to the appropriate government enforcement agency, as shown in Exhibit 5–8.
- If all else fails, sue the creditor. If you win, you can receive actual damages and punitive damages of up to $10,000. You can also recover reasonable attorneys' fees and court costs.

Exhibit 5–8   Federal Government Agencies that Enforce the Consumer Credit Laws

If you think you've been discriminated against by:	You may file a complaint with the following agency:
Consumer reporting agencies, creditors and others not listed below	Federal Trade Commission: Consumer Response Center - FCRA Washington, DC 20580 1-877-382-4357
National banks, federal branches/agencies of foreign banks (word "National" or initials "N.A." appear in or after bank's name)	Office of the Comptroller of the Currency Compliance Management, Mail Stop 6-6 Washington, DC 20219 800-613-6743
Federal Reserve System member banks (except national banks, and federal branches/agencies of foreign banks)	Federal Reserve Board Division of Consumer & Community Affairs Washington, DC 20551 202-452-3693
Savings associations and federally chartered savings banks (word "Federal" or initials "F.S.B." appear in federal institution's name)	Office of Thrift Supervision Consumer Complaints Washington, DC 20552 800-842-6929
Federal credit unions (words "Federal Credit Union" appear in institution's name)	National Credit Union Administration 1775 Duke Street Alexandria, VA 22314 703-519-4600
State-chartered banks that are not members of the Federal Reserve System	Federal Deposit Insurance Corporation Consumer Response Center, 2345 Grand Avenue, Suite 100 Kansas City, MO 64108-2638 1-877-275-3342

The law gives you certain rights as a consumer of credit. *What types of complaints about a creditor might you report to these government agencies?*

Managing Your Debts

A sudden illness or the loss of your job may prevent you from paying your bills on time. If you find you cannot make your payments, contact your creditors at once and try to work out a modified payment plan with them.

Warning Signs of Debt Problems

Chris is in his late 20s. A college graduate, he has a steady job and earns an annual income of $40,000. With the latest model sports car parked in the driveway of his new home, it would appear that Chris has the ideal life.

However, Chris is deeply in debt. He is drowning in a sea of bills. Almost all his income is tied up in debt payments. The bank has already begun foreclosure proceedings on his home, and several stores have court orders to repossess practically all of his new furniture and electronic gadgets. His current car payment is overdue, and he is behind in payments on all his credit cards. If he doesn't come up with a plan of action, he'll lose everything.

Chris's situation is all too common. Some people who seem to be wealthy are just barely keeping their heads above water financially. Generally, the problem they share is financial immaturity. They lack self-discipline and don't control their impulses. They use poor judgment or fail to accept responsibility for managing their money.

Chris and others like him aren't necessarily bad people. They simply haven't thought about their long-term financial goals. Someday you could find yourself in a situation similar to Chris's. Here are some warning signs that you may be in financial trouble:

- You make only the minimum monthly payment on credit cards.
- You're having trouble making even the minimum monthly payment on your credit card bills.
- The total balance on your credit cards increases every month.

- You miss loan payments or often pay late.
- You use savings to pay for necessities such as food and utilities.
- You receive second and third payment due notices from creditors.
- You borrow money to pay off old debts.
- You exceed the credit limits on your credit cards.
- You've been denied credit because of a bad credit bureau report.

If you are experiencing two or more of these warning signs, it's time for you to rethink your priorities before it's too late.

Debt Collection Practices

The Federal Trade Commission enforces the Fair Debt Collection Practices Act (FDCPA). This act prohibits certain practices by debt collectors—businesses that collect debts for creditors. The act does not erase the legitimate debts that consumers owe, but it does control the ways in which debt collection agencies may do business.

Financial Counseling Services

If you're having trouble paying your bills and need help, you have several options. You can contact your creditors and try to work out an adjusted repayment plan, or you can contact a nonprofit financial counseling program.

CONSUMER CREDIT COUNSELING SERVICES   The Consumer Credit Counseling Service (CCCS) is a nonprofit organization affiliated with the National Foundation for Consumer Credit (NFCC). Local branches of the CCCS provide debt-counseling services for families and individuals with serious financial problems. The CCCS is not a charity, a lending institution, or a government agency. CCCS counseling is usually free. However, when the organization supervises a debt repayment plan, it sometimes charges a small fee to help pay administrative costs.

According to the NFCC, millions of consumers contact CCCS offices each year for help with their personal financial problems. To find an office near you, check the white pages of your local telephone directory under Consumer Credit Counseling Service, or call 1-800-388-CCCS. All information is kept confidential.

Credit counselors know that most individuals who are overwhelmed with debt are basically honest people who want to clear up their unmanageable *indebtedness,* the condition of being deeply in debt. Too often, such problems arise from the lack of planning or a miscalculation of earnings. The CCCS is concerned with preventing problems as much as it is with solving them. As a result, its activities are divided into two parts:

- Aiding families with serious debt problems by helping them to manage their money better and set up a realistic budget.
- Helping people prevent indebtedness by teaching them the importance of budget planning, educating them about the pitfalls of unwise credit buying, and encouraging credit institutions to withhold credit from people who cannot afford it.

Key Web Site for Credit Counseling

www.uscourts.gov

See the accompanying Personal Finance in Practice box for help in choosing a credit counselor.

OTHER COUNSELING SERVICES   In addition to the CCCS, universities, credit unions, military bases, and state and federal housing authorities sometimes provide nonprofit credit counseling services. These organizations usually charge little or nothing for their assistance. You can also check with your bank or local consumer protection office to see whether it has a listing of reputable financial counseling services, such as the Debt Counselors of America.

DEBT | The feds weed out bogus counseling services. Where to find good advice.

Credit CRACKDOWN

WHEN Congress passed a new bankruptcy law, lawmakers also required filers to get credit counseling. With more than two million personal-bankruptcy filings last year, consumers clearly need guidance. But it turns out that the solution is often worse than the problem.

The IRS recently audited 41 credit counselors, representing the revenue of more than 40% of the agencies in the field, and found that almost all of them were fronts for debt collectors that took advantage of unwary debtors. As a result, the IRS revoked the firms' tax-exempt status.

The agency that oversees bankruptcy case administration is reviewing the IRS's findings to see if any of the organizations can remain on its approved list.

As legitimate advice gets scarce, employers may fill the void. Human-resources consultants say an increasing number of companies are adding debt-management help to their employee assistance programs. Aflac, the insurance company, offers its employees weekly Lunch and Learn sessions, during which outside experts talk about personal-finance topics. Financial planners who charge reasonable hourly fees or donate their time can be another resource.

1. Why does the new bankruptcy law require filers to get credit counseling?

_____

_____

_____

2. Why did the IRS revoke the tax-exempt status of several credit counseling agencies?

_____

_____

_____

3. Do you believe that employers should offer debt-management counseling to their employees? Why or why not?

_____

_____

_____

Personal Finance in Practice

› Choosing a Credit Counselor

Reputable credit counseling organizations employ counselors who are certified and trained in consumer credit, debt management, and budgeting. Here are a few important questions to ask when choosing a credit counselor:

1. **What services do you offer?** Look for an organization that offers a range of services, including budget counseling, savings and debt management classes, and trained certified counselors.

2. **Are you licensed to offer services in my state?** Many states require that a credit counseling agency register or obtain a license before offering their services.

3. **Do you offer free information?** Avoid organizations that charge for information about the nature of their services.

4. **Will I have a formal written agreement or contract with you?** Don't commit to participate in a debt management program over the telephone. Get all the verbal promises in writing. Read all documents carefully before you sign them. If you are told you need to act immediately, consider finding another organization.

5. **What are the qualifications of your counselors?** Are they accredited or certified by an outside organization? Which one? If not, how are they trained? Try to use an organization whose counselors are trained by an outside organization that is not affiliated with creditors.

6. **Have other consumers been satisfied with the service they received?** Once you have identified credit counseling organizations that suit your needs, check them out with your state attorney general, local consumer protection agency, and Better Business Bureau.

7. **What are your fees? Are there set-up and/or monthly fees?** Get a detailed quote in writing, and specifically ask whether all fees are covered in the quote. If an organization won't help you because you can't afford to pay, look elsewhere for help.

8. **How are your employees paid? Are the employees or the organization paid more if I sign up for certain services, pay a fee, or make a contribution to your organization?** Employees who are counseling you to purchase certain services may receive a commission if you choose to sign up for those services. Many credit counseling organizations receive additional compensation from creditors if you enroll in a debt management program.

9. **What do you do to keep personal information about your clients (for example, name, address, phone number, financial information) confidential and secure?** Credit counseling organizations handle your most sensitive financial information. The organization should have safeguards in place to protect the privacy of this information and prevent misuse.

Declaring Personal Bankruptcy

What if a debtor suffers from an extreme case of financial woes? Can there be any relief? The answer is bankruptcy proceedings. *Bankruptcy* is a legal process in which some or all of the assets of a debtor are distributed among the creditors because the debtor is unable to pay his or her debts. Bankruptcy may also include a plan for the debtor to repay creditors on an installment basis. Declaring bankruptcy is a last resort because it severely damages your credit rating.

Anita Singh illustrates the face of bankruptcy. A 43-year-old freelance photographer from California, she was never in serious financial trouble until she began running up big medical costs. She reached for her credit cards to pay the bills. Because Anita didn't have health insurance, her debt quickly mounted and soon reached $17,000—too much to pay off with her $25,000-a-year income. Her solution was to declare personal bankruptcy and enjoy the immediate freedom it would bring from creditors' demands.

THE U.S. BANKRUPTCY ACT OF 1978 Exhibit 5–9 illustrates the rate of personal bankruptcy in the United States. The vast majority of bankruptcies in the United States, like Anita Singh's, are filed under a part of U.S. bankruptcy code known as Chapter 7. You have two choices in declaring personal bankruptcy: Chapter 7 (a

Exhibit 5–9   **U.S. Consumer Bankruptcy Filings, 1980–2005**
Consumer bankruptcies have increased significantly over the past 25 years. Consumer bankruptcy filings rose from about 287,000 in 1980 to more than 2 million as of December 31, 2005, about a 609 percent increase over the last 25 years.

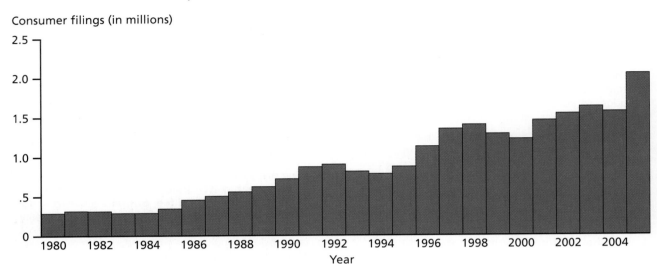

Consumer filings (in millions)

Source: Administrative Office of the United States Courts; www.uscourts.gov/press-releases/bankruptcyfilings032406.html, accessed January 11, 2007.

straight bankruptcy) and Chapter 13 (a wage earner plan bankruptcy). Both choices are undesirable, and neither should be considered an easy way to get out of debt.

Chapter 7 Bankruptcy   In a Chapter 7 bankruptcy, an individual is required to draw up a petition listing his or her assets and liabilities. A person who files for relief under the bankruptcy code is called a *debtor*. The debtor submits the petition to a U.S. district court and pays a filing fee.

Chapter 7 is a straight bankruptcy in which many, but not all, debts are forgiven. Most of the debtor's assets are sold to pay off creditors. Certain assets, however, receive some protection. Among the assets usually protected are Social Security payments, unemployment compensation, and the net value of your home, vehicle, household goods and appliances, tools used in your work, and books.

The release from debt does not affect alimony, child support, certain taxes, fines, certain debts arising from educational loans, or debts that you fail to disclose properly to the bankruptcy court. Furthermore, debts arising from fraud, driving while intoxicated, or certain other acts or crimes may also be excluded.

The Bankruptcy Abuse Prevention and Consumer Protection Act of 2005   On April 20, 2005, President George W. Bush signed the Bankruptcy Abuse Prevention and Consumer Protection Act, which is perhaps the largest overhaul of the Bankruptcy Code since it was enacted in 1978. Signing the bill, the president declared, "Bankruptcy should always be the last resort in our legal system. In recent years too many people have abused the bankruptcy laws. Under the new law, Americans who have the ability to pay will be required to pay back at least a portion of their debts. The law will help make credit more affordable, because when bankruptcy is less common, credit can be extended to more people at better rates. Debtors seeking to erase all debts will now have to wait eight years from their last bankruptcy before they can file again. The law will also allow us to clamp down on bankruptcy mills that make their money by advising abusers on how to game the system."

Among other provisions, the law requires that:

- The director of the Executive Office for U.S. Trustees develop a financial management training curriculum to educate individual debtors on how to better manage their finances; and test, evaluate, and report to Congress on the curriculum's effectiveness.
- Debtors complete an approved instructional course in personal financial management.
- The clerk of each bankruptcy district maintains a list of credit counseling agencies and instructional courses on personal financial management.

Furthermore, the law may require that states should develop personal finance curricula designed for use in elementary and secondary schools.

The bottom line: the new law made it more difficult for consumers to file a Chapter 7 bankruptcy and forces them into a Chapter 13 repayment plan.

Chapter 13 Bankruptcy   In Chapter 13 bankruptcy, a debtor with a regular income proposes a plan for using future earnings or assets to eliminate his or her debts over a period of time. In such a bankruptcy, the debtor normally keeps all or most of his or her property.

During the period when the plan is in effect, which can be as long as five years, the debtor makes regular payments to a Chapter 13 trustee, or representative, who then distributes the money to the creditors. Under certain circumstances, the bankruptcy court may approve a plan that permits the debtor to keep all property, even though he or she repays less than the full amount of the debts.

EFFECTS OF BANKRUPTCY   People have varying experiences in obtaining credit after they file for bankruptcy. Some find the process more difficult, whereas others find it easier because they have removed the burden of prior debts or because creditors know that they cannot file another bankruptcy case for a certain period of time. Obtaining credit may be easier for people who file a Chapter 13 bankruptcy and repay some of their debts than for those who file a Chapter 7 bankruptcy and make no effort to repay any of their debts.

✓ CONCEPT CHECK 5–5

1 What steps might you take if there is a billing error in your monthly statement?

_____

_____

2 What steps would you take if someone stole your identity?

_____

_____

_____

3 How might you protect your credit information on the Internet?

_____

_____

(continued)

4 What are some warning signs of debt problems?

_____

_____

_____

5 Distinguish between Chapter 7 and Chapter 13 bankruptcy.

_____

_____

_____

back to Getting Personal

Reconsider your responses to the Getting Personal questions at the beginning of the chapter. What did you learn in this chapter that might affect your answers to these questions in the future?

Scoring: Give yourself 3 points for each *a*, 2 points for each *b*, and 1 point for each *c*, Add up the number of points.

If you scored 6–9 points, you might want to take a closer look at how credit works before you get over your head in debt.

If you scored 10–13 points, you are off to a good start, but be sure you know the pitfalls of opening a credit account.

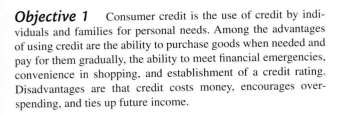

Chapter Summary

Objective 1 Consumer credit is the use of credit by individuals and families for personal needs. Among the advantages of using credit are the ability to purchase goods when needed and pay for them gradually, the ability to meet financial emergencies, convenience in shopping, and establishment of a credit rating. Disadvantages are that credit costs money, encourages overspending, and ties up future income.

Objective 2 Closed-end and open-end credit are two types of consumer credit. With closed-end credit, the borrower pays back a one-time loan in a stated period of time and with a specified number of payments. With open-end credit, the borrower is permitted to take loans on a continuous basis and is billed for partial payments periodically.

The major sources of consumer credit are commercial banks, savings and loan associations, credit unions, finance companies, life insurance companies, and family and friends. Each of these sources has unique advantages and disadvantages.

Parents or family members are often the source of the least expensive loans. They may charge you only the interest they would have earned had they not made the loan. Such loans, however, can complicate family relationships.

Objective 3 Two general rules for measuring credit capacity are the debt payments-to-income ratio and the debt-to-equity ratio. In reviewing your creditworthiness, a creditor seeks information from one of the three national credit bureaus or a regional credit bureau.

Creditors determine creditworthiness on the basis of the five Cs: character, capacity, capital, collateral, and conditions.

Objective 4
Compare the finance charge and the annual percentage rate (APR) as you shop for credit. Under the Truth in Lending Act, creditors are required to state the cost of borrowing so that you can compare credit costs and shop for credit.

Objective 5
If a billing error occurs on your account, notify the creditor in writing within 60 days. If the dispute is not settled in your favor, you can place your version of it in your credit file. You may also withhold payment on any defective goods or services you have purchased with a credit card as long as you have attempted to resolve the problem with the merchant.

If you have a complaint about credit, first try to deal directly with the creditor. If that fails, you can turn to the appropriate consumer credit law. These laws include the Truth in Lending Act, the Consumer Leasing Act, the Equal Credit Opportunity Act, the Fair Credit Billing Act, the Fair Credit Reporting Act, and the Consumer Credit Reporting Reform Act.

If you cannot meet your obligations, contact your creditors immediately. Also, contact your local Consumer Credit Counseling Service or other debt counseling organizations.

A debtor's last resort is to declare bankruptcy, permitted by the U.S. Bankruptcy Act of 1978. Consider the financial and other costs of bankruptcy before taking this extreme step. A debtor can declare Chapter 7 (straight) bankruptcy or Chapter 13 (wage earner plan) bankruptcy.

Key Terms

annual percentage rate (APR) 156	conditions 150	line of credit 143
capacity 149	consumer credit 139	open-end credit 142
capital 149	credit 139	revolving check credit 143
character 149	Fair Credit Billing Act (FCBA) 161	simple interest 158
closed-end credit 142	finance charge 146	
collateral 150	interest 143	

Problems

1. A few years ago, Michael Tucker purchased a home for $100,000. Today the home is worth $150,000. His remaining mortgage balance is $50,000. Assuming Michael can borrow up to 80 percent of the market value of his home, what is the maximum amount he can borrow?

2. Louise McIntyre's monthly gross income is $2,000. Her employer withholds $400 in federal, state, and local income taxes and $160 in Social Security taxes per month. Louise contributes $80 per month for her IRA. Her monthly credit payments for Visa, MasterCard, and Discover cards are $35, $30, and $20, respectively. Her monthly payment on an automobile loan is $285. What is Louise's debt payments-to-income ratio? Is Louise living within her means? Explain.

3. Robert Thumme owns a $140,000 townhouse and still has an unpaid mortgage of $110,000. In addition to his mortgage, he has the following liabilities:

Visa	$ 565
MasterCard	480
Discover card	395
Education loan	920
Personal bank loan	800
Auto loan	4,250
Total	$7,410

Robert's net worth (not including his home) is about $21,000. This equity is in mutual funds, an automobile, a coin collection, furniture, and other personal property. What is Robert's debt-to-equity ratio? Has he reached the upper limit of debt obligations? Explain.

4. Kim Lee is trying to decide whether she can afford a loan she needs in order to go to chiropractic school. Right now Kim is living at home and works in a shoe store, earning a gross income of $820 per month. Her employer deducts a total of $145 for taxes from her monthly pay. Kim also pays $95 on several credit card debts each month. The loan she needs for chiropractic school will cost an additional $120 per month. Help Kim make her decision by calculating her debt payments-to-income ratio with and without the college loan. (Remember the 20 percent rule.)

5. Dave borrowed $500 for one year and paid $50 in interest. The bank charged him a $5 service charge. What is the finance charge on this loan?

6. In problem 5, Dave borrowed $500 on January 1, 2009, and paid it all back at once on December 31, 2009. What was the APR?

7. If Dave paid the $500 in 12 equal monthly payments, what was the APR?

8. Sidney took a $200 cash advance by using checks linked to her credit card account. The bank charges a 2 percent cash advance fee on the amount borrowed and offers no grace period on cash advances. Sidney paid the balance in full when the bill arrived. What was the cash advance fee? What was the interest for one month at an 18 percent APR? What was the total amount she paid? What if she had made the purchase with her credit card and paid off the bill in full promptly?

9. Dorothy lacks cash to pay for a $600 dishwasher. She could buy it from the store on credit by making 12 monthly payments of $52.74. The total cost would then be $632.88. Instead, Dorothy decides to deposit $50 a month in the bank until she has saved enough money to pay cash for the dishwasher. One year later, she has saved $642—$600 in deposits plus interest. When she goes back to the store, she finds the dishwasher now costs $660. Its price has gone up 10 percent, the current rate of inflation. Was postponing her purchase a good trade-off for Dorothy?

10. You have been pricing a compact disk player in several stores. Three stores have the identical price of $300. Each store charges 18 percent APR, has a 30-day grace period, and sends out bills on the first of the month. On further investigation, you find that store A calculates the finance charge by using the average daily balance method, store B uses the adjusted balance method, and store C uses the previous balance method. Assume you purchased the disk player on May 5 and made a $100 payment on June 15. What will the finance charge be if you made your purchase from store A? From store B? From store C?

11. What are the interest cost and the total amount due on a six-month loan of $1,500 at 13.2 percent simple annual interest?

12. After visiting several automobile dealerships, Richard selects the used car he wants. He likes its $10,000 price, but financing through the dealer is no bargain. He has $2,000 cash for a down payment, so he needs an $8,000 loan. In shopping at several banks for an installment loan, he learns that interest on most automobile loans is quoted at add-on rates. That is, during the life of the loan, interest is paid on the full amount borrowed even though a portion of the principal has been paid back. Richard borrows $8,000 for a period of four years at an add-on interest rate of 11 percent. What is the total interest on Richard's loan? What is the total cost of the car? What is the monthly payment? What is the annual percentage rate (APR)?

Questions

1. Vicky is trying to decide whether to finance her purchase of a used Mustang convertible. What questions should Vicky ask herself before making her decision?

2. List advantages and disadvantages of using credit.

3. To finance a sofa for his new apartment, Caleb signed a contract to pay for the sofa in six equal installments. What type of consumer credit is Caleb using?

4. Alka plans to spend $5,000 on plasma television and a home theater system. She is willing to spend some of her $9,000 in savings. However, she wants to finance the rest and pay it off in small monthly installments out of the $400 a month she earns working part-time. How might she obtain a low interest rate and make low monthly payments?

5. What factors would you consider in assessing the choices in declaring personal bankruptcy? Why should personal bankruptcy be the choice of last resort?

Internet Connection

COMPARING CREDIT SOURCES AND COSTS

Credit is available from many sources. Becoming aware of the differences among financial institutions related to borrowing costs and other factors while wisely managing your debt will help you avoid financial difficulties.

1. Using www.cardtrak.com and www.ramsearch.com, evaluate your current use of credit cards. Compare various credit card offers related to APR, annual fee, grace period, and other fees.

2. Using www.bankrate.com and www.banx.com, compare credit sources for loans related to various financial needs.

3. Using www.nfcc.org, myvesta.org, and www.nccs.org, investigate actions commonly taken to avoid debt problems.

4. Prepare a spending plan to minimize the use of credit, using www.centura.com and www.finance-center.com.

Case in Point

FINANCING SUE'S HYUNDAI EXCEL

After shopping around, Sue Wallace decided on the car of her choice, a used Hyundai Excel. The dealer quoted her a total price of $8,000. Sue decided to use $2,000 of her savings as a down payment and borrow $6,000. The salesperson wrote this information on a sales contract that Sue took with her when she set out to find financing.

When Sue applied for a loan, she discussed loan terms with the bank lending officer. The officer told her that the bank's policy was to lend only 80 percent of the total price of a used car. Sue showed the officer her copy of the sales contract, indicating that she had agreed to make a $2,000, or 25 percent, down payment on the $8,000 car, so this requirement caused her no problem. Although the bank was willing to make 48-month loans at an annual percentage rate of 15 percent on used cars, Sue chose a 36-month repayment schedule. She believed she could afford the higher payments, and she knew she would not have to pay as much interest if she paid off the loan at a faster rate. The bank lending officer provided Sue with a copy of the Truth-in-Lending Disclosure Statement shown here.

Truth-in-Lending Disclosure Statement (Loans)

Annual Percentage Rate	Finance Charge	Amount Financed	Total of Payments 36
The cost of your credit as a yearly rate.	The dollar amount the credit will cost you.	The amount of credit provided to you or on your behalf.	The amount you will have paid after you have made all payments as scheduled.
15%	$1,487.64	$6,000.00	$7,487.64

You have the right to receive at this time an itemization of the Amount Financed.

❑ I want an itemization.   ❑ I do not want an itemization.

Your payment schedule will be:

Number of Payments	Amount of Payments	When Payments Are Due
36	$207.99	1st of each month

Sue decided to compare the APR she had been offered with the APR offered by another bank, but the 20 percent APR of the second bank (bank B) was more expensive than the 15 percent APR of the first bank (bank A). Here is her comparison of the two loans:

	Bank A 15% APR	Bank B 20% APR
Amount financed	$6,000.00	$6,000.00
Finance charge	1,487.64	2,027.28
Total of payments	7,487.64	8,027.28
Monthly payments	207.99	222.98

The 5 percent difference in the APRs of the two banks meant Sue would have to pay $15 extra every month if she got her loan from the second bank. Of course, she got the loan from the first bank.

Questions

1. What is perhaps the most important item shown on the disclosure statement? Why?

2. What is included in the finance charge?

3. What amount will Sue receive from the bank?

4. Should Sue borrow from bank A or bank B? Why?

Continuing Case

CREDIT DECISIONS

Life Situation	*Financial Data*	
Recently married couple	Monthly income	$5,840
Pam, 26	Assets	$13,500
Josh, 28	Liabilities	$4,800
Renting an apartment	Living expenses	$3,900
	Emergency fund	$1,000

In an effort to make wise use of credit, the Brocks have examined various sources that could serve their current and future financial needs. In the assessment process, they compared the APR along with various fees and potential charges.

Josh and Pam are also learning about various actions that might be useful if they encounter credit troubles. Their discussions with friends and money management advisers provided expanded knowledge of credit counseling and bankruptcy alternatives.

Questions

1. List other actions that the Brocks might consider to reduce the cost of using credit.

2. What information sources might be useful when comparing various sources of credit?

3. Explain ways in which *Your Personal Financial Plan* sheets 15 and 16 could be useful to the Brocks.

Video Case

CREDIT CARD CHECK UP

Tips for paying off holiday credit card use is up 11 percent this holiday season over the previous year. If you haven't already received your holiday credit card bills, they are certainly on the way soon. Before the debt becomes too much to handle, BusinessWeek experts have tips on which bills to pay first, how to prepare for next year, and how to save while paying off debt.

Questions

1. According to Valerie Adelman, a Certified Financial Planner, what steps can you take to get your financial house back in order?

2. How do people get themselves into a credit card debt?

3. What percentage of credit card debt is paid back in full?

Spending Diary

"I ADMIRE PEOPLE WHO ARE ABLE TO PAY OFF THEIR CREDIT CARDS EACH MONTH."

Directions

Your ability to monitor spending and credit use is a fundamental success for wise money management and long-term financial security. Use the "Daily Spending Diary" sheets provided at the end of the book to record all of your spending in the categories provided. Be sure to indicate the use of a credit card with (CR).

Questions

1. Describe any aspects of your spending habits that might indicate an overuse of credit.

2. How might your Daily Spending Diary provide information for wise credit use?

www.mhhe.com/kdh

15

Your Personal Financial Plan

Name: _____ **Date:** _____

Consumer Credit Usage Patterns

Financial Planning Activities: Record account names, numbers, and payments for current consumer debts.

Suggested Web Sites: www.finance-center.com   www.ftc.gov

Automobile, Education, Personal, and Installment Loans

Financial institution	Account number	Current balance	Monthly payment
_____	_____	_____	_____
_____	_____	_____	_____
_____	_____	_____	_____
_____	_____	_____	_____
_____	_____	_____	_____

Charge Accounts and Credit Cards

_____	_____	_____	_____
_____	_____	_____	_____
_____	_____	_____	_____
_____	_____	_____	_____
_____	_____	_____	_____

Other Loans (overdraft protection, home equity, life insurance loan)

_____	_____	_____	_____
_____	_____	_____	_____
_____	_____	_____	_____
_____	_____	_____	_____
		Totals	_____	_____

$$\text{Debt payment-to-income ratio} = \frac{\text{Total monthly payments}}{\text{net (after-tax) income}}$$

What's Next for Your Personal Financial Plan?

- Survey three or four individuals to determine their uses of credit.
- Talk to several people to determine how they first established credit.

Credit Card/Charge Account Comparison

Financial Planning Activities: Analyze ads and credit applications and contact various financial institutions to obtain the information requested below.

Suggested Web Sites: www.bankrate.com   www.banx.com

16

Your Personal Financial Plan

Type of credit/charge account			
Name of company/account			
Address/phone			
Web site			
Type of purchases that can be made			
Annual fee (if any)			
Annual percentage rate (APR) (interest calculation information)			
Credit limit for new customers			
Minimum monthly payment			
Other costs: • credit report • late fee • other _____			
Restrictions (age, minimum annual income)			
Other information for consumers to consider			
Frequent flyer or other bonus points			

What's Next for Your Personal Financial Plan?

- Make a list of the pros and cons of using credit or debit cards.
- Contact a local credit bureau to obtain information on the services provided and the fees charged.

Consumer Loan Comparison

Financial Planning Activities: Contact or visit a bank, credit union, and consumer finance company to obtain information on a loan for a specific purpose.

Suggested Web Sites: www.eloan.com   www.centura.com

Type of financial institution			
Name			
Address			
Phone			
Web site			
Amount of down payment			
Length of loan (months)			
What collateral is required?			
Amount of monthly payment			
Total amount to be repaid (monthly amount × number of months + down payment)			
Total finance charge/cost of credit			
Annual percentage rate (APR)			
Other costs • credit life insurance • credit report • other _____			
Is a cosigner required?			
Other information			

What's Next for Your Personal Financial Plan?

* Ask several individuals how they would compare loans at different financial institutions.
* Survey several friends and relatives to determine if they ever cosigned a loan. If yes, what were the consequences of cosigning?

6 Consumer Purchasing Strategies and Wise Buying of Motor Vehicles

Getting Personal

For each of the following shopping behaviors, circle "agree," "neutral," or "disagree" to indicate your attitude toward this action.

1. Getting very good quality is very important to me.	Agree	Neutral	Disagree
2. Well-known national brands are best for me.	Agree	Neutral	Disagree
3. I buy as much as possible at "sale" prices.	Agree	Neutral	Disagree
4. I should plan my shopping more carefully than I do.	Agree	Neutral	Disagree
5. I have favorite brands I buy over and over.	Agree	Neutral	Disagree
6. Lower priced products are usually my choice.	Agree	Neutral	Disagree

After studying this chapter, you will be asked to reconsider your responses to these items.

Consumer Purchasing Strategies and Wise Buying of Motor Vehicles

Getting Personal

For each of the following shopping behaviors, circle "agree," "neutral," or "disagree" to indicate your attitude toward this action.

1. Getting very good quality is very important to me.	Agree	Neutral	Disagree
2. Well-known national brands are best for me.	Agree	Neutral	Disagree
3. I buy as much as possible at "sale" prices.	Agree	Neutral	Disagree
4. I should plan my shopping more carefully than I do.	Agree	Neutral	Disagree
5. I have favorite brands I buy over and over.	Agree	Neutral	Disagree
6. Lower priced products are usually my choice.	Agree	Neutral	Disagree

After studying this chapter, you will be asked to reconsider your responses to these items.

Objectives

In this chapter, you will learn to:

1. Identify strategies for effective consumer buying.
2. Implement a process for making consumer purchases.
3. Describe steps to take to resolve consumer problems.
4. Evaluate legal alternatives available to consumers.

Why is this important?

Unplanned and careless buying will reduce your potential for long-term financial security. Impulse buying activities of a few dollars a week can cost you thousands of dollars in just a couple of years.

Consumer Buying Activities

OBJECTIVE 1
Identify strategies for effective consumer buying.

Daily buying decisions involve a trade-off between current spending and saving for the future. A wide variety of economic, social, and personal factors affect daily buying habits. These factors are the basis for spending, saving, investing, and achieving personal financial goals. In very simple terms, the only way you can have long-term financial security is to not spend all of your current income. In addition, overspending leads to misuse of credit and financial difficulties.

Practical Purchasing Strategies

Comparison shopping is the process of considering alternative stores, brands, and prices. In contrast, *impulse buying* is unplanned purchasing, which can result in financial problems. Several buying techniques are commonly suggested for wise buying.

TIMING PURCHASES Certain items go on sale the same time each year. You can obtain bargains by buying winter clothing in mid- or late winter, or summer clothing in mid- or late summer. Many people save by buying holiday items and other products at reduced prices in late December and early January.

STORE SELECTION Your decision to use a particular retailer is probably influenced by location, price, product selection, and services available. Competition and technology have changed retailing with superstores, specialty shops, and online buying. This expanded shopping environment provides consumers with greater choice, potentially lower prices, and the need to carefully consider buying alternatives.

did you know?

A problem with compulsive shopping can be revealed by these questions: Do you have an overwhelming desire to buy things? Do you buy to change your mood? Do your shopping habits hurt your relationships? Does overshopping damage your finances?

BRAND COMPARISON   Food and other products come in various brands. *National-brand* products are highly advertised items available in many stores. *Store-brand* and *private-label* products, sold by one chain of stores, are low-cost alternatives to famous-name products. Since store-brand products are frequently manufactured by the same companies that produce brand-name items, these lower cost alternatives can result in extensive savings. The use of one or more of the many product comparison Web sites can assist you in this process.

LABEL INFORMATION   Certain label information is helpful; however, other information is nothing more than advertising. Federal law requires that food labels contain certain information. Product labeling for appliances includes information about operating costs to assist you in selecting the most energy-efficient models. *Open dating* describes the freshness or shelf life of a perishable product. Phrases such as "Use before May 2009" or "Not to be sold after October 8" appear on most grocery items.

Apply *Yourself!*

Objective 1

Conduct a survey regarding brand loyalty. For what products are people most brand loyal? What factors (price, location, information) may influence their selection of another brand?

PRICE COMPARISON   *Unit pricing* uses a standard unit of measurement to compare the prices of packages of different sizes. To calculate the unit price, divide the price of the item by the number of units of measurement, such as ounces, pounds, gallons, or number of sheets (for items such as paper towels and facial tissues). Then compare the unit prices for various sizes, brands, and stores.

Coupons and rebates also provide better pricing for wise consumers. A family saving about $8 a week on their groceries by using coupons will save $416 over a year and $2,080 over five years (not counting interest). Coupons are available online at www.coolsavings.com, www.centsoff.com, and www.couponsurfer.com. A *rebate* is a partial refund of the price of a product.

When comparing prices, remember that

- More store convenience (location, hours, sales staff) usually means higher prices.
- Ready-to-use products have higher prices.
- Large packages are usually the best buy; however, compare using unit pricing.
- "Sale" may not always mean saving money.
- The use of online sources can save time.

Exhibit 6–1 summarizes techniques that can assist you in your buying decisions.

Warranties

warranty A written guarantee from the manufacturer or distributor of a product that specifies the conditions under which the product can be returned, replaced, or repaired.

Most products come with some guarantee of quality. A **warranty** is a written guarantee from the manufacturer or distributor that specifies the conditions under which the product can be returned, replaced, or repaired. An *express warranty,* usually in written form, is created by the seller or manufacturer and has two forms: the full warranty and the limited warranty. A *full warranty* states that a defective product can be fixed or replaced during a reasonable amount of time.

A *limited warranty* covers only certain aspects of the product, such as parts, or requires the buyer to incur part of the costs for shipping or repairs. An *implied warranty* covers a product's intended use or other basic understandings that are not in writing. For example, an implied *warranty of title* indicates that the seller has the right to sell the product. An implied *warranty of merchantability* guarantees that the product is fit for the ordinary uses for which it is intended: A toaster must toast bread, and a stereo must play CDs or tapes. Implied warranties vary from state to state.

USED-CAR WARRANTIES   The Federal Trade Commission (FTC) requires used cars to have a buyer's guide sticker telling whether the vehicle comes with a warranty and, if so, what protection the dealer will provide. If no warranty is offered, the

Exhibit 6–1

Wise Buying Techniques:
A Summary

✔ Compare brands of similar products to determine which is best for your intended use.

✔ Compare stores and online sources with regard to prices, services offered, product quality, and return privileges.

✔ Read and evaluate label information.

✔ Use coupons for products that you buy regularly or are trying out.

✔ Use unit pricing to compare packages of different sizes.

✔ Obtain "rain checks" for out-of-stock advertised specials that you can use for purchase later.

✔ Use open dating to determine the freshness and shelf life of perishable products.

✔ Use various consumer information sources to assist you with your buying decisions.

✔ Consider the nutritional value and health aspects of the foods you buy.

✔ Evaluate and compare the warranties of different brands.

✔ Read product testing reports to determine which items are the safest and of the highest quality.

✔ Plan your purchases to take advantage of sales and special offers.

✔ Consider the time and effort it takes to evaluate alternatives and go to different stores.

car is sold "as is" and the dealer assumes no responsibility for any repairs, regardless of any oral claims. FTC used-car regulations do not apply to vehicles purchased from private owners.

While a used car may not have an express warranty, most states have implied warranties to protect used-car buyers. An implied warranty of merchantability means the product is guaranteed to do what it is supposed to do. The used car is guaranteed to run—at least for a while!

NEW-CAR WARRANTIES
New-car warranties provide buyers with an assurance of quality. These warranties vary in the time, mileage, and parts they cover. The main conditions of a new-car warranty are (1) coverage of basic parts against defects; (2) power train coverage for the engine, transmission, and drive train; and (3) the corrosion warranty, which usually applies only to holes due to rust, not to surface rust. Other important conditions of a warranty are a statement regarding whether the warranty is transferable to other owners of the car and details about the charges, if any, that will be made for major repairs in the form of a *deductible*.

SERVICE CONTRACTS
A **service contract** is an agreement between a business and a consumer to cover the repair costs of a product. Frequently called *extended warranties,* they are not warranties. For a fee, they insure the buyer against losses due to

Key Web Sites for Warranties
www.ftc.gov
www.consumerautomotive
research.com

service contract An agreement between a business and a consumer to cover the repair costs of a product.

Sheet 18
Consumer Purchase Comparison

the cost of certain repairs. Automotive service contracts can cover repairs not included in the manufacturer's warranty. Service contracts range from $400 to more than $1,000; however, they do not always include everything you might expect. These contracts usually cover failure of the engine cooling system; however, some contracts exclude coverage of such failures if caused by overheating.

Because of costs and exclusions, service contracts may not be a wise financial decision. You can minimize your concern about expensive repairs by setting aside a fund of money to pay for them. Then, if you need repairs, the money to pay for them will be available.

Research-Based Buying

Major buying decisions should be based on a specific decision-making process, which may be viewed in four phases.

PHASE 1: PRESHOPPING ACTIVITIES
Start the buying process with actions that include:

- Problem identification to set a goal and focus your purchasing activities.
- Information gathering to benefit from the buying experiences of others.

PHASE 2: EVALUATING ALTERNATIVES
With every decision, consider various options:

- Attribute assessment with a comparison of product features.
- Price analysis including consideration of the costs at various buying locations.
- Comparison shopping activities to evaluate shopping locations.

PHASE 3: SELECTION AND PURCHASE
When making your final choice, actions may include:

- Negotiation activities to obtain lower price or added quality.
- Payment alternatives including use of cash and various credit plans.
- Assessment of acquisition and installation that might be encountered.

Key Web Sites for Online Comparison Shopping
www.bizrate.com
www.shopzilla.com
www.pricegrabber.com
www.pricescan.com

PHASE 4: POSTPURCHASE ACTIVITIES
After making a purchase, several actions are encouraged:

- Proper maintenance and operation.
- Identification and comparison of after-sale service alternatives.
- Resolution of any purchase concerns that may occur.

✓ CONCEPT CHECK 6–1

1 What types of brands are commonly available to consumers?

_____

_____

2 In what situations can comparing prices help in purchasing decisions?

_____

_____

3 How does a service contract differ from a warranty?

_____

_____

4 Match the following descriptions with the warranties listed here. Write your answer in the space provided.

express warranty   limited warranty

full warranty   service contact

implied warranty

a. _____ covers only aspects of the item purchased.

b. _____ is commonly referred to as an extended warranty.

c. _____ usually is in a written form.

d. _____ covers a product's intended use; it may not be in writing.

e. _____ covers fixing or replacement of a product for a set time period.

Major Consumer Purchases: Buying Motor Vehicles

As shown in Exhibit 6–2, the steps for effective purchasing can be used for wise buying of motor vehicles.

Phase 1: Preshopping Activities

First define your needs and obtain relevant product information. These activities are the foundation for buying decisions to help you achieve your goals.

OBJECTIVE 2
Implement a process for making consumer purchases.

Exhibit 6–2   A Research-Based Approach for Purchasing a Motor Vehicle

1 Preshopping Activities
• Problem identification
• Information gathering

2 Evaluating Alternatives
• Selecting vehicle options
• Comparing used vehicles
• Leasing a vehicle

3 Determining Purchase Price
• Used-car price negotiations
• Price bargaining for new cars
• Comparing financing alternatives

4 Postpurchase Activities
• Automobile operation costs
• Motor vehicle maintenance

Purchasing a Motor Vehicle

PROBLEM IDENTIFICATION   Effective decision making should start with an open mind. Some people always buy the same brand when another brand at a lower price would also serve their needs, or when another brand at the same price may provide better quality. A narrow view of the problem is a weakness in problem identification. You may think the problem is "I need to have a car" when the real problem is "I need transportation."

INFORMATION GATHERING   Information is power. The better informed you are, the better buying decisions you will make. Some people spend very little time gathering and evaluating buying information. At the other extreme are people who spend much time obtaining consumer information. While information is necessary for wise purchasing, too much information can create confusion and frustration. The following information sources are frequently helpful:

Key Web Sites for Consumer Product Information:

www.consumer.gov
www.consumerreports.org
www.consumerworld.org
http://clarkhoward.com

1. *Personal contacts* allow you to learn about product performance, brand quality, and prices from others.
2. *Business organizations* offer advertising, product labels, and packaging that provide information about price, quality, and availability.
3. *Media information* (television, radio, newspapers, magazines, Web sites) can provide valuable information with purchasing advice.
4. *Independent testing organizations,* such as Consumers Union, provide information about the quality of products and services each month in *Consumer Reports.*
5. *Government agencies,* local, state, and federal, provide publications, toll-free telephone numbers, Web sites, and community programs.
6. *Online sources* offer extensive product information and shopping suggestions.

Apply *Yourself!*

Objective 2

Compare the prices charged by different automotive service locations for a battery, tune-up, oil change, and tires.

Phase 2: Evaluating Alternatives

Every purchasing situation usually has several acceptable alternatives. Ask yourself: Is it possible to delay the purchase or to do without the item? Should I pay for the item with cash or buy it on credit? Which brands should I consider? How do the price, quality, and service compare at different stores? Is it possible to rent the item instead of buying it? Considering such alternatives will result in more effective purchasing decisions.

Research shows that prices can vary for all types of products. For a camera, prices may range from under $100 to well over $500. The price of aspirin may range from less than $1 to over $3 for 100 five-grain tablets. While differences in quality and attributes may exist among the cameras, the aspirin are the same in quantity and quality.

Many people view comparison shopping as a waste of time. Although this may be true in certain situations, comparison shopping can be beneficial when (1) buying expensive or complex items; (2) buying items that you purchase often; (3) comparison shopping can be done easily, such as with advertisements, catalogs, or online; (4) different sellers offer different prices and services; and (5) product quality or prices vary greatly.

SELECTING VEHICLE OPTIONS   Optional equipment for cars may be viewed in three categories: (1) mechanical devices to improve performance, such as a larger engine, the transmission, power steering, power brakes, and cruise control; (2) convenience options, including power seats, air conditioning, stereo systems, power locks, rear window defoggers, and tinted glass; and (3) aesthetic features that add to the vehicle's visual appeal, such as metallic paint, special trim, and upholstery.

 CAUTION!

Every year, more than 450,000 people buy used vehicles with mileage gauges rolled back. According to the National Highway Traffic Safety Administration, consumers pay an average of $2,336 more than they should for vehicles with fraudulent mileage totals.

COMPARING USED VEHICLES   The average used car costs about $10,000 less than the average new car. Common sources of used cars include:

- New-car dealers, which offer late-model vehicles and may give you a warranty. Prices usually are higher than at other sources.
- Used-car dealers, which usually have older vehicles. Warranties, if offered, will be limited. However, lower prices may be available.
- Individuals selling their own cars. This can be a bargain if the vehicle was well maintained, but few consumer protection regulations apply to private-party sales. Caution is suggested.
- Auctions and dealers that sell automobiles previously owned by businesses, auto rental companies, and government agencies.
- Used-car superstores, such as CarMax, which offer a large inventory of previously owned vehicles.

Sheet 19
Used-Car Purchase Comparison

Key Web Site for Used Cars

www.dealernet.com

Certified preowned (CPO) vehicles are nearly new cars that come with the original manufacturer's guarantee of quality. The rigorous inspection and repair process means a higher price than other used vehicles. CPO programs were originally created to generate demand for the many low-mileage vehicles returned at the end of a lease.

The appearance of a used car can be deceptive. A well-maintained engine may be inside a body with rust; a clean, shiny exterior may conceal major operational problems. Therefore, conduct a used-car inspection as outlined in Exhibit 6–3. Have a trained and trusted mechanic of *your* choice check the car to estimate the costs of potential repairs. This service will help you avoid surprises.

LEASING A MOTOR VEHICLE   *Leasing* is a contractual agreement with monthly payments for the use of an automobile over a set time period, typically three,

Exhibit 6–3   Checking Out a Used Car

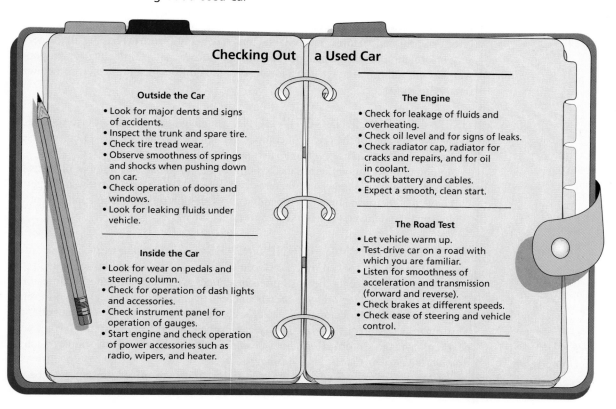

Checking Out | a Used Car

Outside the Car
- Look for major dents and signs of accidents.
- Inspect the trunk and spare tire.
- Check tire tread wear.
- Observe smoothness of springs and shocks when pushing down on car.
- Check operation of doors and windows.
- Look for leaking fluids under vehicle.

Inside the Car
- Look for wear on pedals and steering column.
- Check for operation of dash lights and accessories.
- Check instrument panel for operation of gauges.
- Start engine and check operation of power accessories such as radio, wipers, and heater.

The Engine
- Check for leakage of fluids and overheating.
- Check oil level and for signs of leaks.
- Check radiator cap, radiator for cracks and repairs, and for oil in coolant.
- Check battery and cables.
- Expect a smooth, clean start.

The Road Test
- Let vehicle warm up.
- Test-drive car on a road with which you are familiar.
- Listen for smoothness of acceleration and transmission (forward and reverse).
- Check brakes at different speeds.
- Check ease of steering and vehicle control.

four, or five years. At the end of the lease term, the vehicle is usually returned to the leasing company.

Leasing offers several advantages: (1) only a small cash outflow may be required for the security deposit, whereas buying can require a large down payment; (2) monthly lease payments are usually lower than monthly financing payments; (3) the lease agreement provides detailed records for business purposes; and (4) you are usually able to obtain a more expensive vehicle, more often.

Leasing also has major drawbacks: (1) you have no ownership interest in the vehicle; (2) you must meet requirements similar to qualifying for credit; and (3) additional costs may be incurred for extra mileage, certain repairs, turning the car in early, or even a move to another state.

When leasing, you arrange for the dealer to sell the vehicle through a financing company. As a result, be sure you know the true cost, including

1. The *capitalized cost,* which is the price of the vehicle. The average car buyer pays about 92 percent of the list price for a vehicle; the average leasing arrangement has a capitalized cost of 96 percent of the list price.
2. The *money factor,* which is the interest rate being paid on the capitalized cost.
3. The *payment schedule,* which is the amount paid monthly and the number of payments.
4. The *residual value,* or the expected value of the vehicle at the end of the lease.

After the final payment, you may return, keep, or sell the vehicle. If the current market value is greater than the residual value, you may be able to sell it for a profit. If the residual value is less than the market value (which is the typical case), returning the vehicle to the leasing company is usually the best decision.

Phase 3: Determining Purchase Price

Once you've done your research and evaluations, other activities and decisions may be appropriate. Products such as real estate or automobiles may be purchased using price negotiation. Negotiation may also be used in other buying situations to obtain a lower price or additional features. Two vital factors in negotiation are (1) having all the necessary information about the product and buying situation and (2) dealing with a person who has the authority to give you a lower price or additional features, such as the owner or store manager.

USED-CAR PRICE NEGOTIATION   Begin to determine a fair price by checking newspaper ads for the prices of comparable vehicles. Other sources of current used-car prices are *Edmund's Used Car Prices* and the *Kelley Blue Book.*

A number of factors influence the basic price of a used car. The number of miles the car has been driven, along with features and options, affect price. A low-mileage car will have a higher price than a comparable car with high mileage. The condition of the vehicle and the demand for the model also affect price.

PRICE BARGAINING FOR NEW CARS   An important new-car price information source is the *sticker price* label, printed on the vehicle with the suggested retail price. This label presents the base price of the car with costs of added features. The dealer's cost, or *invoice price,* is an amount less than the sticker price. The difference between the sticker price and the dealer's cost is the range available for negotiation. This range is larger for full-size, luxury cars; subcompacts usually do not have a wide negotiation range. Information about dealer's cost is available from sources such as *Edmund's New Car Prices* and *Consumer Reports.*

Set-price dealers use no-haggling car selling with the prices presented to be accepted or rejected as stated. *Car-buying services* are businesses that help buyers obtain a

Key Web Sites for Leasing
www.leasesource.com
www.leaseguide.com

Sheet 20
*Buying vs.
Leasing an
Automobile*

Key Web Sites for Used Car Prices
www.edmunds.com
www.kbb.com

Key Web Sites for New Cars
www.edmunds.com
www.consumerreports.org

Figure It Out!

› Buying versus Leasing an Automobile

To compare the costs of purchasing and leasing a vehicle, use the following framework.

PURCHASE COSTS	EXAMPLE	YOUR FIGURES
Total vehicle cost, including sales tax ($22,000)		
Down payment (or full amount if paying cash)	$2,000	$_____
Monthly loan payment: $469.70 × 48-month length of financing (this item is zero if vehicle is not financed)	22,545	_____
Opportunity cost of down payment (or total cost of the vehicle if bought for cash): $2,000 × 4 years of financing/ownership × 3 percent	240	_____
Less: Estimated value of vehicle at end of loan term/ownership period	−6,000	−_____
Total cost to buy	$18,785	_____

LEASING COSTS	EXAMPLE	YOUR FIGURES
Security deposit ($370)		
Monthly lease payments: $300 × 48-month length of lease	$17,760	$_____
Opportunity cost of security deposit: $300 security deposit × 4 years × 3 percent	36	_____
End-of-lease charges (if applicable)*	800	_____
Total cost to lease	$18,596	_____

*With a closed-end lease, charges for extra mileage or excessive wear and tear; with an open-end lease, end-of-lease payment if appraised value is less than estimated ending value.

specific new car at a reasonable price. Also referred to as an *auto broker,* these businesses offer desired models with options for prices ranging between $50 and $200 over the dealer's cost. First, the auto broker charges a small fee for price information on desired models. Then, if you decide to buy a car, the auto broker arranges the purchase with a dealer near your home.

To prevent confusion in determining the true price of the new car, do not mention a trade-in vehicle until the cost of the new car has been settled. Then ask how much the dealer is willing to pay for your old car. If the offer price is not acceptable, sell the old car on your own. A typical negotiating conversation might go like this:

Customer: "I'm willing to give you $15,600 for the car. That's my top offer."

Auto salesperson: "Let me check with my manager." After returning, "My manager says $16,200 is the best we can do."

Customer (who should be willing to walk out at this point): "I can go to $15,650."

Auto salesperson: "We have the car you want, ready to go. How about $15,700?"

If the customer agrees, the dealer has gotten $100 more than the customer's "top offer."

Other sales techniques you should avoid include:

* *Lowballing,* when quoted a very low price that increases when add-on costs are included at the last moment.

did you know?

One study found that just 9 percent of car buyers drawn in by 0 percent financing promotions actually obtained that rate.

- *Highballing,* when offered a very high amount for a trade-in vehicle, with the extra amount made up by increasing the new-car price.
- The question "How much can you afford per month?" Be sure to also ask how many months.
- The offer to hold the vehicle for a small deposit only. Never leave a deposit unless you are ready to buy a vehicle or are willing to lose that amount.
- Unrealistic statements, such as "Your price is only $100 above our cost." Usually, hidden costs have been added in to get the dealer's cost.
- Sales agreements with preprinted amounts. Cross out numbers you believe are not appropriate for your purchase.

COMPARING FINANCING ALTERNATIVES   You may pay cash; however, most people buy cars on credit. Auto loans are available from banks, credit unions, consumer finance companies, and other financial institutions. Many lenders will *preapprove* you for a certain loan amount, which separates financing from negotiating the car price. Until the new-car price is set, you should not indicate that you intend to use the dealer's credit plan.

The lowest interest rate or the lowest payment does not necessarily mean the best credit plan. Also consider the loan length. Otherwise, after two or three years, the value of your car may be less than the amount you still owe; this situation is referred to as *upside-down* or *negative equity.* If you default on your loan or sell the car at this time, you will have to pay the difference.

Automobile manufacturers frequently present opportunities for low-interest financing. They may offer rebates at the same time, giving buyers a choice between a rebate and a low-interest loan. Carefully compare low-interest financing and the rebate. Special rebates are sometimes offered to students, teachers, credit union members, real estate agents, and other groups.

Phase 4: Postpurchase Activities

Maintenance and ownership costs are associated with most major purchases. Correct use can result in improved performance and fewer repairs. When you need repairs not covered by a warranty, follow a pattern similar to that used when making the original purchase. Investigate, evaluate, and negotiate a variety of servicing options.

In the past, when major problems occurred with a new car and the warranty didn't solve the difficulty, many consumers lacked a course of action. As a result, all 50 states and the District of Columbia enacted *lemon laws* that require a refund for the vehicle after the owner has made repeated attempts to obtain servicing. These laws apply to situations in which a person has made four attempts to get the same problem corrected or situations in which the vehicle has been out of service for more than 30 days within 12 months of purchase or the first 12,000 miles. The terms of the state laws vary.

Key Web Site for Lemon Laws
www.lemonlawamerica.com

AUTOMOBILE OPERATION COSTS   Over your lifetime, you can expect to spend more than $200,000 on automobile-related expenses. Your driving costs will vary based on two main factors: the size of your automobile and the number of miles you drive. These costs involve two categories:

Fixed Ownership Costs	Variable Operating Costs
Depreciation	Gasoline and oil
Interest on auto loan	Tires
Insurance	Maintenance and repairs
License, registration, taxes, and fees	Parking and tolls

ABCs of a great CAR LOAN

IN THE Internet age, finding new-car data to use as haggling ammo is easy. But many buyers who spend days whittling the sticker price let down their guard and hand the savings back when they accept a dealer's car-loan rate. It's easy to see why. The rate you get depends on information that's not always easy to come by. Plus, dealers put their most talented closers in the financing-and-insurance office, where you are subjected to a rash of offers for extended warranties and other add-ons as well as a blizzard of paperwork that can exhaust you into submission.

Dealers have also been known to bump the rate above what you should pay based on your credit history. If you qualify for a 6.5% rate but the dealer charges 8% on a 60-month, $20,000 car loan, you pay $900 more in interest. That's extra profit for the dealer.

Where do you stand? The interest rate you pay depends on the credit "tier" you fall into. Tier A and sometimes tier B borrowers get the best rates; E borrowers pay up to 30% interest. On five-year loans, A-credit customers shopping for a new vehicle could recently command rates of 6% to 7%, or as low as 0% on vehicles sporting low-rate incentives.

The tier you fall into depends mostly on your credit score, so the first thing you should do is research that number. You can get a free credit report once a year from each of the big-three credit bureaus at www.annualcreditreport.com, but you usually have to pay $6 or so to get your credit *score*. FICO scores, the most popular flavor, range from 300 to 850. About half of all car buyers who finance a vehicle have a score above 720 (tier A), according to a study by the Consumer Banker's Association.

Another 25% beat 680 (tier B). If you have a borderline score, you could be boosted into a higher tier if you make a sizable down payment or shorten the loan term.

In the U.S., the average down payment for a car is $2,400, the average amount financed is $24,864, and the average monthly payment is $479, according to Edmunds.com. The most popular loan term is now a payment-stretching six years.

Avoid the traps. A few simple strategies will prevent you from being fleeced in the dealer's finance office. Your best bet is to have a good loan rate in the bag before you even set foot on the car lot. First, find out the annual percentage rate you qualify for, and then get pre-qualified for a loan from your bank, your credit union or an online lender. If the dealership can't beat the rate, politely decline its loan.

A corollary is to keep all transactions—price of the car, value of the trade-in and financing—separate. If you let the dealer merge them, it's tough to know if you're getting the best deal on each one. And a dealer who knows how much you'd like your monthly payment to be can play with the price, options, trade-in value and interest rate to come up with what you budgeted—often by extending the loan term.

Should you take a low-rate-financing incentive instead of a cash rebate? Zero percent is hard to beat, but if your loan rate is low, say 4.9%, the decision is tougher. One rule of thumb is to take the cash if you plan to keep the vehicle less than three years.

Writing a check from your deductible home-equity line of credit isn't always a good strategy. It's probably better to keep the home-equity funds intact for other financial needs.

Source: Reprinted by permission from the February issue of *Kiplinger's Personal Finance*. Copyright © 2007 The Kiplinger Washington Editors, Inc.

from the pages of . . . **Kiplinger's Personal Finance**

1. Describe how your FICO score might affect your motor vehicle financing decision.

2. What actions should be taken to avoid various traps when accepting financing from a car dealer?

3. What information is available at www.kiplinger.com that might be useful when buying and financing a car?

Exhibit 6–4   Extended Vehicle Life with Proper Maintenance

- Get regular oil changes.
- Check fluids (brake, power steering, transmission).
- Inspect hoses and belts for wear.
- Get a tune-up (new spark plugs, fuel filter, air filter) 12,000–15,000 miles.
- Check and clean battery cables and terminals.
- Check spark plug wires after 50,000 miles.
- Flush radiator and service transmission every 25,000 miles.
- Keep lights, turn signals, and horn in good working condition.
- Check muffler and exhaust pipes.
- Check tires for wear; rotate tires every 7,500 miles.
- Check condition of brakes.

The largest fixed expense associated with a new automobile is *depreciation,* the loss in the vehicle's value due to time and use. Since money is not paid out for depreciation, many people do not consider it an expense. However, this decreased value is a cost that owners incur. Well-maintained vehicles and certain high-quality, expensive models, such as BMW and Lexus, depreciate at a slower rate.

Costs such as gasoline, oil, and tires increase with the number of miles driven. Planning expenses is easier if the number of miles you drive is fairly constant. Unexpected trips and vehicle age will increase such costs.

MOTOR VEHICLE MAINTENANCE   People who sell, repair, or drive automobiles for a living stress the importance of regular care. While owner's manuals and articles suggest mileage or time intervals for certain servicing, more frequent oil changes or tune-ups can minimize major repairs and maximize vehicle life. Exhibit 6–4 suggests maintenance areas to consider.

AUTOMOBILE SERVICING SOURCES   The following businesses offer automobile maintenance and repair service:

- Car dealers provide a service department with a wide range of car care services. Service charges at a car dealer may be higher than those of other repair businesses.
- Service stations can provide convenience and reasonable prices for routine maintenance and repairs. However, the number of full-service stations has declined in recent years.
- Independent auto repair shops can service your vehicle at fairly competitive prices. Since the quality of these repair shops varies, talk with previous customers.
- Mass merchandise retailers, such as Sears and Wal-Mart, may emphasize sale of tires and batteries as well as brakes, oil changes, and tune-ups.
- Specialty shops offer brakes, tires, automatic transmissions, and oil changes at a reasonable price with fast service.

To avoid unnecessary expenses, be aware of the common repair frauds presented in Exhibit 6–5. Remember to deal with reputable auto service businesses. Be sure to get a written, detailed estimate in advance as well as a detailed, paid receipt for the service completed. Studies of consumer problems consistently rank auto repairs as one of the top consumer ripoffs. Many people avoid problems and minimize costs by working on their own vehicles.

Exhibit 6–5   Common Automobile Repair Frauds

The majority of automobile servicing sources are fair and honest. Sometimes, however, consumers waste dollars when they fall prey to the following tricks:

- When checking the oil, the attendant puts the dipstick only partway down and then shows you that you need oil.

- An attendant cuts a fan belt or punctures a hose. Watch carefully when someone checks under your hood.

- A garage employee puts some liquid on your battery and then tries to convince you that it is leaking and you need a new battery.

- Removing air from a tire instead of adding air to it can make an unwary driver open to buying a new tire or paying for an unneeded patch on a tire that is in perfect condition.

- The attendant puts grease near a shock absorber or on the ground and then tells you your present shocks are dangerous and you need new ones.

- You are charged for two gallons of antifreeze with a radiator flush when only one gallon was put in.

Dealing with reputable businesses and a basic knowledge of your automobile are the best methods of avoiding deceptive repair practices.

✓ CONCEPT CHECK 6–2

1 What are the major sources of consumer information?

_____

_____

2 What actions are appropriate when buying a used car?

_____

_____

3 When might leasing a motor vehicle be appropriate?

_____

_____

4 What maintenance activities could reduce the life of your vehicle?

_____

_____

5 The following abbreviations appeared in an ad for selling used cars. Interpret these abbreviations.

AC _____   pwr mrrs _____

ABS _____   P/S   _____

Resolving Consumer Complaints

OBJECTIVE 3
Describe steps to take to resolve consumer problems.

Most customer complaints result from defective products, low quality, short product lives, unexpected costs, deceptive pricing, and poor repairs. Federal consumer agencies estimate annual consumer losses from fraudulent business activities at $10 billion to $40 billion for telemarketing and mail order, $3 billion for credit card fraud and credit "repair" scams, and $10 billion for investment swindles. In addition, consumers commonly encounter problems with motor vehicles, mail-order purchases, work-at-home opportunities, dry cleaning, travel services, magazine subscriptions, contests, and sweepstakes.

People do not anticipate problems with purchases but should be prepared for them. Exhibit 6–6 outlines the process for resolving differences. To help ensure success, keep a file of receipts, names of people you talked to, dates of attempted repairs, copies of letters you wrote, and costs incurred. An automobile owner kept detailed records and receipts for all gasoline purchases, oil changes, and repairs. When a warranty dispute occurred, the owner was able to prove proper maintenance and received a refund for the defective vehicle.

Apply *Yourself!*

Objective 3

Conduct online research to determine the most frequent sources of consumer complaints.

Key Web Site for Company Addresses

www.consumeraction.gov

Step 1: Return to Place of Purchase

Most consumer complaints are resolved at the original sales location. As you talk with the salesperson, customer service person, or store manager, avoid yelling, threatening a lawsuit, or demanding unreasonable action. A calm, rational, yet persistent approach is recommended.

did you know?

An AARP study reports that just over half of consumers (52 percent) said they would go back to the source when they have a complaint about a product or service. A third (34 percent) would report the company to the Better Business Bureau, while fewer than one in five (17 percent) said they would contact the manufacturer or company headquarters.

Step 2: Contact Company Headquarters

Express your dissatisfaction to the corporate level if a problem is not resolved at the local store. Use a letter or e-mail such as the one in Exhibit 6–7. You can obtain addresses of companies at www.consumeraction.gov or in reference books at your library. The Web sites of companies usually provide information for contacting the organization. You can obtain a company's consumer hotline number by calling 1-800-555-1212, the toll-free information number. Many companies print the toll-free hotline number and Web site information on product packages.

Exhibit 6–6

Suggested Steps for Resolving Consumer Complaints

Step 1   Local communication…

Step 2   Higher-level communication…

Step 3   Third-party involvement…

Step 4   Litigation…

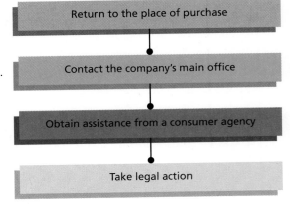

Return to the place of purchase

Contact the company's main office

Obtain assistance from a consumer agency

Take legal action

Exhibit 6–7   Sample Complaint Letter or E-mail

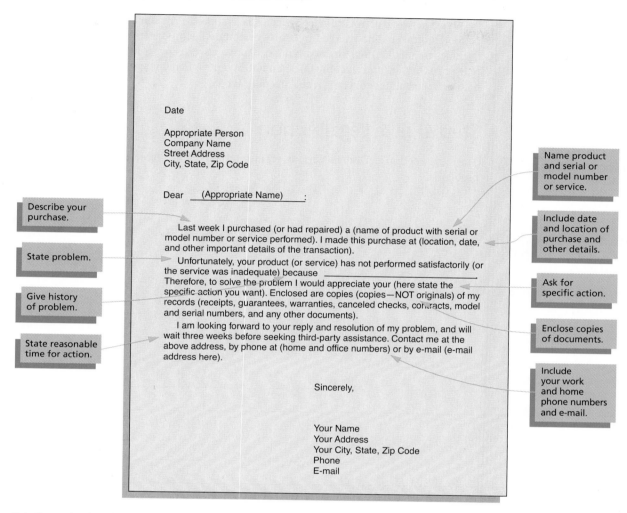

Describe your purchase.

State problem.

Give history of problem.

State reasonable time for action.

Date

Appropriate Person
Company Name
Street Address
City, State, Zip Code

Dear   (Appropriate Name)   :

    Last week I purchased (or had repaired) a (name of product with serial or model number or service performed). I made this purchase at (location, date, and other important details of the transaction).
    Unfortunately, your product (or service) has not performed satisfactorily (or the service was inadequate) because _____
    Therefore, to solve the problem I would appreciate your (here state the specific action you want). Enclosed are copies (copies—NOT originals) of my records (receipts, guarantees, warranties, canceled checks, contracts, model and serial numbers, and any other documents).
    I am looking forward to your reply and resolution of my problem, and will wait three weeks before seeking third-party assistance. Contact me at the above address, by phone at (home and office numbers) or by e-mail (e-mail address here).

                              Sincerely,

                              Your Name
                              Your Address
                              Your City, State, Zip Code
                              Phone
                              E-mail

Name product and serial or model number or service.

Include date and location of purchase and other details.

Ask for specific action.

Enclose copies of documents.

Include your work and home phone numbers and e-mail.

Note: Keep copies of your letter and all related documents and information.

Source: *Consumer's Resource Handbook* (www.pueblo.gsa.gov).

mediation The attempt by an impartial third party to resolve a difference between two parties through discussion and negotiation.

Step 3: Obtain Consumer Agency Assistance

If you do not receive satisfaction from the company, organizations are available to assist with automobiles, appliances, health care, and other consumer concerns. **Mediation** involves the use of a third party to settle grievances. In mediation, an impartial person—the *mediator*—tries to resolve a conflict between a customer and a business through discussion and negotiation. Mediation is a nonbinding process. It can save time and money compared to other dispute settlement methods.

    Arbitration is the settlement of a difference by a third party—the *arbitrator*—whose decision is legally binding. After both sides agree to arbitration, each side presents its case. Arbitrators are selected from volunteers

CAUTION!

Without realizing it, many consumers sign contracts with provisions that stipulate arbitration as the method to resolve disputes. As a result, consumers face various risks, including rules vastly different from a jury trial, higher costs for the arbitrator's time, and selection of an arbitrator by the defendant.

arbitration The settlement of a difference by a third party whose decision is legally binding.

trained for this purpose. Most major automobile manufacturers and many industry organizations have arbitration programs to resolve consumer complaints.

A vast network of government agencies is available. Problems with local restaurants or food stores may be handled by a city or county health department. Every state has agencies to handle problems involving deceptive advertising, fraudulent business practices, banking, insurance companies, and utility rates. Federal agencies are available to help with consumer concerns (see Appendix B).

Step 4: Take Legal Action

The next section considers various legal alternatives available to resolve consumer problems.

Key Web Sites for Consumer Concerns

www.consumer.gov

www.complaints.com

www.bbbonline.org/consumer/complaint.asp

✔ CONCEPT CHECK 6–3

1 What are common causes of consumer problems and complaints?

_____

_____

2 How can most consumer complaints be resolved?

_____

_____

3 How does arbitration differ from mediation?

_____

_____

Legal Options for Consumers

OBJECTIVE 4
Evaluate legal alternatives available to consumers.

If the previous actions fail to resolve your complaint, one of the following may be appropriate.

Small Claims Court

small claims court A court that settles legal differences involving amounts below a set limit and employs a process in which the litigants usually do not use a lawyer.

In **small claims court,** a person may file a claim involving amounts below a set dollar limit. The maximum varies from state to state, ranging from $500 to $10,000; most states have a limit of between $1,500 and $3,000. The process usually takes place without a lawyer, although in many states attorneys are allowed in small claims court. To effectively use small claims court, experts suggest that you:

- Become familiar with court procedures and filing fees (usually from $5 to $50).
- Observe other cases to learn about the process.
- Present your case in a polite, calm, and concise manner.

› Is It Legal?

The following situations are common problems for consumers. How would you respond to the question at the end of each situation?

	Yes	No

1. A store advertised a bottle of shampoo as "the $1.79 size, on sale for 99¢." If the store never sold the item for $1.79 but the manufacturer's recommended price was $1.79, was this a legitimate price comparison? ___ ___

2. You purchase a stereo system for $650. Two days later, the same store offers the same item for $425. Is this legal? ___ ___

3. You receive an unordered sample of flower seeds in the mail. You decide to plant them to see how well they will grow in your yard. A couple of days later, you receive a bill for the seeds. Do you have to pay for the seeds? ___ ___

4. A store has a "going out of business sale—everything must go" sign in its window. After six months, the sign is still there. Is this a deceptive business practice? ___ ___

5. A 16-year-old injured while playing ball at a local park is taken to a hospital for medical care. The parents refuse to pay the hospital since they didn't request the service. Can the parents be held legally responsible for the charges? ___ ___

6. You purchase a shirt for a friend. The shirt doesn't fit, but when you return it to the store, you are offered an exchange since the store policy is no cash refunds. Is this legal? ___ ___

7. A manufacturer refuses to repair a motorcycle that is still under warranty. The manufacturer can prove that the motorcycle was used improperly. If this is true, must the manufacturer honor the warranty? ___ ___

8. An employee of a store incorrectly marks the price of an item at a lower amount. Is the store obligated to sell the item at the lower price? ___ ___

Circumstances, interpretations of the law, and store policies, as well as state and local laws, can affect the above situations. The generally accepted answers are *no* for 1, 3, 7, and 8; *yes* for 2, 4, 5, and 6.

- Submit evidence such as photographs, contracts, receipts, and other documents.
- Use witnesses who can testify on your behalf.

class-action suit A legal action taken by a few individuals on behalf of all the people who have suffered the same alleged injustice.

Class-Action Suits

Occasionally a number of people have the same complaint. A **class-action suit** is a legal action taken by a few individuals on behalf of all the people who have suffered the same alleged injustice. These people are represented by one or more lawyers. Once a situation qualifies as a class-action suit, all of the affected parties must be notified. A person may decide not to participate in the class-action suit and instead file an individual lawsuit. Recent class-action suits included auto owners who were sold unneeded replacement parts for their vehicles and a group of investors who sued a brokerage company for unauthorized buy-and-sell transactions that resulted in high commission charges.

did you know?

A class-action suit can be expensive. After winning $2.19 in back interest, Dexter J. Kamilewicz also noted a $91.33 "miscellaneous deduction" on his mortgage escrow account. This charge was his portion for lawyers he never knew he hired to win a class-action suit.

Apply *Yourself!*

Objective 4

Interview someone who has had a consumer complaint. What was the basis of the complaint? What actions were taken? Was the complaint resolved in a satisfactory manner?

legal aid society One of a network of publicly supported community law offices that provide legal assistance to consumers who cannot afford their own attorney.

Key Web Sites for Legal Questions

www.nolo.com

www.smallclaimscourt.com

Sheet 21
Legal Services Cost Comparison

Using a Lawyer

In some situations, you may seek the services of an attorney. Common sources of lawyers are referrals from friends, advertisements, and the local division of the American Bar Association.

In general, straightforward legal situations such as appearing in small claims court, renting an apartment, or defending yourself on a minor traffic violation may not need legal counsel. More complicated matters such as writing a will, settling a real estate purchase, or suing for injury damages will likely require the services of an attorney.

When selecting a lawyer, consider several questions: Is the lawyer experienced in your type of case? Will you be charged on a flat fee basis, at an hourly rate, or on a contingency basis? Is there a fee for the initial consultation? How and when will you be required to make payment for services?

Other Legal Alternatives

Legal services can be expensive. A **legal aid society** is one of a network of publicly supported community law offices that provide legal assistance to people who cannot afford their own attorney. These community agencies provide this assistance at a minimal cost or without charge.

Prepaid legal services provide unlimited or reduced-fee legal assistance for a set fee. Some programs provide basic services, such as telephone consultation and preparation of a simple will, for an annual fee. Prepaid legal programs are designed to prevent minor troubles from becoming complicated legal problems.

✓ CONCEPT CHECK 6–4

1 In what types of situations would small claims court and class-action suits be helpful?

_____

_____

2 Describe situations in which you might use the services of a lawyer.

_____

_____

3 For the following situations, identify the legal action that would be most appropriate to take.

a. _____ A low-income person wants to obtain the services of a lawyer to file a product-liability suit.

b. _____ A person is attempting to obtain a $150 deposit for catering that was never returned.

c. _____ A consumer wants to settle a dispute out of court with the use of a legally binding third party.

d. _____ A group of telephone customers were overcharged by $1.10 a month over the past 22 months.

back to *Getting Personal*

1. Reconsider your responses to the Getting Personal questions at the beginning of the chapter. Which items might have different answers now or in the future as a result of studying this chapter?

_____

_____

2. What buying strategies learned in this chapter could be of value to you in the future?

_____

_____

3. Identify a major consumer purchase you might make in the future. Describe possible actions for each phase of the buying process that you might take for that item.

Research–Buying Process	Actions for Buying _____
Phase 1: Preshopping Activities Problem identification Information gathering	
Phase 2: Evaluating Alternatives Attribute assessment Price analysis Comparison shopping	
Phase 3: Selection and Purchase Negotiation activities Payment alternatives Acquisition and installation	
Phase 4: Postpurchase Activities Proper maintenance, operation After-sale service alternatives Resolving any purchase concerns	

www.mhhe.com/kdh

Chapter Summary

Objective 1   Timing purchases, comparing stores and brands, using label information, computing unit prices, and evaluating warranties are common strategies for effective purchasing.

Objective 2   A research-based approach to consumer buying involves (1) preshopping activities, such as problem identification and information gathering; (2) evaluating alternatives; (3) determining the purchase price; and (4) postpurchase activities, such as proper operation and maintenance.

Objective 3   Most consumer problems can be resolved by following these steps: (1) return to the place of purchase; (2) contact the company's main office; (3) obtain assistance from a consumer agency; and (4) take legal action.

Objective 4   Small claims court, class-action suits, the services of a lawyer, legal aid societies, and prepaid legal services are legal means for handling consumer problems that cannot be resolved through communication with the company involved or with help from a consumer protection agency.

Key Terms

arbitration   196

class-action suit   197

legal aid society   198

mediation   195

service contract   183

small claims court   196

warranty   182

Problems

1. An online buying club offers a membership for $175, for which you will receive a 10 percent discount on all brand-name items you purchase. How much would you have to buy to cover the cost of the membership?

2. John Walters is comparing the cost of credit to the cash price of an item. If John makes a $60 down payment and pays $32 a month for 24 months, how much more will that amount be than the cash price of $685?

3. Calculate the unit price of each of the following items:

   a. Motor oil—2.5 quarts for $1.95   _____ cents/quart

   b. Cereal—15 ounces for $2.17   _____ cents/ounce

   c. Canned fruit—13 ounces for 89 cents   _____ cents/ounce

   d. Facial tissue—300 tissues for $2.25   _____ cents/100 tissues

4. A service contract for new video television projection system costs $120 a year. You expect to use the system for five years. Instead of buying the service contract, what would be the future value of these annual amounts after five years if you earn 4 percent on your savings?

5. Based on financial and opportunity costs, which of the following do you believe would be the wiser purchase?

   Vehicle 1: A three-year-old car with 45,000 miles, costing $6,700 and requiring $385 of immediate repairs.

   Vehicle 2: A five-year-old car with 62,000 miles, costing $4,500 and requiring $760 of immediate repairs.

6. A work-at-home opportunity is available in which you will receive 3 percent of the sales for customers you refer to the company. The cost of your "franchise fee" is $840. How much would your customers have to buy to cover the cost of this fee?

7. Based on the following data, prepare a financial comparison of buying and leasing a motor vehicle with a $24,000 cash price:

   Down payment (to finance vehicle), $4,000   Down payment for lease, $1,200
   Monthly loan payment, $560   Monthly lease payment, $440
   Length of loan, 48 months   Length of lease, 48 months
   Value of vehicle at end of loan, $7,200   End-of-lease charges, $600

   What other factors should a person consider when choosing between buying and leasing?

8. What would be the net present value of a microwave oven that costs $159 and will save you $68 a year in time and food away from home? Assume an average return on your savings of 4 percent for five years. (Hint: Calculate the present value of the annual savings, then subtract the cost of the microwave.)

9. Based on the data provided here, calculate the items requested:

Annual depreciation, $2,500

Current year's loan interest, $650

Insurance, $680

Average gasoline price, $2.10 per gallon

Parking/tolls, $420

Annual mileage, 13,200

Miles per gallon, 24

License and registration fees, $65

Oil changes/repairs, $370

  a. The total annual operating cost of the motor vehicle.

  b. The operating cost per mile.

10. A class-action suit against a utility company resulted in a settlement of $1.2 million for 62,000 customers. If the legal fees, which must be paid from the settlement, are $300,000, what amount will each plaintiff receive?

Questions

1. Describe how advertisements, news articles, online sources, and personal observations might be used to make wiser buying decisions.

2. When using the research-based approach for purchasing described in this chapter, which actions do you believe are overlooked by most shoppers?

3. What are potential concerns associated with obtaining furniture, appliances, and other items from a rent-to-own business?

4. What is a "certified preowned" vehicle? What are the benefits and drawbacks of this type of purchase?

5. What actions would you recommend to a person when evaluating and comparing automobile prices?

Internet Connection

OBTAINING CONSUMER PROTECTION ASSISTANCE

A variety of local, state, and federal government agencies provide consumer information and assistance. In addition, many other organizations provide consumer assistance. Conduct a Web search to locate a local, state, and federal agency or organization available to assist consumers.

Consumer assistance agency or organization	Local (city or county) agency	State agency	Federal agency
Name of agency or organization			
Phone			
Web address			
Main purpose, services provided			
Types of assistance provided; types of consumer problems			
Publications or information provided online			

Case in Point

BUYING ONLINE WITHOUT GOING OUT OF YOUR MIND

Amie Carver needed a birthday gift for her mother. She knew of several online sites with items her mother would like. Amie saw a sweater her mother would probably like. "This looks very nice," she thought. "And it's quite reasonably priced."

Amie placed an order online using her credit card. Within a week, she received the sweater. But when she opened the package, she noticed the style of the sweater was different than it looked online. "Oh no, this isn't what I wanted," she thought.

Amie called the company to find out how to return the item. The company told her to send the sweater back for a refund. While the company would pay the return postage, Amie was not refunded the original shipping and handling charges.

Later that day, Amie saw a table lamp for sale online. "This is a nice gift for Mother," she thought. After putting the item in her online shopping cart, she received a message notice that the item would not be available for four to six weeks.

With more than 70 percent of Internet users buying online, there will be problems. One study revealed that one in five survey respondents had a problem with online shopping. A major concern is getting something different from what was expected. While consumers have a strong concern about being charged for something they never agreed to, only a very small percentage of online shoppers have this problem.

Some online shopping Web sites charge a "restocking" fee for an item that is returned. Most will also make the consumer pay for the shipping when returning a product. Carefully check the company's return policies.

Questions

1. What benefits and drawbacks are associated with online shopping?

2. What actions might a consumer take before making an online purchase?

3. Conduct an Internet search to obtain suggestions for action to avoid online shopping problems.

Continuing Case

PURCHASING CHOICES

Life Situation	Financial Data	
Young married couple	Monthly income	$3,600
Pam, 30	Assets	$33,850
Josh, 32	Living expenses	$3,125
Two children, ages 1 and 3	Liabilities	$1,520

The Brocks now have two preschool-age children. Their household income has declined with Pam providing full-time care for the children. To compensate for their lower monthly income, Pam and Josh have cut back to spend money on basics only. As a result of this action, the Brocks have managed to pay down their liabilities over the past four years.

The Brocks are considering purchasing a second automobile. Currently, Pam must drive Josh to the train station (creating many inconveniences for her and the children) if she wants to use the car for various business and education activities.

Questions

1. What major factors could affect the Brocks' spending habits?

2. What transportation alternatives should the Brocks consider? If they decide that they need a second motor vehicle, how should they finance it?

3. Describe how various elements of *Your Personal Financial Plan* sheets 18–21 could be useful to the Brocks when making various purchasing decisions.

Video Case

BUYING CARS ONLINE

Today, most car shoppers obtain various types of information online before going to the dealer. Although most purchases are still being made in person, Web sites are becoming increasingly available to finalize the sale through the Internet. Soon, buying a motor vehicle online is expected to be almost as easy as buying books, videos, and other consumer products.

Questions

1. How is the Internet best used when buying a motor vehicle?

2. What are the benefits and drawbacks of using the Web site of an automobile manufacturer?

3. Locate a Web site that might be used when buying a car. What features would be most useful in the car buying process?

Spending Diary

"USING THE DAILY SPENDING DIARY HAS HELPED ME CONTROL IMPULSE BUYING. WHEN I HAVE TO WRITE DOWN EVERY AMOUNT, I'M MORE CAREFUL WITH MY SPENDING. I CAN NOW PUT MORE IN SAVINGS."

Directions

Start (or continue) your Daily Spending Diary or use your own format to record and monitor spending in various categories. Most people who have participated in this activity have found it beneficial for monitoring and controlling their spending habits.

Questions

1. What daily spending items are amounts that might be reduced or eliminated to allow for higher savings amounts?

2. How might a Daily Spending Diary result in wiser consumer buying and more saving for the future?

www.mhhe.com/kdh

Consumer Purchase Comparison

Financial Planning Activities: When considering the purchase of a major consumer item, use ads, catalogs, the Internet, store visits, and other sources to obtain the information below.

Suggested Web Sites: www.consumerreports.org   www.consumer.gov   http://clarkhoward.com

Product

Exact description (size, model, features, etc.)

Research the item in consumer periodicals and online for information regarding your product

article/periodical _____   **Web site** _____

date/pages _____   **date** _____

What buying suggestions are presented in the articles?

Which brands are recommended in these articles? Why?

Contact or visit two or three stores that sell the product to obtain the following information:

	Store 1	Store 2	Store 3
Company			
Address			
Phone/Web site			
Brand name/cost			
Product difference from item above			
Warranty (describe)			
Which brand and at which store would you buy this product? Why?			

What's Next for Your Personal Financial Plan?

- Which consumer information sources are most valuable for your future buying decisions?

- List guidelines to use in the future when making major purchases.

Used-Car Purchase Comparison

Financial Planning Activities: When considering a used car purchase, use advertisements, online sources, and visits to new- and used-car dealers to obtain the information below.

Suggested Web Sites: www.carbuyingtips.com   www.kbb.com

Automobile (year, make, model)			
Name			
Address			
Phone			
Web site (if applicable)			
Cost			
Mileage			
Condition of auto			
Condition of tires			
Radio			
Air conditioning			
Other options			
Warranty (describe)			
Items in need of repair			
Inspection items: • Rust, major dents?			
• Oil or fluid leaks?			
• Condition of brakes?			
• Proper operation of heater, wipers, other accessories?			
Other information			

What's Next for Your Personal Financial Plan?

- Maintain a record of automobile operating costs.
- Prepare a plan for regular maintenance of your vehicle.

Buying vs. Leasing an Automobile

Financial Planning Activities: Obtain cost information to compare leasing and buying a vehicle.

Suggested Web Sites: www.leasesource.com   www.kiplinger.com/tools

Purchase Costs

Total vehicle cost, including sales tax ($ _____)

Down payment (or full amount if paying cash) $ _____

Monthly loan payment: $ _____ times _____ month loan
(this item is zero if vehicle is not financed) $ _____

Opportunity cost of down payment (or total cost of the vehicle if bought
for cash):

$ _____ times number of years of financing/ownership times _____
percent (interest rate which funds could earn) $ _____

Less: estimated value of vehicle at end of loan term/ownership $ _____

Total cost to buy . . . . $ _____

Leasing Costs

Security deposit $ _____

Monthly lease payments: $ _____ times _____ months $ _____

Opportunity cost of security deposit: $ _____ times years
times _____ percent $ _____

End-of-lease charges (if applicable*) $ _____

Total cost to lease . . . . $ _____

*With a closed-end lease, charges for extra mileage or excessive wear and tear; with an open-end lease, end-of-lease payment if appraised value is less than estimated ending value.

What's Next for Your Personal Financial Plan?

- Prepare a list of future actions to use when buying, financing, and leasing a car.
- Maintain a record of operating costs and maintenance actions for your vehicle.

Legal Services Cost Comparison

Financial Planning Activities: Contact various sources of legal services (lawyer, prepaid legal service, legal aid society) to compare costs and available services.

Suggested Web Sites: www.nolo.com   www.abanet.org

Type of legal service			
Organization name			
Address			
Phone			
Web site			
Contact person			
Recommended by			
Areas of specialization			
Cost of initial consultation			
Cost of simple will			
Cost of real estate closing			
Cost method for other services—flat fee, hourly rate, or contingency basis			
Other information			

What's Next for Your Personal Financial Plan?

• Determine the best alternative for your future legal needs.
• Maintain a file of legal documents and other financial records.

7 Selecting and Financing Housing

Your Personal Financial Plan Sheets

22. Renting vs. Buying Housing
23. Apartment Rental Comparison
24. Housing Affordability and Mortgage Qualification
25. Mortgage Company Comparison

Objectives

In this chapter, you will learn to:

1. Assess costs and benefits of renting.
2. Implement the home-buying process.
3. Determine costs associated with purchasing a home.
4. Develop a strategy for selling a home.

Why is this important?

While most people take out a 30-year mortgage, paying off the loan faster can save you thousands of dollars. Paying an additional $25 a month can shorten your loan by eight years or more and save you over $10,000.

Evaluating Renting and Buying Alternatives

OBJECTIVE 1
Assess costs and benefits of renting.

As you walk around various neighborhoods, you are likely to see a variety of housing types. When assessing housing alternatives, start by identifying factors that will influence your choice.

Your Lifestyle and Your Choice of Housing

Although the concept of *lifestyle*—how you spend your time and money—may seem intangible, it materializes in consumer purchases. Every buying decision is a statement about your lifestyle. Personal preferences are the foundation of a housing decision, but financial factors may modify the final choice.

Traditional financial guidelines suggest that "you should spend no more than 25 or 30 percent of your take-home pay on housing" or "your home should cost about 2½ times your annual income." Changes in various economic and social conditions have resulted in revised guidelines. Your budgeting activities and other financial records will provide information to determine an appropriate amount for your housing expenses.

Renting versus Buying Housing

The choice between renting and buying your residence should be analyzed based on lifestyle and financial factors. Mobility is a primary motivator of renters, whereas buyers usually want permanence (see Exhibit 7–1). As you can see in the Figure It Out box, the choice between renting and buying may not be clear-cut. In general, renting is less costly in the short run, but home ownership usually has long-term financial advantages.

Figure It Out!

› Renting versus Buying Your Place of Residence

Comparing the costs of renting and buying involves consideration of a variety of factors. The following framework and example provide a basis for assessing these two housing alternatives. The apartment in the example has a monthly rent of $1,250, and the home costs $200,000. A 28 percent tax rate is assumed.

Although the numbers in this example favor buying, remember that in any financial decision, calculations provide only part of the answer. You should also consider your needs and values and assess the opportunity costs associated with renting and buying.

	Example	Your Figures
Rental Costs		
Annual rent payments	$ 15,000	$_____
Renter's insurance	210	_____
Interest lost on security deposit (amount of security deposit times after-tax savings account interest rate)	36	_____
Total annual cost of renting	$ 15,246	_____
Buying Costs		
Annual mortgage payments	$15,168	_____
Property taxes (annual costs)	4,800	_____
Homeowner's insurance (annual premium)	600	_____
Estimated maintenance and repairs (1%)	2,000	_____
After-tax interest lost on down payment and closing costs	750	_____
Less (financial benefits of home ownership):		
Growth in equity	−1,120	−_____
Tax savings for mortgage interest (annual mortgage interest times tax rate)	−3,048	−_____
Tax savings for property taxes (annual property taxes times tax rate)	−1,344	−_____
Estimated annual appreciation (1.5%)*	−3,000	−_____
Total annual cost of buying	$ 14,806	_____

*This is a nationwide average; actual appreciation of property will vary by geographic area and economic conditions.

Exhibit 7–1   Comparing Renting and Buying of Housing

Advantages	Disadvantages
RENTING	
• Easy to move	• No tax benefits
• Fewer responsibilities for maintenance	• Limitations regarding remodeling
• Minimal financial commitment	• Restrictions regarding pets, other activities
BUYING	
• Pride of ownership	• Financial commitment
• Financial benefits	• Higher living expenses than renting
• Lifestyle flexibility	• Limited mobility

Exhibit 7–2   Housing Rental Activities

1 The Search
- Select an area and rental amount.
- Compare costs and facilities of comparable units.
- Talk to current and past residents.

2 Before Signing a Lease
- Verify lease starting date, costs, and facilities.
- Talk to a lawyer about unclear aspects of the lease.
- Note in writing, signed by the owner, the condition of the rental unit.
- Remember, if two names are on the lease, one person can be held responsible for the full rent.

3 Living in Rental Property
- Keep all facilities in good condition.
- Contact the owners regarding needed repairs.
- Respect the rights of others regarding noise.
- Obtain renter's insurance for personal belongings and liability situations (see Chapter 8).

4 At the End of the Lease
- Clean the apartment; leave it in the same condition as when you moved in.
- Tell landlord where to send your security deposit.
- Require that any deductions from your security deposit be documented.

Housing Rental Activities

Rental Activities

Are you interested in a "2-bd. garden apt, a/c, crptg, mod bath, lndry, sec $850"? Not sure? Translated, this means a two-bedroom garden apartment (at or below ground level) with air conditioning, carpeting, a modern bath, and laundry facilities. An $850 security deposit is required.

At some point in your life, you are likely to rent. As a tenant, you pay for the right to live in a residence owned by someone else. Exhibit 7–2 presents the activities involved in finding and living in a rental unit.

Sheet 22
Renting vs. Buying Housing

SELECTING A RENTAL UNIT   An apartment is the most common type of rental housing. Apartments range from modern, luxury units with extensive recreational facilities to simple one- and two-bedroom units in quiet neighborhoods. If you need more room, consider renting a house. If less space is needed, rent a room in a private house. The main information sources for rental units are newspaper ads, real estate and rental offices, and people you know. When comparing rental units, consider the factors in Exhibit 7–3.

ADVANTAGES OF RENTING   Renting offers mobility when a location change is necessary or desirable. Renters have fewer responsibilities than homeowners since they usually do not have to be concerned with maintenance and repairs. Taking possession of a rental unit is less expensive than buying a home.

DISADVANTAGES OF RENTING   Renters do not enjoy the financial advantages of homeowners. Tenants cannot take tax deductions for mortgage interest and

Exhibit 7–3

Selecting an Apartment

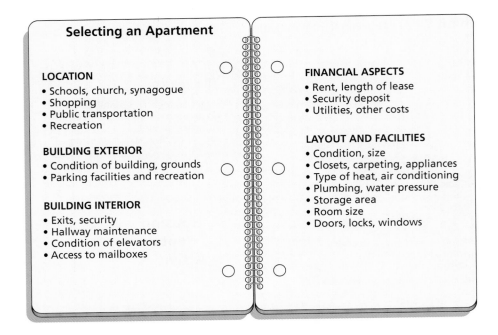

Selecting an Apartment

LOCATION
• Schools, church, synagogue
• Shopping
• Public transportation
• Recreation

BUILDING EXTERIOR
• Condition of building, grounds
• Parking facilities and recreation

BUILDING INTERIOR
• Exits, security
• Hallway maintenance
• Condition of elevators
• Access to mailboxes

FINANCIAL ASPECTS
• Rent, length of lease
• Security deposit
• Utilities, other costs

LAYOUT AND FACILITIES
• Condition, size
• Closets, carpeting, appliances
• Type of heat, air conditioning
• Plumbing, water pressure
• Storage area
• Room size
• Doors, locks, windows

lease A legal document that defines the conditions of a rental agreement.

property taxes or benefit from the increased real estate value. Renters are generally limited in the types of activities they can pursue in their place of residence. Noise from a stereo system or parties may be monitored closely. Tenants are often subject to restrictions regarding pets and decorating.

Apply *Yourself!*

Objective 1

Interview a tenant and a landlord to obtain their views about potential problems associated with renting. How do their views on tenant–landlord relations differ?

LEGAL DETAILS   Most tenants sign a **lease,** a legal document that defines the conditions of a rental agreement. This document presents:

- A description of the property, including the address.
- The name and address of the owner/landlord (the *lessor*).
- The name of the tenant (the *lessee*).
- The effective date of the lease, and the length of the lease.
- The amount of the security deposit, and amount and due date of the monthly rent.
- The date and amount due of charges for late rent payments.
- A list of the utilities, appliances, furniture, or other facilities that are included in the rental amount.
- Restrictions regarding certain activities (pets, remodeling); tenant's right to sublet.
- Charges for damages or for moving out of the rental unit later (or earlier) than the lease expiration date.
- The conditions under which the landlord may enter the apartment.

Standard lease forms include conditions you may not want to accept. Negotiate with the landlord about lease terms you consider unacceptable. Some leases give you the right to *sublet* the rental unit. Subletting may be necessary if you must vacate the premises before the lease expires. Subletting allows you to have another person take over rent payments and live in the rental unit.

While most leases are written, oral leases are also valid. In those situations, one party must give a 30-day written notice to the other party before terminating the lease or imposing a rent increase. A lease provides protection to both landlord and tenant. The tenant is protected from rent increases unless the lease contains a provision allowing an increase. The lease gives the landlord the right to take legal action against a tenant for nonpayment of rent or destruction of property.

Sheet 23
Apartment Rental Comparison

COSTS OF RENTING   A *security deposit*, frequently required when you sign a lease, is usually one month's rent. This money is held by the landlord to cover the cost of any damages. Some state and local laws may require that landlords pay interest on a security deposit if they own buildings with a certain number of rental units. After you vacate the rental unit, your security deposit should be refunded within a reasonable time. If money is deducted, you have the right to an itemized list of repair costs.

As a renter, you will incur other expenses. For many apartments, water is covered by the rent; however, other utilities may not be included. If you rent a house, you will probably pay for heat, electricity, water, telephone, and cable television. When you rent, be sure to obtain insurance coverage on your personal property.

CAUTION!

Renter's insurance is one of the most overlooked expenses of apartment dwellers. Damage or theft of personal property (clothing, furniture, stereo equipment, jewelry) usually is not covered by the landlord's insurance policy.

✓ CONCEPT CHECK 7–1

1 What are the main benefits and drawbacks of renting a place of residence?

_____

_____

2 Which components of a lease are likely to be most negotiable?

_____

_____

3 For the following situations, would you recommend that the person rent or buy housing? (Circle your answer)

   a. A person who desires to reduce income taxes paid.   rent   buy

   b. A person who expects to be transferred for work soon.   rent   buy

   c. A person with few assets for housing expenses.   rent   buy

---

Home-Buying Activities

Many people dream of having a place of residence they can call their own. Home ownership is a common financial goal. Exhibit 7–4 (on page 215) presents the process for achieving this goal.

OBJECTIVE 2
Implement the home-buying process.

Step 1: Determine Home Ownership Needs

In the first phase of this process, consider the benefits and drawbacks of this major financial commitment. Also, evaluate the types of housing units and determine the amount you can afford.

EVALUATE HOME OWNERSHIP   Stability of residence and a personalized living location are important motives of many home buyers. One financial benefit is the deductibility of mortgage interest and real estate tax payments, reducing federal income taxes.

PORTFOLIO DOCTOR | Buying a house isn't a no-brainer after all. *By Jeffrey R. Kosnett*

Sometimes, it makes sense to RENT

PAOLO and Lediya Beltran have a rare southern California housing deal. They pay $700 a month and perform routine maintenance to rent a small, 50-year-old house in Lakewood, near Long Beach. But Paolo and Lediya, both 29, want to start a family within a year and are eager to have a place that's larger—and their own. "We think we've been losing out on price appreciation and equity by renting," says Paolo.

But Paolo is also missing out on mortgage-rate adjustments (possibly), rising property taxes (probably) and repair bills (almost certainly). Paolo, a city administrator in Lakewood, and Lediya, human-resources director for a domestic-violence agency, are undeterred. The couple earn $130,000 combined, so they figure that they can afford monthly payments of $3,000.

In much of the U.S., that would buy a château. In the Los Angeles area, it gets you little more than a shack. Should the Beltrans even be thinking about buying? Or should they rent a larger place and invest the difference to pay for education and retirement?

Pros and cons. Avid savers, Paolo and Lediya would almost certainly qualify for a large mortgage. They have accumulated $100,000 in various Vanguard funds for a down payment, and they have also saved $130,000 for retirement. With their excellent credit histories, the Beltrans could probably obtain a $425,000 loan. At 6%, that would mean payments of $2,500 a month, excluding taxes and insurance.

But there's more to this decision than numbers. Paolo doesn't want to take on so much debt that he might be forced to change careers. Paolo, who has an MBA, derives satisfaction from public service. Plus, municipalities are less likely than private employers to lay off people and chop benefits. That's key because Lediya may cut back once the couple have children.

Financial planners don't often advise renting, but in this case it makes sense. Rick Mayers, a planner in Carlsbad, Cal., says that buying in southern California today can be twice as costly as renting, even after various deductions. He says the couple should rent for now. They can buy, he says, "when they have more savings and the housing market is right."

There are other factors to consider. The tax benefits of homeownership aren't as valuable if the family slides into a lower tax bracket. There are the forgone investment opportunities on down-payment money and taxes on the gains they'd generate to raise the payment. Paolo and Lediya would also give up large sums if they needed to trim retirement-plan contributions because of mortgage costs and upkeep. Paolo now views things in a new light. "When you see all this calculated out, it makes you think differently," he says.

1. What factors discussed in this article might assist you when comparing whether to rent or buy a home?

2. Would you support the recommended action presented for Paolo and Lediya? Explain your decision.

3. Describe various situations in which renting may be preferred to home buying.

Exhibit 7–4   The Home-Buying Process

A disadvantage of home ownership is financial uncertainty. Obtaining money for a down payment and securing mortgage financing may be problems. Changing property values in an area can affect your financial investment. Home ownership does not provide ease of changing living location as does renting. If changes in your situation necessitate selling your home, doing so may be difficult.

Owning your place of residence can be expensive. The homeowner is responsible for maintenance and costs of repainting, repairs, and home improvements. Real estate taxes are a major expense of homeowners. Higher property values and increased tax rates mean higher real estate taxes.

TYPES OF HOUSING AVAILABLE   Home buyers generally choose from the following options:

1. *Single-family dwellings* include previously owned houses, new houses, and custom-built houses.
2. *Multiunit dwellings* are dwellings with more than one living unit. A *duplex* is a building with separate homes. A *townhouse* may contain two, four, or six living units.
3. **Condominiums** are individually owned housing units in a building. Ownership does not include *common areas,* such as hallways, outside grounds, and recreational facilities. These areas are owned by the condominium association, which oversees the management and operation. Condominium owners pay a monthly fee for maintenance, repairs, improvements, and insurance of the building and common areas. A condominium is not the building structure; it is a legal form of home ownership.

condominium An individually owned housing unit in a building with several such units.

cooperative housing A form of housing in which a building containing a number of housing units is owned by a nonprofit organization whose members rent the units.

4. **Cooperative housing** is a form of housing in which the units in a building are owned by a nonprofit organization. The shareholders purchase stock to obtain the right to live in a unit in the building. While the residents do not own the units, they have the legal right to occupy a unit for as long as they own stock in the cooperative association. The title for the property belongs to the co-op. This ownership arrangement is different from condominiums, in which residents own the individual living unit.

5. *Manufactured homes* are assembled in a factory and then moved to the living site. *Prefabricated homes* have components built in a factory and then assembled at the housing site. *Mobile home* is not a completely accurate term since very few are moved from their original sites. Although typically smaller than 1,000 square feet, they can offer features such as a fully equipped kitchen, fireplace, cathedral ceiling, and whirlpool bath. The site for a mobile home may be either purchased or leased.

6. *Building a home* is for people who want certain specifications. Before starting such a project, be sure you possess the necessary knowledge, money, and perseverance. When choosing a contractor to coordinate the project, consider (*a*) the contractor's experience and reputation; (*b*) the contractor's relationship with the architect, materials suppliers, electricians, plumbers, carpenters, and other personnel; and (*c*) payment arrangements during construction. Your written contract should include a time schedule, cost estimates, a description of the work, and a payment schedule.

DETERMINE WHAT YOU CAN AFFORD   The amount you spend on housing is affected by funds available for a down payment, your income, and your current living expenses. Other factors you should consider are current mortgage rates, the potential future value of the property, and your ability to make monthly payments. To determine how much you can afford to spend on a home, have a loan officer at a mortgage company or other financial institution *prequalify* you. This service is provided without charge.

did you know?

The CLUE® (Comprehensive Loss Underwriting Exchange) report provides a five-year history of insurance losses at a property that a home buyer is considering for purchase. This disclosure report is an independent source of information. You can find further information at www.choicetrust.com.

You may not get all the features you want in your first home, but financial advisers suggest getting into the housing market by purchasing what you can afford. As you move up in the housing market, your second or third home can include more of the features you want.

While the home you buy should be in good condition, you may wish to buy a *handyman's special*—a home that needs work and that you are able to get at a lower price. You will then need to put more money into the house for repairs and improvements or do some of the work yourself.

Step 2: Find and Evaluate a Home

Next, select a location, consider using the services of a real estate agent, and conduct a home inspection.

zoning laws Restrictions on how the property in an area can be used.

SELECT A LOCATION   Location is considered the most important factor when buying a home. You may prefer an urban, a suburban, or a rural setting. Or perhaps you want to live in a small town or in a resort area. Be aware of **zoning laws,** restrictions on how the property in an area can be used. The location of businesses and future construction projects may influence your decision.

If you have a family, assess the school system. Educators recommend that schools be evaluated on program variety, achievement level of students, percentage of students who go on to college, dedication of faculty members, facilities, school funding, and involvement of parents. Homeowners without children also benefit from strong schools, since the educational advantages of a community help maintain property values.

SERVICES OF REAL ESTATE AGENTS   Real estate agents have information about housing in areas of interest to you. Their main services include (1) showing you homes to meet your needs; (2) presenting your offer to the seller; (3) negotiating a settlement price; (4) assisting you in obtaining financing; and (5) representing you at the closing. A real estate agent may also recommend lawyers, insurance agents, home inspectors, and mortgage companies to serve your needs.

Since the home seller usually pays the commission, a buyer may not incur a direct cost. However, this expense is reflected in the price paid for the home. In some states, the agent could be working for the seller. In others, the agent may be working for the buyer, the seller, or as a *dual agent,* working for both the buyer and the seller. When dual agency exists, some states require that buyers sign a disclosure acknowledging that they are aware the agent is working for both buyer and seller. Many states have *buyer agents* who represent the buyer's interests and may be paid by either the seller or the buyer.

Apply *Yourself!*

Objective 2

Talk with a real estate agent about the process involved in selecting and buying a home. Ask about housing prices in your area and the services the agent provides.

THE HOME INSPECTION   An evaluation by a trained home inspector can minimize future problems. Being cautious will save you headaches and unplanned expenses. Exhibit 7–5 presents a detailed format for inspecting a home. Some states, cities, and lenders require inspection documents for pests, radon, or mold. The mortgage company will usually conduct an *appraisal,* which is not a home inspection but an assessment of the market value of the property.

Exhibit 7–5   Conducting a Home Inspection

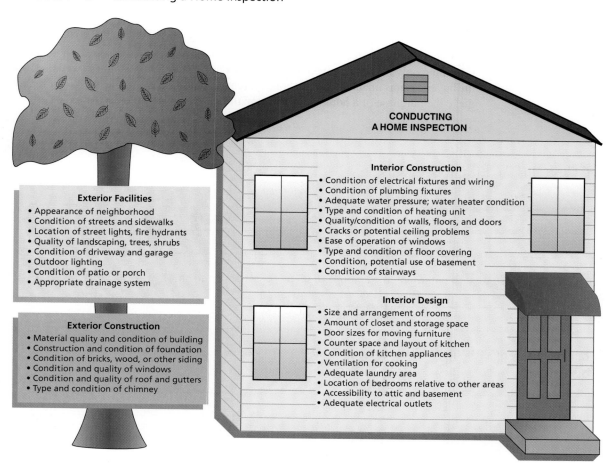

CONDUCTING A HOME INSPECTION

Interior Construction
- Condition of electrical fixtures and wiring
- Condition of plumbing fixtures
- Adequate water pressure; water heater condition
- Type and condition of heating unit
- Quality/condition of walls, floors, and doors
- Cracks or potential ceiling problems
- Ease of operation of windows
- Type and condition of floor covering
- Condition, potential use of basement
- Condition of stairways

Exterior Facilities
- Appearance of neighborhood
- Condition of streets and sidewalks
- Location of street lights, fire hydrants
- Quality of landscaping, trees, shrubs
- Condition of driveway and garage
- Outdoor lighting
- Condition of patio or porch
- Appropriate drainage system

Exterior Construction
- Material quality and condition of building
- Construction and condition of foundation
- Condition of bricks, wood, or other siding
- Condition and quality of windows
- Condition and quality of roof and gutters
- Type and condition of chimney

Interior Design
- Size and arrangement of rooms
- Amount of closet and storage space
- Door sizes for moving furniture
- Counter space and layout of kitchen
- Condition of kitchen appliances
- Ventilation for cooking
- Adequate laundry area
- Location of bedrooms relative to other areas
- Accessibility to attic and basement
- Adequate electrical outlets

Step 3: Price the Property

After selecting a home, determine an offer price and negotiate a final buying price.

DETERMINE THE HOME PRICE   The amount you offer will be affected by recent selling prices in the area, current demand for housing, the time the home has been on the market, the owner's need to sell, financing options, and features and condition of the home. Each of these factors can affect your offer price. For example, you will have to offer a higher price in times of low interest rates and high demand for homes. On the other hand, a home that has been on the market for over a year could mean an opportunity to offer a lower price. Your offer will be in the form of a *purchase agreement,* or contract, which is your legal offer to purchase the home.

did you know?

A two-story addition, a remodeled bathroom, an updated kitchen, addition of a deck, and a refinished basement are the home upgrades most likely to add value to a home.

NEGOTIATE THE PURCHASE PRICE   If your initial offer is accepted, you have a valid contract. If your offer is rejected, you have several options. A *counteroffer* from the owner indicates a willingness to negotiate a price. If the counteroffer is only slightly lower than the asking price, you are expected to move closer to that price with your next offer. If the counteroffer is quite a bit off the asking price, you are closer to arriving at the purchase price. If no counteroffer is forthcoming, you may wish to make another offer to see whether the seller is willing to do any negotiating. Negotiations may involve things other than price, such as closing date or inclusion of existing items, such as appliances.

earnest money A portion of the price of a home that the buyer deposits as evidence of good faith to indicate a serious purchase offer.

As part of the offer, the buyer must present **earnest money,** a portion of the purchase price deposited as evidence of good faith. At the closing of the home purchase, the earnest money is applied toward the down payment. This money is returned if the sale cannot be completed due to circumstances beyond the buyer's control.

Home purchase agreements may contain a *contingency clause,* stating the agreement is binding only if a certain event occurs. For example, the contract may be valid only if the buyer obtains financing for the home purchase within a certain time period, or it may make the purchase of a home contingent on the sale of the buyer's current home.

✓ CONCEPT CHECK 7–2

1   What are the advantages and disadvantages of owning a home?

_____

_____

2   What guidelines can be used to determine the amount to spend for a home purchase?

_____

_____

3   How can the quality of a school system benefit even homeowners in a community who do not have school-age children?

_____

_____

The Finances of Home Buying

After you have decided to purchase a specific home and have agreed on a price, you will probably obtain a loan.

Step 4: Obtain Financing

THE DOWN PAYMENT   The amount of cash available for a down payment affects the size of the mortgage required. If you can make a large down payment, say, 20 percent or more, you will obtain a mortgage relatively easily. Personal savings, sales of investments or other assets, and assistance from relatives are common down payment sources. Parents can help their children purchase a home by giving them a cash gift or a loan.

Private mortgage insurance (PMI) is usually required if the down payment is less than 20 percent. This protects the lender from financial loss due to default. After building up 20 percent equity in a home, a home buyer should contact the lender to cancel PMI. The Homeowners Protection Act of 1998 requires that a PMI policy be terminated automatically when a homeowner's equity reaches 22 percent of the property value at the time the mortgage was executed. Homeowners can request termination earlier if they can provide proof that the equity in the home has grown to 22 percent of the current market value. Some home buyers apply for a second mortgage to obtain down payment funds and to avoid PMI.

THE MORTGAGE   A **mortgage** is a long-term loan on a specific piece of property such as a home or other real estate. Payments on a mortgage are usually made over 15, 20, or 30 years. Applying for a mortgage involves three main phases:

1. You complete the mortgage application and meet with the lender to present evidence of employment, income, ownership of assets, and amounts of existing debts.
2. The lender obtains a credit report and verifies your application and financial status.
3. The mortgage is either approved or denied, with the decision based on your financial history and an evaluation of the home you want to buy.

This process will indicate the maximum mortgage for which you qualify. As shown in Exhibit 7–6, the major factors that affect the affordability of your mortgage are your income, other debts, the amount available for a down payment, the length of the loan, and current mortgage rates. The results of this calculation are (*a*) the monthly mortgage payment you can afford, (*b*) the mortgage amount you can afford, and (*c*) the home purchase price you can afford.

These sample calculations are typical of those most financial institutions use; the actual qualifications for a mortgage may vary by lender and by the type of mortgage. The loan commitment is the financial institution's decision to provide the funds needed to purchase a specific property. The approved mortgage application usually *locks in* an interest rate for 30 to 90 days.

The mortgage loan for which you can qualify is larger when interest rates are low than when they are high. For example, a person who can afford a monthly mortgage payment of $700 will qualify for a 30-year loan of

$130,354 at 5 percent	$95,368 at 8 percent
$116,667 at 6 percent	$86,956 at 9 percent
$105,263 at 7 percent	$79,726 at 10 percent

As interest rates rise, fewer people are able to afford the cost of an average-priced home.

did you know?

Today, with a strong credit score (700 or higher), a person can obtain home financiing without a down payment. This high credit score will also likely result in a lower mortgage rate and less required paperwork to process the loan.

Key Web Site for Private Mortgage Insurance
www.privateemi.com

mortgage   A long-term loan on a specific piece of property such as a home or other real estate.

Sheet 24
Housing Affordability and Mortgage Qualification

Exhibit 7–6   Housing Affordability and Mortgage Qualification Amounts

	Example A	Example B
Step 1: Determine your monthly gross income (annual income divided by 12).	$48,000 ÷ 12	$48,000 ÷ 12
Step 2: With a down payment of at least 10 percent, lenders use 33 percent of monthly gross income as a guideline for PITI (principal, interest, taxes, and insurance) and 38 percent of monthly gross income as a guideline for PITI plus other debt payments.	$ 4,000 × .38 $ 1,520	$ 4,000 × .33 $ 1,320
Step 3: Subtract other debt payments (e.g., payments on an auto loan) and an estimate of the monthly costs of property taxes and homeowner's insurance.	−380 −300	— −300
(a) Affordable monthly mortgage payment	$ 840	$ 1,020
Step 4: Divide this amount by the monthly mortgage payment per $1,000 based on current mortgage rates—an 8 percent, 30-year loan, for example (see Exhibit 7–7)—and multiply by $1,000.	÷ $ 7.34 × $ 1,000	÷ $ 7.34 × $ 1,000
(b) Affordable mortgage amount	$114,441	$138,965
Step 5: Divide your affordable mortgage amount by 1 minus the fractional portion of your down payment (e.g., 1 − .1 with a 10 percent down payment).	÷ .9	÷ .9
(c) Affordable home purchase price	$127,157	$154,405

Note: The two ratios lending institutions use (step 2) and other loan requirements may vary based on a variety of factors, including the type of mortgage, the amount of the down payment, your income level, credit score, and current interest rates.

points Prepaid interest charged by the lender.

When comparing mortgage companies, remember that the interest rate you are quoted is not the only factor to consider. The required down payment and the points charged will affect the interest rate. **Points** are prepaid interest charged by the lender. Each *discount point* is equal to 1 percent of the loan amount and should be viewed as a premium you pay for obtaining a lower mortgage rate. In deciding whether to take a lower rate with more points or a higher rate with fewer points, consider the following guidelines:

- If you plan to live in your home a long time (over five years), the lower mortgage rate is probably the best action.
- If you plan to sell your home in the next few years, the higher mortgage rate with fewer discount points may be better.

Exhibit 7–7

Mortgage Payment Factors (principal and interest factors per $1,000 of loan amount)

TERM RATE	30 YEARS	25 YEARS	20 YEARS	15 YEARS
5.0%	$5.37	$5.85	$ 6.60	$ 7.91
5.5	5.68	6.14	6.88	8.17
6.0	6.00	6.44	7.16	8.43
6.5	6.32	6.67	7.45	8.71
7.0	6.65	7.06	7.75	8.98
7.5	6.99	7.39	8.06	9.27
8.0	7.34	7.72	8.36	9.56
8.5	7.69	8.05	8.68	9.85
9.0	8.05	8.39	9.00	10.14
9.5	8.41	8.74	9.32	10.44
10.0	8.78	9.09	9.65	10.75
10.5	9.15	9.44	9.98	11.05
11.0	9.52	9.80	10.32	11.37

Online research may be used to compare current mortgage rates, and you can apply for a mortgage online.

FIXED-RATE, FIXED-PAYMENT MORTGAGES

As Exhibit 7–8 shows, fixed-rate, fixed-payment mortgages are a major type of mortgage. The *conventional mortgage* usually has equal payments over 15, 20, or 30 years based on a fixed interest rate. Mortgage payments are set to allow **amortization** of the loan; that is, the balance

amortization The reduction of a loan balance through payments made over a period of time.

Exhibit 7–8   Types of Mortgages

Loan Type	Benefits	Drawbacks
FIXED-RATE, FIXED-PAYMENT		
1. Conventional 30-year mortgage.	• Fixed monthly payments for 30 years provide certainty of principal and interest payments.	• Higher initial rates than adjustables.
2. Conventional 15- or 20-year mortgage.	• Lower rate than 30-year fixed; faster equity buildup and quicker payoff of loan.	• Higher monthly payments.
3. FHA/VA fixed-rate mortgage (30-year and 15-year).	• Low down payment requirements and fully assumable with no prepayment penalties.	• May require additional processing time.
4. "Balloon" loan (3–10-year terms).	• May carry discount rates and other favorable terms, particularly when the home seller provides the loan.	• At the end of the 3- to 10-year term, the entire remaining balance is due in a lump-sum or "balloon" payment, forcing the borrower to find new financing.
ADJUSTABLE-RATE, VARIABLE-PAYMENT		
5. Adjustable-rate mortgage (ARM)—payment changes on 1-year, 3-year, and 5-year schedules.	• Lower initial rates than fixed-rate loans, particularly on the one-year adjustable. Generally assumable by new buyers. Offers possibility of future rate and payment decreases. Loans with rate "caps" may protect borrowers against increases in rates. Some may be convertible to fixed-rate plans.	• Shifts far greater interest rate risk onto borrowers than fixed-rate loans. May push up monthly payments in future years.
6. Graduated-payment mortgage (GPM)—payment increases by prearranged increments during first 5 to 7 years, then levels off.	• Allows buyers with marginal incomes to qualify. Higher incomes over next 5–7 years expected to cover gradual payment increases. May be combined with adjustable-rate mortgage to further lower initial rate and payment.	• May have higher annual percentage rate (APR) than standard fixed-rate or adjustable-rate loans. May involve negative amortization—increasing debt owed to lender. Income may not increase as expected.
7. Growing equity mortgage (GEM)—contributes rising portions of monthly payments to payoff of principal debt. Typically pays off in 15–18 years rather than 30.	• Lower up-front payments, quicker loan payoff than conventional fixed-rate or adjustable-rate loans.	• May have higher effective rates and higher down payments than other loans in the marketplace.
8. Interest-only mortgage	• Lower payments for the first few years; more easily affordable.	• No decrease in amount owed; no building equity.

owed is reduced with each payment. Since the amount borrowed is large, the payments made during the early years of the mortgage are applied mainly to interest, with only small reductions in the loan principal. As the amount owed declines, the monthly payments have an increasing impact on the loan balance. Near the end of the mortgage term, almost all of each payment is applied to the balance.

For example, a $75,000, 30-year, 10 percent mortgage would have monthly payments of $658.18. The payments would be divided as follows:

	Interest		Principal	Remaining Balance
For the first month	$625.00	($75,000 $\times$ 0.10 $\times$ 1/12)	$ 33.18	$74,966.82 ($75,000 − $33.18)
For the second month	624.72	($74,966.82 $\times$ 0.10 $\times$ 1/12)	33.46	74,933.36 ($74,966.82 − $33.46)
For the 360th month	5.41		649.54	−0−

In the past, many conventional mortgages were *assumable*. This feature allowed a home buyer to continue with the seller's original agreement. Assumable mortgages were especially attractive if the mortgage rate was lower than market interest rates at the time of the sale. Today, due to volatile interest rates, assumable mortgages are seldom offered.

Apply *Yourself!*

OBJECTIVE 3

Conduct Web research on various types of mortgages and current rates.

GOVERNMENT-GUARANTEED FINANCING PROGRAMS These include loans insured by the Federal Housing Authority (FHA) and loans guaranteed by the Veterans Administration (VA). These government agencies do not provide the mortgage money; rather, they help home buyers obtain low-interest, low-down-payment loans.

To qualify for an FHA-insured loan, a person must meet certain conditions related to the down payment and fees. Most low- and middle-income people can qualify for the FHA loan program. The VA-guaranteed loan program assists eligible armed services veterans with home purchases. As with the FHA program, the funds for VA loans come from a financial institution or a mortgage company, with the risk reduced by government participation. A VA loan can be obtained without a down payment.

ADJUSTABLE-RATE, VARIABLE-PAYMENT MORTGAGES The **adjustable-rate mortgage (ARM),** also referred to as a *flexible-rate mortgage* or a *variable-rate mortgage,* has an interest rate that increases or decreases during the life of the loan. ARMs usually have a lower initial interest rate than fixed-rate mortgages; however, the borrower, not the lender, bears the risk of future interest rate increases.

adjustable-rate mortgage (ARM) A home loan with an interest rate that can change during the mortgage term due to changes in market interest rates; also called a *flexible-rate mortgage* or a *variable-rate mortgage.*

A *rate cap* restricts the amount by which the interest rate can increase or decrease during the ARM term. This limit prevents the borrower from having to pay an interest rate significantly higher than the one in the original agreement. A *payment cap* keeps the payments on an adjustable-rate mortgage at a given level or limits the amount to which those payments can rise. When mortgage payments do not rise but interest rates do, the amount owed can increase in months in which the mortgage payment does not cover the interest owed. This increased loan balance, called *negative amortization,* means the amount of the home equity is decreasing instead of increasing.

Consider several factors when evaluating adjustable-rate mortgages: (1) determine the frequency of and restrictions on allowed changes in interest rates; (2) consider the frequency of and restrictions on changes in the monthly payment; (3) investigate the possibility that the loan will be extended due to negative amortization, and find out if a limit exists on the amount of negative amortization; and (4) find out what index is used to set the mortgage interest rate.

did you know?

By taking out a 15-year instead of a 30-year mortgage, a home buyer borrowing $200,00 can save more than $150,000 in interest over the life of the loan. The faster equity growth with the shorter mortgage is also a benefit.

CREATIVE FINANCING   *Convertible ARMs* allow the home buyer to change an adjustable-rate mortgage to a fixed-rate mortgage during a certain period, such as the time between the second and fifth year of the loan. A conversion fee, typically between $250 and $500, must be paid to obtain a fixed rate, usually 0.25 to 0.50 percent higher than the current rates for conventional 30-year mortgages.

When mortgage rates are high, a *balloon mortgage,* with fixed monthly payments and a very large final payment, usually after three, five, or seven years, may be used. This financing plan is designed for people who expect to be able to refinance the loan or sell the home before or when the balloon payment is due. Most balloon mortgages allow conversion to a conventional mortgage (for a fee) if certain conditions are met.

A *graduated-payment mortgage (GPM)* is a financing agreement in which payments rise to different levels every 5 or 10 years during the term of the loan. In the early years, the loan payments could lead to a negative amortization with an increase in the amount owed. This type of mortgage is especially beneficial for people who anticipate increases in income in the future.

A *growing-equity mortgage (GEM)* provides for increases in payments that allow the amount owed to be paid off more quickly. With this mortgage, a person would be able to pay off a 30-year home loan in 15 to 18 years.

An *interest-only mortgage* allows a homebuyer to have lower payments for the first few years of the loan. During that time, none of the mortgage payment goes toward the loan amount. Once the initial period ends, the mortgage adjusts to be interest only at the new payment rate. Or, a borrower may obtain a different type of mortgage to start building equity.

CAUTION!

Remember, with an interest-only mortgage, higher payments will occur later in the loan. These are based on the amount of the original loan since no principal has been paid. Interest-only mortgages can be especially dangerous if the value of the property declines.

OTHER FINANCING METHODS   A *buy-down* is an interest rate subsidy from a home builder or a real estate developer that reduces the mortgage payments during the first few years of the loan. This assistance is intended to stimulate sales among home buyers who cannot afford conventional financing. After the buy-down period, the mortgage payments increase to the level that would have existed without the financial assistance.

The *shared appreciation mortgage (SAM)* is an arrangement in which the borrower agrees to share the increased value of the home with the lender when the home is sold. This agreement provides the home buyer with a below-market interest rate and lower payments than a conventional loan.

A *second mortgage,* more commonly called a *home equity loan,* allows a homeowner to borrow on the paid-up value of the property. Lending institutions offer a variety of home equity loans, including a line of credit program that allows the borrower to obtain additional funds. You need to be careful when using a home equity line of credit. This revolving credit plan can keep you continually in debt as you request new cash advances. A home equity loan allows you to deduct the interest on consumer purchases on your federal income tax return. However, it creates the risk of losing the home if required payments on both the first and second mortgages are not made.

Reverse mortgages (also called *home equity conversion mortgages)* provide homeowners who are 62 or older with tax-free income in the form of a loan that is paid back (with interest) when the home is sold or the homeowner dies.

During the term of your mortgage, you may want to *refinance* your home, that is, obtain a new mortgage on your current home at a lower interest rate. Before taking this action, be sure the costs of refinancing do not offset the savings of a lower interest rate.

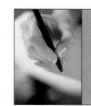

Sheet 25
Mortgage Company Comparison

did you know?

A "portable" mortgage, offered by a few lenders, allows homebuyers to "move" their mortgages to a different home if they buy a different home within the term of the loan.

Another financing decision involves making extra payments on your mortgage. Since this amount will be applied to the loan principal, you will save interest and pay off the mortgage in a shorter time. Paying an additional $25 a month on a $75,000, 30-year, 10 percent mortgage will save you more than $34,000 in interest and enable you to pay off the loan in less than 25 years. Beware of organizations that promise to help you make additional payments on your mortgage. You can do this on your own, without the fee they are likely to charge you.

Step 5: Close the Purchase Transaction

closing costs Fees and charges paid when a real estate transaction is completed; also called *settlement costs*.

title insurance Insurance that, during the mortgage term, protects the owner or the lender against financial loss resulting from future defects in the title and from other unforeseen property claims not excluded by the policy.

Before finalizing the transaction, a *walk-through* allows you to inspect the condition of the home. Use a camera or video recorder to collect evidence for any last-minute items you may need to negotiate.

The *closing* is a meeting of the buyer, seller, and lender of funds, or representatives of each party, to complete the transaction. Documents are signed, last-minute details are settled, and appropriate amounts are paid. A number of expenses are incurred at the closing. The **closing costs**, also referred to as *settlement costs,* are the fees and charges paid when a real estate transaction is completed; these commonly include the items listed in Exhibit 7–9.

Title insurance has two phases. First, the title company defines the boundaries of the property being purchased and conducts a search to determine whether the property is free of claims such as unpaid real estate taxes. Second, during the mortgage term, the title

Exhibit 7–9   Common Closing Costs

At the transaction settlement of a real estate purchase and sale, the buyer and seller will encounter a variety of expenses that are commonly referred to as *closing costs*.

	COST RANGE ENCOUNTERED	
	By the Buyer	**By the Seller**
Title search fee	$50–$150	—
Title insurance	$275–$600	$100–$600
Attorney's fee	$50–$700	$50–$700
Property survey	—	$100–$400
Appraisal fee	$150–$400	—
Recording fees; transfer taxes	$55–$90	$15–$30
Credit report	$5–$20	—
Termite inspection	$70–$150	—
Lender's origination fee	1–3% of loan amount	—
Reserves for home insurance and property taxes	Varies	—
Interest paid in advance (from the closing date to the end of the month) and "points"	Varies	—
Real estate broker's commission	—	5–7% of purchase price

Note: The amounts paid by the buyer are in addition to the down payment.

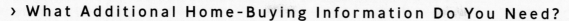
› What Additional Home-Buying Information Do You Need?

For each of the following main aspects of home buying, list questions, additional information, or actions you might need to take. Locate Web sites that provide information for these areas.

- **Location.** Consider the community and geographic region. A $250,000 home in one area may be an average-priced house, while in another part of the country it may be fairly expensive real estate. The demand for homes is largely affected by the economy and the availability of jobs.

- **Down payment.** While making a large down payment reduces your mortgage payments, you will also need the funds for closing costs, moving expenses, repairs, or furniture.

- **Mortgage application.** When applying for a home loan, you will usually be required to provide copies of recent tax returns, a residence and employment history, information about bank and investment accounts, a listing of debts, and evidence of auto and any real estate ownership.

- **Points.** You may need to select between a higher rate with no discount points and a lower rate requiring points paid at closing.

- **Closing costs.** Settlement costs can range from 2 to 6 percent of the loan amount. This means you could need as much as $6,000 to finalize a $100,000 mortgage; this amount is in addition to your down payment.

- **PITI.** Your monthly payment for principal, interest, taxes, and insurance is an important budget item. Beware of buying "too much house" and not having enough for other living expenses.

- **Maintenance costs.** As any homeowner will tell you, owning a home can be expensive. Set aside funds for repair and remodeling expenses.

Web sites to consult:

_____

_____

company protects the owner and the lender against financial loss resulting from future defects in the title and from other unforeseen property claims not excluded by the policy.

Also due at closing time is the deed recording fee. The **deed** is the document that transfers ownership of property from one party to another. With a *warranty deed,* the seller guarantees the title is good. This document certifies that the seller is the true owner of the property, there are no claims against the title, and the seller has the right to sell the property.

The Real Estate Settlement Procedures Act (RESPA) helps home buyers understand the closing process and closing costs. This legislation requires that loan applicants be

deed A document that transfers ownership of property from one party to another.

Key Web Site for RESPA

www.hud.gov

escrow account Money, usually deposited with the lending financial institution, for the payment of property taxes and homeowner's insurance.

given an estimate of the closing costs before the actual closing. Obtaining this information early allows a home buyer to plan for the closing costs.

At the closing and when you make your monthly payments, you will probably deposit money to be used for home expenses. For example, the lender will require that you have property insurance. An **escrow account** is money, usually deposited with the lending institution, for the payment of property taxes and home insurance.

As a new home buyer, you might also consider purchasing an agreement that gives you protection against defects in the home. *Implied warranties* created by state laws may cover some problem areas; other repair costs can occur. Home builders and real estate sales companies offer warranties to buyers. Coverage offered usually provides protection against electrical, plumbing, heating, appliances, and other mechanical defects. Most home warranty programs have various limitations.

Home Buying: A Summary

For most people, buying a home is the most expensive decision they will undertake. As a reminder, the Personal Finance in Practice feature (on page 225) provides an overview of the major elements to consider when making this critical financial decision.

✓ CONCEPT CHECK 7–3

1   What are the main sources of money for a down payment?

_____

_____

2   What factors affect a person's ability to qualify for a mortgage?

_____

_____

3   How do changing interest rates affect the amount of mortgage a person can afford?

_____

_____

4   Under what conditions might an adjustable-rate mortgage be appropriate?

_____

_____

5   For the following situations, select the type of home financing action that would be most appropriate:

   a. A mortgage for a person who desires to finance a home purchase at current interest rates for the entire term of the loan. _____

   b. A homebuyer who wants to reduce the amount of monthly payments since interest rates have declined over the past year. _____

   c. A homeowner who wants to access funds that could be used to remodel the home. _____

   d. A person who served in the military, who does not have money for a down payment. _____

   e. A retired person who wants to obtain income from the value of her home. _____

A Home-Selling Strategy

Most people who buy a home will eventually be on the other side of a real estate transaction. Selling your home requires preparing it for selling, setting a price, and deciding whether to sell it yourself or use a real estate agent.

OBJECTIVE 4
Develop a strategy for selling a home.

Preparing Your Home for Selling

The effective presentation of your home can result in a fast and financially favorable sale. Real estate salespeople recommend that you make needed repairs and paint worn exterior and interior areas. Clear the garage and exterior areas, and keep the lawn cut and the leaves raked. Keep the kitchen and bathroom clean. Remove excess furniture and dispose of unneeded items to make the house, closets, and storage areas look larger. When showing your home, open drapes and turn on lights. This effort will give your property a positive image and make it attractive to potential buyers.

Determining the Selling Price

Putting a price on your home can be difficult. You risk not selling it immediately if the price is too high, and you may not get a fair amount if the price is too low. An **appraisal,** an estimate of the current value of the property, can provide a good indication of the price you should set. An asking price is influenced by recent selling prices of comparable homes in your area, demand in the housing market, and current mortgage rates.

appraisal An estimate of the current value of a property.

   The home improvements you have made may or may not increase the selling price. A hot tub or an exercise room may have no value for potential buyers. Among the most desirable improvements are energy-efficient features, a remodeled kitchen, an additional or remodeled bathroom, added rooms and storage space, a converted basement, a fireplace, and an outdoor deck or patio. Daily maintenance, timely repairs, and home improvements will increase the future sales price.

did you know?

An appraisal is likely to cost between $250 and $350. This expense can help people selling a home on their own to get a realistic view of the property's value.

Sale by Owner

Each year, about 10 percent of home sales are made by the home's owners. If you sell your home without using a real estate agent, advertise in local newspapers and create a detailed information sheet. Distribute the sheet at stores and in other public areas. When selling your home on your own, obtain information about the availability of financing and financing requirements. This will help potential buyers determine whether a sale is possible. Use the services of a lawyer or title company to assist you with the contract, the closing, and other legal matters.

   Require potential buyers to provide names, addresses, telephone numbers, and background information. Show your home only by appointment and only when two or more adults are at home. Selling your own home can save several thousand dollars in commission, but an investment of your time and effort is required.

Apply *Yourself!*

Objective 4

Visit a couple of homes for sale. What features do you believe would appeal to potential buyers? What efforts were made to attract potential buyers to the open houses?

Listing with a Real Estate Agent

If you sell your home with the assistance of a real estate agent, consider the person's knowledge of the community and the agent's willingness to actively market your home.

Personal Finance in Practice

› Lowering Your Property Taxes

Property taxes vary from area to area and usually range from 2 to 4 percent of the market value of the home. Taxes are based on the *assessed value,* the amount that your local government determines your property to be worth for tax purposes. Assessed values normally are lower than the market value, often about half. A home with a market value of $180,000 may be assessed at $90,000. If the tax rate is $60 per $1,000 of assessed value, this would result in annual taxes of $5,400 ($90,000 divided by $1,000 times $60). This rate is 6 percent of the assessed value but only 3 percent of the market value.

Although higher home values are desirable, this increase means higher property assessments. Quickly increasing property taxes are frustrating, but there are actions you can take:

Suggested Action	Your Action
Step 1: Know the appeal deadline. Call the local assessor's office. You will usually have between 14 and 90 days to initiate your appeal. Late requests will most likely not be accepted. Send your appeal by certified mail to have proof that you met the deadline; keep copies of all documents.	
Step 2: Check for mistakes. The assessment office may have incorrect information. Obvious mistakes may include incorrect square footage or an assessment may report a home with four bedrooms when there are only three.	
Step 3: Determine the issues to emphasize. A property tax appeal can be based on a mistake in the assessment or a higher assessment than comparable homes. Note items that negatively affect the value of your home. For example, a bridge is no longer in operation near your home, making your house much less accessible—and less valuable. Or if a garage has been taken down to increase garden space, the home's value likely would be less. Compare your assessment with homes of the same size, age, and general location. Obtain comparisons for 5 to 10 homes.	
Step 4: Prepare for the hearing. Gather your evidence and prepare an organized presentation. Use photos of comparable properties. A spreadsheet can make it easy for the hearing officials to view your evidence. Suggest a specific corrected assessment, and give your reasons. Observe the hearing of another person to become familiar with the process.	

A real estate agent will provide you with various services, such as suggesting a selling price, making potential buyers and other agents aware of your home, providing advice on features to highlight, conducting showings of your home, and handling the financial aspects of the sale. Marketing efforts are likely to include presentation of your home on various Web sites.

A real estate agent can also help screen potential buyers to determine whether they will qualify for a mortgage. Discount real estate brokers are available to assist sellers who are willing to take on certain duties and want to reduce selling costs.

✓ CONCEPT CHECK 7–4

1 What actions are recommended when planning to sell your home?

_____

_____

2 What factors affect the selling price of a home?

_____

_____

3 What should you consider when deciding whether to sell your home on your own or use the services of a real estate agent?

_____

_____

back to *Getting Personal*

1. Reconsider your responses for the Getting Personal questions at the beginning of the chapter. What did you learn in this chapter that might affect your answers to these questions in the future?

_____

_____

2. Describe a financial goal related to housing. What actions will you take to achieve this goal?

_____

_____

Chapter Summary

Objective 1   Assess renting and buying alternatives in terms of their financial and opportunity costs. The main advantages of renting are mobility, fewer responsibilities, and lower initial costs. The main disadvantages of renting are few financial benefits, a restricted lifestyle, and legal concerns.

Objective 2   Home buying involves five major stages: (1) determining home ownership needs, (2) finding and evaluating a property to purchase, (3) pricing the property, (4) financing the purchase, and (5) closing the real estate transaction.

Objective 3   The costs associated with purchasing a home include the down payment; mortgage origination costs; closing costs such as a deed fee, prepaid interest, attorney's fees, payment for title insurance, and a property survey; and an escrow account for homeowner's insurance and property taxes.

Objective 4   When selling a home, you must decide whether to make certain repairs and improvements, determine a selling price, and choose between selling the home yourself and using the services of a real estate agent.

Key Terms

adjustable-rate mortgage (ARM)   222
amortization   221
appraisal   227
closing costs   224
condominium   215

cooperative housing   216
deed   225
earnest money   218
escrow account   226
lease   212

mortgage   219
points   220
title insurance   224
zoning laws   216

Problems

1. Based on the following data, would you recommend buying or renting?

   Rental Costs

   Annual rent, $7,380
   Insurance, $145
   Security deposit, $650
   Insurance/maintenance, $1,050

   Buying Costs

   Annual mortgage payments, $9,800 ($9,575 is interest)
   Property taxes, $1,780
   Down payment/closing costs, $4,500
   Growth in equity, $225
   Estimated annual appreciation, $1,700

   Assume an after-tax savings interest rate of 6 percent and a tax rate of 28 percent.

2. When renting, various move-in costs will be encountered. Estimate the following amounts:

   First month rent $ _____
   Security deposit $ _____
   Security deposit for utilities (if applicable) $ _____
   Moving truck, other moving expenses $ _____
   Household items (dishes, towels, bedding) $ _____
   Furniture and appliances (as required) $ _____
   Renter's insurance $ _____
   Refreshments for friends who helped you move $ _____
   Other items: _____ $ _____

3. Many locations require that renters be paid interest on their security deposits. If you have a security deposit of $1,150, how much would you expect a year at 3 percent?

4. Condominiums usually require a monthly fee for various services. At $160 a month, how much would a homeowner pay over a 10-year period for living in this housing facility?

5. Estimate the affordable monthly mortgage payment, the affordable mortgage amount, and the affordable home purchase price for the following situation (see Exhibit 7–6).
   Monthly gross income, $2,950
   Other debt (monthly payment), $160
   30-year loan at 8 percent

   Down payment to be made—15 percent of purchase price
   Monthly estimate for property taxes and insurance, $210

6. Based on Exhibit 7–7, what would be the monthly mortgage payments for each of the following situations?
   a. A $140,000, 15-year loan at 8.5 percent.

   b. A $215,000, 30-year loan at 7 percent.

   c. A $165,000, 20-year loan at 8 percent.

7. Which mortgage would result in higher total payments?

   Mortgage A: $985 a month for 30 years

   Mortgage B: $780 a month for 5 years and $1,056 for 25 years

8. If an adjustable-rate 30-year mortgage for $120,000 starts at 5.5 percent and increases to 6.5 percent, what is the amount of increase of the monthly payment? (Use Exhibit 7–7)

9. Kelly and Tim Jones plan to refinance their mortgage to obtain a lower interest rate. They will reduce their mortgage payments by $56 a month. Their closing costs for refinancing will be $1,670. How long will it take them to cover the cost of refinancing?

10. You estimate that you can save $3,800 by selling your home yourself rather than using a real estate agent. What would be the future value of that amount if invested for five years at 6 percent?

Questions

1. What do you believe are the most important factors a person should consider when selecting housing?

2. What are some common mistakes a person might make when renting an apartment or other housing?

3. What actions would you recommend to a person who was considering buying a home that needed several improvements?

4. Describe how knowledge of current interest rates would help you better plan when obtaining a mortgage.

5. Prepare a list of actions to take when selling a home.

Internet Connection

COMPARING MORTGAGE RATES ONLINE

Using the three Web sites listed (or others of your choice), obtain the following information:

	www.bankrate.com	www.hsh.com	www.bestrate.com
What is the current rate for a 30-year, fixed-rate mortgage in your geographic area?			
What is the rate for a 15-year, fixed-rate mortgage?			
What is the rate for an adjustable-rate mortgage?			
What is the recent trend (up, down, stable) for mortgage rates?			
What do you believe to be the future prospect for mortgage rates (up, down, stable)?			
In addition to rate information, what additional services are provided on this Web site?			

Case in Point

CAN YOU BUY A HOUSE ONLINE?

When Jamie Covington bought her first home, she did so without ever meeting in person with a mortgage broker or the title insurance representative. She was one of the first home buyers to conduct her real estate transaction completely online.

Jamie started the process by viewing homes on Web sites of various real estate companies and those listed online with various newspapers in her area. Later, Jamie went out to see several of the properties she was considering. The financing process involved several online activities, including:

- The prequalification process to determine the amount of mortgage for which Jamie was eligible.
- Comparing mortgage rates among various lenders both in her area and around the country.
- The mortgage application process in which Jamie was approved for her mortgage within a few hours.

The final negotiations involved a series of e-mail exchanges. Once the buyer and seller agreed on a price, next came the closing, which was conducted completely online. The bank providing Jamie's mortgage prepared the closing documents and sent them electronically over the Internet to the closing agent, who brought them up on a specially equipped computer screen. Jamie signed the documents on the screen. The deed was scanned and delivered by computer image. All completed documents were forwarded to the appropriate parties. Jamie received a CD-ROM with copies of all of the paperwork.

The Electronic Signature in Global and National Commerce Act allowed this process to take place. This law recognizes an *electronic signature* as "an electronic sound, symbol, or process, attached to or logically associated with a contract or other record and executed or adopted by a person with the intent to sign the record."

The time needed for the postclosing process is also reduced. The recording of documents and issuing of the title insurance policy usually takes 45 days. Online, the process was complete in about three hours. This process can result in lower closing costs. Various financial experts estimate that online closings could save businesses and home buyers about $750.

Questions

1. How has technology changed the home-buying process?

2. Based on information at www.homefair.com, describe some advice that should help a person buying a home.

3. What might be some concerns with online home-buying activities? Based on a Web search to obtain additional information on electronic home buying, what other advice would you offer when using the Internet for various phases of the home-buying process?

Continuing Case

HOUSING DECISIONS

Life Situation

Young married couple

Pam, 30

Josh, 32

Two children, ages 1 and 3

Financial Data

Monthly income	$3,600
Assets	$33,850
Living expenses	$3,125
Liabilities	$1,520

Housing needs are changing for the Brocks as their family increases in size. At present, they pay $750 in rent for a two-bedroom apartment. To purchase a home for a comparable monthly payment, the Brocks would have to relocate farther from Josh's place of employment. With a second car and public transportation available, Pam and Josh are starting to consider this home purchase.

Questions

1. Based on a monthly income of $3,600, an estimated $240 per month for property taxes and homeowner's insurance, a current mortgage interest rate of 6 percent, and a down payment of at least 10 percent, what would it cost the Brocks to purchase a home?

2. What tax advantages will the Brocks realize by purchasing a home rather than renting?

3. Explain which sections of *Your Personal Financial Plan* sheets 22–25 could be useful to the Brocks when assessing their housing situation.

Video Case

REAL ESTATE TIPS

The actions of buyers and sellers can enhance the benefits obtained when involved in a home sale transaction. Both parties can prepare for the process in various ways.

Questions

1. What actions can be taken by sellers to improve the sales appeal of their homes?

2. How might a home buyer best prepare for a real estate purchase?

3. Conduct an online search to obtain information about negotiating price when buying or selling a home.

Spending Diary

"AFTER I PAY MY RENT, UTILITIES, AND RENTER'S INSURANCE, I HAVE VERY LITTLE FOR OTHER EXPENSES."

Directions

Your Daily Spending Diary will help you manage your housing expenses to create a better overall spending plan. As you record daily spending, your comments should reflect what you have learned about your spending patterns and help you consider possible changes you might want to make.

Questions

1. What portion of your daily spending involves expenses associated with housing?

2. What types of housing expenses might be reduced with more careful spending habits?

Renting vs. Buying Housing

Financial Planning Activities: To compare the cost of renting and buying your place of residence, obtain estimates for comparable housing units for the data requested below.

Suggested Web Sites: www.homefair.com www.newbuyer.com/homes/ http://finance.move.com
www.dinkytown.net

Rental Costs

Annual rent payments (monthly rent $ _____ × 12) $ _____

Renter's insurance $ _____

Interest lost on security deposit (deposit times after-tax savings account interest rate) $ _____

Total annual cost of renting $

Buying Costs

Annual mortgage payments $ _____

Property taxes (annual costs) $ _____

Homeowner's insurance (annual premium) $ _____

Estimated maintenance and repairs $ _____

After-tax interest lost because of down payment/closing costs $ _____

Less: financial benefits of home ownership

Growth in equity $ – _____

Tax savings for mortgage interest (annual mortgage interest times tax rate) $ – _____

Tax savings for property taxes (annual property taxes times tax rate) $ – _____

Estimated annual depreciation $ – _____

Total annual cost of buying $

What's Next for Your Personal Financial Plan?

- Determine if renting or buying is most appropriate for you at the current time.
- List some circumstances or actions that might change your housing needs.

Apartment Rental Comparison

Financial Planning Activities: Obtain the information requested below to compare costs and facilities of three apartments.

Suggested Web Sites: www.apartments.com   www.apartmentguide.com/

Name of renting person or apartment building			
Address			
Phone			
Monthly rent			
Amount of security deposit			
Length of lease			
Utilities included in rent			
Parking facilities			
Storage area in building			
Laundry facilities			
Distance to schools			
Distance to public transportation			
Distance to shopping			
Pool, recreation area, other facilities			
Estimated utility costs: • Electric • Telephone • Gas • Water			
Other costs			
Other information			

What's Next for Your Personal Financial Plan?

• Which of these rental units would best serve your current housing needs?
• What additional information should be considered when renting an apartment?

Housing Affordability and Mortgage Qualification

Financial Planning Activities: Enter the amounts requested to estimate the amount of affordable mortgage payment, mortgage amount, and home purchase price.

Suggested Web Sites: www.realestate.com   www.kiplinger.com/tools/

Step 1

Determine your monthly gross income (annual income divided by 12)

$ _____

Step 2

With a down payment of at least 10 percent, lenders use 28 percent of monthly gross income as a guideline for TIPI (taxes, insurance, principal, and interest), 36 percent of monthly gross income as a guideline for TIPI plus other debt payments (enter 0.28 or 0.36)

× _____

Step 3

Subtract other debt payments (such as payments on an auto loan), if applicable

− _____

Subtract estimated monthly costs of property taxes and homeowners insurance

− _____

Affordable monthly mortgage payment

$ _____

Step 4

Divide this amount by the monthly mortgage payment per $1,000 based on current mortgage rates (see Exhibit 7–7, text p. 220). For example, for a 10 percent, 30-year loan, the number would be $8.78.

÷ _____

Multiply by $1,000

× _____ $1,000 _____

Affordable mortgage amount

$ _____

Step 5

Divide your affordable mortgage amount by 1 minus the fractional portion of your down payment (for example, 0.9 for a 10 percent down payment).

÷ _____

Affordable home purchase price

$ _____

Note: The two ratios used by lending institutions (Step 2) and other loan requirements are likely to vary based on a variety of factors, including the type of mortgage, the amount of the down payment, your income level, and current interest rates. If you have other debts, lenders will calculate both ratios and then use the one that allows you greater flexibility in borrowing.

What's Next for Your Personal Financial Plan?

- Identify actions you might need to take to qualify for a mortgage.
- Discuss your mortgage qualifications with a mortgage broker or other lender.

Mortgage Company Comparison

Financial Planning Activities: Obtain the information requested below to compare the services and costs for different home mortgage sources.

Suggested Web Sites: www.hsh.com   www.eloan.com

Amount of mortgage:

$ _____	Down payment: $ _____	Years: _____
Company		
Address		
Phone		
Web site		
Contact person		
Application fee, credit report, property appraisal fees		
Loan origination fee		
Other fees, charges (commitment, title, tax transfer)		
Fixed-rate mortgage		
Monthly payment		
Discount points		
Adjustable-rate mortgage		
• Time until first rate charge • Frequency of rate charge		
Monthly payment		
Discount points		
Payment cap		
Interest rate cap		
Rate index used		
Commitment period		
Other information		

What's Next for Your Personal Financial Plan?

- What additional information should be considered when selecting a mortgage?
- Which of these mortgage companies would best serve your current and future needs?

8 Home and Automobile Insurance

Getting Personal

Do you understand the importance of purchasing insurance for your home and automobile? Read the numbered list of possible perils. Then, at the appropriate point along the continuum line following the list, write the number that corresponds to how likely you feel each peril is in your life.

1. You will own a home that will need to be protected against natural disasters, theft, and other adverse occurrences.

2. Your apartment will be robbed.

3. A tornado will destroy your home and automobile.

4. Someone will trip on your sidewalk and sue you.

5. A child of yours will accidentally break a neighbor's window.

6. Your dog will bite someone.

7. Your car will be involved in an accident causing physical injuries to passengers.

8. Your car will be hit by an uninsured motorist.

Most Likely   **Less Likely**

•——•

After studying this chapter, you will be asked to reconsider your priorities.

Objectives

In this chapter, you will learn to:

1. Identify types of risks and risk management methods and develop a risk management plan.
2. Assess the insurance coverage and policy types available to homeowners and renters.
3. Analyze the factors that influence the amount of coverage and cost of home insurance.
4. Identify the important types of automobile insurance coverage.
5. Evaluate factors that affect the cost of automobile insurance.

Why is this important?

Recognizing the importance of insurance and learning how to develop an insurance program can protect you from financial loss. Understanding the factors that affect the cost of insurance will let you get the best insurance value for your money.

Insurance and Risk Management

OBJECTIVE 1
Identify types of risks and risk management methods and develop a risk management plan.

insurance Protection against possible financial loss.

insurance company A risk-sharing firm that assumes financial responsibility for losses that may result from an insured risk.

insurer An insurance company.

policy A written contract for insurance.

policyholder A person who owns an insurance policy.

In today's world of the "strange but true," you can get insurance for just about anything. You might purchase a policy to protect yourself in the event that you're abducted by aliens. Some insurance companies will offer you protection if you think that you have a risk of turning into a werewolf. If you're a fast runner, you might be able to get a discount on a life insurance policy. Some people buy wedding disaster insurance just in case something goes wrong on the big day. You may never need these types of insurance, but you'll certainly need insurance on your home, your vehicle, and your personal property. The more you know about insurance, the better able you will be to make decisions about buying it.

What Is Insurance?

Insurance is protection against possible financial loss. You can't predict the future. However, insurance allows you to be prepared for the worst. It provides protection against many risks, such as unexpected property loss, illness, and injury. Many kinds of insurance exist, and they all share some common characteristics. They give you peace of mind, and they protect you from financial loss when trouble strikes.

An **insurance company,** or **insurer,** is a risk-sharing business that agrees to pay for losses that may happen to someone it insures. A person joins the risk-sharing group by purchasing a contract known as a **policy.** The purchaser of the policy is called a **policyholder.** Under the policy, the insurance company agrees to take on the risk. In return

premium The amount of money a policyholder is charged for an insurance policy.

coverage The protection provided by the terms of an insurance policy.

insured A person covered by an insurance policy.

risk Chance or uncertainty of loss; also used to mean "the insured."

peril The cause of a possible loss.

Key Web Sites for Insurance Company Ratings
www.ambest.com.
www.standardandpoor.com

hazard A factor that increases the likelihood of loss through some peril.

negligence Failure to take ordinary or reasonable care in a situation.

the policyholder pays the company a **premium,** or fee. The protection provided by the terms of an insurance policy is known as **coverage,** and the people protected by the policy are known as the **insured.**

Types of Risk

You face risks every day. You can't cross the street without some danger that a motor vehicle might hit you. You can't own property without running the risk that it will be lost, stolen, damaged or destroyed.

"Risk," "peril," and "hazard" are important terms in insurance. In everyday use, these terms have almost the same meanings. In the insurance business, however, each has a distinct meaning.

Risk is the chance of loss or injury. In insurance it refers to the fact that no one can predict trouble. This means that an insurance company is taking a chance every time it issues a policy. Insurance companies frequently refer to the insured person or property as the risk.

Peril is anything that may possibly cause a loss. It's the reason someone takes out insurance. People buy policies for protection against a wide range of perils, including fire, windstorms, explosions, robbery, and accidents.

Hazard is anything that increases the likelihood of loss through some peril. For example, defective house wiring is a hazard that increases the chance that a fire will start.

The most common risks are personal risks, property risks, and liability risks. *Personal risks* involve loss of income or life due to illness, disability, old age, or unemployment. *Property risks* include losses to property caused by perils, such as fire or theft, and hazards. *Liability risks* involve losses caused by negligence that leads to injury or property damage. **Negligence** is the failure to take ordinary or reasonable care to prevent accidents from happening. If a homeowner doesn't clear the ice from the front steps of her house, for example, she creates a liability risk because visitors could fall on the ice.

Personal risks, property risks, and liability risks are types of *pure,* or *insurable, risk.* The insurance company will have to pay only if some event that the insurance covers actually happens. Pure risks are accidental and unintentional. Although no one can predict whether a pure risk will occur, it's possible to predict the costs that will accrue if one does.

A *speculative risk* is a risk that carries a chance of either loss or gain. Starting a small business that may or may not succeed is an example of speculative risk. Speculative risks are not insurable.

Apply *Yourself!*

Objective 1
Using Web research and discussion with others, develop a risk management plan that best suits your present need for insurance.

Risk Management Methods

Risk management is an organized plan for protecting yourself, your family, and your property. It helps reduce financial losses caused by destructive events. Risk management is a long-range planning process. Your risk management needs will change at various points in your life. If you understand how to manage risks, you can provide better protection for yourself and your family. Most people think of risk management as buying insurance. However, insurance is not the only way of dealing with risk. Four general risk management techniques are commonly used.

RISK AVOIDANCE
You can avoid the risk of a traffic accident by not driving to work. A car manufacturer can avoid the risk of product failure by not introducing new cars. These are both examples of risk avoidance. They are ways to avoid risks, but they require serious trade-offs. You might have to give up your job if you can't get there. The car manufacturer might lose business to competitors who take the risk of producing exciting new cars.

In some cases, though, risk avoidance is practical. By taking precautions in high-crime areas, you might avoid the risk that you will be robbed.

RISK REDUCTION   You can't avoid risks completely. However, you can decrease the likelihood that they will cause you harm. For example, you can reduce the risk of injury in an automobile accident by wearing a seat belt. You can reduce the risk of developing lung cancer by not smoking. By installing fire extinguishers in your home, you reduce the potential damage that could be caused by a fire. Your risk of illness might be lower if you eat properly and exercise regularly.

RISK ASSUMPTION   Risk assumption means taking on responsibility for the negative results of a risk. It makes sense to assume a risk if you know that the possible loss will be small. It also makes sense when you've taken all the precautions you can to avoid or reduce the risk.

When insurance coverage for a particular item is expensive, that item may not be worth insuring. For instance, you might decide not to purchase collision insurance on an older car. If an accident happens, the car may be wrecked, but it wasn't worth much anyway. *Self-insurance* is setting up a special fund, perhaps from savings, to cover the cost of a loss. Self-insurance does not eliminate risks, but it does provide a way of covering losses as an alternative to an insurance policy. Some people self-insure because they can't obtain insurance from an insurance company.

Key Web Sites for Managing Risk
www.insure.com
www.insweb.com

RISK SHIFTING   The most common method of dealing with risk is to shift it. That simply means to transfer it to an insurance company. In exchange for the fee you pay, the insurance company agrees to pay for your losses.

Most insurance policies include deductibles. Deductibles are a combination of risk assumption and risk shifting. A **deductible** is the set amount that the policyholder must pay per loss on an insurance policy. For example, if a falling tree damages your car, you may have to pay $200 toward the repairs. Your insurance company will pay the rest.

Exhibit 8–1 summarizes various risks and effective ways of managing them.

deductible The set amount that the policyholder must pay per loss on an insurance policy.

Planning an Insurance Program

Your personal insurance program should change along with your needs and goals. Dave and Ellen are a young couple. How will they plan their insurance program to meet their needs and goals?

Exhibit 8–2 outlines the steps in developing a personal insurance program.

STEP 1: SET INSURANCE GOALS   Dave and Ellen's main goal should be to minimize personal, property, and liability risks. They also need to decide how they will cover costs resulting from a potential loss. Income, age, family size, lifestyle, experience, and responsibilities will be important factors in the goals they set. The insurance they buy must reflect those goals. Dave and Ellen should try to come up with a basic risk management plan that achieves the following:

did you know?

Deductibles are a combination of risk assumption and risk shifting. The insured person assumes part of the risk, paying the first $100, $250, or $500 of a claim. The majority of the risk for a large claim is shifted to another party, the insurance company.

- Reduces possible loss of income caused by premature death, illness, accident, or unemployment.
- Reduces possible loss of property caused by perils, such as fire or theft, or hazards.
- Reduces possible loss of income, savings, and property because of personal negligence.

Exhibit 8–1   Examples of Risks and Risk Management Strategies

RISKS		STRATEGIES FOR REDUCING FINANCIAL IMPACT		
Personal Events	**Financial Impact**	**Personal Resources**	**Private Sector**	**Public Sector**
Disability	Loss of one income Loss of services Increased expenses	Savings, investments Family observing safety precautions	Disability insurance	Disability insurance

Illness	Loss of one income
	Catastrophic hospital
	    expenses
		Health-enhancing
		    behavior
			Health insurance
			Health maintenance
			    organizations
				Military health care
				Medicare, Medicaid

Death	Loss of one income
	Loss of services
	Final expenses
		Estate planning
		Risk reduction
			Life insurance	Veteran's life
				    insurance
				Social Security
				    survivor's benefits

Retirement	Decreased income
	Unplanned living
	    expenses
		Savings
		Investments
		Hobbies, skills
			Retirement and/or
			    pensions
				Social Security
				Pension plan for
				    government
				    employees

Property loss	Catastrophic storm
	    damage to
	    property
	Repair or
	    replacement cost
	    of theft
		Property repair and
		    upkeep
		Security plans
			Automobile
			    insurance
			Homeowner's
			    insurance
			Flood insurance (joint
			    program with
			    government)
				Flood insurance (joint
				    program with
				    business)

Liability	Claims and
	    settlement costs
	Lawsuits and legal
	    expenses
	Loss of personal
	    assets and income
		Observing safety
		    precautions
		Maintaining property
			Homeowner's
			    insurance
			Automobile
			    insurance
			Malpractice insurance	

Key Web Sites for Insurance Planning Assistance

http://insweb.com

www.insure.com

STEP 2: DEVELOP A PLAN TO REACH YOUR GOALS   Planning is a way of taking control of life instead of just letting life happen to you. Dave and Ellen need to determine what risks they face and what risks they can afford to take. They also have to determine what resources can help them reduce the damage that could be caused by serious risks.

Furthermore, they need to know what kind of insurance is available. The cost of different kinds of insurance and the way the costs vary among companies will be the key factors in their plan. Finally, this couple needs to research the reliability record of different insurance companies.

Dave and Ellen must ask four questions as they develop their risk management plan:

- What do they need to insure?
- How much should they insure it for?
- What kind of insurance should they buy?
- Who should they buy insurance from?

STEP 3: PUT YOUR PLAN INTO ACTION   Once they've developed their plan, Dave and Ellen need to follow through by putting it into action. During this process they might discover that they don't have enough insurance protection. If that's the

Exhibit 8–2   Creating a Personal Insurance Program

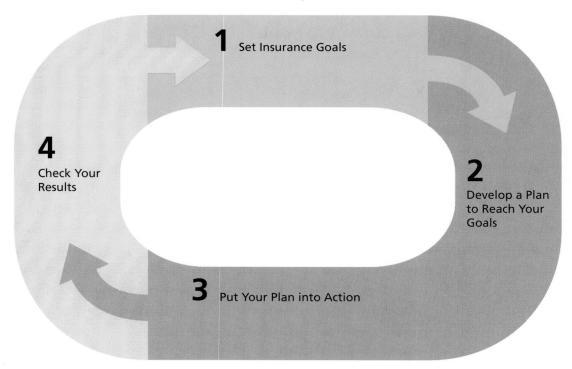

1 Set Insurance Goals

2 Develop a Plan to Reach Your Goals

3 Put Your Plan into Action

4 Check Your Results

case, they could purchase additional coverage or change the kind of coverage they have. Another alternative would be to adjust their budget to cover the cost of additional insurance. Finally, Dave and Ellen might expand their savings or investment programs and use those funds in the case of an emergency.

The best risk management plans will be flexible enough to allow Dave and Ellen to respond to changing life situations. Their goal should be to create an insurance program that can grow or shrink as their protection needs change.

STEP 4: CHECK YOUR RESULTS   Dave and Ellen should take the time to review their plan every two or three years, or whenever their family circumstances change.

Until recently, Dave and Ellen were satisfied with the coverage provided by their insurance policies. However, when the couple bought a house six months ago, the time had come for them to review their insurance plan. With the new house the risks became much greater. After all, what would happen if a fire destroyed part of their home?

The needs of a couple renting an apartment differ from those of a couple who own a house. Both couples face similar risks, but their financial responsibility differs greatly. When you're developing or reviewing a risk management plan, ask yourself if you're providing the financial resources you'll need to protect yourself, your family, and your property. The nearby Personal Finance in Practice feature suggests several guidelines to follow in planning your insurance programs.

Sheet 26
Current
Insurance
Policies
and Needs

Property and Liability Insurance in Your Financial Plan

Major natural disasters have caused catastrophic amounts of property loss in the United States and other parts of the world. In 2005 Hurricanes Katrina, Rita, and Wilma caused $50 billion in damages. In 1992 Hurricane Andrew resulted in $22.3 billion worth of insurance **claims,** or requests for payment to cover financial losses. In the Midwest in 1993, floods caused more than $2 billion worth of damage.

claim A request for payment to cover financial losses.

Personal Finance in Practice

› How Can You Plan an Insurance Program?

Did you:	Yes	No
• Seek advice from a competent and reliable insurance adviser?	☐	☐
• Determine what insurance you need to provide your family with sufficient protection if you die?	☐	☐
• Consider what portion of the family protection is met by Social Security and by group insurance?	☐	☐
• Decide what other needs insurance must meet (funeral expenses, savings, retirement annuities, etc.)?	☐	☐
• Decide what types of insurance best meet your needs?	☐	☐
• Plan an insurance program and implement it except for periodic reviews of changing needs and changing conditions?	☐	☐
• Avoid buying more insurance than you need or can afford?	☐	☐
• Consider dropping one policy for another that provides the same coverage for less money?	☐	☐

Note: *Yes* answers reflect wise actions for insurance planning.

Most people invest large amounts of money in their homes and motor vehicles. Therefore, protecting these items from loss is extremely important. Each year homeowners and renters in the United States lose billions of dollars from more than 3 million burglaries, 500,000 fires, and 200,000 cases of damage from other perils. The cost of injuries and property damage caused by vehicles is also enormous.

Think of the price you pay for home and motor vehicle insurance as an investment in protecting your most valuable possessions. The cost of such insurance may seem high. However, the financial losses from which it protects you are much higher. (Read the accompanying box from the pages of Kiplinger's Personal Finance.)

Two main types of risk are related to your home and your car or other vehicle. One is the risk of damage to or loss of your property. The second type involves your responsibility for injuries to other people or damage to their property.

POTENTIAL PROPERTY LOSSES   People spend a great deal of money on their houses, vehicles, furniture, clothing, and other personal property. Property owners face two basic types of risk. The first is physical damage caused by perils such as fire, wind, water, and smoke. These perils can damage or destroy property. For example, a windstorm might cause a large tree branch to smash the windshield of your car. You would have to find another way to get around while it was being repaired. The second type of risk is loss or damage caused by criminal behavior such as robbery, burglary, vandalism, and arson.

LIABILITY PROTECTION   You also need to protect yourself from liability. **Liability** is legal responsibility for the financial cost of another person's losses or injuries. You can be held legally responsible even if the injury or damage was not your fault. For example, suppose that Terry falls and gets hurt while playing in her friend Lisa's yard. Terry's family may be able to sue Lisa's parents even though Lisa's parents did nothing wrong. Similarly, suppose that Sanjay accidentally damages a valuable painting while helping Ed move some furniture. Ed may take legal action against Sanjay to pay the cost of the painting.

Usually, if you're found liable, or legally responsible, in a situation, it's because negligence on your part caused the mishap. Examples of such negligence include letting

liability Legal responsibility for the financial cost of another person's losses or injuries.

Key Web Sites for State Insurance Regulatory Agencies:

www.naic.org
www.ircweb.org

INSURANCE | Homeowners on the East Coast will pay a steep price for last year's storms. *By Kimberly Lankford*

HURRICANE alley?

INSURERS PAID OUT more than $50 billion in claims for hurricanes Katrina, Rita and Wilma in 2005, swamping the previous record of $27.3 billion in 2004. With the streak of storms predicted to continue, homeowners in the affected areas shouldn't be surprised to see their insurance rates surge this year by 20% to 40% or more, says Robert Hartwig, chief economist for the Insurance Information Institute.

But it may come as a shock to residents of Westchester County, N.Y., just outside New York City and 1,300 miles north of New Orleans, that they'll also be paying for the heavy weather. "We're very concerned that we could see a major hurricane in the Northeast sooner rather than later," says Ken Reeves, director of forecasting operations at AccuWeather.com.

"The storm could take a path like the 'Long Island Express' of 1938, which grazed North Carolina, went up the Eastern seaboard and caused damage of Long Island and in New England."

Allstate, with one-fourth of the market share in the densely populated and expensive New York area, is taking the threat seriously. It has stopped issuing new policies to residents of the Westchester suburbs, as well as to residents of New York's five boroughs and two counties on Long Island. It also plans to drop about 36,000 of the 450,000 New York–area customers whose policies come up for renewal this year.

Risk averse. Insurers can't raise rates in other parts of the U.S. to subsidize their losses in the Southeast. But companies are looking more closely at their risk exposure and scaling back.

Several regional insurers are abandoning the Massachusetts coast and dropping thousands of customers. Of those companies that remain, many are asking for rate increases of 25% to 50% this year.

Flood insurance, however, is still relatively inexpensive, so even residents of inland areas should consider buying it. "I've been telling my customers that they need to think about flood insurance," says independent agent JoAnne Murray of Tarrytown, N.Y., in Westchester County.

To keep premiums down—and coverage in place—all homeowners should also raise their deductible to at least $1,000 to avoid the temptation to file small claims. "People with a claims history are clearly a target for non-renewal," says George Yates, an agent in East Hampton, N.Y.

Storms' wake. Not surprisingly, the situa-tion is even worse in Florida, where residents filed nearly three million hurricane claims in 2004 and 2005. Since December 2004, 12 insurers have stopped writing homeowners coverage in the state entirely, and some large insurers that still do business in the area have dropped tens of thousands of policyholders. Florida Citizens, the state's high-risk pool, is now its second-largest insurer. Nearly 175 companies have filed for rate hikes in the first four months of 2006. One of them, Florida Peninsula Insurance Co., asked for an average increase of 92%.

Meanwhile, if you don't live along the Atlantic or Gulf coasts, consider yourself fortunate when it comes to insurance. Hartwig expects homeowners-insurance premiums to increase by just 2% to 4% in the rest of the country, primarily because of higher construction costs.

1. Why has Allstate stopped issuing new policies in New York?

---

2. What can homeowners do to keep premiums down and coverage in place?

---

3. Why should you feel lucky if you don't live along the Atlantic or Gulf coast?

---

young children swim in a pool without supervision or cluttering a staircase with things that could cause someone to slip and fall.

✓ CONCEPT CHECK 8–1

1   What are the three types of risk? Give an example for each.

_____

_____

_____

2   What are the four methods of managing risks? Give an example for each.

_____

_____

_____

_____

3   List the four steps in planning for your insurance program.

_____

_____

_____

_____

4   Give an example of each kind of risk—personal, property, and liability.

_____

Home and Property Insurance

OBJECTIVE 2

Assess the insurance coverage and policy types available to homeowners and renters.

homeowner's insurance
Coverage for a place of residence and its associated financial risks.

Your home and personal belongings are probably a major portion of your assets. Whether you rent your dwelling or own a home, property insurance is vital. **Homeowner's insurance** is coverage for your place of residence and its associated financial risks, such as damage to personal property and injuries to others (see Exhibit 8–3).

Homeowner's Insurance Coverages

A homeowner's insurance policy provides coverage for the following:

- The building in which you live and any other structures on the property.
- Additional living expenses.
- Personal property.
- Personal liability and related coverage.
- Specialized coverage.

BUILDING AND OTHER STRUCTURES   The main purpose of homeowner's insurance is to protect you against financial loss in case your home is damaged or destroyed. Detached structures on your property, such as a garage or toolshed, are also covered. Homeowner's coverage even includes trees, shrubs, and plants.

Exhibit 8–3   Home Insurance Coverage

Building and other structures | **Personal property** | **Loss of use/additional living expenses while home is uninhabitable** | **Personal liability and related coverages**

ADDITIONAL LIVING EXPENSES
If a fire or other event damages your home, additional living expense coverage pays for you to stay somewhere else. For example, you may need to stay in a motel or rent an apartment while your home is being repaired. These extra living expenses will be paid by your insurance. Some policies limit additional living expense coverage to 10 to 20 percent of the home's coverage amount. They may also limit payments to a maximum of six to nine months. Other policies may pay additional living expenses for up to a year.

PERSONAL PROPERTY
Homeowner's insurance covers your household belongings, such as furniture, appliances, and clothing, up to a portion of the insured value of the home. That portion is usually 55, 70, or 75 percent. For example, a home insured for $80,000 might have $56,000 (70 percent) worth of coverage for household belongings.

Personal property coverage typically limits the payout for the theft of certain items, such as $5,000 for jewelry. It provides protection against the loss or damage of articles that you take with you when you are away from home. For example, items you take on vacation or use at college are usually covered up to the policy limit. Personal property coverage even extends to property that you rent, such as a rug cleaner, while it's in your possession.

Most homeowner's policies include optional coverage for personal computers, including stored data, up to a certain limit. Your insurance agent can determine whether the equipment is covered against data loss and damage from spilled drinks or power surges.

If something does happen to your personal property, you must prove how much it was worth and that it belonged to you. To make the process easier, you can create a household inventory. A **household inventory** is a list or other documentation of personal belongings, with purchase dates and cost information. You can get a form for such an inventory from an insurance agent. Exhibit 8–4 provides a list of items you might include if you decide to compile your own inventory. For items of special value, you should have receipts, serial numbers, brand names, and proof of value.

Your household inventory can include a video recording or photographs of your home and its contents. Make sure that the closet and storage area doors are photographed open. On the back of the photographs, indicate the date and the value of the objects. Update your inventory, photos, and related documents on a regular basis. Keep a copy of each document in a secure location, such as a safe deposit box.

If you own valuable items, such as expensive musical instruments, or need added protection for computers and related equipment, you can purchase a personal property floater. A **personal property floater** is additional property insurance that covers the damage or loss of a specific item of high value. The insurance company will require a detailed description of the item and its worth. You'll also need to have the item appraised, or evaluated by an expert, from time to time to make sure that its value hasn't changed.

household inventory A list or other documentation of personal belongings, with purchase dates and cost information.

personal property floater Additional property insurance to cover the damage or loss of a specific item of high value.

Exhibit 8–4   Household Inventory Contents

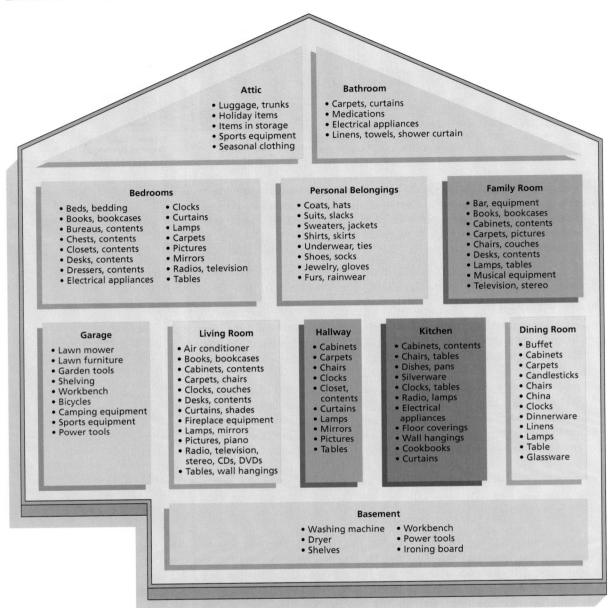

Attic
- Luggage, trunks
- Holiday items
- Items in storage
- Sports equipment
- Seasonal clothing

Bathroom
- Carpets, curtains
- Medications
- Electrical appliances
- Linens, towels, shower curtain

Bedrooms
- Beds, bedding
- Books, bookcases
- Bureaus, contents
- Chests, contents
- Closets, contents
- Desks, contents
- Dressers, contents
- Electrical appliances
- Clocks
- Curtains
- Lamps
- Carpets
- Pictures
- Mirrors
- Radios, television
- Tables

Personal Belongings
- Coats, hats
- Suits, slacks
- Sweaters, jackets
- Shirts, skirts
- Underwear, ties
- Shoes, socks
- Jewelry, gloves
- Furs, rainwear

Family Room
- Bar, equipment
- Books, bookcases
- Cabinets, contents
- Carpets, pictures
- Chairs, couches
- Desks, contents
- Lamps, tables
- Musical equipment
- Television, stereo

Garage
- Lawn mower
- Lawn furniture
- Garden tools
- Shelving
- Workbench
- Bicycles
- Camping equipment
- Sports equipment
- Power tools

Living Room
- Air conditioner
- Books, bookcases
- Cabinets, contents
- Carpets, chairs
- Clocks, couches
- Desks, contents
- Curtains, shades
- Fireplace equipment
- Lamps, mirrors
- Pictures, piano
- Radio, television, stereo, CDs, DVDs
- Tables, wall hangings

Hallway
- Cabinets
- Carpets
- Chairs
- Clocks
- Closet, contents
- Curtains
- Lamps
- Mirrors
- Pictures
- Tables

Kitchen
- Cabinets, contents
- Chairs, tables
- Dishes, pans
- Silverware
- Clocks, tables
- Radio, lamps
- Electrical appliances
- Floor coverings
- Wall hangings
- Cookbooks
- Curtains

Dining Room
- Buffet
- Cabinets
- Carpets
- Candlesticks
- Chairs
- China
- Clocks
- Dinnerware
- Linens
- Lamps
- Table
- Glassware

Basement
- Washing machine
- Dryer
- Shelves
- Workbench
- Power tools
- Ironing board

Sheet 27
Home Inventory

PERSONAL LIABILITY AND RELATED COVERAGE   Every day people face the risk of financial loss due to injuries to other people or their property. The following are examples of this risk:

- A guest falls on a patch of ice on the steps to your home and breaks his arm.
- A spark from the barbecue in your backyard starts a fire that damages a neighbor's roof.
- Your son or daughter accidentally breaks an antique lamp while playing at a neighbor's house.

In each of these situations, you could be held responsible for paying for the damage. The personal liability portion of a homeowner's policy protects you and members of your family if others sue you for injuries they suffer or damage to their property. This coverage includes the cost of legal defense.

Not all individuals who come to your property are covered by your liability insurance. Friends, guests, and babysitters are probably covered. However, if you have regular employees, such as a housekeeper, a cook, or a gardener, you may need to obtain worker's compensation coverage for them.

Most homeowner's policies provide basic personal liability coverage of $100,000, but often that's not enough. An **umbrella policy,** also called a *personal catastrophe policy,* supplements your basic personal liability coverage. This added protection covers you for all kinds of personal injury claims. For instance, an umbrella policy will cover you if someone sues you for saying or writing something negative or untrue or for damaging his or her reputation. Extended liability policies are sold in amounts of $1 million or more and are useful for wealthy people. If you are a business owner, you may need other types of liability coverage as well.

umbrella policy Supplementary personal liability coverage; also called a *personal catastrophe policy.*

Medical payments coverage pays the cost of minor accidental injuries to visitors on your property. It also covers minor injuries caused by you, members of your family, or even your pets, away from home. Settlements under medical payments coverage are made without determining who was at fault. This makes it fast and easy for the insurance company to process small claims, generally up to $5,000. If the injury is more serious, the personal liability portion of the homeowner's policy covers it. Medical payments coverage does not cover injury to you or the other people who live in your home.

medical payments coverage Home insurance that pays the cost of minor accidental injuries on one's property.

If you or a family member should accidentally damage another person's property, the supplementary coverage of homeowner's insurance will pay for it. This protection is usually limited to $500 or $1,000. Again, payments are made regardless of fault. If the damage is more expensive, however, it's handled under the personal liability coverage.

did you know?

For $50 to $80 a year, homeowners can obtain $10,000 for sewage and drain backup damage. Heavy rains that clog a sewer line can cause damage to furniture and other items in a finished basement.

SPECIALIZED COVERAGE   Homeowner's insurance usually doesn't cover losses from floods and earthquakes. If you live in an area that has frequent floods or earthquakes, you need to purchase special coverage. In some places the National Flood Insurance Program makes flood insurance available. This protection is separate from a homeowner's policy. An insurance agent or the Federal Emergency Management Agency (FEMA) of the Federal Insurance Administration can give you additional information about this coverage.

You may be able to get earthquake insurance as an **endorsement**—addition of coverage—to a homeowners' policy or through a state-run insurance program. The most serious earthquakes occur in the Pacific Coast region. However, earthquakes can happen in other regions, too. If you plan to buy a home in an area that has high risk of floods or earthquakes, you may have to buy the necessary insurance in order to be approved for a mortgage loan.

endorsement An addition of coverage to a standard insurance policy.

Renter's Insurance

For people who rent, home insurance coverage includes personal property protection, additional living expenses coverage, and personal liability and related coverage. Renter's insurance does not provide coverage on the building or other structures.

There are two standard renter's insurance policies. The *broad form* covers your personal property against perils specified in the policy, such as fires and thefts, and the *comprehensive form* protects your personal property against all perils not specifically excluded in the policy. When shopping for renter's insurance, be aware that these policies

- Normally pay only the actual cash value of your losses. Replacement cost coverage is available for an extra premium.

- Fully cover your personal property only at home. When traveling, your luggage and other personal items are protected up to a certain percentage of the policy's total amount of coverage.
- Automatically provide liability coverage if someone is injured on your premises.
- May duplicate other coverage. For instance, if you are still a dependent, your personal property may be covered by your parents' homeowner's policy. This coverage is limited, however, to an amount equal to a certain percentage of the total personal property coverage provided by the policy.

did you know?

While more than 9 out of 10 homeowners have property insurance, only about 4 out of 10 renters are covered.

The most important part of renter's insurance is the protection it provides for your personal property. Many renters believe that they are covered under the landlord's insurance. In fact, that's the case only when the landlord is proved liable for some damage. For example, if bad wiring causes a fire and damages a tenant's property, the tenant may be able to collect money from the landlord. Renter's insurance is relatively inexpensive and provides many of the same kinds of protection as a homeowner's policy.

Home Insurance Policy Forms

Home insurance policies are available in several forms. The forms provide different combinations of coverage. Some forms are not available in all areas.

Apply Yourself!

Objective 2

You are about to rent your first apartment. You have approximately $10,000 worth of personal belongings. Contact an insurance agent to find out the cost of renter's insurance.

The basic form (HO-1) protects against perils such as fire, lightning, windstorms, hail, volcanic eruptions, explosions, smoke, theft, vandalism, glass breakage, and riots.

The broad form (HO-2) covers an even wider range of perils, including falling objects and damage from ice, snow, or sleet.

The special form (HO-3) covers all basic- and broad-form risks, plus any other risks except those specifically excluded from the policy. Common exclusions are flood, earthquake, war, and nuclear accidents. Personal property is covered for the risks listed in the policy.

The tenant's form (HO-4) protects the personal property of renters against the risks listed in the policy. It does not include coverage on the building or other structures.

The comprehensive form (HO-5) expands the coverage of the HO-3. The HO-5 includes endorsements for items such as replacement cost coverage on contents and guaranteed replacement cost coverage on buildings.

Condominium owner's insurance (HO-6) protects personal property and any additions or improvements made to the living unit. These might include bookshelves, electrical fixtures, wallpaper, or carpeting. The condominium association purchases insurance on the building and other structures.

CAUTION!

Computers and other equipment used in a home-based business are not usually covered by a home insurance policy. Contact your insurance agent to obtain needed coverage.

Manufactured housing units and mobile homes usually qualify for insurance coverage with conventional policies. However, some mobile homes may need special policies with higher rates because the way they are built increases their risk of fire and wind damage. The cost of mobile home insurance coverage depends on the home's location and the way it's attached to the ground. Mobile home insurance is quite expensive: A $40,000 mobile home can cost as much to insure as a $120,000 house.

Exhibit 8–5   Not Everything Is Covered

CERTAIN PERSONAL PROPERTY IS NOT COVERED BY HOMEOWNERS INSURANCE:

- Items insured separately, such as jewelry, furs, boats, or expensive electronic equipment

- Animals, birds, or fish

- Motorized vehicles not licensed for road use, except those used for home maintenance

- Sound devices used in motor vehicles, such as radios and CD players

- Aircraft and parts

- Property belonging to tenants

- Property contained in a rental apartment

- Property rented by the homeowner to other people

- Business property

Separate coverage may be available for personal property that is not covered by a homeowners insurance policy.

In addition to the risks previously discussed, home insurance policies include coverage for:

- Credit card fraud, check forgery, and counterfeit money.
- The cost of removing damaged property.
- Emergency removal of property to protect it from damage.
- Temporary repairs after a loss to prevent further damage.
- Fire department charges in areas with such fees.

Not everything is covered by home insurance (see Exhibit 8–5).

✓ CONCEPT CHECK 8–2

1 Define the following terms in the spaces below:

a. Homeowner's insurance _____

b. Household inventory _____

c. Personal property floater _____

d. Renter's insurance _____

2 Identify the choice that best completes the statement or answers the question:

a. The personal liability portion of a homeowner's insurance policy protects the insured against financial loss when his or her (i) house floods, (ii) jewelry is stolen, (iii) guests injure themselves, (iv) reputation is damaged.

b. Renter's insurance includes coverage for all of the following except (i) the building, (ii) personal property, (iii) additional living expenses, (iv) personal liability.

c. The basic home insurance policy form protects against several perils, including (i) sleet, (ii) lightning, (iii) flood, (iv) earthquake.

3 Define the following terms in the spaces below:

a. Umbrella policy _____

b. Medical payments coverage _____

c. Endorsement _____

(continued)

4 List at least four personal property items that are not covered by a homeowner's insurance policy.

_____

_____

Home Insurance Cost Factors

How Much Coverage Do You Need?

You can get the best insurance value by choosing the right coverage amount and knowing the factors that affect insurance costs (see Exhibit 8–6). Your insurance should be based on the amount of money you would need to rebuild or repair your house, not the amount you paid for it. As construction costs rise, you should increase the amount of coverage. In fact, today most insurance policies automatically increase coverage as construction costs rise.

In the past, many homeowner's policies insured the building for only 80 percent of the replacement value. If the building were destroyed, the homeowner would have to pay for part of the cost of replacing it, which could be expensive. Today most companies recommend full coverage.

If you are borrowing money to buy a home, the lender will require that you have property insurance. Remember, too, that the amount of insurance on your home determines the coverage on your personal belongings. Coverage for personal belongings is usually from 55 to 75 percent of the insurance amount on your home.

Insurance companies base claim settlements on one or two methods. Under the **actual cash value (ACV)** method, the payment you receive is based on the replacement cost of an item minus depreciation. Depreciation is the loss of value of an item as it gets older. This means you would receive less for a five-year-old bicycle than you originally paid for it.

actual cash value (ACV) A claim settlement method in which the insured receives payment based on the current replacement cost of a damaged or lost item, less depreciation.

Exhibit 8–6   Determining the Amount of Home Insurance You Need

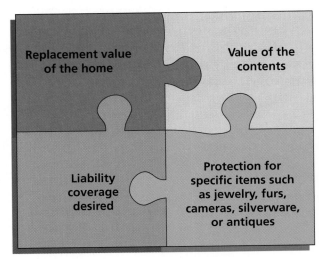

Under the **replacement value** method for settling claims, you receive the full cost of repairing or replacing an item. Depreciation is not considered. Many companies limit the replacement cost to 400 percent of the item's actual cash value. Replacement value coverage is more expensive than actual cash value coverage.

replacement value A claim settlement method in which the insured receives the full cost of repairing or replacing a damaged or lost item.

Factors That Affect Home Insurance Costs

The cost of your home insurance will depend on several factors, such as the location of the building and the type of building and construction materials. The amount of coverage and type of policy you choose will also affect the cost of home insurance. Furthermore, different insurance companies offer different rates.

LOCATION OF HOME   The location of your home affects your insurance rates. Insurance companies offer lower rates to people whose homes are close to a water supply or fire hydrant or located in an area that has a good fire department. On the other hand, rates are higher in areas where crime is common. People living in regions that experience severe weather, such as tornadoes and hurricanes, may also pay more for insurance.

TYPE OF STRUCTURE   The type of home and its construction influence the price of insurance coverage. A brick house, for example, will usually cost less to insure than a similar structure made of wood. However, earthquake coverage is more expensive for a brick house than for a wood dwelling because a wooden house is more likely to survive an earthquake. Also, an older house may be more difficult to restore to its original condition. That means that it will cost more to insure.

COVERAGE AMOUNT AND POLICY TYPE   The policy and the amount of coverage you select affect the premium you pay. Obviously, insuring a $300,000 home costs more than insuring a $100,000 home.

The deductible amount in your policy also affects the cost of your insurance. If you increase the amount of your deductible, your premium will be lower because the company will pay out less in claims. The most common deductible amount is $250. Raising the deductible from $250 to $500 or $1,000 can reduce the premium you pay by 15 percent or more.

HOME INSURANCE DISCOUNTS   Most companies offer discounts if you take action to reduce risks to your home. Your premium may be lower if you have smoke detectors or a fire extinguisher. If your home has dead-bolt locks and alarm systems, which make a break-in harder for thieves, insurance costs may be lower. Some companies offer discounts to people who don't file any claims for a certain number of years.

COMPANY DIFFERENCES   You can save up to 25 percent on homeowner's insurance by comparing rates from several companies. Some insurance agents work for only one company. Others are independent agents who represent several different companies. Talk to both types of agent. You'll get the information you need to compare rates.

Don't select a company on the basis of price alone; also consider service and coverage. Not all companies settle claims in the same way. Suppose that all homes on Evergreen Terrace are dented on one side by large hail. They all have the same kind of siding. Unfortunately, the homeowners discover that this type of siding is no longer available so all the siding on all of the houses will need to be replaced. Some insurance companies will pay to replace all the siding. Others will pay only to replace the damaged parts.

Sheet 28
Determining Needed Property Insurance

Key Web Sites for Comparing Coverage and Costs

www.quotesmith.com

www.accuquote.com

did you know?

In some areas, a home can be automatically rejected for insurance coverage if it has had two or three claims of any sort in the past three years. Homes that have encountered water damage, storm damage, and burglaries are most vulnerable to rejection.

Key Web Site for Flood Insurance

www.fema.gov/nfip

Sheet 29
Apartment/ Home Insurance Comparison

Personal Finance in Practice

› How to Lower the Cost of Insurance

How can you lower your cost of homeowner's and renter's insurance? Shop around and compare the cost. Here are a few tips that can save you hundreds of dollars annually.

1. *Consider a higher deductible.* Increasing your deductible by just a few hundred dollars can make a big difference in your premium.

2. *Ask your insurance agent about discounts.* You may be able to secure a lower premium if your home has safety features such as dead-bolt locks, smoke detectors, an alarm system, storm shutters, or fire retardant roofing material. Persons over 55 years of age or long-term customers may also be offered discounts.

3. *Insure your house, **not** the land under it.* After a disaster, the land is still there. If you don't subtract the value of the land when deciding how much homeowner's insurance to buy, you will pay more than you should.

4. *Make certain you purchase enough coverage to replace what is insured.* "Replacement" coverage gives you the money to rebuild your home and replace its contents. An actual cash value policy is cheaper but pays only what your property is worth at the time of the loss—your cost minus depreciation.

5. *Ask about special coverage you might need.* You may have to pay extra for computers, cameras, jewelry, art, antiques, musical instruments, stamp collections, and other items.

6. *Remember that flood and earthquake damage are not covered by a standard homeowners policy.* The cost of a separate earthquake policy will depend on the likelihood of earthquakes in your area. Homeowners who live in areas prone to flooding should take advantage of the National Flood Insurance Program. Call 1-888-CALLFLOOD or visit www.floodalert.fema.gov.

7. *If you are a renter do **NOT** assume your landlord carries insurance on your personal belongings.* Purchase a special policy for renters.

Key Web Sites for Home and Auto Insurance

www.independentagent.com
www.trustedchoice.com

State insurance commissions and consumer organizations can give you information about different insurance companies. *Consumer Reports* rates insurance companies on a regular basis.

Read the accompanying Personal Finance in Practice box to learn how you can lower the cost of homeowner's and renter's insurance.

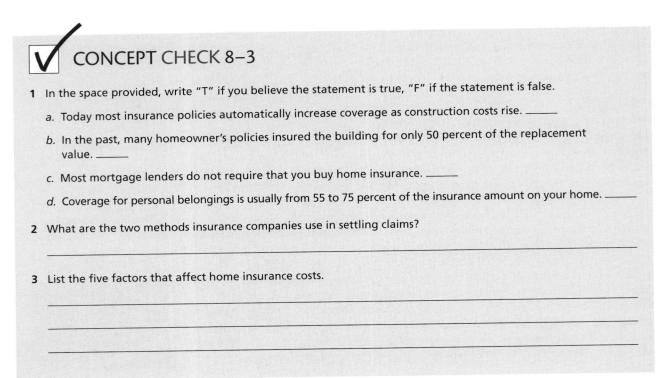

✓ CONCEPT CHECK 8–3

1 In the space provided, write "T" if you believe the statement is true, "F" if the statement is false.

  a. Today most insurance policies automatically increase coverage as construction costs rise. _____

  b. In the past, many homeowner's policies insured the building for only 50 percent of the replacement value. _____

  c. Most mortgage lenders do not require that you buy home insurance. _____

  d. Coverage for personal belongings is usually from 55 to 75 percent of the insurance amount on your home. _____

2 What are the two methods insurance companies use in settling claims?

  _____

3 List the five factors that affect home insurance costs.

  _____

  _____

  _____

Automobile Insurance Coverages

Motor vehicle crashes cost more than $240 billion in lost wages and medical bills every year. Traffic accidents can destroy people's lives physically, financially, and emotionally. Buying insurance can't eliminate the pain and suffering that vehicle accidents cause. It can, however, reduce the financial impact.

Every state in the United States has a **financial responsibility law,** a law that requires drivers to prove that they can pay for damage or injury caused by an automobile accident. Recently, more than 45 states had laws requiring people to carry motor vehicle insurance. In the remaining states, most people buy motor vehicle insurance by choice. Very few people have the money they would need to meet financial responsibility requirements on their own.

The coverage provided by motor vehicle insurance falls into two categories. One is protection for bodily injury. The other is protection for property damage (see Exhibit 8–7).

> **OBJECTIVE 4**
> Identify the important types of automobile insurance coverage.

financial responsibility law State legislation that requires drivers to prove their ability to cover the cost of damage or injury caused by an automobile accident.

Motor Vehicle Bodily Injury Coverages

Most of the money that motor vehicle insurance companies pay out in claims goes for legal expenses, medical expenses, and other costs that arise when someone is injured. The main types of bodily injury coverage are bodily injury liability, medical payments, and uninsured motorist's protection.

BODILY INJURY LIABILITY   **Bodily injury liability** is insurance that covers physical injuries caused by a vehicle accident for which you were responsible. If pedestrians, people in other vehicles, or passengers in your vehicle are injured or killed, bodily injury liability coverage pays for expenses related to the crash.

Liability coverage is usually expressed by three numbers, such as 100/300/50. These amounts represent thousands of dollars of coverage. The first two numbers refer to bodily injury coverage. In the example above, $100,000 is the maximum amount that the insurance company will pay for the injuries of any one person in any one accident. The second number, $300,000, is the maximum amount the company will pay all injured parties (two or more) in any one accident. The third number, $50,000, indicates the limit for payment for damage to the property of others (see Exhibit 8–8).

bodily injury liability Coverage for the risk of financial loss due to legal expenses, medical costs, lost wages, and other expenses associated with injuries caused by an automobile accident for which the insured was responsible.

MEDICAL PAYMENTS COVERAGE   **Medical payments coverage** is insurance that applies to the medical expenses of anyone who is injured in your vehicle, including you. This type of coverage also provides additional medical benefits for you and members of your family; it pays medical expenses if you or your family members are injured while riding in another person's vehicle or if any of you are hit by a vehicle.

medical payments coverage Automobile insurance that covers medical expenses for people injured in one's car.

Exhibit 8–7   Two Major Categories of Automobile Insurance

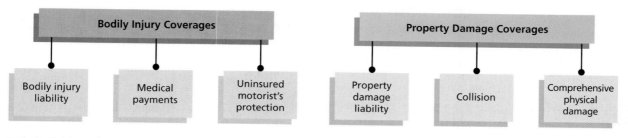

Buying bodily injury and property damage coverage can reduce the financial impact of an accident. *What type of expenses would be paid for by bodily injury liability coverage?*

Exhibit 8–8

Automobile Liability
Insurance Coverage

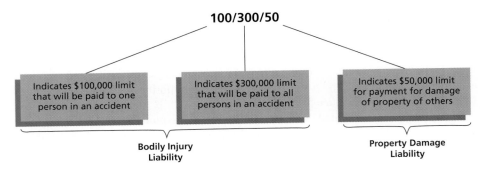

100/300/50

Indicates $100,000 limit that will be paid to one person in an accident

Indicates $300,000 limit that will be paid to all persons in an accident

Indicates $50,000 limit for payment for damage of property of others

**Bodily Injury
Liability**

**Property Damage
Liability**

The three numbers used to describe liability coverage refer to the limits on different types of payments. *Why do you think the middle number is the highest?*

UNINSURED MOTORIST'S PROTECTION   Unfortunately, you cannot assume that everyone who is behind the wheel is carrying insurance. How can you guard yourself and your passengers against the risk of getting into an accident with someone who has no insurance? The answer is uninsured motorist's protection.

Uninsured motorist's protection is insurance that covers you and your family members if you are involved in an accident with an uninsured or hit-and-run driver. In most states it does not cover damage to the vehicle itself. Penalties for driving uninsured vary by state, but they generally include stiff fines and suspension of driving privileges.

Underinsured motorist's coverage protects you when another driver has some insurance, but not enough to pay for the injuries he or she has caused.

uninsured motorist's protection Automobile insurance coverage for the cost of injuries to a person and members of his or her family caused by a driver with inadequate insurance or by a hit-and-run driver.

Motor Vehicle Property Damage Coverage

One afternoon, during a summer storm, Carrie was driving home from her job as a hostess at a pancake house. The rain was coming down in buckets, and she couldn't see very well. As a result, she didn't realize that the car in front of her had stopped to make a left turn, and she hit the car. The crash totaled Carrie's new car. Fortunately, she had purchased property damage coverage. Property damage coverage protects you from financial loss if you damage someone else's property or if your vehicle is damaged. It includes property damage liability, collision, and comprehensive physical damage.

property damage liability Automobile insurance coverage that protects a person against financial loss when that person damages the property of others.

collision Automobile insurance that pays for damage to the insured's car when it is involved in an accident.

Apply *Yourself!*

Objective 4

Research the make and model of vehicles that are most frequently stolen, consequently resulting in higher insurance rates.

PROPERTY DAMAGE LIABILITY   **Property damage liability** is motor vehicle insurance that applies when you damage the property of others. In addition, it protects you when you're driving another person's vehicle with the owner's permission. Although the damaged property is usually another car, the coverage also extends to buildings and to equipment such as street signs and telephone poles.

COLLISION   **Collision** insurance covers damage to your vehicle when it is involved in an accident. It allows you to collect money no matter who was at fault. However, the amount you can collect is limited to the actual cash value of your vehicle at the time of the accident. If your vehicle has many extra features, make sure that you have a record of its condition and value.

COMPREHENSIVE PHYSICAL DAMAGE   Comprehensive physical damage coverage protects you if your vehicle is damaged in a nonaccident situation. It covers your vehicle against risks such as fire, theft, falling objects, vandalism, hail, floods, tornadoes, earthquakes, and avalanches.

No-Fault Insurance

To reduce the time and cost of settling vehicle injury cases, various states are trying a number of alternatives. Under the **no-fault system,** drivers who are involved in accidents collect money from their own insurance companies. It doesn't matter who caused the accident. Each company pays the insured up to the limits of his or her coverage. Because no-fault systems vary by state, you should investigate the coverage of no-fault insurance in your state.

no-fault system An automobile insurance program in which drivers involved in accidents collect medical expenses, lost wages, and related injury costs from their own insurance companies.

Other Coverages

Several other kinds of motor vehicle insurance are available to you. *Wage loss insurance* pays for any salary or income you might have lost because of being injured in a vehicle accident. Wage loss insurance is usually required in states with a no-fault insurance system. In other states it's available by choice.

Emergency road service coverage pays for mechanical assistance in the event that your vehicle breaks down. This can be helpful on long trips or during bad weather. If necessary, you can get your vehicle towed to a service station. However, once your vehicle arrives at the repair shop, you are responsible for paying the bill. If you belong to an automobile club, your membership may include towing coverage. If that's the case, paying for emergency road service coverage could be a waste of money. *Rental reimbursement coverage* pays for a rental car if your vehicle is stolen or being repaired.

✔ CONCEPT CHECK 8–4

1 List the three main types of bodily injury coverage.

_____

_____

2 In the space provided, write "T" if the statement is true, "F" if it is false.

a. Financial responsibility law requires drivers to prove that they can pay for damage or injury caused by an automobile accident. _____

b. Insurance that covers physical injuries caused by a vehicle accident for which you were responsible is called uninsured motorist's protection. _____

c. Automobile liability coverage is usually expressed by three numbers 100/300/50. _____

d. The first two numbers in 100/300/50 refer to the limit for payment for damage to the property of others. _____

e. Uninsured motorist's protection is insurance that covers you and your family members if you are involved in an accident with an uninsured motorist or hit-and-run driver. _____

f. Collision insurance covers damage to your vehicle when it is involved in an accident. _____

3 What is no-fault insurance? What is its purpose?

_____

_____

4 List at least three other kinds of automobile insurance that are available to you.

_____

_____

Automobile Insurance Costs

Sheet 30
Automobile Insurance Cost Comparison

Motor vehicle insurance is not cheap. The average household spends more than $1,200 for motor vehicle insurance yearly. The premiums are related to the amount of claims insurance companies pay out each year. Your automobile insurance cost is directly related to coverage amounts and factors such as the vehicle, your place of residence, and your driving record.

Amount of Coverage

The amount you will pay for insurance depends on the amount of coverage you require. You need enough coverage to protect yourself legally and financially.

LEGAL CONCERNS   As discussed earlier, most people who are involved in motor vehicle accidents cannot afford to pay an expensive court settlement with their own money. For this reason, most drivers buy liability insurance.

In the past, bodily injury liability coverage of 10/20 was usually enough. However, some people have been awarded millions of dollars in recent cases, so coverage of 100/300 is usually recommended.

PROPERTY VALUES   Just as medical expenses and legal settlements have increased, so has the cost of vehicles. Therefore, you should consider a policy with a limit of $50,000 or even $100,000 for property damage liability.

Motor Vehicle Insurance Premium Factors

Vehicle type, rating territory, and driver classification are three other factors that influence insurance costs.

VEHICLE TYPE   The year, make, and model of a vehicle will affect insurance costs. Vehicles that have expensive replacement parts and complicated repairs will cost more to insure. Also, premiums will probably be higher for vehicle makes and models that are frequently stolen.

RATING TERRITORY   In most states your rating territory is the place of residence used to determine your vehicle insurance premium. Different locations have different costs. For example, rural areas usually have fewer accidents and less frequent occurrences of theft. Your insurance would probably cost less there than if you lived in a large city.

DRIVER CLASSIFICATION   Driver classification is based on age, sex, marital status, driving record, and driving habits. In general, young drivers (under 25) and elderly drivers (over 70) have more frequent and more serious accidents. As a result these

---

did you know?

Foods and drinks that were reported as the most common distractions in auto accidents: coffee, hot soup, tacos, chili-covered foods, hamburgers, chicken, jelly- or cream-filled doughnuts, and soft drinks.

---

did you know?

An automobile insurance company once paid $3,600 for damages to a car in an accident caused by a mouse. The critter apparently got into the car while it was parked and then crawled up the driver's pants leg while the car was on an interstate highway. The driver lost control of the vehicle and crashed into a roadside barrier. Another claim resulted when a barbecued steak fell off a 17th-floor balcony and dented a car.

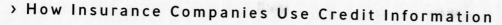

Personal Finance in Practice

› How Insurance Companies Use Credit Information

The Fair Credit Reporting Act (FCRA, discussed in Chapter 5) allows insurance companies to examine your credit report without your permission. These companies believe that consumers who are financially responsible have fewer and less costly losses and therefore should pay less for their insurance. Insurance companies use credit scores in two ways:

- *Underwriting*—deciding whether to issue you a new policy or to renew your existing policy. Some state laws prohibit insurance companies from refusing to issue you a new policy or from renewing your existing policy based solely on information obtained from your credit report. In addition, some state laws prohibit insurance companies from using your credit information as the sole factor in accepting you and placing you into a specific company within their group of companies.

- *Rating*—deciding what price to charge you for your insurance, either by placing you into a specific

rating tier, or level, or by placing you into a specific company within their group of companies. Some insurance companies use credit information along with other more traditional rating factors such as motor vehicle records and claims history. Where permitted by state law, some insurance companies may use credit reports only to determine your rate.

The FCRA requires an insurance company to tell you if it has taken "adverse action" against you because of your credit report information. If the company tells you that you have been adversely affected, it must also tell you the name of the national credit bureau that supplied the information so you can get a free copy of your credit report. The best way to know for sure if your credit score is affecting your acceptance with an insurer for the best policy at the best rate is to ask.

groups pay higher premiums. Your driving record will also influence your insurance premiums. If you have accidents or receive tickets for traffic violations, your rates will increase.

The cost and number of claims that you file with your insurance company will also affect your premium. If you file expensive claims, your rates will increase. If you have too many claims, your insurance company may cancel your policy. You will then have more difficulty getting coverage from another company. To deal with this problem, every state has an assigned risk pool. An **assigned risk pool** includes all the people who can't get motor vehicle insurance. Some of these people are assigned to each insurance company operating in the state. These policyholders pay several times the normal rates, but they do get coverage. Once they establish a good driving record, they can reapply for insurance at regular rates.

Insurance companies may also consider your credit score when deciding whether to sell, renew, or cancel a policy and what premium to charge. However, an insurer cannot refuse to issue you a home or auto insurance policy solely based on your credit report. Read the accompanying Personal Finance in Practice box to understand how insurance companies use credit information.

assigned risk pool Consists of people who are unable to obtain automobile insurance due to poor driving or accident records and must obtain coverage at high rates through a state program that requires insurance companies to accept some of them.

Reducing Vehicle Insurance Premiums

Two ways in which you can reduce your vehicle insurance costs are by comparing companies and taking advantage of discounts.

COMPARING COMPANIES   Rates and services vary among motor vehicle insurance companies. Even among companies in the same area, premiums can vary by as much

Apply *Yourself!*

Objective 5

Using Web research, find the laws in your state regarding uninsured motorist's protection.

Figure It Out!

› Motor Vehicle Insurance—How Much Will It Cost?

Before Mario bought the car he wanted, he needed to be sure he could afford the insurance for it. In this example he chose low liability, uninsured motorist coverage, and high deductibles to keep his insurance payments as low as possible. Clearly insurer B offered a lower price for the same coverage.

Investigating Insurance Companies		
	Insurer A	Insurer B
Bodily Injury Coverage:		
• Bodily injury liability $50,000 each person; $100,000 each accident	$472	$358
• Uninsured motorist's protection	208	84
• Medical payments coverage: $2,000 each person	48	46
Property Damage Coverage:		
• Property damage liability $50,000 each accident	182	178
• Collision with $500 deductible	562	372
• Comprehensive physical damage with $500 deductible	263	202
Car rental	40	32
Discounts: good driver, air bags, garage parking	(165)	
Annual total	$1,610	$1,272

RESEARCH

Identify a make, model, and year of a vehicle you might like to own. Research two insurance companies and get prices using this example. You can get their rates by telephone. Many also have Web sites. Using your workbook or on a separate sheet of paper, record your findings. How do they compare? Which company would you choose and why?

as 100 percent. You should compare the service and rates of local insurance agents. Most states publish this type of information. Furthermore, you can check a company's reputation with sources such as *Consumer Reports* or your state insurance department.

CAUTION!

Your insurance company may charge an extra fee if you are involved in an accident or cited for a serious traffic violation. Worse, the insurer may not renew your insurance policy.

PREMIUM DISCOUNTS The best way for you to keep your rates down is to maintain a good driving record by avoiding accidents and traffic tickets. In addition, most insurance companies offer various discounts. If you are under 25, you can qualify for reduced rates by taking a driver training program or maintaining good grades in college.

Furthermore, installing security devices will decrease the chance of theft and lower your insurance costs. Being a nonsmoker can qualify you for lower motor vehicle insurance premiums as well. Discounts are also offered for insuring two or more vehicles with the same company. Increasing the amounts of deductibles will also lead to a lower premium. If you have an old car that's not worth much, you may decide not to pay for collision and comprehensive coverage. However, before you make this move, you should compare the value of your car for getting to college or work with the cost of these coverages. The nearby Figure It Out box presents motor vehicle insurance cost comparison.

✔ CONCEPT CHECK 8–5

1 In the space provided, write "A" if you agree with the statement, "D" if you disagree.

   a. Motor vehicle insurance is not cheap. _____

   b. The average household spends less than $500 for motor vehicle insurance yearly. _____

   c. Most people who are involved in an automobile accident can afford to pay an expensive court settlement with their own money. _____

   d. Liability coverage of 100/300 is usually recommended. _____

   e. You should consider a policy with a limit of $50,000 or even $100,000 for property damage liability. _____

   f. The year, make, and model of a vehicle do not affect insurance costs. _____

   g. Your automobile insurance would probably cost more in rural areas than if you lived in a large city. _____

2 List the five factors that determine driver classification.

   _____

   _____

3 What are the two ways by which you can reduce your vehicle insurance costs?

   _____

   _____

back to *Getting Personal*

1. Reconsider your responses to the Getting Personal questions at the beginning of the chapter. Have any of your answers changed as a result of what you learned in this chapter?

_____

_____

2. What risk management methods learned in this chapter can you use to protect yourself against the many perils?

_____

_____

3. In what ways can you incorporate property and liability insurance in your financial plan?

_____

_____

4. Which homeowner's insurance coverage will you purchase and why?

_____

_____

5. What automobile insurance coverages are important to you and why? How can you reduce the costs of homeowner's and auto insurance?

_____

_____

_____

Chapter Summary

Objective 1   The main types of risk are personal risk, property risk, and liability risk. Risk management methods include avoidance, reduction, assumption, and shifting.

Planning an insurance program is a way to manage risks.

Property and liability insurance protect your homes and motor vehicles against financial loss.

Objective 2   A homeowner's policy provides coverage for buildings and other structures, additional living expenses, personal property, personal liability and related coverages, and specialized coverages.

Renter's insurance provides many of the same kinds of protection as homeowner's policies.

Objective 3   The factors that affect home insurance coverage and costs include the location, the type of structure, the coverage amount and policy type, discounts, and the choice of insurance company.

Objective 4   Motor vehicle bodily injury coverages include bodily injury liability, medical payments coverage, and uninsured motorist's protection.

Motor vehicle property damage coverages include property damage liability, collision, and comprehensive physical damage.

Objective 5   Motor vehicle insurance costs depend on the amount of coverage you need as well as vehicle type, rating territory, and driver classification.

Key Terms

actual cash value (ACV)   252

assigned risk pool   259

bodily injury liability   255

claim   243

collision   256

coverage   240

deductible   241

endorsement   249

financial responsibility law   255

hazard   240

homeowner's insurance   246

household inventory   247

insurance   239

insurance company   239

insured   240

insurer   239

liability   244

medical payments coverage   249, 255

negligence   240

no-fault system   257

peril   240

personal property floater   247

policy   239

policyholder   239

premium   240

property damage liability   256

replacement value   253

risk   240

umbrella policy   249

uninsured motorist's protection   256

Problems

1. Most home insurance policies cover jewelry for $1,000 and silverware for $2,500 unless items are covered with additional insurance. If $3,500 worth of jewelry and $3,800 worth of silverware were stolen from a family, what amount of the claim would not be covered by insurance?

2. What amount would a person with actual cash value (ACV) coverage receive for two-year-old furniture destroyed by a fire? The furniture would cost $1,000 to replace today and had an estimated life of five years.

3. What would it cost an insurance company to replace a family's personal property that originally cost $18,000? The replacement costs for the items have increased 15 percent.

4. If Carissa Dalton has a $130,000 home insured for $100,000, based on the 80 percent coinsurance provision, how much would the insurance company pay on a $5,000 claim?

5. For each of the following situations, what amount would the insurance company pay?

   a. Wind damage of $785; the insured has a $500 deductible.

   b. Theft of a stereo system worth $1,300; the insured has a $250 deductible.

   c. Vandalism that does $375 of damage to a home; the insured has a $500 deductible.

6. Becky Fenton has 25/50/10 automobile insurance coverage. If two other people are awarded $35,000 each for injuries in an auto accident in which Becky was judged at fault, how much of this judgment would the insurance cover?

7. Kurt Simmons has 50/100/15 auto insurance coverage. One evening he lost control of his vehicle, hitting a parked car and damaging a storefront along the street. Damage to the parked car was $5,400, and damage to the store was $12,650. What amount will the insurance company pay for the damages? What amount will Kurt have to pay?

8. Beverly and Kyle Nelson currently insure their cars with separate companies, paying $450 and $375 a year. If they insured both cars with the same company, they would save 10 percent on the annual premiums. What would be the future value of the annual savings over 10 years based on an annual interest rate of 6 percent?

9. When Carolina's house burned down, she lost household items worth a total of $25,000. Her house was insured for $80,000 and her homeowner's policy provided coverage for personal belongings up to 55 percent of the insured value of the house. Calculate how much insurance coverage Carolina's policy provides for her personal possessions and whether she will receive payment for all of the items destroyed in the fire.

10. Matt and Kristin are newly married and living in their first house. The yearly premium on their homeowner's insurance policy is $450 for the coverage they need. Their insurance company offers a 5 percent discount if they install dead-bolt locks on all exterior doors. The couple can also receive a 2 percent discount if they install smoke detectors on each floor. They have contacted a locksmith, who will provide and install dead-bolt locks on the two exterior doors for $60 each. At the local hardware store, smoke detectors cost $8 each, and the new house has two floors. Kristin and Matt can install them themselves.

    a. What discount will Matt and Kristin receive if they install the dead-bolt locks? If they install smoke detectors?

    b. Assuming their insurance rates remain the same, how many years will it take them to earn back in discounts the cost of the dead-bolts? The cost of the smoke detectors?

    c. Would you recommend Matt and Kristin invest in the safety items? Why or why not?

Questions

1. Survey friends and relatives to determine the types of insurance coverages they have. Also, obtain information about the process used to select these coverages.

2. Outline a personal insurance plan with the following phases: *(a)* identify personal, financial, and property risks; *(b)* set goals you might achieve when obtaining needed insurance coverages; and *(c)* describe actions you might take to achieve these insurance goals.

3. Talk to a financial planner or an insurance agent about the financial difficulties faced by people who lack adequate home and auto insurance. What common coverages do many people overlook?

4. Contact two or three insurance agents to obtain information about home or renter's insurance. Use *Your Personal Financial Plan* sheet 29 to compare the coverages and costs.

5. Examine a homeowner's or renter's insurance policy. What coverages does the policy include? Does the policy contain unclear conditions or wording?

Internet Connection

CREATING AN INSURANCE PLAN (INCLUDING APPROPRIATE COVERAGE FOR YOUR HOME, PERSONAL PROPERTY, AND MOTOR VEHICLES)

For these three major insurance coverages, obtain current information and determine how you can get the appropriate coverage at the best rates.

Home/Renter's Insurance

Web sources: _____

Current findings: _____

Possible influence on your insurance decision: _____

Automobile Insurance

Web sources: _____

Current findings: _____

Possible influence on your insurance decision: _____

Case in Point

WE RENT, SO WHY DO WE NEED INSURANCE?

"Have you been down in the basement?" Nathan asked his wife, Erin, as he entered their apartment.

"No, what's up?" responded Erin.

"It's flooded because of all that rain we got last weekend!" he exclaimed.

"Oh no! We have the extra furniture my mom gave us stored down there. Is everything ruined?" Erin asked.

"The couch and coffee table are in a foot of water; the loveseat was the only thing that looked OK. Boy, I didn't realize the basement of this building wasn't waterproof. I'm going to call our landlady to complain."

As Erin thought about the situation, she remembered that when they moved in last fall, Kathy, their landlady, had informed them that her insurance policy covered the building but not the property belonging to each tenant. Because of this, they had purchased renter's insurance. "Nathan, I think our renter's insurance will cover the damage. Let me give our agent a call."

When Erin and Nathan purchased their insurance, they had to decide whether they wanted to be insured for cash value or for replacement costs. Replacement was more expensive, but it

meant they would collect enough to go out and buy new household items at today's prices. If they had opted for cash value, the couch for which Erin's mother had paid $1,000 five years ago would be worth less than $500 today.

Erin made the call and found out their insurance did cover the furniture in the basement, and at replacement value after they paid the deductible. The $300 they had invested in renter's insurance last year was well worth it!

Not every renter has as much foresight as Erin and Nathan. Fewer than 4 in 10 renters have renter's insurance. Some aren't even aware they need it. They may assume they are covered by the landlord's insurance, but they aren't. This mistake can be costly.

Think about how much you have invested in your possessions and how much it would cost to replace them. Start with your stereo equipment or the color television and DVD that you bought last year. Experts suggest that people who rent start thinking about these things as soon as they move into their first apartment. Your policy should cover your personal belongings and provide funds for living expenses if you are dispossessed by a fire or other disaster.

Questions

1. Why is it important for people who rent to have insurance?

2. Does the building owner's property insurance ever cover the tenant's personal property?

3. What is the difference between cash value and replacement value?

4. When shopping for renter's insurance, what coverage features should you look for?

Continuing Case

PROPERTY INSURANCE

Life Situation

Pam, 36

Josh, 38

Three children, ages 9, 7, and 4

Financial Data

Monthly income $4,300

Assets $150,850

Living expenses $4,075

Liabilities $99,520

Both Pam and Josh Brock are pleased with their lives and various family activities. They now have three children, are enjoying their home, and are more financially secure than six years ago. Yet the Brocks still have financial needs they must address.

Several changes have affected their financial planning. The value of their home has increased due to inflation and home improvements. They have purchased a used car to meet additional transportation needs. These situations must be considered in relation to insurance needs for the Brock household.

Questions

1. How should the Brocks determine whether they have enough insurance coverage for their home?

2. What factors should the Brocks consider in deciding whether to purchase collision insurance coverage for their used car?

3. Describe the possible use of *Your Personal Financial Plan* sheets 26–30 by the Brocks.

Video Case

STORM INSURANCE: WHAT TO LOOK FOR IN RENEWING YOUR POLICY

The 2005 hurricane season, the costliest in the U.S. history, resulted in record insurance losses. The year's three most devastating hurricanes—Katrina, Rita, and Wilma—resulted in at least $45 billion in insured property losses and produced a record 2.8 million claims. Consequently, homeowner's insurance premiums have doubled or tripled for millions of policyholders in recent years.

Questions

1. Does everyone need a flood insurance policy? Why or why not?

2. Where can one obtain a flood insurance policy?

3. Why is reading the "fine print" in your homeowner's insurance policy important?

www.mhhe.com/kdh

Spending Diary

"MY SPENDING TAKES MOST OF MY MONEY. SO AFTER PAYING FOR CAR INSURANCE, MY BUDGET IS REALLY TIGHT."

Directions

As you continue (or start using) Your Daily Spending Diary sheets, you should be able to make better choices for your spending priorities. The financial data you develop will help you better understand your spending patterns and help you plan for achieving financial goals.

Questions

1. What information from your Daily Spending Diary might encourage you to use your money differently?

2. How can your spending habits be developed to ensure that you will be able to afford appropriate home and auto insurance coverage?

Current Insurance Policies and Needs

Financial Planning Activities: Establish a record of current and needed insurance coverage. List current insurance policies and areas where new or additional coverage is needed.

Suggested Web Sites: www.insure.com   www.insweb.com

Your Personal Financial Plan

Current Coverage	Needed Coverage
Property	
Company _____	
Policy No. _____	
Coverage amounts _____	
Deductible _____	
Annual premium _____	
Agent _____	
Address _____	
Phone _____	
Web site _____	
Automobile Insurance	
Company _____	
Policy No. _____	
Coverage amounts _____	
Deductible _____	
Annual premium _____	
Agent _____	
Address _____	
Phone _____	
Web site _____	
Disability Income Insurance	
Company _____	
Policy No. _____	
Coverage _____	
Contact _____	
Phone _____	
Web site _____	
Health Insurance	
Company _____	
Policy No. _____	
Policy provisions _____	
Contact _____	
Phone _____	
Web site _____	
Life Insurance	
Company _____	
Policy No. _____	
Type of policy _____	
Amount of coverage _____	
Cash value _____	
Agent _____	
Phone _____	
Web site _____	

What's Next for Your Personal Financial Plan?

- Talk with friends and relatives to determine the types of insurance coverage they have.
- Locate Web sites that provide additional useful information for company various insurance coverages.

Name: _____   **Date:** _____

Home Inventory

Financial Planning Activities: Create a record of personal belongings for use when settling home insurance claims. For areas of the home, list your possessions including a description (model, serial number), cost, and date of acquisition.

Suggested Web Sites: www.ireweb.com   http://money.com

Item, Description	Cost	Date Acquired

Attic

_____

_____

Bathroom

_____

_____

Bedrooms

_____

_____

Family room

_____

_____

Living room

_____

_____

Hallways

_____

_____

Kitchen

_____

_____

Dining room

_____

_____

Basement

_____

_____

Garage

_____

_____

Other items

_____

_____

What's Next for Your Personal Financial Plan?

- Survey others about the areas of insurance they have and other coverages they are considering.
- Talk to a local insurance agent to point out the areas of protection that many people tend to overlook.

Determining Needed Property Insurance

Financial Planning Activities: Determine property insurance needed for a home or apartment. Estimate the value and your needs for the categories below.

Suggested Web Sites: www.iii.org   www.quicken.com

Real Property (this section not applicable to renters)

Current replacement value of home $ _____

Personal Property

Estimated value of appliances, furniture, clothing and other household $ _____
items (conduct an inventory)

Type of coverage for personal property (check one)

Actual cash value [ ]

Replacement value [ ]

Additional coverage for items with limits on standard personal property coverage such as jewelry, firearms, silverware, and photographic, electronic, and computer equipment

Item	Amount
_____	_____
_____	_____
_____	_____

Personal Liability

Amount of additional personal liability coverage desired for $ _____
possible personal injury claims

Specialized Coverages

If appropriate, investigate flood or earthquake coverage excluded from $ _____
home insurance policies

Note: Use Sheet 29 to compare companies, coverages, and costs for apartment or home insurance.

What's Next for Your Personal Financial Plan?

• Outline the steps involved in planning an insurance program.

• Outline special types of property and liability insurance such as personal computer insurance, trip cancellation insurance, and liability insurance.

Name: _____ **Date:** _____

Apartment/Home Insurance Comparison

Financial Planning Activities: Research and compare companies, coverages, and costs for apartment or home insurance. Contact three insurance agents to obtain the information requested below.

Suggested Web Sites: www.freeinsurancequotes.com   www.insure.com

Type of building: ☐ apartment   ☐ home   ☐ condominium

Location: _____

Type of construction _____ Age of building _____

Company name			
Agent's name, address, and phone			
Coverage: Dwelling $ Other structure $ (does not apply to apartment/condo coverage)	Premium	Premium	Premium
Personal property $			
Additional living expenses $			

Personal liability
   Bodily injury
   $
   Property damage
   $			

Medical payments
   Per person
   $
   Per accident
   $			

Deductible amount			
Other coverage $			
Service charges or fees			
Total Premium			

What's Next for Your Personal Financial Plan?

- Talk to an insurance agent or claim adjuster to determine the type of documentation required for a claim settlement.
- List the reasons most commonly given by renters for not having renter's insurance.

Automobile Insurance Cost Comparison

Financial Planning Activities: Research and compare companies, coverages, and costs for auto insurance. Contact three insurance agents to obtain the information requested below.

Suggested Web Sites: www.autoinsuranceindepth.com   www.progressive.com

Automobile (year, make, model, engine size) _____
_____

Driver's age _____ Sex _____   Total miles driven in a year _____

Full- or part-time driver? _____   Total miles driven in a year _____

Driver's education completed? _____

Accidents or violations within the past three years? _____
_____

Company name			
Agent's name, address, and phone			
Policy length (6 months, 1 year)			
Coverage: Bodily injury liability Per person $ Per accident $	**Premium**	**Premium**	**Premium**
Property damage liability per accident $			
Collision deductible $			
Comprehensive deductible $			
Medical payments per person $			
Uninsured motorist liability Per person $ Per accident $			
Other coverage			
Service charges			
Total Premium			

What's Next for Your Personal Financial Plan?

• Make a list of some arguments in favor of and against mandatory auto insurance.
• Talk to friends, relatives, and insurance agents to determine methods of reducing the cost of auto insurance.

9 Health and Disability Income Insurance

Getting Personal

Should you be concerned about health insurance? Disability income insurance? For each of the following statements, select "yes" or "no" to indicate your behavior regarding these health insurance and disability insurance statements.

	Yes	No
1. Since I am a young adult, I don't really need health insurance.	——	——
2. Since I am a healthy adult, I don't need to worry about disability income insurance.	——	——
3. If my employer does not provide health insurance, I can easily and inexpensively purchase my own insurance.	——	——
4. I am aware of some of the trade-offs of different health insurance policies.	——	——
5. I am aware of health care plans offered by private companies and by the government.	——	——

After studying this chapter, you will be asked to reassess health and disability income insurance and to reconsider your responses to these items.

Your Personal Financial Plan Sheets

31. Assessing Current and Needed Health Care Insurance
32. Disability Income Insurance Needs

Objectives	Why is this important?

In this chapter, you will learn to:

1. Recognize the importance of health insurance in financial planning.
2. Analyze the costs and benefits of various types of health insurance coverage as well as major provisions in health insurance policy.
3. Assess the trade-offs of different health insurance plans.
4. Evaluate the differences among health care plans offered by private companies and by the government.
5. Explain the importance of disability income insurance in financial planning and identify its sources.
6. Explain why the costs of health insurance and health care have been increasing.

Knowing how to determine the type of health and disability income insurance that you need can help you meet your financial goals even when dealing with unexpected medical costs and inability to work.

Health Insurance and Financial Planning

OBJECTIVE 1

Recognize the importance of health insurance in financial planning.

What Is Health Insurance?

Health insurance is a form of protection that eases the financial burden people may experience as a result of illness or injury. You pay a *premium,* or fee, to the insurer. In return the company pays most of your medical costs. Although plans vary in what they cover, they may reimburse you for hospital stays, doctors' visits, medications, and sometimes vision and dental care.

Health insurance includes both medical expense insurance, as discussed above, and disability income insurance. *Medical expense insurance* typically pays only the actual medical costs. *Disability income insurance* provides payments to make up for some of the income of a person who cannot work as a result of injury or illness. In this chapter the term "health insurance" refers to medical expense insurance.

Health insurance plans can be purchased in several different ways: group health insurance, individual health insurance, and COBRA.

GROUP HEALTH INSURANCE Most people who have health insurance are covered under group plans. Typically, these plans are employer sponsored. This means that the employer offers the plans and usually pays some or all of the premiums. Other

Apply *Yourself!*

organizations, such as labor unions and professional associations, also offer group plans. Group insurance plans cover you and your immediate family. The Health Insurance Portability and Accountability Act of 1996 set new federal standards to ensure that workers would not lose their health insurance if they changed jobs. As a result, a parent with a sick child, for example, can move from one group health plan to another without a lapse in coverage. Moreover, the parent will not have to pay more for coverage than other employees do.

The cost of group insurance is relatively low because many people are insured under the same *policy*—a contract with a risk-sharing group, or insurance company. However, group insurance plans vary in the amount of protection that they provide. For example, some plans limit the amount that they will pay for hospital stays and surgical procedures. If your plan does not cover all of your health insurance needs, you have several choices.

If you are married, you may be able to take advantage of a coordination of benefits (COB) provision, which is included in most group insurance plans. This provision allows you to combine the benefits from more than one insurance plan. The benefits received from all the plans are limited to 100 percent of all allowable medical expenses. For example, a couple could use benefits from one spouse's group plan and from the other spouse's plan up to 100 percent.

If this type of provision is not available to you, or if you are single, you can buy individual health insurance for added protection.

INDIVIDUAL HEALTH INSURANCE Some people do not have access to an employer-sponsored group insurance plan because they are self-employed. Others are simply dissatisfied with the coverage that their group plan provides. In these cases individual health insurance may be the answer. You can buy individual health insurance directly from the company of your choice. Plans usually cover you as an individual or cover you and your family. Individual plans can be adapted to meet your own needs. You should comparison shop, however, because rates can vary.

did you know?

You can receive *A Consumer Guide for Getting and Keeping Health Insurance* for your state from Georgetown University Health Policy Institute. Visit www.healthinsuranceinfo.net.

Key Web Sites for Health Insurance Information

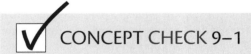

www.insure.com
www.life-line.org

COBRA Hakeem had a group insurance plan through his employer, but he was recently laid off. He wondered how he would be able to get medical coverage until he found a new job. Fortunately for Hakeem, the Consolidated Omnibus Budget Reconciliation Act of 1986, known as COBRA, allowed him to keep his former employer's group coverage for a set period of time. He had to pay the premiums himself, but at least the coverage wasn't canceled. When he found a new job, he was then able to switch to that employer's group plan with no break in coverage.

Not everyone qualifies for COBRA. You have to work for a private company or state or local government to benefit.

✓ CONCEPT CHECK 9–1

1 What is health insurance?

_____

2 What are the three ways of purchasing health insurance?

_____

3 For each of the following statements, circle "T" for true or "F" for false.

  a. Health insurance is available only as a benefit from an employer.   T   F

  b. You can continue your health insurance even if you leave a job.   T   F

Health Insurance Coverage

Several types of health insurance coverage are available, either through a group plan or through individual purchase. Some benefits are included in nearly every health insurance plan; other benefits are seldom offered.

> **OBJECTIVE 2**
> Analyze the costs and benefits of various types of health insurance coverage as well as major provisions in health insurance policy.

Types of Health Insurance Coverage

BASIC HEALTH INSURANCE COVERAGE   **Basic health insurance coverage** includes hospital expense coverage, surgical expense coverage, and physician expense coverage.

Hospital Expense   **Hospital expense coverage** pays for some or all of the daily costs of room and board during a hospital stay. Routine nursing care, minor medical supplies, and the use of other hospital facilities are covered as well. For example, covered expenses would include anesthesia, laboratory fees, dressings, X-rays, local ambulance service, and the use of an operating room.

Be aware, though, that most policies set a maximum amount they will pay for each day you are in the hospital. They may also limit the number of days they will cover. Recall from Chapter 8 that many policies require a deductible. A **deductible** is a set amount that the policyholder must pay toward medical expenses before the insurance company pays benefits.

Surgical Expense   **Surgical expense coverage** pays all or part of the surgeon's fees for an operation, whether it is done in a hospital or in the doctor's office. Policies often have a list of the services that they cover, which specifies the maximum payment for each type of operation. For example, a policy might allow $500 for an appendectomy. If the entire surgeon's bill is not covered, the policyholder has to pay the difference. People often buy surgical expense coverage in combination with hospital expense coverage.

Physician Expense   **Physician expense coverage** meets some or all the costs of physician care that do not involve surgery. This form of health insurance covers treatment in a hospital, a doctor's office, or even a patient's home. Plans may cover routine doctor visits, X-rays, and lab tests. Like surgical expense, physician expense specifies maximum benefits for each service. Physician expense coverage is usually combined with surgical and hospital coverage in a package called basic health insurance.

Major Medical Expense Insurance Coverage   Most people find that basic health insurance meets their usual needs. The cost of a serious illness or accident, however, can quickly go beyond the amounts that basic health insurance will pay. Chen had emergency surgery, which meant an operation, a two-week hospital stay, a number of lab tests, and several follow-up visits. He was shocked to discover that his basic health insurance paid less than half of the total bill, leaving him with debts of more than $10,000.

---

basic health insurance coverage Hospital expense insurance, surgical expense insurance, and physician expense insurance.

hospital expense insurance Pays part or all of hospital bills for room, board, and other charges.

deductible An amount the insured must pay before benefits become payable by the insurance company.

surgical expense insurance Pays part or all of the surgeon's fees for an operation.

physician expense insurance Provides benefits for doctors' fees for nonsurgical care, X-rays, and lab tests.

INSURANCE | Earning a diploma often means losing medical coverage.

HEALTHY choices

Although finding a job may be the top priority for most new college graduates, parents are often more concerned about continuing their children's health coverage. Insurers typically drop kids from their parents' health plan once they grab that diploma (or by the time they turn 25).

Sandy D'Annunzio, a nurse in Sterling Heights, Mich., bought short-term health-insurance policies from Golden Rule (www.goldenrule.com) for her two daughters, Jennifer and Kelly. D'Annunzio pays about $57 a month for each policy, both of which have a $1,000 deductible and 20% co-insurance (meaning the insurer picks up 80% of a claim after the deductible is met). "If one of them broke a leg, it could cost 70 times as much," says D'Annunzio.

Most short-term policies last six months to a year, after which you may reapply, as long as you remain healthy. But they don't typically cover preventive care or preexisting conditions, so they're really just a temporary fix.

For longer coverage, consider an individual policy with a high deductible. For a policy with a $1,500 deductible and 20% co-insurance, a young female nonsmoker would pay $124 per month in Chicago. That's more expensive than short-term insurance, but it covers many of the medical expenses that short-term policies exclude.

If graduation is still a few months away, buying student health insurance may be a cheaper way to go. But don't delay. Assurant Health, a major provider of such plans, requires that coverage begin at least 31 days *before* a student graduates.

Like short-term health insurance, student health coverage has a long list of exclusions. But in most cases, it is less expensive than a short-term policy and is renewable. For example, a 22-year-old female non-smoker in Chicago would pay $66 a month for a student health policy with a $1,000 deductible and 20% co-insurance through eHealthInsurance.com. A similar short-term policy would cost $104 a month.

If your child has a medical condition, such as asthma or depression, buying individual health insurance can be tough. In that case, take advantage of COBRA; the law allows your adult child to remain on your policy for up to 36 months. COBRA coverage isn't cheap because you have to pay both the employer share and the employee share of your group premium, but it can serve as a safety net while you look into other options. A number of states are taking steps to extend coverage for young adults.

—THOMAS M. ANDERSON

1. Why do parents worry when their children graduate from college or by the time they turn 25?

   _____

   _____

2. What type of health insurance policy is desirable for longer coverage?

   _____

   _____

3. Go to www.kiplinger.com to obtain information about COBRA.

   _____

   _____

Chen would have been better protected if he had had major medical expense insurance. This coverage pays the large costs involved in long hospital stays and multiple surgeries. In other words, it takes up where basic health insurance coverage leaves off. Almost every type of care and treatment prescribed by a physician, in and out of a hospital, is covered. Maximum benefits can range from $5,000 to more than $1 million per illness per year.

Of course, this type of coverage isn't cheap. To control premiums, most major medical plans require a deductible. Some plans also include a coinsurance provision. **Coinsurance** is the percentage of the medical expenses the policyholder must pay in addition to the deductible amount. Many policies require policyholders to pay 20 or 25 percent of expenses after they have paid the deductible.

Ariana's policy includes an $800 deductible and a coinsurance provision requiring her to pay 20 percent of all bills. If her bill total is $3,800, for instance, the company will first exclude $800 from coverage, which is Ariana's deductible. It will then pay 80 percent of the remaining $3,000, or $2,400. Therefore, Ariana's total costs are $1,400 ($800 for the deductible and $600 for the coinsurance).

Some major medical policies contain a stop-loss provision. **Stop-loss** is a provision that requires the policyholder to pay all costs up to a certain amount, after which the insurance company pays 100 percent of the remaining expenses, as long as they are covered in the policy. Typically, the policyholder will pay between $3,000 and $5,000 in out-of-pocket expenses before the coverage begins.

Major medical expense insurance may be offered as a single policy with basic health insurance coverage, or it can be bought separately. Comprehensive major medical insurance is a type of complete insurance that helps pay hospital, surgical, medical, and other bills. It has a low deductible, usually $400 to $800. Many major medical policies set limits on the benefits they will pay for certain expenses, such as surgery and hospital room and board.

HOSPITAL INDEMNITY POLICIES

A hospital indemnity policy pays benefits when you're hospitalized. Unlike most of the other plans mentioned, however, these policies don't directly cover medical costs. Instead you are paid in cash, which you can spend on medical or nonmedical expenses as you choose. Hospital indemnity policies are used as a supplement to—and not a replacement for—basic health or major medical policies. The average person who buys such a policy, however, usually pays much more in premiums that he or she receives in payments.

DENTAL EXPENSE INSURANCE

Dental expense insurance provides reimbursement for the expenses of dental services and supplies. It encourages preventive dental care. The coverage normally provides for oral examinations (including X-rays and cleanings), fillings, extractions, oral surgery, dentures, and braces. As with other insurance plans, dental insurance may have a deductible and a coinsurance provision, stating that the policyholder pays from 20 to 50 percent after the deductible.

VISION CARE INSURANCE

An increasing number of insurance companies are including vision care insurance as part of group plans. Vision care insurance may cover eye examinations, glasses, contact lenses, eye surgery, and the treatment of eye diseases.

DREAD DISEASE POLICIES

Dread disease, trip accident, death insurance, and cancer policies are usually sold through the mail, in newspapers and magazines, or by

Apply Yourself!

Objective 2

Raj is thinking about buying major medical insurance to supplement his basic health insurance from work. Describe a situation in which Raj would need major medical.

coinsurance A provision under which both the insured and the insurer share the covered losses.

stop-loss A provision under which an insured pays a certain amount, after which the insurance company pays 100 percent of the remaining covered expenses.

did you know?

The Coalition against Insurance Fraud provides "scam alerts" on phony health coverage, including a list of 10 warning signs. Visit www.insurancefraud.org.

door-to-door salespeople. These kinds of policy play upon unrealistic fears, and they are illegal in many states. They cover only specific conditions, which are already fully covered if you are insured under a major medical plan.

LONG-TERM CARE INSURANCE **Long-term care insurance (LTC)** provides coverage for the expense of daily help that you may need if you become seriously ill or disabled and are unable to care for yourself. It is useful whether you require a lengthy stay in a nursing home or just need help at home with daily activities such as dressing, bathing, and household chores. Annual premiums range from less than $1,000 to over $16,000, depending on your age and extent of the coverage. The older you are when you enroll, the higher your annual premium. Typically, individual insurance plans are sold to the 50-to-80 age group, pay benefits for a maximum of two to six years, and carry a dollar limit on the total benefits they will pay. The nearby Personal Finance in Practice box can help you compare the features of long-term care policies.

Explore services available in your community to help meet long-term care needs. Care given by family members can be supplemented by visiting nurses, home health aides, friendly visitor programs, home-delivered meals, chore services, adult day care centers, and respite services for caregivers who need a break from daily responsibilities.

These services are becoming more widely available. Some or all of them may be found in your community. Your local area Agency on Aging or Office on Aging can help you locate the services you need. Call the Eldercare Locator at 1-800-677-1116 to locate your local office.

Major Provisions in a Health Insurance Policy

All health insurance policies have certain provisions in common. You have to be sure that you understand what your policy covers. What are the benefits? What are the limits? The following are details of provisions that are usually found in health insurance policies:

- *Eligibility:* The people covered by the policy must meet specified eligibility requirements, such as family relationship and, for children, a certain age.
- *Assigned benefits:* You are reimbursed for payments when you turn in your bills and claim forms. When you assign benefits, you let your insurer make direct payments to your doctor or hospital.
- *Internal limits:* A policy with internal limits sets specific levels of repayment for certain services. Even if your hospital room costs $400 a day, you won't be able to get more than $250 if an internal limit specifies that maximum.
- *Copayment:* A **copayment** is a flat fee that you pay every time you receive a covered service. The fee is usually between $10 and $15, and the insurer pays the balance of the cost of the service. This is different from coinsurance, which is the percentage of your medical costs for which you are responsible after paying your deductible.
- *Service benefits:* Policies with this provision list coverage in terms of services, not dollar amounts: You're entitled to X-rays, for instance, not $40 worth of X-rays per visit. Service benefits provisions are always preferable to dollar amount coverage because the insurer will pay all the costs.
- *Benefit limits:* This provision defines a maximum benefit, either in terms of a dollar amount or in terms of number of days spent in the hospital.
- *Exclusions and limitations:* This provision specifies services that the policy does not cover. It may include preexisting conditions (a condition you were diagnosed with before your insurance plan took effect), cosmetic surgery, or more.
- *Guaranteed renewable:* This provision means that the insurer can't cancel the policy unless you fail to pay the premiums. It also forbids insurers to raise premiums unless they raise all premiums for all members of your group.

long-term care insurance (LTC) Provides day-in, day-out care for long-term illness or disability.

Key Web Site for Long-Term Care

www.longtermcareinsurance.org

copayment A provision under which the insured pays a flat dollar amount each time a covered medical service is received after the deductible has been met.

Personal Finance in Practice

› Long-Term Care Policy Checklist

The following checklist will help you compare LTC policies you may be considering:

	Policy A	Policy B
1. What services are covered?		
Skilled care	_____	_____
Intermediate care	_____	_____
Custodial care	_____	_____
Home health care	_____	_____
Adult day care	_____	_____
Other	_____	_____
2. How much does the policy pay per day?		
For skilled care	_____	_____
For intermediate care	_____	_____
For custodial care	_____	_____
For home health care	_____	_____
For adult day care	_____	_____
3. How long will benefits last?		
In a nursing home for:		
Skilled nursing care	_____	_____
Intermediate nursing care	_____	_____
Custodial care	_____	_____
At home:	_____	_____
4. Does the policy have a maximum lifetime benefit? If so, what is it?		
For nursing home care	_____	_____
For home health care	_____	_____
5. Does the policy have a maximum length of coverage for each period of confinement? If so, what is it?		
For nursing home care	_____	_____
For home health care	_____	_____
6. How long must I wait before preexisting conditions are covered?	_____	_____
7. How many days must I wait before benefits begin?		
For nursing home care	_____	_____
For home health care	_____	_____

	Policy A	Policy B
8. Are Alzheimer's disease and other organic mental and nervous disorders covered?	_____	_____
9. Does this policy require:		
Physician certification of need?	_____	_____
An assessment of activities of daily living?	_____	_____
A prior hospital stay for:		
Nursing home care?	_____	_____
Home health care?	_____	_____
A prior nursing home stay for home health care coverage?	_____	_____
Other?	_____	_____
10. Is the policy guaranteed renewable?	_____	_____
11. What is the age range of enrollment?	_____	_____
12. Is there a waiver-of-premium provision:		
For nursing home care?	_____	_____
For home health care?	_____	_____
13. How long must I be confined before premiums are waived?	_____	_____
14. Does the policy offer an inflation adjustment feature? If so:		
What is the rate of increase?	_____	_____
How often is it applied?	_____	_____
For how long?	_____	_____
Is there an additional cost?	_____	_____
15. What does the policy cost:		
Per year?	_____	_____
With inflation feature	_____	_____
Without inflation feature	_____	_____
Per month?	_____	_____
With inflation feature	_____	_____
Without inflation feature	_____	_____
16. Is there a 30-day free look?	_____	_____

Source: *Guide to Long-Term Care Insurance* (Washington, DC: Health Insurance Association of America, 1994), pp. 11–12.

- *Cancellation and termination:* This provision explains the circumstances under which the insurer can cancel your coverage. It also explains how you can convert your group contract into an individual contract.

✓ CONCEPT CHECK 9–2

1 What three types of coverage are included in the basic health insurance?

_____

2 What benefits are provided by

  a. Hospital expense coverage? _____

_____

  b. Surgical expense coverage? _____

_____

  c. Physician expense coverage? _____

_____

3 Match the following terms with an appropriate statement.

coinsurance   *a.* Requires the policyholder to pay all costs up to a certain amount. _____

stop-loss   *b.* The percentage of the medical expenses you must pay. _____

hospital indemnity policy   *c.* A policy used as a supplement to basic health or major medical policies.

_____

exclusion and limitations   *d.* Defines who is covered by the policy. _____

copayment   *e.* Specifies services that the policy does not cover. _____

eligibility   *f.* A flat fee that you pay every time you receive a covered service. _____

Health Insurance Trade-Offs

OBJECTIVE 3
Assess the trade-offs of different health insurance plans.

Different health insurance policies may offer very different benefits. As you decide which insurance plan to buy, consider the following trade-offs.

REIMBURSEMENT VERSUS INDEMNITY   A reimbursement policy pays you back for actual expenses. An indemnity policy provides you with specific amounts, regardless of how much the actual expenses may be.

Katie and Seth are both charged $200 for an office visit to the same specialist. Katie's reimbursement policy has a deductible of $300. Once she has met the deductible, the policy will cover the full cost of such a visit. Seth's indemnity policy will pay him $125, which is what his plan provides for a visit to any specialist.

INTERNAL LIMITS VERSUS AGGREGATE LIMITS   A policy with internal limits will cover only a fixed amount for an expense, such as the daily cost of room and board during a hospital stay. A policy with aggregate limits will limit only the total amount of coverage (the maximum dollar amount paid for all benefits in a year), such as $1 million in major expense benefits, or it may have no limits.

DEDUCTIBLES AND COINSURANCE   The cost of a health insurance policy can be greatly affected by the size of the deductible (the set amount that the policyholder must pay toward medical expenses before the insurance company pays benefits). It can also be affected by the terms of the *coinsurance provision* (which states what percentage of the medical expenses the policyholder must pay in addition to the deductible amount).

OUT-OF-POCKET LIMITS   Some policies limit the amount of money you must pay for the deductible and coinsurance. After you have reached that limit, the insurance company covers 100 percent of any additional costs. Out-of-pocket limits help you lower your financial risk, but they also increase your premiums.

BENEFITS BASED ON REASONABLE AND CUSTOMARY CHARGES
Some policies consider the average fee for a service in a particular geographical area. They then use the amount to set a limit on payments to policyholders. If the standard cost of a certain procedure is $1,500 in your part of the country, then your policy won't pay more than that amount.

Which Coverage Should You Choose?

Now that you are familiar with the available types of health insurance and some of their major provisions, how do you choose one? The type of coverage you choose will be affected by the amount you can afford to spend on the premiums and the level of benefits that you feel you want and need. It may also be affected by the kind of coverage your employer offers, if you are covered through your employer.

You can buy basic health coverage, major medical coverage, or both basic and major medical coverage. Any of these three choices will take care of at least some of your medical expenses. Ideally, you should get a basic plan and a major medical supplement. Another option is to purchase a comprehensive major medical policy that combines the value of both plans in a single policy. Exhibit 9–1 describes the most basic features you should look for.

Apply *Yourself!*

Objective 3

Prepare a list of trade-offs that are important to you in a health insurance policy.

did you know?

The Employee Benefits Security Administration (EBSA) provides *Health Benefits Education for Consumers* and *Health Insurance Tips.* Call toll-free 866-444-3272 or visit www.dol.gov/ebsa.

Sheet 31
Assessing Current and Needed Health Care Insurance.

A health insurance plan should:

- Offer basic coverage for hospital and doctor bills

- Provide at least 120 days' hospital room and board in full

- Provide at least a $1 million lifetime maximum for each family member

- Pay at least 80 percent for out-of-hospital expenses after a yearly deductible of $500 per person or $1,000 per family

- Impose no unreasonable exclusions

- Limit your out-of-pocket expenses to no more than $3,000 to $5,000 a year, excluding dental, vision care, and precription costs

Although health insurance plans vary greatly, all plans should have the same basic features. *Would you add anything to this list of must-haves?*

Exhibit 9–1

Health Insurance Must-Haves

✓ CONCEPT CHECK 9–3

1 As you decide which health insurance plan to buy, what trade-offs would you consider?

_____

_____

2 Match the following terms with an appropriate statement.

reimbursement   *a.* A policy that will cover only a fixed amount of an expense. _____

indemnity   *b.* A policy that pays you back for actual expenses. _____

internal limits   *c.* A policy that provides you with specific amounts, regardless of how much the actual expenses may be. _____

deductible   *d.* After you have reached a certain limit, the insurance company covers 100 percent of any additional cost. _____

out-of-pocket limit *e.* The set amount that you must pay toward medical expenses before the insurance company pays benefits. _____

3 What basic features should be included in your health insurance plan?

_____

_____

Private Health Care Plans and Government Health Care Programs

Private Health Care Plans

OBJECTIVE 4
Evaluate the differences among health care plans offered by private companies and by the government.

Most health insurance in the United States is provided by private organizations rather than by the government. Private health care plans may be offered by a number of sources: private insurance companies; hospital and medical service plans; health maintenance organizations; preferred provider organizations; home health care agencies; and employer self-funded health plans.

PRIVATE INSURANCE COMPANIES   Several hundred private insurance companies are in the health insurance business. They provide mostly group health plans to employers, which in turn offer them to their employees as a benefit. Premiums may be fully or partially paid by the employer, with the employee paying any remainder. These policies typically pay you for medical costs you incur, or they send the payment directly to the doctor, hospital, or lab that provides the services.

Blue Cross An independent nonprofit membership corporation that provides protection against the cost of hospital care.

Blue Shield An independent nonprofit membership corporation that provides protection against the cost of surgical and medical care.

HOSPITAL AND MEDICAL SERVICE PLANS   Blue Cross and Blue Shield are statewide organizations similar to private health insurance companies. Each state has its own Blue Cross and Blue Shield. The "Blues" provide health insurance to millions of Americans. **Blue Cross** provides hospital care benefits. **Blue Shield** provides benefits for surgical and medical services performed by physicians.

HEALTH MAINTENANCE ORGANIZATIONS

Rising health care costs have led to an increase in managed care plans. According to a recent industry survey, 23 percent of employed Americans are enrolled in some form of managed care. **Managed care** refers to prepaid health plans that provide comprehensive health care to their members. Managed care is designed to control the cost of health care services by controlling how they are used. Managed care is offered by health maintenance organizations (HMOs), preferred provider organizations (PPOs), and point-of-service plans (POSs).

Health maintenance organizations are an alternative to basic health insurance and major medical expense insurance. A **health maintenance organization (HMO)** is a health insurance plan that directly employs or contracts with selected physicians and other medical professionals to provide health care services in exchange for a fixed, prepaid monthly premium.

HMOs are based on the idea that preventive services will minimize future medical problems. Therefore, these plans typically cover routine immunizations and checkups, screening programs, and diagnostic tests. They also provide customers with coverage for surgery, hospitalization, and emergency care. If you have an HMO, you will usually pay a small copayment for each covered service. Supplemental services may include vision care and prescription services, which are typically available for an additional fee.

When you first enroll in an HMO, you must choose a plan physician from a list of doctors provided by the HMO. The physician provides or arranges for all of your health care services. You must receive care through your plan physician; if you don't, you are responsible for the cost of the service. The only exception to this rule is in the case of a medical emergency. If you experience a sudden illness or injury that would threaten your life or health if not treated immediately, you may go to the emergency room of the nearest hospital. All other care must be provided by hospitals and doctors under contract with the HMO.

HMOs are not for everyone. Many HMO customers complain that their HMO denies them necessary care. Others feel restricted by the limited choice of doctors.

Exhibit 9–2 provides some tips on using and choosing an HMO: Because HMOs require you to use only certain doctors, you should make sure that these doctors are near your home or office. You should also be able to change doctors easily if you don't like your first choice. Similarly, second opinions should always be available at the HMO's expense, and you should be able to appeal any case in which the HMO denies care. Finally, look at the costs and benefits: Will you incur out-of-pocket expenses or copayments? What services will the plan provide?

PREFERRED PROVIDER ORGANIZATIONS

A variation on the HMO is a **preferred provider organization (PPO),** a group of doctors and hospitals that agree to provide specified medical services to members at prearranged fees. PPOs offer these discounted services to employers either directly or indirectly through an insurance company. The premiums for PPOs are slightly higher than the premiums for HMOs.

PPO plan members often pay no deductibles and may make minimal copayments. Whereas HMOs require members to receive care from HMO providers only, PPOs allow members greater flexibility. Members can either visit a preferred provider (a physician whom you select from a list, as in an HMO) or go to their own physicians. Patients who decide to use their own doctors do not lose coverage as they would with an HMO. Instead they must pay deductibles and larger copayments.

Increasingly, the difference between PPOs and HMOs is becoming less clear. A **point-of-service (POS) plan** combines features of both HMOs and PPOs. POSs use a network of participating physicians and medical professionals who have contracted to

---

did you know?

The National Association of Insurance Commissioners provides a useful brochure, *Protect Yourself against Illegal Health Plans.* Visit www.naic.org/pressroom/consumer_alerts/.

---

managed care Prepaid health plans that provide comprehensive health care to members.

health maintenance organization (HMO) A health insurance plan that provides a wide range of health care services for a fixed, prepaid monthly premium.

Key Web Sites for Health Insurance Articles

www.money.cnn.com
www.kiplinger.com

preferred provider organization (PPO) A group of doctors and hospitals that agree to provide health care at rates approved by the insurer.

point-of-service (POS) plan A network of selected contracted, participating providers; also called an *HMO-PPO hybrid* or *open-ended HMO.*

Exhibit 9–2 Tips on Using and Choosing an HMO

How to Use an HMO

When you first enroll in an HMO, you must choose a plan physician (family practitioner, internist, pediatrician, or obstetrician-gynecologist) who provides or arranges for all of your health care services. It is extremely important that you receive your care through the plan physician. If you don't, you are responsible for the cost of the service rendered.

The only exceptions to the requirement that care be received through the plan physician are medical emergencies. A medical emergency is a sudden onset of illness or a sudden injury that would jeopardize your life or health if not treated immediately. In such instances, you may use the facilities of the nearest hospital emergency room. All other care must be provided by hospitals and doctors under contract with the HMO.

How to Choose an HMO

If you decide to enroll in an HMO, you should consider these additional factors:

1. *Accessibility.* Since you must use plan providers, it is extremely important that they be easily accessible from your home or office.

2. *Convenient office hours.* Your plan physician should have convenient office hours.

3. *Alternative physicians.* Should you become dissatisfied with your first choice of a physician, the HMO should allow you the option to change physicians.

4. *Second opinions.* You should be able to obtain second opinions.

5. *Type of coverage.* You should compare the health care services offered by various HMOs, paying particular attention to whether you will incur out-of-pocket expenses or copayments.

6. *Appeal procedures.* The HMO should have a convenient and prompt system for resolving problems and disputes.

7. *Price.* You should compare the prices various HMOs charge to ensure that you are getting the most services for your health care dollar.

What to Do When an HMO Denies Treatment or Coverage

- *Get it in writing.* To better defend your case, ask for a letter detailing the clinical reasons your claim was denied and the name and medical expertise of the HMO staff member responsible.

- *Know your rights.* The plan document or your HMO's member services department will tell you how experimental treatments are defined and covered and how the appeals process works.

- *Keep records.* Make copies of any correspondence, including payments and any reimbursements. Also, keep a written log of all conversations relevant to your claim.

- *Find advocates.* Enlist the help of your doctor, employer, and state insurance department to lobby your case before the HMO.

Source: Reprinted from the May 18, 1997, issue of *BusinessWeek* by special permission. © 1999 McGraw-Hill Companies, Inc.

provide services for certain fees. As with your HMO, you choose a plan physician who manages your care and controls referrals to specialists. As long as you receive care from a plan provider, you pay little or nothing, just as you would with an HMO. However, you're allowed to seek care outside the network at a higher charge, as with a PPO.

HOME HEALTH CARE AGENCIES Rising hospital costs, new medical technology, and the increasing number of elderly people have helped make home care one of the fastest growing areas of the health care industry. Home health care consists of home health agencies; home care aide organizations; and hospices, facilities that care for the terminally ill. These providers offer medical care in a home setting in agreement with a medical order, often at a fraction of the cost hospitals would charge for a similar service.

EMPLOYER SELF-FUNDED HEALTH PLANS Some companies choose to self-insure. The company runs its own insurance plan, collecting premiums from employees and paying medical benefits as needed. However, these companies must cover any costs that exceed the income from premiums. Unfortunately, not all corporations have the financial assets necessary to cover these situations, which can mean a financial disaster for the company and its employees.

Key Web Site for Health Insurance Information
www.healthfinder.gov

Personal Finance in Practice

› HSAs: How They Work

1. Your company offers a health insurance policy with an annual deductible of at least $1,100.

2. You can put pretax dollars into an HSA each year, up to the amount of the deductible—but no more than $5,650 for family coverage or $2,850 for individual coverage.

3. You withdraw the money from your HSA tax-free, but it can be used only for your family's medical expenses. After the deductible and copays are met, insurance still typically covers 80 percent of health costs.

4. HSA plans are required to have maximum out-of-pocket spending limits, $5,500 for individuals, $11,000 for families. That's when your company's insurance kicks in again at 100 percent coverage.

5. Your company can match part or all of your HSA contributions if it wishes, just as it does with 401(k)s.

6. You can invest your HSA in stocks, bonds, or mutual funds. Unused money remains in your account at the end of the year and grows tax free.

7. You can also take your HSA with you if you change jobs or retire.

8. To help you shop for health care now that you're spending your own money, employers say they will give you detailed information about prices and quality of doctors and hospitals in your area.

Source: U.S. Department of the Treasury, www.ustreas.gov/offices/public-affairs/hsa07IndexedAmounts.Shtml, accessed February 15, 2007.

NEW HEALTH CARE ACCOUNTS Health savings accounts (HSAs), which Congress authorized in 2003, are the newest addition to the alphabet soup of health insurance available to American workers. Now you and your employer must sort through HSAs, health reimbursement accounts (HRAs), and flexible spending accounts (FSAs). Each has its own rules about how money is spent, how it can be spent, and how it is taxed.

How to FSAs, HRAs, and HSAs differ? FSAs allow you to contribute pretax dollars to an account managed by your employer. You use the money for health care spending but forfeit anything left over at the end of the year.

HRAs are tied to high-deductible policies. They are funded *solely* by your employer and give you a pot of money to spend on health care. You can carry over unspent money from year to year, but you lose the balance if you switch jobs. Premiums tend to be lower than for traditional insurance but higher than for HSAs. You can invest the funds in stocks, bonds, and mutual funds. The money grows tax-free but can be spent only on health care.

HSAs allow you to contribute money to a tax-free account that can be used for out-of-pocket health care expenses if you buy high-deductible health insurance policies to cover catastrophic expenses. In 2007 up to 80 percent of U.S. employers are expected to offer HSAs as a major weapon in the fight against rising health care costs. Read the accompanying Personal Finance in Practice feature to learn how HSAs will work.

In addition to the private sources of health insurance and health care discussed in this section, government health care programs cover over 46 million people. The next section discusses these programs.

CAUTION!

HSA versus FSA

Don't confuse an HSA with the more familiar flexible-spending account (FSA), or flex account. Like an HSA, a flex account lets you set aside tax-free dollars you can use to pay for medical expenses that aren't covered by insurance. Unlike an HSA, a flex account isn't tied to a high-deductible policy. Also unlike an HSA, money left over in a flex account can't be carried over—if you don't use it, you lose it.

Source: *Kiplinger's Personal Finance*, October 2006, p. 90.

Personal Finance in Practice

› A Brief Look at Medicare

Medicare is health insurance for people age 65 or older, under age 65 with certain disabilities, and any age with end-stage renal disease (permanent kidney failure requiring dialysis or a kidney transplant).

Most people get their Medicare health care coverage in one of two ways. Your costs vary depending on your plan, coverage, and the services you use.

ORIGINAL MEDICARE PLAN	
Part A **(Hospital)**	**Part B** **(Medical)**
Medicare provides this coverage. Part B is optional. You have your choice of doctors. Your costs may be higher than in Medicare Advantage Plans.	

or

MEDICARE ADVANTAGE PLANS LIKE HMOs AND PPOs
Called "Part C," this option combines your Part A (Hospital) and Part B (Medical)
Private insurance companies approved by Medicare provide this coverage. Generally, you must see doctors in the plan. Your costs may be lower than in the Original Medicare Plan, and you may get extra benefits.

+

Part D (Prescription Drug Coverage)
You can choose this coverage. Private companies approved by Medicare run these plans. Plans cover different drugs. Medically necessary drugs must be covered.

+

Part D (Prescription Drug Coverage)
Most Part C plans cover prescription drugs. If they don't, you may be able to choose this coverage. Plans cover different drugs. Medically necessary drugs must be covered.

+

Medigap (Medicare Supplement Insurance) Policy
You can choose to buy this private coverage (or an employer or union may offer similar coverage) to fill in gaps in Part A and Part B coverage. Costs vary by policy and company.

For information about Medicare, visit www.medicare.gov or call 1-800-MEDICARE (1-800-633-4227).

Source: *Medicare & You* (Washington, DC: The Centers for Medicare and Medicaid Services, 2007).

Government Health Care Programs

The health insurance coverage discussed thus far is normally purchased through private companies. Some consumers, however, are eligible for health insurance coverage under programs offered by federal and state governments.

Apply *Yourself!*

Objective 4

Talk to several people covered by Medicare and Medicaid to obtain information on the coverage provided and the difficulties sometimes faced.

MEDICARE Perhaps the best-known government health program is Medicare. *Medicare* is a federally funded health insurance program available mainly to people over 65 and to people with disabilities. Medicare has two parts: hospital insurance (Part A) and medical insurance (Part B). Medicare hospital insurance is funded by part of the Social Security payroll tax. Part A helps pay for inpatient hospital care, inpatient care in a skilled nursing facility, home health care, and hospice care. Program participants pay a single annual deductible.

Part B helps pay for doctors' services and a variety of other medical services and supplies not covered or not fully covered by Part A. Part B has a deductible and a 20 percent coinsurance provision. Medicare medical insurance is a supplemental program paid for by individuals who feel that they need it. A regular monthly premium is charged. The federal government matches this amount. For a brief summary of Medicare Parts A, B, C, and D, see the nearby Personal Finance in Practice feature.

Medicare is constantly in financial trouble. Health care costs continue to grow, and the proportion of senior citizens in society is rising. This situation puts Medicare in danger of running out of funds. According to projections in 2007, the program will be bankrupt by the year 2019 if no changes are made.

The Balanced Budget Act of 1997 created the new Medicare Choice program. This program allows many Medicare members to choose a managed care plan in addition to their Medicare coverage. For some additional costs, members can receive greater benefits. Exhibit 9–3 compares features of different Medicare options.

did you know?

Medicare pays over $330 billion a year to more than 1 million health care providers to help more than 42 million elderly.

What Is Not Covered by Medicare?   Although Medicare is very helpful for meeting medical costs, it does not cover everything. In addition to the deductibles and coinsurance payments, Medicare will not cover some medical expenses at all. These are certain types of skilled or long-term nursing care, out-of-hospital prescription drugs, routine checkups, dental care, and most immunizations. Medicare also severely limits the types of services it will cover and the amount it will pay for those services. If your doctor does not accept Medicare's approved amount as payment in full, you're responsible for the difference.

Key Web Site for Medicare Information

www.ssa.gov

Medigap   Those eligible for Medicare who would like more coverage may buy **MEDIGAP (MedSup) insurance.** MEDIGAP insurance supplements Medicare by filling the gap between Medicare payments and medical costs not covered by Medicare. It is offered by private companies.

medigap (MedSup) insurance Supplements Medicare by filling the gap between Medicare payments and medical costs not covered by Medicare.

MEDICAID   The other well-known government health program is *Medicaid*, a medical assistance program offered to certain low-income individuals and families. Medicaid is administered by states, but it is financed by a combination of state and federal funds. Unlike Medicare, Medicaid coverage is so comprehensive that people with Medicaid do not need supplemental insurance. Typical Medicaid benefits include physicians' services, inpatient and outpatient hospital services, lab services, skilled nursing and home health services, prescription drugs, eyeglasses, and preventive care for people under the age of 21.

GOVERNMENT CONSUMER HEALTH INFORMATION WEB SITES

The Department of Health and Human Services operates more than 60 Web sites with a wealth of reliable information related to health and medicine. For example,

- *Healthfinder:* Healthfinder includes links to more than 1,000 Web sites operated by government and nonprofit organizations. It lists topics according to subject (www.hhs.gov).
- *MedlinePlus:* Medline Plus is the world's largest collection of published medical information. It was originally designed for health professionals and researchers, but it's also valuable for students and others who are interested in health care and medical issues (www.nlm.nih.gov/medlineplus).

Exhibit 9–3   A Comparison of Various Medicare Plans

	Current Options	New Options (Medicare and Choice)	Plan Description
Original Medicare	✔	✔	• You choose your health care providers. • Medicare pays your providers for covered services. • Most beneficiaries choose Medicare supplemental insurance to cover deductible and copayments.
Medicare health maintenance organization (HMO)	✔	✔	• You must live in the plan's service area. • You agree to use the plan network of doctors, hospitals, and other health providers, except in an emergency. • Medicare pays the HMO to provide all medical services.
Preferred provider organization (PPO)		✔	• Works like an HMO, except you have the choice to see a health provider out of the network. • If you do see an out-of-network provider, you will pay a higher cost.
Provider-sponsored organization (PSO)		✔	• Works like a Medicare HMO, except the networks are managed by health care providers (doctors and hospitals) rather than an insurance company.
Private fee for service		✔	• Medicare pays a lump sum to a private insurance health plan. • Providers can bill more than what the plan pays; you are responsible for paying the balance. • The plan may offer more benefits than original Medicare.
Medical savings account (MSA)		✔	• Medicare MSAs are a special type of savings account that can be used to pay medical bills. • CMS will make an annual lump-sum deposit into enrollee's account (only Medicare can deposit funds into this account). • MSAs work with a special private insurance company and carry a very high deductible. • Funds withdrawn for nonmedical purposes are taxable and subject to a penalty.

Source: *Medicare & You* (Washington, DC: The Centers for Medicare and Medicaid Services, 2007).

- *NIH Health Information Page:* The National Institutes of Health (NIH) operates a Web site called the NIH Health Information Page, which can direct you to the consumer health information in NIH publications and on the Internet (www.nih.gov).
- *FDA:* The Food and Drug Administration (FDA) also runs a Web site. This consumer protection agency's site provides information about the safety of various foods, drugs, cosmetics, and medical devices (www.fda.gov).

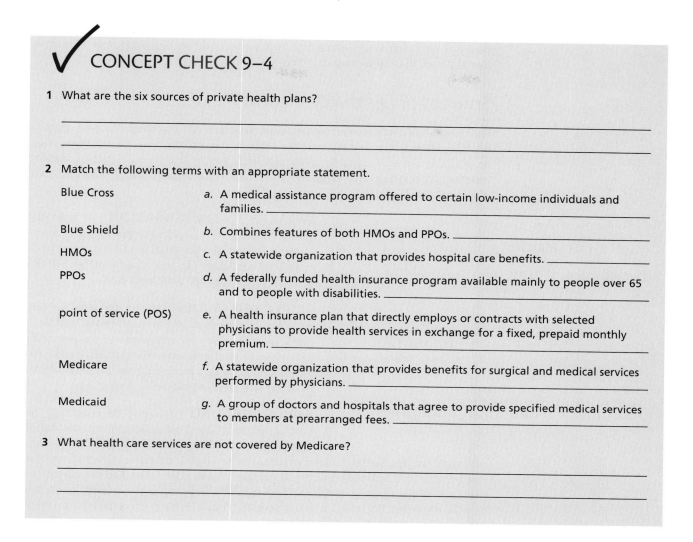

✔ CONCEPT CHECK 9–4

1 What are the six sources of private health plans?

_____

_____

2 Match the following terms with an appropriate statement.

Blue Cross   *a.* A medical assistance program offered to certain low-income individuals and families. _____

Blue Shield   *b.* Combines features of both HMOs and PPOs. _____

HMOs   *c.* A statewide organization that provides hospital care benefits. _____

PPOs   *d.* A federally funded health insurance program available mainly to people over 65 and to people with disabilities. _____

point of service (POS)   *e.* A health insurance plan that directly employs or contracts with selected physicians to provide health services in exchange for a fixed, prepaid monthly premium. _____

Medicare   *f.* A statewide organization that provides benefits for surgical and medical services performed by physicians. _____

Medicaid   *g.* A group of doctors and hospitals that agree to provide specified medical services to members at prearranged fees. _____

3 What health care services are not covered by Medicare?

_____

_____

Disability Income Insurance

The Need for Disability Income

Before disability insurance existed, people who were ill lost more money from missed paychecks than from medical bills. Disability income insurance was set up to protect against such loss of income. This kind of coverage is very common today, and several hundred insurance companies offer it.

Disability income insurance provides regular cash income when you're unable to work because of a pregnancy, a non-work-related accident, or an illness. It protects your earning power, your most valuable resource.

The exact definition of a disability varies from insurer to insurer. Some insurers will pay you when you are unable to work at your regular job. Others will pay only if you are so ill or badly hurt that you can't work at any job. A violinist with a hand injury, for instance, might have trouble doing his or her regular work but might be able to perform a range of other jobs. A good disability income insurance plan pays you if you can't work at your regular job. A good plan will also pay partial benefits if you are able to work only part-time.

Many people make the mistake of ignoring disability insurance, not realizing that it's very important insurance to have. Disability can cause even greater financial problems

> **OBJECTIVE 5**
> Explain the importance of disability income insurance in financial planning and identify its sources.

disability income insurance Provides payments to replace income when an insured person is unable to work.

than death. Disabled persons lose their earning power but still have to meet their living expenses. In addition, they often face huge costs for the medical treatment and special care that their disabilities require.

Sources of Disability Income

Before you buy disability income insurance from a private insurance company, remember that you may already have some form of insurance of this kind. This coverage may be available through worker's compensation if you're injured on the job. Disability benefits may also be available through your employer or through Social Security in case of a long-term disability.

WORKER'S COMPENSATION   If your disability is a result of an accident or illness that occurred on the job, you may be eligible to receive worker's compensation benefits in your state. Benefits will depend on your salary and your work history.

EMPLOYER PLANS   Many employers provide disability income insurance through group insurance plans. In most cases your employer will pay part or all of the cost of such insurance. Some policies may provide continued wages for several months only, whereas others will give you long-term protection.

SOCIAL SECURITY   Social Security may be best known as a source of retirement income, but it also provides disability benefits. If you're a worker who pays into the Social Security system, you're eligible for Social Security funds if you become disabled. How much you get depends on your salary and the number of years you've been paying into Social Security. Your dependents also qualify for certain benefits. However, Social Security has very strict rules. Workers are considered disabled if they have a physical or mental condition that prevents them from working and that is expected to last for at least 12 months or to result in death. Benefits start at the sixth full month the person is disabled. They stay in effect as long as the disability lasts.

Apply *Yourself!*

Objective 5

Contact an insurance agent to obtain cost information for an individual disability income insurance policy.

PRIVATE INCOME INSURANCE PROGRAMS Privately owned insurance companies offer many policies to protect people from loss of income resulting from illness or disability. Disability income insurance gives weekly or monthly cash payments to people who cannot work because of illness or accident. The amount paid is usually 40 to 60 percent of a person's normal income. Some plans, however, pay as much as 75 percent.

Disability Income Insurance Trade-Offs

As with the purchase of health insurance, you must make certain trade-offs when you decide among different private disability insurance policies. Keep the following in mind as you look for a plan that is right for you.

WAITING OR ELIMINATION PERIOD   Benefits won't begin the day you become disabled. You'll have to wait anywhere between one and six months before you can begin collecting. The span of time is called an elimination period. Usually a policy with a longer elimination period charges lower premiums.

DURATION OF BENEFITS   Every policy names a specified period during which benefits will be paid. Some policies are valid for only a few years. Others are automatically canceled when you turn 65. Still others continue to make payments for life. You should look for a policy that pays benefits for life. If your policy stops payments when you turn 65, then permanent disability could be a major financial as well as physical loss.

AMOUNT OF BENEFITS   You should aim for a benefit amount that, when added to other sources of income, will equal 70 to 80 percent of your take-home pay. Of course, the greater the benefit, the greater the cost, or premium.

ACCIDENT AND SICKNESS COVERAGE   Some disability policies pay only for accidents. Coverage for sickness is important, though. Accidents are not the only cause of disability.

GUARANTEED RENEWABILITY   If your health becomes poor, your disability insurer may try to cancel your coverage. Look for a plan that guarantees coverage as long as you continue to pay your premiums. The cost may be higher, but it's worth the extra security and peace of mind. You may even be able to find a plan that will stop charging the premiums if you become disabled, which is an added benefit.

Your Disability Income Needs

Once you have found out what your benefits from the numerous public and private sources would be, you should determine whether those benefits would meet your disability income needs. Ideally, you'll want to replace all the income you otherwise would have earned. This should enable you to pay your day-to-day expenses while you're recovering. You won't have work-related expenses and your taxes will be lower during the time you are disabled. In some cases you may not have to pay certain taxes at all. Use Exhibit 9–4 to determine how much income you will have available if you become disabled.

Sheet 32
Disability Income Insurance Needs.

	Monthly Amount	After Waiting:	For a Period of:
Sick leave or short-term disability	_____	_____	_____
Group long-term disability	_____	_____	_____
Social Security	_____	_____	_____
Other government programs	_____	_____	_____
Individual disability insurance	_____	_____	_____
Credit disability insurance	_____	_____	_____
Other income:	_____	_____	_____
Savings	_____	_____	_____
Spouse's income	_____	_____	_____
Total monthly income while disabled:	$ _____		

Exhibit 9–4

Calculating Disability Income
How much income will you have available if you become disabled?

✓ CONCEPT CHECK 9–5

1 What is the purpose of disability income insurance?

_____

_____

2 What are the four sources of disability income?

_____

_____

3 Match the following terms with an appropriate statement. _____

waiting or elimination period

a. A specified period during which benefits are paid.

duration of benefits

b. A plan that guarantees coverage as long as you continue to pay your premiums. _____

guaranteed renewability

c. A period of one to six months that must elapse before benefits can be collected. _____

High Medical Costs

OBJECTIVE 6

Explain why the costs of health insurance and health care have been increasing.

Affordable health care has become one of the most important social issues of our time. News broadcasts abound with special reports on "America's health care crisis" or politicians demanding "universal health insurance."

What do an aging and overweight population, the cost of prescription drugs, the growing number of uninsured, and advancements in medical technology have in common? These and other factors all add up to rising health costs. The United States has the highest per capita medical expenditures of any country in the world. We spend twice as much on health care as the average for the 24 industrialized countries in Europe and North America. The average per employee cost for health care was more than $8,000 in 2006. It seems that, year after year, U.S. citizens can be sure of one thing besides death and taxes: higher health costs.

Health care costs were estimated at $2.2 trillion in 2006 (see Exhibit 9–5). Since 1993, health care spending as a percentage of gross domestic product (GDP) has remained relatively constant at 13.6 percent, except in 1997, when it fell to 13.4 percent, and in 2005, when it increased to 15.7 percent. The latest projections from The Centers of Medicare and Medicaid Services show that over the next 8 years annual health care spending is expected to grow to over $3.6 trillion, or 19.2 percent of GDP. Yet 47 million people, or 15.7 percent of our population, have no health insurance.

RAPID INCREASE IN MEDICAL EXPENDITURES Since federally sponsored health care began in 1965, U.S. health care expenditures rose from $41.6 billion, or about 6 percent of GDP, to $2.2 trillion in 2006, about 15.7 percent of GDP.

HIGH ADMINISTRATIVE COSTS In the United States, administrative costs consume nearly 26 percent of health care dollars, compared to 1 percent under Canada's socialized system. These costs include activities such as enrolling beneficiaries in a health plan, paying health insurance premiums, checking eligibility, obtaining

Exhibit 9–5   U.S. National Health Expenditures, 1960–2006

Billions of dollars

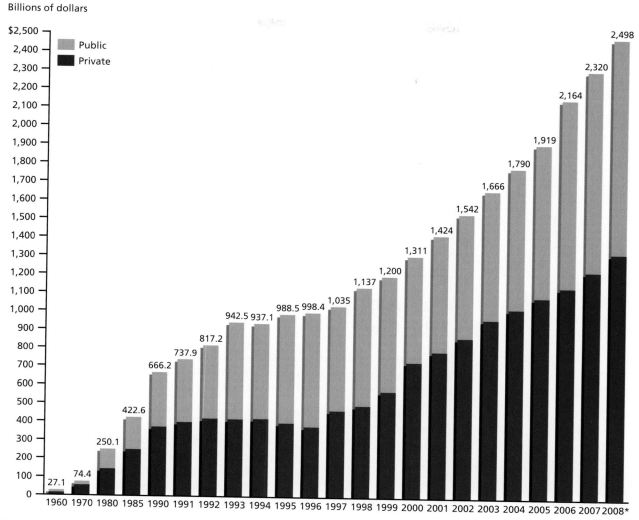

Sources: U.S. Department of Health and Human Services. The Centers for Medicare and Medicaid Services; *Statistical Abstract of the United States, 2004–2005*, Table 116, p. 93; *BusinessWeek*, January 10, 2005, p. 115, www.census.gov/compendia/statab/tables/07s0120.xls, accessed May 16,2007.
* Projected

authorizations for specialist referrals, and filing reimbursement claims. More than 1,100 different insurance forms are now in use in the United States.

Why Does Health Care Cost So Much?

The high and rising costs of health care are attributable to many factors, including

- The use of sophisticated, expensive technologies.
- Duplication of tests and sometimes duplication of technologies that yield similar results.
- Increases in the variety and frequency of treatments, including allegedly unnecessary tests.
- The increasing number and longevity of elderly people.
- Regulations that result in cost shifting rather than cost reduction.
- The increasing number of accidents and crimes that require emergency medical services.

- Limited competition and restrictive work rules in the health care delivery system.
- Labor intensiveness and rapid average earnings growth for health care professionals and executives.
- Using more expensive medical care than necessary, such as going to an emergency room with a bad cold.
- Built-in inflation in the health care delivery system.
- Aging baby boomers use of more health care services, whether they're going to the doctor more often, or snapping up pricier drugs, from Celebrex to Viagra.
- Other major factors that cost billions of dollars each year, including fraud, administrative waste, malpractice insurance, excessive surgical procedures, a wide range of prices for similar services, and double health coverage.

According to the Government Accountability Office, fraud and abuse account for nearly 10 percent of all dollars spent on health care. In 2006, that was a loss of more than $25 billion to Medicare.

Because third parties—private health insurers and government—pay such a large part of the nation's health care bill, hospitals, doctors, and patients often lack the incentive to make the most economical use of health care services.

What Is Being Done about the High Costs of Health Care?

In the private sector, concerned groups such as employers, labor unions, health insurers, health care professionals, and consumers have undertaken a wide range of innovative activities to contain the costs of health care. These activities include

- Programs to carefully review health care fees and charges and the use of health care services.

CAUTION!

For $60, a thief can buy your health records— and use them to get costly care. Guess who gets the bill? *You!*

Source: *BusinessWeek,* January 8, 2007, p. 30.

- The establishment of incentives to encourage preventive care and provide more services out of hospitals, where this is medically acceptable.
- Involvement in community health planning to help achieve a better balance between health needs and health care resources.
- The encouragement of prepaid group practices and other alternatives to fee-for-service arrangements.
- Community health education programs that motivate people to take better care of themselves.
- Physicians encouraging patients to pay cash for routine medical care and lab tests.

What Can You Do to Reduce Personal Health Care Costs?

The best way to avoid the high cost of illness is to stay well. The prescription is the same as it has always been:

1. Eat a balanced diet and keep your weight under control.
2. Avoid smoking and don't drink to excess.

Personal Finance in Practice

› Medical ID Theft

How to find out where you stand:

- Most patients toss out those "Explanation of Benefits" letters unopened. You should read them carefully to make sure no unauthorized treatment was performed in your name.
- Each year, ask your insurer for a "history of disclosures" from your doctor or insurer. This lists what medical information of yours was disclosed, as well as when, why, and to whom it was given, and can help spot fraud.
- Check your credit report periodically. Some victims learn of ID theft from collection notices for care they didn't get.

What to do if you're a victim:

- File theft reports with both the police and your insurer.
- Contact the Federal Trade Commission, which provides helpful resources on resolving identity theft (877-438-4338 or consumer.gov/idtheft/).
- Request a copy of your medical records from your doctor or hospital. If either refuses, file a complaint with the Office of Civil Rights at Health & Human Services (800-368-1019 or hhs.gov/ocr/privacyhowtofile.htm).

Source: Dean Foust, "Diagnosis: Identity Theft," *BusinessWeek*, January 8, 2007, p. 32.

3. Get sufficient rest, relaxation, and exercise.
4. Drive carefully and watch out for accident and fire hazards in the home.
5. Protect yourself from medical ID theft. (Read the accompanying Personal Finance in Practice box.)

Apply *Yourself!*

Create a list of personal actions that you can take to reduce the costs of health care.

✓ CONCEPT CHECK 9–6

1 What are the reasons for rising health care expenditures?

_____

_____

_____

2 What are various groups doing to curb the high costs of health care?

_____

_____

_____

3 What can individuals do to reduce health care costs?

_____

_____

_____

back to *Getting Personal*

1. Reconsider your responses to the Getting Personal questions at the beginning of the chapter. Which statements might have different responses now or in the future as a result of studying this chapter?

_____

_____

2. Why do young adults need health insurance?

_____

_____

3. Even if you are a healthy adult, why you still need disability income insurance?

_____

_____

4. Can you easily and inexpensively purchase your own health insurance?

_____

_____

5. List a few trade-offs of different health insurance policies.

_____

_____

6. List health care plans offered by private companies and by the government.

_____

_____

_____

Chapter Summary

Objective 1   Health insurance is protection that provides payments of benefits for a covered sickness or injury. Health insurance should be a part of your overall insurance program to safeguard your family's economic security. Health insurance plans can be purchased through group health insurance, individual health insurance, and COBRA.

Objective 2   Four basic types of health insurance are available under group and individual policies: hospital expense insurance, surgical expense insurance, physician's expense insurance, and major medical expense insurance.

   Major provisions of a health insurance policy include eligibility requirements, assigned benefits, internal limits, copayment, service benefits, benefit limits, exclusions and limitations, guaranteed renewability, and cancellation and termination.

Objective 3   Health insurance policy trade-offs include reimbursement versus indemnity, internal limits versus aggregate limits, deductibles and coinsurance, out-of-pocket limits, and benefits based on reasonable and customary charges.

Objective 4   Health insurance and health care are available from private insurance companies, hospital and medical service plans such as Blue Cross/Blue Shield, health maintenance organizations (HMOs), preferred provider organizations (PPOs),

point-of-service plans (POSs), home health care agencies, and employer self-funded health plans.

   The federal and state governments offer health coverage in accordance with laws that define the premiums and benefits. Two well-known government health programs are Medicare and Medicaid.

Objective 5   Disability income insurance provides regular cash income lost by employees as the result of an accident, illness, or pregnancy. Sources of disability income insurance include the employer, Social Security, worker's compensation, and private insurance companies.

Objective 6   Health care costs, except during 1994–1996, have gone up faster than the rate of inflation. Among the reasons for high and rising health care costs are the use of expensive technologies, duplication of tests and sometimes technologies, increases in the variety and frequency of treatments, unnecessary tests, the increasing number and longevity of elderly people, regulations that shift rather than reduce costs, the increasing number of accidents and crimes requiring emergency services, limited competition and restrictive work rules in the health care delivery system, rapid earnings growth among health care professionals, and built-in inflation in the health care delivery system.

Key Terms

basic health insurance coverage   275

Blue Cross   282

Blue Shield   282

coinsurance   277

copayment   278

deductible   275

disability income insurance   289

health maintenance organization
(HMO)   283

hospital expense insurance   275

long-term care insurance (LTC)   278

managed care   283

medigap (MedSup) insurance   287

physician expense insurance   275

point-of-service (POS) plan   283

preferred provider organization
(PPO)   283

stop-loss   277

surgical expense insurance   275

Problems

1. The Kelleher family has health insurance coverage that pays 80 percent of out-of-hospital expenses after a $500 deductible per person. If one family member has doctor and prescription medication expenses of $1,100 what amount would the insurance company pay?

2. A health insurance policy pays 65 percent of physical therapy costs after a $200 deductible. In contrast, an HMO charges $15 per visit for physical therapy. How much would a person save with the HMO if he or she had 10 physical therapy sessions costing $50 each?

3. Sarah's comprehensive major medical health insurance plan at work has a deductible of $750. The policy pays 85 percent of any amount above the deductible. While on a hiking trip, Sarah contracted a rare bacterial disease. Her medical costs for treatment, including medicines, tests, and a six-day hospital stay, totaled $8,893. A friend told her that she would have paid less if she had a policy with a stop-loss feature that capped her out-of-pocket expenses at $3,000. Was her friend correct? Show your computations. Then determine which policy would have cost Sarah less and by how much.

4. Georgia Braxton, a widow, has take-home pay of $600 a week. Her disability insurance coverage replaces 70 percent of her earnings after a four-week waiting period. What amount would she receive in disability benefits if an illness kept Georgia from work for 16 weeks?

5. Stephanie was injured in a car accident and was rushed to the emergency room. She received stitches for a facial wound and treatment for a broken finger. Under Stephanie's PPO plan, emergency room care at a network hospital is 80 percent covered after the member has met a $300 annual deductible. Assume that Stephanie went to a hospital within her PPO network. Her total emergency room bill was $850. What amount did Stephanie have to pay? What amount did the PPO cover?

Questions 6, 7, and 8 are based on the following scenario:

Ronald Roth started his new job as controller with Aerosystems today. Carole, the employee benefits clerk, gave Ronald a packet that contains information on the company's health insurance options. Aerosystems offers its employees the choice between a private insurance company plan (Blue Cross/Blue Shield), an HMO, and a PPO. Ronald needs to review the packet and make a decision on which health care program fits his needs. The following is an overview of that information.

a. *Blue Cross/Blue Shield plan:* The monthly premium cost to Ronald will be $42.32. For all doctor office visits, prescriptions, and major medical charges, Ronald will be responsible for 20 percent and the insurance company will cover 80 percent of covered charges. The annual deductible is $500.

b. The HMO is provided to employees free of charge. The copayment for doctors' office visits and major medical charges is $10. Prescription copayments are $5. The HMO pays 100 percent after the Ronald's copayment. No annual deductible.

c. The POS requires that the employee pay $24.44 per month to supplement the cost of the program with the company's payment. If Ron uses health care providers within the plan, he pays the copayments as described above for the HMO. He can also choose to use a health care provider out of the service and pay 20 percent of all charges after he pays a $500 deductible. The POS will pay for 80 percent of those covered visits. No annual deductible.

Ronald decided to review his medical bills from the previous year to see what costs he had incurred and to help him evaluate his choices. He visited his general physician four times during the year at a cost of $125 for each visit. He also spent $65 and $89 on prescriptions during the year. Using these costs as an example, what would Ron pay for each of the plans described above? (For the purposes of the POS computation, assume that Ron visited a physician outside of the network plan. Assume he had his prescriptions filled at a network-approved pharmacy.

6. What annual medical costs will Ronald pay using the sample medical expenses provided if he were to enroll in the Blue Cross/ Blue Shield plan?

7. What total costs will Ronald pay if he enrolls in the HMO plan?

8. If Ronald selects the POS plan, what would annual medical costs be?

9. In 1995, Joelle spent $3,600 on her health care. If this amount increased by 5 percent per year, what would be the amount Joelle spent in 2005 for the same health care? (Hint: Use the time value of money table in Chapter 1.)

10. As of 2006, per capita spending on health care in the United States was about $8,000. If this amount increased by 5 percent a year, what would be the amount of per capita spending for health care in 10 years? (Hint: Use the time value of money table in Chapter 1.)

Questions

1. Larry and Liz are a young couple both working full time and earning about $50,000 a year. They recently purchased a house and took out a large mortgage. Since both of them work, they own two cars and are still making payments on them. Liz has major medical health insurance through her employer, but Larry's coverage is inadequate. They have no children, but they hope to start a family in about three years. Liz's employer provides disability income insurance, but Larry's employer does not. Analyze the need for health and disability insurance for Liz and Larry.

2. Pam is 31 and recently divorced, with children ages 3 and 6. She earns $28,000 a year as a secretary. Her employer provides her with basic health insurance coverage. She receives child support from the children's father, but he misses payments often and is always behind in payments. Her ex-husband, however, is responsible for the children's medical bills. Analyze the need for health and disability insurance for Pam.

3. List the benefits included in your employee benefit package, such as health insurance, disability income insurance, and life insurance. Discuss the importance of such a benefit package to the consumer.

4. Visit the Social Security Administration's Web page to determine your approximate monthly Social Security disability benefits should you become disabled in the current year. Or call your Social Security office to request the latest edition of *Social Security: Understanding the Benefits.*

5. Obtain sample health insurance policies from insurance agents or brokers, and analyze the policies for definitions, coverage, exclusions, limitations on coverage, and amounts of coverage. In what ways are the policies similar? In what ways do they differ?

www.mhhe.com/kdh

Internet Connection

RESEARCHING HEALTH INSURANCE STATISTICS

The U.S. Census Bureau collects a wide variety of data about the people and economy of the United States. Health insurance coverage is one of the many surveys the bureau completes each year.

Locate the Health Insurance section of the U.S. Census Bureau Web site. Complete the worksheet below and answer the questions that follow.

Results	
U.S. Census Bureau Web site address	
For what year is the most recent health insurance coverage survey presented?	
In the most recent health insurance survey, how many people in the United States were without health insurance coverage?	
What populations (age or race) are less likely to have health insurance?	
How many children under the age of 18 have no health insurance according to the most recent health insurance survey?	

Case in Point

BUYING ADEQUATE HEALTH INSURANCE COVERAGE

Kathy Jones was a junior at Glenbard High School. She had two younger brothers. Her father, the assistant manager of a local supermarket, had take-home pay of $3,000 a month. He had a group health insurance policy and a $30,000 life insurance policy. He said that he could not afford to buy additional insurance. All of his monthly salary was used to meet current expenses, including car and house payments, food, clothing, transportation, children's allowances, recreation and entertainment, and vacation trips.

One evening, Kathy was talking with her father about insurance, which she was studying in an economics course. She asked what kind of insurance program her father had for their family. The question started Mr. Jones thinking about how well he was planning for his wife and children. Since the family had always been in good health, Mr. Jones felt that additional health and life insurance was not essential. Maybe after he received a raise in

his salary and after his daughter was out of high school, he could afford to buy more insurance.

Questions

1. Do you think Kathy's father was planning wisely for the welfare of his family? Can you suggest ways in which this family could have cut monthly expenses and thus set aside some money for more insurance?

2. Although Mr. Jones's salary was not big enough to buy insurance for all possible risks, what protection do you think he should have had at this time?

3. Suppose Mr. Jones had been seriously injured and unable to work for at least one year. What would his family have done? How might this situation have affected his children?

Continuing Case

HEALTH INSURANCE

Life Situation

Pam, 36

Josh, 38

Financial Data

Monthly income $4,300

Living expenses $4,075

Three children, ages 9, 7, and 4   Assets $150.850

                                                     Liabilities $99.520

The Brocks are assessing their health insurance coverages. Since Josh's current employer offers him only 30 days of sick leave, they need to consider this factor when assessing disability insurance plans.

Since Pam's work activities have varied, the family is dependent on Josh's health insurance. In recent weeks, his company is considering several types of plans. These alternatives include traditional health insurance programs and HMOs, with a wide variety of coverage and cost differences.

Questions

1. When considering disability income insurance, what length of waiting period and duration of benefits should the Brocks consider?

2. What types of health insurance coverages would be recommended for the Brocks?

3. How might the Brocks use *Your Personal Financial Plan* sheets 31 and 32 to select health and disability insurance?

Video Case

CORPORATE HEALTH: CORPORATIONS BUILDING HEALTH FACILITIES

As medical costs rise, corporations are building facilities like in-house clinics, pharmacies, and gyms, and serving more nutritious meals to encourage healthy living. Corporations such as Pitney Bowes have been focusing on teaching healthy lifestyle choices to their employees in the workplace. Employers are offering day-long health seminars, nutrition and weight-loss programs, on-site pharmacies, flu shots, and gyms. These proactive companies believe that healthier employees are happier, more productive, and less expensive employees.

Questions

1. What can corporations do to encourage their employees to be healthy?

2. Why are corporations spending billions of dollars building in-house clinics, pharmacies, and gyms and serving more nutritious meals to encourage healthy living?

Spending Diary

"SOME OF MY EATING HABITS NOT ONLY WASTE MONEY BUT ARE ALSO NOT BEST FOR MY HEALTH."

Directions

Continue your Daily Spending Diary to record and monitor spending in various categories. Your comments should reflect what you have learned about your spending patterns and help you consider possible changes you might want to make in your spending habits.

Questions

1. What spending actions might directly or indirectly affect your health and physical well-being?

2. What amounts (if any) are currently required from your spending for the cost of health and disability insurance?

Assessing Current and Needed Health Care Insurance

Financial Planning Activities: Assess current and needed medical and health care insurance. Investigate your existing medical and health insurance, and determine the need for additional coverages.

Suggested Web Sites: www.insure.com www.life-line.org

Insurance company _____

Address _____

Type of coverage ☐ individual health policy ☐ group health policy
☐ HMO ☐ PPO ☐ other

Premium amount (monthly/quarter/semiannual/annual) _____

Main coverages _____

Amount of coverage for _____

• Hospital costs _____

• Surgery costs _____

• Physicians' fees _____

• Lab tests _____

• Outpatient expenses _____

• Maternity _____

• Major medical _____

Other items covered/amounts _____

Policy restrictions (deductible, coinsurance, maximum limits) _____

Items not covered by this insurance _____

Of items not covered, would supplemental coverage be appropriate for your personal situation? _____

What actions related to your current (or proposed additional) coverage are necessary? _____

What's Next for Your Personal Financial Plan?

• Talk to others about the impact of their health insurance on other financial decisions.

• Contact an insurance agent to obtain cost information for an individual health insurance plan.

Disability Income Insurance Needs

Financial Planning Activities: Determine financial needs and insurance coverage related to employment disability situations. Use the categories below to determine your potential income needs and disability insurance coverage.

Suggested Web Sites: www.ssa.gov   www.insweb.com

Monthly Expenses

	Current	When Disabled
Mortgage (or rent)	$ _____	$ _____
Utilities	$ _____	$ _____
Food	$ _____	$ _____
Clothing	$ _____	$ _____
Insurance payments	$ _____	$ _____
Debt payments	$ _____	$ _____
Auto/transportation	$ _____	$ _____
Medical/dental care	$ _____	$ _____
Education	$ _____	$ _____
Personal allowances	$ _____	$ _____
Recreation/entertainment	$ _____	$ _____
Contributors, donations	$ _____	$ _____
Total monthly expenses when disabled		$ _____

Substitute Income

Monthly Benefit*

	Monthly Benefit*
Group disability insurance	$ _____
Social Security	$ _____
State disability insurance	$ _____
Worker's compensation	$ _____
Credit disability insurance (in some auto loan or home mortgages)	$ _____
Other income (investments, etc.)	$ _____
Total projected income when disabled	$ _____

If projected income when disabled is less than expenses, additional disability income insurance should be considered.

*Most disability insurance programs have a waiting period before benefits start, and they may have a limit as to how long benefits are received.

What's Next for Your Personal Financial Plan?

- Survey several people to determine if they have disability insurance.

- Talk to an insurance agent to compare the costs of disability income insurance available from several insurance companies.

10 Financial Planning with Life Insurance

Should you be concerned about life insurance? For each of the following statements, select "yes" or "no" to indicate your behavior regarding these life insurance statements.

	Yes	No
1. I need life insurance because someone depends on me for financial support.	____	____
2. My survivors can use the life insurance benefits to cover my funeral expenses or other financial obligations.	____	____
3. I should start budgeting for my life insurance premiums while I am still young and healthy.	____	____
4. My life insurance premiums will be lower if I buy a policy at a younger age.	____	____
5. I can determine my average life expectancy with some certainty.	____	____
6. I am aware of several different types of life insurance.	____	____
7. I can decide who receives the benefits of my life insurance policy.	____	____

After studying this chapter, you will be asked to use what you learned about the purpose of life insurance and types of life insurance policies and to reconsider your responses to these items.

Your Personal Financial Plan Sheets

33. Determining Life Insurance Needs
34. Life Insurance Policy Comparison

Objectives	Why is this important?
In this chapter, you will learn to: 1. Define life insurance and determine your life insurance needs. 2. Distinguish between the types of life insurance companies and analyze various life insurance policies these companies issue. 3. Select important provisions in life insurance contracts and create a plan to buy life insurance. 4. Recognize how annuities provide financial security.	Life insurance helps protect the people who depend on you. Deciding whether you need it and choosing the right policy take time, research, and careful thought.

What Is Life Insurance?

OBJECTIVE 1
Define life insurance and determine your life insurance needs.

Even though putting a price on your life is impossible, you probably own some life insurance—through a group plan where you work, as a veteran, or through a policy you bought. Life insurance is one of the most important and expensive purchases you may ever make; therefore, it is important that you budget for this need. Deciding whether you need it and choosing the right policy from dozens of options take time, research, and careful thought. This chapter will help you make decisions about life insurance. It describes what life insurance is and how it works, the major types of life insurance coverage, and how you can use life insurance to protect your family.

When you buy life insurance, you're making a contract with the company issuing the policy. You agree to pay a certain amount of money—the premium—periodically. In return the company agrees to pay a death benefit, or a stated sum of money upon your death, to your beneficiary. A **beneficiary** is a person named to receive the benefits from an insurance policy.

beneficiary A person designated to receive something, such as life insurance proceeds, from the insured.

The Purpose of Life Insurance

Most people buy life insurance to protect the people who depend on them from financial losses caused by their death. Those people could include a spouse, children, an aging parent, or a business partner or corporation. Life insurance benefits may be used to:

- Pay off a home mortgage or other debts at the time of death.
- Provide lump-sum payments through an endowment for children when they reach a specified age.

Apply *Yourself!*

- Provide an education or income for children.
- Make charitable donations after death.
- Provide a retirement income.
- Accumulate savings.
- Establish a regular income for survivors.
- Set up an estate plan.
- Pay estate and gift taxes.

The Principle of Life Insurance

No one can say with any certainty how long a particular person will live. Still, insurance companies are able to make some educated guesses. Over the years they've compiled tables that show about how long people live. Using these tables, the company will make a rough guess about a person's life span and charge him or her accordingly. The sooner a person is likely to die, the higher the premiums he or she will pay.

did you know?

Japan spends more per capita on life insurance than any other nation. Next: Switzerland, the United States, Great Britain, and the Netherlands.

How Long Will You Live?

If history is a guide, you'll live longer than your ancestors did. In 1900 an American male could be expected to live 46.3 years. By 2000, in contrast, life expectancy had risen to 74 years for men and 80 for women. Exhibit 10–1 shows about how many years a person can be expected to live today. For instance, a 30-year-old woman can be expected to live another 50.6 years. That doesn't mean that she has a high probability of dying at age 80.6. This just means that 50.6 is the average number of additional years a 30-year-old woman may expect to live.

Exhibit 10–1   Life Expectancy Tables, All Races, 2000

Age	Both Sexes	Male	Female	Age	Both Sexes	Male	Female
0	76.9	74.1	79.5	45	34.4	32.2	36.3
1	76.4	73.7	79.0	50	30.0	27.9	31.8
5	72.5	69.8	75.1	55	24.7	23.8	27.4
10	67.6	64.9	70.1	60	21.6	19.9	23.1
15	62.6	59.9	65.2	65	17.9	16.3	19.2
20	57.8	55.2	60.3	70	14.4	13.0	15.5
25	53.1	50.6	55.4	75	11.3	10.1	12.1
30	48.3	45.9	50.6	80	8.6	7.6	9.1
35	43.6	41.3	45.8	85	6.3	5.6	6.7
40	38.9	36.7	41.0				

This table helps insurance companies determine insurance premiums. *Use the table to find the average number of additional years a 15-year-old male and female are expected to live.*

Do You Need Life Insurance?

Before you buy life insurance, you'll have to decide whether you need it at all. Generally, if your death would cause financial hardship for somebody, then life insurance is a wise purchase. Households with children usually have the greatest need for life insurance. Single people who live alone or with their parents, however, usually have little or no need for life insurance unless they have a great deal of debt or want to provide for their parents, a friend, relative, or charity.

Estimating Your Life Insurance Requirements

In estimating your life insurance requirements, consider the insurance coverage that your employer offers you as a fringe benefit. Most employers provide employees with life insurance coverage equal to their yearly salary. For example, if you earn $35,000 per year, you may receive $35,000 of insurance coverage. Some employers offer insurance of two or more times the salary with increased contributions from employees. The premiums are usually lower than premiums for individual life insurance policies, and you don't have to pass a physical exam.

There are four general methods for determining the amount of insurance you may need: the easy method, the DINK method, the "nonworking" spouse method, and the "family need" method.

THE EASY METHOD   Simple as this method is, it is remarkably useful. It is based on the insurance agent's rule of thumb that a "typical family" will need approximately 70 percent of your salary for seven years before they adjust to the financial consequences of your death. In other words, for a simple estimate of your life insurance needs, just multiply your current gross income by 7 (7 years) and 0.70 (70 percent).

EXAMPLE

$30,000 current income × 7 = $210,000 × 0.70 = $147,000

EXAMPLE FROM YOUR LIFE

$ _____ current income × 7 = $ _____ × 0.70 = $ _____

This method assumes your family is "typical." You may need more insurance if you have four or more children, if you have above-average family debt, if any member of your family suffers from poor health, or if your spouse has poor employment potential. On the other hand, you may need less insurance if your family is smaller.

THE DINK (DUAL INCOME, NO KIDS) METHOD   If you have no dependents and your spouse earns as much or more than you do, you have very simple insurance needs. Basically, all you need to do is ensure that your spouse will not be unduly burdened by debts should you die. Here is an example of the DINK method:

EXAMPLE

	Example	Your Figures
Funeral expenses	$ 5,000	$ _____
One-half of mortgage	60,000	_____
One-half of auto loan	7,000	_____
One-half of credit card balance	1,500	_____
One-half of personal debt	1,500	_____
Other debts	1,000	_____
Total insurance needs	$76,000	$ _____

This method assumes your spouse will continue to work after your death. If your spouse suffers poor health or is employed in an occupation with an uncertain future, you should consider adding an insurance cushion to see him or her through hard times.

THE "NONWORKING" SPOUSE METHOD   Insurance experts have estimated that extra costs of up to $10,000 a year may be required to replace the services of a homemaker in a family with small children. These extra costs may include the cost of a housekeeper, child care, more meals out, additional carfare, laundry services, and so on. They do not include the lost potential earnings of the surviving spouse, who often must take time away from the job to care for the family.

To estimate how much life insurance a homemaker should carry, simply multiply the number of years before the youngest child reaches age 18 by $10,000:

EXAMPLE

Youngest child's age = 8 years
10 years × $10,000 = $100,000

EXAMPLE FROM YOUR LIFE

_____ years × $10,000 = $ _____

If there are teenage children, the $10,000 figure can be reduced. If there are more than two children under age 13, or if anyone in the family suffers poor health or has special needs, the $10,000 figure should be adjusted upward.

THE "FAMILY NEED" METHOD   The first three methods assume you and your family are "typical" and ignore important factors such as Social Security and your liquid assets. The nearby Figure It Out box provides a detailed worksheet for making a thorough estimate of your life insurance needs.

Although this method is quite thorough, if you believe it does not address all of your special needs, you should obtain further advice from an insurance expert or a financial planner.

As you determine your life insurance needs, don't forget to consider the life insurance you may already have. You may have ample coverage through your employer and through any mortgage and credit life insurance you purchased.

Before you consider types of life insurance policies, you must decide what you want your life insurance to do for you and your dependents. First, how much money do you want to leave to your dependents should you die today? Will you require more or less insurance protection to meet their needs as time goes on? Second, when would you

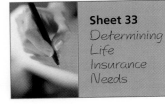

Sheet 33
Determining Life Insurance Needs

Key Web Sites for Life Insurance Planning
www.ircweb.org
www.iiaa.com

Figure It Out!

› A Worksheet to Calculate Your Life Insurance Needs

1. Five times your personal yearly income _____ (1)

2. Total approximate expenses above and beyond your daily living costs for you and your dependents (e.g. tuition, care for a disabled child or parent) amount to = _____ (2)

3. Your emergency fund (3 to 6 months of living expenses) amounts to = _____ (3)

4. Estimated amount for your funeral expenses (U.S. average is $5,000 to $10,000) + _____ (4)

5. Total estimate of your family's financial needs (add lines 1 through 4) = _____ (5)

6. Your total liquid assets (e.g. savings accounts, CDs, money market funds, existing life insurance both individual and group, pension plan death benefits, and Social Security benefits) − _____ (6)

7. Subtract line 6 from line 5 and enter the difference here. = _____ (7)

The net result (line 7) is an estimate of the shortfall your family would face upon your death. Remember, these are just rules of thumb. For a complete analysis of your needs, consult a professional.

Sources: *About Life Insurance*, Metropolitan Life Insurance Company, February 1997, p. 3; *The TIAA Guide to Life Insurance Planning for People in Education* (New York: Teachers Insurance and Annuity Association, January 1997), p. 3.

like to be able to retire? What amount of income do you believe you and your spouse would need then? Third, how much will you be able to pay for your insurance program? Are the demands on your family budget for other living expenses likely to be greater or lower as time goes on?

When you have considered these questions and developed some approximate answers, you are ready to select the types and amounts of life insurance policies that will help you accomplish your objectives.

✓ CONCEPT CHECK 10–1

1 What is life insurance? What is its purpose?

_____

_____

2 For each of the following statements, indicate your response by writing "T" or "F".

  a. Life insurance is one of the least important and inexpensive purchases. _____

  b. A beneficiary is a person named to receive the benefits from the insurance policy. _____

  c. Life insurance benefits may be used to pay off a home mortgage or other debts at the time of death. _____

  d. The sooner a person is likely to die, the higher the premiums he or she will pay. _____

  e. All people need to purchase a life insurance policy. _____

3 What are the four methods of determining life insurance needs?

_____

_____

Types of Life Insurance Companies and Policies

OBJECTIVE 2

Distinguish between the types of life insurance companies and analyze various types of life insurance policies these companies issue.

nonparticipating policy Life insurance that does not provide policy dividends; also called a *nonpar policy.*

participating policy Life insurance that provides policy dividends; also called a *par policy.*

Types of Life Insurance Companies

You can purchase the new or extra life insurance you need from two types of life insurance companies: stock life insurance companies, owned by shareholders, and mutual life insurance companies, owned by policyholders. About 95 percent of the U.S. life insurance companies are stock companies, and about 5 percent are mutual.

Stock companies generally sell **nonparticipating** (or *nonpar*) **policies,** while mutual companies specialize in the sale of **participating** (or *par*) **policies.** A participating policy has a somewhat higher premium than a nonparticipating policy, but a part of the premium is refunded to the policyholder annually. This refund is called the *policy dividend.*

A long debate about whether stock companies or mutual companies offer less expensive life insurance has been inconclusive. You should check with both stock and mutual companies to determine which type offers the best policy for your particular needs at the lowest price.

If you wish to pay exactly the same premium each year, you should choose a nonparticipating policy with its guaranteed premiums. However, you may prefer life insurance whose annual price reflects the company's experience with its investments, the health of its policyholders, and its general operating costs, that is, a participating policy.

Nevertheless, as with other forms of insurance, price should not be your only consideration in choosing a life insurance policy. You should consider the financial stability of and service provided by the insurance company.

Types of Life Insurance Policies

Both mutual insurance companies and stock insurance companies sell two basic types of life insurance: temporary and permanent insurance. Temporary insurance can be term, renewable term, convertible term, or decreasing term insurance. Permanent insurance is known by different names, including whole life, straight life, ordinary life, and cash value life insurance. As you will learn in the next section, permanent insurance can be limited payment, variable, adjustable, or universal life insurance. Other types of insurance policies—group life and credit life insurance—are generally temporary forms of insurance. Exhibit 10–2 lists major types and subtypes of life insurance.

term insurance Life insurance protection for a specified period of time; sometimes called *temporary life insurance.*

TERM LIFE INSURANCE   **Term insurance,** sometimes called *temporary life insurance,* provides protection against loss of life for only a specified term, or period of time. A term insurance policy pays a benefit only if you die during the period it covers, which may be 1, 5, 10, or 20 years, or up to age 70. If you stop paying the premiums, your coverage stops. Term insurance is often the best value for customers. You need insurance coverage most while you are raising children. As your children become

Exhibit 10–2

Major Types and Subtypes of Life Insurance

Term (temporary)	Whole, Straight, or Ordinary Life	Other Types
• Renewable term	• Limited payment	• Group life
• Multiyear level term	• Variable life	• Credit life
• Convertible term	• Adjustable life	• Endowment life
• Decreasing term	• Universal life	
• Return of Premium		

independent and your assets increase, you can reduce your coverage. Term insurance comes in many different forms. Here are some examples.

Renewable Term   The coverage of term insurance ends at the conclusion of the term, but you can continue it for another term—five years, for example—if you have a renewable option. However, the premium will increase because you will be older. It also usually has an age limit; you cannot renew after you reach a certain age.

Multiyear Level Term   A multiyear level term, or *straight term,* policy guarantees that you will pay the same premium for the duration of your policy.

Conversion Term   This type of policy allows you to change from term to permanent coverage. This will have a higher premium.

Decreasing Term   Term insurance is also available in a form that pays less to the beneficiary as time passes. The insurance period you select might depend on your age or on how long you decide that the coverage will be needed. For example, if you have a mortgage on a house, you might buy a 25-year decreasing term policy as a way to make sure that the debt could be paid if you died. The coverage would decrease as the balance on the loan decreased.

Return-of-Premium Term   Recently, insurance companies began to sell return-of-premium term life policies. These policies return all the premiums if you survive to the end of the policy term. Premiums are higher than the regular term policy but you do get all your money back. Is return-of-premium a good investment? Read the nearby From the Pages of *Kiplinger's Personal Finance* feature.

WHOLE LIFE INSURANCE

The other major type of life insurance is known as whole life insurance (also called a *straight life policy,* a *cash-value policy,* or an *ordinary life policy*). **Whole life insurance** is a permanent policy for which you pay a specified premium each year for the rest of your life. In return the insurance company pays your beneficiary a stated sum when you die. The amount of your premium depends mostly on the age at which you purchase the insurance.

Whole life insurance can also serve as an investment. Part of each premium you pay is set aside in a savings account. When and if you cancel the policy, you are entitled to the accumulated savings, which is known as the **cash value.** Whole life policies are popular because they provide both a death benefit and a savings component. You can borrow from your cash value if necessary, although you must pay interest on the loan. Cash-value policies may make sense for people who intend to keep the policies for the long term or for people who want a more structured way to save. However, the Consumer Federation of America Insurance Group suggests that you explore other savings and investment strategies before investing your money in a permanent policy.

The premium of a term insurance policy will increase each time you renew your insurance. In contrast, whole life policies have a higher annual premium at first, but the rate remains the same for the rest of your life. Several types of whole life policies have been developed to meet the needs of different customers. These include the limited payment policy, the variable life policy, the adjustable life policy and universal life insurance.

whole life insurance An insurance plan in which the policyholder pays a specified premium each year for as long as he or she lives; also called a *straight life policy,* a *cash-value life policy,* or an *ordinary life policy.*

cash value The amount received after giving up a life insurance policy.

did you know?

A Harris interactive poll reported 8 percent of Americans bought more disability insurance and 6 percent bought or increased their life insurance within one month of September 11, 2001.

Limited Payment Policy   Limited payment policies charge premiums for only a certain length of time, usually 20 or 30 years or until the insured reaches a certain age. At the end of this time, the policy is "paid up," and the policyholder remains insured for life. When the policyholder dies, the beneficiary receives the full death benefit. The annual

INSURANCE | With return-of-premium policies, you bet your life you'll get money back.
By Kimberly Lankford

REFUND guaranteed

JORGE RAMIREZ is expecting a life-insurance payout *before* he dies. If he lives another 20 years, he'll get a windfall of more than $26,000. Last year Ramirez, 42, bought a term-life policy with an interesting new twist: If he survives to the end of the policy term, he gets back all of the money he paid in premiums.

Return-of-premium, or ROP, policies are becoming a popular alternative to standard term-life insurance, for which you pay the lowest premiums but get nothing back if you outlive the term. Ramirez wanted coverage that would last until his children, 14-year-old Susana and 8-year-old Jorge Jr.,

were grown. When he went to shop for a policy, he found that insurers were charging up to $1,500 for ordinary term-life policies providing $500,000 worth of coverage. At $1,332 per year, AIG's return-of-premium policy was still in the ballpark, and Ramirez figured he'd get back the money just as he was about to retire. "If I take care of myself, I'll probably be around in 20 years," he says. "I was looking to see if I could get something back while I'm still alive."

A good investment?
A check for $26,000 (or whatever you paid in premiums) sounds like a great deal. But you may not be getting the biggest bang for your buck.

Ramirez could have paid $405 a year (instead of $1,332) for the same coverage with a regular 20-year term policy and invested the $927 difference in premiums. As long as his investments returned more than 3.1% per year, he would have come out ahead.

A 30-year ROP policy can be a better deal if you need insurance for a longer time, because the premium differential between the two kinds of term policies is much smaller. For example, a healthy 41-year-old man would pay a premium of $930 a year for a regular 30-year, $500,000 term policy and $1,425 for a return-of-premium version. If he invested the annual difference

of $495 himself, his investments would have to return at least 6.2% a year to accumulate more than the nearly $43,000 he'd get in returned premiums.

If you drop an ROP policy before the term is up, you may get some of your money back. But payout amounts vary from company to company, says Byron Udell, CEO of AccuQuote. His favorite policies right now are from insurance giants AIG and Genworth Financial. Genworth offers the best deal on early payouts, he says: 60% of the premiums you've paid if you drop a 30-year policy after 15 years.

1. What is a return-of-premium (ROP) term life insurance policy?

_____

_____

_____

2. Is a return-of-premium term life policy a good investment? Why or why not?

_____

_____

_____

3. Why did Jorge Ramirez purchase a return-of-premium policy?

_____

_____

_____

premiums are higher for limited payment policies because the premiums have to be paid within a shorter period of time.

Variable Life Policy   With a variable life policy, your premium payments are fixed. As with a cash value policy, part of your premium is placed in a separate account; this money is invested in a stock, bond, or money market fund. The death benefit is guaranteed, but the cash value of the benefit can vary considerably according to the ups and downs of the stock market. Your death benefit can also increase, depending on the earnings of that separate fund.

Adjustable Life Policy   An adjustable life policy allows you to change your coverage as your needs change. For example, if you want to increase or decrease your death benefit, you can change either the premium payments or the period of coverage.

Universal Life   **Universal life insurance** is essentially a term policy with a cash value. Part of your premium goes into an investment account that grows and earns interest. You are able to borrow or withdraw your cash value. Unlike a traditional whole life policy, a universal life policy allows you to change your premium without changing your coverage. Exhibit 10–3 compares the important features of term life, whole life, and universal life insurance.

universal life insurance A whole life policy that combines term insurance and investment elements.

Exhibit 10–3   Comparing the Major Types of Life Insurance

	Term Life	**Whole Life**	**Universal Life**
Premium	Lower initially, increasing with each renewal.	Higher initially than term; normally doesn't increase.	Flexible premiums.
Protects for	A specified period.	Entire life if you keep the policy.	A flexible time period.
Policy benefits	Death benefits only.	Death benefits and eventually a cash and loan value.	Flexible death benefits and eventually a cash and loan value.
Advantages	Low outlay. Initially, you can purchase a larger amount of coverage for a lower premium.	Helps you with finanicial discipline. Generally fixed premium amount. Cash value accumulation. You can take loan against policy.	More flexibility. Takes advantages of current interest rates. Offers the possibility of improved mortality rates (increased life expectancy because of advancements in medicine, which may lower policy costs).
Disadvantages	Premium increases with age. No cash value.	Costly if you surrender early. Usually no cash value for at least three to five years. May not meet short-term needs.	Same as whole life. Greater risks due to program flexibility. Low interest rates can affect cash value and premiums.
Options	May be renewable or convertible to a whole life policy.	May pay dividends. May provide a reduced paid-up policy. Partial cash surrenders permitted.	May pay dividends. Minimum death benefit. Partial cash surrenders permitted.

OTHER TYPES OF LIFE INSURANCE POLICIES   Other types of life insurance policies include group life insurance, credit life insurance, and endowment life insurance.

Group Life Insurance   Group life insurance is basically a variation of term insurance. It covers a large number of people under a single policy. The people included in the group do not need medical examinations to get the coverage. Group insurance is usually offered through employers, who pay part or all of the costs for their employees, or through professional organizations, which allow members to sign up for the coverage. Group plans are easy to enroll in, but they can be much more expensive than similar term policies.

Credit Life Insurance   Credit life insurance is used to pay off certain debts, such as auto loans or mortgages, in the event that you die before they are paid in full. These types of policies are not the best buy for the protection that they offer. Decreasing term insurance is a better option.

Key Web Sites for Life Insurance Information
www.iii.org
www.insweb.com

Endowment Life Insurance   Endowment is life insurance that provides coverage for a specific period of time and pays an agreed-upon sum of money to the policyholder if he or she is still living at the end of the endowment period. If the policyholder dies before that time, the beneficiary receives the money.

✔ CONCEPT CHECK 10–2

1 What are the two types of life insurance companies?

_____

2 For each of the following statements, indicate your response by writing "T" or "F."

    a. Stock life insurance companies generally sell participating (or par) policies. ___

    b. Mutual life insurance companies specialize in the sale of nonparticipating (nonpar) policies. ___

    c. If you wish to pay exactly the same premium each year, you should choose a nonpar policy. ___

    d. Permanent insurance is known as whole life, straight life, ordinary life, and cash-value life insurance. ___

    e. Term life insurance is the most expensive type of policy. ___

3 What are the five forms of term insurance?

_____

_____

4 What are the four forms of whole life insurance?

_____

_____

5 Define the following types of life insurance policies:

    a. Group life insurance _____

    b. Credit life insurance _____

    c. Endowment life insurance _____

Selecting Provisions and Buying Life Insuarance

Key Provisions in a Life Insurance Policy

Study the provisions in your policy carefully. The following are some of the most common features.

OBJECTIVE 3
Select important provisions in life insurance contracts and create a plan to buy life insurance.

NAMING YOUR BENEFICIARY   You decide who receives the benefits of your life insurance policy: your spouse, your child, or your business partner, for example. You can also name contingent beneficiaries, those who will receive the money if your primary beneficiary dies before or at the same time as you do. Update your list of beneficiaries as your needs change.

INCONTESTABILITY CLAUSE   The incontestability clause says that the insurer can't cancel the policy if it's been in force for a specified period, usually two years. After that time the policy is considered valid during the lifetime of the insured. This is true even if the policy was gained through fraud. The incontestability clause protects the beneficiaries from financial loss in the event that the insurance company refuses to meet the terms of the policy.

THE GRACE PERIOD   When you buy a life insurance policy, the insurance company agrees to pay a certain sum of money under specified circumstances and you agree to pay a certain premium regularly. The *grace period* allows 28 to 31 days to elapse, during which time you may pay the premium without penalty. After that time, the policy lapses if you have not paid the premium.

POLICY REINSTATEMENT   A lapsed policy can be put back in force, or reinstated, if it has not been turned in for cash. To reinstate the policy, you must again qualify as an acceptable risk, and you must pay overdue premiums with interest. There is a time limit on reinstatement, usually one or two years.

NONFORFEITURE CLAUSE   One important feature of the whole life policy is the **nonforfeiture clause.** This provision prevents the forfeiture of accrued benefits if you choose to drop the policy. For example, if you decide not to continue paying premiums, you can exercise specified options with your cash value.

nonforfeiture clause A provision that allows the insured not to forfeit all accrued benefits.

MISSTATEMENT OF AGE PROVISION   The misstatement of age provision says that if the company finds out that your age was incorrectly stated, it will pay the benefits your premiums would have bought if your age had been correctly stated. The provision sets forth a simple procedure to resolve what could otherwise be a complicated legal matter.

Apply *Yourself!*

Objective 3

Examine your life insurance policies and the policies of other members of your family. Note the contractual provisions of each policy. What does the company promise to do in return for premiums?

POLICY LOAN PROVISION   A loan from the insurance company is available on a whole life policy after the policy has been in force for one, two, or three years, as stated in the policy. This feature, known as the *policy loan provision,* permits you to borrow any amount up to the cash value of the policy. However, a policy loan reduces the death benefit by the amount of the loan plus interest if the loan is not repaid.

SUICIDE CLAUSE   In the first two years of coverage, beneficiaries of someone who dies by suicide receive only the amount of the premiums paid. After two years beneficiaries receive the full value of death benefits.

RIDERS TO LIFE INSURANCE POLICIES

rider A document attached to a policy that modifies its coverage.

An insurance company can change the conditions of a policy by adding a rider to it. A **rider** is a document attached to a policy that changes its terms by adding or excluding specified conditions or altering its benefits.

Waiver of Premium Disability Benefit   One common rider is a waiver of premium disability benefit. This clause allows you to stop paying premiums if you're totally and permanently disabled before you reach a certain age, usually 60. The company continues to pay the premiums at its own expense.

double indemnity A benefit under which the company pays twice the face value of the policy if the insured's death results from an accident.

Accidental Death Benefit   Another common rider to life insurance is an accidental death benefit, sometimes called **double indemnity.** Double indemnity pays twice the value of the policy if you are killed in an accident. Again, the accident must occur before a certain age, generally 60 to 65. Experts counsel against adding this rider to your coverage. The benefit is very expensive, and your chances of dying in an accident are slim.

Guaranteed Insurability Option   A third important rider is known as a guaranteed insurability option. This rider allows you to buy a specified additional amount of life insurance at certain intervals without undergoing medical exams. This is a good option for people who anticipate needing more life insurance in the future.

Cost-of-Living Protection   This special rider is designed to help prevent inflation from eroding the purchasing power of the protection your policy provides. A *loss, reduction,* or *erosion of purchasing power* refers to the impact inflation has on a fixed amount of money. As inflation increases the cost of goods and services, that fixed amount will not buy as much in the future as it does today. Exhibit 10–4 shows the effects of inflation on a $100,000 life insurance policy. However, your insurance needs are likely to be smaller in later years.

Accelerated Benefits   *Accelerated benefits,* also known as *living benefits,* are life insurance policy proceeds paid to the policyholder who is terminally ill before he or she dies. The benefits may be provided for directly in the policies, but more often they are added by riders or attachments to new or existing policies. A representative list of

Exhibit 10–4

Effects of Inflation on a $100,000 Life Insurance Policy

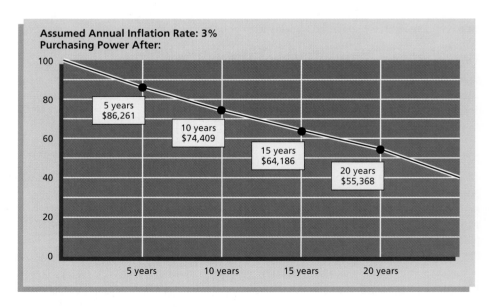

Source: *The TIAA Guide to Life Insurance Planning for People in Education* (New York: Teachers Insurance and Annuity Association, January 1997), p. 8.

insurers that offer accelerated benefits is available from the National Insurance Consumer Helpline (NICH) at 800-942-4242. Although more than 150 companies offer some form of accelerated benefits, not all plans are approved in all states. NICH cannot tell you whether a particular plan is approved in any given state. For more information, check with your insurance agent or your state department of insurance.

Second-to-Die Option   A *second-to-die life insurance policy,* also called *survivorship life,* insures two lives, usually husband and wife. The death benefit is paid when the second spouse dies. Usually a second-to-die policy is intended to pay estate taxes when both spouses die. However, some attorneys claim that with the right legal advice, you can minimize or avoid estate taxes completely.

Now that you know the various types of life insurance policies and the major provisions of and riders to such policies, you are ready to make your buying decisions.

Buying Life Insurance

You should consider a number of factors before buying life insurance. As discussed earlier in this chapter, these factors include your present and future sources of income, other savings and income protection, group life insurance, group annuities (or other pension benefits), Social Security, and, of course, the financial strength of the company.

CAUTION!

Each rating agency uses its own criteria to determine financial ratings. Even though all use an "A," "B," or "C" grading system, what is "A" for one might be "AA+" or "Aa1" for another.

FROM WHOM TO BUY?   Look for insurance coverage from financially strong companies with professionally qualified representatives. It is not unusual for a relationship with an insurance company to extend over a period of 20, 30, or even 50 years. For that reason alone you should choose carefully when deciding on an insurance company or an insurance agent. Fortunately, you have a choice of sources.

Sources   Protection is available from a wide range of private and public sources, including insurance companies and their representatives; private groups such as employers, labor unions, and professional or fraternal organizations; government programs such as Medicare and Social Security; and financial institutions and manufacturers offering credit insurance.

Rating Insurance Companies   Some of the strongest, most reputable insurance companies in the nation provide excellent insurance coverage at reasonable costs. In fact, the financial strength of an insurance company may be a major factor in holding down premium costs for consumers.

Locate an insurance company by checking the reputations of local agencies. Ask members of your family, friends, or colleagues about the insurers they prefer. Exhibit 10–5 describes the rating systems used by A. M. Best and the other big four rating agencies.

Choosing Your Insurance Agent   An insurance agent handles the technical side of insurance. However, that's only the beginning. The really important part of the agent's job is to apply his or her knowledge of insurance to help you select the proper kind of protection within your financial boundaries.

Choosing a good agent is among the most important steps in building your insurance program. How do you find an agent?

did you know?

Life insurance salespeople who pass examinations and meet other requirements are awarded the Chartered Life Underwriter (CLU) designation.

did you know?

Buying a $4.00 pack of cigarettes every day for 15 years will cost you about $22,000 and almost double your life insurance premiums.

Exhibit 10–5

Rating Systems of Major
Rating Agencies: You Should
Deal with Companies Rated
Superior or Excellent

	A. M. Best	Standard & Poor's Duff & Phelps	Moody's	Weiss Research
Superior	A++ A+	AAA	Aaa	A+
Excellent	A A−	AA+ AA AA−	Aa1 Aa2 Aa3	A A− B+
Good	B++ B+	A+ A A−	A1 A2 A3	B B− C+
Adequate	B B−	BBB+ BBB BBB−	Baa1 Baa2 Baa3	C C− D+
Below average	C++ C+	BB+ BB BB−	Ba1 Ba2 Ba3	D D− E+
Weak	C C− D	B+ B B−	B1 B2 B3	E E−
Nonviable	E F	CCC CC C, D	Caa Ca C	F

Key Web Sites for Insurance Company Ratings

www.standardandpoor.com
http://infoseek.go.com/
www.ambest.com
www.moodys.com

One of the best ways to begin is by asking your parents, friends, neighbors, and others for their recommendations. The Personal Finance in Practice feature on page 319 offers guidelines for choosing an insurance agent.

COMPARING POLICY COSTS   Each life insurance company designs the policies it sells to make them attractive and useful to many policyholders. One policy may have features another policy doesn't; one company may be more selective than another company; one company may get a better return on its investments than another company. These and other factors affect the prices of life insurance policies.

In brief, five factors affect the price a company charges for a life insurance policy: the company's cost of doing business, the return on its investments, the mortality rate it expects among its policyholders, the features the policy contains, and competition among companies with comparable policies.

interest-adjusted index A method of evaluating the cost of life insurance by taking into account the time value of money.

Ask your agent to give you interest-adjusted indexes. An **interest-adjusted index** is a method of evaluating the cost of life insurance by taking into account the time value of money. Highly complex mathematical calculations and formulas combine premium payments, dividends, cash-value buildup, and present value analysis into an index number that makes possible a fairly accurate cost comparison among insurance companies. The lower the index number, the lower the cost of the policy. The Figure It Out box on page 320 shows how to use an interest-adjusted index to compare the costs of insurance.

Personal Finance in Practice

› Checklist for Choosing an Insurance Agent

	Yes	No
1. Is your agent available when needed? Clients sometimes have problems that need immediate answers.	☐	☐
2. Does your agent advise you to have a financial plan? Each part of the plan should be necessary to your overall financial protection.	☐	☐
3. Does your agent pressure you? You should be free to make your own decisions about insurance coverage.	☐	☐
4. Does your agent keep up with changes in the insurance field? Agents often attend special classes or study on their own so that they can serve their clients better.	☐	☐
5. Is your agent happy to answer questions? Does he or she want you to know exactly what you are paying for an insurance policy?	☐	☐

OBTAINING AND EXAMINING A POLICY A life insurance policy is issued after you submit an application for insurance and the insurance company accepts the application. The company determines your insurability by means of the information in your application, the results of a medical examination, and the inspection report. When you receive a life insurance policy, read every word of the contract and, if necessary, ask your agent for a point-by-point explanation of the language. Many insurance companies have rewritten their contracts to make them more understandable. These are legal documents, and you should be familiar with what they promise, even though they use technical terms.

After you buy new life insurance, you have a 10-day "free-look" period during which you can change your mind. If you do so, the company will return your premium without penalty.

Key Web Sites for Comparing Rates
www.accuquote.com
www.iquote.com

CAUTION!

Never buy coverage you don't understand. It is the agent's responsibility to explain your coverage in terms you can understand.

CHOOSING SETTLEMENT OPTIONS Selecting the appropriate settlement option is an important part of designing a life insurance program. The most common settlement options are lump-sum payment, limited installment payment, life income option, and proceeds left with the company.

Lump-Sum Payment The insurance company pays the face amount of the policy in one installment to the beneficiary or to the estate of the insured. This form of settlement is the most widely used option.

Limited Installment Payment This option provides for payment of the life insurance proceeds in equal periodic installments for a specified number of years after your death.

Life Income Option Under the life income option, payments are made to the beneficiary for as long as she or he lives. The amount of each payment is based primarily on the sex and attained age of the beneficiary at the time of the insured's death.

Proceeds Left with the Company The life insurance proceeds are left with the insurance company at a specified rate of interest. The company acts as trustee and pays the interest to the beneficiary. The guaranteed minimum interest rate paid on the proceeds varies among companies.

Sheet 34
Life Insurance Policy Comparison

Figure It Out!

› Determining the Cost of Insurance

In determining the cost of insurance, don't overlook the time value of money. You must include as part of that cost the interest (opportunity cost) you would earn on money if you did not use it to pay insurance premiums. For many years, insurers did not assign a time value to money in making their sales presentations. Only recently has the insurance industry widely adopted interest-adjusted cost estimates.

If you fail to consider the time value of money, you may get the false impression that the insurance company is giving you something for nothing. Here is an example. Suppose you are 35 and have a $10,000 face amount, 20-year, limited-payment, participating policy. Your annual premium is $210, or $4,200 over the 20-year period. Your dividends over the 20-year payment period total $1,700, so your total net premium is $2,500 ($4,200 – $1,700). Yet the cash value of your policy at the end of 20 years is $4,600. If you disregard the interest your premiums could otherwise have earned, you might get the impression that the insurance company is giving you $2,100 more than you paid ($4,600 – $2,500). But if you consider the time value of money (or its opportunity cost), the insurance company is not giving you

$2,100. What if you had invested the annual premiums in a conservative stock mutual fund? At an 8 percent annual yield, your account would have accumulated to $6,180 in 20 years. Therefore, instead of having received $2,100 from the insurance company, you have paid the company $1,580 for 20 years of insurance protection:

Premiums you paid over 20 years	$4,200	
Time value of money	1,980	($6,180 – $4,200)
Total cost	6,180	
Cash value	4,600	
Net cost of insurance	1,580	($6,180 – $4,600)

Be sure to request interest-adjusted indexes from your agent; if he or she doesn't give them to you, look for another agent. As you have seen in the example, you can compare the costs among insurance companies by combining premium payments, dividends, cash value buildup, and present value analysis into an index number.

Key Web Sites for Life Insurance Information

www.accuquote.com
www.quickquote.com

SWITCHING POLICIES   Think twice if your agent suggests that you replace the whole life or universal life insurance you already own. Before you give up this protection, make sure you are still insurable (check medical and any other qualification requirements). Ask your agent or company for an opinion about the new proposal to get both sides of the argument. The Personal Finance in Practice feature on page 321 presents 10 important guidelines for purchasing life insurance.

✓ CONCEPT CHECK 10–3

1 What are the key provisions in a life insurance policy?

_____

_____

2 What is a rider?

_____

_____

3 What are the various riders in a life insurance policy?

_____

_____

Personal Finance in Practice

› Ten Golden Rules of Buying Life Insurance

Remember that your need for life insurance coverage will change over time. Your income may go up or down, or your family size might change. Therefore, it is wise to review your coverage periodically to ensure that it keeps up with your changing needs.

Follow these rules when buying life insurance	Done
1. Understand and know what your life insurance needs are before you make any purchase, and make sure the company you choose can meet those needs.	☐
2. Buy your life insurance from a company that is licensed in your state.	☐
3. Select an agent who is competent, knowledgeable, and trustworthy.	☐
4. Shop around and compare costs.	☐
5. Buy only the amount of life insurance you need and can afford.	☐
6. Ask about lower premium rates for nonsmokers.	☐
7. Read your policy and make sure you understand it.	☐
8. Inform your beneficiaries about the kinds and amount of life insurance you own.	☐
9. Keep your policy in a safe place at home, and keep your insurance company's name and your policy number in a safe deposit box.	☐
10. Check your coverage periodically, or whenever your situation changes, to ensure that it meets your current needs.	☐

Source: American Council of Life Insurance, 1001 Pennsylvania Avenue NW, Washington, DC 20004-2599.

---

4 What factors do you consider in choosing an insurance agent?

_____

_____

5 What are the four most common settlement options?

_____

_____

6 Match the following terms with the appropriate definition:

endowment

a. A person named to receive the benefits from an insurance policy. _____

beneficiary

b. Provides coverage for a specific period of time and pays an agreed-upon sum of money to the policyholder if he or she is still living at the end of the period.

_____

whole life insurance

c. A permanent policy for which the policyholder pays a specified premium for the rest of his or her life. _____

double indemnity

d. A rider to a life insurance policy that pays twice the value of the policy if the policyholder is killed in an accident. _____

Financial Planning with Annuities

annuity A contract that provides a regular income for as long as the person lives.

As you have seen so far, life insurance provides a set sum of money at your death. However, if you want to enjoy benefits while you are still alive, you might consider annuities. An annuity protects you against the risk of outliving your assets.

An **annuity** is a financial contract written by an insurance company that provides you with regular income. Generally, you receive the income monthly, often with payments arranged to continue for as long as you live. The payments may begin at once (*immediate annuity*) or at some future date (*deferred annuity*).

As with the life insurance principle, discussed earlier, the predictable mortality experience of a large group of individuals is fundamental to the annuity principle. By determining the average number of years a large number of persons in a given age group will live, the insurance company can calculate the annual amounts to pay to each person in the group over his or her entire life.

Because the annual payouts per premium amount are determined by average mortality experience, annuity contracts are more attractive for people whose present health, living habits, and family mortality experience suggest that they are likely to live longer than average. As a general rule, annuities are not advisable for people in poor health, although exceptions to this rule exist.

Why Buy Annuities?

A primary reason for buying an annuity is to give you retirement income for the rest of your life. You should fully fund your IRAs, Keoghs, and 401(k)s before considering annuities. We discuss retirement income in Chapter 14.

Although people have been buying annuities for many years, the appeal of variable annuities increased during the mid-1990s due to a rising stock market. A *fixed annuity* states that the annuitant (the person who is to receive the annuity) will receive a fixed amount of income over a certain period or for life. With a *variable annuity*, the monthly payments vary because they are based on the income received from stocks or other investments.

Some of the growth in the use of annuities can be attributed to the passage of the Employee Retirement Income Security Act (ERISA) of 1974. Annuities are often purchased for individual retirement accounts (IRAs), which ERISA made possible. They may also be used in Keogh-type plans for self-employed people. As you will see in Chapter 14, contributions to both IRA and Keogh plans are tax deductible up to specified limits.

Tax Considerations

When you buy an annuity, the interest on the principal, as well as the interest compounded on that interest, builds up free of current income tax. The Tax Reform Act of 1986 preserves the tax advantage of annuities (and insurance) but curtails deductions for IRAs. With an annuity, there is no maximum annual contribution. Also, if you die during the accumulation period, your beneficiary is guaranteed no less than the amount invested.

Exhibit 10–6 shows the difference between an investment in an annuity and an investment in a certificate of deposit (CD). Remember, federal income tax on an annuity is deferred, whereas the tax on interest earned on a CD must be paid currently.

As with any other financial product, the advantages of annuities are tempered by drawbacks. In the case of variable annuities, these drawbacks include reduced flexibility and fees that lower investment return.

Exhibit 10–6   Tax-Deferred Annuity versus Taxable CD (a 30-year projection
of performance; single deposit of $30,000)

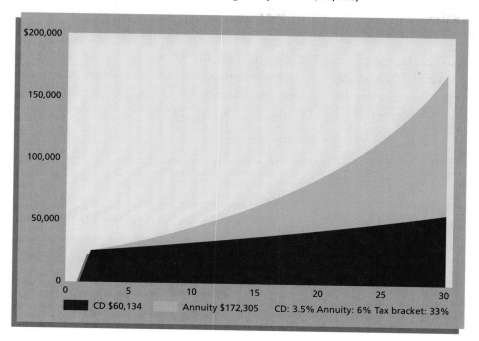

CD $60,134   Annuity $172,305   CD: 3.5% Annuity: 6% Tax bracket: 33%

✓ CONCEPT CHECK 10–4

1 What is an annuity?

_____

_____

2 What is the difference between an immediate and a deferred annuity?

_____

_____

3 As a general rule, are annuities advisable for people in poor health?

_____

Why or why not? _____

4 What are fixed and variable annuities?

_____

_____

back to *Getting Personal*

1. Reconsider your responses to the Getting Personal questions at the beginning of the chapter. Which statements might have different responses now or in the future as a result of studying this chapter?

_____

_____

_____

2. In your own words, describe why and under what circumstances single individuals should purchase life insurance.

_____

_____

_____

3. Proceeds from life insurance can be used for a variety of purposes. List the various uses of life insurance benefits that may be personally beneficial to you and your family.

_____

_____

_____

4. For each of the major types of life insurance policies, what might be the advantages and disadvantages in your own situation?

_____

_____

_____

_____

Type of Policy	Advantages	Disadvantages
a. Term life		
b. Whole life		
c. Universal life		

Chapter Summary

Objective 1   Life insurance protects the people who depend on you from financial losses caused by your death. You can use the easy method, the DINK method, the "nonworking" spouse method, or the "family need" method to determine your life insurance need.

Objective 2   Two types of insurance companies—stock and mutual—sell nonparticipating and participating policies. Both sell two basic types of insurance: term life and whole life. Many variations and combinations of these types are available.

Objective 3   Most life insurance policies have standard features. An insurance company can change the conditions of a policy by adding a rider to it.

Before buying life insurance, consider all your present and future sources of income, then compare the costs and choose appropriate settlement options.

Objective 4   An annuity pays while you live, whereas life insurance pays when you die. With a fixed annuity, you receive a fixed amount of income over a certain period or for life. With a variable annuity, the monthly payments vary because they are based on the income received from stocks or other investments.

Key Terms

annuity   322
beneficiary   305
cash value   311
double indemnity   316

interest-adjusted index   318
nonforfeiture clause   315
nonparticipating policy   310
participating policy   310

rider   316
term insurance   310
universal life insurance   313
whole life insurance   311

Problems

1. You are the wage earner in a "typical family," with $40,000 gross annual income. Use the easy method to determine how much insurance you should carry.

2. You and your spouse are in good health and have reasonably secure careers. Each of you makes about $28,000 annually. You own a home with an $80,000 mortgage, and you owe $10,000 on car loans, $5,000 in personal debts, and $3,000 on credit card loans. You have no other debts. You have no plans to increase the size of your family in the near future. Estimate your total insurance needs using the DINK method.

3. Tim and Allison are married and have two children, ages 4 and 7. Allison is a "nonworking" spouse who devotes all of her time to household activities. Estimate how much life insurance Tim and Allison should carry.

4. Obtain premium rates for $25,000 whole life, universal life, and term life policies from local insurance agents. Compare the costs and provisions of these policies.

5. Use the Figure It Out worksheet on page 320 to calculate your own life insurance needs.

6. You currently hold a variable annuity with an account value of $20,000, which is no longer subject to surrender charges. You exchange that annuity for a new variable annuity, which pays 4 percent bonus credit and has a surrender charge period of eight years, with surrender charges beginning at 9 percent of purchase payments in the first year. Your account value in this new variable annuity is now $20,800. During the first year you hold the new annuity, you decide to withdraw all of your account value because of an emergency situation. Assuming that your account value has not increased or decreased because of the investment performance, how much will you receive from the insurance company? Was it a better deal or not? Explain.

7. You own a variable annuity that offers a death benefit equal to the greater of the account value or the total purchase payments minus withdrawals. You have made purchase payments totaling $50,000. In addition, you have withdrawn $5,000 from your account. Because of these withdrawals and investment losses, your account value is currently $40,000. If you die, what will your designated beneficiary receive?

8. You purchase a variable annuity contract with a $10,000 purchase payment. The contract has a schedule of surrender charges, beginning with a 7 percent charge in the first year and declining by 1 percent each year. In addition, you are allowed to withdraw 10 percent of your contract value each year free of surrender charges. In the first year, you decide to withdraw $5,000, or one-half of your contract value of $10,000 (assuming that your contract value has not increased or decreased because of investment performance). What amount can you withdraw without surrender charges? What is the total surrender charge you will have to pay?

9. Your variable annuity has a mortality and expense risk charge at an annual rate of 1.25 percent of account value. Your average account value during the year is $20,000. What is your mortality and expense risk charge for the year?

10. Your variable annuity charges administrative fees at an annual rate of 0.15 percent of account value. Your average account value during the year is $50,000. What is the administrative fee for the year?

Questions

1. Choose a current issue of *Money, Kiplinger's Personal Finance Magazine, Consumer Reports,* or *Worth* and summarize an article that provides information on human life expectancy and how life insurance may provide financial security.

2. Analyze the four methods of determining life insurance requirements. Which method is best, and why?

3. Visit a few Web sites of companies such as Metropolitan Life, New York Life, Transamerica Life, Lincoln Benefit Life, or others of your choice. Then summarize the various types of insurance coverage available from these companies.

4. Contact your state insurance department to get information about whether your state requires interest-adjusted cost disclosure. Summarize your findings.

5. Review the settlement options on your family's life insurance policies, and discuss with your family which option would be the best choice for them at this time.

Internet Connection

BUYING LIFE INSURANCE

Providing for the financial needs of dependents is the primary goal of a life insurance program. Comparing policy types, coverage amounts, and other provisions will help you meet this financial purpose. Visit Web sites of two reputable insurance companies of your choice and compare the following:

Company A Web address _____

Company B Web address _____

Type of Policy	Company A	Company B
20-year term insurance $100,000		
Monthly premium		
Total premiums, 20 years		
Cash value at 20 years	None	None
Whole life insurance $100,000		
Monthly premium		
Total premiums, 20 years		
Cash value at 20 years		

1. Which is less expensive, term insurance or whole life insurance?

   _____ term   _____ whole life

2. Which company would you select for your purchase of life insurance? Why?

   _____

   _____

   _____

   _____

Case in Point

LIFE INSURANCE FOR THE YOUNG MARRIED

Jeff and Ann are both 28 years old. They have been married for three years, and they have a son who is almost 2. They expect their second child in a few months.

Jeff is a teller in a local bank. He has just received a $30-a-week raise. His income is $480 a week, which, after taxes, leaves him with $1,648 a month. His company provides $20,000 of life insurance, a medical/hospital/surgical plan, and a major medical plan. All of these group plans protect him as long as he stays with the bank.

When Jeff received his raise, he decided that part of it should be used to add to his family's protection. Jeff and Ann talked to their insurance agent, who reviewed the insurance Jeff obtained through his job. Under Social Security, they also had some basic protection against the loss of Jeff's income if he became totally disabled or if he died before the children were 18.

But most of this protection was only basic, a kind of floor for Jeff and Ann to build on. For example, monthly Social Security payments to Ann would be approximately $1,250 if Jeff died leaving two children under age 18. Yet the family's total expenses would soon be higher after the birth of the second baby. Although the family's expenses would be lowered if Jeff died, they would be at least $250 a month more than Social Security would provide.

Questions

1. What type of policy would you suggest for Jeff and Ann? Why?

2. In your opinion do Jeff and Ann need additional insurance? Why or why not?

Continuing Case

LIFE INSURANCE

Life Situation

Pam, 36

Josh, 38

Three children, ages 9, 7, and 4

Financial Goals

Monthly income $4,300

Living expenses $4,075

Assets $150,850

Liabilities $99,520

With three dependent children, the Brocks are assessing their life insurance. Pam has $5,000 of coverage. Josh has life insurance coverage equal to approximately eight times his annual salary.

Questions

1. Do you think Pam and Josh have enough life insurance? If not, describe changes you would recommend for the Brocks.

2. Explain which sections of *Your Personal Financial Plan* sheets 33 and 34 could be useful to the Brocks.

Video Case

LIFE INSURANCE: HOW MUCH DO YOU NEED?

How much life insurance is right for you? There is no precise formula to determine the amount of life insurance a person needs. Some consumer groups recommend buying coverage in the amount of 5 times your annual household income; some insurance industry organizations recommend 10 times your income. To decide the amount that's right for you, consider your family's current and anticipated financial obligations and the amount of time your beneficiaries may have to meet these obligations. Another important consideration is the value of services provided by non–wage earners. For example, a stay-at-home parent's duties of child care and household management should be included. *BusinessWeek Money Talks* reports on a formula that helps determine exactly what you need.

Questions

1. What are some important questions to ask before deciding on the amount of life insurance to buy?

2. How can you determine if you are under- or overinsured?

Spending Diary

"I'M NOT SURE SPENDING FOR LIFE INSURANCE IS NECESSARY FOR MY LIFE SITUATION."

Directions

As you continue to record and monitor spending in various categories, be sure to consider how various decisions will affect your long-term financial security. Various comments you record might remind you to consider possible changes you might want to make in your spending habits.

Questions

1. Are there any spending amounts or items that you might consider reducing or eliminating?

2. What actions might you consider now or in the future regarding spending on life insurance?

Determining Life Insurance Needs

Financial Planning Activities: Estimate life insurance coverage needed to cover expected expenses and future family living costs.

Suggested Web Sites: www.insure.com   www.kiplinger.com/tools/

Household expenses to be covered

Final expenses (funeral, estate taxes, etc.)	1 $ _____
Payment of consumer debt amounts	2 $ _____
Emergency fund	3 $ _____
College fund	4 $ _____

Expected living expenses:

Average living expense	$ _____
Spouse's income after taxes	$ _−_____
Annual Social Security benefits	$ _−_____
Net annual living expenses	$ _____
Years until spouse is 90	$ _____
Investment rate factor (see below)	$ _____

Total living expenses

(net annual expenses times investment rate factor)	5 $ _____
Total monetary needs (1 + 2 + 3 + 4 + 5)	$ _____
Less: Total current investments	$ _____
Life insurance needs	$ _____

Investment rate factors

Years until spouse is 90	25	30	35	40	45	50	55	60
Conservative investment	20	22	25	27	30	31	33	35
Aggressive investment	16	17	19	20	21	21	22	23

Note: Use Sheet 34 to compare life insurance policies.

What's Next for Your Personal Financial Plan?

- Survey several people to determine their reasons for buying life insurance.
- Talk to an insurance agent to compare the rates charged by different companies and for different age categories.

Life Insurance Policy Comparison

Financial Planning Activities: Research and compare companies, coverages, and costs for different life insurance policies. Analyze ads and contact life insurance agents to obtain the information requested below.

Suggested Web Sites: www.quotesmith.com   www.accuquote.com

Age:			
Company			
Agent's name, address, and phone			
Type of insurance (term, straight/whole, limited payment, endowment, universal)			
Type of policy (individual, group)			
Amount of coverage			
Frequency of payment (monthly, quarterly, semiannual, annual)			
Premium amount			
Other costs: • Service charges • Physical exam			
Rate of return (annual percentage increase in cash value; not applicable for term policies)			
Benefits of insurance as stated in ad or by agent			
Potential problems or disadvantages of this coverage			

What's Next for Your Personal Financial Plan?

- Talk to a life insurance agent to obtain information on the methods he or she suggests for determining the amount of life insurance a person should have.
- Research the differences in premium costs between a mutual and a stock company.

11 Investing Basics and Evaluating Bonds

Why invest? For each of the following statements, select "yes" or "no" to indicate your behavior regarding these investing activities:

	Yes	No
1. My investment goals are written down.	___	___
2. I have enough money to begin an investment program.	___	___
3. I am aware of various risk factors that may affect my investment program.	___	___
4. When making investment decisions, I understand how asset allocation can affect the choice of investments.	___	___
5. I know why people invest in bonds and other conservative investments.	___	___

After studying this chapter, you will be asked to reconsider your responses to these items.

Your Personal Financial Plan Sheets

35. Establishing Investment Goals
36. Assessing Risk for Investments
37. Evaluating Corporate Bonds

In this chapter, you will learn to:

1. Explain why you should establish an investment program.
2. Describe how safety, risk, income, growth, and liquidity affect your investment program.
3. Identify the factors that can reduce investment risk.
4. Understand why investors purchase government bonds.
5. Recognize why investors purchase corporate bonds.
6. Evaluate bonds when making an investment.

While many people dream of being rich, dreaming doesn't make anything happen. You have to want to establish an investment program—especially since no one is going to make you save the money you need to fund an investment plan.

Preparing for an Investment Program

OBJECTIVE 1

Explain why you should establish an investment program.

The old saying goes "I've been rich and I've been poor, but believe me, rich is better." While being rich doesn't guarantee happiness, the accumulation of money does provide financial security. And yet, just dreaming of being rich doesn't make it happen. In fact, it takes planning, research, and continued evaluation of existing investments to establish an investment program that will help you accomplish your goals. By studying the material in this chapter, along with the information on stocks and mutual funds in Chapters 12 and 13, you can create an investment plan that is custom-made for you.

Like other decisions, the decision to start an investment plan is one you must make for yourself. No one is going to make you save the money you need to fund an investment plan. In fact, the *specific* goals you want to accomplish must be the driving force behind your investment plan.

Establishing Investment Goals

Sheet 35
Establishing Investment Goals

Some financial planners suggest that investment goals be stated in terms of money: By December 31, 2014, I will have total assets of $120,000. Other financial planners believe investors are more motivated to work toward goals that are stated in terms of the particular things they desire: By January 1, 2015, I will have accumulated enough money to purchase a second home in the mountains. To be useful, investment goals must be specific and measurable. They must also be tailored to your particular financial needs. The following questions will help you establish valid investment goals:

1. What will you use the money for?
2. How much money do you need to satisfy your investment goals?

3. How will you obtain the money?
4. How long will it take you to obtain the money?
5. How much risk are you willing to assume in an investment program?
6. What possible economic or personal conditions could alter your investment goals?
7. Considering your economic circumstances, are your investment goals reasonable?
8. Are you willing to make the sacrifices necessary to ensure that you meet your investment goals?
9. What will the consequences be if you don't reach your investment goals?

Your investment goals are always oriented toward the future. In Chapter 1, we classified goals as short term (less than two years), intermediate (two to five years), or long term (over five years). These same classifications are also useful in planning your investment program. For example, you may establish a short-term goal of accumulating $3,000 in a savings account over the next 18 months. You may then use the $3,000 to purchase stocks or mutual funds to help you obtain your intermediate or long-term investment goals.

Performing a Financial Checkup

Before beginning an investment program, your personal financial affairs should be in good shape. In this section, we examine several factors you should consider before making your first investment.

Apply *Yourself!*

Objective 1

Visit the Consumer Credit Counseling Service Web site (www.cccs.net) and describe the services available to individuals who need help managing their finances.

WORK TO BALANCE YOUR BUDGET   Many individuals regularly spend more than they make. They purchase items on credit and then must make monthly installment payments and pay finance charges ranging between 12 and 18 percent or higher. With this situation, starting an investment program makes no sense until credit card and installment purchases, along with the accompanying finance charges, are reduced or eliminated. Therefore, you should limit credit purchases to only the necessities or to purchases required to meet emergencies. A good rule of thumb is to limit consumer credit payments to 20 percent of your net (after-tax) income. Eventually, the amount of cash remaining after the bills are paid will increase and can be used to start a savings program or finance investments.

OBTAIN ADEQUATE INSURANCE PROTECTION   We discussed insurance in detail in Chapters 8, 9, and 10 and will not cover that topic again here. However, it is essential that you consider insurance needs. Before you start investing, examine the amount of your insurance coverage for life insurance, hospitalization, your home and other real estate holdings, automobiles, and any other assets that may need coverage.

emergency fund An amount of money you can obtain quickly in case of immediate need.

START AN EMERGENCY FUND   Before beginning an investment program, most financial planners suggest that you establish an emergency fund. An **emergency fund** is an amount of money you can obtain quickly in case of immediate need. This money should be deposited in a savings account paying the highest available interest rate or in a money market mutual fund that provides immediate access to cash if needed.

The amount of money to be put away in the emergency fund varies from person to person. However, most financial planners agree that an amount equal to at least three months' living expenses is reasonable. For example, if your monthly expenses total $1,800, before you can begin investing, you must save at least $5,400 ($1,800 × 3 months = $5,400) in a savings account or other near-cash investments to meet emergencies.

line of credit A short-term loan that is approved before the money is actually needed.

HAVE ACCESS TO OTHER SOURCES OF CASH FOR EMERGENCY NEEDS   You may also want to establish a line of credit at a commercial bank, savings and loan association, or credit union. A **line of credit** is a short-term loan that is approved

PORTFOLIO DOCTOR | How much would it take to cut back early?
By Jeffrey R. Kosnett

Looking for your magic NUMBER

LINDSAY Bennett seems to have it made. With a six-figure income, she earns enough selling corporate software to sock away $19,000 a year in retirement accounts and still have money to spare. She has more than $135,000 in IRAs and a 401(k) plan, and $50,000 in the bank. Plus, she owns a home in Boston. But Lindsay, who is 30 and single, wants to do more than accumulate wealth. Within 15 or 20 years, she'd like to move to the not-for-profit world. That will almost certainly mean a big cut in pay.

Lindsay is better able than most to imagine downsizing. The key is how large a nest egg she needs to amass to manage reduced earnings without exhausting her savings too soon. "What is the magic number for something like this?" she asks.

Hidden costs. Retiring—or dramatically cutting back—in your mid forties requires a vastly different calculus than retiring in your mid sixties. At normal retirement age, you're covered by Social Security and Medicare, and your life expectancy is perhaps 20 years. But if you exit at 45, you could easily live another 40 years. You may stop contributing to retirement accounts, and if you tap them early, you'll have to pay penalties as well as income taxes. You will also forgo much potential growth.

But because Lindsay is off to a fast start, she may be able to pull it off. She needs to build a nest egg outside of retirement accounts that's large enough—*the magic number*—to produce principal and income that, when combined with a lower salary, offsets expenses, says Jim Corbeau, of Maas Capital Advisors, in Eugene, Ore. That way, she can leave her retirement accounts intact for old age.

Estimating the magic number requires making assumptions. Lindsay says her expenses are $55,000 a year. In 15 years, assuming 3% annual inflation, her yearly costs would total $85,000. If Lindsay can live on 20% less and gross $45,000 a year ($30,000 in today's dollars) in a new career, she'll still have to take about $4,500 a month from investments (assuming a 25% tax bracket).

To draw that much for 22 years—from 45 until her normal retirement age of 67—Lindsay will need to accumulate at least $750,000 and probably $1 million, based on the same tax and inflation projections.

To reach the target, Cheryl Hancock, of Rinehart & Associates, in Charlotte, N.C., advises Lindsay to "save as much as you can while you're making the big bucks." Starting with the $50,000 in the bank, Lindsay should add $27,000 this year, then boost her contribution by 3% each year. If she earns 8% a year on her nest egg and emphasizes tax-efficient investments, she'll approach $1 million. A menu of low-cost index funds or exchange-traded funds, most focusing on stocks, should do the trick. A similar plan for her retirement accounts should ensure a comfortable lifestyle when Lindsay calls it quits altogether.

from the pages of . . . **Kiplinger's Personal Finance**

1. Lindsay Bennett, 30, is working so she can quit her highly paid job selling corporate software and work for a not-for-profit organization in 15 to 20 years. Would this type of career change appeal to you? Justify your answer.

2. Often people must sacrifice immediate purchases to save for the future. Would you be willing to make the sacrifices necessary to retire early?

3. While many people dream of retiring before the age of 50, this takes planning. What steps could help you accumulate enough money to retire early?

before you actually need the money. Because the paperwork has already been completed and the loan has been preapproved, you can later obtain the money as soon as you need it.

The cash advance provision offered by major credit card companies can also be used in an emergency. However, both lines of credit and credit cards have a ceiling, or maximum dollar amount, that limits the amount of available credit. If you have already exhausted both of these sources of credit on everyday expenses, they will not be available in an emergency.

Getting the Money Needed to Start an Investment Program

Once you have established your investment goals and completed your financial checkup, it's time to start investing—assuming you have enough money to finance your investments. Unfortunately, the money doesn't automatically appear.

PRIORITY OF INVESTMENT GOALS How badly do you want to achieve your investment goals? Are you willing to sacrifice some purchases to provide financing for your investments? The answers to both questions are extremely important. Take Rita Johnson, a 32-year-old nurse in a large St. Louis hospital. As part of a divorce settlement in 2004, she received a cash payment of almost $55,000. At first, she was tempted to spend this money on a new BMW and new furniture. But after some careful planning, she decided to save $25,000 in a certificate of deposit and invest the remainder in a conservative mutual fund. On May 31, 2007, these investments were valued at $79,000.

What is important to you? What do you value? Each of these questions affects your investment goals. At one extreme are people who save or invest as much of each paycheck as they can. The satisfaction they get from attaining their intermediate and long-term financial goals is more important than the more immediate satisfaction of spending a large part of their paychecks on new clothes, a meal at an expensive restaurant, or a weekend getaway. At the other extreme are people who spend everything they make and run out of money before their next paycheck. Most people find either extreme unacceptable and take a more middle-of-the-road approach. These people often spend money on the items that make their lives more enjoyable and still save enough to fund an investment program. Suggestions to help you obtain the money you need to fund an investment program are listed in the nearby Personal Finance in Practice feature.

For many people, the easiest way to begin an investment program is to participate in an employer-sponsored retirement account—often referred to as a 401(k) or a 403(b) account. Many employers will match part or all of your contributions to retirement accounts. For example, an employer may contribute $0.25 for every $1.00 the employee contributes. And while the amount of the "match" varies, some employers still match $1.00 for every $1.00 employees contribute up to a certain percentage of their annual salary. More information on different types of retirement accounts is provided in Chapter 14.

The Value of Long-Term Investment Programs

Many people never start an investment program because they have only small sums of money. But even small sums grow over a long period of time. Mary and Peter Miller, for example, began their investment program by investing $2,000 *each year* when they were in their 20s; yet they expect their investment portfolio to be worth more than $1 million

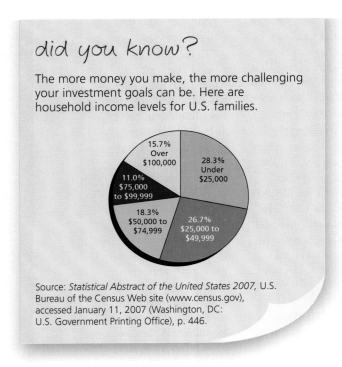

did you know?

The more money you make, the more challenging your investment goals can be. Here are household income levels for U.S. families.

- 15.7% Over $100,000
- 28.3% Under $25,000
- 11.0% $75,000 to $99,999
- 18.3% $50,000 to $74,999
- 26.7% $25,000 to $49,999

Source: *Statistical Abstract of the United States 2007,* U.S. Bureau of the Census Web site (www.census.gov), accessed January 11, 2007 (Washington, DC: U.S. Government Printing Office), p. 446.

Rate of Return	BALANCE AT END OF YEAR					
	1	5	10	20	30	40
2%	$2,000	$10,408	$21,900	$48,594	$81,176	$ 120,804
3	2,000	10,618	22,928	53,740	95,150	150,802
4	2,000	10,832	24,012	59,556	112,170	190,052
5	2,000	11,052	25,156	66,132	132,878	241,600
6	2,000	11,274	26,362	73,572	158,116	309,520
7	2,000	11,502	27,632	81,990	188,922	399,280
8	2,000	11,734	28,974	91,524	226,560	518,120
9	2,000	11,970	30,386	102,320	272,620	675,780
10	2,000	12,210	31,874	114,550	328,980	885,180
11	2,000	12,456	33,444	128,406	398,040	1,163,660
12	2,000	12,706	35,098	144,104	482,660	1,534,180

Exhibit 11–1

Growth Rate for $2,000 Invested at the End of Each Year at Various Rates of Return for Different Time Periods

by the time Peter reaches age 65. How did they do it? Simple: They took advantage of the time value of money. You can achieve the same type of result. For instance, if you invest $2,000 each year for 40 years at a 6 percent annual rate of return, your investment will grow to $309,520. The rate of return and the length of time your money is invested *do* make a difference. Exhibit 11–1 shows how much your investment portfolio will be worth at the end of selected time periods and with different rates of return.

Notice that the value of your investments increases each year because of two factors. First, it is assumed you will invest another $2,000 each year. For example, at the end of 40 years, you will have invested a total of $80,000 ($2,000 × 40 years). Second, all investment earnings are allowed to accumulate and are added to your yearly deposits. In the above example, you earned $229,520 ($309,520 total return − $80,000 yearly contributions = $229,520 accumulated earnings).

Also, notice that if investments earn a higher rate of return, total portfolio values increase dramatically. For example, a $2,000 annual investment that earns 10 percent a year is worth $885,180 at the end of 40 years. The search for higher returns is one reason many investors choose stocks, mutual funds, and other investments that offer higher potential returns compared to certificates of deposit or savings accounts.

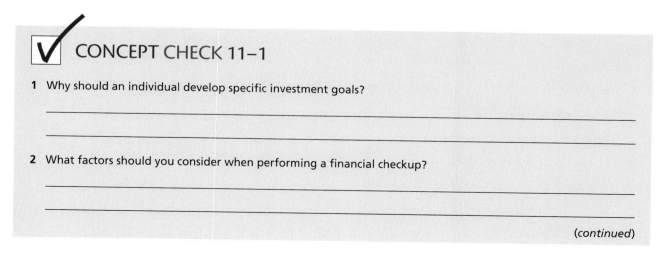

✔ CONCEPT CHECK 11–1

1 Why should an individual develop specific investment goals?

_____

_____

2 What factors should you consider when performing a financial checkup?

_____

_____

(continued)

Personal Finance in Practice

Here are some suggestions for obtaining the money you need to fund an investment program

1. **Pay yourself first.** Each month, pay your monthly bills, save or invest a reasonable amount of money, and use whatever money is left over for personal expenses such as new clothes or entertainment.

   How could this suggestion help you fund an investment program?

   _____

   _____

   _____

   _____

2. **Take advantage of employer-sponsored retirement programs.** Many employers will match part or all of the contributions you make to a retirement program in accounts often referred to as 401(k)s or 403(b)s.

   How could this suggestion help you fund an investment program?

   _____

   _____

   _____

   _____

3. **Participate in an elective savings program.** You can elect to have money withheld from your paycheck each payday and automatically deposited in a savings or investment account.

How could this suggestion help you fund an investment program?

_____

_____

_____

_____

4. **Make a special savings effort one or two months each year.** Many financial planners recommend that you cut back to the basics for one or two months each year.

   How could this suggestion help you fund an investment program?

   _____

   _____

   _____

   _____

5. **Take advantage of gifts, inheritances, and windfalls.** Use money from unexpected sources to fund an investment program.

   How could this suggestion help you fund an investment program?

   _____

   _____

   _____

   _____

---

3   Why should you participate in an employer-sponsored 401(k) or 403(b) retirement plan?

_____

_____

4   In your own words, describe the time value of money concept and how it could affect your investment program.

_____

_____

5   How can using a spending diary help you accumulate the money needed to fund an investment program?

_____

_____

Factors Affecting the Choice of Investments

Millions of Americans buy stocks, bonds, or mutual funds or make similar investments. And they all have reasons for investing their money. Some people want to supplement their retirement income when they reach age 65, while others want to become millionaires before age 40. Although each investor may have specific, individual goals for investing, all investors must consider a number of factors before choosing an investment alternative.

OBJECTIVE 2
Describe how safety, risk, income, growth, and liquidity affect your investment program.

Safety and Risk

The safety and risk factors are two sides of the same coin. Safety in an investment means minimal risk or loss. On the other hand, risk in an investment means a measure of uncertainty about the outcome. Investments range from very safe to very risky. At one end of the investment spectrum are very safe investments that attract conservative investors. Investments in this category include government bonds, savings accounts, certificates of deposit, and certain corporate bonds, stocks, and mutual funds. Real estate may also be a very safe investment. Investors pick such investments because they know there is very little chance that investments of this kind will become worthless.

Many investors choose conservative investments because of the individual life situations in which they find themselves. As people approach retirement, for example, they usually choose more conservative investments with less chance of losing a large part of their nest egg. Some people choose to invest one-time windfalls or inheritances in a conservative investment because they know it may be impossible to replace the money if it is lost. Finally, some investors simply dislike the risk associated with investments that promise larger returns.

Sheet 36
Assessing Risk for Investments

At the other end of the investment spectrum are speculative investments. A **speculative investment** is a high-risk investment made in the hope of earning a relatively large profit in a short time. Such investments offer the possibility of a larger dollar return, but if they are unsuccessful, you may lose most or all of your initial investment. Speculative stocks, certain bonds, some mutual funds, and some real estate, commodities, options, precious metals, precious stones, and collectibles are risk-oriented investments.

speculative investment A high-risk investment made in the hope of earning a relatively large profit in a short time.

From an investor's standpoint, one basic rule sums up the relationship between the factors of safety and risk: *The potential return on any investment should be directly related to the risk the investor assumes.* For example, Ana Luna was injured in a work-related accident three years ago. After a lengthy lawsuit, she received a great deal of money that could be invested to provide a steady source of income for the remainder of her life. Having never invested before, she quickly realized her tolerance for risk was minimal. She had to conserve her $420,000 settlement. Eventually, after much discussion with professionals and her own research, she chose to save about half of her money in certificates of deposit. For the remaining half, she chose three stocks that offered a 3 percent average dividend, a potential for growth, and a high degree of safety because of the financial stability of the corporations that issued the stocks.

Often beginning investors are afraid of the risk associated with many investments. But remember that without the risk, obtaining the larger returns that really make an investment program grow is impossible. The key is to determine how much risk you are willing to assume, and then choose quality investments that offer higher returns without an unacceptably high risk. To help you determine how much risk you are willing to assume, take the test for risk tolerance presented in Exhibit 11–2.

Components of the Risk Factor

The risk factor associated with a specific investment does change from time to time. For example, the stock of Computer-Tabulating-Recording Company was once considered

Exhibit 11–2   A Quick Test to Measure Investment Risk

The following quiz, adapted from one prepared by the T. Rowe Price group of mutual funds, can help you discover how comfortable you are with varying degrees of risk. Other things being equal, your risk tolerance score is a useful guide in deciding how heavily you should weight your portfolio toward safe investments versus more risk-oriented, speculative investments.

1. You're the winner on a TV game show. Which prize would you choose?
    ☐ $2,000 in cash (1 point).
    ☐ A 50 percent chance to win $4,000 (3 points).
    ☐ A 20 percent chance to win $10,000 (5 points).
    ☐ A 2 percent chance to win $100,000 (9 points).

2. You're down $500 in a poker game. How much more would you be willing to put up to win the $500 back?
    ☐ More than $500 (8 points).
    ☐ $500 (6 points).
    ☐ $250 (4 points).
    ☐ $100 (2 points).
    ☐ Nothing—you'll cut your losses now (1 point).

3. A month after you invest in a stock, it suddenly goes up 15 percent. With no further information, what would you do?
    ☐ Hold it, hoping for further gains (3 points).
    ☐ Sell it and take your gains (1 point).
    ☐ Buy more—it will probably go higher (4 points).

4. Your investment suddenly goes down 15 percent one month after you invest. Its fundamentals still look good. What would you do?
    ☐ Buy more. If it looked good at the original price, it looks even better now (4 points).

☐ Hold on and wait for it to come back (3 points).
☐ Sell it to avoid losing even more (1 point).

5. You're a key employee in a start-up company. You can choose one of two ways to take your year-end bonus. Which would you pick?
    ☐ $1,500 in cash (1 point).
    ☐ Company stock options that could bring you $15,000 next year if the company succeeds, but will be worthless if it fails (5 points).

Your total score: _____

Scoring

5–18 points You are a more conservative investor. You prefer to minimize financial risks. The lower your score, the more cautious you are. When you choose investments, look for high credit ratings, well-established records, and an orientation toward stability. In stocks, bonds, and real estate, look for a focus on income.

19–30 points You are a less conservative investor. You are willing to take more chances in pursuit of greater rewards. The higher your score, the bolder you are. When you invest, look for high overall returns. You may want to consider bonds with higher yields and lower credit ratings, the stocks of newer companies, and real estate investments that use mortgage debt.

A primer on the ABCs of investing is available from T. Rowe Price, 100 E. Pratt St., Baltimore, MD 21202 (800-638-5660).

a high-risk investment. Then this company changed its name to IBM and eventually became a leader in the computer industry. By the early 1980s, many conservative investors were purchasing IBM stock because of its safety and earnings potential. But in the early 1990s, many of these same investors sold their IBM stock because changes in the computer industry had brought financial problems for IBM. IBM was once again considered too risky for many investors. Today, as a result of solving many of its financial problems, IBM is once again considered an excellent choice for conservative investors. At the same time, many more risk-oriented investors are purchasing IBM stock, anticipating potential larger gains because of the importance of the computer industry to the world's economy.

When choosing an investment, you must carefully evaluate changes in the risk factor. In fact, the overall risk factor can be broken down into four components.

INFLATION RISK   As defined in Chapter 1, inflation (an economic condition that is common for most economies) is a rise in the general level of prices. During periods of high inflation, there is a risk that the financial return on an investment will not keep pace with the inflation rate. To see how inflation reduces your buying power, let's assume you have deposited $10,000 in a savings account at 2 percent interest. At the end of one year, your money will have earned $200 in interest ($10,000 × 2% = $200). Assuming an inflation rate of 5 percent, it will cost you an additional $500 ($10,000 × 5% = $500), or a total of $10,500, to purchase the same amount of goods you could have purchased for $10,000 a year earlier. Thus, even though you earned $200, you lost $300 in purchasing power. And after paying taxes on the $200 interest, your loss of purchasing power is even greater.

INTEREST RATE RISK   The interest rate risk associated with preferred stocks or government or corporate bonds is the result of changes in the interest rates in the economy. The value of these investments decreases when overall interest rates increase. In contrast, the value of these same investments rises when overall interest rates decrease. For example, suppose you purchase a $1,000 corporate bond issued by AMR, the parent company of American Airlines, that matures in 2016 and pays 9 percent interest until maturity. If bond interest rates for comparable bonds increase to 10 percent, the market value of your 9 percent bond will decrease. No one will be willing to purchase your bond at the price you paid for it, since a comparable bond that pays 10 percent can be purchased for $1,000. As a result, you will have to sell your bond for less than $1,000 or hold it until maturity.

Of course, if overall interest rates declined, your bond would increase in value. Let's assume that interest rates on comparable corporate bonds declined to 8 percent. As a result, the value of your AMR bond that pays 9 percent would increase in value.

To reduce the effects of interest-rate risk, both the federal government and corporations are now issuing inflation-protected bonds. Adjustments are made to the amount of interest the investor receives and in some cases to the principal and are based on changes in the consumer price index (CPI). Typically maturities for corporate inflation-protected bonds are 5, 7, or 10 years. The maturities for inflation-protected securities issued by the federal government are 5, 10, or 20 years.

BUSINESS FAILURE RISK   The risk of business failure is associated with investments in stock and corporate bonds. With each of these investments, you face the possibility that bad management, unsuccessful products, competition, or a host of other factors will cause the business to be less profitable than originally anticipated. Lower profits usually mean lower dividends or no dividends at all. If the business continues to operate at a loss, even interest payments and repayment of corporate bonds may be questionable. The business may even fail and be forced to file for bankruptcy, in which case your investment may become totally worthless. Before ignoring the possibility of business failure, consider the plight of employees and investors who owned stock in Enron. Of course, the best way to protect yourself against such losses is to carefully evaluate the companies that issue the stocks and bonds you purchase and then continue to evaluate your investment after the purchase. Purchasing stock or bonds in more than one company or purchasing shares in a mutual fund can also help diversify your investments and protect against losses.

MARKET RISK   Economic growth is not as systematic and predictable as most investors might believe. Generally, a period of rapid expansion is followed by a period of recession. During periods of recession, it may be quite difficult to sell investments such as real estate. Fluctuations in the market price for stocks and bonds may have nothing to do with the fundamental changes in the financial health of corporations. Such fluctuations may be caused by political or social conditions. For example, the price of petroleum stocks may increase or decrease as a result of political activity in the Middle East.

Investment Income

Investors sometimes purchase certain investments because they want a predictable source of income. The safest investments—passbook savings accounts, certificates of deposit, and securities issued by the United States government—are also the most predictable sources of income. With these investments, you know exactly how much income will be paid on a specific date.

If investment income is a primary objective, you can also choose government bonds, corporate bonds, preferred stocks, utility stocks, or selected common stock issues. Other investments that may provide income potential are mutual funds and real estate rental property.

Investment Growth

To investors, *growth* means their investments will increase in value. Often the greatest opportunity for growth is an investment in common stock. During the 1990s, investors found that stocks issued by corporations in the electronics, technology, energy, and health care industries provided the greatest growth potential. And yet, many corporations in those same industries encountered financial problems, lower profits, or even losses during the first part of the 21st century. In fact, many firms—especially technology firms—failed during this same time period. Since 2003, the U.S. economy has shown signs of stability and even improvement. While many analysts debate whether economic growth will continue, one factor is certain: Investors still like the potential that is offered by growth investments.

Companies with earnings potential, sales revenues that are increasing, and managers who can solve the problems associated with rapid expansion are often considered to be growth companies. These same companies generally pay little or no dividends. For most growth companies, profits that would normally be paid to stockholders in the form of dividends are reinvested in the companies in the form of *retained earnings*. The money the companies keep can provide at least part of the financing they need for future growth and expansion and control the cost of borrowing money. As a result, they grow at an even faster pace.

Other investments that may offer growth potential include mutual funds and real estate. For example, many mutual funds are referred to as growth funds or aggressive growth funds because of the growth potential of the individual securities included in the fund.

Apply *Yourself!*

Objective 2

Why would an investor choose an investment for income? Why would an investor choose an investment for growth?

Investment Liquidity

Liquidity is the ability to buy or sell an investment quickly without substantially affecting the investment's value. Investments range from near-cash investments to frozen investments from which it is virtually impossible to get your money. Interest-bearing checking and savings accounts are very liquid because they can be quickly converted to cash. Certificates of deposit impose penalties for withdrawing money before the maturity date. With other investments, you may be able to sell quickly, but market conditions, economic conditions, or many other factors may prevent you from regaining the amount you originally invested.

liquidity The ability to buy or sell an investment quickly without substantially affecting the investment's value.

✓ CONCEPT CHECK 11–2

1 Why are safety and risk two sides of the same coin?

_____

_____

2 In your own words, describe each of the four components of the risk factor.

Inflation risk:	
Interest rate risk:	
Business failure risk:	
Market risk:	

3 How do income, growth, and liquidity affect the choice of an investment?

_____

_____

Factors that Reduce Investment Risk

By now, you are probably thinking, how can I choose the right investment for me? Good question. To help answer that question, consider the following: Since 1926—more than 80 years—stocks have returned approximately 11 percent a year. During the same period, U.S. government bonds earned 5 percent.[1] These facts suggest that everyone should invest in stocks because they offer the largest returns. In reality, stocks may have a place in your investment portfolio, but establishing an investment program is more than just picking a bunch of stocks or mutual funds that invest in stocks. Before making the decision to purchase stocks, consider the factors of portfolio management and asset allocation.

> **OBJECTIVE 3**
> Identify the factors that can reduce investment risk.

Portfolio Management and Asset Allocation

Earlier in this chapter, we examined how safety, risk, income, growth, and liquidity affect your investment choices. Now let's compare the factors that affect the choice of investments with each investment alternative. Exhibit 11–3 ranks each alternative in terms of safety, risk, income, growth, and liquidity. More information on each investment alternative is provided later in this chapter and in Chapters 12 and 13.

ASSET ALLOCATION   **Asset allocation** is the process of spreading your assets among several different types of investments to lessen risk. The term *asset allocation* is a fancy way of saying you need to diversify and avoid the pitfall of putting all your eggs in one basket. Asset allocation is often expressed in percentages. For example, what percentage of my assets do I want to put in stocks and mutual funds? What percentage do I want to put in bonds or certificates of deposit? To help answer these questions, many brokerage firms construct model portfolios like those illustrated in

asset allocation The process of spreading your assets among several different types of investments to lessen risk.

[1]Motley Fool Web site (www.fool.com), January 4, 2007, The Motley Fool, 123 N. Pitt Street, Alexandria, VA 22314.

Exhibit 11–3

Factors Used to Evaluate Traditional Investment Alternatives

Type of Investment	FACTORS TO BE EVALUATED				
	Safety	Risk	Income	Growth	Liquidity
Common stock	Average	Average	Average	High	Average
Preferred stock	Average	Average	High	Average	Average
Corporate bonds	Average	Average	High	Low	Average
Government bonds	High	Low	Low	Low	High
Mutual funds	Average	Average	Average	Average	Average
Real estate	Average	Average	Average	Average	Low

Exhibit 11–4 to help investors find the appropriate balance between risk and return. Some brokerage firms take the next step and suggest specific bonds, stocks, or mutual funds that are contained in each portfolio. In fact, some brokerage firms even allow you to purchase the securities in the portfolio as a package—a concept often referred to as *portfolio investing.*

Take a moment and look at each portfolio illustrated in Exhibit 11–4. Then ask yourself: Which portfolio is the best one for me? The answer to that question is often tied to your tolerance for risk. Remember the basic rule presented earlier in this chapter: *The potential return on any investment should be directly related to the risk the investor assumes.* While investors often say they want larger returns, they must be willing to assume larger risks to obtain larger returns. For example, the aggressive growth portfolio illustrated in Exhibit 11–4 promises the largest return. It also has more potential risk when compared to the other portfolios. In addition to asset allocation, other factors you should consider before investing are the time your investments will work for you and your age.

THE TIME FACTOR   The amount of time that your investments have to work for you is another important factor when managing your investment portfolio. Recall the investment returns presented earlier in this section. Since 1926, stocks have returned

Exhibit 11–4

Five Different Investment Portfolios Suggested by Merrill Lynch

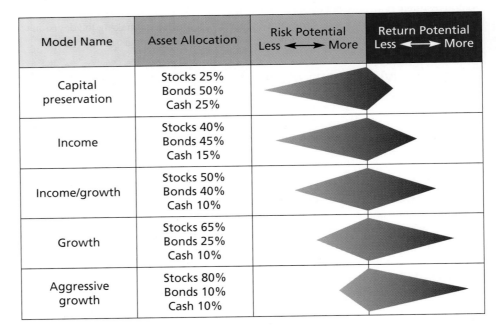

Model Name	Asset Allocation	Risk Potential Less ⟷ More	Return Potential Less ⟷ More
Capital preservation	Stocks 25% Bonds 50% Cash 25%		
Income	Stocks 40% Bonds 45% Cash 15%		
Income/growth	Stocks 50% Bonds 40% Cash 10%		
Growth	Stocks 65% Bonds 25% Cash 10%		
Aggressive growth	Stocks 80% Bonds 10% Cash 10%		

Source: The Merrill Lynch Web site (www.merrill.ml.com), accessed January 12, 2007.

approximately 11 percent a year and returned more than other investment alternatives. And yet, during the same period, there were years when stocks decreased in value.[2] The point is that if you invested at the wrong time and then couldn't wait for the investment to recover, you would lose money.

The amount of time you have before you need your investment money is crucial. If you can leave your investments alone and let them work for 5 to 10 years or more, then you can invest in stocks and mutual funds. On the other hand, if you need your investment money in two years or less, you should probably invest in short-term government bonds, highly rated corporate bonds, or certificates of deposit. By taking a more conservative approach for short-term investments, you reduce the possibility of having to sell your investments at a loss because of depressed market value or a staggering economy.

YOUR AGE   A final factor to consider when choosing an investment is your age. As mentioned earlier in this chapter, younger investors tend to invest a large percentage of their nest egg in growth-oriented investments. If their investments take a nosedive, they have time to recover. On the other hand, older investors tend to be more conservative and invest in government bonds, high-quality corporate bonds, and very safe corporate stocks or mutual funds. As a result, a smaller percentage of their nest egg is placed in growth-oriented investments. For example, younger investors might choose the growth or aggressive growth portfolio illustrated in Exhibit 11–4 because they are willing to take more risks in order to obtain the larger returns that will help their investment portfolio grow. On the other hand, older investors might choose the capital preservation or income portfolio illustrated in Exhibit 11–4 because they want the safety provided by more conservative investments.

Financial experts like Suze Orman, author of *The Road to Wealth* and other personal finance self-help books, suggest that you subtract your age from 110, and the difference is the percentage of your assets that should be invested in growth investments. For example, if you are 40 years old, subtract 40 from 110, which gives you 70. Therefore, 70 percent of your assets should be invested in growth-oriented investments while the remaining 30 percent should be kept in safer, conservative investments.[3]

Apply *Yourself!*

Objective 3

Use the Suze Orman method to determine the percentage of your investments that should be invested in growth investments.

Your Role in the Investment Process

Successful investors continually evaluate their investments. They never sit back and let their investments manage themselves. Some factors to consider when choosing different investments are described next.

EVALUATE POTENTIAL INVESTMENTS   Let's assume you have $25,000 to invest. Also assume your investment will earn a 10 percent return the first year. At the end of one year, you will have earned $2,500 and your investment will be worth $27,500. Not a bad return on your original investment! Now ask yourself: How long would it take to earn $2,500 if I had to work for this amount of money at a job? For some people, it might take a month; for others, it might take longer. The point is that if you want this type of return, you should be willing to work for it, but the work takes a different form than a job. When choosing an investment, the work you invest is the time needed to research different investments so that you can make an informed decision.

Some people invest large sums of money and never research the investments they purchase. Obviously, this is a flawed approach that can lead to large dollar losses. On

[2]Motley Fool Web site (www.fool.com), accessed January 4, 2007, The Motley Fool, 123 N. Pitt Street, Alexandria, VA 22314.

[3]Suze Orman, *The Road to Wealth* (New York: Riverbend Books, 2001), p. 371.

Figure It Out!

› Charting the Value of Your Investment

To monitor the value of their investments, many investors use a simple chart like the one illustrated here. To construct a chart like this one, place the original purchase price of your investment in the middle on the side of the chart. Then use price increments of a logical amount to show increases and decreases in dollar value.

Place individual dates along the bottom of the chart. For stocks, bonds, mutual funds, and similar investments, you may want to graph every two weeks and chart current values on, say, a Friday. For longer term investments like real estate, you can chart current values every six months. *It is also possible to use computer software to chart the value of your investments.*

A WORD OF CAUTION

If an investment is beginning to have a large increase or decrease in value, you should watch that investment more closely. You can still continue to chart at regular intervals, but you may want to check dollar values more frequently—in some cases, daily.

PRACTICE MAKES PERFECT!

Using the dates and dollar amounts below, construct a graph to illustrate the price movements for a share of stock issued by Chesapeake Manufacturing.

Date	Price
June 1	$19
June 15	$16
June 29	$17
July 13	$20
July 27	$24
August 10	$25
August 24	$23

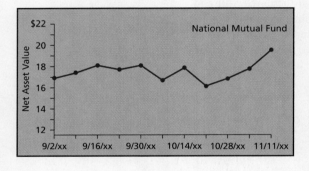

the other hand, an informed investor has a much better chance of choosing the types of investments that will increase in value. Later in this chapter, and then in Chapters 12 and 13, you will learn how to evaluate bond, stock, and mutual fund investments.

MONITOR THE VALUE OF YOUR INVESTMENTS   Would you believe that some people invest large sums of money and don't know if their investments have increased or decreased in value. They don't know if they should sell their investments or continue to hold them. A much better approach is to monitor the value of your investments. If you choose to invest in stocks, bonds, mutual funds, commodities, or options, you can determine the value of your holdings by looking at the price quotations reported on the Internet and in newspapers. Your real estate holdings may be compared with similar properties currently for sale in the surrounding area. Finally, you can determine the value of your precious metals, gemstones, and collectibles by checking with reputable dealers and investment firms. Regardless of which type of investment you choose, close surveillance will keep you informed of whether your investment increases or decreases in value. The nearby Figure It Out box presents further information on monitoring the value of your investments.

KEEP ACCURATE AND CURRENT RECORDS   Accurate recordkeeping can help you spot opportunities to maximize profits or reduce dollar losses when you sell your investments. Accurate recordkeeping can also help you decide whether you want to invest additional funds in a particular investment. At the very least, you should keep purchase records for each of your investments that include the actual dollar cost of the investment, plus any commissions or fees you paid. It is also useful to keep a list of the sources of information (Internet addresses, business periodicals, research publications, etc.), along with copies of the material you used to evaluate each investment. Then, when it is time to reevaluate an existing investment, you will know where to begin your search for current information. Finally, accurate recordkeeping is also necessary for tax purposes.

OTHER FACTORS THAT IMPROVE INVESTMENT DECISIONS   To achieve their financial goals, many people seek professional help. In many cases, they turn to stockbrokers, lawyers, accountants, bankers, or insurance agents. However, these professionals are specialists in one specific field and may not be qualified to provide the type of advice required to develop a thorough financial plan. Another source of investment help is a financial planner who has had training in securities, insurance, taxes, real estate, and estate planning.

Whether you are making your own decisions or have professional help, you must consider the tax consequences of selling your investments. Taxes were covered in Chapter 3, and it is not our intention to cover them again. And yet, it is your responsibility to determine how taxes affect your investment decisions. You may want to review the material on dividend, interest, and rental income and on capital gains and capital losses that result from selling an investment. You may also want to read the material on tax-deferred investment income and retirement planning presented in Chapter 14.

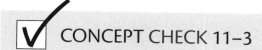

CONCEPT CHECK 11–3

1 Assume you must choose an investment that will help you obtain your investment goals. Rank the following investments from 1 (low) to 6 (high) and then justify your choice for your investment portfolio. (See Exhibit 11–3 for help evaluating each investment.)

Investment	Rank (1 = low; 6 = high)	Justification
Common stocks		
Preferred stocks		
Corporate bonds		
Government bonds		
Mutual funds		
Real estate		

2 Why should investors be concerned with asset allocation and the time their investments have to work for them?

_____

_____

3 Why should you monitor the value of your investments?

_____

_____

Conservative Investment Options: Government Bonds

OBJECTIVE 4
Understand why investors purchase government bonds.

As noted in the last section, stocks have outperformed other investment alternatives over the past 80 years. Nevertheless, smart investors sometimes choose other investments. Answer the following questions to see if more conservative investments may be right for you:

Question	Yes	No
1. Stocks seem to be overpriced and will probably go down in the next 12 to 18 months.	_____	_____
2. I need to convert my investments to cash in a short period of time.	_____	_____
3. I'm afraid I will lose the money invested in speculative investments.	_____	_____

If you answered yes to any of these questions, you may want to consider the more conservative investments described in this section and the next section.

As discussed in Chapter 4, savings accounts, certificates of deposit, money market accounts, and savings bonds provide a safe place to invest your money. Unfortunately, they don't offer a lot of growth or income potential. Other conservative investments that may offer more potential include bonds and debt securities issued by the U.S. government and state and local governments.

Government Bonds and Debt Securities

government bond The written pledge of a government or a municipality to repay a specified sum of money, along with interest.

The U.S. government and state and local governments issue bonds to obtain financing. A **government bond** is a written pledge of a government or a municipality to repay a specified sum of money, along with interest. In this section, we discuss bonds issued by each level of government and look at why investors purchase these bonds.

U.S. TREASURY BILLS, NOTES, AND BONDS
The main reason investors choose U.S. government securities is that most investors consider them risk free. Because they are backed by the full faith and credit of the U.S. government and carry a decreased risk of default, they offer lower interest rates than corporate bonds. Today, the U.S. Treasury Department issues four principal types of securities: Treasury bills, Treasury notes, Treasury bonds, and Treasury Inflation-Protected Securities (TIPS). These securities can be purchased through Treasury Direct at www.treasurydirect.com. Treasury Direct conducts auctions to sell Treasury securities, and buyers interested in purchasing these securities at such auctions may bid competitively or noncompetitively. If they bid competitively, they must specify the rate or interest yield they are willing to accept. If they bid noncompetitively, they are willing to accept the interest rate or yield determined at auction. Treasury securities may also be purchased through banks or brokers, which charge a commission.

U.S. government securities can be held until maturity or sold/redeemed before maturity. Interest paid on U.S. government securities is taxable for federal income tax purposes but is exempt from state and local taxation.

Treasury Bills   A *Treasury bill,* sometimes called a *T-bill,* is sold in a minimum unit of $1,000 with additional increments of $1,000 above the minimum. Currently the Treasury Department sells T-bills with 4-week, 13-week, and 26-week maturities only. T-bills are discounted securities, and the actual purchase price you pay is less than the maturity value of the T-bill. At maturity, the government repays the $1,000 face value.

Treasury Notes   A *Treasury note* is issued in $1,000 units with a maturity of more than 1 year but not more than 10 years. Typical maturities are 2, 5, and 10 years. Interest rates for Treasury notes are slightly higher than those for Treasury bills, because investors must wait longer to get their money back and therefore demand higher interest. Interest for Treasury notes is paid every six months.

Treasury Bonds   The Treasury Department resumed issuing 30-year Treasury bonds in February 2006. A *Treasury bond* is issued in minimum units of $1,000 and has a 30-year maturity. Interest rates for Treasury bonds are generally higher than those for either Treasury bills or Treasury notes. Again, the primary reason for the higher interest rates is the length of time investors must hold Treasury bonds. Like interest on Treasury notes, interest on Treasury bonds is paid every six months.

Treasury Inflation-Protected Securities (TIPS)   *Treasury inflation-protected securities (TIPS)* are sold in minimum units of $1,000 with additional increments of $1,000 above the minimum. Currently, TIPS are sold with 5-, 10-, or 20-year maturities. The principal of TIPS securities increases with inflation and decreases with deflation, as measured by the consumer price index. When TIPS mature, you are paid the adjusted principal or original principal, whichever is greater. TIPS also pay interest twice a year, at a fixed rate. Interest income and growth in principal are exempt from state and local income taxes, but are subject to federal income tax.

FEDERAL AGENCY DEBT ISSUES

In addition to the bonds and securities issued by the Treasury Department, debt securities are issued by federal agencies and quasi-federal agencies. Although these debt issues are, for practical purposes, risk free, they offer a slightly higher interest rate than government securities issued by the Treasury Department. The minimum investment may be as high as $25,000. Securities issued by federal agencies usually have maturities ranging from 15 to 30 years, with an average life of about 12 years.

STATE AND LOCAL GOVERNMENT SECURITIES

A **municipal bond** is a debt security issued by a state or local government. Such securities are used to finance the ongoing activities of state and local governments and major projects such as airports, schools, toll roads, and toll bridges, and may be purchased directly from the government entity that issued them or through account executives.

State and local securities are classified as either general obligation bonds or revenue bonds. A **general obligation bond** is backed by the full faith, credit, and unlimited taxing power of the government that issued it. A **revenue bond** is repaid from the income generated by the project it is designed to finance. Although both general obligation and revenue bonds are relatively safe, defaults have occurred in recent years.

If the risk of default worries you, you can purchase insured municipal bonds. A number of states offer to guarantee payments on selected securities. Three large private insurers—MBIA, Inc.; the Financial Security Assurance Corporation (FSA); and AMBAC, Inc. (American Municipal Bond Assurance Corporation)—also insure municipal bonds. Even if a municipal bond issue is insured, however, financial experts worry about the insurer's ability to pay off in the event of default on a large bond issue. Most advise investors to determine the underlying quality of a bond whether or not it is insured.

One of the most important features of municipal bonds is that the interest on them may be exempt from federal taxes. Whether or not the interest on municipal bonds is tax exempt often depends on how the funds obtained from their sale are used. *You are responsible, as an investor, to determine whether or not interest on municipal bonds is taxable.* Municipal bonds exempt from federal taxation are generally exempt from state and local taxes only in the state where they are issued. Although the interest on

municipal bond A debt security issued by a state or local government.

general obligation bond A bond backed by the full faith, credit, and unlimited taxing power of the government that issued it.

revenue bond A bond that is repaid from the income generated by the project it is designed to finance.

Exhibit 11–5

Yields for Tax-Exempt
Investments

The following information can be used to compare the return on tax-exempt investments with the returns offered by taxable investments.

	EQUIVALENT YIELDS FOR TAXABLE INVESTMENTS				
Tax-Exempt Yield	15% Tax Rate	25% Tax Rate	28% Tax Rate	33% Tax Rate	35% Tax Rate
4%	4.71%	5.33%	5.56%	5.97%	6.15%
5	5.88	6.67	6.94	7.46	7.69
6	7.06	8.0	8.33	8.96	9.23
7	8.24	9.33	9.72	10.45	10.77

municipal bonds may be exempt from taxation, a *capital gain* that results when you sell a municipal bond before maturity *and* at a profit may be taxable just like capital gains on other investments sold at a profit.

Because of their tax-exempt status, the interest rates on municipal bonds are lower than those on taxable bonds. By using the following formula, you can calculate the *taxable equivalent yield* for a municipal security:

$$\text{Taxable equivalent yield} = \frac{\text{Tax-exempt yield}}{1.0 - \text{Your tax rate}}$$

For example, the taxable equivalent yield on a 5 percent, tax-exempt municipal bond for a person in the 28 percent tax bracket is 6.94 percent, as follows:

$$\text{Taxable equivalent yield} = \frac{0.05}{1.0 - 0.28} = 0.0694, \text{ or } 6.94 \text{ percent}$$

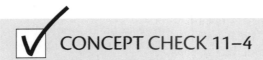

Apply *Yourself!*

Objective 4

You may want to practice calculating taxable equivalent yield using the formula in this section.

If this taxpayer had been in the 35 percent tax bracket, the taxable equivalent yield for a 5 percent, tax-exempt investment would increase to 7.69 percent. Once you have calculated the taxable equivalent yield, you can compare the return on tax-exempt securities with the return on taxable investments. Exhibit 11–5 illustrates the yields for tax-exempt investments and their taxable equivalent yields.

✓ CONCEPT CHECK 11–4

1 What is the difference between a Treasury bill, a Treasury note, and federal agency debt issues?

_____

_____

2 Explain the difference between a general obligation bond and a revenue bond.

_____

_____

3 Calculate the taxable equivalent yield in the following situations:

Tax-Exempt Yield	Equivalent Yield for a Taxpayer in the 25% Tax Bracket	Equivalent Yield for a Taxpayer in the 28% Tax Bracket	Equivalent Yield for a Taxpayer in the 33% Tax Bracket
4.5%			
5.5%			
6.5%			

Conservative Investment Options: Corporate Bonds

OBJECTIVE 5

Recognize why investors purchase corporate bonds.

A **corporate bond** is a corporation's written pledge to repay a specified amount of money with interest. The face value is the dollar amount the bondholder will receive at the bond's maturity. The usual face value of a corporate bond is $1,000. Between the time of purchase and the maturity date, the corporation pays interest to the bondholder. For example, assume you purchase a $1,000 bond issued by American Electric Power (AEP) Company. The interest rate for this bond is 5.25 percent. Using the following formula, you can calculate the annual interest amount for this AEP corporate bond:

corporate bond A corporation's written pledge to repay a specified amount of money with interest.

$$\text{Amount of annual interest} = \text{Face value} \times \text{Interest rate}$$
$$= \$1,000 \times 5.25 \text{ percent}$$
$$= \$1,000 \times 0.0525$$
$$= \$52.50$$

Typically, the interest is paid semiannually, or every six months, in $26.25 ($52.50 ÷ 2 = $26.25) installments until the bond matures.

The **maturity date** of a corporate bond is the date on which the corporation is to repay the borrowed money. On the maturity date, the bondholder returns the bond to the corporation and receives cash equal to the bond's face value. Maturity dates for bonds generally range from 1 to 30 years after the date of issue.

maturity date For a corporate bond, the date on which the corporation is to repay the borrowed money.

The actual legal conditions for a corporate bond are described in a bond indenture. A **bond indenture** is a legal document that details all of the conditions relating to a bond issue. Since corporate bond indentures are very difficult for the average person to read and understand, a corporation issuing bonds appoints a trustee. The **trustee** is a financially independent firm that acts as the bondholders' representative. Usually the trustee is a commercial bank or some other financial institution. If the corporation fails to live up to all the provisions in the indenture agreement, the trustee may bring legal action to protect the bondholders' interests.

bond indenture A legal document that details all of the conditions relating to a bond issue.

trustee A financially independent firm that acts as the bondholders' representative.

Why Corporations Sell Corporate Bonds

Corporations borrow when they don't have enough money to pay for major purchases—much as individuals do. Bonds can also be used to finance a corporation's ongoing business activities. In addition, corporations often sell bonds when it is difficult or impossible to sell stock. The sale of bonds can also improve a corporation's financial leverage—the use of borrowed funds to increase the corporation's return on investment. Finally, the interest paid to bond owners is a tax-deductible expense and thus can be used to reduce the taxes the corporation must pay to the federal and state governments.

Corporate bonds are a form of *debt financing*. Bond owners must be repaid at a future date, and interest payments on bonds are required. Finally, in the event of bankruptcy, bondholders have a claim to the assets of the corporation prior to that of stockholders. Before issuing bonds, a corporation must decide what type of bond to issue and how the bond issue will be repaid.

TYPES OF BONDS   Most corporate bonds are debentures. A **debenture** is a bond that is backed only by the reputation of the issuing corporation. If the corporation fails to make either interest payments or repayment at maturity, debenture bondholders become general creditors, much like the firm's suppliers.

To make a bond issue more appealing to conservative investors, a corporation may issue a mortgage bond. A **mortgage bond** (sometimes referred to as a *secured bond*) is a corporate bond secured by various assets of the issuing firm. Because of this added security, interest rates on mortgage bonds are usually lower than interest rates on unsecured debentures.

CONVERTIBLE BONDS   A special type of bond a corporation may issue is a convertible bond. A **convertible bond** can be exchanged, at the owner's option, for a specified number of shares of the corporation's common stock. This conversion feature allows investors to enjoy the lower risk of a corporate bond but also take advantage of the speculative nature of common stock. For example, Walt Disney Corporation's $1,000 bond issue with a 2023 maturity date is convertible. Each bond can be converted to 33.94 shares of the company's common stock. This means you could convert the bond to common stock whenever the price of the company's common stock is $29.46 ($1,000 ÷ 33.94 = $29.46) or higher.

In reality, there is no guarantee that Walt Disney bondholders will convert to common stock even if the market value of the common stock does increase to $29.46 or higher. The reason for choosing not to exercise the conversion feature in this example is quite simple. As the market value of the common stock increases, the market value of the convertible bond *also* increases. By not converting to common stock, bondholders enjoy the added safety of the bond and interest income in addition to the increased market value of the bond caused by the price movement of the common stock. Generally, the interest rate on a convertible bond is 1 to 2 percent lower than that on traditional bonds. Convertible bonds, like all potential investments, must be carefully evaluated. Remember, not all convertible bonds are quality investments.

PROVISIONS FOR REPAYMENT   Today most corporate bonds are callable. A **call feature** allows the corporation to call in, or buy, outstanding bonds from current bondholders before the maturity date. In most cases, corporations issuing callable bonds agree not to call them for the first 5 to 10 years after the bonds have been issued. The money needed to call a bond may come from the firm's profits, the sale of additional stock, or the sale of a new bond issue that has a lower interest rate.

A corporation may use one of two methods to ensure that it has sufficient funds available to redeem a bond issue at maturity. First, the corporation may establish a sinking fund. A **sinking fund** is a fund to which annual or semiannual deposits are made for the purpose of redeeming a bond issue. To repay a $250 million bond issue, J.C. Penney agreed to make $12.5 million annual sinking fund payments prior to the bond issue's maturity in 2021.

Second, a corporation may issue serial bonds. **Serial bonds** are bonds of a single issue that mature on different dates. For example, Seaside Productions used a 20-year, $100 million bond issue to finance its expansion. None of the bonds mature during the first 10 years. Thereafter, 10 percent of the bonds mature each year until all the bonds are retired at the end of the 20-year period.

Detailed information about provisions for repayment, along with other vital information (including maturity date, interest rate, bond rating, call provisions, trustee, and details about security) is available from Moody's Investors Service, Standard & Poor's Corporation, and

---

debenture A bond that is backed only by the reputation of the issuing corporation.

mortgage bond A corporate bond secured by various assets of the issuing firm.

convertible bond A bond that can be exchanged, at the owner's option, for a specified number of shares of the corporation's common stock.

call feature A feature that allows the corporation to call in, or buy, outstanding bonds from current bondholders before the maturity date.

sinking fund A fund to which annual or semiannual deposits are made for the purpose of redeeming a bond issue.

serial bonds Bonds of a single issue that mature on different dates.

Personal Finance in Practice

› The "How To" of Researching a Bond

How do you find out whether or not a corporate bond is callable? Where can you find out who the trustee for a specific bond issue is? These are only two of the multitude of questions that concern investors who are trying to evaluate bond investments. Fortunately, the answers are easy to obtain if you know where to look.

Today the most readily available source of detailed information about a corporation, including information about its bond issues, is Mergent's *Manuals.* Individual subscriptions to this series of publications are too expensive for most investors, but the series is available at both college and public libraries. It includes individual manuals on industrial companies, public utilities, banks and financial institutions, and transportation companies. Each manual contains detailed information on major companies, including the company's history, operations, products, and bond issues.

The following data on a corporate bond issued by Halliburton Company will give you an idea of the contents of the "Long-Term Debt" section of a Mergent's report.

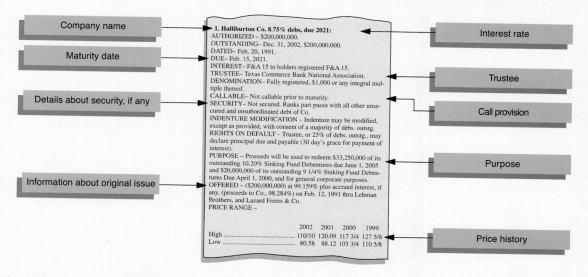

Company name		Interest rate
Maturity date	**1. Halliburton Co. 8.75% debs, due 2021:** AUTHORIZED – $200,000,000. OUTSTANDING– Dec. 31, 2002, $200,000,000. DATED– Feb. 20, 1991. DUE– Feb. 15, 2021.	
Details about security, if any	INTEREST– F&A 15 to holders registered F&A 15. TRUSTEE– Texas Commerce Bank National Association. DENOMINATION– Fully registered, $1,000 or any integral multiple thereof. CALLABLE– Not callable prior to maturity. SECURITY– Not secured. Ranks pari passu with all other unsecured and unsubordinated debt of Co. INDENTURE MODIFICATION – Indenture may be modified, except as provided, with consent of a majority of debs. outstg. RIGHTS ON DEFAULT – Trustee, or 25% of debs. outstg., may declare principal due and payable (30 day's grace for payment of interest).	Trustee
Information about original issue	PURPOSE – Proceeds will be used to redeem $33,250,000 of its outstanding 10.20% Sinking Fund Debentures due June 1, 2005 and $20,000,000 of its outstanding 9 1/4% Sinking Fund Debentures Due April 1, 2000, and for general corporate purposes. OFFERED – ($200,000,000) at 99.159% plus accrued interest, if any, (proceeds to Co., 98.284%) on Feb. 12, 1991 thru Lehman Brothers, and Lazard Freres & Co. PRICE RANGE –	Call provision

Details about security, if any — CALLABLE– Not callable prior to maturity.

Purpose

	2002	2001	2000	1999
High	110/10	120.09	117 3/4	127 5/8
Low	80.58	88.12	103 3/4	110 5/8

Price history

Source: The information for the Halliburton Company corporate bond was taken from Mergent's *Industrial Manual* (New York: Mergent, 2006), p. 1620.

---

other financial service companies. Take a look at the information provided by Mergent's *Industrial Manual* for a bond issued by the Halliburton Company—a global engineering and construction company—in the nearby Personal Finance in Practice feature.

Why Investors Purchase Corporate Bonds

Investors often consider many corporate and government bonds a safer investment when compared to stocks or mutual funds. Bonds are also considered a "safe harbor" in troubled economic times. For example, many stock investors lost money during the period from 2002 to 2003 because of the economic downturn. As an alternative to leaving your money in stocks, assuming that you thought the stock market was headed for a period of decline, you could have moved money into corporate or government bonds. And investors sometimes purchase bonds as a way to diversify their investment portfolio.

Instead of purchasing individual bonds, some investors prefer to purchase bond funds. Bond funds are an indirect way of owning bonds and other securities issued by the U.S. Treasury; city, state, and local governments; and corporations. Many financial experts recommend bond funds for small investors because they offer diversification and professional management. The advantages and disadvantages of bond funds are discussed in more detail in Chapter 13.

did you know?

Bond yields for high-grade corporate bonds:

Source: *Statistical Abstract of the United States 2007,* U.S. Bureau of the Census Web site (www.census.gov), accessed January 13, 2007 (Washington, DC: U.S. Government Printing Office), p. 744.

registered bond A bond that is registered in the owner's name by the issuing company.

registered coupon bond A bond that is registered for principal only, and not for interest.

bearer bond A bond that is not registered in the investor's name.

zero-coupon bond A bond that is sold at a price far below its face value, makes no annual or semiannual interest payments, and is redeemed for its face value at maturity.

Basically, investors purchase corporate bonds for three reasons: (1) interest income, (2) possible increase in value, and (3) repayment at maturity.

INTEREST INCOME As mentioned earlier in this section, bondholders normally receive interest payments every six months. Because interest income is so important to bond investors, let's review this calculation. If IBM issues a 7 percent bond with a face value of $1,000, the investor will receive $70 ($1,000 × 7% = $70) a year, paid in installments of $35 at the end of each six-month period.

The method used to pay bondholders their interest depends on whether they own registered bonds, registered coupon bonds, bearer bonds, or zero-coupon bonds. A **registered bond** is registered in the owner's name by the issuing company. Interest checks for registered bonds are mailed directly to the bondholder of record. A variation of a registered bond is the registered coupon bond. A **registered coupon bond** is registered for principal only, not for interest. To collect interest payments on a registered coupon bond, the owner must present one of the detachable coupons to the issuing corporation or the paying agent.

A third type of bond is a **bearer bond,** which is not registered in the investor's name. As with a registered coupon bond, the owner of a bearer bond must detach a coupon and present it to the issuing corporation or the paying agent to collect interest payments. *Be warned:* If you own a bearer bond, you can be out of luck if it is lost or stolen. While some bearer bonds are still in circulation, U.S. corporations no longer issue them. Bearer bonds are generally issued by corporations in foreign countries.

A **zero-coupon bond** is sold at a price far below its face value, makes no annual or semiannual interest payments, and is redeemed for its face value at maturity. With a zero-coupon bond, the buyer receives a return based on the bond's increased market value as its maturity date approaches. For example, assume you purchased a General Mills zero-coupon bond for $690 in 2006 and General Mills will pay you $1,000 when the bond matures in 2022.

Before investing in zero-coupon bonds, you should consider at least two factors. First, even though all of the interest on these bonds is paid at maturity, the IRS requires you to report interest each year—that is, as you earn it, not when you actually receive it. Second, zero-coupon bonds are often more volatile than other types of bonds.

DOLLAR APPRECIATION OF BOND VALUE Most beginning investors think that a $1,000 bond is always worth $1,000. In reality, the price of a corporate bond may fluctuate until the maturity date. Changes in overall interest rates in the economy are the primary cause of most bond price fluctuations. Changing bond prices that result from changes in overall interest rates in the economy are an example of interest rate risk, discussed earlier in this chapter. When IBM issued the bond mentioned earlier, the 7 percent interest rate was competitive with the interest rates offered by other corporations issuing bonds at that time. If overall interest rates fall, the IBM bond will go up in market value due to its higher, 7 percent, interest rate. On the other hand, if overall interest rates rise, the market value of the IBM bond will fall due to its lower, 7 percent, interest rate.

When a bond is selling for less than its face value, it is said to be selling at a *discount.* When a bond is selling for more than its face value, it is said to be selling at a *premium.* It is possible to approximate a bond's market value using the following formula:

$$\text{Approximate market value} = \frac{\text{Dollar amount of annual interest}}{\text{Comparable interest rate}}$$

For example, assume you purchase a Verizon New Jersey bond that pays 5.875 percent or annual interest of $58.75 and has a face value of $1,000. Also assume new corporate bond issues of comparable quality are currently paying 7 percent. The approximate market value is $839.29, as follows:

$$\text{Approximate market value} = \frac{\text{Dollar amount of annual interest}}{\text{Comparable interest rate}} = \frac{\$58.75}{7\%}$$

$$= \$839.29$$

The market value of a bond may also be affected by the financial condition of the company or government unit issuing the bond, the factors of supply and demand, an upturn or downturn in the economy, and the proximity of the bond's maturity date.

BOND REPAYMENT AT MATURITY   Corporate bonds are repaid at maturity. After you purchase a bond, you have two options: You may keep the bond until maturity and then redeem it, or you may sell the bond to another investor. In either case, the value of your bond is closely tied to the corporation's ability to repay its bond indebtedness. For example, Delta Airlines filed for reorganization under the provisions of the U.S. Bankruptcy Act. As a result, the bonds issued by Delta dropped in value due to questions concerning the prospects for bond repayment at maturity.

> ## Apply *Yourself!*
>
> **Objective 5**
>
> Why would investors choose corporate bonds for an investment program?

A Typical Bond Transaction

Most bonds are sold through full-service brokerage firms, discount brokerage firms, or the Internet. If you use a full-service brokerage firm, your account executive should provide both information and advice about bond investments. As with other investments, the chief advantage of using a discount brokerage firm or trading online is lower commissions, but you must do your own research. As you will see later in this chapter, many sources of information can be used to evaluate bond investments.

Generally, if you purchase a $1,000 corporate bond through an account executive or brokerage firm, you should expect to pay a minimum commission of between $5 and $35. If you purchase more bonds, the commission usually drops to $2 to $20 per bond. Commissions on governments bonds are often less than those on corporate bonds. You should also expect to pay commissions when you sell bonds.

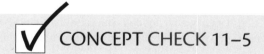 CONCEPT CHECK 11–5

1 Calculate the annual interest and the semiannual interest payment for corporate bond issues with a face value of $1,000.

Annual Interest Rate	Annual Interest	Semiannual Interest Payment
6%		
6.5%		
7%		
7.5%		

(continued)

2 In your own words, describe why corporations issue corporate bonds.

_____

_____

3 List the three reasons investors purchase corporate bonds.

_____

_____

The Decision to Buy or Sell Bonds

> **OBJECTIVE 6**
> Evaluate bonds when making an investment

One basic principle we have stressed throughout this chapter is the need to evaluate any potential investment. Certainly corporate _and_ government bonds are no exception. As you will see in this section, a number of sources of information can be used to evaluate bond investments.

Apply _Yourself!_

Objective 6

Visit one of the bond Web sites listed in this section and describe the type of information available to investors.

The Internet

By accessing a corporation's Web page and locating the topics "financial information," "annual report," or "investor relations," you can find many of the answers to the questions asked in Your Personal Financial Plan Sheet 37.

When investing in bonds, you can use the Internet in three other ways. First, you can obtain price information on specific bond issues to track your investments. Especially if you live in a small town or rural area without access to newspapers that provide bond coverage, the Internet can be a welcome source of current bond prices. Second, it is possible to trade bonds online and pay lower commissions than you would pay a full-service or discount brokerage firm. Third, you can get research about a corporation and its bond issues (including recommendations to buy or sell) by accessing specific bond Web sites. _Be warned:_ Bond Web sites are not as numerous as Web sites that provide information on stocks, mutual funds, or other investment alternatives. And many of the better bond Web sites charge a fee for their research and recommendations.

You may want to visit the Moody's Web site (www.moodys.com) and the Standard & Poor's Web site (www.standardpoors.com) to obtain detailed information about both corporate and government bonds.

Web Sites for Bond Investor Information

www.bondsonline.com
www.bondsearch123.com
www.treasurydirect.gov
http://bonds.yahoo.com

Sheet 37
Evaluating Corporate Bonds

Financial Coverage for Bond Transactions

In bond quotations, prices are given as a percentage of the face value, which is usually $1,000. Thus, to find the actual market price for a bond, you must multiply the face value ($1,000) by the bond quotation. For example, a price quoted as 84 means a selling price of $1,000 × 84% = $840.

While _The Wall Street Journal, Barron's,_ and some metropolitan newspapers publish information on bonds, most bond investors use the Internet to obtain detailed information on bond issues. Detailed information obtained from the Yahoo! Finance Web site (http://bonds.yahoo.com) for a $1,000 Sears Roebuck Acceptance Corporation bond, which pays 6.50 percent interest and matures in 2028, is provided in Exhibit 11.6.

SEARS ROEBUCK ACCEP CORP	
Overview	
1. Price:	95.82
2. Coupon (%):	6.500
3. Maturity Date:	1-Dec-2028
4. Yield to Maturity (%):	6.871
5. Current Yield (%):	6.783
6. Fitch Ratings:	BB
7. Coupon Payment Frequency:	Semi-Annual
8. First Coupon Date:	1-Jun-1999
9. Type:	Corporate
10. Callable:	No

1. Price quoted as a percentage of the face value: $1,000 × 95.82 = $958.20

2. Coupon (%) is the rate of interest: 6.50 percent

3. Maturity Date is the date when bondholders will receive repayment of the face value: December 1, 2028

4. Yield to Maturity (%) takes into account the relationship among a bond's maturity value, the time to maturity, the current price, and the amount of interest: 6.871 percent

5. Current Yield (%) is determined by dividing the dollar amount of annual interest by the current price of the bond: $65 ÷ $958.20 = 6.783 percent

6. Fitch Ratings is issued by Fitch Bond Ratings and is used to assess the risk associated with this bond: BB

7. Coupon Payment Frequency tells bondholders how often they will receive interest payments: Semi-Annual

8. First Coupon Date: June 1, 1999

9. Type: Corporate

10. Callable tells the bondholder if the bond is callable or not: No

Exhibit 11–6

Bond Information Available by Accessing the Yahoo! Bond Web Site

Source: The Yahoo! Finance bond Web site (http://bonds.yahoo.com), accessed January 13, 2007.

For government bonds, most financial publications include two price quotations. The first price quotation, or the *bid price,* is the price a dealer is willing to pay for a government security. The bid price represents the amount that a seller could receive for a government bond. The second price quotation, or the *asked price,* represents the price at which a dealer is willing to sell a government security. The asked price represents the amount for which a buyer could purchase the security.

Bond Ratings

To determine the quality and risk associated with bond issues, investors rely on the bond ratings provided by Moody's Investors Service, Inc., Standard & Poor's Corporation, and Fitch Ratings. All three companies rank thousands of corporate and municipal bonds.

As Exhibit 11–7 illustrates, bond ratings range from AAA (the highest) to D (the lowest) for Standard & Poor's and Aaa (the highest) to C (the lowest) for Moody's. Fitch Ratings are similar to the bond ratings provided by Standard & Poor's and Moody's. For both Moody's and Standard & Poor's, the first four individual categories represent

Exhibit 11–7   Description of Bond Ratings Provided by Moody's Investors Service and Standard & Poor's Corporation

Quality	Moody's	Standard & Poor's	Description
High-grade	Aaa	AAA	Bonds that are judged to be of the best quality.
	Aa	AA	Bonds that are judged to be of high quality by all standards. Together with the first group, they comprise what are generally known as *high-grade* bonds.
Medium-grade	A	A	Bonds that possess many favorable investment attributes and are to be considered upper-medium-grade obligations.
	Baa	BBB	Bonds that are considered medium-grade obligations; i.e., they are neither highly protected nor poorly secured.
Speculative	Ba	BB	Bonds that are judged to have speculative elements; their future cannot be considered well assured.
	B	B	Bonds that generally lack characteristics of the desirable investment.
Default	Caa	CCC	Bonds that are of poor standing.
	Ca	CC	Bonds that represent obligations that are highly speculative.
	C		Bonds that are regarded as having extremely poor prospects of attaining any real investment standing.
		C	Standard & Poor's rating given to bonds where a bankruptcy petition has been filed.
		D	Bond issues in default.

Source: Mergent, Inc., *Mergent Industrial Manual* (New York: Mergent, 2006), pp. 3–4, and Standard & Poor's Corporation, *Standard & Poor's Bond Guide*, December 2006, p. 4.

investment-grade securities. Investment-grade securities are suitable for conservative investors who want a safe investment that provides a predictable source of income. Bonds in the next two individual categories are considered speculative in nature. Finally, the C and D categories are used to rank bonds where there are poor prospects of repayment or even continued payment of interest. Bonds in these categories may be in default.

Generally, U.S. government securities issued by the Treasury Department and various federal agencies are not graded because they are risk free for practical purposes. The rating of municipal bonds is similar to that of corporate bonds.

Bond Yield Calculations

yield The rate of return earned by an investor who holds a bond for a stated period of time.

For a bond investment, the **yield** is the rate of return earned by an investor who holds a bond for a stated period of time. The **current yield** is determined by dividing the yearly dollar amount of interest by the bond's current market value. The following formula may help you complete this calculation:

$$\text{Current yield} = \frac{\text{Annual interest amount}}{\text{Current market value}}$$

current yield Determined by dividing the yearly dollar amount of interest by the bond's current market value.

For example, assume you own an AT&T corporate bond that pays 6.5 percent interest on an annual basis. This means that each year you will receive $65 ($1,000 × 6.5% = $65). Also assume the current market price of the AT&T bond is $1,040. Because the current market value is more than the bond's face value, the current yield decreases to 6.25 percent, as follows:

$$\text{Current yield} = \frac{\$65}{\$1,040}$$

$$= 0.0625 = 6.25\%$$

This calculation allows you to compare the yield on a bond investment with the yields of other investment alternatives, which include savings accounts, certificates of deposit, common stock, preferred stock, and mutual funds. Naturally, the higher the current yield, the better! A current yield of 8 percent is better than a current yield of 6.25 percent.

Other Sources of Information

Investors can use two additional sources of information to evaluate potential bond investments. First, business periodicals can provide information about the economy and interest rates and detailed financial information about a corporation or government entity that issues bonds. You can locate many of these periodicals at your college or public library or on the Internet.

Second, a number of federal agencies provide information that may be useful to bond investors in either printed form or on the Internet. Reports and research published by the Federal Reserve System, the U.S. Treasury, and the Department of Commerce may be used to assess the nation's economy. You can also obtain information that corporations have reported to the Securities and Exchange Commission by accessing the SEC Web site. Finally, state and local governments will provide information about specific municipal bond issues.

Key Web Sites for Bond Investors

www.federalreserve.gov
www.treasury.gov
www.commerce.gov
www.sec.gov

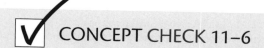

CONCEPT CHECK 11–6

1 What type of information about bonds is found on the Internet? How could this information be used to evaluate a bond issue?

_____

_____

2 Calculate the current market value for the following bonds:

Face Value	Bond Quotation	Current Market Value
$1,000	84	
$1,000	92	
$1,000	77.5	

3 Explain what the following bond ratings mean for investors.

Bond Rating	Explanation
Aaa	
BBB	
B	
CC	

back to *Getting Personal*

1. Reconsider your responses to the Getting Personal questions at the beginning of the chapter. Have any of your answers changed as a result of studying this chapter?

   _____

   _____

2. How can you obtain the money needed to establish an emergency fund and an investment program?

   _____

   _____

3. How do asset allocation and age affect your investment program?

   _____

   _____

4. Would you consider either government bonds or corporate bonds for your investment program? Explain your answer.

   _____

   _____

   _____

Chapter Summary

Objective 1   Investment goals must be specific and measurable. In addition to developing investment goals, you must make sure your personal financial affairs are in order. The next step is the accumulation of an emergency fund equal to at least three months' living expenses. Then, and only then, is it time to save the money needed to establish an investment program.

Objective 2   Although each investor may have specific, individual reasons for investing, all investors must consider the factors of safety, risk, income, growth, and liquidity. Especially important is the relationship between safety and risk. Basically, this relationship can be summarized as follows: The potential return for any investment should be directly related to the risk the investor assumes. In addition to safety and risk, investors choose investments that provide income, growth, or liquidity.

Objective 3   Before making the decision to purchase an investment, you should consider the factors of asset allocation, the time your investments will work for you, and your age. Asset allocation is the process of spreading your assets among several different types of investments to lessen risk. In addition to asset allocation, the amount of time before you need your money is a critical component in the type of investments you choose. Finally, your age is a factor that influences investment choices. Younger investors tend to invest a large percentage of their nest egg in growth-oriented investments. On the other hand, older investors tend to be more conservative. You can also improve your investment returns by evaluating all potential investments, monitoring the value of your investments, and keeping accurate and current records.

Objective 4   Conservative investments include savings accounts, certificates of deposit, money market accounts, savings bonds, and government securities. Generally, U.S. government securities are chosen because most investors consider them risk free. Although the level of risk can be higher for federal agency debt issues and municipal bonds, they are also chosen as a conservative investment. Municipal bonds may also provide tax-exempt income.

Objective 5   Bonds are issued by corporations to raise capital. Investors purchase corporate bonds for three reasons: (1) interest income, (2) possible increase in value, and (3) repayment at maturity. Bonds also can be an excellent way to diversify a portfolio. The method used to pay bondholders interest depends on whether they own registered bonds, registered coupon bonds, bearer bonds, or zero-coupon bonds. Most corporate bonds are bought and sold through full-service brokerage firms, discount brokerage firms, or the Internet. Investors pay commissions when bonds are bought and sold.

Objective 6   Today it is possible to obtain information and trade bonds online via the Internet. In addition to the Internet, *The Wall Street Journal, Barron's*, and some local newspapers provide investors with information they need to evaluate a bond issue. To determine the quality of a bond issue, most investors study the ratings provided by Standard & Poor's, Moody's, and Fitch Ratings. Investors can also calculate a current yield to evaluate a decision to buy or sell bond issues. Finally, business periodicals and government sources can be used to evaluate bonds and the economy.

Key Terms

asset allocation   343

bearer bond   354

bond indenture   351

call feature   352

convertible bond   352

corporate bond   351

current yield   358

debenture   352

emergency fund   334

general obligation bond   349

government bond   348

line of credit   334

liquidity   342

maturity date   351

mortgage bond   352

municipal bond   349

registered bond   354

registered coupon bond   354

revenue bond   349

serial bonds   352

sinking fund   352

speculative investment   339

trustee   351

yield   358

zero-coupon bond   354

Problems

1. Jane and Bill Collins have total take-home pay of $3,900 a month. Their monthly expenses total $2,800. Calculate the minimum amount this couple needs to establish an emergency fund.

2. Using Exhibit 11–1, complete the following table.

Annual Deposit	Rate of Return	Number of Years	Investment Value at the End of Time Period	Total Amount of Investment	Total Amount of Interest
$2,000	3%	10			
$2,000	9%	10			
$2,000	5%	30			
$2,000	11%	30			

3. Based on the following information, construct a graph that illustrates price movement for a Washington Utilities bond fund.

January	$16.50	July	$14.00
February	$15.50	August	$13.10
March	$17.20	September	$15.20
April	$18.90	October	$16.70
May	$19.80	November	$18.40
June	$16.50	December	$19.80

4. Use the following table to compare U.S. Treasury bills, notes, bonds, and TIPS.

	Minimum Amount	Maturity	How Interest Is Paid
Treasury bill			
Treasury note			
Treasury bond			
TIPS			

5. Assume you are in the 35 percent tax bracket and purchase a 5.25 percent municipal bond. Use the formula presented in this chapter to calculate the taxable equivalent yield for this investment.

6. Assume you are in the 28 percent tax bracket and purchase a 4.25 percent municipal bond. Use the formula presented in this chapter to calculate the taxable equivalent yield for this investment.

7. Assume that three years ago you purchased a corporate bond that pays 6.5 percent. The purchase price was $1,000. What is the annual dollar amount of interest that you receive from your bond investment?

8. Twelve months ago, you purchased a 30-year treasury bond with a face value of $1,000. The interest rate is 5.10 percent. What is the annual dollar amount of interest you will receive each year?

9. Assume that you purchased a $1,000 convertible corporate bond. Also assume the bond can be converted to 35.714 shares of the firm's stock. What is the dollar value that the stock must reach before investors would consider converting to common stock?

10. Five years ago, you purchased a $1,000 corporate bond issued by General Electric. The interest rate for the bond was 5 percent. Today comparable bonds are paying 7 percent.
    a. What is the approximate dollar price for which you could sell your General Electric bond?

    b. In your own words, describe why your bond decreased in value.

11. In 1990, you purchased a 30-year, $1,000 corporate bond issued by AMR, the parent company of American Airlines. At the time, the interest rate for the bond was 9 percent. Today, comparable bonds are paying 7 percent.
    a. What is the approximate dollar price for which you could sell your AMR bond?

    b. In your own words, describe why your bond increased in value.

12. Determine the current yield on a corporate bond investment that has a face value of $1,000, pays 7 percent interest, and has a current market value of $820.

13. Determine the current yield on a corporate bond investment that has a face value of $1,000, pays 7.25 percent, and has a current market value of $1,080.

14. Choose a corporate bond that you would consider purchasing. Then, using information obtained on the Internet or in the library, answer the questions in Your Personal Financial Plan Sheet 37. Based on your research, would you still purchase this bond?

Questions

1. After performing a financial checkup, you realize that you have too much credit card debt. What steps can you take to reduce the amount of money you owe on your credit cards?

2. Choose a current issue of *Kiplinger's Personal Finance Magazine, Money,* or *Consumer Reports* and summarize an article that provides suggestions on how you could use your money more effectively.

3. Many people would like to start investing, but they never have enough money to begin. What steps can you take to get the money needed to start an investment program?

4. Explain the following statement: The potential return on any investment should be directly related to the risk the investor assumes.

5. List three personal factors that might lead some investors to emphasize income rather than growth in their investment planning.

6. List three personal factors that might lead some investors to emphasize growth rather than income in their investment planning.

7. Choose one of the model portfolios illustrated in Exhibit 11–4 and explain how it could help you obtain your investment goals.

8. Assume that you are choosing an investment for your retired parents. Would you choose a bond issued by the federal government or a bond issued by a state or local government? Justify your answer.

9. What is the difference between a debenture bond, a mortgage bond, and a convertible bond?

10. Why would investors care if a bond is callable or not?

11. In what circumstances would a $1,000 corporate bond be worth more than $1,000? In what circumstances would the corporate bond be worth less than $1,000?

12. You are considering two different corporate bonds. One is rated AAA by Standard & Poor's and pays 5.8 percent annual interest. The other bond is rated B by Standard & Poor's and pays 7.5 percent annual interest. What do these ratings mean? Which bond would you choose and why?

Internet Connection

RESEARCHING INVESTMENT PLANNING AND CONSERVATIVE INVESTMENTS

Use the Internet to research the following topics, determine the type of information that is available, and determine how it might affect your investment decisions.

Investment Planning

Web sources _____

Type of information available _____

_____

Possible influence on your investment decisions _____

_____

Corporate and Government Bonds

Web sources _____

Type of information available _____

_____

Possible influence on your investment decisions _____

_____

Case in Point

YOU'D BE A FOOL IF YOU DIDN'T USE THE MOTLEY FOOL WEB SITE!

Ten years ago, Penny and Jim Tilson opened a brokerage account, and each month they contributed what they could afford. Over the years, they had managed to invest almost $30,000 in high-tech dot-com companies. Because their investments increased in value, the value of their investment portfolio had grown to just over $100,000 by January 2000. And yet, by January 2004, the value of their investments had dropped to a little less than $55,000. They had lost almost half the value of their investments in just four years. What happened?

To answer that question, you must understand that the Tilsons were like a lot of people investing in the high-tech surge. They chose high-tech stocks because they offered great returns. Computers were popular, and who would even dream that the bubble would eventually burst? Now the Tilsons admit that they didn't know how to research stocks, mutual funds, or other potential investments. In fact, they didn't even bother to open the statements that their brokerage firm sent out each month. They just assumed that their investments would keep increasing in value. Unfortunately, their wake-up call came when they opened their January 2004 statement in order to obtain some information they needed to file their tax return. That's when they realized how much money they had lost. That's also when they decided that if they were going to continue to invest their money, they needed to learn how to invest.

The Tilsons began their search for educational materials by using their home computer to find investment Web sites. According to Penny, there were many sites offering investment information, but they chose the Motley Fool Web site because they felt pretty foolish after losing so much money. Started by David and Tom Gardner, the goal of the Motley Fool is to help average people make the best decisions about every dollar that they spend, save, and invest. Although just one of many investment Web sites, the Motley Fool is an excellent choice for beginning investors like the Tilsons as well as more experienced investors.

While the Tilsons looked at other Web sites, they kept coming back to the Motley Fool because this site offered investment advice that the average person could understand. According to Jim, learning about the investments was not only rewarding, but also fun. For the first time since they began their investment program, they actually knew how to evaluate their investment options.

Questions

1. The Tilsons lost almost half of the value of their investment portfolio in just four years. What did they do wrong?

2. Visit the Motley Fool Web site at www.fool.com. Describe the type of investment information that is available.

3. If you were beginning an investment program, would you use the information provided by the Motley Fool or similar Web sites? Explain your answer.

Continuing Case

INVESTMENT FOUNDATIONS

Life Situation

  Pam, 43

  Josh, 45

  Children ages 16, 14, and 11

Financial Data

  Monthly income $4,900

  Living expenses $4,450

  Emergency fund $5,000

  Assets $262,700

  Liabilities $84,600

With approximately 20 years to retirement, Pam and Josh Brock want to establish a more aggressive investment program to accumulate funds for their long-term financial needs. Josh does have a retirement program at work. This money, about $110,000, is invested in various conservative mutual funds.

In addition, the Brocks established their own investment program about four years ago, and today they have about $36,000 invested in conservative stocks and mutual funds. In addition to their investment program, the Brocks have accumulated $11,000 to help pay for the children's college educations. Also, they have $5,000 tucked away in a savings account that serves as the family's emergency fund. Finally, both will qualify for Social Security when they reach retirement age.

Questions

1. What would you view as the strengths and weaknesses of the Brocks' financial situation at this stage in their lives?

2. Given that Pam is 43 and Josh is 45 and they have three children who will soon begin their college educations, what investment goals would be most appropriate?

3. Describe a preliminary investment portfolio for the Brocks. Suggest *specific* investments and explain risks associated with each.

4. Describe how the Brocks might use *Your Personal Financial Plan* sheets 35–37 for planning investments.

Video Case

INVESTING IN STOCKS AND BONDS

Why would investors choose to invest in bonds when the stock market is performing at record levels? Good question! The fact is that bonds are more conservative investments that may have a place in your portfolio if you want diversification or a steady income stream of interest payments.

Questions

1. At the time of publication, the Dow Jones Industrial Average was 13,326. What is the current Dow Jones Industrial Average? What does an increase or decrease in this average mean for investors?

2. From the investor's viewpoint, what is the difference between a stockholder and a bondholder?

3. Why would a young investor purchase bonds? Why would an older investor purchase bonds?

4. Why do some experts recommend purchasing bond funds instead of purchasing individual bonds?

Spending Diary

"WHILE I HAVE A FAIRLY LARGE AMOUNT IN A SAVINGS ACCOUNT, I SHOULD THINK ABOUT INVESTING SOME OF THIS MONEY IN OTHER WAYS."

Directions

The use of your Daily Spending Diary can provide an important foundation for monitoring and controlling spending. This will allow the possibility of wiser use of money now and in the future.

Questions

1. Explain how the use of a Daily Spending Diary could result in starting an investment program.

2. Based on your Daily Spending Diary, describe actions that you might take to identify and achieve various financial goals.

Name: _____ Date: _____

Establishing Investment Goals

Financial Planning Activities: Determine specific goals for an investment program. Based on short- and long-term objectives for your investment efforts, enter the items requested below.

Suggested Web Sites: www.fool.com   www.money.cnn.com

Description of investment goal	Dollar amount	Date needed	Level of acceptable risk (high, medium, low)	Possible investments to achieve this goal

Note: Sheets 37, 38, and 41 may be used to implement specific investment plans to achieve these goals.

What's Next for Your Personal Financial Plan?

- Use the suggestions listed in this chapter to perform a financial checkup.
- Discuss the importance of investment goals and financial planning with other household members.

Name: _____ Date: _____

Assessing Risk for Investments

Financial Planning Activities: Assess the risk of various investments in relation to your personal risk tolerance and financial goals. List various investments you are considering based on the type and level of risk associated with each.

Suggested Web Sites: http://moneycentral.msn.com/investor/calcs/n_riskq/main.asp.   www.fool.com

Type of Investment	Loss of market value (market risk)	Type of Risk		
		Inflation risk	Interest rate risk	Liquidity risk
High risk				
Moderate risk				
Low risk				

What's Next for Your Personal Financial Plan?

- Identify current economic trends that might increase or decrease the risk associated with your choice of investments.
- Based on the risk associated with the investments you chose, which investment would you choose to obtain your investment goals?

Name: _____   Date: _____

Evaluating Corporate Bonds

Financial Planning Activities: No checklist can serve as a foolproof guide for choosing a corporate bond. However, the following questions will help you evaluate a potential bond investment.

Suggested Web Sites: http://bonds.yahoo.com   www.bondsonline.com

Category 1: Information about the Corporation

1. What is the corporation's name, address, and phone number? _____

_____

2. What type of products or services does this firm provide? _____

_____

3. Briefly describe the prospects for this company. (Include significant factors like product development, plans for expansion, plans for mergers, etc.)

_____

_____

_____

Category 2: Bond Basics

4. What type of bond is this? _____
5. What is the face value for this bond? _____
6. What is the interest rate for this bond? _____
7. What is the dollar amount of annual interest for this bond? _____
8. When are interest payments made to bondholders?

_____

9. Is the corporation currently paying interest as scheduled?   ☐ Yes ☐ No
10. What is the maturity date for this bond? _____
11. What is Moody's rating for this bond? _____
12. What is Standard & Poor's rating for this bond?

_____

13. What do these ratings mean? _____

_____

_____

14. What was the original issue date? _____

_____

15. Who is the trustee for this bond issue? _____

_____

16. Is the bond callable? If so, when? _____

_____

17. Is the bond secured with collateral? If so, what?
☐ Yes ☐ No

_____

Category 3: Financial Performance

18. What are the firm's earnings per share for the last year? _____
19. Have the firm's earnings increased over the past five years? _____
20. What are the firm's projected earnings for the next year? _____
21. Do the analysts indicate that this is a good time to invest in this company?

_____

_____

22. Briefly describe any other information that you obtained from Moody's, Standard & Poor's, or other sources of information.

_____

_____

A Word of Caution

The above checklist is not a cure-all, but it does provide some very sound questions that you should answer before making a decision to invest in bonds. If you need other information, *you* are responsible for obtaining it and for determining how it affects your potential investment.

What's Next for Your Personal Financial Plan?

- Talk with various people who have invested in government, municipal, or corporate bonds.
- Discuss with other household members why bonds might be a logical choice for your investment program.

12 Investing in Stocks

Getting Personal

Why invest in stocks? For each of the following statements, select "yes" or "no" to indicate your behavior regarding these investing activities:

	Yes	No
1. I understand the three ways investors can profit from stock investments.	___	___
2. I have an investment plan and it includes some growth stocks.	___	___
3. I know how to evaluate a stock issue.	___	___
4. I know the difference between long-term and short-term investment techniques.	___	___

After studying this chapter, you will be asked to reconsider your responses to these questions.

Objectives

Why is this important?

In this chapter, you will learn to:

1. Identify the most important features of common and preferred stock.
2. Explain how you can evaluate stock investments.
3. Analyze the numerical measures that cause a stock to increase or decrease in value.
4. Describe how stocks are bought and sold.
5. Explain the trading techniques used by long-term investors and short-term speculators.

Today, financial planners recommend that investors who want their investments to grow choose stocks or mutual funds that contain growth-oriented stocks. This chapter provides the information you need to become a better stock investor.

Common and Preferred Stock

OBJECTIVE 1

Identify the most important features of common and preferred stock.

Many investors face two concerns when they begin an investment program. First, they don't know where to get the information they need to evaluate potential investments. In reality, more information is available than most investors can read. Yet, as crazy as it sounds, some investors invest in stocks without doing any research at all. As we begin this chapter, you should know that there is no substitute for researching a potential investment. *Simply put, good investors know something about the company before they invest their money in the company's stock.*

Second, beginning investors sometimes worry that they won't know what the information means when they do find it. Yet common sense goes a long way when evaluating potential investments. For example, consider the following questions:

1. Is an increase in sales revenues a healthy sign for a corporation? (Answer: yes)
2. Should a firm's net income increase or decrease over time? (Answer: increase)
3. Should a corporation's earnings per share increase or decrease over time? (Answer: increase)

Although the answers to these questions are obvious, you will find more detailed answers to these and other questions in this chapter. In fact, that's what this chapter is all about. We want you to learn how to evaluate a stock and to make money from your investment decisions.

Today a lot of people buy and sell stocks. Why? The most obvious answer is simple: They want larger returns than more conservative investments offer. Although stocks have returned on average about 11 percent a year since 1926—substantially more than

U.S. Treasury bills or bonds—there are periods when stocks have declined in value.[1] For proof, just ask any long-term investor what happened for the two-year period beginning in 2002. In fact, the key to success with any investment program is often allowing your investments to work for you over a long period of time. In short, a long-term investment program allows you to ride through the rough times and enjoy the good times. However, before you decide to invest in stocks, you should realize that this type of investment involves more risk and greater potential for loss.

Since common stockholders are the actual owners of the corporation, they share in its success. But before investing your money, it helps to understand why corporations issue common stock and why investors purchase that stock.

Why Corporations Issue Common Stock

common stock The most basic form of ownership for a corporation; owners elect the board of directors and may vote on important corporate matters.

Common stock is the most basic form of ownership for a corporation; owners of common stock elect the board of directors and may vote on important corporate matters. Corporations issue common stock to finance their business start-up costs and help pay for expansion and their ongoing business activities. Corporate managers prefer selling common stock as a method of financing for several reasons.

equity financing Money received from the owners or from the sale of shares of ownership in a business.

A FORM OF EQUITY   *Important point:* Stock is equity financing. **Equity financing** is money received from the sale of shares of ownership in a business. One reason corporations prefer selling stock is because the money obtained from equity financing doesn't have to repaid and the company doesn't have to buy back shares from the stockholders. On the other hand, a stockholder who buys common stock may sell his or her stock to another individual. The selling price is determined by how much a buyer is willing to pay for the stock. Simply put, if the demand for a particular stock increases, the market value of the stock will increase. If the demand for a particular stock decreases, the market value of the stock will decrease. Demand for a stock changes when information about the firm or its future prospects is released to the general public. For example, information about expected sales revenues, earnings, expansions or mergers, or other important developments within the firm can increase or decrease the demand for, and ultimately the market value of, the firm's stock.

dividend A distribution of money, stock, or other property that a corporation pays to stockholders.

DIVIDENDS NOT MANDATORY   *Important point:* Dividends are paid out of profits, and dividend payments must be approved by the corporation's board of directors. A **dividend** is a distribution of money, stock, or other property that a corporation pays to stockholders. Dividend policies vary among corporations, but most firms distribute between 30 and 70 percent of their earnings to stockholders. However, some corporations follow a policy of smaller or no dividend distributions to stockholders. In general, these are rapidly growing firms, like Amazon (online sales) or Bankrate, Inc. (online banking), that retain a large share of their earnings for research and development, expansion, or major projects. On the other hand, utility companies, such as American Electric Power (AEP), and other financially secure enterprises may distribute 80 to 90 percent of their earnings. Always remember that if a corporation has had a bad year, dividend payments may be reduced or omitted.

proxy A legal form that lists the issues to be decided at a stockholders' meeting and requests that stockholders transfer their voting rights to some individual or individuals.

VOTING RIGHTS AND CONTROL OF THE COMPANY   In return for the financing provided by selling common stock, management must make concessions to stockholders that may restrict corporate policies. For example, corporations are required by law to have an annual meeting at which stockholders have a right to vote, usually casting one vote per share of stock. Stockholders may vote in person or by proxy. A **proxy** is a legal form

---

[1]The Motley Fool Web site (www.fool.com), accessed January 17, 2007, The Motley Fool, 2000 Duke Street, Fourth Floor, Alexandria, VA 22314.

that lists the issues to be decided at a stockholders' meeting and requests that stockholders transfer their voting rights to some individual or individuals. The common stockholders elect the board of directors and must approve major changes in corporate policies.

Why Investors Purchase Common Stock

How do you make money by buying common stock? Basically, there are three ways: income from dividends, dollar appreciation of stock value, and the *possibility* of increased value from stock splits.

INCOME FROM DIVIDENDS   While the corporation's board members are under no legal obligation to pay dividends, most board members like to keep stockholders happy (and prosperous). Few things will unite stockholders into a powerful opposition force more rapidly than omitted or lowered dividends. Therefore, board members usually declare dividends if the corporation's after-tax profits are sufficient for them to do so. Since dividends are a distribution of profits, investors must be concerned about future after-tax profits.

Corporate dividends for common stock may take the form of cash, additional stock, or company products. However, the last type of dividend is extremely unusual. If the board of directors declares a cash dividend, each common stockholder receives an equal amount per share. Although dividend policies vary, most corporations pay dividends on a quarterly basis.

Notice in Exhibit 12–1 that Washington Mutual declared a quarterly dividend of $0.54 per share to stockholders who own the stock on the record date of January 31, 2007. The **record date** is the date on which a stockholder must be registered on the corporation's books in order to receive dividend payments. When a stock is traded around the record date, the company must determine whether the buyer or the seller is entitled to the dividend. To solve this problem, this rule is followed: *Dividends remain with the stock until two business days before the record date.* On the second day before the record date, the stock begins selling *ex-dividend.* Investors who purchase an ex-dividend stock are not entitled to receive dividends for that quarter, and the dividend is paid to the previous owner of the stock.

For example, Washington Mutual declared a quarterly dividend of $0.54 per share to stockholders who owned its stock on Wednesday, January 31, 2007. The stock went ex-dividend on Monday, January 29, 2007, two *business* days before the January 31 date. A stockholder who purchased the stock on January 29 or after was not entitled to this quarterly dividend payment. The actual dividend payment was paid on February 15 to stockholders who owned the stock on the record date. Investors are generally very conscious of the date on which a stock goes ex-dividend, and the dollar value of the stock may go down by the value of the quarterly dividend.

DOLLAR APPRECIATION OF STOCK VALUE   In most cases, you purchase stock and then hold onto that stock for a period of time. If the market value of the stock increases, you must decide whether to sell the stock at the higher price or continue to hold it. If you decide to sell the stock, the dollar amount of difference between the purchase price and the selling price represents your profit.

Let's assume that on January 18, 2005, you purchased 100 shares of Procter & Gamble stock at a cost of $55 a share. Your cost for the stock was $5,500 plus $55 in commission

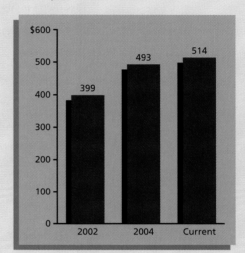

did you know?

One reason investors purchase stocks is because of dividend income. (amounts in billions)

Year	Amount
2002	399
2004	493
Current	514

Source: *Statistical Abstract of the United States, 2007*, U.S. Bureau of the Census Web site (www.census.gov), accessed January 17, 2007 (Washington, DC: U.S. Government Printing Office), p. 514.

record date The date on which a stockholder must be registered on the corporation's books in order to receive dividend payments.

Exhibit 12–1

Typical Information on Corporate Dividends as Presented in *The Wall Street Journal*

Dividend announcements from January 17.

DIVIDEND CHANGES				
Company/ Symbol		**Yield (%)**	**Amount New/Old**	**Payable/ Record**
Increased				
Archston-Smith	ASN	2.9	.45/.43	Q Feb 28/Feb 13
Colonial BancGrp	CNB	3.0	.19/.17	Q Feb 09/Jan 26
Cmnwlth Bkshr	CWBS	1.0	.06/.055	Q Feb 28/Feb 19
Green County Bnc	GCBC	3.3	.25/.23	SA Mar 01/Feb 15
Kinder Morgan En	KMP	6.8	.83/.81	Q Feb 14/Jan 31
Kinder Morgan Mg	KMR	6.9	.83/.81	Q Feb 14/Jan 31
Linear Technolog	LLTC	2.3	.18/.15	Q Feb 14/Jan 26
Marsh & McLennan	MMC	2.5	.19/.17	Q Feb 15/Jan 24
Peoples Banctrus	PBTC	2.0	.13/.12	Q Mar 13/Feb 27
Washington Mutua	WM	4.9	.54/.53	Q Feb 15/Jan 31

Source: Republished with permission of Dow Jones, Inc., from *The Wall Street Journal*, January 18, 2007; permission conveyed through Copyright Clearance Center, Inc.

charges, for a total investment of $5,555. (Note: Commissions, a topic covered later in this chapter, are charged when you purchase stock *and* when you sell stock.) Let's also assume you held your 100 shares until January 18, 2007, and then sold them for $65 a share. During the investment period you owned Procter & Gamble, the company paid dividends totaling $2.05 a share. Exhibit 12–2 shows your return on the investment. In this case,

Exhibit 12–2

Sample Stock Transaction for Procter & Gamble

Assumptions			
100 shares of common stock purchased January 18, 2005, sold January 18, 2007; dividends of $2.05 per share for the investment period.			
Costs when Purchased		**Return when Sold**	
100 shares @ $55 =	$5,500	100 shares @ $65 =	$6,500
Plus commission	+ 55	Minus commission	– 55
Total investment	$5,555	Total return	$6,445

Transaction Summary	
Total return	$6,445
Minus total investment	– 5,555
Profit from stock sale	$ 890
Plus dividends	+ 205
Total return for the transaction	$1,095

Personal Finance in Practice

› When Should You Sell a Stock?

Here are some suggestions for deciding when you should sell a stock.

1. *Follow your stock's value.* Too often, investors purchase a stock and then forget about it. A much better approach is to graph the dollar value of your stock every two weeks.

How could this suggestion help you decide if it is time to sell a stock?

_____

_____

2. *Watch the company's financials.* Smart investors evaluate a stock investment before they make it. The smartest investors use all the available information to continuously evaluate their stocks.

How could this suggestion help you decide if it is time to sell a stock?

_____

_____

3. *Track the firm's product line.* If the firm's products become obsolete and the company fails to introduce state-of-the-art new products, its sales—and, ultimately, profits—may take a nosedive.

How could this suggestion help you decide if it is time to sell a stock?

_____

_____

4. *Monitor economic developments.* An economic recession or an economic recovery may cause the value of a stock investment to increase or decrease. Also, watch the unemployment rate, inflation rate, interest rates, productivity rates, and similar economic indicators.

How could this suggestion help you decide if it is time to sell a stock?

_____

_____

5. *Be patient.* The secret of success for making money with stocks is time. As pointed out earlier in this chapter, stocks have returned on average 11 percent before adjusting for inflation each year since 1926. Assuming you purchase *quality* stocks, your investments will eventually increase in value.

How could this suggestion help you decide if it is time to sell a stock?

_____

_____

---

you made money because of dividend distributions and through an increase in stock value from $55 to $65 per share. As Exhibit 12–2 shows, your total return is $1,095. Of course, if the stock's value should decrease, or if the firm's board of directors reduces or votes to omit dividends, your return may be less than the original investment. For help in deciding if it's time to sell stock, read the nearby Personal Finance in Practice feature.

POSSIBILITY OF INCREASED VALUE FROM STOCK SPLITS

Investors can also increase potential profits through a stock split. A **stock split** is a procedure in which the shares of stock owned by existing stockholders are divided into a larger number of shares. In 2006, for example, the board of directors of Emerson Electric Company, a Missouri-based company that employs 128,000, approved a 2-for-1 stock split. After the stock split, a stockholder who had previously owned 100 shares now owned 200 shares. The most common stock splits are 2-for-1 or 3-for-1.

Why do corporations split their stock? In many cases, a firm's management has a theoretical ideal price range for the firm's stock. If the market value of the stock rises above the

stock split A procedure in which the shares of stock owned by existing stockholders are divided into a larger number of shares.

Apply *Yourself!*

Objective 1

Use the Internet to identify a stock split. Then graph the price of the stock each day for a week before the split and each day for a week after the split. Describe your findings.

ideal range, a stock split brings the market value back in line. In the case of Emerson Electric, the 2-for-1 stock split reduced the market value to one-half of the stock's value on the day prior to the split. The lower market value for each share of stock was the result of dividing the dollar value of the company by a larger number of shares of common stock. Also, a decision to split a company's stock and the resulting lower market value make the stock more attractive to the investing public. This attraction is based on the belief that most corporations split their stock only when their financial future is improving and on the upswing.

Be warned: There are no guarantees that a stock's market value will go up after a split. This is important to understand, because investors often think that a stock split leads to immediate profits. Nothing could be further from the truth. Here's why. The total market capitalization—the value of the company's stock multiplied by the number of shares outstanding—does not change because a corporation splits its stock. A company that has a market capitalization of $100 million before a 2-for-1 stock split is still worth $100 million after the split. Simply put, there is twice as much stock, but each share is worth half of its previous value before the stock split occurred. If a stock's value does increase after a stock split, it increases because of the firm's financial performance after the split and not just because there are more shares of stock.

Preferred Stock

preferred stock A type of stock that gives the owner the advantage of receiving cash dividends before common stockholders are paid any dividends.

par value An assigned (and often arbitrary) dollar value that is printed on a stock certificate.

In addition to or instead of purchasing common stock, you may purchase preferred stock. **Preferred stock** is a type of stock that gives the owner the advantage of receiving cash dividends before common stockholders are paid any dividends. This is the most important priority an investor in preferred stock enjoys. Unlike the amount of the dividend on common stock, the dollar amount of the dividend on preferred stock is known before the stock is purchased. The dividend amount is either a stated amount of money for each share of preferred stock or a certain percentage of the par value of the stock. The **par value** is an assigned (and often arbitrary) dollar value that is printed on a stock certificate. For example, if the par value for a preferred stock issue is $50 and the dividend rate is 4 percent, the dollar amount of the dividend is $2 ($50 × 4% = $2).

Preferred stocks are often referred to as "middle" investments because they represent an investment midway between common stock (an ownership position for the stockholder) and corporate bonds (a creditor position for the bondholder). When compared to corporate bonds, the yield on preferred stocks is often smaller than the yield on bonds. When compared to common stocks, preferred stocks are safer investments that offer more secure dividends. They are often purchased by individuals who need a predictable source of income greater than offered by common stock investments. They are also purchased by other corporations, because corporations receive a tax break on the dividend income. For all other investors, preferred stocks lack the growth potential that common stocks offer and the safety of many corporate bond issues.

When compared to corporations selling common stock, preferred stock is issued less often by only a few corporations. Yet it is an alternative method of financing that may attract investors who do not wish to buy common stock. Preferred stock, like common stock, is equity financing that does not have to be repaid. And dividends on preferred stock, as on common stock, may be omitted by action of the board of directors. While preferred stock does not represent a legal debt that must be repaid, if the firm is dissolved or declares bankruptcy, preferred stockholders do have first claim to the corporation's assets after creditors (including bondholders). To make preferred stock issues more attractive, some corporations may offer two additional features.

One way preferred stockholders can protect themselves against omitted dividends is to purchase cumulative preferred stock. *Cumulative preferred stock* is stock whose unpaid dividends accumulate and must be paid before any cash dividend is paid to the common stockholders. If a corporation does not pay dividends to the cumulative preferred stockholders during one dividend period, the amount of the missed dividends is added to the following period's preferred dividends. If you own noncumulative preferred stock, an omitted dividend will not be made up later.

The second feature that makes preferred stock attractive is the conversion feature. *Convertible preferred stock* can be exchanged, at the stockholder's option, for a specified number of shares of common stock. The conversion feature provides the investor with the added safety of preferred stock and the possibility of greater speculative gain through conversion to common stock. For example, assume Martin & Martin Manufacturing has issued a convertible preferred stock. Each share of preferred stock is convertible into two shares of common stock. Assume the market price of Martin & Martin's convertible preferred stock is $24 and the stock pays an annual dividend of $1.60 a share. Also assume the market price of the company's common stock is $9 and the common stock currently pays an annual dividend of $0.54 a share. Under these circumstances, you would keep the preferred stock. If the market price of the common stock increased to above $12 a share, however, you would have an incentive to exercise the conversion option.

The decision to convert preferred stock to common stock is complicated by three factors. First, the dividends paid on preferred stock are more secure than the dividends paid on common stock. Second, the amount of the dividend for preferred stock is generally higher than the amount of the dividend for common stock. Third, because of the conversion option, the market value of convertible preferred stock usually increases as the market value of common stock increases.

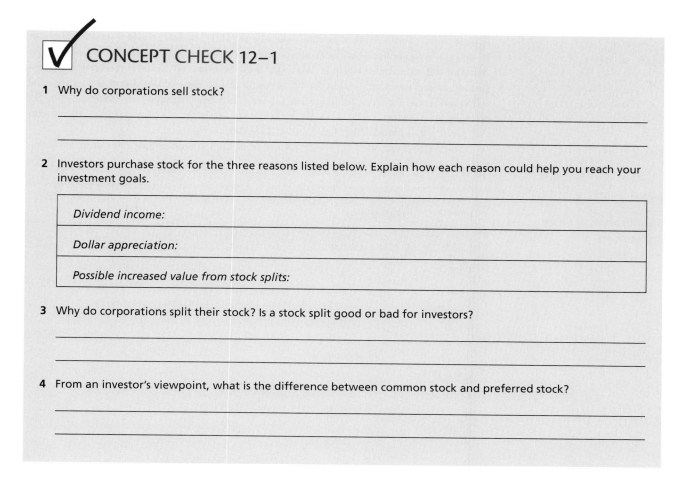

✓ CONCEPT CHECK 12–1

1 Why do corporations sell stock?

_____

_____

2 Investors purchase stock for the three reasons listed below. Explain how each reason could help you reach your investment goals.

Dividend income:
Dollar appreciation:
Possible increased value from stock splits:

3 Why do corporations split their stock? Is a stock split good or bad for investors?

_____

_____

4 From an investor's viewpoint, what is the difference between common stock and preferred stock?

_____

_____

Evaluating a Stock Issue

OBJECTIVE 2

Explain how you
can evaluate stock
investments.

Many investors expect to earn a 10 percent or higher return on their investments, yet they are unwilling to spend the time required to become a good investor. In fact, many people purchase investments without doing *any* research. They wouldn't buy a car without a test drive or purchase a home without comparing different houses, but for some unknown reason they invest without doing their homework. The truth is that there is no substitute for a few hours of detective work when choosing an investment. This section explains how to evaluate a potential stock investment. In reality, it is important to evaluate not only the corporation that issues the individual stock you are interested in purchasing, but also the industry in which the corporation operates. For example, when the hi-tech and computer industries encountered problems beginning in the late 1990s, most companies within these industries found that increasing sales and profits was difficult if not impossible. Also, keep in mind that the nation's and even the world's economy—the big picture—may impact the way a corporation operates and cause a corporate stock to increase or decrease in value.

A wealth of information is available to stock investors, and a logical place to start the evaluation process for stock is with the classification of different types of stock investments described in Exhibit 12–3. Once you have identified a type of stock that may help you obtain your investment goals, you may want to use the Internet to evaluate a potential investment.

The Internet

In this section, we examine some Web sites that are logical starting points when evaluating a stock investment, but there are many more than those described. Let's begin with information about the corporation that is available on the Internet.

Today most corporations have a Web site, and the information these pages provide is especially useful. First, it is easily accessible. All you have to do is type in the corporation's URL address or use a search engine to locate the corporation's home page. Second, the information on the Web site may be more up to date and thorough than printed material obtained from the corporation or outside sources. Look at the financial information on the investor page for General Electric displayed in Exhibit 12–4. By clicking on a button, you can access information on the firm's earnings and other financial factors that could affect the value of the company's stock.

You can also use Web sites like Yahoo! and other search engines to obtain information about stock investments. Take a look at a small portion of the opening page of the

Exhibit 12–3

Classification of Stock
Investments

When evaluating a stock investment, investors often classify stocks into the following eight categories.	
Type of Stock	**Characteristics of This Type of Investment**
Blue chip	A safe investment that generally attracts conservative investors.
Income	An investment that pays higher-than-average dividends.
Growth	A stock issued by a corporation that has the potential of earning profits above the average profits of all firms in the economy.
Cyclical	A stock that follows the business cycle of advances and declines in the economy.
Defensive	A stock that remains stable during declines in the economy.
Large cap	A stock issued by a corporation that has a large amount of capitalization in excess of $5 billion.
Small cap	A stock issued by a company that has a capitalization of $500 million or less.
Penny	A stock that typically sells for less than $1 per share.

Exhibit 12–4   Financial Information Available on General Electric's Investor Communications Web Page

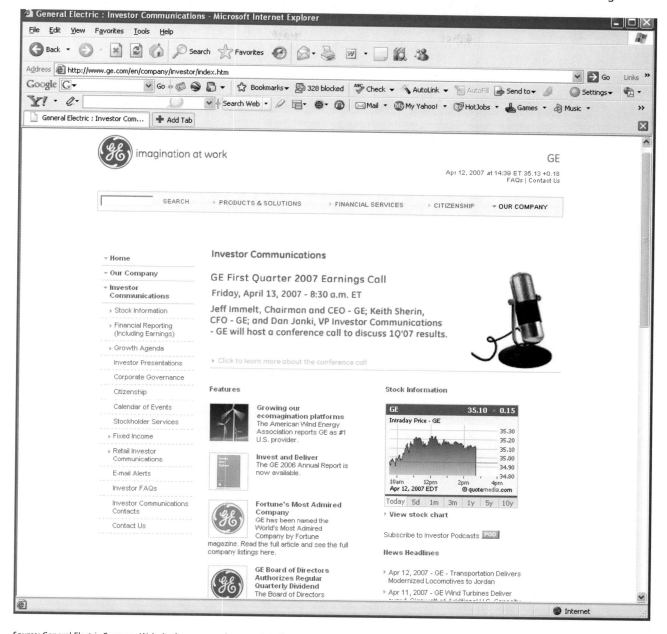

Source: General Electric Company Web site (www.ge.com), accessed April 12, 2007. General Electric Company, 3135 Easton Turnpike, Fairfield, CT 06431.

Yahoo! Finance Web site (http://finance.yahoo.com) in Exhibit 12–5. The entire Web site provides a wealth of information. For example, under the stock research category, there is a stock screener that will help you pick stock investments. You can also get current market values by entering a corporation's stock symbol and clicking on the Get Quotes button at the top of the page. If you don't know the symbol, just click on Symbol Lookup and follow the directions. In addition to the current market value, the Yahoo! Finance Web site provides even more specific information about a particular company. By clicking on the buttons under the headings for the quotes, charts, news and info, analyst coverage, ownership and financials that are part of the screen for each corporation, you can obtain even more information. How about picking a company like Texas Instruments (symbol TXN) or Coca-Cola (symbol KO) and going exploring on the Internet? To begin, enter the Web address for Yahoo! Finance (http://finance.yahoo.com). Then

Exhibit 12–5   A Portion of the Opening Page for the Yahoo! Finance Web Site

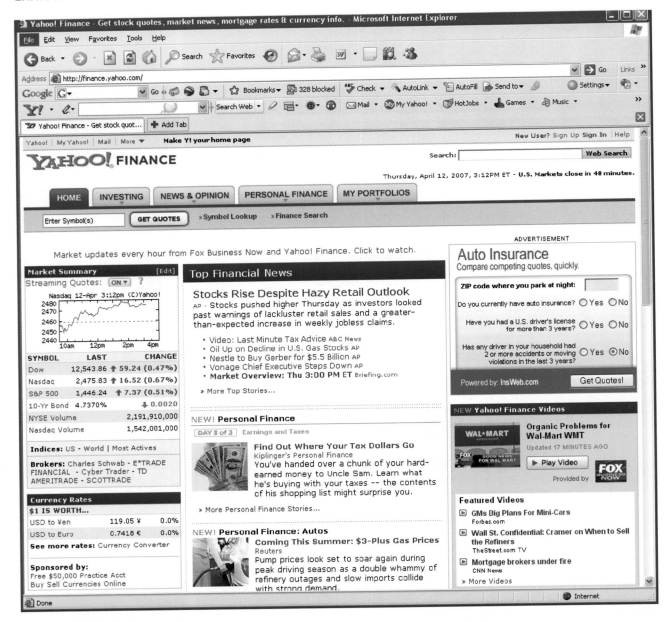

enter the symbol for one of the above corporations in the Quotes section. You'll be surprised at the amount of information you can obtain with a click of your mouse.

You can also use professional advisory services like Standard & Poor's Financial Information Services (www2.standardpoors.com), Mergent Online (www.fisonline.com), and Value Line (www.valueline.com). While some of the information provided by these services is free, there is a charge for the more detailed information you may need to evaluate a stock investment. For more information about professional advisory services and the type of information they provide, read the next section.

In addition to Internet search engines and professional advisory services, you can access personal finance Web sites like *SmartMoney* (www.smartmoney.com) and *Kiplinger's Personal Finance* (www.kipliner.com). Both Web sites provide a wealth of information for the stock investor. Additional Web sites that can help you learn more about investing in stocks are included in the nearby Key Web Sites for Investing Advice feature.

Stock Advisory Services

In addition to the Internet, sources of information you can use to evaluate potential stock investments are the printed materials provided by stock advisory services. The information ranges from simple alphabetical listings to detailed financial reports.

Standard & Poor's reports, Value Line, and Mergent are three widely used advisory services that provide detailed research for stock investors. Here we will examine a detailed report for PepsiCo, the global beverage company, that is published in *Mergent's Handbook of Common Stocks* (see Exhibit 12–6).

Key Web Sites for Investing Advice

www.businessweek.com
http://money.cnn.com
www.thestreet.com

Exhibit 12–6

Mergent's Report for PepsiCo, Inc.

PEPSICO INC.

Exchange	Symbol	Price	52Wk Range	Yield	P/E	Div Acheiver
NYS	PEP	$60.46 (5/31/2006)	60.66-52.58	1.96	25.09	34 Years

*7 Year Price Score 94.86   *NYSE Composite Index=100   *12 Month Price Score 95.09

Interim Earnings (Per Share)

Qtr.	Mar	Jun	Aug	Dec
2003	0.45	0.58	0.62	0.41
2004	0.46	0.61	0.79	0.58
2005	0.53	0.70	0.51	0.65
2006	0.60	...	...	...

Interim Dividends (Per Share)

Amt	Decl	Ex	Rec	Pay
0.26Q	7/22/2005	9/7/2005	9/9/2005	9/30/2005
0.26Q	11/18/2005	12/7/2005	12/9/2005	1/3/2006
0.26Q	2/3/2006	3/8/2006	3/10/2006	3/31/2006
0.30Q	5/3/2006	6/7/2006	6/9/2006	6/30/2006

Indicated Div: $1.20 (Div. Reinv. Plan)

Valuation Analysis / **Institutional Holding**

Forecast P/E	17.01	No of Institutions
	(6/10/2006)	1202
Market Cap	$100.1 Billion	Shares
Book Value	14.8 Billion	1,083,386,368
Price/Book	6.76	% Held
Price/Sales	3.07	65.56

TRADING VOLUME (thousand shares)

1997 1998 1999 2000 2001 2002 2003 2004 2005 2006

Business Summary: Food (MIC: 4.1 SIC: 2086 NAIC: 312111)
PepsiCo is a global snack and beverage company. Co. manufactures, markets and sells a variety of salty, convenient, sweet and grain-based snacks, carbonated and non-carbonated beverages and foods. Co.'s Frito-Lay North America division's brands include Lay's potato chips, Fritos corn chips, Quaker Chewy granola bars and Rold Gold pretzels. PepsiCo Beverages North America brands include Pepsi, Mountain Dew, Sierra Mist, Mug, SoBe, Gatorade, Tropicana Pure Premium and Propel. PepsiCo International brands include Sabritas in Mexico, Walkers in the UK, and Smith's in Australia. Quaker Foods North America's products include Quaker oatmeal and Cap'n Crunch and Life ready-to-eat cereals.

Recent Developments: For the twelve weeks ended Mar 25 2006, net income increased 11.7% to $1.02 billion compared with $912.0 million in the corresponding year-earlier period. Revenues were $7.21 billion, up 9.4% from $6.59 billion the year before. Operating income was $1.35 billion versus $1.25 billion in the prior-year quarter, an increase of 8.1%. Direct operating expenses rose 10.8% to $3.18 billion from $2.87 billion in the comparable period the year before. Indirect operating expenses increased 8.5% to $2.68 billion from $2.47 billion in the equivalent prior-year period.

Prospects: Co. continues to see strong revenue momentum across all its businesses, which is being driven by product innovation and strong marketplace execution. For instance, Co.'s net revenue in its Pepsico Beverages North America division is reflecting volume growth, a positive mix effect from the strong performance of its non-carbonated beverage portfolio, increased pricing, and the timing of concentrate shipments to bottlers. In addition, Co. is benefiting from solid profit performance despite continued pressure from inflation in some of its key input costs. Looking ahead to full-year 2006, Co. expects earnings of at least $2.93 per share.

Financial Data
(US$ in Thousands)

	3 Mos	12/31/2005	12/25/2004	12/27/2003	12/28/2002	12/29/2001	12/30/2000	12/25/1999
Earnings Per Share	2.41	2.39	2.44	2.05	1.85	1.47	1.48	1.37
Cash Flow Per Share	3.16	3.45	2.99	2.53	2.65	2.39	2.66	2.07
Tang Book Value Per Share	5.50	5.20	4.84	3.82	4.93	2.17	1.91	1.47
Dividends Per Share	1.040	1.010	0.850	0.630	0.595	0.575	0.555	0.535
Dividend Payout %	43.15	42.26	34.84	30.73	32.16	39.12	37.50	39.05
Income Statement								
Total Revenue	7,205,000	32,562,000	29,261,000	26,971,000	25,112,000	26,935,000	20,438,000	20,367,000
EBITDA	1,718,000	7,732,000	6,848,000	6,269,000	6,077,000	5,189,000	4,209,000	4,843,000
Depn & Amortn	286,000	1,253,000	1,209,000	1,165,000	1,067,000	1,008,000	854,000	942,000
Income Before Taxes	1,415,000	6,382,000	5,546,000	4,992,000	4,868,000	4,029,000	3,210,000	3,656,000
Income Taxes	396,000	2,304,000	1,372,000	1,424,000	1,555,000	1,367,000	1,027,000	1,606,000
Net Income	1,019,000	4,078,000	4,212,000	3,568,000	3,313,000	2,662,000	2,183,000	2,050,000
Average Shares	1,695,000	1,706,000	1,729,000	1,739,000	1,789,000	1,807,000	1,475,000	1,496,000
Balance Sheet								
Total Assets	30,994,000	31,727,000	27,987,000	25,327,000	23,474,000	21,695,000	18,339,000	17,551,000
Current Liabilities	8,160,000	9,406,000	6,752,000	6,415,000	6,052,000	4,998,000	3,935,000	3,788,000
Long-Term Obligations	2,288,000	2,313,000	2,397,000	1,702,000	2,187,000	2,651,000	2,346,000	2,812,000
Total Liabilities	16,253,000	17,476,000	14,464,000	13,453,000	14,183,000	13,021,000	11,090,000	10,670,000
Stockholders' Equity	14,812,000	14,320,000	13,572,000	11,896,000	9,298,000	8,648,000	7,249,000	6,881,000
Shares Outstanding	1,656,000	1,656,000	1,679,000	1,705,000	1,722,000	1,756,000	1,446,000	1,455,000
Statistical Record								
Return on Assets %	13.74	13.44	15.84	14.66	14.71	13.34	11.97	10.22
Return on Equity %	28.49	28.77	33.17	33.76	37.02	33.58	30.40	30.95
EBITDA Margin %	23.84	23.75	23.40	23.24	24.20	19.26	20.59	23.78
Net Margin %	14.14	12.52	14.39	13.23	13.19	9.88	10.68	10.07
Asset Turnover	1.09	1.07	1.10	1.11	1.11	1.35	1.12	1.02
Current Ratio	1.16	1.11	1.28	1.08	1.06	1.17	1.17	1.10
Debt to Equity	0.15	0.16	0.18	0.14	0.24	0.31	0.32	0.41
Price Range	60.49-52.29	59.90-51.57	55.55-45.39	48.71-37.30	53.12-35.50	50.28-41.26	49.75-30.50	41.81-30.50
P/E Ratio	25.10-21.70	25.06-21.58	22.77-18.60	23.76-18.20	28.71-19.19	34.20-28.07	33.61-20.61	30.52-22.26
Average Yield %	1.83	1.82	1.66	1.43	1.29	1.25	1.36	1.46

Address: 700 Anderson Hill Road, Purchase, NY 10577-1444 **Telephone:** 914-253-2000 **Fax:** 914-253-2070	**Web Site:** www.pepsico.com **Officers:** Steven S. Reinemund - Chmn., C.E.O. Indra K. Nooyi - Pres., C.F.O.	**Auditors:** KPMG LLP **Investor Contact:** 914-253-3035 **Transfer Agents:** The Bank of New York

597

Source: *Mergent's Handbook of Common Stocks,* Summer 2006 (New York: Mergent, 2006).

The basic report illustrated in Exhibit 12–6 consists of six main sections. The top section provides information about stock prices, earnings, and dividends. The Business Summary describes the company's major operations in detail. The next section, Recent Developments, provides current information about the company's net income and sales revenue. The Prospects section describes the company's outlook. The Financial Data section provides important data on the company for the past 7 years plus the last 3-month reporting period. Among the topics included in this section are total revenues, earnings per share, dividends per share, return on equity, and net income. The final section of the report states, among other things, who its auditors are, where its principal office is located, who its transfer agent is, and who its main corporate officers are. While other stock advisory services provide basically the same types of information as that in Exhibit 12–6, it is the investor's job to interpret such information and decide whether the company's stock is a good investment.

How to Read the Financial Section of the Newspaper

Although some newspapers have eliminated or reduced the amount of financial coverage, *The Wall Street Journal* and most metropolitan newspapers still contain some information about stocks listed on the New York Stock Exchange, the American Stock Exchange, other major stock exchanges, and the Nasdaq over-the-counter market. Although not all newspapers print exactly the same information, they usually provide the basic information. Stocks are listed alphabetically, so your first task is to move down the table to find the stock you're interested in. Then, to read the stock quotation, you simply read across the table. The fourth line in Exhibit 12–7 provides information about Wal-Mart.

Corporate News

The federal government requires corporations selling new issues of securities to disclose in a prospectus information about corporate earnings, assets and liabilities, products

Exhibit 12–7

Financial Information about Common Stocks

Reproduced at the top of the exhibit is an enlarged portion of the stock quotations reported in *The Wall Street Journal.* The numbers above each of the columns correspond to the numbered entries in the list of explanations that appear at the bottom of the exhibit.

1 STOCK	2 SYM	3 CLOSE	4 NET CHG
Wachovia	WB	56.56	−0.11
WadlRed A	WDR	26.56	−0.18
Walgreen	WAG	46.51	0.42
WalMart	WMT	48.20	−0.11

1. Name (often abbreviated) of the company: Wal-Mart

2. Ticker symbol or letters that identify a stock for trading: WMT

3. Price paid in the last transaction of the day: $48.20

4. Difference between the price paid for the last share sold today and the price paid for the last share sold on the previous day: $0.11 (In Wall Street terms, Wal-Mart "closed down $0.11" on this day.)

Source: Republished with permission of Dow Jones, Inc., from *The Wall Street Journal*, January 18, 2007; permission conveyed through Copyright Clearance Center, Inc.

or services, and the qualifications of top management. In addition to a prospectus, all publicly owned corporations send their stockholders an annual report that contains detailed financial data. Even if you're not a stockholder, you can obtain an annual report from the corporation. For most corporations, all it takes is a call to a toll-free phone number, a written request to the corporation's headquarters, or a visit to a corporation's Web site.

In addition to corporate publications, you can access the Securities and Exchange Commission Web site (www.sec.gov) to obtain financial and other important information that a corporation has supplied to the federal government. Finally, many periodicals, including *BusinessWeek, Fortune, Forbes, Money, Kiplinger's Personal Finance Magazine,* and similar publications contain information about stock investing.

✓ CONCEPT CHECK 12–2

1 Assume that you are considering a $2,500 investment in common stock issued by Microsoft. How would you go about researching your potential investment?

_____

_____

2 Describe how each of the following sources of investment information could help you evaluate a stock investment.

Source of Information	Type of Information	How Could This Help
The Internet		
Professional advisory services		
A newspaper		
Government publications		
Business periodicals		

3 What is the difference between a prospectus and an annual report?

_____

_____

4 Using Exhibit 12–6, pick three financial measures and describe how they could help you evaluate a corporate stock.

_____

_____

Numerical Measures That Influence Investment Decisions

How do you determine whether the time is right to buy or sell a particular stock? Good question! Unfortunately, there is no simple answer. In addition to the material in the last section, Evaluating a Stock Issue, many investors rely on numerical measures to decide when to buy or sell a stock. We begin this section by examining the relationship between a stock's price and a corporation's earnings.

> **OBJECTIVE 3**
> Analyze the numerical measures that cause a stock to increase or decrease in value.

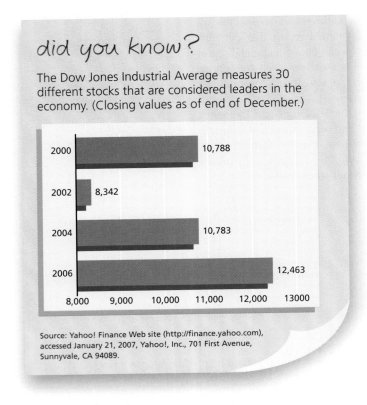

earnings per share A corporation's after-tax earnings divided by the number of outstanding shares of a firm's common stock.

price-earnings (PE) ratio The price of a share of stock divided by the corporation's earnings per share of stock.

Why Corporate Earnings Are Important

Many analysts believe that a corporation's ability or inability to generate earnings in the future may be one of the most significant factors that account for an increase or decrease in the value of a stock. Simply put, higher earnings generally equate to higher stock value. Unfortunately, the reverse is also true. If a corporation's earnings decline, generally the stock's value will also decline. Corporate earnings are reported in the firm's annual report. You can also obtain information about a corporation's current earnings by using a professional advisory service or accessing the Yahoo! Finance Web site or one of the other Web sites described in the last section.

In addition, many investors also calculate earnings per share to evaluate the financial health of a corporation. **Earnings per share** are a corporation's after-tax earnings divided by the number of outstanding shares of a firm's common stock. For example, assume that in 2007, XYZ Corporation has after-tax earnings of $2,500,000. Also assume that XYZ has 5,000,000 shares of common stock. This means XYZ's earnings per share are $0.50, as illustrated below.

$$\text{Earnings per share} = \frac{\text{After-tax income}}{\text{Number of shares outstanding}}$$

$$= \frac{\$2,500,000}{5,000,000}$$

$$= \$0.50$$

Most stockholders consider the amount of earnings per share important because it is a measure of the company's profitability. No meaningful average for this measure exists, mainly because the number of shares of a firm's stock is subject to change via stock splits and stock dividends. *As a general rule, however, an increase in earnings per share is a healthy sign for any corporation and its stockholders.*

Another calculation, the price-earnings ratio, can be used to evaluate a potential stock investment. The **price-earnings (PE) ratio** is the price of a share of stock divided by the corporation's earnings per share of stock. For example, assume XYZ Corporation's common stock is selling for $10 a share. As determined earlier, XYZ's earnings per share are $0.50. XYZ's price-earnings ratio is, therefore, 20, as illustrated below.

$$\text{Price-earnings (PE) ratio} = \frac{\text{Price per share}}{\text{Earnings per share}}$$

$$= \frac{\$10.00}{\$0.50}$$

$$= 20$$

The price-earnings ratio is a key factor that serious investors use to evaluate stock investments. *A low price-earnings ratio indicates that a stock may be a good investment, and a high price-earnings ratio indicates that it may be a poor investment.* Generally, you should study the price-earnings ratio for a corporation over a period of time. For example, if XYZ's price-earnings ratio has ranged from 17 to 45 over the past five years, its current

Figure It Out!

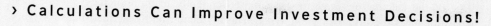

› Calculations Can Improve Investment Decisions!

Numbers, numbers, numbers! The truth is that if you are going to be a good investor, you must learn the numbers game. As mentioned in the text, many calculations can help you gauge the value of a potential stock investment. These same calculations can help you decide if the time is right to sell a stock investment.

Now it's your turn. Use the following financial information for Bozo Oil Company to calculate the earnings per share, price-earnings (PE) ratio, and dividend yield:

After-tax income, $6,250,000
Dividend amount, $0.60
Price per share, $30
Number of shares outstanding, 5,000,000

Calculation	Calculation Formula	Your Answer	Indications
Earnings per share			
Price-earnings (PE) ratio			
Dividend yield			

Answers: earnings per share (EPS) = $1.25; price-earnings ratio (PE) = 24; dividend yield = 0.02 = 2%.

---

ratio of 20 indicates that it is a potentially good investment. If XYZ's current price-earnings ratio was 45—at the high end of the range—it might be a poor investment at this time. It is also possible to use price-earnings ratios to compare firms within the same industry. *Generally, the firm with the lowest PE ratio is the better investment.*

Both earnings per share and the price-earnings ratio are based on historical numbers. In other words, this is what the company has done in the past. With this fact in mind, many investors will also look at earnings estimates for a corporation. The Yahoo! Finance Web site or similar financial Web sites provide earnings estimates for major corporations. At the time of publication, for example, Yahoo! Finance provided the following earnings estimates for General Mills, one of the largest manufacturer of packaged consumer foods in the United States.[2]

Apply *Yourself!*

Objective 3

Use the Yahoo Finance Web site (http://finance.yahoo.com) to locate the current price for a share of stock and earnings per share for Microsoft, (symbol MSFT) and 3M Company (symbol MMM).

General Mills	This Year	Next Year
Yearly earnings estimates	$3.15 per share	$3.40 per share

From an investor's standpoint, a projected increase in earnings from $3.15 per share to $3.40 per share is a good sign. In the case of General Mills, these estimates were determined by surveying different analysts who track General Mills, Inc. By using the same projected earnings amount, it is possible to calculate a projected price-earnings ratio or a projected price per share of stock. Of course, you should remember that these are estimates and are not "etched in stone." An increase or decrease in interest rates, higher or lower unemployment rates, terrorist attacks, and changes that affect the economy, industry, or company's sales and profit amounts could cause analysts to revise the above estimates.

[2]Yahoo! Finance Web site (http://finance.yahoo.com), accessed January 21, 2007, Yahoo!, Inc., 701 First Avenue, Sunnyvale, CA 94089.

Other Factors That Influence the Price of a Stock

One of the calculations investors use most frequently to monitor the value of their investments is the dividend yield. *Note:* The dividend yield described below is very similar to the current yield calculation presented in Chapter 11. The difference is that the term "annual interest amount" used in the current yield calculation has been changed to "annual dividend amount" because stocks often pay dividends to investors and provide dividend income. The **dividend yield** is the yearly dollar amount of dividend generated by an investment divided by the investment's current market value. For example, assume you purchase stock in Boeing Company. Also assume Boeing pays an annual dividend of $1.40 per share and is currently selling for $87.50 a share. The current dividend yield is 1.60 percent, calculated as follows:

dividend yield The yearly dollar amount of dividend generated by an investment divided by the investment's current market value.

$$\text{Dividend yield} = \frac{\text{Annual dividend amount}}{\text{Current market value}}$$

$$= \frac{\$1.40}{\$87.50}$$

$$= 0.0160, \text{ or } 1.60 \text{ percent}$$

As a general rule, an increase in dividend yield is a healthy sign for any investment. A dividend yield of 3 percent is better than a 1.6 percent dividend yield.

Although the dividend yield calculation is useful, you should also consider whether the investment is increasing or decreasing in dollar value. **Total return** is a calculation that includes not only the yearly dollar amount of dividend but also any increase or decrease in the original purchase price of the investment. The following formula is used to calculate total return:

total return A calculation that includes the yearly dollar amount of dividend as well as any increase or decrease in the original purchase price of the investment.

$$\text{Total return} = \text{Dividends} + \text{Capital gain}$$

While this concept may be used for any investment, let's illustrate it by using the assumptions for the Boeing stock presented in the preceding example. Assume, in addition, that you own 100 shares of the stock that you purchased for $67.50 a share and hold your stock for one year before deciding to sell it at the current market price of $87.50 a share. Your total return for this investment would be $2,140, calculated as follows:

$$\text{Total return} = \text{Dividends} + \text{Capital gain}$$

$$\$2,140 = \$140 + \$2,000$$

The dividends of $140 results from the payment of dividends for one year ($1.40 per-share dividend × 100 shares). The capital gain of $2,000 results from the increase in the stock price from $67.50 a share to $87.50 a share ($20 per-share increase × 100 shares = $2,000). (Of course, commissions to buy and sell your stock, a topic covered in the next section, would reduce your total return.)

Sheet 38
*Evaluating
Corporate
Stocks*

Although little correlation may exist between the market value of a stock and its book value, book value is widely reported in financial publications. Therefore, it deserves mention. The **book value** for a share of stock is determined by deducting all liabilities from the corporation's assets and dividing the remainder by the number of outstanding shares of common stock. For example, assume XYZ Corporation has assets of $60 million and liabilities of $20 million and has issued 5,000,000 shares of common stock. In this situation, the book value for a share of XYZ stock is $8 per share, as follows:

book value Determined by deducting all liabilities from the corporation's assets and dividing the remainder by the number of outstanding shares of common stock.

$$\text{Book value} = \frac{\text{Assets} - \text{Liabilities}}{\text{Shares outstanding}}$$

$$= \frac{\$60,000,000 - \$20,000,000}{5,000,000 \text{ shares of stock}} = \$8 \text{ per share}$$

Some investors believe they have found a bargain when a stock's market value is about the same as or lower than its book value. *Be warned:* Book value calculations may be misleading, because the dollar amount of assets used in the above formula may be understated or overstated on the firm's financial statements. From a practical standpoint, most financial experts suggest that book value is just one piece of the puzzle and you must consider other factors along with book value when evaluating a possible stock investment.

✓ CONCEPT CHECK 12–3

1 Explain the relationship between corporate earnings and a stock's market value.

_____

_____

2 Why are earnings per share and price-earnings ratios important?

_____

_____

3 Write the formula for the following stock calculations, and then describe how this formula could help you make a decision to buy or sell a stock.

Calculation	What Is the Formula?	Why Is This Calculation Useful?
Earnings per share		
Price-earnings (PE) ratio		
Dividend yield		
Total return		
Book value		

Buying and Selling Stocks

To purchase a pair of Levi Strauss jeans, you simply walk into a store that sells Levi's, choose a pair, and pay for your purchase. To purchase common or preferred stock, you generally have to work through a brokerage firm. In turn, your brokerage firm must buy the stock in either the primary or secondary market. In the **primary market,** you purchase financial securities, via an investment bank or other representative, from the issuer of those securities. An **investment bank** is a financial firm that assists corporations in raising funds, usually by helping to sell new security issues.

New security issues sold through an investment bank can be issued by corporations that have sold stocks and bonds before and need to sell new issues to raise additional financing. The new securities can also be initial public offerings. An **initial public offering (IPO)** occurs when a corporation sells stock to the general public for the first time. Companies that have used IPOs to raise capital include Burger King ($425 million), Chipotle Mexican Grill ($173 million), and J. Crew ($376 million).[3] Investors bought these stocks through brokerage firms acting as agents for an investment banking firm, and the money they paid for common stock flowed to the corporations that issued the stock. Because these companies used the financing obtained through IPOs wisely,

OBJECTIVE 4
Describe how stocks are bought and sold.

primary market A market in which an investor purchases financial securities, via an investment bank or other representative, from the issuer of those securities.

investment bank A financial firm that assists corporations in raising funds, usually by helping to sell new security issues.

[3]"2006 Annual Deal List," the IPO Home Web site (www.ipohome.com), accessed January 21, 2007.

initial public offering (IPO) Occurs when a corporation sells stock to the general public for the first time.

they have grown and prospered, and investors have profited from their IPO investments. However, not all companies that use IPOs to raise capital are good investments.

Be warned: The promise of quick profits often lures investors to purchase IPOs. An IPO is generally classified as a high-risk investment—one made in the hope of earning a relatively large profit in a short time. Depending on the corporation selling the new security, IPOs are usually too speculative for most people.

After a stock has been sold through the primary market, it is traded through the secondary market. The **secondary market** is a market for existing financial securities that are currently traded among investors. Once the stocks are sold in the primary market, they can be sold time and again in the secondary market. The fact that stocks can be sold in the secondary market improves the liquidity of stock investments because the money you pay for stock goes to the seller of the stock.

secondary market A market for existing financial securities that are currently traded among investors.

Secondary Markets for Stocks

To purchase common or preferred stock, you usually have to work with an employee of a brokerage firm who will buy or sell for you at a securities exchange or through the over-the-counter market.

securities exchange A marketplace where member brokers who represent investors meet to buy and sell securities.

SECURITIES EXCHANGES   A **securities exchange** is a marketplace where member brokers who represent investors meet to buy and sell securities. The securities sold at a particular exchange must first be listed, or accepted for trading, at that exchange. Generally, the securities issued by nationwide corporations are traded at either the New York Stock Exchange or the American Stock Exchange. The securities of regional corporations are traded at smaller, regional exchanges. These exchanges are located in Philadelphia, Boston, and several other cities. The securities of very large corporations may be traded at more than one exchange. American firms that do business abroad may also be listed on foreign securities exchanges—in Tokyo, London, or Paris, for example.

The New York Stock Exchange (NYSE) is one of the largest securities exchanges in the world. This exchange lists stocks for about 2,750 corporations with a total market value of about $25 trillion. The NYSE has 1,366 members, or *seats*.[4] Most of these members represent brokerage firms that charge commissions on security trades made by their representatives for their customers. Other members are called *specialists* or *specialist firms*. A **specialist** buys *or* sells a particular stock in an effort to maintain a fair and orderly market.

specialist Buys or sells a particular stock in an effort to maintain an orderly market.

Before a corporation's stock is approved for listing on the NYSE, the corporation must meet specific listing requirements. The American Stock Exchange (AMEX) and various regional exchanges also have listing requirements, but typically these are less stringent than the NYSE requirements. The stock of corporations that cannot meet the NYSE requirements, find it too expensive to be listed on the NYSE, or choose not to be listed on the NYSE is often traded on the American Stock Exchange, on one of the regional exchanges, or through the over-the-counter market.

over-the-counter (OTC) market A network of dealers who buy and sell the stocks of corporations that are not listed on a securities exchange.

THE OVER-THE-COUNTER MARKET   Not all securities are traded on organized exchanges. Stocks issued by several thousand companies are traded in the over-the-counter market. The **over-the-counter (OTC) market** is a network of dealers who buy and sell the stocks of corporations that are not listed on a securities exchange. Today these stocks are not really traded over the counter. The term was coined more than 100 years ago when securities were sold "over the counter" in stores and banks.

Nasdaq An electronic marketplace for stocks issued by 3,200 different companies.

Most over-the-counter securities are traded through Nasdaq (pronounced "nazzdack"). **Nasdaq** is an electronic marketplace for stocks issued by approximately 3,200 different

[4]New York Stock Exchange Web site (www.nyse.com), accessed January 22, 2007.

companies.[5] In addition to providing price information, this computerized system allows investors to buy and sell shares of companies traded on Nasdaq. When you want to buy or sell shares of a company that trades on Nasdaq—say, Microsoft—your account executive sends your order into the Nasdaq computer system, where it shows up on the screen with all the other orders from people who want to buy or sell Microsoft. Then a Nasdaq dealer (sometimes referred to as a *market maker*) sitting at a computer terminal matches buy and sell orders for Microsoft. Once a match is found, your order is completed.

Begun in 1971, Nasdaq is known for its innovative, forward-looking growth companies. Although many securities are issued by smaller companies, some large firms, including Intel, Microsoft, and Cisco Systems, also trade on Nasdaq.

Apply *Yourself!*

Objective 4

Prepare a list of at least five questions that could help you interview a prospective account executive.

Brokerage Firms and Account Executives

An **account executive,** or *stockbroker,* is a licensed individual who buys or sells securities for his or her clients. (Actually, *account executive* is the more descriptive title because such individuals handle all types of securities, not just stocks.) While all account executives can buy or sell stock for clients, most investors expect more from their account executives. Ideally, an account executive should provide information and advice to be used in evaluating potential investments. Many investors begin their search for an account executive by asking friends or business associates for recommendations. This is a logical starting point, but remember that some account executives are conservative while others are more risk oriented.

Before choosing an account executive, you should have already determined your short-term and long-term financial objectives. Then you must be careful to communicate those objectives to the account executive so that he or she can do a better job of advising you. Needless to say, account executives may err in their investment recommendations. To help avoid a situation in which your account executive's recommendations are automatically implemented, you should be *actively* involved in the decisions related to your investment program and you should never allow your account executive to use his or her discretion without your approval. Watch your account for signs of churning. **Churning** is excessive buying and selling of securities to generate commissions. From a total dollar return standpoint, this practice usually leaves the client worse off or at least no better off. Churning is illegal under the rules established by the Securities and Exchange Commission; however, it may be difficult to prove. Finally, keep in mind that account executives generally are not liable for client losses that result from their recommendations. In fact, most brokerage firms require new clients to sign a statement in which they promise to submit any complaints to an arbitration board. This arbitration clause generally prevents a client from suing an account executive or a brokerage firm.

account executive A licensed individual who buys or sells securities for clients; also called a *stockbroker.*

Sheet 39
Investment Broker Comparison

churning Excessive buying and selling of securities to generate commissions.

Should You Use a Full-Service or a Discount Brokerage Firm?

Today a healthy competition exists between full-service, discount, and online brokerage firms. While the most obvious difference between full-service, discount, and online firms is the amount of the commissions they charge when you buy or sell stock and other securities, there are at least three other factors to consider. First, consider how much

---

[5]The Nasdaq Web site (www.nasdaq.com), accessed January 22, 2007.

research information is available and how much it costs. All three types of brokerage firm offer excellent research materials, but you are more likely to pay extra for information if you choose a discount or online brokerage firm.

Second, consider how much help you need when making an investment decision. Many full-service brokerage firms argue that you need a professional to help you make important investment decisions. While this may be true for some investors, most account executives employed by full-service brokerage firms are too busy to spend unlimited time with you on a one-on-one basis, especially if you are investing a small amount. On the other side, many discount and online brokerage firms argue that you alone are responsible for making your investment decisions. They are quick to point out that the most successful investors are the ones involved in their investment programs. And they argue that they have both personnel and materials dedicated to helping you learn how to become a better investor. Although there are many exceptions, the information below may help you decide whether to use a full-service, discount, or online brokerage firm.

- Full service   Beginning investors with little or no experience.
                   Individuals who are uncomfortable making investment decisions.
                   Individuals who are uncomfortable trading stocks online.
- Discount   People who understand the "how to" of researching stocks and prefer to make their own decisions.
                   Individuals who are uncomfortable trading stocks online.
- Online   People who understand the "how to" of researching stocks and prefer to make their own decisions.
                   Individuals who are comfortable trading stocks online.

Finally, consider how easy it is to buy and sell stock and other securities when using a full-service, discount, or online brokerage firm. Questions to ask include:

1. Can I buy or sell stocks over the phone?
2. Can I trade stocks online?
3. Where is your nearest office located?
4. Do you have a toll-free telephone number for customer use?
5. How often do I get statements?
6. Is there a charge for statements, research reports, and other financial reports?
7. Are there any fees in addition to the commissions I pay when I buy or sell stocks?

CAUTION!

Whether you are a beginner or have been investing for many years doesn't matter; it's never too early or too late to ask questions—especially about

- Specific stocks and other investment products.
- An account executive.
- A brokerage firm.

To find out if other investors have lodged complaints about an account executive or a brokerage firm and for information about investment frauds, go to the Securities and Exchange Commission Web site at www.sec.gov.

Computerized Transactions

Many people still prefer to use telephone orders to buy and sell stocks, but a growing number are using computers to complete security transactions. To meet this need, online, discount, and many full-service brokerage firms allow investors to trade online.

As a rule of thumb, the more active the investor is, the more sense it makes to use computers to trade online. Other reasons that justify using a computer include

1. The size of your investment portfolio.
2. The ability to manage your investments closely.
3. The capability of your computer and the software package.

While computers can make the investment process easier and faster, you should real-ize that *you* are still responsible for analyzing the information and making the final deci-sion to buy or sell a security. All the computer does is provide more information and, in most cases, complete transactions more quickly and economically.

A Sample Stock Transaction

Once you and your account executive have decided on a particular transaction, it is time to execute an order to buy or sell. Let's begin by examining three types of orders used to trade stocks.

A **market order** is a request to buy or sell a stock at the current market value. Since the stock exchange is an auction market, the account executive's representative will try to get the best price available and the transaction will be completed as soon as possible. Payment for stocks is generally required within three business days after the transac-tion. Then, in about four to six weeks, a stock certificate is sent to the purchaser of the stock, unless the securities are left with the brokerage firm for safekeeping. Today it is common practice for investors to leave stock certificates with a brokerage firm. Because the stock certificates are in the broker's care, transfers when the stock is sold are much easier. The phrase "left in the street name" is used to describe investor-owned securities held by a brokerage firm.

A **limit order** is a request to buy or sell a stock at a specified price. When you pur-chase stock, a limit order ensures that you will buy at the best possible price but not above a specified dollar amount. When you sell stock, a limit order ensures that you will sell at the best possible price, but not below a specified dollar amount. For example, if you place a limit order to buy General Motors common stock for $35 a share, the stock will not be purchased until the price drops to $35 a share or lower. Likewise, if your limit order is to sell General Motors for $35 a share, the stock will not be sold until the price rises to $35 a share or higher. *Be warned:* Limit orders are executed if and when the specified price or better is reached and *all* other previously received orders have been fulfilled.

Many stockholders are certain they want to sell their stock if it reaches a specified price. A limit order does not guarantee this will be done. With a limit order, as men-tioned above, orders by other investors may be placed ahead of your order. If you want to guarantee that your order will be executed, you place a special type of limit order known as a stop order. A **stop order** (sometimes called a *stop-loss order*) is an order to sell a particular stock at the next available opportunity after its market price reaches a specified amount. This type of order is used to protect an investor against a sharp drop in price and thus stop the dollar loss on a stock investment. For example, assume you purchased General Motors common stock at $35 a share. Two weeks after you made that investment, General Motors is facing multiple product liability lawsuits. Fearing that the market value of your stock will decrease, you enter a stop order to sell your General Motors stock at $28. This means that if the price of the stock decreases to $28 or lower, the account executive will sell it. While a stop order does not guarantee that your stock will be sold at the price you specified, it does guarantee that it will be sold at the next available opportunity. Both limit and stop orders may be good for one day, one week, one month, or good until canceled (GTC).

market order A request to buy or sell a stock at the current market value.

limit order A request to buy or sell a stock at a specified price.

stop order An order to sell a particular stock at the next available opportunity after its market price reaches a specified amount.

Commission Charges

Most brokerage firms have a minimum commission ranging from $7 to $55 for buying and selling stock. Additional commission charges are based on the number of shares and the value of stock bought and sold.

Exhibit 12–8

Typical Commission
Charges for Online Stock
Transactions in Which 1,000
Shares Are Bought or Sold

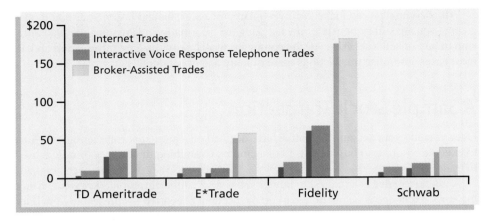

Source: TD Ameritrade Web site (www.tdameritrade.com), accessed January 23, 2007, TD Ameritrade, Inc., 4211 South 102nd Street, Omaha, NE 68127.

Exhibit 12–8 shows typical commissions charged by discount and online brokerage firms. Generally, full-service and discount brokerage firms charge higher commissions than those charged by online brokerage firms. As a rule of thumb, full-service brokers may charge as much as 1 to 2 percent of the transaction amount. In return for charging higher commissions, full-service brokers usually spend more time with each client, help make investment decisions, and provide free research information.

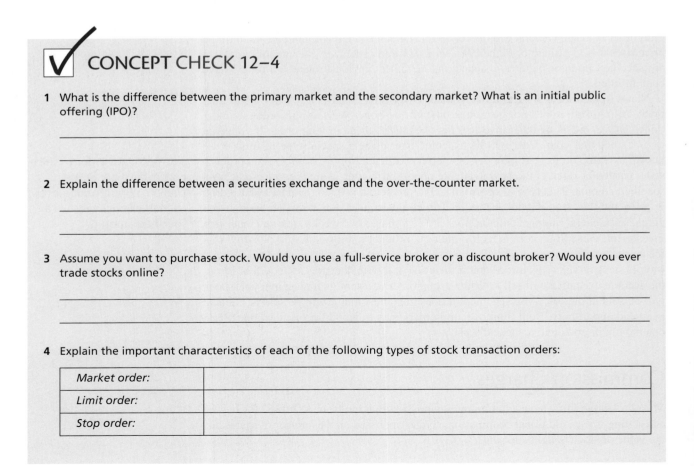

✓ CONCEPT CHECK 12–4

1 What is the difference between the primary market and the secondary market? What is an initial public offering (IPO)?

_____

_____

2 Explain the difference between a securities exchange and the over-the-counter market.

_____

_____

3 Assume you want to purchase stock. Would you use a full-service broker or a discount broker? Would you ever trade stocks online?

_____

_____

4 Explain the important characteristics of each of the following types of stock transaction orders:

Market order:	
Limit order:	
Stop order:	

Although full-service brokerage firms usually charge higher commissions, on some occasions a discount brokerage firm may charge higher commissions. This generally occurs when the transaction is small, involving a total dollar amount of less than $1,000, and the investor is charged the discount brokerage firm's minimum commission charge.

Long-Term and Short-Term Investment Strategies

Once you purchase stock, the investment may be classified as either long term or short term. Generally, individuals who hold an investment for a long period of time are referred to as *investors*. Typically, long-term investors hold their investments for at least a year or longer. Individuals who routinely buy and then sell stocks within a short period of time are called *speculators* or *traders*.

> **OBJECTIVE 5**
> Explain the trading techniques used by long-term investors and short-term speculators.

Long-Term Techniques

In this section, we discuss the long-term techniques of buy and hold, dollar cost averaging, direct investment programs, and dividend reinvestment programs.

BUY-AND-HOLD TECHNIQUE   Many long-term investors purchase stock and hold onto it for a number of years. When they do this, their investment can increase in value in three ways. First, they are entitled to dividends if the board of directors approves dividend payments to stockholders. Second, the price of the stock may go up. Third, the stock may be split. Although there are no guarantees, stock splits may increase the future value of a stock investment over a long period of time.

DOLLAR COST AVERAGING   **Dollar cost averaging** is a long-term technique used by investors who purchase an equal dollar amount of the same stock at equal intervals. Assume you invest $2,000 in Johnson & Johnson's common stock each year for a period of three years. The results of your investment program are illustrated in Exhibit 12–9. Notice that when the price of the stock increased in 2006 and 2007, you purchased fewer shares. The average cost for a share of stock, determined by dividing the total investment ($6,000) by the total number of shares, is $60.98 ($6,000 ÷ 98.4 = $60.98). Other applications of dollar cost averaging occur when employees purchase shares of their company's stock through a payroll deduction plan or as part of an employer-sponsored retirement plan over an extended period of time.

dollar cost averaging   A long-term technique used by investors who purchase an equal dollar amount of the same stock at equal intervals.

Year	Investment	Stock Price	Shares Purchased
2005	$2,000	$56	35.7
2006	2,000	60	33.3
2007	2,000	68	29.4
Total	$6,000		98.4

Average cost = Total investment ÷ Total shares

= $6,000 ÷ 98.4

= $60.98

Exhibit 12–9

Dollar Cost Averaging for Johnson & Johnson

The two goals of dollar cost averaging are to minimize the average cost per share and to avoid the common pitfall of buying high and selling low. In the situation shown in Exhibit 12–9, you would lose money only if you sold your stock at less than the average cost of $60.98. Thus, with dollar cost averaging, you can make money if the stock is sold at a price higher than the average cost for a share of stock.

DIRECT INVESTMENT AND DIVIDEND REINVESTMENT PLANS

direct investment plan A plan that allows stockholders to purchase stock directly from a corporation without having to use an account executive or a brokerage firm.

dividend reinvestment plan A plan that allows current stockholders the option to reinvest or use their cash dividends to purchase stock of the corporation.

Today a large number of corporations offer direct investment plans. A **direct investment plan** allows you to purchase stock directly from a corporation without having to use an account executive or a brokerage firm. Similarly, a **dividend reinvestment plan** (often called a DRIP) allows you the option to reinvest your cash dividends to purchase stock of the corporation. For stockholders, the chief advantage of both types of plans is that these plans enable them to purchase stock without paying a commission charge to a brokerage firm. (*Note:* A few companies may charge a small fee for direct and dividend reinvestment plans, but the fee is less than the commissions most brokerage firms charge.) The fees, minimum investment amounts, rules, and features for both direct investment and dividend reinvestment vary from one corporation to the next. To learn more about direct investing or dividend reinvestment plans, visit www.dripcentral.com or www.directinvesting.com. Also, with the direct investment and dividend reinvestment plans, you can take advantage of dollar cost averaging, discussed in the last section. For corporations, the chief advantage of both types of plans is that they provide an additional source of capital. As an added bonus, they are providing a service to their stockholders.

Short-Term Techniques

In addition to the long-term techniques presented in the preceding section, investors sometimes use more speculative, short-term techniques. In this section, we discuss buying stock on margin, selling short, and trading in options. *Be warned:* The methods presented in this section are risky; do not use them unless you fully understand the underlying risks. Also, you should not use them until you have experienced success using the more traditional long-term techniques described above.

margin A speculative technique whereby an investor borrows part of the money needed to buy a particular stock.

BUYING STOCK ON MARGIN   When buying stock on **margin,** you borrow part of the money needed to buy a particular stock. The margin requirement is set by the Federal Reserve Board and is subject to periodic change. The current margin requirement is 50 percent and a $2,000 minimum. This requirement means you may borrow up to half of the total stock purchase price as long as you have at least $2,000 in your brokerage firm account. Although margin is regulated by the Federal Reserve, margin requirements and the interest charged on the loans used to fund margin transactions may vary among brokers and dealers. Usually the brokerage firm either lends the money or arranges the loan with another financial institution.

Investors buy on margin because the financial leverage created by borrowing money can increase the return on an investment. Because they can buy up to twice as much stock by buying on margin, they can earn larger returns. Suppose you expect the market price of a share of ExxonMobil to *increase* in the next three to four months. Let's say you have enough money to purchase 100 shares of the stock. However, if you buy on margin, you can purchase an additional 100 shares for a total of 200 shares. If the price of ExxonMobil's stock increases by $7 a share, your profit will be $700 ($7 × 100 shares = $700) if you pay cash. But it will be $1,400 ($7 × 200 shares = $1,400) if you buy on margin. That is, buying more shares on margin, you will earn double the profit (less the interest you pay on the borrowed money and customary commission charges).

If the value of a margined stock decreases to approximately one-half of the original price, you will receive a *margin call* from the brokerage firm. After the margin call, you must pledge additional cash or securities to serve as collateral for the loan. If you don't have acceptable collateral or cash, the margined stock is sold and the proceeds are used to repay the loan. The exact price at which the brokerage firm issues the margin call is determined by the amount of money you borrowed when you purchased the stock. Generally, the more money you borrow, the sooner you will receive a margin call if the value of the margined stock drops.

In addition to facing the possibility of larger dollar losses, you must pay interest on the money borrowed to purchase stock on margin. Most brokerage firms charge 1 to 3 percent above the prime rate. Normally, economists define the prime rate as the interest rate that the best business customers must pay. Interest charges can absorb the potential profits if the value of margined stock does not increase rapidly enough and the margined stocks must be held for long periods of time.

SELLING SHORT
Your ability to make money by buying and selling securities is related to how well you can predict whether a certain stock will increase or decrease in market value. Normally, you buy stocks and assume they will increase in value, a procedure referred to as *buying long*. But not all stocks increase in value. In fact, the value of a stock may decrease for many reasons, including lower sales, lower profits, reduced dividends, product failures, increased competition, and product liability lawsuits. With this fact in mind, you may use a procedure called *selling short* to make money when the value of a stock is expected to decrease in value. **Selling short** is selling stock that has been borrowed from a brokerage firm and must be replaced at a later date. When you sell short, you sell today, knowing you must buy or *cover* your short transaction at a later date. To make money in a short transaction, you must take these steps:

selling short Selling stock that has been borrowed from a brokerage firm and must be replaced at a later date.

1. Arrange to *borrow a stock certificate* for a certain number of shares of a particular stock from a brokerage firm.
2. *Sell the borrowed* stock, assuming it will drop in value in a reasonably short period of time.
3. *Buy the stock at a lower price* than the price it sold for in step 2.
4. Use the stock purchased in step 3 to *replace the stock borrowed from the brokerage firm* in step 1.

When selling short, your profit is the difference between the amount received when the stock is sold in step 2 and the amount paid for the stock in step 3. For example, assume that you think Walt Disney stock is overvalued at $35 a share. You also believe the stock will *decrease* in value over the next four to six months. You call your broker and arrange to borrow 100 shares of Walt Disney stock (step 1). The broker then sells your borrowed Disney stock for you at the current market price of $35 a share (step 2). Also assume that four months later Disney stock drops to $27 a share. You instruct your broker to purchase 100 shares of Disney stock at the current lower price (step 3). The newly purchased Disney stock is given to the brokerage firm to repay the borrowed stock (step 4). In this example, you made $800 profit by selling short ($3,500 selling price − $2,700 purchase price = $800 profit). Remember, the $800 profit must be reduced by the commissions you paid to the broker for buying and selling the Disney stock.

There is usually no special or extra brokerage charge for selling short, since the brokerage firm receives its regular commission when the stock is bought and sold. Before selling short, consider two factors. First, since the stock you borrow from your broker is actually owned by another investor, you must pay any dividends the stock earns before you replace the stock. After all, you borrowed the stock and then sold the borrowed stock. Eventually, dividends can absorb the profits from your short transaction if the price of the stock does not decrease rapidly enough. Second, to make money selling short, you must be correct in predicting that a stock will decrease in value. If the value of the stock increases, you lose.

Apply *Yourself!*

Objective 5

In a short paragraph, describe why you would use a long-term technique or a short-term technique to achieve your investment goals.

option The right to buy or sell a stock at a predetermined price during a specified period of time.

TRADING IN OPTIONS An **option** gives you the right to buy or sell a stock at a predetermined price during a specified period of time. Options are usually available for three-, six-, or nine-month periods. If you think the market price of a stock will increase during a short period of time, you may decide to purchase a call option. A *call option* is sold by a stockholder and gives the purchaser the right to *buy* 100 shares of a stock at a guaranteed price before a specified expiration date. With a call option, the purchaser is betting that the price of the stock will increase in value before the expiration date.

It is also possible to purchase a put option. A *put option* is the right to sell 100 shares of a stock at a guaranteed price before a specified expiration date. With a put option, the purchaser is betting that the price of the stock will decrease in value before the expiration date. If these price movements do not occur before the expiration date, you lose the money you paid for your call or put option.

Because of the increased risk involved in option trading, a more detailed discussion of how you profit or lose money with options is beyond the scope of this book. *Be warned:* Amateurs and beginning investors should stay away from options unless they fully understand all of the risks involved. For the rookie, the lure of large profits over a short period of time may be tempting, but the risks are real.

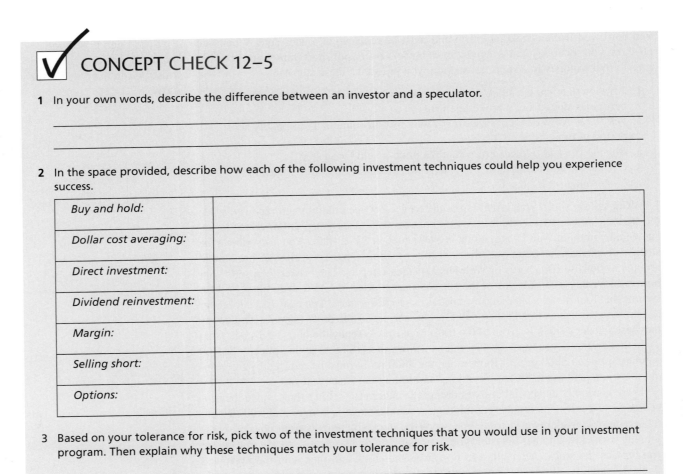

✓ CONCEPT CHECK 12–5

1 In your own words, describe the difference between an investor and a speculator.

_____

_____

2 In the space provided, describe how each of the following investment techniques could help you experience success.

Buy and hold:	
Dollar cost averaging:	
Direct investment:	
Dividend reinvestment:	
Margin:	
Selling short:	
Options:	

3 Based on your tolerance for risk, pick two of the investment techniques that you would use in your investment program. Then explain why these techniques match your tolerance for risk.

_____

_____

back to *Getting Personal*

1. Reconsider your responses to the Getting Personal questions at the beginning of the chapter. Have any of your answers changed as a result of studying this chapter?

_____

_____

2. In your own words, describe why corporations sell stock to obtain financing. Why do investors purchase stock?

_____

_____

3. Why should an investor evaluate a stock investment?

_____

_____

4. Why is it important for your investment portfolio to include some growth stocks?

_____

_____

5. A number of different long-term and short-term investment techniques were described in this chapter. Indicate below which techniques you would use to obtain your investment goals. Then explain why you made each decision.

Investment Technique	Long-Term or Short-Term Technique	Would I Use This Technique?	Explanation for My Choice
Buy and hold			
Dollar cost averaging			
Direct investment			
Dividend reinvestment			
Margin			
Selling short			
Options			

www.mhhe.com/kdh

Chapter Summary

Objective 1   Corporations sell stock (a form of equity) to finance their business start-up costs and help pay for their ongoing business activities. In return for providing the money needed to finance the corporation, stockholders have the right to elect the board of directors. They must also approve major changes to corporate policies.

People invest in stock because of dividend income, appreciation of value, and the *possibility* of gain through stock splits. In addition to common stock, a few corporations may issue preferred stock. The most important priority an investor in preferred stock enjoys is receiving cash dividends before any cash dividends are paid to common stockholders. Still, dividend distributions to both preferred and common stockholders must be approved by the board of directors.

Objective 2   A wealth of information is available to stock investors. A logical place to start the evaluation process is with the classification of different types of stock investments that range from very conservative to very speculative—see Exhibit 12–3. Today, many investors use the information available on the Internet to evaluate individual stocks. Information is also available from professional advisory services, the newspaper, business and personal finance periodicals, and government publications.

Objective 3   Many analysts believe that a corporation's ability or inability to generate earnings in the future may be one of the most significant factors that account for an increase or decrease in the value of a stock. Generally, higher earnings equate to higher stock value, and lower earnings equate to lower stock value. In addition to the total amount of earnings reported by the corporation, investors can calculate earnings per share and a price-earnings ratio to evaluate a stock investment. Whereas both earnings per share and price-earnings ratio are historical numbers based on what a corporation has already done, investors can obtain earnings estimates for most corporations. Other calculations that help evaluate stock investments include dividend yield, total return, and book value.

Objective 4   A corporation may sell a new stock issue with the help of an investment banking firm. Once the stock has been sold in the primary market, it can be sold time and again in the secondary market. In the secondary market, investors purchase stock listed on a securities exchange or traded in the over-the-counter market. Many securities transactions are made through an account executive who works for a full-service brokerage firm, but a growing number of investors are using a discount brokerage firm or are completing security transactions online. Whether you trade online or not, you must decide if you want to use a market, limit, or stop order to buy or sell stock. Most brokerage firms charge a minimum commission for buying or selling stock. Additional commission charges are based on the number and value of the stock shares bought or sold and if you use a full-service or discount broker or trade online.

Objective 5   Purchased stock may be classified as either a long-term investment or a speculative investment. Long-term investors typically hold their investments for at least a year or longer; speculators (sometimes referred to as traders) usually sell their investments within a shorter time period. Traditional trading techniques long-term investors use include the buy-and-hold technique, dollar cost averaging, direct investment plans, and dividend reinvestment plans. More speculative techniques include buying on margin, selling short, and trading in options.

Key Terms

account executive   389
book value   386
churning   389
common stock   372
direct investment plan   394
dividend   372
dividend reinvestment plan   394
dividend yield   386
dollar cost averaging   393
earnings per share   384
equity financing   372

initial public offering (IPO)   388
investment bank   387
limit order   391
margin   394
market order   391
Nasdaq   388
option   396
over-the-counter (OTC) market   388
par value   376
preferred stock   376
price-earnings (PE) ratio   384

primary market   387
proxy   372
record date   373
secondary market   388
securities exchange   388
selling short   395
specialist   388
stock split   375
stop order   391
total return   386

Problems

1. Jamie and Peter Dawson own 250 shares of IBM common stock. IBM's quarterly dividend is $0.30 per share. What is the amount of the dividend check the Dawson couple will receive for this quarter?

2. During the four quarters for 2009, the Browns received two quarterly dividend payments of $0.18, one quarterly payment of $0.20, and one quarterly payment of $0.22. If they owned 200 shares of stock, what was their total dividend income for 2009?

3. Jim Johansen noticed that a corporation he is considering investing in is about to pay a quarterly dividend. The record date is March 15. In order for Jim to receive this quarterly dividend what is the last date that he could purchase stock in this corporation and receive this quarter's dividend payment?

4. Sarah and James Hernandez purchased 100 shares of Cisco Systems stock at $18.50 a share. One year later, they sold the stock for $26.35 a share. She paid a broker a $32 commission when she purchased the stock and a $40 commission when she sold the stock. During the 12-month period the couple owned the stock, Cisco Systems paid no dividends. Calculate the Hernandez's total return for this investment.

5. Wanda Sotheby purchased 150 shares of Home Depot stock at $32.25 a share. One year later, she sold the stock for $40.10 a share. She paid her broker a $34 commission when she purchased the stock and a $42 commission when she sold it. During the 12 months she owned the stock, she received $135 in dividends. Calculate Wanda's total return on this investment.

6. Wallace Davis purchased 200 shares of Ford stock at $9.50 a share. One year later, he sold the stock for $8.42 a share. He paid his broker a $22 commission when he purchased the stock and a $24 commission when he sold it. During the 12 months he owned the stock, he received $40 in dividends. Calculate Wallace's total return on this investment.

7. In September, stockholders of Chaparral Steel approved a 2-for-1 stock split. After the split, how many shares of Chaparral Steel stock will an investor have if he or she owned 360 shares before the split?

8. Bill Martin owns Ohio Utility preferred stock. If this preferred stock issue pays 3.5 percent based on a par value of $50, what is the dollar amount of the dividend for one share of Ohio Utility?

9. As a stockholder of Kentucky Gas and Oil, you receive its annual report. In the financial statements, the firm reported after-tax earnings of $1,200,000 and has issued 1,500,000 shares of common stock. The stock is currently selling for $24 a share.
   a. Calculate the earnings per share for Kentucky Gas and Oil.

   b. Calculate the price-earnings (PE) ratio for Kentucky Gas and Oil.

10. Michelle Townsend owns stock in National Computers. Based on information in its annual report, National Computers reported after-tax earnings of $4,850,000 and has issued 3,500,000 shares of common stock. The stock is currently selling for $32 a share.
    a. Calculate the earnings per share for National Computers.

    b. Calculate the price-earnings (PE) ratio for National Computers.

11. Analysts for Citigroup, one of the nation's largest providers of financial services, estimate that Citigroup's earnings per share will increase from $4.49 in the current year to $4.97 next year.
    a. What is the amount of the increase?

    b. What effect, if any, should this increase have on the value of the corporation's stock?

12. Currently, Johnson & Johnson pays an annual dividend of $1.50. If the stock is selling for $68, what is the dividend yield?

www.mhhe.com/kdh

13. Casper Energy Exploration reports that the corporation's assets are valued at $185,000,000, its liabilities are $80,000,000, and it has issued 6,000,000 shares of stock. What is the book value for a share of Casper stock?

14. For four years, Marty Campbell invested $4,000 each year in Newsome Golf Apparel. The stock was selling for $32 in 2005, $45 in 2006, $35 in 2007, and $50 in 2008.
    a. What is Marty's total investment in Newsome Golf?

    b. After four years, how many shares does Marty own?

    c. What is the average cost per share of Marty's investment?

15. Bob Orleans invested $3,000 and borrowed $3,000 to purchase shares in Verizon Communications. At the time of his investment, Verizon was selling for $30 a share.
    a. If Bob paid a $30 commission, how many shares could he buy if he used *only* his own money and did not use margin?

    b. If Bob paid a $60 commission, how many shares could he buy if he used his $3,000 and borrowed $3,000 on margin to buy Verizon stock?

    c. Assuming Bob did use margin, paid a $60 total commission to buy his Verizon stock and another $60 to sell his stock, and sold the stock for $39 a share, how much profit did he make on his Verizon stock investment?

16. After researching General Motors common stock, Sandra Pearson is convinced the stock is overpriced. She contacts her account executive and arranges to sell short 200 shares of General Motors. At the time of the sale, a share of common stock has a value of $32. Three months later, General Motors is selling for $23 a share, and Sandra instructs her broker to cover her short transaction. Total commissions to buy and sell the stock were $65. What is her profit for this short transaction?

Questions

1. Why would a corporation sell common or preferred stock to raise equity financing?

2. In your own words, describe how an investment in common stock could help you obtain your investment goals.

3. What is the difference between common and preferred stock? What type of investor would invest in preferred stock?

4. Assume you have $5,000 to invest and that you are trying to decide between investing in Ford Motor Company or Coca-Cola. Describe how the Internet could help you decide which investment is the right one for you. What other sources of information could help you evaluate these companies?

5. Explain the relationship between earnings per share, projected earnings, and the market value for a stock.

6. What is the difference between the dividend yield and total return calculations that were described in this chapter?

7. Stock can be sold in the primary market or the secondary market. What is the difference between these two markets?

8. Explain the difference between a securities exchange and the over-the-counter market.

9. Prepare a list of questions you could use to interview an account executive about career opportunities in the field of finance and investments.

10. Today, you can use a full-service brokerage firm, a discount brokerage firm, or trade online to buy and sell stocks. Which type of brokerage firm would you use? Justify your answer.

11. Prepare a chart that describes the similarities and differences among the buy-and-hold investment technique, dollar cost averaging, direct investment, and dividend reinvestment.

12. Why would a speculator use margin? Why would a speculator sell short?

Internet Connection

RESEARCHING STOCK INVESTMENTS

Visit the following Web sites and describe the type of information provided by each site.

Sponsor	Web Site	Type of Information	How Could This Site Help Me Invest?
SmartMoney	www.smartmoney.com		
Motley Fool	www.fool.com		
Nasdaq	www.nasdaq.com		
New York Stock Exchange	www.nyse.com		
Yahoo! Finance	http://finance.yahoo.com		

Case in Point

RESEARCH INFORMATION AVAILABLE FROM MERGENT

This chapter stressed the importance of evaluating potential investments. Now it's your turn to try your skill at evaluating a potential investment in PepsiCo, Inc. Assume you could invest $10,000 in the common stock of this company. To help you evaluate this potential investment, carefully examine Exhibit 12–6, which reproduces the research report on PepsiCo from *Mergent's Handbook of Common Stocks*. The report was published in the summer of 2006.

Questions

1. Based on the research provided by Mergent, would you buy PepsiCo stock? Justify your answer.

2. What other investment information would you need to evaluate PepsiCo common stock? Where would you obtain this information?

www.mhhe.com/kdh

3. On January 26, 2007, PepsiCo common stock was selling for $64.45 a share. Using the Internet or a newspaper, determine the current price for a share of PepsiCo. Based on this information, would your PepsiCo investment have been profitable? (*Hint:* PepsiCo stock is listed on the New York Stock Exchange and its stock symbol is PEP.)

4. Assuming you purchased PepsiCo stock on January 26, 2007, and based on your answer to question 3, how would you decide if you want to hold or sell your PepsiCo stock? Explain your answer.

Continuing Case

STOCK INVESTMENTS

Life Situation

Pam, 43

Josh, 45

Children ages 16, 14, and 11

Financial Data

Monthly income $4,900

Assets $262,700

Liabilities $84,600

Living expenses $4,450

Emergency fund $5,000

As previously noted, the Brocks have some of their investment portfolio in conservative stocks. These equities have had very slow growth while regularly paying a small dividend.

Pam and Josh have received several e-mails recently with suggestions about various biotechnology, retailing, and environmental companies. The investment advisers believe that these industries would provide an opportunity for strong long-term financial gains.

Questions

1. According to Pam, "We both know we should have started our investment program sooner, but we always seemed to have 'emergencies' that took what extra money we had." To what extent should the Brocks invest in stocks as a major portion of their investment portfolio?

2. Research the industries recommended by the investment advisers. What are some industries and specific stocks you would recommend for the Brocks?

3. How might *Your Personal Financial Plan* sheets 38 and 39 be useful to the Brocks?

Video Case

SAFER STOCKS

For stock investors, the goal is to find investments that offer low risk and high returns. And while it may be impossible to find the "perfect" investment, factors like market share, strong competitive advantage, and even patent protection for a firm's products may improve a stock's performance in both a down market and an up market.

Questions

1. Investors are often tempted to ignore the risk factor and choose investments that offer higher returns. Describe why this may be a flawed approach—especially when the stock market is declining.

2. What specific factors make corporations like Wrigley, Wal-Mart, and Johnson & Johnson attractive investments for both a down and an up market?

3. Internet Web sites like MSN (http://moneycentral.msn.com/investor/finder/customstocksdl.asp) provide a stock screener to help you research specific stocks. Take a look at the MSN site or a similar site and describe how using a stock screener could help you choose better stock investments.

Spending Diary

"INVESTING IN STOCK IS NOT POSSIBLE. I'M BARELY ABLE TO PAY MY VARIOUS LIVING EXPENSES."

Directions

Your Daily Spending Diary will help you manage your expenses to create a better overall spending plan. Once you know and try to control your spending, you will likely be able to have funds available for various types of investments.

Questions

1. What information from your daily spending records help you better achieve financial goals?

2. Based on your observations of our society and the economy, what types of stocks might you consider for investing now or in the near future?

Evaluating Corporate Stocks

Financial Planning Activities: No checklist can serve as a foolproof guide for choosing a common or preferred stock. However, the following questions will help you evaluate a potential stock investment. Use stock Web sites on the Internet and/or use library materials to answer these questions about a corporate stock that you believe could help you obtain your investment goals.

Suggested Web Sites: http://finance.yahoo.com   www.smartmoney.com

Category 1: The Basics

1. What is the corporation's name? _____
_____

2. What are the corporation's address and telephone number? _____
_____

3. Have you requested the latest annual report and quarterly report?   ☐ Yes ☐ No

4. What information about the corporation is available on the Internet? _____
_____

5. Where is the stock traded? _____
_____

6. What types of products or services does this firm provide? _____
_____

7. Briefly describe the prospects for this company. (Include significant factors like product development, plans for expansion, plans for mergers, etc.)
_____

Category 2: Dividend Income

8. Is the corporation currently paying dividends? If so, how much? _____
_____

9. What is the dividend yield for this stock? _____
_____

10. Has the dividend payout increased or decreased over the past three years? _____
_____

11. How does the yield for this investment compare with those for other potential investments?
_____

Category 3: Financial Performance

12. What are the firm's earnings per share for the last year? _____
_____

13. Have the firm's earnings increased over the past three years? _____
_____

14. What is the firm's current price-earnings ratio?
_____

15. How does the firm's current price-earnings ratio compare with firms in the same industry?
_____

16. Describe trends for the firm's price-earnings ratio over the past three years. Do these trends show improvement (lower PE ratio) or decline in investment value (higher PE ratio)?
_____

17. What are the firm's projected earnings for the next year? _____
_____

18. Have sales increased over the last five years? _____
_____

19. What is the stock's current price? _____
_____

20. What are the 52-week high and low for this stock?
_____

21. Do the analysts indicate that this is a good time to invest in this stock? _____
_____

22. Briefly describe any other information that you obtained from Mergent, Value Line, Standard & Poor's, or other sources of information.
_____
_____

A Word of Caution

When you use a checklist, there is always a danger of overlooking important relevant information. Quite simply, it is a place to start only. If you need other information, *you* are responsible for obtaining it and for determining how it affects your potential investment.

What's Next for Your Personal Financial Plan?

- Identify additional factors that may affect your decision to invest in this corporation's stock.
- Develop a plan for monitoring an investment's value once a stock(s) is purchased.

Name: _____ **Date:** _____

Investment Broker Comparison

Financial Planning Activities: To compare the benefits and costs of different investment brokers, compare the services of an investment broker based on the factors listed below.

Suggested Web Sites: www.scottrade.com   www.placeatrade.com

	Broker Number 1	Broker Number 2
Broker's name		
Brokerage firm		
Address		
Phone		
Web site		
Years of experience		
Education and training		
Areas of specialization		
Certifications and licenses held		
Employer's stock exchange and financial market affiliations		
Information services offered		
Minimum commission charge		
Commission on 100 shares of stock at $50/share		
Fees for other investments: • Corporate bonds • Government bonds • Mutual funds		
Other fees: • Annual account fee • Inactivity fee • Other		

What's Next for Your Personal Financial Plan?

- Using the information you obtained, choose a brokerage firm that you feel will help you attain your investment goals.
- Access the Web site for the brokerage firm you have chosen and answer the questions on page 390 in your text.

13 Investing in Mutual Funds

Getting Personal

Why invest in mutual funds? For each of the following statements, select "yes" or "no" to indicate your behavior regarding these investment activities.

	Yes	No
1. I understand the reasons investors choose mutual funds.	____	____
2. I understand the different charges and fees associated with mutual fund investments.	____	____
3. I can identify the types of mutual funds that will help me achieve my investment goals.	____	____
4. I know how to evaluate a mutual fund.	____	____
5. I understand the purchase and withdrawal options for mutual funds.	____	____

After studying this chapter, you will be asked to reconsider your responses to these questions.

Objectives

In this chapter, you will learn to:

1. Describe the characteristics of mutual fund investments.
2. Classify mutual funds by investment objective.
3. Evaluate mutual funds.
4. Describe how and why mutual funds are bought and sold.

Why is this important?

For many investors, mutual funds have become the investment of choice. Yet even though mutual funds offer professional management and diversification, investors still need to evaluate mutual funds before investing their money.

mutual fund An investment chosen by people who pool their money to buy stocks, bonds, and other financial securities selected by professional managers who work for an investment company.

investment company An organization that invests the pooled shareholder dollars in securities appropriate to the organization's investment objective.

If you ever thought about buying stocks or bonds but decided not to, your reasons were probably like most other people's: You didn't know enough to make a good decision, and you lacked enough money to diversify your investments among several choices. These same two reasons explain why people invest in mutual funds. By pooling your money with money from other investors, a mutual fund can do for you what you can't do on your own. Specifically, a **mutual fund** is an investment chosen by people who pool their money to buy stocks, bonds, and other financial securities selected by professional managers who work for investment companies. The Investment Company Institute defines an **investment company** as an organization that invests the pooled shareholder dollars in securities appropriate to the organization's investment objective.[1] Mutual funds are an excellent choice for many individuals. In many cases, they can also be used for retirement accounts, including traditional individual retirement accounts, Roth IRAs, and 401(k) and 403(b) retirement accounts. For example, many employees contribute a portion of their salary to a 401(k) retirement account. And in many cases, the employer matches the employee's contribution. A common match would work like this: For every $1.00 the employee invests, the employer contributes an additional $0.50. All monies—both the employee's and employer's contributions—are often invested in mutual funds that are selected by the employee. *Hint:* During a job interview, ask the prospective employer about the firm's 401(k) plan and what investment options are available for retirement funds.

An investment in mutual funds is based on the concept of opportunity costs, which we have discussed throughout this text. Simply put, you have to be willing to take some chances if you want to get larger returns on your investments. Before deciding whether mutual funds are the right investment for you, read the material presented in the next section.

[1]Investment Company Institute Web site (www.ici.org), accessed February 14, 2007, Investment Company Institute, 1401 H Street, NW, Washington, DC 20005.

Why Investors Purchase Mutual Funds

The following statistics illustrate how important mutual fund investments are to both individuals and the nation's economy:

1. An estimated 91 million individuals own mutual funds in the United States.[2]
2. The number of funds grew from 361 in 1970 to over 9,200 in 2005.[3]
3. The combined value of assets owned by investment companies in the United States totals $9.5 trillion.[4]

No doubt about it, the mutual fund industry is big business. And yet, you may be wondering why so many people invest in mutual funds.

The major reasons investors purchase mutual funds are *professional management* and *diversification.* Most investment companies do everything possible to convince you that they can do a better job of picking securities than you can. Sometimes these claims are true, and sometimes they are just so much hot air. Still, investment companies do have professional fund managers with years of experience who devote large amounts of time to picking just the "right" securities for their funds' portfolios. *Be warned:* Even the best portfolio managers make mistakes. So you, the investor, must be careful!

The diversification mutual funds offer spells safety, because an occasional loss incurred with one investment contained in a mutual fund is usually offset by gains from other investments in the fund. For example, consider the diversification provided in the portfolio of the AIM Basic Value Fund, shown in Exhibit 13–1. An investment in the $5 billion AIM Basic Value Fund represents ownership in at least 10 different industries, as seen at the top of Exhibit 13–1. In addition, the companies in the fund's portfolio, as seen at the bottom of the exhibit, offer long-term earnings potential. With a total of almost 50 different companies included in the fund's investment portfolio, investors enjoy diversification coupled with AIM's stock-selection expertise. For beginning investors or investors without a great deal of money to invest, the diversification offered by funds is especially important because there is no other practical way to purchase the individual stocks issued by a large number of corporations. A mutual fund like the AIM Basic Value fund, on the other hand, can provide a practical way for investors to obtain diversification because the fund can use the pooled funds of a large number of investors to purchase a large number of shares of many different companies.

Characteristics of Mutual Funds

Today mutual funds may be classified as closed-end funds, exchange-traded funds, or open-end funds.

CLOSED-END, EXCHANGE-TRADED, OR OPEN-END MUTUAL FUNDS

closed-end fund A mutual fund whose shares are issued by an investment company only when the fund is organized.

Approximately 7 percent of all mutual funds are closed-end funds offered by investment companies. A **closed-end fund** is a mutual fund whose shares are issued by an investment company only when the fund is organized. As a result, only a certain number of shares are available to investors. After all the shares originally issued have been sold, an investor can purchase shares only from another investor who is willing to sell. Closed-end funds are actively managed by professional fund managers and shares are traded on the floors of stock exchanges, including the New York Stock Exchange, or in the over-the-counter market (Nasdaq). Like the prices of stocks, the prices of shares for closed-end funds are determined by the factors of supply and demand, by the

[2]Ibid.
[3]Ibid.
[4]Ibid.

Top Ten Industries* as of 12/31/2006	
1 Pharmaceuticals	7.58%
2 Other diversified financial services	6.69
3 Industrial conglomerates	6.63
4 Advertising	6.31
5 Investment banking and brokerage	5.27
6 Data processing and outsourced services	4.63
7 Systems software	4.44
8 Oil and gas equipment and services	4.21
9 Managed health care	4.18
10 Health care distributors	4.15

Top Ten Equity Holdings as of 12/31/2006	
1 Unitedhealth Group Inc.	4.18%
2 Tyco Intl Ltd.	4.02
3 JPMorgan Chase & Co.	3.85
4 Cardinal Health Inc.	3.68
5 Fannie Mae	3.43
6 Cemex Sab de CV Adr.	3.22
7 Interpublic Group Co. Inc.	3.20
8 Omnicom Group Inc.	3.11
9 Target Corp.	2.89
10 Dell Inc.	2.86

Holdings are subject to change.

Source: The AIM Investments Company Web site (www.aiminvestments.com), accessed February 14, 2007, AIM Investment Services, Inc., 11 Greenway Plaza, Suite 100, Houston, TX 77046.

value of stocks and other investments contained in the fund's portfolio, and by investor expectations. A special section of *The Wall Street Journal* provides information about closed-end funds.

An **exchange-traded fund (ETF)** is a fund that invests in the stocks contained in a specific stock index, like the Standard & Poor's 500 stock index, the Dow Jones Industrial Average, or the Nasdaq Composite index, and whose shares are traded on a stock exchange or over the counter. With both a closed-end fund and an exchange-traded fund, an investor can purchase as little as one share of a fund, because both types are traded on a stock exchange or over-the-counter market like individual corporate stock issues. Although exchange-traded funds are similar to closed-end funds, there is an important difference. Most closed-end funds are actively managed, with portfolio managers making the selection of stocks and other securities contained in a closed-end fund. An exchange-traded fund, on the other hand, invests in the stocks included in a specific stock index. Exchange-traded funds tend to mirror the performance of the index, moving up or down as the individual stocks contained in the index move up or down. Therefore, there is less need for a portfolio manager to make investment decisions. Because of passive management,

exchange-traded fund (ETF) A fund that invests in the stocks contained in a specific stock index, like the Standard & Poor's 500 stock index, and whose shares are traded on a stock exchange or over the counter.

fees associated with owning shares are generally lower than those of both closed-end and open-end funds. In addition to lower fees, other advantages to investing in ETFs include.

- No minimum investment amount, because shares are traded on an exchange and not purchased from an investment company, which often requires a minimum investment of $500, $1,000, or more.
- Shares can be bought or sold through a broker or online any time during regular market hours at the current price. With mutual funds, the price you pay for shares or the price you receive when you sell shares is calculated once a day—usually at the end of the trading day.
- You can use limit orders and the more speculative techniques of selling short and margin—all discussed in Chapter 12—to buy and sell ETF shares.

Although increasing in popularity, there are only about 200 exchange-traded funds. Like closed-end funds, ETFs are reported in a special section of *The Wall Street Journal.*

open-end fund A mutual fund whose shares are issued and redeemed by the investment company at the request of investors.

Approximately 90 percent of all mutual funds are open-end funds. An **open-end fund** is a mutual fund whose shares are issued and redeemed by the investment company at the request of investors. Investors are free to buy and sell shares at the net asset value. The **net asset value (NAV)** per share is equal to the current market value of securities contained in the mutual fund's portfolio minus the mutual fund's liabilities divided by the number of shares outstanding:

net asset value (NAV) The current market value of the securities contained in the mutual fund's portfolio minus the mutual fund's liabilities divided by the number of shares outstanding.

$$\text{Net asset value} = \frac{\text{Value of the fund's portfolio} - \text{Liabilities}}{\text{Number of shares outstanding}}$$

For example, assume the portfolio of all investments contained in the New American Frontiers Mutual Fund has a current market value of $975 million. The fund also has liabilities totaling $10 million. If this mutual fund has 20 million shares outstanding, the net asset value per share is $48.25:

$$\text{Net asset value} = \frac{\text{Value of the fund's portfolio} - \text{Liabilities}}{\text{Number of shares outstanding}}$$

$$= \frac{\$975 \text{ million} - \$10 \text{ million}}{20 \text{ million shares}}$$

$$= \$48.25 \text{ per share}$$

For most mutual funds, the net asset value is calculated at the close of trading each day.

In addition to buying and selling shares on request, most open-end funds provide their investors with a wide variety of services, including payroll deduction programs, automatic reinvestment programs, automatic withdrawal programs, and the option to change shares in one fund to another fund within the same fund family—all topics discussed later in this chapter.

COST: LOAD FUNDS COMPARED TO NO-LOAD FUNDS
Before investing in mutual funds, you should compare the cost of this type of investment with the cost of other investment alternatives, such as stocks or bonds. With regard to cost, mutual funds are classified as load funds or no-load funds. A **load fund** (sometimes referred to as an *A fund*) is a mutual fund in which investors pay a commission every time they purchase shares. The commission, often referred to as the *sales charge,* may be as high as 8.5 percent of the purchase price for investments under $10,000. (Typically, this fee declines for investments over $10,000.)

load fund A mutual fund in which investors pay a commission (as high as 8.5 percent) every time they purchase shares.

Many exceptions exist, but the average load charge for mutual funds is between 3 and 5 percent. Let's assume you decide to invest $10,000 in the Davis Opportunity mutual fund. This fund charges a sales load of 4.75 percent that you must pay when you purchase shares. The dollar amount of the sales charge on your $10,000 investment is \$475 (\$10,000 $\times$ 4.75% = \$475). After paying the \$475, the amount available for investment is reduced to \$9,525 (\$10,000 − \$475 = \$9,525). Typically, load funds must be purchased through brokerage firms or registered representatives. The "stated" advantage of a load fund is that the fund's sales force (account executives, financial planners, or brokerage divisions of banks and other financial institutions) will explain the mutual fund to investors, help determine which fund will help investors achieve their financial objective, and offer advice as to when shares of the fund should be bought or sold.

A **no-load fund** is a mutual fund in which the individual investor pays no sales charge. No-load funds don't charge commissions when you buy shares because they have no salespeople. If you want to buy shares of a no-load fund, you must make your own decisions and deal directly with the investment company. The usual means of contact is by telephone, the Internet, or mail. You can also purchase shares in a no-load fund from many discount brokers, including Charles Schwab, Ameritrade, and E*Trade.

no-load fund A mutual fund in which the individual investor pays no sales charge.

As an investor, you must decide whether to invest in a load fund or a no-load fund. Some investment salespeople have claimed that load funds outperform no-load funds. But many financial analysts suggest there is generally no significant difference between mutual funds that charge commissions and those that do not.[5] *Since no-load funds offer the same investment opportunities load funds offer, you should investigate them further before deciding which type of mutual fund is best for you.* Although the sales commission should not be the decisive factor, the possibility of saving a sales commission of up to 8.5 percent is a factor to consider.

Instead of charging investors a fee when they purchase shares in a mutual fund, some mutual funds charge a **contingent deferred sales load** (sometimes referred to as a *back-end load,* a *B fund,* or a *redemption fee*). These fees range from 1 to 5 percent, depending on how long you own the mutual fund before making a withdrawal. For example, assume you withdraw \$5,000 from B shares that you own in the Franklin Growth mutual fund within a year of your original purchase date. You must pay a 4 percent contingent deferred sales fee. Your fee is \$200 (\$5,000 $\times$ 4% = \$200). After the fee is deducted from your \$5,000 withdrawal, you will receive \$4,800 (\$5,000 − \$200 = \$4,800). *Generally,* the contingent deferred sales load declines until there is no withdrawal charge if you own the shares in the fund for more than five years.

contingent deferred sales load A 1 to 5 percent charge that shareholders pay when they withdraw their investment from a mutual fund.

COSTS: MANAGEMENT FEES AND OTHER CHARGES   In evaluating a specific mutual fund, you should consider ongoing management fees and a number of other charges. Fees are important because they reduce your investment return and are a major factor to consider when choosing a mutual fund. The investment companies that sponsor mutual funds charge management fees. This fee, which is disclosed in the fund's prospectus, is a fixed percentage of the fund's net asset value on a predetermined date. Today annual management fees range between 0.25 and 1.5 percent of the fund's net asset value. While fees vary considerably, the average is 0.5 to 1 percent of the fund's net asset value.

The investment company may also levy a **12b-1 fee** (sometimes referred to as a *distribution fee*) to defray the costs of advertising and marketing a mutual fund and commissions paid to a broker who sold you shares in the mutual fund. Approved by the Securities and Exchange Commission, annual 12b-1 fees are calculated on the value of a fund's assets and cannot exceed 1 percent of a fund's assets per year. *Note:* For a fund to be called a "no-load" fund, its 12b-1 fee must not exceed 0.25 percent of its assets.

12b-1 fee A fee that an investment company levies to defray the costs of advertising and marketing a mutual fund.

Unlike the one-time sales load fees that mutual funds charge to purchase or sell shares, the 12b-1 fee is often an ongoing fee that is charged on an annual basis. Note that 12b-1 fees can cost you a lot of money over a period of years. Assuming there is no difference in performance offered by two different mutual funds, one of which charges a 12b-1 fee while the other doesn't, choose the latter fund. The 12b-1 fee is so lucrative

[5]The Investopedia Web site (www.investopedia.com), accessed February 15, 2007, Investopedia, Inc., Suite 605, 10080 Jasper Avenue, Edmonton, Alberta T5J1V9.

expense ratio The amount that investors pay for all of a mutual fund's management fees and operating costs.

for investment companies that a number of them have begun selling Class C shares that charge a higher 12b-1 fee and no sales load or contingent deferred sales fee to attract new investors. When compared to Class A shares (commissions charged when shares are purchased) and Class B shares (commissions charged when withdrawals are made over the first five years), Class C shares, with their ongoing, higher 12b-1 fees, may be more expensive over a long period of time.

Together, all the different management fees and fund operating costs are often referred to as an **expense ratio.** Since it is important to keep fees and costs as low as possible, you should examine a fund's expense ratio as one more fact to consider when evaluating a mutual fund.

CAUTION!

Many financial planners recommend that you choose a mutual fund with an expense ratio of 1 percent or less.

By now, you are probably asking yourself, "Should I purchase Class A shares, Class B shares, or Class C shares?" There are no easy answers, but your professional financial adviser or broker can help you determine which class of shares of a particular mutual fund best suits your financial needs. You can also do your own research to determine which fund is right for you. Factors to consider include whether you want to invest in a load fund or no-load fund, management fees, and expense ratios. As you will see later in this chapter, a number of sources of information can help you evaluate investment decisions.

The investment company's prospectus must provide all details relating to management fees, sales fees, 12b-1 fees, and other expenses. Exhibit 13–2 reproduces the summary of expenses (sometimes called a *fee table*) taken from the Davis Opportunity Fund. Notice that this fee table has three separate parts. The first part describes shareholder transaction expenses. For this fund, the maximum sales charge is 4.75 percent. The second part describes the fund's annual operating expenses. For this fund, the expense ratio is 1.15 percent for Class A shares. The third part illustrates the total fees and expenses you would pay on a $10,000 investment, assuming a 5 percent annual return and redemption at the end of 1, 3, 5, and 10 years.

Exhibit 13–3 summarizes information for load charges, no-load charges, and Class A, Class B, and Class C shares. In addition, it reports typical management fees, contingent deferred sales loads, and 12b-1 charges.

Apply *Yourself!*

Objective 1

Use the Internet to find a fund you are interested in for investment purposes. Then determine the fund's load charge (if any), management fee, and expense ratio.

Classifications of Mutual Funds

OBJECTIVE 2
Classify mutual funds by investment objective.

The managers of mutual funds tailor their investment portfolios to the investment objectives of their customers. Usually a fund's objectives are plainly disclosed in its prospectus. For example, the objective and strategy of the Fidelity Capital Appreciation Mutual Fund are described as follows:

Objective
Seeks capital appreciation

Strategy
Normally invests primarily in common stocks of domestic and foreign issuers. Invests in either "growth" stocks or "value" stocks or both. Uses fundamental analysis of each issuer's financial condition and industry position and market and economic conditions to select instruments.[6]

---

[6]Fidelity Investments Web site (www.fidelity.com), accessed February 15, 2007, Fidelity Investments, Inc., 82 Devonshire St., Boston, MA 02109.

Exhibit 13–2   Summary of Expenses Paid to Invest in the Davis Opportunity Fund

	Class A Shares	Class B Shares	Class C Shares
Fees You May Pay As a Davis Funds Shareholder *paid directly from your investment*			
Maximum sales charge (load) imposed on purchases *as a percentage of offering price*	4.75%	None	None
Maximum deferred sales charge (load) imposed on redemptions *as a percentage of the lesser of the net asset value of the shares redeemed or the total cost of such shares*	0.75%	4.00%	1.00%
Maximum sales charge (load) imposed on reinvested dividends	None	None	None
Exchange fee	None	None	None
Davis Opportunity Fund Annual Operating Expenses *deducted from the fund's assets*			
Management fees	0.67%	0.67%	0.67%
Distribution (12b-1) fees	0.25%	1.00%	1.00%
Other expenses	0.23%	0.25%	0.24%
Total annual operating expenses	1.15%	1.92%	1.91%

Expenses may very in future years.

Expense Example

This example is intended to help you compare the cost of investing in the fund with the cost of investing in other mutual funds.

The example assumes that you invest $10,000 in the fund for the time periods indicated. The example also assumes that your investment has a 5% return each year and that the fund's operating expenses remain the same. Although your actual costs may be higher or lower, your costs, based on these assumptions, would be:

If You Sell Your Shares In . . .	1 Year	3 Years	5 Years	10 Years
Class A shares	$587	$823	$1,078	$1,806
Class B shares	$595	$903	$1,237	$2,043
Class C shares	$294	$600	$1,032	$2,233

If You Still Hold Your Shares after . . .	1 Year	3 Years	5 Years	10 Years
Class A shares	$587	$823	$1,078	$1,806
Class B shares	$195	$603	$1,037	$2,043
Class C shares	$194	$600	$1,032	$2,233

Note: Class B shares' expenses for the 10-year period include 2 years of Class A shares' expenses since Class B shares automatically convert to Class A shares after 8 years.

Source: Excerpted from the Davis Opportunity Fund Prospectus, Davis Funds Web site (www.davisfunds.com), accessed February 15, 2007, Davis Funds, P.O. Box 8406, Boston, MA 02266.

Exhibit 13–3

Typical Fees Associated with Mutual Fund Investments

Type of Fee or Charge	Customary Amount
Load fund	Up to 8.5 percent of the purchase.
No-load fund	No sales charge.
Contingent deferred sales load	1 to 5 percent of withdrawals, depending on how long you own shares in the fund before making a withdrawal.
Management fee	0.25 to 1.5 percent per year of the fund's net asset value on a predetermined date.
12b-1 fee	Cannot exceed 1 percent of the fund's assets per year.
Expense ratio	The amount investors pay for all fees and operating costs.
Class A shares	Commission charge when shares are purchased.
Class B shares	Commission charge when money is withdrawn during the first five years.
Class C shares	No commission to buy or sell shares of a fund, but higher, ongoing 12b-1 fees.

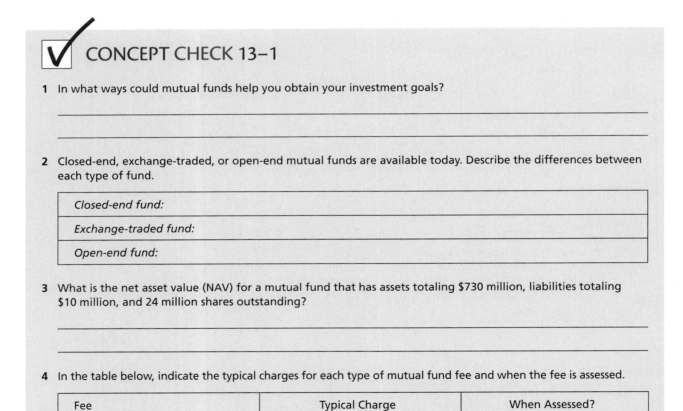

✓ CONCEPT CHECK 13–1

1 In what ways could mutual funds help you obtain your investment goals?

_____

_____

2 Closed-end, exchange-traded, or open-end mutual funds are available today. Describe the differences between each type of fund.

Closed-end fund:	
Exchange-traded fund:	
Open-end fund:	

3 What is the net asset value (NAV) for a mutual fund that has assets totaling $730 million, liabilities totaling $10 million, and 24 million shares outstanding?

_____

_____

4 In the table below, indicate the typical charges for each type of mutual fund fee and when the fee is assessed.

Fee	Typical Charge	When Assessed?
Load fund		
Contingent deferred sales load		
Management fee		
12b-1 fee		

5 What is an expense ratio? Why is it important?

_____

_____

Although categorizing over 9,200 funds may be helpful, note that different sources of investment information may use different categories for the same mutual fund. In most cases, the name of the category gives a pretty good clue to the types of investments included within the category. The *major* fund categories are described in alphabetical order as follows:

Stock Funds

- *Aggressive growth funds* seek rapid growth by purchasing stocks whose prices are expected to increase dramatically in a short period of time. Turnover within an aggressive growth fund is high because managers are buying and selling stocks of small, growth companies. Investors in these funds experience wide price swings because of the underlying speculative nature of the stocks in the fund's portfolio.
- *Equity income funds* invest in stocks issued by companies with a long history of paying dividends. The major objective of these funds is to provide income to shareholders. These funds are attractive investment choices for conservative or retired investors.
- *Global stock funds* invest in stocks of companies throughout the world, including the United States.
- *Growth funds* invest in companies expecting higher-than-average revenue and earnings growth. While similar to aggressive growth funds, growth funds tend to invest in larger, well-established companies. As a result, the prices for shares in a growth fund are less volatile compared to aggressive growth funds.
- *Index funds* invest in the same companies included in an index like the Standard & Poor's 500 stock index or Russell 3000 Index. Since fund managers pick the stocks issued by the companies included in the index, an index fund should provide approximately the same performance as the index. Also, since index funds are cheaper to manage, they often have lower management fees and expense ratios.
- *International funds* invest in foreign stocks sold in securities markets throughout the world; thus, if the economy in one region or nation is in a slump, profits can still be earned in others. Unlike global funds, which invest in stocks issued by companies in both foreign nations and the United States, a true international fund invests outside the United States.
- *Large-cap funds* invest in the stocks of companies with total capitalization of $5 billion or more. Large-capitalization stocks are generally stable, well-established companies and are likely to have minimal fluctuation in their value.
- *Lifecycle funds* (sometimes referred to as *lifestyle funds*) are popular with investors planning for retirement by a specific date. Typically, these funds

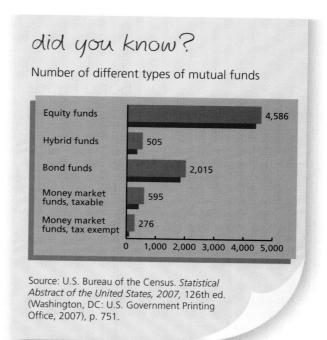

did you know?

Number of different types of mutual funds

Type	Number
Equity funds	4,586
Hybrid funds	505
Bond funds	2,015
Money market funds, taxable	595
Money market funds, tax exempt	276

Source: U.S. Bureau of the Census. *Statistical Abstract of the United States, 2007,* 126th ed. (Washington, DC: U.S. Government Printing Office, 2007), p. 751.

initially invest in more risk-oriented companies and become increasingly conservative and income oriented as the specified date approaches and investors are closer to retirement.

- *Midcap funds* invest in companies with total capitalization of $1 to $5 billion whose stocks offer more security than small-cap funds and more growth potential than funds that invest in large corporations.
- *Regional funds* seek to invest in stock traded within one specific region of the world, such as the European region, the Latin American region, and the Pacific region.
- *Sector funds* invest in companies within the same industry. Examples of sectors include Health and Biotech, Science & Technology, and Natural Resources.
- *Small-cap funds* invest in smaller, lesser-known companies with a total capitalization of less than $500 million. Because these companies are small and innovative, these funds offer higher growth potential. They are more speculative than funds that invest in larger, more established companies.
- *Socially responsible funds* avoid investing in companies that may cause harm to people, animals, and the environment. Typically, these funds do not invest in companies that produce tobacco, nuclear energy, or weapons or in companies that have a history of discrimination.

Bond Funds

- *High-yield (junk) bond funds* invest in high-yield, high-risk corporate bonds.
- *Intermediate corporate bond funds* invest in investment-grade corporate debt with maturities between 5 and 10 years.
- *Intermediate U.S. government bond funds* invest in U.S. Treasury securities with maturities between 5 and 10 years.
- *Long-term corporate bond funds* invest in investment-grade corporate bond issues with maturities in excess of 10 years.
- *Long-term (U.S.) government bond funds* invest in U.S. Treasury securities with maturities in excess of 10 years.
- *Municipal bond funds* invest in municipal bonds that provide investors with tax-free interest income.
- *Short-term corporate bond funds* invest in investment-grade bond issues with maturities between 1 and 5 years.
- *Short-term (U.S.) government bond funds* invest in U.S. Treasury issues with maturities between 1 and 5 years.

Apply *Yourself!*

Objective 2

Use *The Wall Street Journal, BusinessWeak,* or *Kiplinger's Personal Finance Magazine* to identify one stock fund, one bond fund, and a balanced fund or asset allocation fund.

Other Funds

- *Asset allocation funds* invest in various asset classes, including stocks, bonds, fixed-income securities, and money market instruments. These funds seek high total return by maintaining precise amounts within each type of asset.
- *Balanced funds* invest in both stocks and bonds with the primary objectives of conserving principal, providing income, and providing long-term growth. Often the percentage of stocks and bonds is stated in the fund's prospectus.
- *Money market funds* invest in certificates of deposit, government securities, and other safe and highly liquid investments.

family of funds A group of mutual funds managed by one investment company.

A **family of funds** exists when one investment company manages a group of mutual funds. Each fund within the family has a different financial objective. For instance, one fund may be a long-term government bond fund and another a growth stock fund. Most investment companies offer exchange privileges that enable shareholders to switch among the mutual funds in a fund family. For example, if you own shares in the Franklin growth fund, you may, at your discretion, switch to the Franklin income fund. Generally, investors may give instructions to switch from one fund to another within the same family in writing, over the telephone, or via the Internet. The family-of-funds concept allows shareholders to conveniently switch their investments among funds as different funds offer more potential, financial reward, or security. Charges for exchanges, if any, generally are small for each transaction. For funds that do charge, the fee may be as low as $5 per transaction.

✔ CONCEPT CHECK 13–2

1   How important is the investment objective as stated in a mutual fund's prospectus?

_____

_____

2   Identify one mutual fund in each of the three categories (stocks, bonds, and other) and describe the characteristics of the fund you select and the type of investor who would invest in that type of fund.

General Fund Type	Fund Name	Characteristics of Fund	Typical Investor
Stock			
Bond			
Other			

3   Explain the family-of-funds concept. How is it related to shareholder exchanges?

_____

_____

How to Make a Decision to Buy or Sell Mutual Funds

Often the decision to buy or sell shares in mutual funds is "too easy" because investors assume they do not need to evaluate these investments. Why question what the professional portfolio managers decide to do? Yet professionals do make mistakes. The responsibility for choosing the right mutual fund rests with *you*. After all, you are the only one who knows how much risk you are willing to assume and how a particular mutual fund can help you achieve your goals.

Fortunately, a lot of information is available to help you evaluate a specific mutual fund. Unfortunately, you can get lost in all the facts and figures and forget your ultimate goal: to choose a mutual fund that will help you achieve your financial goals. To help you sort out all the research, statistics, and information about mutual funds and give you some direction as to what to do first, answer the questions in the nearby Personal Finance in Practice feature. Then answer one basic question: Do you want a managed fund or an index fund?

OBJECTIVE 3
Evaluate mutual funds.

Personal Finance in Practice

› Mutual Funds: Getting Started

Here are some suggestions for beginning a mutual fund investment program.

1. *Perform a financial checkup.* Before investing, you should make sure your budget is balanced, you have adequate insurance protection, and you have established an emergency fund.

How could this suggestion help you prepare for an investment program?

_____

_____

2. *Obtain the money you need to purchase mutual funds.* Although the amount will vary, $250 to $3,000 or more is usually required to open an account with a brokerage firm or an investment company.

How can I obtain the money needed to fund my investment program?

_____

_____

3. *Determine your investment goals.* Without investment goals, you cannot know what you want to accomplish. For more information on the importance of goals, review the material in Chapter 11.

How could this suggestion help you establish a mutual fund investment program?

_____

_____

4. *Find a fund with an objective that matches your objective. The Wall Street Journal, Barron's,* and personal finance magazines may help you identify funds with objectives that match your investment objectives.

Why is a "match" between your investment objective and a fund's objective important?

_____

_____

5. *Evaluate, evaluate, and evaluate any mutual fund before buying or selling.* Possible sources of information include the Internet, professional advisory services, the fund's prospectus, the fund's annual report, financial publications, and newspapers—all sources described in the remainder of this section.

Since mutual funds provide professional management, why is evaluation important?

_____

_____

Managed Funds versus Index Funds

Most mutual funds are managed funds. In other words, there is a professional fund manager (or team of managers) who chooses the securities that are contained in the fund. The fund manager also decides when to buy and sell securities in the fund. One important question is how long the present fund manager has been managing the fund. If a fund has performed well under its present manager over a 5-year, 10-year, or longer period, there is a strong likelihood that it will continue to perform well under that manager in the future. On the other hand, if the fund has a new manager, his or her decisions may affect the performance of the fund. The decisions made by a new manager are often untested and may or may not stand the test of time. Managed funds may be open-end funds or closed-end funds.

Instead of investing in a managed fund, some investors choose to invest in an index fund. Why? The answer to that question is simple: Over many years, the majority of managed mutual funds fail to outperform the Standard & Poor's 500 stock index. The exact statistics vary, depending on the year, but on average, anywhere from 50 percent to 80 percent of managed funds are beaten by

CAUTION!

Don't forget the role of the fund manager in determining a fund's success.

the index each year.[7] If the individual securities included in an index like the Standard & Poor's 500, the Nasdaq Composite, the Russell 2000, or similar indexes increase in value, the index goes up.

Because an index mutual fund is a mirror image of a specific index, the dollar value of a share in an index fund also increases when the index increases. Unfortunately, the reverse is true. If the index goes down, the value of a share in an index fund goes down. Index funds, sometimes called "passive" funds, have managers, but they simply buy the stocks or bonds contained in the index. A second reason why investors choose index funds is the lower expense ratio charged by these passively managed funds. As mentioned earlier in this chapter, the total fees charged by a mutual fund is called the expense ratio. If a fund's expense ratio is 1.25 percent, then the fund has to earn at least that amount on its investment holdings just to break even each year. With very few exceptions, typical expense ratios for an index fund are 0.50 percent or less. Index funds may be open-end funds, closed-end funds, or exchange-traded funds.

Which type of fund is best? Good question. The answer depends on which managed mutual fund you choose. If you pick a managed fund that has better performance than an index, then you made the right choice. If, on the other hand, the index (and the index fund) outperforms the managed fund—which happens 50 to 80 percent of the time—an index fund is a better choice. With both investments, the key is how well you can research a specific investment alternative using the sources of information that are described in the remainder of this section.

The Internet

Many investors have found a wealth of information about mutual fund investments on the Internet. Basically, you can access information three ways. First, you can obtain current market values for mutual funds by using one of the Internet search engines, such as Yahoo! The Yahoo! Finance page (http://finance.yahoo.com) has a box where you can enter the symbol of the mutual fund you want to research. If you don't know the symbol, you can enter in the name of the mutual fund in the symbol lookup box. The Yahoo! Finance Web site will respond with the correct symbol. In addition to current market values, you can obtain a price history for a mutual fund, a profile including research information about current holdings, performance data, comparative data, risk level, and purchase information.

Second, most investment companies that sponsor mutual funds have a Web page. To obtain information, all you have to do is access one of the Internet search engines and type in the name of the fund or enter the investment company's Internet address (URL) in your computer. Generally, statistical information about performance of individual funds, procedures for opening an account, promotional literature, and different investor services are provided. *Be warned:* Investment companies want you to become a shareholder. As a result, the Web sites for *some* investment companies read like a sales pitch. Read between the glowing descriptions and look at the facts before investing your money.

Finally, professional advisory services, covered in the next section, offer online research reports for mutual funds. A sample of the information available from the Morningstar Web site for the Dodge and Cox Balanced Fund is illustrated in Exhibit 13–4. Note that information about the fund symbol, current NAV, Morningstar Rating, and past returns is provided. You can also obtain more detailed information by clicking on the appropriate button on the left side of the Web site. In many cases, more detailed information is provided by companies like Morningstar, Inc.

Apply *Yourself!*

Objective 3

Use the Yahoo! Finance Web site (http://finance.yahoo.com) to locate a mutual fund with a five-star Morningstar rating. What does the five-star rating mean?

Key Web Sites for Investing Advice

www.morningstar.com
www.lipperweb.com
www.valueline.com
www.smartmoney.com
www.mfea.com

[7]The Investopedia Web site (www.investopedia.com), accessed February 16, 2007, Investopedia, Inc., Suite 605, 10080 Jasper Avenue, Edmonton, Alberta 75J1V9.

Exhibit 13–4   Information about the Dodge and Cox Balanced Fund Available from the Morningstar Web Site

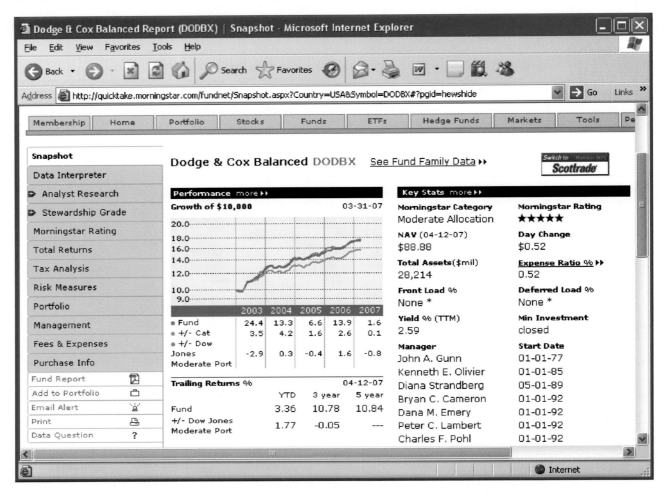

Source: Morningstar Web site (www.morningstar.com), accessed April 12, 2007, Morningstar, Inc., 225 W. Wacker Drive, Chicago, IL 60606.

(www.morningstar.com) and Lipper Analytical Services, Inc. (www.lipperweb.com) for a small fee. While the information is basically the same as that in the printed reports described later in this section, the ability to obtain up-to-date information quickly without having to wait for research materials to be mailed or to make a trip to the library is a real selling point.

Professional Advisory Services

A number of subscription services provide detailed information on mutual funds. Lipper Analytical Services, Morningstar, Inc., and Value Line are three widely used sources of such information. Exhibit 13–5 illustrates the type of information provided by Morningstar, Inc., for the T. Rowe Price Growth Stock Fund. Although the Morningstar report is just one page long, it provides a wealth of information designed to help you decide if this is the right fund for you. Notice that the information is divided into various sections. At the top, a small box entitled "Historical Profile" contains information about financial return, risk, and rating. Notice that T. Rowe Price Growth Stock Fund is rated five stars, Morningstar's highest rating. The report also provides statistical information over the past 12 years. The middle section of the report provides information about the fund's performance, risk analysis, and portfolio analysis. The last section at the very bottom

Exhibit 13–5   Mutual Fund Research Information Provided by Morningstar, Inc.

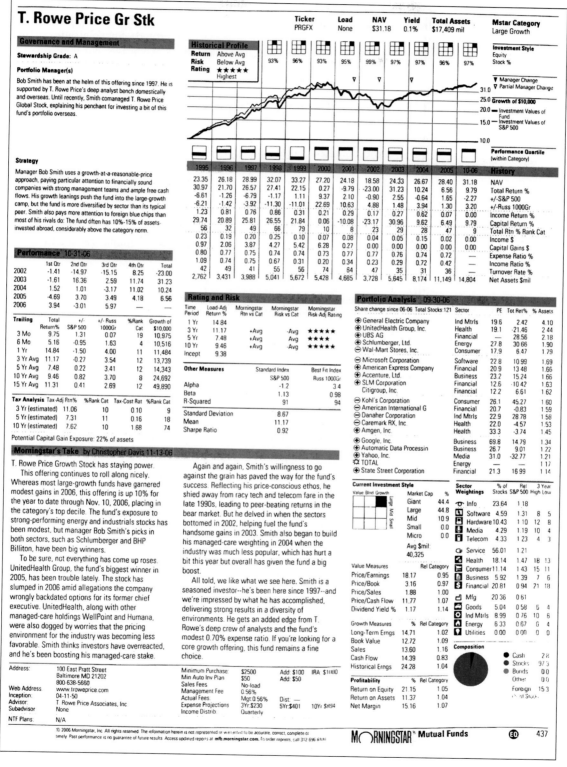

describes the investment philosophy of the fund. Generally, the "Morningstar's Take" section summarizes the analyst's research.

As you can see, the research information for this fund is pretty upbeat. However, other research firms like Lipper Analytical Services and Value Line, as well as Morningstar, Inc., will also tell you if a fund is a poor performer that offers poor investment potential.

In addition, various mutual fund newsletters provide financial information to subscribers for a fee. All of these sources are rather expensive, but their reports may be available from brokerage firms or libraries.

The Mutual Fund Prospectus

An investment company sponsoring a mutual fund must give potential investors a prospectus. You can also request a prospectus by mail, by calling a toll-free phone number, or by accessing the investment company Web site.

According to financial experts, the prospectus is usually the first piece of information investors receive, and they should read it completely before investing. Although it may look foreboding, a commonsense approach to reading a fund's prospectus can provide valuable insights. In fact, most investors find that a fund's prospectus offers a wealth of information. As pointed out earlier, the prospectus summarizes the fund's objective. Also, the fee table summarizes the fees a fund charges. In addition to information about objectives and fees, the prospectus should provide the following:

- A statement describing the risk factor associated with the fund.
- A description of the fund's past performance.
- A statement describing the type of investments contained in the fund's portfolio.
- Information about dividends, distributions, and taxes.
- Information about the fund's management.
- Information on limitations or requirements, if any, the fund must honor when choosing investments.
- The process investors can use to buy or sell shares in the fund.
- A description of services provided to investors and fees for services, if any.
- Information about how often the fund's investment portfolio changes (sometimes referred to as its *turnover ratio*).

Finally, the prospectus provides information about how to open a mutual fund account with the investment company.

The Mutual Fund Annual Report

If you are a prospective investor, you can request an annual report by mail, a toll-free telephone number, or the Internet. A fund's annual report contains a letter from the president of the investment company, from the fund manager, or both. The annual report also contains detailed financial information about the fund's assets and liabilities, statement of operations, and statement of changes in net assets. Next, the annual report includes a schedule of investments. Finally, the fund's annual report should include a letter from the fund's independent auditors that provides an opinion as to the accuracy of the fund's financial statements.

Financial Publications

Investment-oriented magazines like *BusinessWeek, Forbes, Kiplinger's Personal Finance Magazine,* and *Money* are other sources of information about mutual funds. Each of these publications provides information on mutual fund investing. Depending on the publication, coverage ranges from detailed articles that provide in-depth information to simple listings of which funds to buy or sell. And many personal finance magazines now provide information on the Internet about mutual funds. The material in Exhibit 13–6 was obtained from the *BusinessWeek* "Mutual Fund Scoreboard." Although the information seems complicated at first glance, much of the information is self-explanatory for an investor who takes the time to evaluate the information supplied in each column. For example, information is provided about

- The fund type.
- Overall and category rating of the fund.
- Fund category.
- Value of assets in the fund.
- Sales charge, if any.
- Expense ratio.
- Returns for 1 month, 3 months, year to date, 12 months, 3-year, 5-year, and 10-year periods.
- Turnover of investments in the fund.
- Risk level associated with the fund.

An investor can also compare the information for one fund with the same data for other funds. In most cases, all you have to do to get started is to enter the name of the fund or the trading symbol for the fund.

In addition to mutual fund information in financial publications, a number of mutual fund guidebooks are available at your local bookstore or public library.

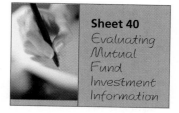

Sheet 40
*Evaluating
Mutual
Fund
Investment
Information*

Newspapers

Most large metropolitan newspapers, *The Wall Street Journal,* and *Barron's* provide information about mutual funds. Typical coverage includes information about net asset value,

Exhibit 13–6   Information Provided by the "Mutual Fund Scoreboard" on the *BusinessWeek* Web Site

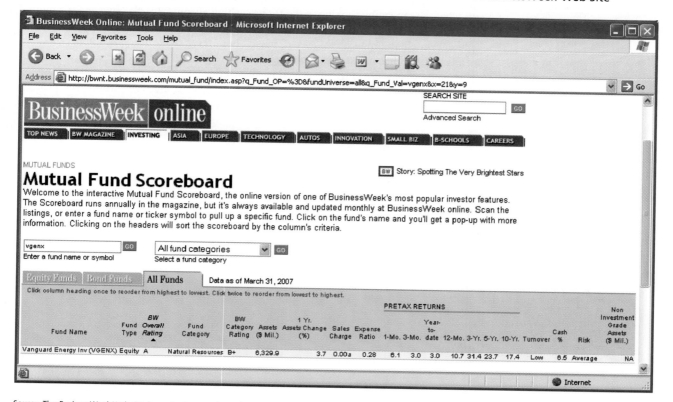

Source: The *BusinessWeek* Web site (www.businessweek.com), accessed March 31, 2007. Used by special permission © 2007 McGraw-Hill Companies, Inc.

Exhibit 13-7

Financial Information about Mutual Funds Available in *The Wall Street Journal*

1 FUND	2 NAV	3 NET CHG	4 YTD % RET
Fidelity Invest			
AggrGr r	19.85	−0.03	2.4
AMgr50%	16.29	0.06	1.1
AMgr70%	16.48	0.07	1.4
Balanc	19.75	0.11	1.6

1. **FUND:** The name of the fund is the Fidelity Balanced fund.

2. **NAV:** Net asset value. For the Fidelity Balanced fund, the NAV is $19.75 per share.

3. **NET CHG:** Net change is the difference between the price paid for the last share today and the price paid for the last share on the previous trading day. The Fidelity Balanced fund closed $0.11 higher than yesterday's closing price.

4. **YTD % RET:** The year-to-date percentage of increase or decrease for a fund. This Fidelity fund has gained 1.6 percent of its value since January 1.

Source: Republished by permission of Dow Jones Inc. from *The Wall Street Journal*, February 1, 2007, p. C14; permission conveyed through the Copyright Clearance Center, Inc.

Sheet 41
Evaluation of a Mutual Fund

net change, the fund family and fund name, and total return over selected time periods. The last line in Exhibit 13–7 provides detailed information for the Fidelity Balanced fund. Each numbered entry in the list below the exhibit refers to a numbered column in the mutual fund table. Much of this same information is also available on the Internet.

The letters beside the name of a specific fund can be very informative. You can find out what they mean by looking at the footnotes that accompany the newspaper's mutual fund quotations. Generally, "p" means a 12b-1 distribution fee is charged, "r" means a redemption charge may be made, "t" means both the p and r footnotes apply, and "s" means the fund has had a stock split or paid a dividend.

The newspaper coverage described in this section is a good means of monitoring the value of your mutual fund investments. However, other sources of information provide a more complete basis for evaluating mutual fund investments.

✓ CONCEPT CHECK 13–3

1   In your own words, describe the difference between a managed fund and an index fund. Which one do you think could help you achieve your investment goals?

_____

_____

2   Assume you are considering a $5,000 investment in a growth mutual fund. How would you go about researching your potential mutual fund investment?

_____

_____

3 Describe how each of the following sources of investment information could help you evaluate a mutual fund investment.

Source of Information	Type of Information	How This Could Help
The Internet		
Professional advisory services		
Mutual fund prospectus		
Mutual fund annual report		
Financial publications		
Newspapers		

The Mechanics of a Mutual Fund Transaction

For many investors, mutual funds have become the investment of choice. In fact, you probably either own shares or know someone who owns shares in a mutual fund—they're that popular! They may be part of a 401(k) or 403(b) retirement account, a SEP IRA, a Roth IRA, or a traditional IRA retirement account, all topics discussed in Chapter 14. They can also be owned outright by purchasing shares through a registered sales representative who works for a bank or brokerage firm or an investment company that sponsors a mutual fund. As you will see later in this section, it's easy to purchase shares in a mutual fund. For $250 to $3,000 or more, you can open an account and begin investing. And there are other advantages that encourage investors to purchase shares in funds. Unfortunately, there are also disadvantages. Exhibit 13–8 summarizes the advantages and disadvantages of fund investments.

One advantage of any investment is the opportunity to make money on it. In the next section, we examine how you can make money by investing in closed-end funds, exchange-traded funds, or open-end funds. We consider how taxes affect your fund investments. Then we look at the options used to purchase shares in a mutual fund. Finally, we examine the options used to withdraw money from a mutual fund.

OBJECTIVE 4
Describe how and why mutual funds are bought and sold.

Return on Investment

As with other investments, the purpose of investing in a closed-end fund, exchange-traded fund, or open-end fund is to earn a financial return. Shareholders in such funds can receive a return in one of three ways. First, all three types of funds pay income dividends. **Income dividends** are the earnings a fund pays to shareholders from its dividend and interest income. Second, investors may receive capital gain distributions. **Capital gain distributions** are the payments made to a fund's shareholders that result from the sale of securities in the fund's portfolio. Both amounts generally are paid once a year. Note: Exchange-traded funds don't usually pay end-of-the-year capital gain distributions. Third, as with stock and bond investments, you can buy shares in funds at a low price and then sell them after the price has increased. For example, assume you purchased shares in the Fidelity Stock Selector Fund at $29.00 per share and sold your shares two years later at $33.50 per share. In this case, you made $4.50 ($33.50 selling price minus $29.00 purchase price) per share. With this financial information and the dollar amounts for income dividends and capital gain distributions, you can calculate a total return for your mutual fund investment. Before completing this section, you may

income dividends The earnings a fund pays to shareholders from its dividend and interest income.

capital gain distributions The payments made to a fund's shareholders that result from the sale of securities in the fund's portfolio.

Exhibit 13–8

Advantages and Disadvantages of Investing in Mutual Funds

Advantages

- Diversification.
- Professional management.
- Ease of buying and selling shares.
- Multiple withdrawal options.
- Distribution or reinvestment of dividends and capital gains.
- Switching privileges within the same fund family.
- Services that include toll-free telephone numbers, complete records of all transactions, and savings and checking accounts.

Disadvantages

- Purchase/withdrawal costs.
- Ongoing management fees and 12b-1 fees.
- Poor performance that may not match the Standard & Poor's 500 stock index or some other index.
- Inability to control when capital gain distributions occur and complicated tax-reporting issues.
- Potential market risk associated with all investments.
- Some sales personnel are aggressive and/or unethical.

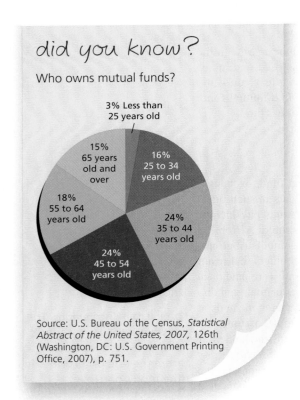

did you know?

Who owns mutual funds?

- 3% Less than 25 years old
- 15% 65 years old and over
- 16% 25 to 34 years old
- 18% 55 to 64 years old
- 24% 35 to 44 years old
- 24% 45 to 54 years old

Source: U.S. Bureau of the Census, *Statistical Abstract of the United States, 2007,* 126th (Washington, DC: U.S. Government Printing Office, 2007), p. 751.

want to examine the actual procedure used to calculate the dollar amount of total return and percentage of total return in the nearby Figure It Out box.

When shares in a mutual fund are sold, the profit that results from an increase in value is referred to as a *capital gain.* Note the difference between a capital gain distribution and a capital gain. A capital gain distribution occurs when *the fund* distributes profits that result from *the fund* selling securities in the portfolio at a profit. On the other hand, a capital gain is the profit that results when *you* sell your shares in the mutual fund for more than you paid for them. Of course, if the price of a fund's shares goes down between the time of your purchase and the time of sale, you incur a capital loss.

Taxes and Mutual Funds

Income dividends, capital gain distributions, and financial gains and losses from the sale of closed-end, exchange-traded, or open-end funds are subject to taxation. At the end of each year, investment companies are required to send each shareholder a statement specifying how much he or she received in dividends and capital gain distributions. Although investment companies may provide this information as part of their year-end statement, most funds use IRS Form 1099 DIV.

Figure It Out!

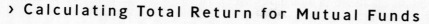

› Calculating Total Return for Mutual Funds

In Chapter 12, we defined total return as a calculation that includes not only the yearly dollar amount of income but also any increase or decrease in market value from the original purchase price of an investment. For mutual funds, you can use the following calculation to determine the dollar amount of total return:

Income dividends
+ Capital gain distributions
+ Change in share market value when sold
—————————————————————————
Dollar amount of total return

For example, assume you purchased 100 shares of Majestic Growth Fund for $12.20 per share for a total investment of $1,220. During the next 12 months, you received income dividends of $0.45 a share and capital gain distributions of $0.90 a share. Also, assume you sold your investment at the end of 12 months for $13.40 a share. As illustrated below, the dollar amount for total return is $255:

Income dividends = 100 × $0.45 = $ 45
Capital gain distributions = 100 × $0.90 =   + 90
Change in share value = $13.40 − $12.20
    = $1.20 × 100 =   + 120
                                       ———
Dollar amount of total return $ 255

To calculate the percentage of total return, divide the dollar amount of total return by the original cost of your mutual fund investment. The percentage of total return for the above example is 20.9 percent, as follows:

$$\text{Percent of total return} = \frac{\text{Dollar amount of total return}}{\text{Original cost of your investment}}$$

$$= \frac{\$255}{\$1,220}$$

$$= 0.209, \text{ or } 20.9\%$$

Now it's your turn. Use the following financial information for the Northeast Utility fund to calculate the dollar amount of total return and percent of total return over a 12-month period.

Number of shares, 100
Purchase price, $14.00 a share
Income dividends, $0.30 a share
Capital gain distribution, $0.60 a share
Sale price, $15.25 a share

Calculation	Calculation Formula	Your Answer
Dollar amount of total return		
Percent of total return		

Answers: The total return is $215 and the percent of total return is 15.4%.

The following information provides general guidelines on how mutual fund transactions are taxed:

- Income dividends are reported, along with all other dividend amounts you have received, on your federal tax return and are taxed as dividend income
- Capital gain distributions that result from the fund selling securities in the fund's portfolio at a profit are reported on Schedule D as part of your federal tax return and on the 1040.
- Capital gains or losses that result from your selling shares in a mutual fund are reported on Schedule D and the 1040. How long you hold the shares determines if your gains or losses are taxed as a short-term or long-term capital gain. (See Chapter 3 for more information on capital gains and capital losses.)

Two specific problems develop with taxation of mutual funds. First, almost all investment companies allow you to reinvest income dividends and capital gain distributions from the fund to purchase additional shares instead of receiving cash. Even though you didn't receive cash because you chose to reinvest such distributions, they are still taxable and must be reported on your federal tax return as current income. Second, when you purchase shares of stock, corporate bonds, or other investments and use the buy-and-hold technique described in Chapter 12, you decide when you sell. Thus, you can pick the tax year when you pay tax on capital gains or deduct capital losses. Mutual funds, on the other hand, buy and sell securities within the

turnover ratio A ratio that measures the percentage of a fund's holdings that have changed or "been replaced" during a 12-month period of time.

fund's portfolio on a regular basis during any 12-month period. At the end of the year, profits that result from the mutual fund's buying and selling activities are paid to shareholders in the form of capital gain distributions. Because income dividends and capital gain distributions are taxable, one factor to consider when choosing a mutual fund is its turnover. For a mutual fund, the **turnover ratio** measures the percentage of a fund's holdings that have changed or "been replaced" during a 12-month period of time. Simply put, it is a measure of a fund's trading activity. *Caution:* Unless you are using the fund in a 401(k) or 403(b) retirement account, or some type of individual retirement account, a mutual fund with a high turnover ratio can result in higher income tax bills. A higher turnover ratio can also result in higher transaction costs and fund expenses. Unlike the investments that you manage, you have no control over when the mutual fund sells securities and when you will be taxed on capital gain distributions.

To ensure having all of the documentation you need for tax reporting purposes, it is essential that *you* keep accurate records. The same records will help you monitor the value of your mutual fund investments and make more intelligent decisions with regard to buying and selling these investments.

Purchase Options

You can buy shares of a closed-end fund or exchange-traded fund through a stock exchange or in the over-the-counter market. You can purchase shares of an open-end, no-load fund by contacting the investment company that manages the fund. You can purchase shares of an open-end, load fund through a salesperson who is authorized to sell them or through an account executive of a brokerage firm.

You can also purchase both no-load and load funds from mutual fund supermarkets available through brokerage firms. A mutual fund supermarket offers at least two advantages. First, instead of dealing with numerous investment companies that sponsor mutual funds, you can make one toll-free phone call or use the Internet to obtain information, purchase shares, and sell shares in a large number of mutual funds. Second, you receive one statement from one brokerage firm instead of receiving a statement from each investment company or brokerage firm you deal with. One statement can be a real plus because it provides the information you need to monitor the value of your investments in one place and in the same format.

Because of the unique nature of open-end fund transactions, we will examine how investors buy and sell shares in this type of mutual fund. To purchase shares in an open-end mutual fund, you may use four options: regular account transactions, voluntary savings plans, contractual savings plans, and reinvestment plans. The most popular and least complicated method of purchasing shares in an open-end fund is through a regular account transaction. When you use a regular account transaction, you decide how much money you want to invest and when you want to invest, and simply buy as many shares as possible.

The chief advantage of the voluntary savings plan is that it allows you to make smaller purchases than the minimum purchases required by the regular account method described above. At the time of the initial purchase, you declare an intent to make regular minimum purchases of the fund's shares. Although there is no penalty for not making purchases, most investors feel an "obligation" to make purchases on a periodic basis, and, as pointed out throughout this text, small monthly investments are a great way to save for long-term objectives. For most voluntary savings plans, the minimum purchase ranges from $25 to $100 for each purchase after the initial investment. Funds try to make investing as easy as possible. Most offer payroll deduction plans, and many will deduct, upon proper shareholder authorization, a specified amount from a shareholder's bank account. Also, many investors can choose mutual funds as a vehicle to invest money that is contributed to a 401(k), 403(b), or individual retirement account.

As mentioned earlier, Chapter 14 provides more information on the tax advantages of different types of retirement accounts.

Contractual savings plans require you to make regular purchases over a specified period of time, usually 10 to 15 years. These plans are sometimes referred to as *front-end load plans* because almost all of the commissions are paid in the first few years of the contract period. Also, you may incur penalties if you do not fulfill the purchase requirements. For example, if you drop out of a contractual savings plan before completing the purchase requirements, you sacrifice the prepaid commissions. Many financial experts and government regulatory agencies are critical of contractual savings plans. As a result, the Securities and Exchange Commission and many states have imposed new rules on investment companies offering contractual savings plans.

You may also purchase shares in an open-end fund by using the fund's reinvestment plan. A **reinvestment plan** is a service provided by an investment company in which income dividends and capital gain distributions are automatically reinvested to purchase additional shares of the fund. Most reinvestment plans allow shareholders to use reinvested money to purchase shares without having to pay additional sales charges or commissions. *Reminder:* When your dividends or capital gain distributions are reinvested, you must still report these transactions as taxable income.

All four purchase options allow you to buy shares over a long period of time. As a result, you can use the principle of *dollar cost averaging,* which was explained in Chapter 12. Dollar cost averaging allows you to average many individual purchase prices over a long period of time. This method helps you avoid the problem of buying high and selling low. With dollar cost averaging, you can make money if you sell your mutual fund shares at a price higher than their *average* purchase price.

Apply *Yourself!*

Objective 4

In a short paragraph, describe which purchase option and which withdrawal option appeal to you. Explain your answer.

reinvestment plan A service provided by an investment company in which shareholder income dividends and capital gain distributions are automatically reinvested to purchase additional shares of the fund.

Withdrawal Options

Because closed-end funds and exchange-traded funds are listed on stock exchanges or traded in the over-the-counter market, an investor may sell shares in such a fund to another investor. Shares in an open-end fund can be sold on any business day to the investment company that sponsors the fund. In this case, the shares are redeemed at their net asset value. All you have to do is give proper notification and the fund will send you a check. With some funds, you can even write checks to withdraw money from the fund.

In addition, most funds have provisions that allow investors with shares that have a minimum net asset value (usually at least $5,000) to use four options to systematically withdraw money. First, you may withdraw a specified, fixed dollar amount each investment period until your fund has been exhausted. Normally, an investment period is three months.

A second option allows you to liquidate or "sell off" a certain number of shares each investment period. Since the net asset value of shares in a fund varies from one period to the next, the amount of money you receive will also vary.

A third option allows you to withdraw a fixed percentage of asset growth. For example, assume you arrange to receive 60 percent of the asset growth of your investment, and the asset growth of your investment amounts to $1,200 in a particular investment period. For that period, you will receive a check for $720 ($1,200 × 60% = $720). If no asset growth occurs, no payment is made to you. Under this option, your principal remains untouched.

A final option allows you to withdraw all income dividends and capital gain distributions earned by the fund during an investment period. Under this option, your principal remains untouched.

✓ CONCEPT CHECK 13–4

1 In your own words, describe the advantages and disadvantages of mutual fund investments.

_____

_____

2 In the table below indicate how each of the key terms affects a mutual fund investment and how each would be taxed.

Key Term	Effect on a Mutual Fund Investment	Type of Taxation
Income dividends		
Capital gain distributions		
Capital gains		
Capital losses		

3 Whom would you contact to purchase a closed-end fund? An exchange-traded fund?

_____

_____

4 What options can you use to purchase shares in an open-end mutual fund from an investment company?

_____

_____

5 What options can you use to withdraw money from an open-end mutual fund?

_____

_____

back to Getting Personal

1. Reevaluate your Getting Personal answers at the beginning of the chapter. Have any of your answers changed as a result of studying this chapter?

_____

_____

2. In your own words, describe why you would choose mutual funds to help you obtain your investment goals.

_____

_____

3. Mutual funds charge investors a number of different fees and charges. In the table below indicate the typical fee or charge and when it is assessed.

Charge or Fee	Typical Fee	When Assessed
Front-end load		
Contingent deferred sales load		
12b-l fee		
Management fee		

4. In this chapter, mutual funds were divided into three different categories: stock funds, bond funds, and other funds. Choose a specific type of fund described in one of the three categories. Then explain how that fund seems to match your investment goals.

_____

_____

Chapter Summary

Objective 1 The major reasons investors choose mutual funds are professional management and diversification. Mutual funds are also a convenient way to invest money—especially for retirement accounts offered by some employers. There are three types of funds: closed-end funds, exchange-traded funds, and open-end funds. A closed-end fund is a mutual fund whose shares are issued only when the fund is organized. An exchange-traded fund (ETF) is a fund that invests in the stocks contained in a specific stock index like the Standard & Poor's 500 stock index, the Dow Jones Industrial Average, or the Nasdaq Composite Index. Both closed-end and exchange-traded funds are traded on a stock exchange or in the over-the-counter market. An open-end fund is a mutual fund whose shares are sold and redeemed by the investment company at the net asset value (NAV) at the request of investors.

Mutual funds can also be classified as A shares (commissions charged when shares are purchased), B shares (commissions charged when money is withdrawn during the first five years), and C shares (no commission to buy or sell shares, but higher, ongoing fees). Other possible fees include management fees and 12b-1 fees. Together all the different management fees and operating costs are referred to as an expense ratio.

Objective 2 The major categories of stock mutual funds, in terms of the types of securities in which they invest, are aggressive growth, equity income, global, growth, index, international, large cap, lifecycle, midcap, regional, sector, small cap, and socially responsible. There are also bond funds that include

high-yield (junk), intermediate corporate, intermediate U.S. government, long-term corporate, long-term U.S. government, municipal, short-term corporate, and short-term U.S. government. Finally, other funds invest in a mix of different stocks, bonds, and other investment securities that include asset allocation funds, balanced funds, and money market funds. Today many investment companies use a family-of-funds concept, which allows shareholders to switch among funds as different funds offer more potential, financial reward, or security.

Objective 3 The responsibility for choosing the "right" mutual fund rests with you, the investor. Fortunately, a lot of information is available to help you evaluate a specific mutual fund. Often, the first question investors must answer is whether they want a managed fund or an index fund. With a managed fund, a professional fund manager (or team of managers) chooses the securities that are contained in the fund. Some investors choose to invest in an index fund, because over many years, index funds have outperformed 50 to 80 percent of all managed funds. If the individual securities included in an index increase in value, the index goes up. On the other hand, if the securities included in the index go down, the index goes down. Because an index mutual fund is a mirror image of a specific index, the dollar value of a share in an index fund also increases or decreases when the index increases or decreases. To help evaluate different mutual funds, investors can use the information on the Internet, from professional advisory services, from the fund's prospectus and annual report, in financial publications, and in newspapers.

Objective 4   The advantages and disadvantages of mutual funds have made mutual funds the investment of choice for many investors. For $250 to $3,000 or more, you can open an account and begin investing. The shares of a closed-end fund or exchange-traded fund are bought and sold on organized stock exchanges or the over-the-counter market. The shares of an open-end fund may be purchased through a salesperson who is authorized to sell them, through an account executive of a brokerage firm, from a mutual fund supermarket, or from the investment company that sponsors the fund. The shares in an open-end fund can be sold to the investment company that sponsors the fund. Shareholders in mutual funds can receive a return in one of three ways: income dividends, capital gain distributions when the fund buys and sells securities in the fund's portfolio at a profit, and capital gains when the shareholder sells shares in the mutual fund at a higher price than the price paid. Income dividends, capital gain distributions, and capital gains are subject to taxation. A number of purchase and withdrawal options are available for mutual fund investors.

Key Terms

capital gain distributions 425	income dividends 425	open-end fund 410
closed-end fund 408	investment company 407	reinvestment plan 429
contingent deferred sales load 411	load fund 410	turnover ratio 428
exchange-traded fund (ETF) 409	mutual fund 407	12b-1 fee 411
expense ratio 412	net asset value (NAV) 410	
family of funds 416	no-load fund 411	

Problems

1. Given the following information, calculate the net asset value for the Boston Equity mutual fund:
   Total assets, $225,000,000
   Total liabilities, 5,000,000
   Total number of shares, 4,400,000

2. The Western Capital Growth mutual fund has
   Total assets, $750,000,000
   Total liabilities, 7,200,000
   Total number of shares, 24,000,000
   What is the fund's net asset value (NAV)?

3. Jan Throng invested $15,000 in the AIM Charter Mutual Fund. The fund charges a 5.50 percent commission when shares are purchased. Calculate the amount of commission Jan must pay.

4. As Bill Salvatore approached retirement, he decided the time had come to invest some of his nest egg in a conservative bond fund. He chose the American Century Municipal Bond Fund. If he invests $80,000 and the fund charges a 4.50 percent load when shares are purchased, what is the amount of commission that Bill must pay?

5. Mary Canfield purchased the New Dimensions Global Growth Fund. This fund doesn't charge a front-end load, but it does charge a contingent deferred sales load of 4 percent for any withdrawals during the first five years. If Mary withdraws $6,000 during the second year, how much is the contingent deferred sales load?

6. Mike Jackson invested a total of $8,500 in the ABC Mutual Fund. The management fee for this particular fund is 0.70 percent of the total asset value. Calculate the management fee Mike must pay this year.

7. Betty and James Holloway invested $34,000 in the Financial Vision Social Responsibility Fund. The management fee for this fund is 0.60 percent of the total asset value. Calculate the management fee the Holloways must pay.

8. As part of his 401(k) retirement plan at work, Ken Lowery invests 5 percent of his salary each month in the Capital Investments Lifecycle Fund. At the end of the year, Ken's 401(k) account has a dollar value of $21,800. If the fund charges a 12b-1 fee of 0.80 percent, what is the amount of the fee?

9. When Jill Thompson received a large settlement from an automobile accident, she chose to invest $120,000 in the Vanguard 500 Index Fund. This fund has an expense ratio of 0.18 percent. What is the amount of the fees that Jill will pay this year?

10. The Yamaha Aggressive Growth Fund has a 2.13 percent expense ratio.
    a. If you invest $25,000 in this fund, what is the dollar amount of fees that you would pay this year?

    b. Based on the information in this chapter and your own research, is this a low, average, or high expense ratio?

11. Three years ago, James Matheson bought 200 shares of a mutual fund for $21 a share. During the three-year period, he received total income dividends of 0.70 per share. He also received total capital gain distributions of $1.40 per share. At the end of three years, he sold his shares for $25 a share. What was his total return for this investment?

12. Assume that one year ago, you bought 100 shares of a mutual fund for $15 a share, you received a $0.55 per-share capital gain distribution during the past 12 months, and the market value of the fund is now $17 a share.
    a. Calculate the total return for your $1,500 investment.

    b. Calculate the percentage of total return for your $1,500 investment.

Questions

1. For many investors, mutual funds have become the investment of choice. In your own words, describe why investors purchase mutual funds.

2. Describe the type of fees that you would pay to purchase a load fund. What annual fees would you typically pay for your mutual fund investment?

3. This chapter explored a number of different classifications of mutual funds.
    a. Based on your age and current financial situation, which type of mutual fund seems appropriate for your investment needs? Explain your answer.

    b. As people get closer to retirement, their investment goals often change. Assume you are now 45 and have accumulated $110,000 in a retirement account. In this situation, what type of mutual funds would your choose? Why?

    c. Assume you are now 60 years of age and have accumulated $400,000 in a retirement account. Also assume you would like to retire when you are 65. What type of mutual funds would you choose to help you reach your investment goals? Why?

4. Choose either the AIM Charter (symbol CHTRX) mutual fund or the Fidelity Fifty (symbol FFTYX) mutual fund. Then describe how each of the following sources of information could help you evaluate one of these funds.
    a. The Internet.

    b. Professional advisory services.

    c. The fund's prospectus.

   d. The fund's annual report.

   e. Financial publications.

   f. Newspapers.

5. Visit the Yahoo! Finance Web site and evaluate one of the following mutual funds. To complete this activity, follow these steps:

   a. Go to http://finance.yahoo.com.

   b. Choose one of the following three funds, enter its symbol, and click on the "Get Quotes" button: Oakmark I fund (OAKMX), Janus High Yield fund (JAHYX), and American Funds Washington Mutual fund (AWSHX).

   c. Print out the information for the mutual fund that you chose to evaluate.

   d. Based on the information included in this research report, would you invest in this fund? Explain your answer.

6. Obtain a mutual fund prospectus to determine the options you can use to purchase and redeem shares.

   a. Which purchase option would appeal to you? Why?

   b Assuming you are now of retirement age, which withdrawal option would appeal to you?

Internet Connection

RESEARCHING MUTUAL FUND INVESTMENTS

Visit the following Web sites and describe the types of information provided by each site. Then describe how this site could help you invest.

Sponsor	Web Site	Type of Information	How Could This Site Help Me Invest?
Bloomberg	www.Bloomberg.com		
CNNMoney	www.money.com		
Motley Fool	www.fool.com		
Kiplinger	www.kiplinger.com		
SmartMoney	www.smartmoney.com		

Case in Point

RESEARCH INFORMATION AVAILABLE FROM MORNINGSTAR

This chapter stressed the importance of evaluating potential investments. Now it is your turn to try your skill at evaluating a potential investment in the T. Rowe Price Growth Stock Fund. Assume you could invest $10,000 in shares of this fund. To help you evaluate this potential investment, carefully examine Exhibit 13–5, which reproduces the Morningstar research report for the T. Rowe Price Growth Stock Fund. The report was published December 6, 2006.

Questions

1. Based on the research provided by Morningstar, would you buy shares in the T. Rowe Price Growth Stock Fund? Justify your answer.

2. What other investment information would you need to evaluate this fund? Where would you obtain this information?

3. On February 26, 2007, shares in the T. Rowe Price Growth Stock Fund were selling for $32.55 per share. Using the Internet or a newspaper, determine the current price for a share of this fund. Based on this information, would your investment have been profitable? (*Hint:* The symbol for this fund is PRGFX.)

4. Assuming you purchased shares in the T. Rowe Price Growth Stock Fund on February 26, 2007, and based on your answer to question 3, how would you decide if you want to hold or sell your shares? Explain your answer.

Continuing Case

MUTUAL FUND INVESTMENTS

Life Situation

Pam, 43

Josh, 45

Children ages 16, 14, and 11

Financial Data

Monthly income $4,900

Assets $262,700

Living expenses $4,450

Liabilities $84,600

Emergency fund $5,000

In recent years, the Brocks have made extensive use of mutual funds in their investment portfolio. However, they are concerned that their selection of the funds may not be coordinated. With over 9,200 different mutual funds available, this financial marketplace is confusing.

The Brocks start the evaluation process by connecting various types of mutual funds to their investments goals. Next, they assess the past performance and management of the funds. Finally, they talk with various financial advisers and other investors to gather additional information.

Questions

1. How might Pam and Josh use mutual funds for various investment goals?

2. What types of mutual funds might be considered by the Brocks for their investment portfolio?

3. How could *Your Personal Financial Plan* Sheets 40 and 41 be used by the Brocks?

Video Case

INVESTING IN MUTUAL FUNDS

Often the people who sell mutual funds stress that they make investing easy because fund managers make the decisions about what securities are included in the fund and when to buy and sell those securities. And while mutual funds do provide professional management and diversification, the truth is that you must still pick the funds that can help you reach your investment goals. While the investment companies that sponsor mutual funds make investing as easy as possible, the decision is complicated by the fees and the potential risk associated with fund investments.

Questions

1. Why should an investor consider the fund's objective, risk associated with the fund, and historical performance when choosing a mutual fund?

2. According to the video, the average fund investor paid $93 for every $10,000 invested last year. Is the professional management worth the added cost?

3. With a 15.3 percent return over the last three years, managed funds have outperformed index funds. And yet, over the 20-year period from 1985 to 2005, index funds have outperformed managed funds. Given these facts, would you choose a managed fund or an index fund? What factors would affect your decision?

Spending Diary

"I MUST CHOOSE BETWEEN SPENDING MONEY ON SOMETHING NOW OR INVESTING FOR THE FUTURE."

Directions

Monitoring your daily spending will allow you to better consider financial planning alternatives. You will have better information and the potential for better control if you use your spending information for making wiser choices.

Questions

1. Are there any spending items that you might consider revising to allow you to increase the amount you invest?

2. Based on your investment goals and the amount available to invest, what types of mutual funds would you consider?

Evaluating Mutual Fund Investment Information

Financial Planning Activities: To identify and assess the value of various investment information sources, obtain samples of several items of investment information that you might consider to guide you in your investment decisions.

Suggested Web Sites: www.morningstar.com   www.mfea.com

Criteria Evaluation	Item 1	Item 2	Item 3
Location (address, phone)			
Web site			
Overview of information provided (main features)			
Cost, if any			
Ease of access			
Evaluation • Reliablility • Clarity • Value of information compared to cost			

What's Next for Your Personal Financial Plan?

• Talk with friends and relatives to determine what sources of information they use to evaluate mutual funds.
• Choose one source of information and describe how the information could help you obtain your investment goals.

Evaluation of a Mutual Fund

Financial Planning Activities: No checklist can serve as a foolproof guide for choosing a mutual fund. However, the following questions will help you evaluate a potential investment in a specific fund. Use mutual fund Web sites on the Internet and/or library materials to answer these questions about a mutual fund that you believe could help you obtain your investment goals.

Suggested Web Sites: www.morningstar.com   http://finance.yahoo.com

Category 1: Fund Characteristics

1. What is the fund's name?
   _____

2. What is this fund's Morningstar rating?
   _____

3. What is the minimum investment?
   _____

4. Does the fund allow telephone or Internet exchanges? ☐ Yes ☐ No

5. Is there a fee for exchanges? ☐ Yes ☐ No

Category 2: Costs

6. Is there a front-end load charge? If so, how much is it?
   _____

7. Is there a redemption fee? If so, how much is it?
   _____

8. How much is the annual management fee?
   _____

9. Is there a 12b-1 fee? If so, how much is it?
   _____

10. What is the fund's expense ratio?
    _____

Category 3: Diversification

11. What is the fund's objective?
    _____

12. What types of securities does the fund's portfolio include?
    _____

13. How many different securities does the fund's portfolio include?
    _____

14. How many types of industries does the fund's portfolio include?
    _____

15. What are the fund's five largest holdings?
    _____

Category 4: Fund Performance

16. How long has the fund manager been with the fund?
    _____

17. How would you describe the fund's performance over the past 12 months?
    _____

18. How would you describe the fund's performance over the past five years?
    _____

19. How would you describe the fund's performance over the past 10 years?
    _____

20. What is the current net asset value for this fund?
    _____

21. What is the high net asset value for this fund over the last 12 months?
    _____

22. What is the low net asset value for this fund over the last 12 months?
    _____

23. What do the experts say about this fund?
    _____

Category 5: Conclusion

24. Based on the above information, do you think an investment in this fund will help you achieve your investment goals? ☐ Yes ☐ No

25. Explain your answer to question 24.
    _____

A Word of Caution

When you use a checklist, there is always a danger of overlooking important relevant information. This checklist is not a cure-all, but it does provide some very sound questions that you should answer before making a mutual fund investment decision. Quite simply, it is a place to start. If you need other information, *you* are responsible for obtaining it and for determining how it affects your potential investment.

What's Next for Your Personal Financial Plan?

- Identify additional factors that may affect your decision to invest in this fund.
- Develop a plan for monitoring an investment's value once a mutual fund(s) is purchased.

14 Retirement and Estate Planning

What are your attitudes toward retirement and estate planning? For each of the following statements, select "agree" or "disagree" to indicate your behavior regarding the following statements:

	Agree	Disagree
1. I have plenty of time to start saving for retirement.	___	___
2. My living expenses will drop when I retire.	___	___
3. I can depend on Social Security and my company pension to pay for my retirement living expenses.	___	___
4. Since I am not married now, I don't need a will.	___	___
5. I believe estate planning is only for the rich and famous.	___	___
6. I can free myself from managing my assets by setting up a trust.	___	___

After studying this chapter, you will be asked to reconsider your responses to these questions.

Objectives

In this chapter, you will learn to:

1. Analyze your current assets and liabilities for retirement and estimate your retirement living costs.
2. Determine your planned retirement income and develop a balanced budget based on your retirement income.
3. Analyze the personal and legal aspects of estate planning.
4. Distinguish among various types of wills and trusts.

Why is this important?

Retirement planning is important because you'll probably spend many years in retirement. Properly estimating your retirement living costs and housing needs will enable you to save or invest enough money to live comfortably during retirement.

Identifying various kinds of wills and trusts will help you devise an estate plan that protects your interests as well as those of your family. Creating an effective estate plan will allow you to prosper during retirement and provide for your loved ones when you die.

Planning for Retirement: Start Early

OBJECTIVE 1

Analyze your current assets and liabilities for retirement and estimate your retirement living costs.

Your retirement years may seem a long way off right now. However, the fact is, it's never too early to start planning for retirement. Planning can help you cope with sudden changes that may occur in your life and give you a sense of control over your future.

If you haven't done any research on the subject of retirement, you may hold some outdated beliefs about your "golden years." Some common mistaken beliefs include:

- You have plenty of time to start saving for retirement.
- Saving just a little bit won't help.
- You'll spend less money when you retire.
- Your retirement will only last about 15 years.
- You can depend on Social Security and a company pension plan to pay your basic living expenses.
- Your pension benefits will increase to keep pace with inflation.
- Your employer's health insurance plan and Medicare will cover all your medical expenses when you retire.

Some of these statements were once true but are no longer true today. You may live for many years after you retire. If you want your retirement to be a happy and comfortable time of your life, you'll need enough money to suit your lifestyle. You can't count on others to provide for you. That's why you need to start planning and saving as early as possible. It's never too late to start saving for retirement, but the sooner you start, the better off you'll be. (See Exhibit 14–1.)

Apply *Yourself!*

Objective 1

Survey friends, relatives, and other people to get their views on retirement planning. Prepare a written report of your findings.

Exhibit 14–1   Tackling the Trade-Offs: Saving Now versus Saving Later

Get an early start on your plan for retirement.

	SAVER ABE				SAVER BEN		
Age	Years	Contributions	Year-End Value	Age	Years	Contributions	Year-End Value
25	1	$ 2,000	$ 2,188	25	1	$ 0	$ 0
26	2	2,000	4,580	26	2	0	0
27	3	2,000	7,198	27	3	0	0
28	4	2,000	10,061	28	4	0	0
29	5	2,000	13,192	29	5	0	0
30	6	2,000	16,617	30	6	0	0
31	7	2,000	20,363	31	7	0	0
32	8	2,000	24,461	32	8	0	0
33	9	2,000	28,944	33	9	0	0
34	10	2,000	33,846	34	10	0	0
35	11	0	37,021	35	11	2,000	2,188
36	12	0	40,494	36	12	2,000	4,580
37	13	0	44,293	37	13	2,000	7,198
38	14	0	48,448	38	14	2,000	10,061
39	15	0	52,992	39	15	2,000	13,192
40	16	0	57,963	40	16	2,000	16,617
41	17	0	63,401	41	17	2,000	20,363
42	18	0	69,348	42	18	2,000	24,461
43	19	0	75,854	43	19	2,000	28,944
44	20	0	82,969	44	20	2,000	33,846
45	21	0	90,752	45	21	2,000	39,209
46	22	0	99,265	46	22	2,000	45,075
47	23	0	108,577	47	23	2,000	51,490
48	24	0	118,763	48	24	2,000	58,508
49	25	0	129,903	49	25	2,000	66,184
50	26	0	142,089	50	26	2,000	74,580
51	27	0	155,418	51	27	2,000	83,764
52	28	0	169,997	52	28	2,000	93,809
53	29	0	185,944	53	29	2,000	104,797
54	30	0	203,387	54	30	2,000	116,815
55	31	0	222,466	55	31	2,000	129,961
56	32	0	243,335	56	32	2,000	144,340
57	33	0	266,162	57	33	2,000	160,068
58	34	0	291,129	58	34	2,000	177,271
59	35	0	318,439	59	35	2,000	196,088
60	36	0	348,311	60	36	2,000	216,670
61	37	0	380,985	61	37	2,000	239,182
62	38	0	416,724	62	38	2,000	263,807
63	39	0	455,816	63	39	2,000	290,741
64	40	0	498,574	64	40	2,000	320,202
65	41	0	545,344	65	41	2,000	352,427
		$20,000				$62,000	
Value at retirement*			$545,344	Value at retirement*			$ 352,427
Less total contributions			−20,000	Less total contributions			−62,000
Net earnings			$525,344	Net earnings			$ 290,427

*The table assumes a 9 percent fixed rate of return, compounded monthly, and no fluctuation of the principal. Distributions from an IRA are subject to ordinary income taxes when withdrawn and may be subject to other limitations under IRA rules.

Source: *The Franklin investor* (San Mateo, CA: Franklin Distributors Inc., January 1989).

Suppose that you want to have at least $1 million when you retire at age 65. If you start saving for retirement at age 25, you can meet that goal by putting about $127 per month into investment funds that grow at a rate of about 11 percent each year. If you wait until you're 50, the monthly amount skyrockets to $2,244.

As you think about your retirement years, consider your long-range goals. What does retirement mean to you? Maybe it will simply be a time to stop working, sit back, and relax. Perhaps you imagine traveling the world, developing a hobby, or starting a second career. Where do you want to live after you retire? What type of lifestyle would you like to have? Once you've pondered these questions, your first step in retirement planning is to determine your current financial situation. That requires you to analyze your current assets and liabilities.

Key Web Sites for Retirement Planning
www.isrplan.org/
www.asec.org

Conducting a Financial Analysis

As you learned in Chapter 2, an asset is any item of value that you own—cash, property, personal possessions, and investments—including cash in checking and savings accounts, a house, a car, a television, and so on. It also includes the current value of any stocks, bonds, and other investments that you may have as well as the current value of any life insurance and pension funds.

Your liabilities, on the other hand, are the debts you owe: the remaining balance on a mortgage or automobile loan, credit card balances, unpaid taxes, and so on. If you subtract your liabilities from your assets, you get your net worth. Ideally, your net worth should increase each year as you move closer to retirement.

It's a good idea to review your assets on a regular basis. You may need to make adjustments in your saving, spending, and investment in order to stay on track. As you review your assets, consider the following factors: housing, life insurance, and other investments. Each will have an important effect on your retirement income.

HOUSING   A house will probably be your most valuable asset. However, if you buy a home with a large mortgage that prevents you from saving, you put your ability to meet your retirement goal at risk. In that case you might consider buying a smaller, less expensive place to live. Remember that a smaller house is usually easier and cheaper to maintain. You can use the money you save to increase your retirement fund.

LIFE INSURANCE   At some point in the future, you may buy life insurance to provide financial support for your children in case you die while they are still young. As you near retirement, though, your children will probably be self-sufficient. When that time comes, you might reduce your premium payments by decreasing your life insurance coverage. This would give you extra money to spend on living expenses or to invest for additional income.

OTHER INVESTMENTS   When you review your assets, you'll also want to evaluate any other investments you have. When you originally chose these investments, you may have been more interested in making your money grow than in getting an early return from them. When you are ready to retire, however, you may want to use the income from those investments to help cover living expenses instead of reinvesting it.

Estimating Retirement Living Expenses

Next you should estimate how much money you'll need to live comfortably during your retirement years. (See the nearby Personal Finance in Practice feature.) You can't predict exactly how much money you'll need when you retire. You can, however, estimate what your basic needs will be. To do this, you'll have to think about your spending

Exhibit 14–2   How an "Average" Older (65+) Household Spends Its Money

Retired families spend a greater share of their income for food, housing, and medical care than nonretired families.

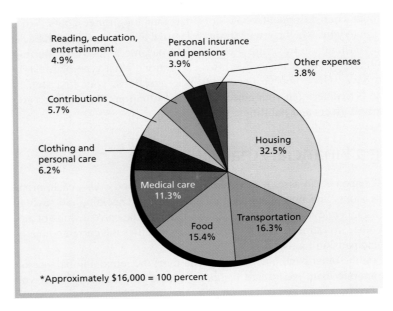

*Approximately $16,000 = 100 percent

Source: U.S. Bureau of Labor Statistics.

patterns and how your living situation will change when you retire. For instance, you probably will spend more money on recreation, health insurance, and medical care in retirement than you do now. At the same time, you may spend less on transportation and clothing. Your federal income taxes may be lower. Also, some income from various retirement plans may be taxed at a lower rate or not at all. As you consider your retirement living expenses, remember to plan for emergencies. Look at Exhibit 14–2 for an example of retirement spending patterns.

Don't forget to take inflation into account. Estimate high when calculating how much the prices of goods and services will rise by the time you retire (see Exhibit 14–3). Even a 3 percent rate of inflation will cause prices to double every 24 years.

Exhibit 14–3   The Effects of Inflation over Time

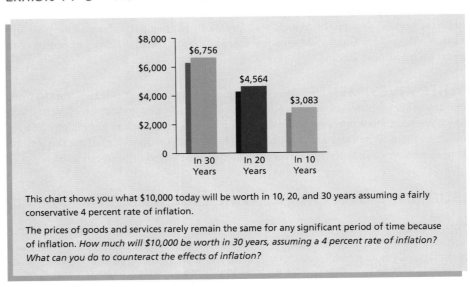

This chart shows you what $10,000 today will be worth in 10, 20, and 30 years assuming a fairly conservative 4 percent rate of inflation.

The prices of goods and services rarely remain the same for any significant period of time because of inflation. *How much will $10,000 be worth in 30 years, assuming a 4 percent rate of inflation? What can you do to counteract the effects of inflation?*

Personal Finance in Practice

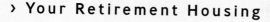

› Your Retirement Housing

The place where you choose to live during retirement can have a significant impact on your financial needs. Use vacations in the years before you retire to explore areas you think you might enjoy. If you find a place you really like, go there at different times of the year. That way you'll know what the climate is like. Meet people who live in the area and learn about activities, transportation, and taxes.

Consider the downside of moving to a new location. You may find yourself stuck in a place you really don't like after all. Moving can also be expensive and emotionally draining. You may miss your children, your grandchildren, and the friends and relatives you leave behind. Be realistic about what you'll have to give up as well as what you'll gain if you move after you retire.

AVOIDING RETIREMENT RELOCATION PITFALLS

Some retired people move to the location of their dreams and then discover that they've made a big mistake financially. Here are some tips from retirement specialists on how to uncover hidden taxes and other costs before you move to a new area:

- Contact the local chamber of commerce to get details on area property taxes and the local economy.

- Contact the state tax department to find out about income, sales, and inheritance taxes as well as special exemptions for retirees.

- Read the Sunday edition of the local newspaper of the city where you're thinking of moving.

- Check with local utility companies to get estimates on energy costs.

- Visit the area in different seasons, and talk to local residents about the various costs of living.

- Rent for a while instead of buying a home immediately.

What are your findings?

_____

_____

_____

✔ CONCEPT CHECK 14–1

1 The three assets you should review on a regular basis during retirement are:

_____

_____

2 What expenses are likely to increase during retirement?

_____

_____

3 What expenses are likely to decrease during retirement?

_____

_____

Your Retirement Income

The four major sources of retirement income are employer pension plans, public pension plans, personal retirement plans, and annuities.

> **OBJECTIVE 2**
> Determine your planned retirement income and develop a balanced budget based on your retirement income.

Figure It Out!

› Saving for Retirement

Calculate how much you would have in 10 years if you saved $2,000 a year at an annual compound interest rate of 10 percent, with the company contributing $500 a year.

	Contributions	10% Interest	Total
Annual contribution of 10% of a $20,000 salary	$2,000.00		
Company annual contribution matching $0.50 of 5% of the salary	500.00		
1st Year			
2nd Year			
3rd Year			
4th Year			
5th Year			
6th Year			
7th Year			
8th Year			
9th Year			
10th Year			
Total			

Employer Pension Plans

A pension plan is a retirement plan that is funded, at least in part, by an employer. With this type of plan, your employer contributes to your retirement benefits, and sometimes you contribute too. (See the nearby Figure It Out feature.) These contributions and earnings remain tax-deferred until you start to withdraw them in retirement.

Private employer pension plans vary. If the company you work for offers one, you should know when you become eligible to receive pension benefits. You'll also need to know what benefits you'll receive. Ask these questions during your interview with a prospective employer and start participating in the plan as soon as possible. Most employer plans are one of two basic types: defined-contribution plans or defined-benefit plans.

defined-contribution plan A plan—profit sharing, money purchase, Keogh, or 401(k)—that provides an individual account for each participant; also called an *individual account plan.*

DEFINED-CONTRIBUTION PLAN A **defined-contribution plan,** sometimes called an *individual account plan,* consists of an individual account of each employee to which the employer contributes a specific amount annually. This type of retirement plan does not guarantee any particular benefit. When you retire and become eligible for benefits, you simply receive the total amount of funds (including investment earnings) that have been placed in your account.

Several types of defined-contribution plans exist. With a money-purchase plan, your employer promises to set aside a certain amount of money for you each year. The amount is generally a percentage of your earnings. Under a stock bonus plan, your employer's contribution is used to buy stock in the company for you. The stock is usually held in trust until you retire. Then you can either keep your shares or sell them. Under a profit-sharing plan, you employer's contribution depends on the company's profits.

In a **401(k) plan,** also known as a *salary-reduction plan,* you set aside a portion of your salary from each paycheck to be deducted from your gross pay and placed in a special account. Your employer will often match your contribution up to a specific dollar amount or percentage of your salary. For example, as one of the retirement benefits, the McGraw-Hill Companies (the publisher of your textbook) offers its employees a 401(k) savings plan. Under this plan, employees can contribute up to 25 percent of their pay with a maximum contribution limit of $15,500 in 2007. The company matches up to 4.5 percent of the first 6 percent of the employee's pretax contributions.

The funds in 401(k) plans are invested in stocks, bonds, and mutual funds. As a result you can accumulate a significant amount of money in this type of account if you begin contributing to it early in your career. In addition, the money that accumulates in your 401(k) plan is tax-deferred, meaning that you don't have to pay taxes on it until you withdraw it.

If you're employed by a tax-exempt institution, such as a hospital or a nonprofit organization, the salary-reduction plan is called a Section 403(b) plan. As in 401(k) plan, the funds in a 403(b) plan are tax-deferred. The amount that can be contributed annually to 401(k) and 403(b) plans is limited by law, as is the amount of annual contributions to money-purchase plans, stock bonus plans, and profit-sharing plans.

Employee contributions to a pension plan belong to you, the employee, regardless of the amount of time that you are with a particular employer. What happens to the contributions that the employer has made to your account if you change jobs and move to another company before you retire? One of the most important aspects of such plans is vesting. **Vesting** is the right to receive the employer's pension plan contributions that you've gained, even if you leave the company before retiring. After a certain number of years with the company, you will become *fully vested,* or entitled to receive 100 percent of the company's contributions to the plan on your behalf. Under some plans, vesting may occur in stages. For example, you might become eligible to receive 20 percent of your benefits after three years and gain another 20 percent each year until you are fully vested.

401(K) plan A plan under which employees can defer current taxation on a portion of their salary; also called a *salary-reduction plan.*

did you know?

The number of 401(k) plans increased from fewer than 8 million in the mid-1980s to about 47 million in 2005. Assets in 401(k) plans increased more than 20-fold during the same period, from less than $100 billion to more than $2 trillion.

Source: U.S. Government Accountability Office, November 2006.

Apply *Yourself!*

Objective 2

Read newspaper or magazine articles to determine what expenses are likely to increase and decrease during retirement. How might this information affect your retirement-planning decisions?

vesting An employee's right to at least a portion of the benefits accrued under an employer pension plan, even if the employee leaves the company before retiring.

DEFINED-BENEFIT PLAN   A **defined-benefit plan** specifies the benefits you'll receive at retirement age, based on your total earnings and years on the job. The plan does not specify how much the employer must contribute each year. Instead your employer's contributions are based on how much money will be needed in the fund as each participant in the plan retires. If the fund is inadequate, the employer will have to make additional contributions.

defined-benefit plan A plan that specifies the benefits the employee will receive at the normal retirement age.

CARRYING BENEFITS FROM ONE PLAN TO ANOTHER   Some pension plans allow *portability,* which means that you can carry earned benefits from one pension plan to another when you change jobs. Workers are also protected by the Employee Retirement Income Security Act of 1974 (ERISA), which sets minimum standards for pensions plans. Under this act the federal government insures part of the payments promised by defined-benefit plans.

Public Pension Plans

Another source of retirement income is Social Security, a public pension plan established by the U.S. government in 1935. The government agency that manages the program is called the Social Security Administration.

CAUTION!

This chart shows the percentage of final earnings Social Security is estimated to replace. Will you have enough to make up the difference?

Your Retirement "Gap"

Preretirement Salary	Percent of Income Replaced by Social Security	The "Gap" You and Your Employer Must Fill
$20,000	45%	35%
30,000	40	40
40,000	33	47
60,000	25	55
$100,000	15	65

Source: TIAA-CREF.

SOCIAL SECURITY   Social Security is an important source of retirement income for most Americans. The program covers 97 percent of all workers, and almost one out of every six Americans currently collects some form of Social Security benefit. Social Security is actually a package of protection that provides benefits to retirees, survivors, and disabled persons. The package protects you and your family while you are working and after you retire. Nevertheless, you should not rely on Social Security to cover all of your retirement expenses. Social Security was never intended to provide 100 percent of your retirement income.

Who Is Eligible for Social Security Benefits?   The amount of retirement benefits you receive from Social Security is based on your earnings over the years. The more you work and the higher your earnings, the greater your benefits, up to a certain maximum amount.

The Social Security Administration provides you an annual history of your earnings and an estimate of your future monthly benefits. The statement includes an estimate, in today's dollars, of how much you will get each month from Social Security when you retire—at age 62, 65, or 70—based on your earnings to date and your projected future earnings.

To qualify for retirement benefits you must earn a certain number of credits. These credits are based on the length of time you work and pay into the system through the Social Security tax, or contribution, on your earnings. You and your employer pay equal amounts of the Social Security tax. Your credits are calculated on a quarterly basis. The number of quarters you need depends on your year of birth. People born after 1928 need 40 quarters to qualify for benefits.

Certain dependents of a worker may receive benefits under the Social Security program. They include a wife or dependent husband aged 62 or older; unmarried children under 18 (or under 19 if they are full-time students no higher than grade 12); and unmarried, disabled children aged 18 or older. Widows or widowers can receive Social Security benefits earlier.

Social Security Retirement Benefits   Most people can begin collecting Social Security benefits at age 62. However, the monthly amount at age 62 will be less than it would be if the person waits until full retirement age. This reduction is permanent.

In the past, people could receive full retirement benefits at age 65. However, because of longer life expectancies, the full retirement age is being increased in gradual steps. For people born in 1960 and later, the full retirement age will be 67. If you postpone applying for benefits beyond your full retirement age, your monthly payments will increase slightly for each year you wait, but only up to age 70.

Social Security Information   For more information about Social Security, you can visit the Social Security Web site. It provides access to forms and publications and gives links to other valuable information. To learn more about the taxability of Social Security benefits, contact the Internal Revenue Service at 800-829-3676 and ask for Publication 554, *Social Security and Equivalent Railroad Retirement Benefits.*

OTHER PUBLIC PENSION PLANS   Besides Social Security, the federal government provides several other special retirement plans for federal government workers and railroad employees. Employees covered under these plans are not covered by Social Security. The Veterans Administration provides pensions for survivors of people who died while in the armed forces. It also offers disability pensions for eligible veterans. Many state and local governments provide retirement plans for their employees as well.

Key Web Sites for Retirement Income
www.quicken.com/retirement
www.moneymag.com

Personal Retirement Plans

In addition to public and employer retirement plans, many people choose to set up personal retirement plans. Such plans are especially important to self-employed people and other workers who are not covered by employer pension plans. Among the most popular personal retirement plans are individual retirement accounts (IRAs) and Keogh accounts.

Key Web Sites for Personal Retirement Plans
www.financialengines.com
http://401k.com

INDIVIDUAL RETIREMENT ACCOUNTS   An **individual retirement account (IRA)** is a special account in which the person sets aside a portion of income for retirement. Several types of IRAs are available:

- **Regular IRA:** A regular (traditional or classic) IRA lets you make annual contributions until age 70½. The contribution limit of up to $4,000 per year through 2007 increased to $5,000 in 2008 and after. Depending on your tax filing status and income, the contribution may be fully or partially tax-deductible. The tax deductibility of a traditional IRA also depends on whether you belong to an employer-provided retirement plan.

- **Roth IRA:** Annual contributions to a Roth IRA are not tax-deductible, but the earnings accumulate tax-free. You may contribute the amounts discussed above if you're a single taxpayer with an adjusted gross income (AGI) of less than $110,000. For married couples the combined AGI must be less than $160,000. You can continue to make annual contributions to a Roth IRA even after age 70½. If you have a Roth IRA, you can withdraw money from the account tax-free and penalty-free after five years if you are at least 59½ years old or plan to use the money to help buy your first home. You may convert a regular IRA to a Roth IRA. Depending on your situation, one type of account may be better for you than the other.

individual retirement account (IRA) A special account in which the employee sets aside a portion of his or her income; taxes are not paid on the principal or interest until money is withdrawn from the account.

CAUTION!

Withdrawals from a regular IRA prior to age 59½ may be subject to a 10 percent penalty. From a Roth IRA, contributions may be withdrawn at any age without penalty if the account has been open for five years.

- **Simplified Employee Pension (SEP) Plan:** A simplified employee pension (SEP) plan, also known as a SEP IRA, is an individual retirement account funded by an employer. Each employee sets up an IRA account at a bank or other financial institution. Then the employer makes an annual contribution of up to $40,000. The employee's contributions, which can vary from year to year, are fully tax-deductible, and earnings are tax-deferred. The SEP IRA is the simplest type of retirement plan if a person is self-employed.

- **Spousal IRA:** A spousal IRA lets you make contributions on behalf of your nonworking spouse if you file a joint tax return. The contributions are the same as for the traditional and Roth IRAs. As with a traditional IRA, this contribution may be fully or partially tax-deductible, depending on your income. This also depends on whether you belong to an employer-provided retirement plan.

- **Rollover IRA:** A rollover IRA is a traditional IRA that lets you roll over, or transfer, all or a portion of your taxable distribution from a retirement plan or other IRA. You may move your money from plan to plan without paying taxes on it. To avoid taxes, however, you must follow certain rules about transferring the money from one plan to another. If you change jobs or retire before age 59½, a rollover IRA may be just what you need. It will let you avoid the penalty you would otherwise have to pay on early withdrawals.
- **Education IRA:** An education IRA, also known as a Coverdell Education Savings Account, is a special IRA with certain restrictions. It allows individuals to contribute up to $2,000 per year toward the education of any child under age 18. The contributions are not tax-deductible. However, they do provide tax-free distributions for education expenses.

Exhibit 14–4 summarizes the various types of IRA.

Whether or not you're covered by another type of pension plan, you can still make IRA contributions that are not tax-deductible. All of the income your IRA earns will compound tax-deferred, until you begin making withdrawals. Remember, the biggest benefit of an IRA lies in its tax-deferred earnings growth. The longer the money accumulates tax-deferred, the bigger the benefit.

IRA Withdrawals   When you retire, you can withdraw the money from your IRA by one of several methods. You can take out all of the money at one time, but the entire amount will be taxed as income. If you decide to withdraw the money from your IRA

Exhibit 14–4

Various Types of IRA

Type of IRA	IRA Features
Regular IRA	• Tax-deferred interest and earnings • Annual limit on individual contributions • Limited eligibility for tax-deductible contributions • Contributions do not reduce current taxes
Roth IRA	• Tax-deferred interest and earnings • Annual limit on individual contributions • Withdrawals are tax-free in specific cases • Contributions do not reduce current taxes
Simplified Employee Pension Plan (SEP IRA)	• "Pay yourself first" payroll reduction contributions • Pretax contributions • Tax-deferred interest and earnings
Spousal IRA	• Tax-deferred interest and earnings • Both working spouse and nonworking spouse can contribute up to the annual limit • Limited eligibility for tax-deductible contributions • Contributions do not reduce current taxes
Rollover IRA	• Traditional IRA that accepts rollovers of all or a portion of your taxable distribution from a retirement plan • You can roll over to a Roth IRA
Education IRA	• Tax-deferred interest and earnings • 10% early withdrawal penalty is waived when money is used for higher-education expenses • Annual limit on individual contributions • Contributions do not reduce current taxes

IRAs can be a good way to save money for retirement. *What are the features of the Education IRA?*

in installments, you will have to pay tax only on the amount that you withdraw. A final alternative would be to place the money that you withdraw in an annuity that guarantees payments over your lifetime. See the discussion of annuities later in this section for further information about this option.

KEOGH PLANS   A **Keogh plan,** also known as an *H.R. 10 plan* or a *self-employed retirement plan,* is a retirement plan specially designed for self-employed people and their employees. Keogh plans have limits on the amount of annual tax-deductible contributions as well as various other restrictions. Keogh plans can be complicated to administer, so you should get professional tax advice before using this type of personal retirement plan.

LIMITS ON PERSONAL RETIREMENT PLANS   With the exception of Roth IRAs, you cannot keep money in most tax-deferred retirement plans forever. When you retire, or by age 70½ at the latest, you must begin to receive "minimum lifetime distributions," withdrawals from the funds you accumulated in the plan. The amount of the distributions is based on your life expectancy at the time the distributions begin. If you don't withdraw the minimum distributions from a retirement account, the IRS will charge you a penalty.

Keogh plan A plan in which tax-deductible contributions fund the retirement of self-employed people and their employees; also called an *H.R. 10 plan* or a *self-employed retirement plan.*

Sheet 42
Retirement Plan Comparison

Annuities

What do you do if you have funded your 401(k), 403(b), Keogh, and profit-sharing plans up to the allowable limits and you want to put away more money for retirement? The answer may be an annuity. You will recall from Chapter 10, an *annuity* is a contract purchased from an insurance company that provides for a sum of money to be paid to a person at regular intervals for a certain number of years or for life.

You might purchase an annuity with the money you receive from an IRA or company pension. You can simply buy an annuity to supplement the income you'll receive from either of these types of plans.

You can choose to purchase an annuity that has a single payment or installment payments. You will also need to decide whether you want the insurance company to send the income from your annuity to you immediately or begin sending it to you at a later date. The payments you receive from an annuity are taxed as ordinary income. However, the interest you earn from the annuity accumulates tax-free until payments begin.

did you know?

Social Security provides only 27 percent of the average retiree's annual income. On average, pension income accounts for about 19 percent, slightly less than that provided by Social Security.

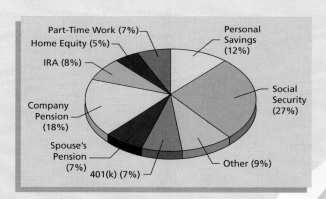

SOURCES OF INCOME IN RETIREMENT

Living on Your Retirement Income

As you plan for retirement, you'll estimate a budget or spending plan. When the time to retire arrives, however, you may find that your expenses are higher than you expected. If that's the case, you'll have some work to do.

First, you'll have to make sure that you're getting all the income to which you're entitled. Are there other programs or benefits for which you might qualify? You'll also need to think about any assets or valuables you might be able to convert to cash or sources of income.

Sheet 43
*Forecasting
Retirement
Income*

You may have to confront the trade-off between spending and saving again. For example, perhaps you can use your skills and time instead of money. Instead of spending money on an expensive vacation, take advantage of free and low-cost recreation opportunities, such as public parks, museums, libraries, and fairs. Retirees often receive special discounts on movie tickets, meals, and more.

WORKING DURING RETIREMENT   Some people decide to work part-time after they retire. Some even take new full-time jobs. Work can provide a person with a greater sense of usefulness, involvement, and self-worth. It may also be a good way to add to your retirement income.

DIPPING INTO YOUR NEST EGG   When should you take money out of your savings during retirement? The answer depends on your financial circumstances, your age, and how much you want to leave to your heirs. (Your *heirs* are the people who will have the legal right to your assets when you die.) Your savings may be large enough to allow you to live comfortably on the interest alone. On the other hand, you may need to make regular withdrawals to help finance your retirement. Dipping into savings isn't wrong. However, you must do so with caution.

If you dip into your retirement nest egg, you should consider one important question: How long will your savings last if you make regular withdrawals? For example, if you have $10,000 in savings that earns 5.5 percent interest, compounded quarterly, you could take out $68 every month for 20 years before reducing those savings to zero. If you have $40,000, you could withdraw $224 every month for 30 years. Whatever your situation is, once your nest egg is gone, it's gone. As shown in Exhibit 14–5, dipping into your nest egg is not wrong, but do so with caution.

Exhibit 14–5   Dipping into Your Nest Egg

Dipping into savings isn't wrong; however, you must do so with caution.

Starting Amount of Nest Egg	You Can Reduce Your Nest Egg to Zero by Withdrawing This Much Each Month for the Stated Number of Years . . .					Or You Can Withdraw This Much Each Month and Leave Your Nest Egg Intact
	10 Years	15 Years	20 Years	25 Years	30 Years	
$ 10,000	$ 107	$ 81	$ 68	$ 61	$ 56	$ 46
15,000	161	121	102	91	84	69
20,000	215	162	136	121	112	92
25,000	269	202	170	152	140	115
30,000	322	243	204	182	168	138
40,000	430	323	272	243	224	184
50,000	537	404	340	304	281	230
60,000	645	485	408	364	337	276
80,000	859	647	544	486	449	368
100,000	1,074	808	680	607	561	460

Note: Based on an interest rate of 5.5 percent per year, compounded quarterly.

Source: Select Committee on Aging, U.S. House of Representatives.

✓ CONCEPT CHECK 14–2

1 What are four major sources of retirement income?

_____

_____

2 What are the two basic types of employer pension plans?

_____

_____

3 What are the most popular personal retirement plans?

_____

_____

4 What is the major difference between a regular IRA and a Roth IRA?

_____

_____

5 What might you do if your expenses during retirement are higher than you expected?

_____

_____

Estate Planning

The Importance of Estate Planning

Many people think of estates as belonging only to the rich or elderly. The fact is, however, everyone has an estate. Simple defined, your **estate** consists of everything you own. During your working years your financial goal is to acquire and accumulate money for both your current and future needs. Many years from now, as you grow older, your point of view will change. Instead of working to acquire assets, you'll start to think about what will happen to your hard-earned wealth after you die. In most cases you'll want to pass that wealth along to your loved ones. That is where estate planning becomes important.

OBJECTIVE 3
Analyze the personal and legal aspects of estate planning.

estate Everything one owns.

What Is Estate Planning?

Estate planning is the process of creating a detailed plan for managing your assets so that you can make the most of them while you're alive and ensure that they're distributed wisely after your death. It's not pleasant to think about your own death. However, it is a part of estate planning. Without a good estate plan, the assets you accumulate during your lifetime might be greatly reduced by various taxes when you die.

Estate planning is an essential part of both retirement planning and financial planning. It has two phases. First, you build your estate through savings, investments, and insurance.

estate planning A definite plan for the administration and disposition of one's property during one's lifetime and at one's death.

Apply *Yourself!*

Sheet 44
Estate
Planning
Activities

Second, you ensure that your estate will be distributed as you wish at the time of your death. If you're married, your estate planning should take into account the needs of your spouse and children. If you are single, you still need to make sure that your financial affairs are in order for your beneficiaries. Your *beneficiary* is a person you've named to receive a portion of your estate after your death.

When you die, your surviving spouse, children, relatives, and friends will face a period of grief and loneliness. At the same time, one or more of these people will probably be responsible for settling your affairs. Make sure that important documents are accessible, understandable, and legally proper.

Legal Documents

An estate plan typically involves various legal documents, one of which is usually a will. When you die, the person who is responsible for handling your affairs will need access to these and other important documents. The documents must be reviewed and verified before your survivors can receive the money and other assets to which they're entitled. If no one can find the necessary documents, your heirs may experience emotionally painful delays. They may even lose part of their inheritance. The important papers you need to collect and organize include:

- Birth certificates for you, your spouse, and your children.
- Marriage certificates and divorce papers.
- Legal name changes (especially important to protect adopted children).
- Military service records.
- Social Security documents.
- Veteran's documents.
- Insurance policies.
- Transfer records of joint bank accounts.
- Safe-deposit box records.
- Automobile registration.
- Titles to stock and bond certificates.

✓ CONCEPT CHECK 14–3

1 What is estate planning?

_____

_____

2 What are the two stages in planning your estate?

_____

_____

3 List some important documents you will need to collect and organize.

_____

_____

Legal Aspects of Estate Planning

Wills

One of the most important documents that every adult should have is a written will. A **will** is the legal document that specifies how you want your property to be distributed after your death. If you die **intestate**—without a valid will—your legal state of residence will step in and control the distribution of your estate without regard for any wishes you may have had.

You should avoid the possibility of dying intestate. The simplest way to do that is to make sure that you have a written will. By having an attorney help you draft your will, you may forestall many difficulties for your heirs. Legal fees for drafting a will vary with the size of your estate and your family situation. A standard will costs between $200 and $350. Make sure that you find an attorney who has experience with wills and estate planning.

Types of Wills

You have several options in preparing a will. The four basic types of wills are the simple will, the traditional marital share will, the exemption trust will, and the stated amount will. The differences among them can affect how your estate will be taxed.

SIMPLE WILL   A simple will leaves everything to your spouse. Such a will is generally sufficient for people with small estates. However, if you have a large or complex estate, a simple will may not meet your objectives. It may also result in higher overall taxation, since everything you leave to your spouse will be taxed as part of his or her estate.

TRADITIONAL MARITAL SHARE WILL   The traditional marital share will leaves one-half of the adjusted gross estate (the total value of the estate minus debts and costs) to the spouse. The other half of the estate may go to children or other heirs. It can also be held in trust for the family. A **trust** is an arrangement by which a designated person, known as a *trustee,* manages assets for the benefit of someone else. A trust can provide a spouse with a lifelong income and would not be taxed at his or her death.

EXEMPTION TRUST WILL   With an exemption trust will, all of your assets go to your spouse except for a certain amount, which goes into a trust. This amount, plus any interest it earns, can provide your spouse with lifelong income that will not be taxed. The tax-free aspect of this type of will may become important if your property value increases considerably after you die.

STATED AMOUNT WILL   The stated amount will allows you to pass on to your spouse any amount that satisfies your family's financial goals. For tax purposes you could pass the exempted amount of $2.00 million (in 2008). However, you might decide to pass on a stated amount related to your family's future income needs or to the value of personal items.

WILLS AND PROBATE   The type of will that is best for your particular needs depends on many factors, including the size of your estate, inflation, your age, and your objectives. No matter what type of will you choose, it's best to avoid probate. **Probate** is the legal procedure of proving a valid or invalid will. It's the process by which your estate is managed and distributed after your death, according to the provisions of your will. A special probate

---

OBJECTIVE 4
Distinguish among various types of wills and trusts.

will The legal declaration of a person's mind as to the disposition of his or her property after death.

intestate Without a valid will.

Key Web Sites for Estate Planning
www.law.cornell.edu
www.nolo.com

trust A legal arrangement through which one's assets are held by a trustee.

did you know?

According to a recent American Association of Retired Persons (AARP) survey, over 40 percent of Americans age 45 or older have not drawn up a will.

probate The legal procedure of proving a valid or invalid will.

court generally validates wills and makes sure that your debts are paid. You should avoid probate because it's expensive, lengthy, and public. As you will read later, a living trust avoids probate and is also less expensive, quicker, and private.

Formats of Wills

Wills may be either holographic or formal. A *holographic will* is a handwritten will that you prepare yourself. It should be written, dated, and signed entirely in your own handwriting. No printed or typed information should appear on its pages. Some states do not recognize holographic wills as legal.

A *formal will* is usually prepared with the help of an attorney. It may be typed, or it may be a preprinted form that you fill out. You must sign the will in front of two witnesses; neither person can be a beneficiary named in the will. The witnesses must then sign the will in front of you.

A *statutory will* is prepared on a preprinted form, available from lawyers or stationery stores. Using preprinted forms to prepare your will presents serious risks. The form may include provisions that are not in the best interests of your heirs. Therefore, it is best to seek a lawyer's advice when you prepare your will.

Sheet 45
Will Planning Sheet

Writing Your Will

Writing a will allows you to express exactly how you want your property to be distributed to your heirs. If you're married, you may think that all the property owned jointly by you and your spouse will automatically go to your spouse after your death. This is true of some assets, such as your house. Even so, writing a will is the only way to ensure that all of your property will end up where you want it.

executor Someone willing and able to perform the tasks involved in carrying out your will.

guardian A person who assumes responsibility for providing children with personal care and managing the deceased's estate for them.

SELECTING AN EXECUTOR   An **executor** is someone who is willing and able to perform the tasks involved in carrying out your will. These tasks include preparing an inventory of your assets, collecting any money due, and paying off your debts. Your executor must also prepare and file all income and estate tax returns. In addition, he or she will be responsible for making decisions about selling or reinvesting assets to pay off debt and provide income for your family while the estate is being settled. Finally, your executor must distribute the estate and make a final accounting to your beneficiaries and to the probate court.

did you know?

Who can be an executor? Any U.S. citizen over 18 who has not been convicted of a felony can be named the executor of a will.

SELECTING A GUARDIAN   If you have children, your will should also name a guardian to care for them in the event that you and your spouse die at the same time and the children cannot care for themselves. A **guardian** is a person who accepts the responsibility of providing children with personal care after their parents' death and managing the parents' estate for the children until they reach a certain age.

ALTERING OR REWRITING YOUR WILL   Sometimes you'll need to change the provisions of your will because of changes in your life or in the law. Once you've made a will, review it frequently so that it remains current. Here are some reasons to review your will:

- You've moved to a new state that has different laws.
- You've sold property that is mentioned in the will.
- The size and composition of your estate have changed.
- You've married, divorced, or remarried.
- Potential heirs have died, or new ones have been born.

Don't make any written changes on the pages of an existing will. Additions, deletions, or erasures on a will that has been signed and witnessed can invalidate the will. If you want to make only a few minor changes, adding a codicil may be the best choice. A **codicil** is a document that explains, adds, or deletes provisions in your existing will.

codicil A document that modifies provisions in an existing will.

A Living Will

At some point in your life you may become physically or mentally disabled and unable to act on your own behalf. If that happens, you'll need a living will. A **living will** is a document in which you state whether you want to be kept alive by artificial means if you become terminally ill and unable to make such a decision. Many states recognize living wills. Exhibit 14–6 is an example of a typical living will.

living will A document that enables an individual, while well, to express the intention that life be allowed to end if he or she becomes terminally ill.

POWER OF ATTORNEY   Related to the idea of a living will is power of attorney. A **power of attorney** is a legal document that authorizes someone to act on your behalf. If you become seriously ill or injured, you'll probably need someone to take care of your needs and personal affairs. This can be done through a power of attorney.

power of attorney A legal document authorizing someone to act on one's behalf.

LETTER OF LAST INSTRUCTION   In addition to a traditional will, it is a good idea to prepare a letter of last instruction. This document is not legally binding, but it can provide your heirs with important information. It should contain your wishes for your funeral arrangements as well as the names of the people who are to be informed of your death.

Exhibit 14–6   A Living Will

Living Will Declaration

Declaration made this _____ day of _____ (month, year)

I, _____, being of sound mind, willfully and voluntarily make known my desire that my dying shall not be artificially prolonged under the circumstances set forth below, do hereby declare

If at any time I should have an incurable injury, disease, or illness regarded as a terminal condition by my physician and if my physician has determined that the application of life-sustaining procedures would serve only to artificially prolong the dying process and that my death will occur whether or not life-sustaining procedures are utilized, I direct that such procedures be withheld or withdrawn and that I be permitted to die with only the administration of medication or the performance of any medical procedure deemed necessary to provide me with comfort care.

In the absence of my ability to give directions regarding the use of such life-sustaining procedures, it is my intention that this declaration shall be honored by my family and physician as the final expression of my legal right to refuse medical or surgical treatment and accept the consequences from such refusal. I understand the full import of this declaration, and I am emotionally and mentally competent to make this declaration.

Signed _____

City, County, and State of Residence _____

The declarant has been personally known to me, and I believe him or her to be of sound mind.

Witness _____

Witness _____

Some people who become terminally ill cannot make decisions on their own behalf.
What is the basic purpose of a living will?

Trusts

Basically, a trust is a legal arrangement that helps manage the assets of your estate for your benefit or that of your beneficiaries. The creator of the trust is called the *trustor,* or *grantor.* The *trustee* might be a person or institution, such as a bank, that administers the trust. A bank charges a small fee for its services in administering a trust. The fee is usually based on the value of the assets in the trust.

Individual circumstances determine whether establishing a trust makes sense. Some of the common reasons for setting up a trust are to:

Key Web Sites for Trusts

www.webtrust.com

http://the.nnepa.com

- Reduce or otherwise provide payment of estate taxes.
- Avoid probate and transfer your assets immediately to your beneficiaries.
- Free yourself from managing your assets while you receive a regular income from the trust.
- Provide income for a surviving spouse or other beneficiary.
- Ensure that your property serves a desired purpose after your death.

Types of Trusts

There are many types of trusts, some of which are described in detail below. You'll need to choose the type of trust that's most appropriate for your particular situation. An estate attorney can advise you about the right type of trust for your personal and family needs.

Apply *Yourself!*

Objective 4

Discuss with your attorney the possibility of establishing a trust as a means of managing your estate.

All trusts are either revocable or irrevocable. A *revocable trust* is one in which you have the right to end the trust or change its terms during your lifetime. An *irrevocable trust* is one that cannot be changed or ended. Revocable trusts avoid the lengthy process of probate, but they do not protect assets from federal or state estate taxes. Irrevocable trusts avoid probate and help reduce estate taxes. However, by law you cannot remove any assets from an irrevocable trust, even if you need them at some later point in your life.

CREDIT-SHELTER TRUST   A credit-shelter trust is one that enables the spouse of a deceased person to avoid paying federal taxes on a certain amount of assets left to him or her as part of an estate. Perhaps the most common estate planning trust, the credit-shelter trust has many other names: bypass trust, "residuary" trust, A/B trust, exemption equivalent trust, or family trust. It is designed to allow married couples, who can leave everything to each other tax free, to take full advantage of the exemption that allows $2 million (in 2006, 2007, and 2008) in every estate to pass free of federal estate taxes.

The Economic Growth and Tax Relief Reconciliation Act of 2001 (EGTRRA) increased the exemption amounts to $3.5 million by the year 2009 as follows:

2006–2008	$2,000,000
2009	$3,500,000
2010	Repeal (no estate tax)
2011	$1,000,000

DISCLAIMER TRUST   A disclaimer trust is appropriate for couples who do not yet have enough assets to need a credit-shelter trust but may have in the future. With a disclaimer trust, the surviving spouse is left everything, but he or she has the right to disclaim, or deny, some portion of the estate. Anything that is disclaimed goes into a credit-shelter trust. This approach allows the surviving spouse to protect wealth from estate taxes.

LIVING TRUST   A living trust, also known as an inter vivos trust, is a property management arrangement that goes into effect while you're alive. It allows you, as a trustor, to receive benefits during your lifetime. To set up a living trust, you simply transfer some of your assets to a trustee. Then you give the trustee instructions for managing the trust while you're alive and after your death. A living trust has several advantages:

- It ensures privacy. A will is a public record; a trust is not.
- The assets held in trust avoid probate at your death. This eliminates probate costs and delays.
- It enables you to review your trustee's performance and make changes if necessary.
- It can relieve you of management responsibilities.
- It's less likely than a will to create arguments between heirs upon your death.
- It can guide your family and doctors if you become terminally ill or unable to make your own decisions.

Setting up a living trust costs more than creating a will. However, depending on your particular circumstances, a living trust can be a good estate planning option.

TESTAMENTARY TRUST   A testamentary trust is one established by your will that becomes effective upon your death. Such a trust can be valuable if your beneficiaries are inexperienced in financial matters. It may also be your best option if your estate taxes will be high. A testamentary trust provides many of the same advantages as a living trust.

Sheet 46
Trust Comparison Sheet

Taxes and Estate Planning

Federal and state governments impose various types of taxes that you must consider in estate planning. The four major types of taxes are estate taxes, estate and trust federal income taxes, inheritance taxes, and gift taxes.

ESTATE TAXES   An estate tax is a federal tax collected on the value of a person's property at the time of his or her death. The tax is based on the fair market value of the deceased person's investments, property, and bank accounts, less an exempt amount of $2 million in 2008 ($3.5 million in 2009); this tax is due nine months after a death.

ESTATE AND TRUST FEDERAL INCOME TAXES   In addition to the federal estate tax return, estates and certain trusts must file federal income tax returns with the Internal Revenue Service. Taxable income for estates and trusts is computed in the same manner as taxable income for individuals. Trusts and estates must pay quarterly estimated taxes.

INHERITANCE TAXES   Your heirs might have to pay a tax for the right to acquire the property that they have inherited. An inheritance tax is a tax collected on the property left by a person in his or her will.

Only state governments impose inheritance taxes. Most states collect an inheritance tax, but state laws differ widely as to exemptions and rates of taxation. A reasonable average for state inheritance taxes would be 4 to 10 percent of whatever the heir receives.

GIFT TAXES   Both the state and federal governments impose a gift tax, a tax collected on money or property valued at more than $12,000 given by one person to another in a single year. One way to reduce the tax liability of your estate is to reduce the size of the estate while you're alive by giving away portions of it as gifts. You're free to make such gifts to your spouse, children, or anyone else at any time. (Don't give away assets if you need them in your retirement!)

✓ CONCEPT CHECK 14–4

1 What is a will?

_____

_____

2 What are the four basic types of wills?

_____

_____

3 What are the responsibilities of an executor?

_____

_____

4 Why should you name a guardian?

_____

_____

5 What is the difference between a revocable and an irrevocable trust?

_____

_____

6 What are the four major types of trusts?

_____

_____

7 What are the four major types of taxes to consider in estate planning?

_____

_____

back to *Getting Personal*

1. Reconsider your responses to the Getting Personal questions at the beginning of the chapter. Have any of your answers changed as a result of studying this chapter?

_____

_____

2. When should one start planning for retirement?

_____

_____

3. Can you depend on Social Security and a company pension plan to pay for your basic living expenses? Explain.

_____

_____

4. In the first column of the following table, list items you'd like to include in your will. Include all financial assets, like cash, savings, stocks, bonds, mutual funds, and other investments you imagine having. Then think about items that may have cost a good deal: a car or bike, computer, stereo system, musical instrument, or sports and hobby equipment. Finally, consider inexpensive items that may have sentimental or other special value to a friend or relative, such as a piece of jewelry, an old letter or photograph, or a favorite memento. In the second column, write to whom you'd like to give the item. In the third column, explain why you've decided to give that item to that particular person. Use extra paper if you need more space.

Financial Assets	To Whom?	Why?
Major possessions		
Items of sentimental or special value		

Chapter Summary

Objective 1   The difference between your assets and your liabilities is your net worth. Review your assets to ensure they are sufficient for retirement. Then estimate your living expenses. Some expenses are likely to decrease while others will increase.

Objective 2   Your possible sources of income during retirement include employer pension plans, public pension plans, personal retirement plans, and annuities. If your income approximates your expenses, you are in good shape; if not, determine additional income needs and sources.

Objective 3   The personal aspects of estate planning depend on whether you are single or married. Never having been married does not eliminate the need to organize your financial affairs. Every adult should have a written will. A will is a way to transfer your property according to your wishes after you die.

Objective 4   The four basic types of wills are the simple will, the traditional marital share will, the exemption trust will, and the stated amount will. Types of trusts include the credit-shelter trust, the disclaimer trust, the living trust, and the testamentary trust.

Federal and state governments impose various types of estate taxes; you can prepare a plan for paying these taxes.

Key Terms

codicil   457

defined-benefit plan   447

defined-contribution plan   446

estate   453

estate planning   453

executor   456

401(k) plan   447

guardian   456

individual retirement
    account (IRA)   449

intestate   455

Keogh plan   451

living will   457

power of attorney   457

probate   455

trust   455

vesting   447

will   455

Problems

1. Janine is 25 and has a good job at a biotechnology company. She currently has $5,000 in an IRA, an important part of her retirement nest egg. She believes her IRA will grow at an annual rate of 8 percent, and she plans to leave it untouched until she retires at age 65. Janine estimates that she will need $875,000 in her *total* retirement nest egg by the time she is 65 in order to have retirement income of $20,000 a year (she expects that Social Security will pay her an additional $15,000 a year).

   a. How much will Janine's IRA be worth when she needs to start withdrawing money from it when she retires? (*Hint:* Use Exhibit A–1 in the appendix to Chapter 1.)

   b. How much money will she have to accumulate in her company's 401(k) plan over the next 40 years in order to reach her retirement income goal?

2. Gene and Dixie, husband and wife (ages 45 and 42), both work. They have an adjusted gross income of $40,000, and they are filing a joint income tax return. What is the maximum IRA contribution they can make? How much of that contribution is tax deductible?

3. Assume your gross pay per pay period is $2,000 and you are in the 33 percent tax bracket. Calculate your net pay and spendable income in the following situations.

   a. You save $200 per pay period after paying income tax on $2,000.

   b. You save $200 per pay period in a tax-sheltered annuity.

4. You have $50,000 in your retirement fund that is earning 5.5 percent per year, compounded quarterly. How many dollars in withdrawals per month would reduce this nest egg to zero in 20 years? How many dollars per month can you withdraw for as long as you live and still leave this nest egg intact? (*Hint:* Use Exhibit 14–5.)

5. In 2008, Joshua gave $11,000 worth of Microsoft stock to his son. In 2010, the Microsoft shares are worth $23,000.

   a. What was the gift tax in 2008?

   b. What is the total amount removed from Joshua's estate in 2010?

   c. What will be the gift tax in 2010?

6. In 2008, you gave a $12,000 gift to a friend. What is the gift tax?

7. Barry and his wife Mary have accumulated over $4 million during their 45 years of marriage. They have three children and five grandchildren. How much money can they gift to their children and grandchildren in 2009 without any gift tax liability?

8. The date of death for a widow was 2008. If the estate was valued at $2,129,000 and the estate was taxed at 47 percent, what was the heir's tax liability?

9. Joe and Rachel are both retired. Married for 50 years, they've amassed an estate worth $2.4 million. The couple has no trusts or other types of tax-sheltered assets. If Joe or Rachel dies in 2006–2008, how much federal estate tax would the surviving spouse have to pay, assuming that the estate is taxed at the 47 percent rate?

Questions

1. How will your spending patterns change during your retirement years? Compare your spending patterns with those shown in Exhibit 14–2.

2. Obtain Form SSA-7004 from your local Social Security office. Complete and mail the form to receive a personal earnings and benefits statement. Use the information in this statement to plan your retirement.

3. Prepare a written report of personal information that would be helpful to you and your heirs. Be sure to include the location of family records, your military service file, and other important papers; medical records; bank accounts; charge accounts; location of your safe-deposit box; U.S. savings bonds, stocks, bonds, and other securities; property owned; life insurance; annuities; and Social Security information.

4. Visit Metropolitan Life Insurance Company's Web page at http://www.lifeadvice.com. Using this information, prepare a report on the following: (*a*) Who needs a will? (*b*) What are the elements of a will (naming a guardian, naming an executor, preparing a will, updating a will, estate taxes, where to keep your will, living will, etc.)? (*c*) How is this report helpful in preparing your own will?

5. Make a list of the criteria you will use in deciding who will be the guardian of your minor children if you and your spouse die at the same time.

Internet Connection

ESTATE PLANNING AND CHARITABLE GIVING

Charitable gifts can be an important tool in estate planning. Giving to charity supports a cause and offers benefits such as reduced taxes and increased interest income.

To find ways to plan an estate and help your favorite charities at the same time, use the Internet to find at least three Web sites that suggest general ways to combine estate planning and charitable giving. At the Web sites, look for specific details about planned giving.

Keywords Used	Site Name	Web Site Addresses	Information Offered

1. What basic approaches to estate planning through charitable giving did you find?

_____

_____

2. Which Web sites suggest using donations in estate planning?

_____

_____

3. Choose a charity that accepts donations from people's wills. How does the charity use these gifts?

_____

_____

Case in Point

PLANNING FOR RETIREMENT

Is a bad day fishing better than a good day at the office? Yes, according to a retired dad, Chuck. With his company pension, at least he didn't have to worry about money. In the good old days, if you had a decent job, you'd hang on to it, and then your company's pension combined with Social Security payments would be enough to live comfortably. Chuck's son, Rob, does not have a company pension and is not sure whether Social Security will even exist when he retires. So when it comes to retirement, the sooner you start saving, the better.

Take Maureen, a salesperson for a computer company, and Therese, an accountant for a lighting manufacturer. Both start their jobs at age 25. Maureen starts saving for retirement right away by investing $300 a month at 9 percent until age 65. But Therese does nothing until age 35. At 35 she begins investing the same $300 a month at 9 percent until age 65. What a shocking difference! Maureen has accumulated $1.4 million, while Therese has only $553,000 in her retirement fund. The moral? The sooner you start, the more you'll have for your retirement. Women especially need to start sooner, because they typically enter the workforce later, have lower salaries, and, ultimately, have lower pensions.

Laura Tarbox, owner and president of Tarbox Equity, explains how to determine your retirement needs and how your budget might change when you retire. Tarbox advises that the old rule of thumb that you need 60 to 70 percent of preretirement income is too low an estimate. She cautions that most people will want to spend very close to what they were spending before retiring. There are some expenses that might be lower, however, such as clothing for work, dry cleaning, and commuting expenses. Other expenses, though, such as insurance, travel, and recreation, may increase during retirement.

Questions

1. In the past, many workers chose to stay with their employers until retirement. What was the major reason for employees' loyalty?

2. How did Maureen amass $1.4 million for retirement, while Therese could accumulate only $553,000?

3. Why do women need to start early to save for retirement?

4. What expenses may increase or decrease during retirement?

Continuing Case

RETIREMENT PLANNING

Life Situation

Pam, 48

Josh, 50

Children ages 21, 19, and 16

Financial Data

Monthly income $6,700

Assets $242,500

Living expenses $5,600

Liabilities $69,100

With two children in college, the Brocks once again find their life situation changing. Compared to five years ago, their total assets have declined due to college expenses. The Brocks' oldest child will graduate next year, but the youngest will enter college in a couple of years. The drain on the family's finances will continue.

While the family's finances are adequate, both Pam and Josh are beginning to think more about retirement. Over the years, Josh has taken advantage of different career opportunities. Today his annual salary is higher than ever. However, his employment changes have resulted in a smaller pension fund than would have been available had he remained with the same organization.

The current value of his pension plan is just over $115,000. The investment program he and Pam started almost 10 years ago is growing and is now worth about $62,000. But they still worry whether they will have enough money to finance their retirement when Josh retires in 15 years.

Questions

1. How would you assess the strengths and weaknesses of the Brocks' financial condition at this stage in their lives?

2. Since Pam is 48 and Josh is 50, what should be their major priorities as they continue planning for retirement?

3. Describe potential uses by the Brocks of *Your Personal Financial Plan* sheets 42–44.

ESTATE PLANNING

Life Situation

Pam, 48

Josh, 50

Children ages 21, 19, and 16

Financial Data

Monthly income $6,700

Living expenses $5,600

Assets $242,500

Liabilities $69,100

Pam and Josh should also be concerned with various estate planning actions. They have talked about a will and investigated the benefits of several types of trusts. However, they have not taken any specific actions.

Questions

1. What types of estate planning activities might be considered by the Brocks at this time?

2. In what ways might *Your Personal Financial Plan* sheets 45–46 be used by the Brocks?

Video Case

THE ROLE OF AN EXECUTOR: A SERIOUS, CHALLENGING JOB

While you may feel honored when asked to serve as the executor of someone's estate, the appointment is really a serious job and a challenging one at that.

Questions

1. What is a role of an executor of an estate?

2. Can you be held liable for mismanaging an estate?

3. Is there any compensation for being an executor?

www.mhhe.com/kdh

Spending Diary

"KEEPING TRACK OF MY DAILY SPENDING GETS ME TO START THINKING ABOUT SAVING AND INVESTING FOR RETIREMENT."

Directions

The consistent use of a Daily Spending Diary can provide you with ongoing information that will help you manage your spending, saving, and investing activities. Taking time to reconsider your spending habits can result in achieving better satisfaction from your available finances.

Analysis Questions

1. What portion of your available finances involve saving or investing for long-term financial security?

2. What types of retirement and estate planning activities might you start to consider at this point of your life?

Retirement Plan Comparison

Financial Planning Activities: Compare benefits and costs for different retirement plans (401K, IRA, Keogh). Analyze advertisements and articles, and contact your employer and financial institutions to obtain the information below.

Suggested Web Sites: www.lifenet.com   www.aarp.org

Type of plan			
Name of financial institution or employer			
Address			
Phone			
Web site			
Type of investments			
Minimum initial deposit			
Minimum additional deposits			
Employer contributions			
Current rate of return			
Service charges/fees			
Safety insured? By whom?			
Amount			
Payroll deduction available			
Tax benefits			
Penalty for early withdrawal: • IRS penalty (10%) • Other penalties			
Other features or restrictions			

What's Next for Your Personal Financial Plan?

- Survey local businesses to determine the types of retirement plans available to employees.
- Talk to representatives of various financial institutions to determine their suggestions for IRA investments.

Forecasting Retirement Income

Financial Planning Activities: Determine the amount needed to save each year to have the necessary funds to cover retirement living costs. Estimate the information requested below.

Suggested Web Sites: www.ssa.gov   www.pensionplanners.com

Estimated annual retirement living expenses

Estimated annual living expenses
if you retired today $ _____

Future value for _____ years until
retirement at expected annual
income of _____ % (use future
value of $1, Exhibit A–1 of
Appendix A)   × _____

**Projected annual retirement living expenses
adjusted for inflation** . . . .   (A) $ _____

Estimated annual income at retirement

Social security income $ _____

Company pension, personal
retirement account income $ _____

Investment and other income $ _____

Total retirement income . . . .   (B) $ _____

Additional retirement plan contributions (if B is less than A)

Annual shortfall of income after
retirement (A − B) $ _____

Expected annual rate of return on
invested funds after retirement,
percentage expressed as a decimal $ _____

Needed investment fund after retirement (A − B) . . . .   (C) $ _____

Future value factor of a series of deposits for _____ years until
retirement and an expected annual rate of return before
retirement of _____ % (Use Exhibit A–2 in Appendix A)   (D) $ _____

**Annual deposit to achieve needed investment fund
(C ÷ D)** . . . . $ _____

What's Next for Your Personal Financial Plan?

- Survey retired individuals or people close to retirement to obtain information on their main sources of retirement income.
- Make a list that suggests the best investment options for an individual retirement account.

Estate Planning Activities

Financial Planning Activities: Develop a plan for estate planning and related financial activities. Respond to the following questions as a basis for making and implementing an estate plan.

Suggested Web Sites: www.nolo.com   www.webtrust.com

Are your financial records, including recent tax forms, insurance policies, and investment and housing documents, organized and easily accessible?	
Do you have a safe-deposit box? Where is it located? Where is the key?	
Location of life insurance policies. Name and address of insurance company and agent.	
Is your will current? Location of copies of your will. Name and address of your lawyer.	
Name and address of your executor	
Do you have a listing of the current value of assets owned and liabilities outstanding?	
Have any funeral and burial arrangements been made?	
Have you created any trusts? Name and location of financial institution.	
Do you have any current information on gift and estate taxes?	
Have you prepared a letter of last instruction? Where is it located?	

What's Next for Your Personal Financial Plan?

- Talk to several individuals about the actions they have taken related to estate planning.
- Create a list of situations in which a will would need to be revised.

Name: _____ Date: _____

Will Planning Sheet

Financial Planning Activities: Compare costs and features of various types of wills. Obtain information for the various areas listed based on your current and future situation; contact attorneys regarding the cost of these wills.

Suggested Web Sites: www.netplanning.com   www.estateplanninglinks.com

Type of will	Features that would be appropriate for my current or future situation	Cost Attorney, Address, Phone

What's Next for Your Personal Financial Plan?

- Create a list of items that you believe would be desirable to include in a will.
- Obtain the cost of a will from a number of different lawyers.

Trust Comparison Sheet

Financial Planning Activities: Identify features of different types of trusts. Research features of various trusts to determine their value to your personal situation.

Suggested Web Sites: www.webtrust.com   www.lifenet.com

Type of trust	Benefits	Possible value for my situation

What's Next for Your Personal Financial Plan?

- Talk to legal and financial planning experts to contrast the cost and benefits of wills and trusts.
- Talk to one or more lawyers to obtain information about the type of trust recommended for your situation.

A
Developing a Career Search Strategy

The average person changes jobs seven times during a lifetime. Most likely, you will reevaluate your work situation on a regular basis. The following information will help you plan and manage your career.

The Career Planning Process

Career planning activities may be viewed using the following steps:

1. *Personal assessment*—to determine interests and values, and to identify talents and abilities.
2. *Employment market analysis*—to assess geographic, economic, technological, and social influences on employment opportunities.
3. *Application process*—in which you prepare a résumé and create a cover letter.
4. *Interview process*—in which you practice your interview skills, research the organization, and send a follow-up message to the organization.
5. *Employment acceptance*—when you assess the salary and other financial factors as well as the organizational environment of your potential employer.
6. *Career development and advancement*—in which you develop plans to enhance career success behaviors and build strong work relationships.

CAREER ACTIVITY 1

For each of the six steps of the career planning process, write: (*a*) a goal you have now or might have in the future and (*b*) an action you might take regarding this career planning area.

Using Career Information Sources to Identify Career Trends

Whereas careers have dwindled in some sectors of our economy, opportunities in other sectors have grown. Service industries that are expected to have the greatest employment potential in the 21st century include computer technology, health care, business services, social and government services, sales and retailing, hospitality and food services, management and human resources, education, and financial services.

Many career information sources are available; these include:

1. *Print and other media sources,* such as the *Occupational Outlook Handbook,* which provides detailed information on many occupations. The employment and business sections of newspapers also publish articles on various career topics.
2. *Online sources* are available to assist you with all aspects of career planning. Consider a Web search to gather information about résumés, effective interviewing, or creating a career portfolio.

3. *Informational interviews* are very effective for obtaining career information. A planned discussion with a person in a field of interest to you will help you learn about the job duties, required training, and the person's feelings about the career. Most people like to talk about their work experiences. Before the interview, plan to ask questions such as:

- How did you get your current position? Did other jobs lead to this one?
- In what ways do you find your work most satisfying? What are your main frustrations?
- What tasks and activities are required in your work?
- What are the most important qualifications for working in this field? What training and education are needed?
- What advice would you give a person who is considering this type of work?

CAREER ACTIVITY 2

Locate a career information source. Prepare a brief summary of key ideas that could be valuable to you in the future.

Obtaining Employment Experience

Most people possess more career skills than they realize. Your involvement in school, community, and work activities provides a foundation for employment experiences. The following opportunities offer work-related training:

1. *Part-time employment* can provide experience and knowledge for a career field.
2. *Volunteer work* in community organizations or agencies can help you acquire skills, establish good work habits, and make contacts.
3. *Internships* allow you to gain experience needed to obtain employment in a field.
4. *Campus projects* offer work-related experiences to help you obtain career skills through campus organizations, course assignments, and research projects.

CAREER ACTIVITY 3

Create a list of your work, volunteer, and school activities. Describe how each could apply to a future work situation.

Identifying Job Opportunities

Some of the most valuable sources of job information include:

1. *Job advertisements* in newspapers and professional periodicals are a common source. However, since over 60 percent of jobs may not be advertised to the public, use other job search activities as well.
2. *Career fairs,* on campus and at convention centers, allow you to contact several firms in a short time. At a career fair, you will be asked a couple of questions to determine if you qualify for a longer interview. Prepare for job fairs by being ready to quickly communicate your potential contributions to an organization. Knowing something about the organization will help distinguish you from other applicants.

3. *Employment agencies* match job hunters with employers. Often the hiring company pays the fee. Be wary when asked to pay a fee in advance. Government employment services may be contacted through your state employment service or state department of labor.
4. *Business contacts* advise people about careers. Friends, relatives, and others are potential business contacts. *Networking* is the process of making and using contacts to obtain and update career information.
5. *Job creation* involves developing a position that matches your skills with organizational needs. As you develop skills you enjoy, you may be able to create a demand for yourself.
6. *Other job search sources* include (*a*) visits to companies to make face-to-face contacts; (*b*) business directories and Web sites to obtain names of organizations that employ people with your qualifications; and (*c*) alumni who work in your field.

CAREER ACTIVITY 4

Using one or more of the sources of available jobs, select a position that you might apply for in the future. How well do your qualifications match those required for the job?

Developing a Résumé

Marketing yourself to prospective employers usually requires a résumé, or personal information sheet.

Résumé Elements

This summary of your education, training, experience, and other qualifications has these main components:

1. *The personal data section* presents your name, address, telephone number, and e-mail address. Do not include your birth date, sex, height, and weight unless this information applies to a specific job qualification.
2. *A career objective* is designed to clearly focus you to a specific employment situation. Your career objective may be omitted from the résumé and communicated in your cover letter. Also, consider a summary section with a synopsis of your main skills and capabilities.
3. *The education section* should include dates, schools attended, fields of study, and degrees earned.
4. *The experience section* lists organizations, dates of involvement, and responsibilities for previous employment, relevant school activities, and community service. Highlight computer skills, technical abilities, and other specific competencies. Use action verbs to connect your experience to the needs of the organization. Focus this information on results and accomplishments.
5. *The related information section* may include honors, awards, and other activities related to your career field.
6. *The references section* lists people who can verify your skills. These individuals may be teachers, past employers, supervisors, or business colleagues. References are usually not included in a résumé; however, have this information available when requested.

Exhibit A–1

Sample Résumé

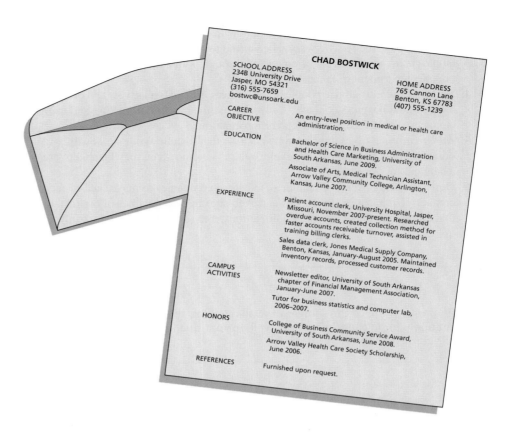

CHAD BOSTWICK

SCHOOL ADDRESS
234B University Drive
Jasper, MO 54321
(316) 555-7659
bostwc@unsoark.edu

HOME ADDRESS
765 Cannon Lane
Benton, KS 67783
(407) 555-1239

CAREER
OBJECTIVE   An entry-level position in medical or health care administration.

EDUCATION

Bachelor of Science in Business Administration and Health Care Marketing, University of South Arkansas, June 2009.

Associate of Arts, Medical Technician Assistant, Arrow Valley Community College, Arlington, Kansas, June 2007.

EXPERIENCE

Patient account clerk, University Hospital, Jasper, Missouri, November 2007-present. Researched overdue accounts, created collection method for faster accounts receivable turnover, assisted in training billing clerks.

Sales data clerk, Jones Medical Supply Company, Benton, Kansas, January-August 2005. Maintained inventory records, processed customer records.

CAMPUS
ACTIVITIES

Newsletter editor, University of South Arkansas chapter of Financial Management Association, January-June 2007.

Tutor for business statistics and computer lab, 2006–2007.

HONORS

College of Business Community Service Award, University of South Arkansas, June 2008.

Arrow Valley Health Care Society Scholarship, June 2006.

REFERENCES   Furnished upon request.

Résumé Preparation

An effective résumé must be presented in a professional manner. Many candidates are disqualified by poor résumés. Limit your résumé to one page. Send a two-page résumé only if you have enough material to fill three pages; then use the most valid information to prepare an impressive two-page presentation.

One key to successful résumé writing is the use of action words to demonstrate what you have accomplished or achieved. Examples of strong action words include:

- Achieved
- Administered
- Coordinated
- Created
- Designed
- Developed
- Directed

- Edited
- Facilitated
- Initiated
- Implemented
- Managed
- Monitored
- Organized

- Planned
- Produced
- Researched
- Supervised
- Trained
- Updated

Other words and phrases that commonly impress prospective employers include foreign language skills, computer experience, achievement, research experience, flexible, team projects, and overseas study or experience. For best results, seek assistance from counselors, the campus placement office, and friends to find errors and suggest improvements.

CAREER ACTIVITY 5

Outline the main sections of a résumé that you might create for a job offer the next couple of years. Conduct a Web search to find a résumé format that you might use.

Creating a Cover Letter

A *cover letter,* designed to express your interest in a specific job, accompanies your résumé and consists of three main sections:

1. The *introductory paragraph* gets the reader's attention. Indicate your reason for writing by referring to the employment position. Communicate what you have to offer the organization. If applicable, mention the name of the person who referred you.

2. The *development paragraphs* highlight aspects of your background that specifically qualify you for the position. At this point, elaborate on experiences and training. Connect your skills and competencies to specific organizational needs.

3. The *concluding paragraph* should request action. Ask for an interview to discuss your qualifications in detail. Include your contact information, such as telephone numbers and the times when available. Close your letter by summarizing your benefits to the organization.

Create a personalized cover letter for each position addressed to the appropriate person in the organization. A poorly prepared cover letter guarantees rejection.

In recent years, job applicants are increasingly using a *targeted application letter* instead of a résumé and cover letter. After researching a position and company, you can communicate how your specific skills and experiences will benefit the organization. Once again, your goal is to emphasize achievements and accomplishments so you will be invited for an interview.

Exhibit A–2   **Sample Cover Letter**

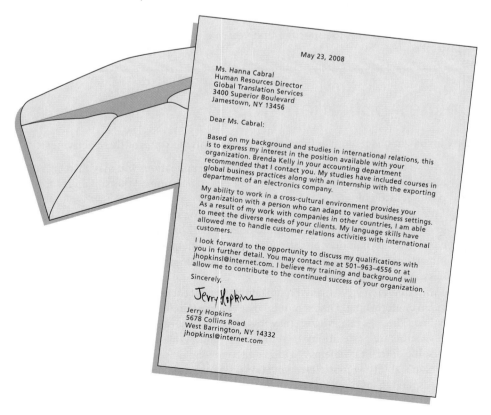

May 23, 2008

Ms. Hanna Cabral
Human Resources Director
Global Translation Services
3400 Superior Boulevard
Jamestown, NY 13456

Dear Ms. Cabral:

Based on my background and studies in international relations, this is to express my interest in the position available with your organization. Brenda Kelly in your accounting department recommended that I contact you. My studies have included courses in global business practices along with an internship with the exporting department of an electronics company.

My ability to work in a cross-cultural environment provides your organization with a person who can adapt to varied business settings. As a result of my work with companies in other countries, I am able to meet the diverse needs of your clients. My language skills have allowed me to handle customer relations activities with international customers.

I look forward to the opportunity to discuss my qualifications with you in further detail. You may contact me at 501–963–4556 or at jhopkinsl@internet.com. I believe my training and background will allow me to contribute to the continued success of your organization.

Sincerely,

Jerry Hopkins

Jerry Hopkins
5678 Collins Road
West Barrington, NY 14332
jhopkinsl@internet.com

> ## CAREER ACTIVITY 6
> Select a potential job. Create a cover letter for that position. Conduct an online search to obtain additional suggestions for effective cover letters.

Career Portfolios

In addition to a résumé, many job applicants prepare a *career portfolio.* This collection of documents and other items provides tangible evidence of your ability and skills. A career portfolio may include the following items:

1. *Documentation*—a résumé, sample interview answers, a competency summary, and letters of recommendation.
2. *Creative works*—ads, product designs, packages, brand, promotions, and video clips on DVD.
3. *Research project samples*—research findings, PowerPoint presentation, Web site designs, marketing plans, and photos of project activities.
4. *Employment accomplishments*—published articles, sales results data, financial charts, and news articles of community activities.

A career portfolio can present your abilities and experiences in a tangible manner. In addition, these materials will communicate your initiative and uniqueness. An electronic portfolio can be developed on a Web site, with various graphics and links. Be sure your home page is not cluttered and is organized to quickly find desired information. Consider sending a CD with your Web site files along with your résumé.

> ## CAREER ACTIVITY 7
> List the various items (be specific) that you might include in your career portfolio.

Online Application Process

Many organizations require online applications involving some of these activities:

1. *Online applications*—in addition to the basic application, you may also be asked to answer some preliminary questions to determine your suitability for the position available.
2. *E-résumés*—when posting your résumé online or sending it by e-mail, be sure to (*a*) use a simple format, avoiding bold, underlines, italics, and tabs; and (*b*) attach no files that may be difficult to open. Remember that an Internet résumé is impersonal, so do not overlook other job search methods—phone calls, ads, job fairs, and personal contacts.
3. *Cyber interviewing*—many organizations conduct screening interviews using video conferencing. Others require that you post preliminary interview responses online. These "e-interviews" may involve questions such as: "Would you rather have structure or flexibility in your work?" and "What approach do you use to solve difficult problems?" Online interviewing may also be used to test a person's ability in job-related situations. For example, an applicant may be asked to respond to tasks such as those that an investment broker or customer service representative might encounter.

> **CAREER ACTIVITY 8**
>
> Go to a Web site that posts résumés. Obtain information on the process involved in posting your résumé online.

The Job Interview

The interview phase is limited to candidates who possess the desired qualifications.

Preparing for the Interview

Prepare by obtaining additional information about the organization. The best sources include the library, the Internet, observations during company visits, analysis of company products, informal conversations with employees, and discussions with people knowledgeable about the company or industry. Research the company's operations, competitors, recent successes, planned expansion, and personnel policies to help you discuss your potential contributions to the company.

Exhibit A–3

Common Interview Questions

Education and Training Questions

What education and training qualify you for this job?

Why are you interested in working for this company?

In addition to going to school, what activities have helped you to expand your interests and knowledge?

What did you like best about school?

What did you like least?

Work and other Experience Questions

In what types of situations have you done your best work?

Describe the supervisors who motivated you most.

Which of your past accomplishments are you proud of?

Have you ever had to coordinate the activities of several people?

Describe some people whom you have found difficult to work with.

Describe a situation in which your determination helped you achieve a specific goal.

What situations frustrate you?

Other than past jobs, what experiences have helped prepare you for this job?

What methods do you consider best for motivating employees?

Personal Qualities Questions

What are your major strengths?

What are your major weaknesses? What have you done to overcome your weaknesses?

(continued)

Personal Qualities Questions
What do you plan to be doing 5 or 10 years from now?
Which individuals have had the greatest influence on you?
What traits make a person successful?
How well do you communicate your ideas orally and in writing?
How would your teachers and your past employers describe you?
What do you do in your leisure time?
How persuasive are you in presenting ideas to others?

Another preinterview activity is preparing questions you will ask during the interview, such as:

- What do employees like most about your organization's working environment?
- What challenges might be encountered by new employees?
- What training opportunities are available to employees who desire advancement?
- What qualities do your most successful employees possess?
- What actions of competitors are likely to affect the company in the near future?

Successful interviewing requires practice. Use a video recorder or work with friends to develop confidence when interviewing. Organize ideas, speak clearly and calmly, and communicate enthusiasm. Prepare specific answers regarding your strengths. Campus organizations and career placement offices may offer opportunities for interview practice.

When interviewing, keep in mind that proper dress and grooming are vital. Dress more conservatively than current employees. A business suit is usually appropriate. Avoid trendy and casual styles, and don't wear too much jewelry.

Confirm the time and location of the interview. Take copies of your résumé, your reference list, and paper for notes. Arrive about 10 minutes earlier than your appointed time.

The Interview Process

Interviews may include situations or questions to determine how you react under pressure. Answer clearly in a controlled manner.

Behavioral interviewing, also called *competency-based interviewing,* is frequently used to evaluate an applicant's on-the-job potential. In these questions, you might be asked how you might handle various work situations. Behavioral interview questions typically begin with "Describe . . ." or "Tell me about . . ." to encourage interviewees to better explain their work style.

In *situational interviewing,* you are asked to participate in role-playing, similar to what may be encountered on the job. For example, you might be asked to resolve a complaint with a customer or negotiate with a supplier. This interview experience is used to evaluate your ability to work in various organizational environments.

Avoid talking too much, but answer each question completely using good eye contact. Stay calm during the interview. Remember, you are being asked questions about a subject about which you are the world's expert—YOU! Finally, thank the interviewer for the opportunity to discuss the job and your qualifications.

After the Interview

Most interviewers conclude by telling you when you can expect to hear from them. While waiting, do two things. First, send a follow-up letter or e-mail within a day or two expressing your appreciation for the opportunity to interview. If you don't get the job, this thank-you letter can make a positive impression to improve your chances for future consideration.

Second, do a self-evaluation of your interview performance. Write down the areas to improve. Try to remember the questions you were asked that differed from your expected questions. Remember, the more interviews you have, the better you will present yourself and the better the chance of being offered a job.

CAREER ACTIVITY 9

Have someone ask you sample interview questions. Have them point out the strengths and weaknesses of your interview skills.

Job Offer Comparison

The financial aspects of a job should be assessed along with some organization factors.

1. *Salary and financial factors*—your rate of pay will be affected by the type of work and your experience. The position may also include employee benefits. These include insurance, retirement plans, vacation time, and other special benefits for employees. Many organizations offer recreational facilities, discounts, and other advantages for workers.
2. *Organizational environment*—while the financial elements of a job are very important, also consider the working environment. Leadership style, dress code, and the social atmosphere should be investigated. Talk with people who have worked in the organization. Advancement potential might also be evaluated. Training programs may be available. These opportunities can be very beneficial for your long-term career success.

CAREER ACTIVITY 10

Prepare a list of factors that you would consider when accepting a job. Talk to other people about what they believe to be important when accepting a job.

Key Web Sites for Career Planning

www.careerjournal.com   www.rileyguide.com
www.ajb.dni.us   www.careerbuilder.com
www.monster.com   www.careerfairs.com
www.bls.gov/oco   www.businessweek.com/careers

B Consumer Agencies and Organizations

The following government agencies and private organizations can offer information and assistance on various financial planning and consumer purchasing areas. These groups can serve your needs when you want to

- Research a financial or consumer topic area.
- Obtain information for planning a purchase decision.
- Seek assistance to resolve a consumer problem.

Section 1 provides an overview of federal, state, and local agencies and other organizations you may contact for information related to various financial planning and consumer topic areas. Section 2 covers state consumer protection offices that can assist you in local matters.

Section 1

Most federal agencies may be contacted through the Internet; several Web sites are noted. In addition, consumer information from several federal government agencies may be accessed at www.consumer.gov.

Exhibit B–1   Federal, State, and Local Agencies and Other Organizations

Topic Area	Federal Agency	State, Local Agency; Other Organizations
Advertising False advertising Product labeling Deceptive sales practices Warranties	Federal Trade Commission 600 Pennsylvania Avenue, NW Washington, DC 20580 1-877-FTC-HELP (www.ftc.gov)	State Consumer Protection Office c/o State Attorney General or Governor's Office National Fraud Information Center Box 65868 Washington, DC 20035 1-800-876-7060 (www.fraud.org)
Air Travel Air safety Airport regulation Airline route	Federal Aviation Administration 800 Independence Avenue, SW Washington, DC 20591 1-800-FAA-SURE (www.faa.gov)	International Airline Passengers Association Box 660074 Dallas, TX 75266 1-800-527-5888 (www.iapa.com)

Exhibit B–1   (*continued*)

Topic Area	Federal Agency	State, Local Agency; Other Organizations
Appliances/Product Safety Potentially dangerous products Complaints against retailers, manufacturers	Consumer Product Safety Commission Washington, DC 20207 1-800-638-CPSC (www.cpsc.gov)	Council of Better Business Bureaus 4200 Wilson Boulevard Arlington, VA 22203 1-800-955-5100 (www.bbb.org)
Automobiles New cars Used cars Automobile repairs Auto safety	Federal Trade Commission (see above) National Highway Traffic Safety Administration 400 Seventh Street, SW Washington, DC 20590 1-800-424-9393 (www.nhtsa.gov)	AUTOCAP/National Automobile Dealers Association 8400 Westpark Drive McLean, VA 22102 1-800-252-6232 (www.nada.org) Center for Auto Safety 2001 S Street, NW Washington, DC 20009 (202) 328-7700 (www.autosafety.org)
Banking and Financial Institutions Checking accounts Savings accounts Deposit insurance Financial services	Federal Deposit Insurance Corporation 550 17th Street, NW Washington, DC 20429 1-877-275-3342 (www.fdic.gov) Comptroller of the Currency 15th Street and Pennsylvania Avenue, NW Washington, DC 20219 (202) 447-1600 (www.occ.treas.gov) Federal Reserve Board Washington, DC 20551 (202) 452-3693 (www.federalreserve.gov) National Credit Union Administration 1775 Duke Street Alexandria, VA 22314 (703) 518-6300 (www.ncua.gov)	State Banking Authority Credit Union National Association Box 431 Madison, WI 53701 (608) 232-8256 (www.cuna.org) American Bankers Association 1120 Connecticut Avenue, NW Washington, DC 20036 (202) 663-5000 (www.aba.com) U.S. savings bond rates 1-800-US-BONDS (www.savingsbonds.gov)
Career Planning Job training Employment information	Coordinator of Consumer Affairs Department of Labor Washington, DC 20210 (202) 219-6060 (www.dol.gov)	State Department of Labor or State Employment Service

Exhibit B–1 (*continued*)

Topic Area	Federal Agency	State, Local Agency; Other Organizations
Consumer Credit Credit cards Deceptive credit advertising Truth-in-Lending Act Credit rights of women, minorities	Federal Trade Commission 600 Pennsylvania Avenue, NW Washington, DC 20580 (202) 326-2222 (www.ftc.gov)	100 Edgewood Avenue (#1800) Atlanta, GA 30303 1-800-251-2227 (www.cccsatl.org) National Foundation for Credit Counseling 801 Roeder Road (#900) Silver Spring, MD 20910 (301) 589–5600 (www.nfcc.org)
Environment Air, water pollution Toxic substances	Environmental Protection Agency Washington, DC 20024 1-800-438-4318 (indoor air quality) 1-800-426-4791 (drinking water safety) (www.epa.gov)	Clean Water Action 4455 Connecticut Avenue, NW Washington, DC 20008 (202) 895-0420 (www.cleanwater.org)

Food
Food grades
Food additives
Nutritional information
	U.S. Department of Agriculture
	Washington, DC 20250
	1-800-424-9121
	(www.usda.gov)
	
	Food and Drug Administration
	5600 Fishers Lane
	Rockville, MD 20857
	1-888-463-6332
	(www.fda.gov)
		Center for Science in the Public
		  Interest
		1875 Connecticut Avenue, NW,
		  Suite 300
		Washington, DC 20009
		(202) 332-9110
		(www.cspinet.org)

Funerals Cost disclosure Deceptive business practices	Federal Trade Commission (see above)	Funeral Service Help Line 13625 Bishop's Drive Brookfield, WI 53005 1-800-228-6332 (www.nfda.org)

Housing and Real Estate
Fair housing practices
Mortgages
Community development
	Department of Housing and Urban
	  Development
	451 Seventh Street, SW
	Washington, DC 20410
	1-800-669-9777
	(www.hud.gov)
		National Association of Realtors
		(www.realtor.com)
		(www.move.com)
		
		National Association of Home
		  Builders
		1201 15th Street, NW
		Washington, DC 20005
		(www.nahb.com)

Exhibit B–1   (*continued*)

Topic Area	Federal Agency	State, Local Agency; Other Organizations
Insurance Policy conditions Premiums Types of coverage Consumer complaints	Federal Trade Commission (see above) National Flood Insurance Program 500 C Street, SW Washington, DC 20472 1-888-CALL-FLOOD	State Insurance Regulator American Council of Life Insurance 1001 Pennsylvania Avenue, NW Washington, DC 20004-2599 (www.acli.com) Insurance Information Institute 110 William Street New York, NY 10038 1-800-331-9146 (www.iii.org)

Investments
Stocks, bonds
Mutual funds
Commodities
Investment brokers
	Securities and Exchange Commission
	100 F Street, NE
	Washington, DC 20549
	(202) 551-6551
	(www.sec.gov)
	
	Commodity Futures Trading
	  Commission
	1155 21st Street, NW
	Washington, DC 20581
	(202) 418-5000
	(www.cftc.gov)
		Investment Company Institute
		1600 M Street, NW
		Washington, DC 20036
		(202) 293-7700
		(www.ici.org)
		
		National Association of Securities
		  Dealers
		1735 K Street, NW
		Washington, DC 20006
		(202) 728-8000
		(www.nasd.com)
		
		National Futures Association
		200 West Madison Street
		Chicago, IL 60606
		1-800-621-3570
		(www.nfa.futures.org)
		
		Securities Investor Protection Corp.
		805 15th Street, NW, Suite 800
		Washington, DC 20005
		(202) 371-8300
		(www.sipc.org)

Legal Matters Consumer complaints Arbitration	Department of Justice Office of Consumer Litigation Washington, DC 20530 (202) 514-2401	American Arbitration Association 140 West 51st Street New York, NY 10020 (212) 484-4000 (www.adr.org) American Bar Association 321 North Clark Street Chicago, IL 60610 1-800-285-2221 (www.abanet.org)

Exhibit B–1   (concluded)

Topic Area	Federal Agency	State, Local Agency; Other Organizations
Mail Order Damaged products Deceptive business practices Illegal use of U.S. mail	U.S. Postal Service Washington, DC 20260-2202 1-800-ASK-USPS (www.usps.gov)	Direct Marketing Association 1120 Avenue of the Americas New York, NY 10036 (212) 768-7277 (www.the-dma.org)
Medical Concerns Prescription medications Over-the-counter medications Medical devices Health care	Food and Drug Administration (see above) Public Health Service 200 Independence Avenue, SW Washington, DC 20201 1-800-336-4797 (www.usphs.gov)	American Medical Association 510 North State Street Chicago, IL 60610 1-800-621-8335 (www.ama-assn.org) Public Citizen Health Research Group 1600 20th Street, NW Washington, DC 20009 (202) 588-1000
Retirement Old-age benefits Pension information Medicare	Social Security Administration 6401 Security Boulevard Baltimore, MD 21235 1-800-772-1213 (www.ssa.gov)	AARP 601 E Street, NW Washington, DC 20049 (202) 434-2277 (www.aarp.org)
Taxes Tax information Audit procedures	Internal Revenue Service 1111 Constitution Avenue, NW Washington, DC 20204 1-800-829-1040 1-800-TAX-FORM (www.irs.gov)	Department of Revenue (in your state capital city) The Tax Foundation 2001 L Street, NW (#1050) Washington, DC 20036 (202) 464-6200 (www.taxfoundation.org) National Association of Enrolled Agents 1120 Connecticut Avenue, NW (#440) Washington, DC 20036 1-800-424-4339 (www.naea.org)
Telemarketing 900 numbers	Federal Communications Commission 445 12th Street, SW Washington, DC 20554 1-888-225-5322 (www.fcc.gov)	National Consumers League 1701 K Street, NW Washington, DC 20006 (202) 835-3323 (www.nclnet.org)
Utilities Cable television Utility rates	Federal Communications Commission 445 12th Street, SW Washington, DC 20554 1-988-225-5322 (www.fcc.gov)	State utility commission (in your state capital)

Information on additional government agencies and private organizations available to assist you may be obtained in the *Consumer Action Handbook,* available at no charge from the Consumer Information Center, Pueblo, CO 81009 or online at www.pueblo.gsa.gov.

Section 2

State, county, and local consumer protection offices provide consumers with a variety of services, including publications and information before buying as well as handling complaints. This section provides contact information for state consumer protection agencies. In addition to the primary offices listed here, agencies regulating banking, insurance, securities, and utilities are available in each state. These may be located through a Web search or by going to the *Consumer's Resource Handbook* at www.pueblo.gsa.gov.

Many state consumer protection offices may be accessed through the Web site of the National Association of Attorneys General at www.naag.org or with a Web search for your state consumer protection office using "*(state)* consumer protection agency."

To save time, call the office before sending in a written complaint. Ask if the office handles the type of complaint you have or if complaint forms are provided. Many offices distribute consumer materials specifically geared to state laws and local issues. Call to obtain available educational information on your problem.

State departments of insurance may be accessed online at www.naic.org/state_web_map.htm.

The Web sites of state tax departments are available at www.taxadmin.org or www.aicpa.org/yellow/yptsgus.htm.

C Daily Spending Diary

Effective short-term money management and long-term financial security are dependent on spending less than you earn. The use of a Daily Spending Diary will provide information to better understand your spending patterns and to help you achieve desired financial goals.

The following sheets should be used to record *every cent* of your spending each day in the categories provided. Or you can create your own format to monitor your spending. You can indicate the use of a credit card with (CR). This experience will help you better understand your spending habits and identify desired changes you might want to make in your spending activities. Your comments should reflect what you have learned about your spending and can assist with changes you might want to make. Ask yourself, "What spending amounts can I reduce or eliminate?"

Many people who take on this task find it difficult at first, and may consider it a waste of time. However, nearly everyone who makes a serious effort to keep a Daily Spending Diary has found it beneficial. The process may seem tedious at first, but after a while recording this information becomes easier and faster. Most important, you will know where your money is going. Then you will be able to better decide if that is truly how you want to spend your available financial resources. A sincere effort with this activity will result in very beneficial information for monitoring and controlling your spending.

Daily Spending Diary

Directions: Record every cent of your spending each day in the categories provided, or create your own format to monitor your spending. You can indicate the use of a credit card with (CR). Comments should reflect what you have learned about your spending patterns and desired changes you might want to make in your spending habits. (Note: As income is received, record in Date column.)

Month: _____   Amount available for spending: $ _____   Amount to be saved: $ _____

Date (Income)	Total Spending	Auto, Transportation	Housing, Utilities	Food (H) Home (A) Away	Health, Personal Care	Education	Recreation, Leisure	Donations, Gifts	Other (note item, amount)	Comments
Example	$83	$20 (gas) (CR)		$47 (H)		$2 (pen)	$4 (DVD rental)	$10 (church)		This takes time but it helps me control my spending
1										
2										
3										
4										
5										
6										
7										
8										
9										
10										
11										
12										
13										
14										
Subtotal										

(continued)

Date (Income)	Total Spending	Auto, Transportation	Housing, Utilities	Food (H) Home (A) Away	Health, Personal Care	Education	Recreation, Leisure	Donations, Gifts	Other (note item, amount)	Comments
15										
16										
17										
18										
19										
20										
21										
22										
23										
24										
25										
26										
27										
28										
29										
30										
31										
Total										

Total Income
$ _____

Total Spending
$ _____

Difference (+/−)
$ _____

Actions: amount to savings, areas for reduced spending, other actions . . .

Daily Spending Diary

Directions: Record *every cent* of your spending each day in the categories provided, or create your own format to monitor your spending. You can indicate the use of a credit card with (CR). Comments should reflect what you have learned about your spending patterns and desired changes you might want to make in your spending habits. (Note: As income is received, record in Date column.)

Month: _____ Amount available for spending: $ _____ Amount to be saved: $ _____

Date (Income)	Total Spending	Auto, Transportation	Housing, Utilities	Food (H) Home (A) Away	Health, Personal Care	Education	Recreation, Leisure	Donations, Gifts	Other (note item, amount)	Comments
1										
2										
3										
4										
5										
6										
7										
8										
9										
10										
11										
12										
13										
14										
Subtotal										

(continued)

Date (Income)	Total Spending	Auto, Transportation	Housing, Utilities	Food (H) Home (A) Away	Health, Personal Care	Education	Recreation, Leisure	Donations, Gifts	Other (note item, amount)	Comments
15										
16										
17										
18										
19										
20										
21										
22										
23										
24										
25										
26										
27										
28										
29										
30										
31										
Total										

Total Income
$ _____

Total Spending
$ _____

Difference (+/−)
$ _____

Actions: amount to savings, areas for reduced spending, other actions . . .

Daily Spending Diary

Directions: Record *every cent* of your spending each day in the categories provided, or create your own format to monitor your spending. You can indicate the use of a credit card with (CR). Comments should reflect what you have learned about your spending patterns and desired changes you might want to make in your spending habits. (Note: As income is received, record in Date column.)

Month: _____   Amount available for spending: $ _____   Amount to be saved: $ _____

Date (Income)	Total Spending	Auto, Transportation	Housing, Utilities	Food (H) Home (A) Away	Health, Personal Care	Education	Recreation, Leisure	Donations, Gifts	Other (note item, amount)	Comments
1										
2										
3										
4										
5										
6										
7										
8										
9										
10										
11										
12										
13										
14										
Subtotal										

(continued)

Date (Income)	Total Spending	Auto, Transportation	Housing, Utilities	Food (H) Home (A) Away	Health, Personal Care	Education	Recreation, Leisure	Donations, Gifts	Other (note item, amount)	Comments
15										
16										
17										
18										
19										
20										
21										
22										
23										
24										
25										
26										
27										
28										
29										
30										
31										
Total										

Total Income
$ _____

Total Spending
$ _____

Difference (+/−)
$ _____

Actions: amount to savings, areas for reduced spending, other actions . . .

Daily Spending Diary

Directions: Record *every cent* of your spending each day in the categories provided, or create your own format to monitor your spending. You can indicate the use of a credit card with (CR). Comments should reflect what you have learned about your spending patterns and desired changes you might want to make in your spending habits. (Note: As income is received, record in Date column.)

Month: _____   Amount available for spending: $ _____   Amount to be saved: $ _____

Date (Income)	Total Spending	Auto, Transportation	Housing, Utilities	Food (H) Home (A) Away	Health, Personal Care	Education	Recreation, Leisure	Donations, Gifts	Other (note item, amount)	Comments
1										
2										
3										
4										
5										
6										
7										
8										
9										
10										
11										
12										
13										
14										
Subtotal										

(continued)

Date (Income)	Total Spending	Auto, Transportation	Housing, Utilities	Food (H) Home (A) Away	Health, Personal Care	Education	Recreation, Leisure	Donations, Gifts	Other (note item, amount)	Comments
15										
16										
17										
18										
19										
20										
21										
22										
23										
24										
25										
26										
27										
28										
29										
30										
31										
Total										

Total Income	Total Spending	Difference (+/−)	*Actions:* amount to savings, areas for reduced spending, other actions . . .
$ _____	$ _____	$ _____	

Index

Page numbers followed by n indicate material found in notes.